W9-AAF-752

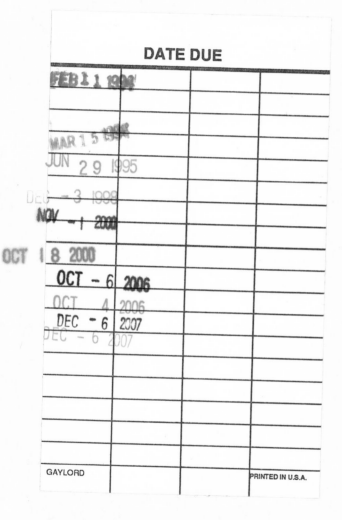

Critical Acclaim for *Shattered Peace*

"[Yergin] is a master of the historian's craft . . . Even more impressive is his judicious treatment of the evidence . . . future historians will have to follow his lead."

ROBERT DIVINE,
American Historical Review

"The volume presents much that is new; it is replete with sparkling vignettes of men and events. Always balanced in its judgments, *Shattered Peace* is narrative history at its best."

NORMAN A. GRAEBNER,
Virginia Quarterly Review

"[Yergin] has largely escaped from the arid conceptual desert of all those revisionist *versus* traditional tracts. He appreciates that neither the orthodox blame-it-on-the-Russians approach, nor the revisionist blame-it-on-the-Americans, even begins to do justice to the complexity and ambiguity of the situation the postwar statesmen faced."

ADAM ROBERTS,
London Sunday *Times*

"This is not just another book on the origins of the cold war. It is an exceptionally well-written study based on the literature, interviews, oral history transcripts, and research in archives."

JOHN GIMBEL,
Political Science Quarterly

"Daniel Yergin . . . has written an interpretation of how the conflict began and ramified [that is] commanding in its iron persuasiveness, in its subtle didactic purpose that seems inescapable and in the masterful control of the sources."

HENRY GRAFF,
Business History Review

"Intelligent, lively, argumentative . . . [Yergin] has grasped those difficult elements — the passage of time and the nature of individual human beings — the way men live in and are formed by their eras — and expresses them with great sensitivity . . . Personality is very much a part of Mr. Yergin's story — a reason that his book is fascinating."

The New Yorker

"A triumph of the historian's art."

Montreal Star

"Undoubtedly will become a classic."

Asian Wall Street Journal

"Daniel Yergin's *Shattered Peace* is beautifully written, exhaustively researched, and several of its central themes — such as the 'Riga axioms,' development of German policy, and the growth of the National Security State under Truman's direction — will henceforth be at the center of the controversy over the Cold War's origins."

WALTER LAFEBER,
author of *America, Russia and the Cold War*

"There have been many accounts of the origins of the Cold War but never one so richly detailed, so powerfully argued, so brilliantly illuminating, and so scrupulously fair. *Shattered Peace* is indispensable to an understanding of the men and forces that shaped the world we live in."

RONALD STEEL,
author of *Pax Americana*

PENGUIN BOOKS

SHATTERED PEACE

Daniel Yergin graduated from Yale in 1968 and as a Marshall Scholar attended Cambridge University, from which he received a Ph.D. in international relations. He was formerly a lecturer at the Harvard Business School and the Kennedy School of Government at Harvard. Since 1982, he has been President of Cambridge Energy Research of Cambridge, Massachusetts and Paris.

He is also author of *The Prize: The Epic Quest for Oil, Money, and Power* and coauthor of *Energy Future: The Report of the Energy Project of the Harvard Business School.* His articles have appeared in many magazines and newspapers around the world.

DANIEL YERGIN

Shattered Peace

The Origins of the Cold War

PENGUIN BOOKS

PENGUIN BOOKS
Published by the Penguin Group
Viking Penguin, a division of Penguin Books USA Inc.,
40 West 23rd Street, New York, New York 10010, U.S.A.
Penguin Books Ltd, 27 Wrights Lane, London W8 5TZ, England
Penguin Books Australia Ltd, Ringwood, Victoria, Australia
Penguin Books Canada Ltd, 2801 John Street,
Markham, Ontario, Canada L3R 1B4
Penguin Books (N.Z.) Ltd, 182–190 Wairau Road,
Auckland 10, New Zealand

Penguin Books Ltd, Registered Offices:
Harmondsworth, Middlesex, England

First published in the United States of America by
Houghton Mifflin Company 1977
First published in Great Britain by Andre Deutsch Limited 1978
This updated and revised edition published in Penguin Books 1990

1 3 5 7 9 10 8 6 4 2

This book was written under the auspices of
the Center for International Affairs,
Harvard University.

LIBRARY OF CONGRESS CATALOGING IN PUBLICATION DATA
Yergin, Daniel.
Shattered peace: the origins of the cold war and the national
security state/Daniel Yergin.
p. cm.
Reprint. Originally published: Boston: Houghton Mifflin, 1977.
Includes bibliographical references.
ISBN 0 14 01.2177 3
1. Cold War. 2. United States—Foreign relations—Soviet Union.
3. Soviet Union—Foreign relations—United States. 4. United
States—National security. I. Title.
D843.Y47 1989
327.73047'09'044—dc20 89-36536

Printed in the United States of America

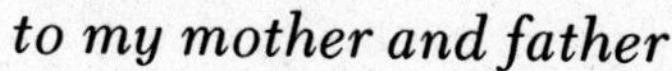

to my mother and father

Never before has there been such utter confusion in the public mind with respect to U.S. foreign policy. The President doesn't understand it; the Congress doesn't understand it; nor does the public, nor does the press. They all wander around in a labyrinth of ignorance and error and conjecture, in which truth is intermingled with fiction at a hundred points, in which unjustified assumptions have attained the validity of premises, and in which there is no recognized and authoritative theory to hold on to. Only the diplomatic historian, working from the leisure and detachment of a later day, will be able to unravel this incredible tangle and to reveal the true aspect of the various factors and issues involved.

— GEORGE KENNAN
Diary entry, 1950

Acknowledgments

IN THE COURSE of this book, I have acquired debts to many people and institutions which I wish to acknowledge — though, of course, the responsibility for the interpretations belongs only to me.

Professor F. H. Hinsley, Fellow of St. John's College, Cambridge, was a wise, judicious, and responsive Ph.D. supervisor. I learned from my many discussions with Michael Vyvyan, Fellow of Trinity College, Cambridge, and my tutor in history. Nicholas X. Rizopoulos, formerly of Yale, now executive director of the Lehrman Institute in New York City, has had — as teacher, friend, and blunt and incisive critic — a marked impact on this project, from inception to conclusion. Professor Ernest May of Harvard kindly helped me as an "informal supervisor" during my research time in Cambridge, Massachusetts, and I found participation in his Cold War Group at the Kennedy Institute of Politics to be most valuable. Professor John Iatrides of Southern Connecticut State College aided me a great deal with the issues involved in the Greek civil war. I also thank Barrington Moore for allowing me to join his stimulating seminar on American foreign policy.

I was very fortunate to have as my editor Grant Ujifusa, who brought insight, commitment, and patience to this project.

There are institutional debts to acknowledge. To the Board of Graduate Studies at Cambridge University, for support during work on my Ph.D. To both the University Consortium for World Order Studies and the Program on Conflict in International Relations of the Rockefeller Foundation, for postdoctoral grants for further work on issues in Soviet-American relations. To the Harry S. Truman Library Institute, which provided grants that enabled me to travel to the Truman Library. To Trinity College, Cambridge, for its assistance. I benefited greatly from participation in two study groups at the Lehrman Institute — Vojtech Mastny's on "Aims and Motives of Soviet Policies, 1944–1945" and Charles Maier's on "The United States and European Reorganization." I thank the principals and the Institute, which, in a few short years, has established itself as one of the foremost centers for the study of international relations, both from a contemporary and a historical point of view. I have worked in so many archives that I could not thank in any complete way all the archivists who helped me, but I do want to single out, since I called so much upon its services, the Truman Library with its outstanding staff, in particular Philip Lagerquist, Dennis Bilger, and Harry Clark.

I want to express special appreciation to the Center for International Affairs at Harvard University, where I have been since 1974, to its director and associate directors, Professors Raymond Vernon and Samuel Huntington, to Professors Robert Bowie and Joseph Nye, to its executive officer, Sally Cox, and to its editor of publications, Peter Jacobsohn. My gratitude goes to Helen Brann and Pat Kavanagh, who have given important support to my writing over what is now a number of years. And I appreciate a new association, the Division of Research at the Harvard Business School, and, in particular, Professor Robert Stobaugh.

In addition to the many of the above who have read all or parts of the manuscript, I thank the following for their readings: Cyril Black, Carl Brauer, Bernard Brodie, Walter Clemens, Sylvia Cleveland, Benjamin V. Cohen, Robert Dallek, Herbert Dinerstein, Robert Fishman, Frank Friedel, Philip Gillette, John Hazard, Jiri Hochman, Michael Janeway, Robert Jervis, Charles Kindleberger, George Kistiakowsky, Stephen Krasner, Thomas Lifka, Eugen Loebl, Mark Lytle, Michael Mandelbaum, Samuel Popkin, Avi Schlaim, Ronald Steel, R. W. Stent, and William Taubman. Special thanks to Jill Danzig.

And I am grateful to those who had the patience to help me in preparation of the manuscript: Terry Dash, Lisa Nekich, Ann Martin, Elizabeth Marvin, and Stephanie Duffill.

Finally, and most important, I should especially like to thank my wife, Angela Stent, of Harvard's Russian Research center — herself a student of the issues at the heart of this book — for her interest, judgment, and encouragement through many seasons.

Cambridge, Massachusetts,
1977

For this new edition of *Shattered Peace*, I would like to express special appreciation to a thoughtful and outstanding editor, Amanda Vaill of Viking Penguin, for her long interest, commitment, and encouragement. I would also like to thank Robert Laubacher, Sue Lena Thompson, and Thomas Schwartz.

Contents

PROLOGUE

The New Lore

Russia and the Balkans! It's already an old story, part of our new lore. The repression of German aggressiveness has been or is about to be accomplished forever, but in the meantime pan-Slavism has been mobilized in the interest of world Marxist revolution.

— MAYNARD BARNES (formerly U.S. minister to Bulgaria), October 1947 [1]

Prologue: The New Lore

ROOSEVELT was the first to arrive. His plane set down on the icy runway at the airport at Saki, on the Crimean peninsula of the Soviet Union, just after noon on February 3, 1945. It had taken nine hours to fly the 1400 miles from the Mediterranean island of Malta, where he had rendezvoused briefly with Churchill the day before. Roosevelt sat in his plane for twenty minutes until the aircraft bearing the Prime Minister landed. The two Westerners then emerged, to be greeted by a Red Army band and a delegation of high Soviet officials.

Roosevelt and Churchill left Saki by car. They drove across the Crimea for more than five hours on a newly paved road, which was guarded by an endless line of soldiers, and which twisted through terrain only recently liberated from the Germans. Later Churchill would remember how sudden was the change as they descended from the chilly, snow-covered mountains toward the coast at Yalta and into the "warm and brilliant sunshine and a most genial climate." Stalin arrived at Yalta the next morning, traveling most of the way from Moscow by train.

The weather remained unseasonably mild through the week that followed. The Russians called it "Roosevelt weather," for it matched the mood of the conference.

With victory and the end of the war already in sight, the three leaders were meeting to lay the groundwork for what they hoped would be a stable peace. For a week, in the ballroom of what once was the Czar's summer palace, they argued, negotiated, reminisced, ruminated, pontificated, postured, traded, and compromised. All three left Yalta basically satisfied with the outcome. Stalin said that the peace could be kept, so long as the three of them lived. But he wondered what would happen in ten years.

Even then the three were already in error on a crucial point — they thought the end of the war was probably still a year or more away.[2] As it happened, the passage into the postwar era was much swifter and more decisively marked than they had imagined. On April 12, two months after the Yalta meeting, Roosevelt died. His successor, Harry Truman, had virtually no experience of foreign affairs. And just as Truman became President, a flood of unprecedented and complex postwar problems was loosed. On April 25, Soviet and American troops linked up for the first time, on the banks of the River Elbe. Germany was sundered and the Thousand-Year Reich had ceased to exist after thirteen. Within days, Hitler was dead, a suicide in the rubble of bombed-out Berlin. By the end of July, the votes in the British general election had been counted, and, in a stunning upset, Winston Churchill was unceremoniously turned out as Prime Minister, replaced by Clement Attlee, who had once been a social worker in the East End of London. On August 6, and then again on August 9, the Americans inaugurated a new age of warfare by dropping atomic bombs on Hiroshima and Nagasaki. On August 14, Japan surrendered.

And so the only wartime leader left was Joseph Stalin. In September 1945, a U.S. senator, Claude Pepper from Florida, called on him at the Kremlin. Stalin emphasized the obvious. The Grand Alliance, he said, had been created by the single circumstance of a common enemy, Adolf Hitler, who had gone to war to gain hegemony over Europe. "That tie no longer exists, and we shall have to find a new basis for our close relations in the future," Stalin observed. "And that will not be easy." But, continued the dictator, once a student in a Russian Orthodox seminary, "Christ said, 'Seek and ye shall find.' "[3]

By 1945, the world had been refashioned by death, destruction, and social upheaval. Germany and Japan, two of the most powerful nations, had been defeated and occupied, and the aging European empires were on the way to disintegration. With the defeat or decline of most of the European states, the old international system collapsed, leaving just two powers dominant, the United States and the Soviet Union. Many basic questions had no clear answers in 1945, and even as Stalin spoke in September of that year, the victor states were already busy assessing each other across the devastated lands and the wreckage of states, anxiously calculating possible gains and losses.

The victors never did find the tie that would hold them together. The Grand Alliance gave way to a global antagonism between two hostile coalitions, one led by the United States and the other by the Soviet Union — those two countries standing opposed to each other as nation-states, as ideologies, and as economic and political systems. After 1945 the two superpowers were able to approximate a state of general mobilization without general war being the consequence.[4]

The confrontation brought about fundamental changes in American life, a permanent military readiness in what passed for peacetime. "We are in a period now I think of the formulation of a mood," Dean Acheson told a group of American policymakers at the end of 1947. "The country is getting serious. It is getting impressed by the fact that the business of dealing with the Russians is a long, long job. People don't say any more why doesn't Mr. Truman get together with Uncle Joe Stalin and fix it up. That used to be a common idea. There is less and less talk even among silly people about dropping bombs on Moscow. They now see it as a long, long pull, and that it can only be done by the United States getting itself together, determining that we cannot maintain a counter-balance to the communistic power without strengthening all those other parts of the world which belong in the system with us. That takes money, imagination, American skill and American technical help and many, many years." Confident that the public was coming to accept this view, Acheson added, "We are going to understand that our functions in the world will require all of the power and all the thought and all the calmness we have at our disposal."[5]

Acheson spoke about the "United States getting itself together." By this, he meant that the country had to become organized for perpetual confrontation and for war. The unified pattern of attitudes, policies, and institutions by which this task was to be effected comprise what I call America's "national security state." It became, in fact, a "state within a state." The attitudes were derived from the two commanding ideas of American postwar foreign policy — anti-communism and a new doctrine of national security. The policies included containment, confrontation, and intervention, the methods by which U.S. leaders have sought to make the world safe for America. The institutions include those government bureaucracies and private organizations that serve in permanent war preparedness. These developments have helped to increase dramatically the power of the Executive branch of the U.S. government, particularly the presidency. For the national security state required, as Charles Bohlen put it in 1948, "a confidence in the Executive where you give human nature in effect a very large blank check." [6]

And so the Second World War was succeeded not by the peace that Yalta had promised, but by a new conflict, the Cold War, an armed truce, precarious and dangerous — and still today, the central and defining fact of international life.

This work is the result of seven years of research and writing. Much use has been made of many archives and private collections of papers that have only recently been opened or are still in the process of being opened.*

This is not a book for those who want a simple story, a morality play, a confirmation of prejudices, or a rationalization for or against present-day policies. It is my hope that the narrative that follows will enable us to penetrate the myths and the polemics so that we might learn how and why the confrontation between the United States and the Soviet Union came about — not as people have chosen to remember it, but as it really happened.

One of the great diplomatic sports between East and West in the latter part of the 1940s was what might be called "onus-shifting" — each side trying to make a record and place blame on the other for the division of Europe and the Cold War itself. In this sense, much of the subsequent writing about the Cold War, both "orthodox" and

* The reader should be aware that Westerners have no access whatsoever to relevant Soviet archives. On the other hand, no country is so open and forthright with its diplomatic materials as the United States — a circumstance of which Soviet scholars have availed themselves in recent years. This disparity leads, in all writing about the Cold War, to an inevitable focus upon the interplay of Western, primarily American, policymaking. No Westerner can know how the Soviet leaders among themselves interpreted and misinterpreted American intentions and capabilities. So the historian today, like the policymaker in the postwar years, must seek to develop a consistent and reasonable interpretation based upon what is available.

"revisionist," has been a continuation of the Cold War by other means. The impulse to apportion blame is understandable simply from the magnitude of the circumstance. But the very name "Cold War" has provided an important additional reason, for historians spend much time tracking responsibilities for the outbreak of wars. The Cold War, however, was something other than a war. If one imagines that this phenomenon had instead become conventionally known as the "global antagonism," as it might have, then it becomes instantly clear how difficult it is to assign guilt in a meaningful way. For how do you blame a single man — whether Stalin, Churchill or Truman — for so complicated a phenomenon, involving events in so many different countries and at so many different levels. Of course, it was hard to resist the impulse during the years when the antagonism was at its sharpest, but perhaps the passage of time has liberated us from the need to apportion blame in the course of explanation.

For the fundamental source of the Cold War, we must turn to the interests and positions of nation-states, which are the basic unit in international politics. As the historian F. H. Hinsley has observed, "In an international system the independent state is unable to abandon its primary concern with advancing the interests of that society in competition with other states, if also by collaboration with them." [7] This imperative applies as much to states that draw their inspiration and legitimacy from Marx as to those based on Locke or divine right. The four-century-old state system that was centered in Europe, and which had been weakened in the First World War, collapsed in the course of the Second. A new system would have to emerge. There was much uncertainty about the shape it would take, and about the two countries that were sure to dominate it. One of them, the United States, had been little involved in the old system; the other, the Union of Soviet Socialist Republics, had been mostly excluded from it in the years between the two world wars. The U.S.A. and the USSR had little in the way of common traditions, no common political vocabulary, precious few links. They looked upon themselves as rival models for the rest of mankind.[8] They shared little except distrust.

In a system of independent states, all nations live rather dangerously.[9] Therefore, the reduction of dangers becomes a nation's objective in international politics. A country will take actions and pursue policies that it considers defensive, but which appear ominous, if not threatening, to rivals. And so a dialectic of confrontation develops.

But why did the Cold War confrontation take the shape it did? Here we must look closely at the diplomacy of the postwar period. For it is central to my argument that diplomacy *did* matter.[10] There has been too much of a tendency to assume that all that happened was of a single piece, foreordained and determined. But how world leaders perceived their interests and acted on those perceptions counted for a very great deal.

The Soviet outlook was not the only significant ideological factor involved in the development of the global antagonism. There was also the American ideology — the ideas and outlook that U.S. leaders brought to international affairs, their *world set.*[11] The understanding American leaders had of events and possibilities controlled their own actions and reactions in the dialectic of confrontation.

We shall pay close attention to three key elements in their world set — Wilsonianism, an interpretation of Soviet objectives, and the new doctrine of national security.

Wilsonianism, an ideology of liberal internationalism, has been at the heart of twentieth-century American foreign policy. It is a powerful vision of how the world might be organized, and of America's role in it. Woodrow Wilson was its most articulate proponent in the years 1917–19, when the United States threw its full weight into the politics of the international system and into the issue at the center of that system — the balance of power in Europe. Wilson sought to project American values into world politics, the values of a liberal society united in a broad Lockean consensus.

Wilson, like many other American leaders then and now, thought that the often brutal anarchy of the international system and the balance of power could be superseded by a juridical international community, committed to due process and common values. The United States would work within the old system only in order to reform it. The Wilsonian program, meant to produce a middle way between reaction and revolution, included national self-determination, representative government, a league of nations, an end to formal empires, nonrecognition of revolutionary change, democratic liberties and human rights, reduction of armaments, a belief in an "enlightened public opinion," and an open-door world economy. The economic objectives were an important element, but only part of the picture. The United States saw itself as a disinterested, innocent power, whose own desires and aims were thought to express the yearnings of all people, and whose responsibilities were to become inescapable and worldwide.[12]

But, almost immediately after the First World War, a disillusioned American polity put aside the pursuit of the program, though not its values. Europe slid into political and economic chaos, and then again into war. The men guiding U.S. policy in the 1940s had witnessed events in their own lifetimes that provided a compelling impetus for once again trying to make Woodrow Wilson's enterprise work. They saw the Great Depression as a very close call for their own kind of liberal capitalist society. The rise of the dictatorships and the experience of two world wars made their quest for a different kind of world order even more urgent. They wanted to fulfill the Wilsonian vision so that, as Secretary of State Cordell Hull told Congress in 1943, "there will no longer be a need for spheres of influence, for alliances, for balance of power, or any other of the special arrangements through which, in the unhappy past, the nations strove to safeguard their security or to promote their interests." These men thought the best of all worlds was a world without nazism, communism, and colonialism. This desire was not cynical. They feared that a world laden with reaction or revolution would be a world dangerous for American society, a rapacious world soon to be embroiled again in war. And autocracy of any kind offended their deepest democratic instincts.

The unhappy past was much with American leaders. "I cannot tell you how much I appreciate your very comforting letter recalling the obstacles of 1919," James Byrnes, who became Secretary of State in 1945, wrote to a friend in December of that year, shortly before flying to Moscow to continue the arid attempts to make a postwar settlement with the Russians. "As I read your letter I recalled the hurdles we had to overcome after World War I . . . It is remarkable how history repeats itself." [13]

But, as it sought to remove conflict and anarchy from international relations, Wilsonianism was truly seeking to abolish the very substance of world politics — balance of power, spheres of influence, power politics. These are the ineluctable features of an international system composed of sovereign nations.[14] It is paradoxical, but in order to achieve his goals, a Wilsonian must be a renegade Wilsonian, like Franklin Roosevelt, facing the world as it is, not as one would wish it to be, using traditional means to achieve Wilsonian ends.

The Soviet leaders, on the other hand, shared none of the Wilsonian values. Though they spoke in the language of Marxism-Leninism, they were primarily concerned with power as traditionally conceived in the international system. They were carving a sphere of influence, a glacis, out of bordering countries. As they did so, a great debate developed within the American policy elite over how to evaluate Soviet intentions and capabilities.[15] Was that sphere all Russia wanted or was it only a first step on a road to world revolution?

Underlying the debate were two related questions that have always confronted those in the West who have to shape policies toward the Soviet Union. They are the same two questions we face today.

The first was raised by the October 1917 Revolution itself. What is the connection between Marxist-Leninist ideology and Soviet foreign policy? The ideology proclaims that communism will inevitably inherit the entire world from capitalism, and calls upon Marxist-Leninists to be the conscious agents of the revolution. But the men who have ruled the Soviet Union were not and are not merely ideologues with many idle hours to dream about tomorrow's utopia. For the most part, they must concern themselves with today, with governing a powerful state that has pressing interests to protect, dangers to avoid, tasks to accomplish, and problems to solve. "There is no revolutionary movement in the West," said Stalin during the debates over the Brest-Litovsk treaty in 1918. "There are no facts; there is only a possibility, and with possibilities we cannot reckon."[16]

The second question was brutally posed by the horrors of Stalinism, in particular by collectivization and the Great Terror of the 1930s. Does a totalitarian practice at home necessarily produce a foreign policy that is totalitarian in intent, committed to overturning the international system and to endless expansion in pursuit of world dominance? The policies of Adolf Hitler seemed to confirm that a powerful relationship did exist between such domestic practice and international behavior.

The changes wrought by the Second World War gave urgent and

highest priority to these questions. What was the American response to be? Within the ensuing debate, there were two sets of generalizations, two interpretations that competed for hegemony in the American policy elite in the middle 1940s. At the heart of the first set was an image of the Soviet Union as a world revolutionary state, denying the possibilities of coexistence, committed to unrelenting ideological warfare, powered by a messianic drive for world mastery. The second set downplayed the role of ideology and the foreign policy consequences of authoritarian domestic practices, and instead saw the Soviet Union behaving like a traditional Great Power within the international system, rather than trying to overthrow it. The first set I call, for shorthand, the Riga axioms; the second, the Yalta axioms.*

The Riga axioms triumphed in American policy circles in the postwar years and provided a foundation for the anticommunist consensus. Charles Bohlen summarized this outlook when he wrote to former Secretary of State Edward Stettinius in 1949. "I am quite convinced myself, and I think all of those who have been working specifically on the problems of relations with the Soviet Union are in agreement," said Bohlen, "that the reasons for the state of tension that exists in the world today between the Soviet Union and the non-Soviet world are to be found in the character and nature of the Soviet state, the doctrines to which it faithfully adheres, and not in such matters as the shutting off of Lend-Lease and the question of a loan." [17]

With a view of this sort, the effort to make a diplomatic settlement became irrelevant, even dangerous, for the Cold War confrontation was thought to be almost genetically preordained in the revolutionary, messianic, predatory character of the Soviet Union.

Though not so named, the Riga and Yalta axioms still today provide the points of reference for the continuing debate about how to organize U.S. relations with the Soviet Union. The Riga axioms help form the outlook of the Cold War. The Yalta axioms underlie détente.[18]

Neither set of axioms had a monopoly on the truth. Both emphasized some aspects of reality, and obscured others. No decent human being, whatever his political values, can be anything but ap-

* To my knowledge no one ever before referred to these two interpretative structures as the Riga and Yalta axioms. My reasons for doing so will become clear as the narrative unfolds.

palled by the monstrous horrors of the Stalinist regime. As Solzhenitsyn has written, the prison camps stretched across the Soviet Union like a great archipelago. As many as twenty million people may have died because of Stalin's tyranny. So awful is the legacy that the Soviet leadership today, a quarter century after the dictator's death, still cannot acknowledge what Khrushchev called Stalin's "crimes." To do so would be to undermine the very legitimacy of the Soviet system.

The terror merely abated during the time of the Grand Alliance. Of her experiences during the war years, Nadezhda Mandelstam, the widow of the poet Osip Mandelstam, writes: "By this time I had talked with many people who had returned from the camps (and most of them were sent back to them in the second half of the forties)." She asks, "What manner of people were they, those who first decreed and then carried out this mass destruction of their own kind?" There is no good answer. But she pleads, "No one should lightly dismiss our experience, as complacent foreigners do, cherishing the hope that with them — who are so clever and cultured — things will be different." [19]

For my part, I do not want to suggest that Stalin's character, intentions, or methods were, by any means, benign or kindly. But in the international arena, Stalin's politics were not those of a single-minded world revolutionist. The truth is that the Soviet Union's foreign policy was often clumsy and brutal, sometimes confused, but usually cautious and pragmatic. The USSR behaved as a traditional Great Power, intent upon aggrandizing itself along the lines of historic Russian goals, favoring spheres of influence, secret treaties, Great Power consortiums, and the other methods and mores from the "old diplomacy." Moreover, if the Soviet Union had harbored ambitions of unlimited expansion, it was hardly in a position to pursue them. Unlike the United States, whose gross national product had actually doubled during the war, it was a ruined, ravaged country in 1945.

American leaders who accepted the Riga axioms misinterpreted both the range and degree of the Soviet challenge and the character of Soviet objectives and so downplayed the possibilities for diplomacy and accommodation. It was the new doctrine of "national security" that led them to believe that the USSR presented an *immediate military* threat to the United States. That doctrine, an expansive interpretation of American security needs, represented a major redefinition of America's relation to the rest of the world.[20]

If American interests were in jeopardy everywhere in the world, the exercise of Soviet power anywhere outside Russian borders appeared ominous. Any form of compromise was therefore regarded as appeasement, already once tried and once failed.

The doctrine of national security also permitted America's postwar leaders to harmonize the conflicting demands of Wilsonianism and realpolitik — to be democratic idealists and pragmatic realists at the same time. So emboldened, American leaders pursued a global, often crusading, foreign policy, convinced that it was made urgent by something more earthy than the missionary impulse of Woodrow Wilson.

History is shaped by the time in which it is written. This work was researched and executed during the latter years of the Vietnam war and the period of what might be called tentative détente. Consequently, two separate questions have informed my inquiry. First, I wanted to determine, if I could, the origins of the ideologies, policies, and institutions that played a major role in the U.S. intervention in Indochina. That is, what gave rise to the national security state? Of course, it would be simplistic to say that the ideology, policies, and institutions that are the subject of this book in themselves *caused* the Vietnam war. Nor do I mean to suggest that the United States alone is "guilty" of possessing a national security state or that, somehow, the national security state is a creature of capitalism. As embedded as the national security state may be in our political and economic system, a national security state is even more firmly entrenched in the Soviet Union, beyond the reach of question. Indeed, the USSR might be called a "total security state."

Détente has called up a different question. Was not some form of détente — some reduction in tensions, some explicit ground rules — possible earlier, much earlier?[21] Why did diplomacy fail and confrontation become a way of life? What are the constraints on coexistence between two such dissimilar systems?

At the Potsdam Conference in July 1945, a British diplomat became involved during lunch in a vigorous conversation with his colleagues. Afterward, he made a diary note, "Debate on the perennial question whether Russia peaceful and wants to join the Western Club but is suspicious of us, or whether she is out to dominate the world and is hoodwinking us. It always seems safer to go on the worse assumption."[22]

People who make policy do not always go on the worst assumptions. Certainly, those in the late 1940s felt that their predecessors in the late 1930s had naïvely failed to do so, with disastrous results. Still, the pressure is so strong on the diplomat in an anarchic world to decide on the basis of the worse or even the worst assumption, that this particular diplomat's phrase is a virtual maxim of decision-making in international politics. But in some circumstances, to so proceed can result in the closing off of choices that might in the longer term produce a more genuine and lasting reduction in danger.

The policymaker and the historian see events from different perspectives, for they have different obligations. The policymaker's duty is to his polity, to minimize the risks it faces in the world. He must look to the future. The consequences of his errors, unlike those of the historian, can sometimes have immediate impact on the lives of millions.

As the historian reconstructs the past, he must recognize this difference. He must be aware of the imperfect knowledge of, and pressures on, those about whom he writes. With that in mind, he may even come to suspect that had he himself been in a position to participate in the events that form his subject, he too might have made choices that now, as a historian, he questions and challenges.

But, of course, the historian has no responsibility to go on the worst assumption. He is freer in that sense. Yet he is bound in another. For his aim is to comprehend, to explain, to unravel, and his singular obligation is to the truth.

PART ONE

The Grand Alliance

Perhaps never before in history — at least in the history that we know about — has there been so deep a cleavage as this.

— DEWITT CLINTON POOLE

MAYNARD BARNES: Our problem is to learn the idiom of dealing with Russia. We know the language already, don't we George?

GEORGE KENNAN: We do.[1]

I

The Breach: The Riga Axioms

BY OCTOBER 1917, the moment was ripe.

Vladimir Ilyich Lenin left his hiding place in Finland and returned to Petrograd, formerly St. Petersburg, despite an order out for his arrest. On October 10, disguising himself with a wig, he made his way to a meeting of the Central Committee of the Bolshevik Party, which, responding to months of taunts and cajolery from him, at last voted 10 to 2 to prepare an armed insurrection against the Provisional Government. Hardly a formidable opponent, the Provisional Government had held power only since the overthrow of the Czar the preceding winter, and it had already lost most of its authority and will to rule. Early on the morning of October 25, the Bolshevik forces, meeting little resistance, seized strategic points in Petrograd. In the afternoon Lenin proclaimed the triumph of the workers' and peasants' revolution. Late in the evening, the Winter Palace, last stronghold of the Provisional Government, fell to the rebels. A new revolutionary state had been born.

Autocracy would give way to totalitarianism. What had been the empire of the Czars was to become the Union of the Soviet Socialist Republics, a change that would, of course, transform the lives of the many nationalities that inhabited that vast territory. It would have, as well, great impact on international politics. But what kind of impact? And what role would the Soviet Union play in the international system? "I will issue a few revolutionary proclamations to the peoples of the world and then shut up shop," announced Leon Trotsky, upon becoming the first People's Commissar for Foreign Affairs. Yet, in April 1922, the second People's Commissar for Foreign Affairs, Georgi Chicherin, showed up at the Genoa Conference wearing the top hat of bourgeois diplomacy and speaking not only fluent French, but also the traditional vocabulary of international politics.[2] Was the USSR a state in the service of an ideology, or an ideology in the service of a state?

That question — which turned on an assessment of the character of this political entity, its objectives and capabilities — emerged in the 1940s as the single most important problem facing those responsible for American foreign policy. It remained such through the 1970s. But for the first two decades after the Great October Revolution, the question was urgent only to a more limited circle of American officials.

When Joseph Grew was a junior secretary in the American embassy in St. Petersburg during 1907–8, he presented himself in full court regalia, including fore-and-aft hat and gold sword, and mixed with his Russian counterparts at the yacht, tennis, and polo clubs. The Bolshevik Revolution rudely shattered these pleasant customs. "Profoundly disgusting" was the way Grew described Western negotiations with the successor to the Czarist state at Genoa and Rapallo in 1922.[3]

During the 1920s, a new "Soviet Service" developed in the State Department; it was anti-Bolshevik and opposed to diplomatic recognition of the USSR. Cohesive, with a strongly articulated sense of identity, this group advocated a policy of sophisticated anticommunism in an axiomatic form. Its outlook was based on personal experience, assessment, study, and pessimism. As U.S. leaders attempted, after World War II, to analyze Soviet policy and select an appropriate American course, this group's position provided one end of the spectrum of the debate. Eventually its axioms triumphed. Or, rather, they triumphed again, for they had held sway during most of the interwar years, when they had little competition, and before the problem of the Soviet Union had moved to the fore.[4]

Initially, American officials saw the Bolshevik Revolution as a double betrayal. The revolutionaries made peace with the Germans at Brest-Litovsk early in 1918 and withdrew from the war, hurting the Allied cause. The Bolsheviks had also destroyed the hopes for the budding Russian democracy by overturning the liberal regime, which in its few months of existence had at last removed the Czarist stigma from the coalition meant to make the world safe for democracy. There was even the possibility of a third betrayal — that Lenin was a German agent.

American policymakers refused to recognize the new regime, in part because they hoped that it would be short-lived. The idea was shared by "practically all of us," recalled DeWitt Clinton Poole, who worked on Russian affairs in the State Department after World War I, "that the cure for Bolshevism was prosperity and good order and that Bolshevism would disappear under those conditions." There was, in Poole's words, a "breach between the Bolsheviks and the rest of the world." In an important memorandum addressed to his superiors in the State Department, in August 1919, Poole marshaled the arguments against giving diplomatic recognition to this "unconstitutional" regime: "Their aim is world-wide revolution . . . Their doctrines aim at the destruction of all governments as now constituted." [5]

This outlook was widely accepted in the government and, instead of recognizing the Bolsheviks, the State Department set up a Division of Russian Affairs, with a mandate unusual for its time: to study and interpret the great mass of often contradictory information that made its way across the breach from this new Russia. It called upon the services of professors like Samuel Harper, of the University of Chicago, one of the first academic experts on Soviet Russia.

The U.S. maintained an observation post in the American mission in the Baltic port city of Riga, which was, through the interwar years, the capital of the independent republic of Latvia. Founded in 1201 by German merchants, tucked into a gulf at the very eastern end of the Baltic Sea, Riga still resembled a city of northern Germany, with narrow cobbled streets, gabled towers, and tiny squares. It was in this mission during the 1920s that much of the research on the Soviet Union was conducted, personnel trained, and fundamental attitudes formed and nurtured; and it was from the mission that there issued constant warnings against the international menace. For these reasons, I have associated place with ideas and linked Riga to the axiomatic outlook of the Soviet Service in the State Department, although the ideas would receive further elaboration and gain new intensity in the latter half of the 1930s.[6]

The new Bolshevik regime, surviving civil war, famine, and intervention, had consolidated its power by the mid-1920s. In 1924 the Russian Division in the State Department was absorbed by the Eastern European Division, which continued to focus on the new state. Robert F. Kelley, who became the chief of the Division in 1926 and directed the creation of the Soviet Service, was the guiding force. A tall, taciturn former military attaché, educated at Harvard and the Sorbonne, Kelley spoke and read Russian flawlessly and was familiar with Russian literature. He felt that any analysis of the new regime should be based upon facts and study, not emotions, and he emphasized academic-style analysis. He oversaw the development of the Russian section at Riga, which eventually prided itself upon being, at least in economic matters, the equal of any of the leading academic research centers.

Even the stabs at humor in Riga tended to be rather grim. "We used to practice our Russian and sharpen our wits," George Kennan once recalled, "by drafting *Pravda* editorials in which we announced the reinstatement of capitalism in Russia and claimed it was a tremendous triumph for socialist construction and maintained only the Soviet system was able to bring to the people of the world the advantages of capitalist initiatives without throwing them open to exploitation."[7]

Though insisting that emotions had no place in analyses, Kelley was known even in the Department for his pronounced antipathy toward the "Boles," as he called them.[8] "The fundamental obstacle" to recognition, Kelley believed, "is the world revolutionary aims and practices of the rulers of that country." Under him, throughout the 1920s, the Division regularly turned out papers against diplomatic recognition. "I trust you noted the two interviews from the White House re our Russian policy," Kelley wrote to Samuel Harper in March 1925. "They could hardly have been more to the point — yet certain *dark forces* persisted in misconstruing them . . . Our policy is not, or was not, a Hughes policy, but a Wilson-Colby-Harding-Hughes-Coolidge-Kellogg one." And two years later he confidently added, "There is no change in our policy toward the Soviet regime — none is under contemplation."[9]

Although Kelley's influence was apparent to all who worked under him, he had special influence on those he referred to as "my boys," the young State Department officers who went through a study program in Russian language, culture, and history that he initiated in 1928.[10] The emphasis was rightly on "Russian," for in many ways the program was an exercise in nineteenth-century nostalgia. He insisted that the two officers chosen for it each year emerge with a background similar to that "of a well-educated Russian of the old, prerevolutionary school." It was not only the education — in Berlin for George Kennan, in Paris for Charles Bohlen and the others — that shaped the outlook of these young officers; their first contacts with Russians were with White refugees. They became friends and identified with these anticommunist but "highly cultured Russian émigrés." They also trained in the Baltic republics which, with large émigré populations, were much more like Czarist Russia than anywhere in the Soviet Union; the ambience underscored for these Department men the existence of the "breach" Poole had described. "The Russian intelligentsia before the Revolution constituted one of the most remarkable collections of men that the world has seen," Bohlen wrote in his memoirs. The new Soviet specialists felt, in some small sense at least, that they themselves were émigrés from this Czarist past.[11]

This left the Americans with an attitude toward the Soviet Union compounded of fascination and distaste, which continued through the decades. In these early years Russia was already the consuming interest not only of their professional lives but of much of their personal lives as well. Nevertheless they generally opposed recognition as an unnecessary concession, even though nonrecognition kept them out in Riga or elsewhere, looking in. Echoing Robert Kelley, Kennan recalled in his memoirs: "Never — neither then nor at any later date — did I consider the Soviet Union a fit ally or associate, actual or potential, for this country." [12]

But with the Roosevelt Administration in 1933 came recognition. For one thing, pressure from market-hungry businessmen had been mounting. For another, both Roosevelt and, more reluctantly, Secretary of State Cordell Hull regarded nonrecognition as anomalous and of doubtful moral utility. The Soviet Union had not disappeared, nor could it be ignored as a factor in world politics. Roosevelt felt that recognition might be useful to the U.S. in dealing with problems in

Europe and, more particularly, in the Far East. The Russians, although they wanted expanded trade, also wanted relations with the United States to help balance the growing Japanese threat in Asia. As early as December 1931, Premier Molotov had characterized the Manchurian situation as the "most important problem of our foreign policy." Roosevelt bypassed State in the actual negotiations, first using William Bullitt, then taking charge himself. In an effort to deflect domestic criticism and "satisfy at least a majority of our people" — if not such implacable opponents as former Secretary of State Bainbridge Colby, who in 1920 had enunciated a powerful nonrecognition stand and now in 1933 denounced Russia as an "enemy state" — Roosevelt obtained from Soviet Foreign Minister Maxim Litvinov a number of guarantees, of which the most important were a Russian promise not to meddle in domestic American politics and a vague "gentleman's agreement," tying a U.S. loan to a Soviet assumption of the debts of Kerensky's Provisional Government. These agreements, however, ended up causing more problems than they solved.[13]

Roosevelt selected Bullitt, who had become a foreign policy adviser during the 1932 campaign, as the first American ambassador to the Soviet Union.

Bullitt was a charming, but restless, ambitious, and erratic man, subject to great swings of emotion, from intense loyalty to profound hatred. He had been a member of the American delegation to the Versailles peace talks after World War I. In February and March 1919, he had journeyed to Russia for secret but officially approved talks with Lenin and other Bolsheviks; he had returned with what he regarded as sound terms for a political truce between the Bolsheviks and the victorious Allies. But Woodrow Wilson and David Lloyd George had repudiated him, and in May 1919 he submitted his resignation. He had been "one of the millions" who had trusted in Wilson, he wrote to the President, adding, "I am sorry you did not fight our fight to the finish." Convinced that he had been personally betrayed, Bullitt attacked Wilson and the Versailles settlement in testimony before the Senate Foreign Relations Committee, then wandered back to Europe to mingle with its upper classes.

He had, for almost fifteen years, lived with the bitter memory. Now, with this new mission, he could prove himself right and Wilson wrong; he could absolve himself and make the great reputation that had been once denied him.

Arriving in Moscow in December 1933, Bullitt had the honor of being greeted in his hotel lobby by Marx — by Harpo Marx, who had arrived in the Russian capital at the same time. Both men were received warmly by the Bolsheviks. Harpo delighted a small audience one evening by "extracting" knives, spoons, and forks from Litvinov's clothes. Bullitt thought he would be able to delight the audience back home by extracting from Litvinov and the rest of the Bolshevik leadership some ill-defined concessions and prizes.[14]

The Americans had arrived at a very curious moment in the history of the Soviet Union. Late 1933 and 1934 provided a respite for the Soviet Union, a break between terrors. It was a pause between the two phases of Stalinization. The revolution mandated from above — industrialization and collectivization — had taken a terrible toll. Collectivization had not only created one of the worst famines in all of Russian history, but had also led to the deportation and deaths of millions of farming people — an "ethnic catastrophe" in Solzhenitsyn's phrase.

But, in these first months of the new American embassy, the pressure on both the land and industry had been reduced. The great famine was easing, the new Five-Year Plan was more realistic, the economy was recovering, and conditions of life improving. Repression was less in evidence.[15]

These changes had effects on diplomacy. The Soviet leaders, Bullitt immediately reported, were "intelligent, sophisticated, vigorous" men, who could not be "persuaded to waste their time with the ordinary conventional diplomatist." Fortunately, they were "extremely eager" for contact with "anyone who had first-rate intelligence and dimension as a human being. They were, for example, delighted by young Kennan, who went in with me." Convinced that he had "the inside track," Bullitt imagined that he was picking up with Stalin where he had left off with Lenin. "I want you to understand that if you want to see me at any time, day or night," Stalin assured him, "you have only to let me know and I will see you at once." Bullitt informed Roosevelt that Stalin was like "a wiry Gipsy with roots and emotions beyond my experience." The ambassador marveled at the "magnificent forehead" of Molotov, who reminded him of a "first-rate French scientist, great poise, kindliness and intelligence."[16]

The intellectual heritage of the Russian experts assumed less importance as the members of the embassy staff, operating under the spell of Bullitt's charm, were caught up in the ambassador's enthusiasm and hopes. During this honeymoon, Moscow appeared colorful, cozy, even pleasurable. Discussion went on endlessly. Russian officials, including prominent Bolsheviks like Nikolai Bukharin and Karl Radek, came to dinner at Spaso House, the ambassador's residence, formerly the home of a rich vodka merchant; and they would stay to watch new films sent from Hollywood at Bullitt's behest. The ambassador also imported polo equipment, to teach the game to Red Army officers and thus win their friendship. The American air attaché, Thomas White, was allowed to keep his plane in Moscow, the only private aircraft in the entire country. Although Kennan asserts in his memoirs that his orientation was firmly fixed before he arrived, the evidence, including his own testimony, indicates that there was indeed a departure from the attitudes of the 1920s: "It was in truth a wonderful exciting time . . . an example of what Soviet-American relations *might*, in other circumstances, have been . . . Most of us look back on those days, I suppose, as the high point of life." [17]

Within a year, the honeymoon ended in bitter squabbles. Stabilization in the Far East removed the need that had been felt by both sides for a major understanding. In December 1934, Sergei Kirov, the Leningrad party leader, was assassinated, setting off a long train of accusations and arrests that culminated in the purges of the Great Terror.[18]

The small American diplomatic colony, however, blamed the deterioration on Russian violations of the Roosevelt-Litvinov agreements. Much time was spent on the essentially trivial matter of Soviet assumption of the Provisional Government's debts, but no conclusion was reached. Roosevelt, who was willing to take "a very liberal view" of any settlement, left most of the negotiating to Bullitt. The ambassador took an opposing stance, however, and became increasingly angry at the Soviet refusal to see the matter his way.* "Any representative of the Soviet Union who suggests [direct credits] should, I think, have his face stamped on promptly," he advised.

* Initially Bullitt did make a distinction between ethnic Russians and a Soviet minority, based upon a certain obvious prejudice. Some official Soviet nastiness, he complained to R. Walton Moore, resulted from "the influence of Mr. Umanski, the wretched little kike . . . The Foreign Office, as you know, has been purged recently of all its non-Jewish members, and it is perhaps only natural that we should find the members of that race more difficult to deal with than the Russians themselves. The Moscow Soviet, which is straight Russian, has been altogether friendly and cooperative." Bullitt was apparently unaware that Stalin shared his prejudice.

The debt question was shelved at the beginning of 1935. Most of the Americans, not recognizing any inconsistency in their own position, blamed the Russians for bad faith.[19]

Bullitt viewed it as a piercing personal insult, as well as a violation of the most important of the agreements, when the Communist Third International, otherwise known as the Comintern, invited a contingent from the American Communist Party to attend its Seventh Congress in Moscow. He failed to see that the convocation, held in Moscow in the summer of 1935, was belated penance for the hostility of the Sixth Congress in 1928, which had attacked social democrats as "social fascists," split the left in Europe, and thus helped open the way for Adolf Hitler's accession to power. This Seventh Congress was meant to change the party line with a call for broad antifascist popular fronts.[20]

Bullitt now swung to the other extreme. He raised with Washington the question of breaking diplomatic relations.[21] He wanted to attack Moscow from Moscow; he encouraged journalists to write anti-Bolshevik articles; he "deviled" the Russians. He no longer had any desire to stay in Russia.[22] He was in ill-health, and feared the psychological consequences of remaining in Moscow. The Polish ambassador had already suffered a nervous breakdown, and the British ambassador seemed close to one on the day he confided to Bullitt, "I feel like a prisoner pacing my garden between banks of snow, unable to escape." In March of 1936, Bullitt wrote plaintively, "Russia is a good country for pine trees, St. Bernard dogs, and polar bears, and I must say frankly I long to be at home again." In the middle of the year he left Moscow for good, and assumed the ambassadorship in Paris.[23]

The repudiation by Wilson and Lloyd George at Versailles now paled before the much greater rejection he felt the Russians had dealt him. It was as though promises made to him personally had been broken. He left, hurt, insulted, embittered. In October 1934, while the honeymoon was still on, in what was an optimistic report about Soviet developments, he had written: "No generalization on the Soviet Union can have more than momentary validity." But within a few months he himself had adopted generalizations to which he would cling for the rest of his life. Before departing Moscow in 1936, he summarized his views. Nothing remained of the Bullitt of 1919: "The problem of relations with the Government of the Soviet Union is, therefore, a subordinate part of the problem presented by communism as a militant faith determined to produce world revolution and the 'liquidation' (that is to say, murder) of all non-believers." In the face of this danger, there was little the United States could do save "to encourage reconciliation between France and Germany." Bullitt, and apparently some of those he left behind in the embassy, believed that only Nazi Germany could stay the advance of Soviet Bolshevism into Europe. "With respect to the Soviet Union," he had written the year before his departure, "the countries of Europe are rapidly falling into the situation of the squabbling city states of Greece with respect to Macedonia. Athens and Sparta, France and Germany, Philip of Macedon — Stalin. I don't like the comparison but can not get it out of my mind."

With Bullitt's departure, the career officers in the embassy dug in. Bullitt's opinions were fully in accord with, and indeed partly shaped by their own, and they were prepared for their little Cold War with the Soviet authorities. Several months after Bullitt's departure, Arthur Bliss Lane, the American minister in Riga, noted that there was no change, "even a particle [in] the policy which was pursued by the former Ambassador since the disillusionment of 1935." The hard line was supported almost wholeheartedly in the embassy. If one had taken a snapshot of the career staff sometime during those first couple of years of relations, it would have shown many of the men who were to become the State Department experts on Soviet and communist affairs in the middle and late 1940s, the era of the origins of the Cold War and the rise of the national security state.[24]

Loy Henderson, one of the founders of the Soviet Service and a major figure in the history of the Foreign Service, was already emerging as the leader of this loosely defined but highly influential group; he was a man of strong opinions, considerable ability, steadfast loyalties, and an integrity that impressed those who worked with him throughout the State Department. As Lane commented: "Mr. Henderson, through his tact, ability, and firmness, has made an enviable reputation for himself." Born in the Ozarks, Henderson always thought of himself as coming from "the old pioneering culture which had to go" but nonetheless resented the "urban blight" that "helped to destroy the code of ethics and ideals." A stiff right arm, the result of boyhood roughhousing, kept him out of the Army during World

War I, so he joined the Red Cross, worked in repatriating Russian prisoners, and then — fearing that the Bolsheviks might capitalize on misery — helped deliver relief assistance to Lithuania in 1919. During the next few years, he was a witness to abortive leftist uprisings in Germany. Almost from the beginning, then, he had concluded that Bolshevik Russia was a threat to world peace and stability. Joining the Foreign Service, he started working on Soviet affairs in 1925 and was assigned to the Riga observation post. He became a fascinated but unsympathetic and, in the Kelley tradition, unemotional student of Soviet affairs. In Moscow he became the senior political officer, and, in effect, embassy administrator as well.[25]

If Henderson was the dominant member of the group, George Kennan was its chief ideologue. The Foreign Service was for him almost a family, a home, and this was important to a man who always tended to feel like an outsider. This feeling had already developed by the time he was a Princeton undergraduate in the early 1920s; indeed, upon reading the description, by fellow Princetonian F. Scott Fitzgerald, in *The Great Gatsby* of a Midwesterner's reaction to the fashionable East, Kennan was moved to tears. He was taken by the notion that he would follow the course of a relative with whom he shared a birthday, another George Kennan — cousin of his grandfather, traveler and diplomat in late Czarist times — and become a major figure in the history of Russia and the West. So he would. Throughout his diplomatic career, the younger George Kennan attached himself as a kind of court intellectual and explicator to men of power. He was known as "Bullitt's bright boy." In 1935, when Kennan was recuperating from an illness in Vienna, Bullitt wrote back to Washington: "He is the best officer I have had here and I could release *two* officers when he returns. But I want to be sure he can stand Moscow. The climate is not easy. It is now May 10 and we have had snow five times this week. I want to have Kennan but not kill him." Troubled by ulcers, with an expression that seemed somewhat ascetic, Kennan struck others as arrogant, high-strung, ambitious, and very bright. A fitness report from Riga in 1933 listed these qualities: "excellent mind, supple and penetrating, and well balanced, save perhaps for a tendency . . . to entertain intellectual concepts rather emotionally, and to be a trifle more enthusiastically idealistic or more hopelessly cynical, than would be the case if he were a little more mature." Kennan liked to think of himself as a realist, with a keen eye for power and the less obvious traits of a man's character; but as one historian has written, "In George Frost Kennan, the Presbyterian elder wrestled with the Bismarckian geopolitician." The struggle within him was joined as well by a romantic who fancied a "mysterious affinity" with Russia and imagined himself friend and heir to the cultured turn-of-the-century intelligentsia, whose way of life had been destroyed by the Bolsheviks.

He cared much about style, in both personal manner and his prose; he had a fondness for the upper classes around the world. Much later in life, he described himself as "a conservative person, a natural-born antiquarian, a firm believer in the need for continuity across the generations in form and ceremony." Like Henderson, he felt that he had not only left and lost his American roots, but that America had left him. And like the White Russians with whom he mixed so happily and nostalgically in Berlin and Riga, he too was an émigré, though his was an exile of the spirit.[26]

Two others in this imaginary snapshot stand out. Charles Bohlen was, in background and approach, the perfect exemplar of the diplomat, a graceful, charming master of technique, less emotional and less committed than his peers, "most capable" but with an "apparently carefree attitude" (in the words of one American in Moscow). His father had been a gentleman of leisure, and he had traveled a good deal in Europe with his mother, receiving part of his education there. His friends at Harvard, from which he was graduated in 1927, became bankers, lawyers, and stockbrokers; Bohlen joined the Foreign Service. Two years after Kennan, he entered the Russian specialization program. Kennan attributes to him "a leading place in the formative influences" on his own understanding of Soviet communism. Yet at first, because he was slightly less in thrall to the Riga heritage, his views were not so well defined; he was more willing to follow the lead of others, neither tied to one position nor feeling the need to take a position, more adaptable to changing lines.[27]

Elbridge Durbrow, a short, energetic, voluble Yale graduate who had served in Rumania and Poland, was skeptical from the beginning. He did not have the same academic training as those from Riga, and was always outspoken, blunt, and categoric in his views. In his first year and a half, as vice consul in Moscow, he listened to perhaps 200 workers from the U.S., either Russian-born or native American, who had been lured to the Soviet Union during the

Depression by the false promise of high-paying jobs. "I learned a lot about the damned place, talking to those guys who were workers and wanted to go back to the U.S.," he recalled. "The Revolution didn't have a good reputation . . . When you once went there and lived and looked out the window and saw what the hell it was like, it confirmed your worst fears."

The American mission was in the new style; continuing the Riga tradition and having little consular work, it allowed its members to engage in study and analysis. The discussions and debates went on daily, endlessly, in the embassy. "There were differences between us," Loy Henderson remembered. "While we all agreed what was the situation in the Soviet Union, the differences were about the extent to which we should allow the situation to affect relations between the U.S. and the USSR." The environment encouraged a common view among the officers; their "education," after the pleasant confusion of the honeymoon, led them back to a simplification, to a restatement of the Riga axioms. Alexander Kirk, Charles Thayer, Edward Page, and others who served there in the 1930s for the most part shared the same ideas. One of the few exceptions was the chief military attaché, Colonel Philip Faymonville. He lived apart, and the opinion in which he was held by the others is suggested by the brief description in Bohlen's memoirs: "pink-faced."[28]

Certain factors reinforced the cohesiveness of the group and its outlook. The living conditions made the embassy staff feel isolated, even embattled; they perceived themselves under siege, as if in rehearsal for the Cold War. Informal socializing with Russians ended, and the American diplomats could not join a sports club. Food was bad, the Russians were truculent, and life was not easy. Harassments of all sorts increased. Observation and spying became so obvious that at one point Kennan recommended against having an ambassador in Moscow at all.[29] It was like living in a land where "you were officially billeted as a sort of representative of the devil, evil and dangerous, and to be shunned," he wrote in a 1938 memoir. "Personal friendship, like some powerful curse, would spell ruin for those to whom it attached itself."

The effects of the purges, with their great trials and sudden disappearances, on the image of the Soviet Union held by the American diplomats cannot be exaggerated. The assassination of Kirov inaugurated a second phase of Stalinism — the orgy of terror, now directed against the apparatus of state and party. The unprecedented and spectacular show trials — conducted not only in the major cities but in almost every *oblast* — delivered their requisite output, an endless series of perfectly outlandish confessions, which "proved" that Trotskyites and foreign agents honeycombed Soviet society with their conspiracies. Millions suffered directly in this holocaust. In the simple words of Roy Medvedev, "Between 1936 and 1938 Stalin broke all records for political terror." Dread became a basic ingredient of Soviet life. By 1939 the purges had helped to establish firmly a highly centralized, bureaucratic, terror-driven totalitarian state, and the entire nation had become the servant of the state and of its ruler.

How could one react to this spectacle, save with shock and horror? The terror accentuated all the fears of the American diplomats; in its total impact, it erased whatever doubts the men in the Soviet Service may have had about the character of the regime. It was as though they were watching some barbaric blood sacrifice. "No one seems to know who will be the next to disappear," Henderson wrote Robert Kelley in April 1937. "Since, during the last ten years, it has been almost impossible for anyone to survive in the Soviet Union unless he broke a law now and then, and since nearly every person at some time or another in an unguarded moment has made statements critical of certain policies or Soviet leaders, there is practically no one who does not have a guilty conscience." Henderson discounted one explanation of the purges; he did not think that Stalin was anti-Semitic, though he did think it likely that Stalin would be "impatient and distrustful of persons with the mentality possessed by so many Eastern European Jews." But he admitted that those in the embassy could not explain the "weird developments" taking place. "It would almost appear as though Stalin is trying to discredit some predecessor who has been ruling the country unwisely for the last 15 years." Still, on balance, Henderson believed at the time that there might be some truth in the charges. "Undoubtedly by this process many thoroughly rotten branches are being lopped off the Soviet tree. One is beginning to wonder, however, how much hacking and pruning will be necessary before good solid wood is to be found."

Well into 1938, the debates continued in the Moscow embassy: Why did the purges start? What was their aim? Was Stalin mad? Did he have some other plan in mind? How much truth was there in the charges? Kennan, assigned back to the State Department in

Washington, occupied himself during much of the hot summer with the hundreds of pages of testimony from the Radek trial, studying everything he could find on opposition activities since the death of Lenin, using note cards and chronologies in an effort to reconstruct something that "made more sense than the monstrous accusations and absurd confessions which were put forward for the edification of the outside world." [30]

The American specialists found their place on the periphery of these events disorienting, even shattering: they lost whatever channels and contacts they once had had into Soviet society. By 1937 the purges had made their isolation virtually complete. Former friends would purposely turn away at the opera. By then it was already well known that the favored method of execution was a bullet in the back of the head. The mysterious "Baron" Boris Steiger, the only trusted informal link to the Kremlin and the conduit for delivering Edgeworth pipe tobacco from the American embassy to Stalin, told Charles Thayer, "It is very dangerous weather, very treacherous. At times like these one must be very careful to protect the back of one's head." Soon after, Steiger was tapped on the shoulder while dining with some Americans at the Hotel Metropole; his execution was announced a short time later. "No arrest in recent years, not even that of the highest Soviet officials, has made such an impression upon the Diplomatic Corps," Henderson reported. Steiger was the only Soviet official who had ever talked with a foreign diplomat "as though he were an intelligent human being," Henderson added. "The others continuously told him things which only a person with a childish intellect could believe."

The Americans learned that, one after another, many of the highest officials — civilian, military, even secret police — were arrested, tried, executed, or had simply disappeared. One of the most searing experiences was the trial whose defendants included the Bolshevik theoretician Bukharin, with whom some of the Americans had found communication possible, even entertaining. Bohlen listened as Bukharin dueled with the prosecutor, Andrei Vyshinsky, in some language he could not understand. When he finally heard the sentences in this trial — "to be shot . . . to be shot . . . to be shot . . ." — he felt dizzy, as though his head were coming off, and for a month after he could not easily sleep.

The Americans felt that those Bolsheviks whom they might in

some ways have respected and talked to — the intellectuals, those that were civilized and cosmopolitan — had all been wiped out. Stalin, in contrast, seemed irrational, fanatical, with a lust for power that knew no bounds, with a ruthlessness that was total and an incapacity for trust that was complete. In his memoirs, Kennan seems to backdate his conclusion, but nevertheless to assess accurately the ultimate impact of the trials: "a sort of liberal education in the horrors of Stalinism." Stalin was not merely a dictator, he was a tyrant. Those who did survive in positions of leadership seemed so mediocre and intimidated, so compromised, that their consciences and minds must have been heavily mortgaged to the General Secretary of the Party. In the most fundamental way, there seemed something totally corrupt about Stalin and his entourage. Ever after, the American specialists could not, no matter what the circumstances, think of Stalin and his associates without recalling the blood on their hands.[31]

Leninism had posed the first of the crucial questions about the Soviet Union — what was the relationship between its ideology and its behavior in the international system? Now Stalinism underlined in a stark fashion the second of the two questions — what was the connection between domestic totalitarianism and Soviet foreign policy? As with the first, there was no easy answer. Certainly, the American diplomats were correct in their judgment about the corruption of the Stalinist system. Indeed, if anything, they were restrained, for they were able to see only the surface of the terror, for it has taken many years since for Westerners to begin to learn the full extent of Stalin's tyranny. Still, those diplomats concluded that the connection between the character of the state and its foreign policy was necessary and complete, that a totalitarian system at home meant a totalitarian foreign policy. If their answer was too categoric, even mistaken, one can understand — seeing what they did of collectivization, of the purges, of the daily life of terror and hypocrisy — why they came to it.

The group's sense of unity was made even stronger by what it felt to be attacks coming from another source as well — Washington, D.C. These "attacks" heightened its feeling of isolation, and confirmed its perception that the New Deal was an enemy. The first blow came in the figure of Joseph Davies, Bullitt's much-resented successor as ambassador. Conventional Cold War history, like the Riga School itself, has portrayed Davies as naïve, muddle-headed, and dishonest — a dangerous, meddling fool. That view is inaccurate.[32] Davies, a Wisconsin lawyer who had made a fortune representing Standard Oil and had married a General Foods heiress, had remained a staunch progressive. As a reward for serving as one of Woodrow Wilson's campaign managers in 1912, he had been offered the Moscow ambassadorship after Wilson's victory, but opted instead for the chairmanship of the Federal Trade Commission. During World War I, he became devoted to the future presidential prospects of Assistant Navy Secretary Franklin D. Roosevelt. Eventually one of the largest contributors to Roosevelt's presidential campaign chests, he was chosen to replace Bullitt in Moscow. Preceded by rumors that he would be accompanied by "5 servants, 25 ice boxes and a thirst for entertaining," he arrived in the Russian capital early in 1937. He opened himself to a certain kind of ridicule — he spent much time on his yacht anchored at Leningrad, and because of a bad stomach he ate frozen foods shipped from abroad. On other matters the ridicule was misspent. He was not completely hoodwinked by the purge trials. His dispatches show the same confusion as did those of the career officers. He found the trials "horrible" and a "shock to our mentality," and declared that "the terror here is a horrifying fact." The Soviet Union, he said, was "a tyranny, without any protection whatever to the Proletariat of 'Life, Liberty and the pursuit of happiness.' "

But Davies' political role clashed with the traditional career mission of Foreign Service officers. He was not sent to Moscow to study and analyze and report facts but, in the context of Roosevelt's growing concern with the European crisis, "to win the confidence of Stalin." His messages were composed not only for an audience in Washington but also for one in Moscow; he was sure the Russians would get wind one way or another of what he was saying. But before Davies got to Moscow, the officers, angered by what they took to be Roosevelt's slighting of the new traditions of the Soviet Service by the dispatch of this "unserious" ambassador, were already making fun of him, raising complaints and planning revolts — to such an extent that Loy Henderson felt the need to send around a sharp memorandum, prior to Davies' arrival, ordering the staff to treat the new ambassador with respect.[33] Although the open complaining was reduced, the basic animosity did not abate. Only Loy Henderson, though convinced that Moscow was not a place for ambassadors "with a political turn of mind," succeeded in establishing a more cordial relationship.*

The others, especially Bullitt's former protégé, George Kennan, resented Davies' close relationship with British and American journalists and his tendency to review developments with them rather than with the staff. Moreover, Davies rejected their outlook: he thought the fundamental tenets of the "revolutionary state" were wrong. He believed that communism by its nature had to fail, that Stalinist Russia had retreated into state socialism, that it was not necessary to fuss about the Comintern because its influence was small in America, and that communism was not a threat to the United States. He also thought Soviet Russia could prove an important factor in the power equation on the European continent. The embassy staff endured all this only with reluctance; they were greatly relieved when he was assigned to Brussels in 1938. Davies thereafter remained for the Soviet specialists the archetype of the fuzzy-minded American liberal who refused to see the truth as they saw it.[34]

The diplomats were also shocked and upset when, in 1937, the State Department's European Division absorbed the Eastern European Division, which had nurtured them and shaped the tradition in which they worked. "We have been liquidated," Robert Kelley wrote. They perceived the amalgamation as a threat to their own expertise, and were dismayed at what seemed to be Kelley's enforced transfer to a post in Turkey. The group suspected a "plot" by left-wing New Dealers, perhaps even Eleanor Roosevelt and Harry Hopkins.[35]

Yet it seems that the Riga group had misconstrued the "plot." The sudden action — it had been effected largely over one weekend — was a coup of sorts, part of a struggle between Assistant Secretary of State Sumner Welles on one side, and, on the other, Hull and R. Walton Moore, also an Assistant Secretary of State.[36] In addition, the Mexican Division had been eliminated a short time before and the dismantling of the Eastern European Division was part of the same effort to make the Department more efficient.

There had been considerable unhappiness with the insularity of the Eastern European Division. Arthur Bliss Lane, for instance,

* Indeed, when Davies died two decades later, Henderson was one of his pallbearers.

whose anticommunist credentials were impeccable, had been complaining for some time that those who worked in it, "as a result of overspecialization on Russian affairs, have come to think in terms of Russia as a separate entity, rather than in terms of Russia's relationship to Europe and the rest of the world." The Division could not comprehend, he declared, "that the Eastern European area (with the possible exception of Russia) is in itself perhaps the least important of all the areas in the world with which the United States has to deal." * "I entirely agree with you as to the narrowness of the system which seems to have grown up in the Eastern European area," James Dunn, a senior official of the European Division and a strong anticommunist himself, wrote to Lane. Conservative men continued to direct the Department's policy toward Russia, and Kennan in fact was brought home to assist in the enterprise.[37]

Such changes, however, were more organizational than ideological. Circumstances and experience had confirmed predispositions and reinvigorated what had been the dominant American diplomatic response to the Bolshevik Revolution. By the end of the 1930s, the image of the revolutionary state and the ideas associated with it had become firmly fixed in the minds of the Soviet specialists and in those of people, like Bullitt, who had "learned" with them. "I am inclined to believe that all of us who have been in close contact with the thing itself gradually come to a common point of view," Henderson observed in 1940. "There are a few exceptions among the chaps who are emotional and likely to become prejudiced." So codified had these beliefs become that we can now lay them out as axioms — though we must be careful not to confuse axioms with blinding dogma.[38]

Doctrine and ideology and a spirit of innate aggressiveness shaped Soviet policy, the specialists believed. Thus, the USSR was committed to world revolution and unlimited expansion. In consequence, the United States, not just the countries around the Russian rim, was under siege and had to be continually vigilant. The "breach" of 1919 was still very real, to be bridged only by a major transformation.[39]

* We shall have occasion to return to this statement when we consider the controversy between the United States and the Soviet Union after World War II.

Curiously, however, for all their fanatical devotion to ideology, the Soviet leaders were cool thinkers, much cooler than their Western counterparts. "They are realists, if ever there are any realists in this world," wrote Ambassador Laurence Steinhardt, Davies' successor, in 1940. The Soviet leaders always set their goals with supreme clarity. To an extent greater than that of most countries, Henderson wrote in 1936, Russian policy "has before it a series of definite objectives." Soviet officials are judged by "the progress" they can make "in the direction of those objectives." The Russians were always surefooted, and were masters of strategy and tactics.

The historian must here observe that the axiomatic notion that the Soviets worked by a foreign affairs plan, derived from ideology and with definite objectives, not only gave them more credit than they deserved, but also proved to be a central weakness in the assessments of Soviet policy after the war. For it led U.S. officials to exaggerate the policy coherence of the Kremlin — the role of ideology and conscious intentions. At the same time they understated the role played by accident, confusion, and uncertainty in Russian policy and also mistook mere reaction for planned action. A similar pattern, no doubt, would exist on the other side; what Americans would regard as their efforts to muddle through, in response to this or that problem, would be seen by the Soviets as part of a larger calculated policy. Indeed, one might even go further and hypothesize that there is a general tendency in international relations to exaggerate the policy coherence of an adversary.

In the eyes of American officials in the 1930s, the Soviet Union was also dangerous and untrustworthy because it was a completely immoral state, placing no value on human life. The effect of Stalin's terror was a powerful one. In 1938, Kennan recalled how he would gaze out from his window on Red Square and the "snow-covered towers . . . with the big Asiatic carrion-crows wheeling overhead against a leaden sky, as though they sense that they were over one of the bloodiest spots in the world." The image of the carrion birds was appropriate in another way, for the Russians were the scavengers of war and international crisis. "War will mean such horrible suffering that it will end in general revolution," Bullitt wrote in 1936. "The only winners will be Stalin and Company." [40]

Underlying all these assumptions was a view of the collective "personality" of the Soviet leaders. Aggressiveness and insecurity coexisted in their minds in such a way that they were geared for permanent warfare. It should be considered "axiomatic," Henderson wrote in 1938, that the Soviet leaders regard the presence of foreign diplomats "as an evil which world conditions force them to endure." Such attitudes on the part of the Russians made impossible almost any kind of constructive relations with them.

The American officials believed that the Soviet outlook reflected a merger of Bolshevik doctrine and practice with Russian national character. In a lecture delivered in 1938, important because it shows the origin of his postwar "Mr. X" article and the Freudian concepts that influenced it, Kennan chose to skip over the "hackneyed question of how far Bolshevism has changed Russia" to take up instead the question of "how far Russia has changed Bolshevism." The natural environment, especially the Asiatic frontier (generating fear, concern for "face," and a "vague feeling of universalism"); the Black Sea civilization; the Byzantine Church (with its adherence to dogma and its intolerance and intrigues); the backwardness of the country as compared to the West — all these had given rise to a state "with a very definite personality." Kennan continued: "After all, nations, like individuals, are largely the products of their environment; and many of their characteristics, their fears and their neuroses, as well as their abilities, are conditioned by the impressions of what we may call their early childhood." He saw powerful continuities, both in internal and foreign affairs, of life under the Czars and under Stalin.[41]

Confronted by such a potential adversary, the United States needed to adopt a stance of wariness and constant vigilance. Great patience and a counterassertiveness, an explicit "toughness," were required to cope with the Russian "personality." Steinhardt wrote to Henderson in October 1940: "Approaches by Britain or the United States must be interpreted here as signs of weakness and the best policy to pursue is one of aloofness, indicating strength . . . As you know from your own experiences, the moment these people here get it into their heads that we are 'appeasing them, making up to them or need them,' they immediately stop being cooperative . . . My experience has been that they respond only to force and if force cannot be applied, then to straight oriental bartering or trading methods . . . That, in my opinion, is the only language they understand and the only language productive of results."[42] The conclusion, therefore, was that diplomacy with the Soviet Union was not merely a questionable venture, but downright dangerous.

By the end of the 1930s, the Soviet specialists and those associated with them held a fully developed image of the Soviet Union as a world revolutionary state. It was an elaboration of the outlook associated with Riga, emerging from the original Wilsonian nonrecognition of the Bolshevik Revolution, but intensified by their experience since recognition, especially by the only partly glimpsed horrors of Stalinism. The diplomats had a language for describing Soviet Russia and its role in international relations, and they had an idiom as well, as Steinhardt had declared, for speaking *to* the Russians.

The Nazi-Soviet nonaggression pact, initialed in Moscow on August 23, 1939, was not the shock to the Soviet specialists that it was to the Popular Front left. As early as May 1937, Henderson had predicted "extremely interesting developments in Soviet-German relations during the next two years." He did not think that the Soviet Union would "formally drop its international revolutionary ideas and adopt a frankly dictatorial form of government" to appease the Nazis, but it might subordinate the German communists to the exigencies of an "understanding" if Hitler would show greater friendship toward Russia and gradually stop "his campaign against international Jewry." Henderson explained: "Please don't gather the impression from the last condition mentioned that I feel that the Soviet Union is being dominated by the Jews. Nevertheless, I am convinced that the Soviet Union realizes that, by and large, the international Jewry is an important supporter of it in international affairs, and I further believe that it would prefer, at the present time at least, to continue to have bad relations with Germany than to allow the internationally-minded Jews of the world to feel that it has left them in the lurch." [43]

The events that followed the 1939 pact — the Soviet role in the partition of Poland, the winter war in Finland, the annexation of the Balkan states and Bessarabia — all of these steps involving deportations and further extension of the terror — confirmed the Riga viewpoint, and gave its advocates the confidence to speak even more categorically. The war with Finland, in general, mobilized anti-Soviet sentiment in the United States and chilled Russo-American relations. The abhorrence that had fed DeWitt Clinton Poole's strictures two decades before returned, and with greater force.[44]

Even at the highest levels the Riga image regained acceptance. In the middle of 1940 Loy Henderson challenged his superiors: "Is the

Government of the United States to apply certain standards of judgment and conduct to aggression by Germany and Japan, and not to Soviet aggression?" The answer came now: Germany and Russia were two of a kind; they were totalitarian dictatorships. Cordell Hull, on the eve of the German invasion of Russia, summarized the knowledge gleaned in the 1930s: "Basing ourselves upon our own experiences and upon observations of the experiences of other governments," U.S. policy toward the Soviet Union called for making "no approaches to the Soviet Government," treating any Soviet approaches with reserve, and rendering "no sacrifices in principle in order to improve relations." [45]

These axioms seemed to explain satisfactorily Russia's role in world politics and to delineate an appropriate course for the United States to follow. They dominated interpretations of events until the German invasion of Russia in the night of June 21–22, 1941.[46] With that, the Riga axioms suffered a startling loss of relevance. A new phase began in Soviet-American relations, which led to an experience radically different from that of the Soviet Service during the interwar years. A fresh image, based upon other assumptions, came to the fore. In addition, procedures were established for handling political problems that bypassed the State Department.[47]

Those who had been on the front lines of the small interwar cold war now found themselves sidetracked. Their interpretations and explanations no longer fitted the situation. The men who had formulated them feared that Roosevelt was a deluded dreamer, that he was following the mistaken and dangerous path of Joseph Davies. But it did not matter what they thought; they had become an ineffective opposition. Henderson fought as hard as he could against the new Roosevelt policy and the practices that would implement it. He did not want to see the United States "scrap these principles [of] normal international intercourse," but he knew that policy was not being devised "by such persons like myself, but by the highest authorities of our Government." He wrote to Samuel Harper in March 1942, "These are interesting times here in Washington, but you may be sure of one thing — it is not the most agreeable situation in which to carry on." Finally, overruled too many times, he decided to carry on no longer. Having asked to be relieved of his duties as head of the Russian section of the European Division in 1943, he was exiled to the post of chief of mission in Iraq.

Charles Bohlen succeeded him in Washington, and, initially at least, continued to argue the Riga view. However, Bohlen was coopted into Roosevelt's immediate foreign policy circle and became liaison man between the State Department and the White House. As such, his attachment to the Riga axioms relaxed, and he found himself accepting with cautious optimism Roosevelt's assumptions. In February 1945, George Kennan wrote Bohlen a personal letter in which he called for a spheres-of-influence division of Europe, but really for the formation of an anti-Soviet bloc. Kennan criticized Soviet influence in Eastern and Central Europe as "so dangerous to everything which we need to see preserved in Europe."

"I don't believe for one minute that there has been any time in this war when we could seriously have done very differently than we did," Bohlen wrote back. "Isn't it a question of realities and not bits of paper? Either our pals intend to limit themselves or they don't. I submit, as the British say, that the answer is not yet clear. But what is clear is that the Soyuz [Soviet Union] is here to stay, as one of the major factors in the world. Quarreling with them would be so easy, but we can always come to that." [48]

Kennan had laid out his own opposition almost four years earlier in a letter to Loy Henderson, two days after the German attack on Russia. In every border country in Europe "Russia is generally more feared than Germany." To welcome Russia "as an associate in defense of democracy" would be to identify the United States with Soviet oppression of Eastern Europe and with the domestic policy of a regime "which is widely feared and detested throughout this part of the world." Kennan was not alarmed, in the early days of the war, by the exercise of German power on the European continent. "It cannot be said that German policy is motivated by any sadistic desire to see other people suffer under German rule," he wrote in April 1941. "On the contrary, Germans are most anxious that their new subjects should be happy in their care; they are willing to make what seems to them important compromises to achieve this result, and they are unable to understand why these measures should not be successful." [49] Kennan was, in fact, primarily occupied with non-Russian subjects during the war, first in Germany (where he was interned for a time after America joined the war), then in Lisbon and London until the summer of 1944.

Elbridge Durbrow did eventually become head of a reconstituted Eastern European Division, and warnings continued to flow from the

State Department, as they had in the time of Kelley, regarding Russia's revolutionary goals, its lust for power and territory, its duplicity, and the dangers of appeasement. The alarms were not heard.

United States policy toward the Soviet Union was now out of the hands of the State Department. In an environment sharply transformed from that of the interwar years, the Riga School was being made obsolete by the bold new span Roosevelt was constructing to bridge the breach between America and Russia in the postwar era.[50]

> . . . the glaring and dangerous defect of nearly all thinking, both academic and popular, about international politics in English-speaking countries from 1919 to 1939 — the almost total neglect of the factor of power.
>
> — E. H. CARR, *The Twenty-Years Crisis*, 1939

> The time had come to be realistic.
>
> — FRANKLIN ROOSEVELT, 1941 [1]

II

The Yalta Axioms: Roosevelt's Grand Design

ONE EVENING in March of 1943, British Foreign Secretary Anthony Eden dined privately at the White House with President Roosevelt and Harry Hopkins. The three fell into a long, ruminating conversation that continued late into the night. With an ease available only to men who number themselves among the handful of arbiters over the world's destiny, they surveyed the outstanding political questions of the entire planet, playing with borders, shifting governments like so many chess pieces, guessing at the political shadings that would color the postwar map. "A conjuror, skillfully juggling with balls of dynamite," was the way Eden remembered Roosevelt from that night. "The big question which rightly dominated Roosevelt's mind was whether it was possible to work with Russia now and after the war," he recalled.

Roosevelt asked Eden what he thought of the "Bullitt Thesis," referring to a lengthy memorandum, based upon the Riga axioms, that Bullitt had sent to the White House several weeks earlier. Bullitt, whose enthusiasms of ten years before had long since soured into fear and alarm, predicted that the Russians would succeed in communizing the Continent — unless the United States and Britain blocked "the flow of the Red amoeba into Europe."

Eden replied that a definite answer to this question was impossible. But "even if these fears were to prove correct," he continued, "we should make the position no worse by trying to work with Russia and by assuming that Stalin meant what he said." Eden agreed with Roosevelt that it would be better to proceed on a premise contrary to Bullitt's — that it would be possible to find some system of working *with*, rather than *against*, the Soviet Union. Roosevelt also did not think that a categoric answer existed. He believed Soviet goals and methods would be partly determined by Stalin's own estimate of American and British intentions and capabilities.[2]

Certainly the most important goal of Roosevelt's wartime diplomacy was the establishment of a basis for postwar cooperation with the Soviet Union. He had a clear conception of the postwar settlement he wanted and how it might be achieved. This conception was also governed by a number of axioms, some of which had predated the war, some of which had emerged in the course of the war. Roosevelt's axioms were always more tentative than those of Riga, but at their center point, there also lay an image — derived from experience, assessment, and optimism — of Soviet Russia.

Secretary of War Henry Stimson once grumbled about Roosevelt's "confounded happy-go-luckiness." [3] This habit of deferral, a tendency to charmingly wave away a problem, was an oft-remarked characteristic of the President. But he had not put off thinking about the postwar world, and early on he had taken as his first premise that this peace would have to be based upon the realities of power.

Shortly after the Eden visit, he had opened a public window on his thinking. A journalist named Forrest Davis had stayed a weekend in the White House, talking with the President about his ideas for the postwar world. The article, checked over in advance by the President, appeared in the *Saturday Evening Post* in the spring of 1943. Word filtered through the State Department that the article was to be regarded as authoritative; it expressed the "Old Man's Grand Design."

This new peace had to be based upon "the factor of power," Davis wrote. The Versailles System had collapsed because of the failure to include power considerations in the post–World War I peace settlement. The League of Nations had been an idealistic dream, without proper foundations. "Aspirations toward a better world" were not Roosevelt's primary concern, but rather, "the cold, realistic techniques, or instruments, needed to make those aspirations work . . . The question was one of power among the victors. How would they use their power?"

Davis made clear Roosevelt's assumption that the United States would participate in the peace. The Soviet Union would also have to be brought in. "With Germany reduced and France in ruins," Davis wrote, "Russia becomes the only first-rate military power on the continent." [4]

Such an approach separated Roosevelt from most American planning for the postwar world, both in and outside government. When he continued to speak of Woodrow Wilson as "my President," he had more in mind than merely his service during World War I as Assistant Secretary of the Navy. For he remained committed to the Wilsonian goals of (as he expressed it) a "better world, an ordered world."

But, as he remarked once, not long after first becoming President, he had also learned Woodrow Wilson's mistakes. He searched for more "realistic" methods with which to solve the major postwar problems of Germany and Japan; of preserving peace, countering aggression, and preventing instability; of maintaining the victors' alliance and calmly settling the inevitable disputes among them. To complicate matters, the machinery had to be agreeable to the American people, for without an adequate popular consensus, the United States could not play the leading role Roosevelt envisioned for it. The thought of creating such machinery delighted him, for he gloried in the manipulation of power. This renegade Wilsonian, for that is what he was — mindful of the lessons of the preceding quarter century, a much more subtle and pragmatic politician than the preceding war President, more sensitive to the nuances of personality and of international relations — planned to use spheres of influence and other more traditional tactics from the "old diplomacy" in order to create a new system.[5]

For that centerpiece of the Wilsonian vision, the League of Nations, he had no patience. Though he had campaigned for the League in 1920, he had dismissed it by 1935 as "nothing more than a debating society and a poor one at that." At the Atlantic Conference in August 1941, he steadfastly refused even to include mention of a new international organization in the Atlantic Charter, despite British entreaties that this omission would be tragic. Such a reference, the President insisted, would only create suspicion and opposition in the United States. "The time had come to be realistic," he said. He might, he allowed, support some organization after a long transition period, but at best such an organization would only be a safety valve, of no political significance.[6]

For Roosevelt, the only sensible way to organize a new international order was on the basis of a consortium of the Great Powers, in which the United States would play an active role. Less than two months after Pearl Harbor, he was complaining that Churchill had not given much thought to the postwar world and to how "the German problem" was to be solved. The United States would have to take a hand "to the extent of joining in the police work for a time." After all, explained the President, "somebody had to be in a position if there were signs of Germany breaking loose again to crack down on them hard." [7]

Soon Roosevelt — with his gift of locating major problems in the idiom of a friendly village, for which, no doubt, he was the country squire — was talking about international "sheriffs" and the Four Policemen — the U.S., Britain, Russia, and China. In 1942 and 1943, he outlined to both Soviet Foreign Minister Molotov (who visited him under the pseudonym "Mr. Brown") and Anthony Eden his vision of the wartime alliance made permanent, in the form of the Four Policemen who "would maintain sufficient armed force to impose peace."

China brought a skeptical reaction from both foreign ministers. Eden thought China might well have to go through a revolution after the war, and he frankly "did not much like the idea of the Chinese running up and down the Pacific." China was one of Roosevelt's great illusions, rather surprising for one fixed upon the idea of power. But he feared that a weak China would give rise to a Spanish Civil War on a grand scale, and hoped that treating it as a Great Power would assist the country in solving its internal problems. He also thought that an Asian policeman was necessary to meet Asian nationalism and help control Japan, and that China could act as a barrier to Soviet influence.[8]

By the time of Eden's visit in the spring of 1943, however, public opinion was already forcing Roosevelt to disguise his Great Power consortium in a Wilsonian garb. He was a President very sensitive to the mood of the populace. During the 1930s, he had regarded the national temper of isolationism as a powerful constraint, preventing him from bringing American influence to bear on the developing conflicts in Europe and Asia. Public opinion hemmed him in. Just two months before Pearl Harbor, the British ambassador, Lord Halifax, reported to Churchill that the President had said "that his perpetual problem is to steer a course between the two factors represented by: (1) the wish of 70% of Americans to keep out of the war (2) the wish of 70% of Americans to do everything to break Hitler, even if it means war. He said that if he asked for a declaration of war he wouldn't get it, and opinion would swing against him. He therefore intended to go on doing whatever he best could to help us, and declarations of war were, he said, out of fashion . . . It pretty well confirms my view, which I think is yours, that he is going to move to the undeclared war rather than the other, although no doubt things could change overnight if the right things were to happen."[9]

Whereas Roosevelt had formerly believed an international organization was unacceptable to the American people, by 1943 he had come to see that failure to create some organization would be unacceptable. There was little choice; to oppose an organization would be like swimming against a powerful flood. It was not that he had regained the Wilsonian faith — but, rather, much of the country had.

By 1943, there had been a vast movement in public opinion that would have considerable effect on policy for the rest of the war and into the Cold War. The American people were in an internationalist phase, a fervent rebirth of Wilsonianism, moved in part, as one historian has written, by a "pervasive feeling of guilt" that the Second World War resulted to a significant degree from the United States' failure to play its proper role after the First. The pollster George Gallup had already detected in the summer of 1942 "a profound change in viewpoint on international affairs" among the American people; by May of 1943, 74 percent endorsed United States participation in an international police force to keep the peace.

Congress mirrored this change. "God damn it, everybody's running around here like a fellow with a tick in his navel, howling about postwar resolutions," Tom Connally, chairman of the Senate Foreign Relations Committee, exploded at one point. Eventually passing the Fulbright and Connally resolutions, both houses went overwhelmingly on record in favor of a postwar organization.[10]

The alteration in public thinking reflected not only guilt, but also a changed environment. Senator Robert Taft had laid out the key isolationist assumption in 1939: "My whole idea of foreign policy is based largely on the position that America can successfully defend itself against the rest of the world." Pearl Harbor and the hostilities that followed destroyed the credibility of that position. The mobilization of the entire nation in the cause of total war further shifted attitudes. The development of bipartisanship — general agreement and cooperation between Congress and the Executive and between the two parties — meant that foreign policy no longer was a divisive, domestic party issue. One of the most significant figures in this development was John Foster Dulles, who was the chief foreign policy adviser of the Republican presidential candidate Thomas Dewey in 1944, and who negotiated with Secretary Hull a bipartisan truce that lasted the duration of that year's presidential campaign.[11]

Even more significant was Arthur Vandenberg, the leading Senate Republican foreign policy spokesman, who managed — streaking trails of purple rhetoric behind him — to embody in himself at one and the same time the transformation of attitudes in public opinion, in the Republican Party, and in the U.S. Senate — and all of this with an appropriate lack of modesty. Once, urged on by her husband, Mrs. Robert Taft tried to "butter Van up" at a dinner party, but was forced to report that she found the task impossible — "he buttered himself so thoroughly that I really couldn't find a single ungreased spot." Before the war, sharing Taft's assumption about American self-defense, he had been an isolationist. After Pearl Harbor, swayed by arguments about air power from his nephew Air Force General Hoyt Vandenberg, swayed also by his desire to move from opposition into policy formation, he had come to accept a major United States role in postwar international affairs. His January 1945 "confession" before the Senate of the errors of isolationism capped the development of a broad internationalist consensus in domestic politics.[12]

By that time, Roosevelt had long since realized that his Grand Design would have to be redrawn, at least superficially, to take into account this great change in American public opinion. Instead of fighting public opinion, he would harness it. He would use a new League of Nations, a United Nations, to assure public support for an active American role in the postwar world, and so legitimize that role and ensure against a return to isolationism. This entailed a duality in his policy that many at the time — and many since — have failed to see.

By the autumn of 1943, he visualized a United Nations composed both of an assembly open to all nations and a more restricted "executive committee," which would be dominated by the Great Powers. At the same time, the Four Policemen would perform their peace-keeping role completely outside the UNO framework.

American opinion continued to be defiantly suspicious of "big power politics." Meanwhile, Roosevelt concluded that an executive committee controlled by the Big Four and the Four Policemen could achieve much the same purpose. In February 1944, he approved a merging of the police department into the executive committee.[13] This change satisfied public and congressional sentiment, but it was more cosmetic than real, for the new organization rested upon a two-tiered structure that assured Great Power primacy. In other words, the United Nations itself represented a yoking together of two separate approaches to the postwar order — a Wilsonian peace, reflected in what became the General Assembly; and a Great Power peace, embodied in what became the Security Council. The genuine tension between these two approaches remained concealed for most of the Second World War. After the war, the conflict became explicit, and a major source of the Cold War.

The slow birth of the United Nations did not shift Roosevelt's underlying assumptions. For him it was axiomatic that the peace had to be based upon the realities of power, which in turn meant that the peace had to be rooted in the Great Powers. The Allies "are about 95 percent together," Roosevelt told a press conference in March 1943. "I wish some people would put that in their pipes and smoke it."[14]

This was only a mildly hyperbolic assessment of Anglo-American relations. There were some sharp differences on such questions as the role of General Charles de Gaulle, China, the European colonial empires, and postwar economic arrangements. Nevertheless, the area of common understanding and agreement was broad. The two countries were joined together not only by their military coordination and common strategic concerns, not merely by the close and comfortable personal relations between Roosevelt and Churchill, but also by deep ties of language, economics, culture, political traditions, and social contacts. On their major political goals, the British stood close to their Atlantic ally. The evidence indicates that Roosevelt, if not all those around him, shared in turn the premise expressed by

Walter Lippmann in 1944: "I take the agreement with Britain not for granted perhaps, but as fundamental." [15]

What held true with Great Britain certainly did not hold true with the Soviet Union. The gap between the U.S. and the USSR — measured in outlook, experience, traditions, habits, and contacts — was very wide. The difference in the relation of the United States to its two partners in the Grand Alliance, though obvious, still bears illustrating. Stimson's diary is studded with his declarations about the primary need to maintain Anglo-American collaboration in the postwar world, matched with the equally fervent assents of senior American and British officials. Indeed, Stimson and many of the English almost seemed members of the same society.

The friendliness and mutual comprehension contrasted sharply with the distance evident in Stimson's account of his first meeting in 1943 with the new Soviet ambassador to Washington, Andrei Gromyko. "I got into a fairly nice human relation with him for a wonder — the first time I have with any of these Russians. I had my Russian map out . . . and then I asked him where he lived and he pointed out a place in the northwestern part of Russia now occupied by the Nazis. The tears came in his eyes when he told me that he hadn't heard from any of his relatives and he didn't know whether they were alive. I told him I hoped that the Russians would find their old capital, Kiev, not altogether battered to pieces but he said he did not have very much hope of it. He is a young man and seemed to be more like a human being than the others that the Soviets have had here." [16]

Of Russia, the Americans could never be sure. The establishment of diplomatic relations in Roosevelt's first term had proved of little value. Roosevelt's own attitudes during the 1930s had been mixed. He had had some curiosity about the Soviet Union, a measured respect for its accomplishments, and a certain sympathy for its goals of social justice, although he doubted that one could attain "Utopia in a day." Such regard did not diminish his abhorrence of the nature of communist rule and its atheism. In October 1933, commenting on an enthusiastic book about Soviet Russia, he complained that it failed to include "enough of the costs in hunger, death and bitterness in uprooted folks that had been paid for in the extraordinary achievements by the Soviet regime in the past fifteen years." He had not thought possible the importation of its revolution into the United States, and he did recognize that as a state power it would become an increasingly important factor in world politics.

The Nazi-Soviet Pact of August 1939 and the subsequent Russian attack on Finland turned his feelings to scorn; he classed Russia with Germany as a totalitarian dictatorship. When extreme left-wing students heckled him at a White House conference in 1940, Roosevelt responded that "everyone who has the courage to face the facts" knows that the Soviet Union "is run by a dictatorship as absolute as any other dictatorship in the world." Yet he still kept open backdoor negotiations with the Russians, for he believed that the Nazi-Soviet Pact was inherently unstable, and, in its failure, might give way to an alliance between the Soviet Union and the West.[17]

The Germans abruptly abrogated the pact with their punishing attack on the Soviet Union in the night of June 21–22, 1941. "It will mean the liberation of Europe from Nazi domination," Roosevelt wrote shortly after, almost happily, to Admiral William Leahy. "And at the same time I do not think we need worry about any possibility of Russian domination."

Although the United States itself was still a half year short of being officially at war, the President, like Churchill, saw instantly that Russia now shared a common enemy with Britain and the United States. Necessity had made the Soviet Union a natural ally of the West, and in such an alliance resided the best hope for victory.[18]

The foundations for what afterward became known as the Grand Alliance were laid by Harry Hopkins, Roosevelt's alter ego in wartime diplomacy, a month after the German invasion.

"An odd creature but a very nice one," Lord Halifax had once mused about Hopkins. Certainly he was the most unlikely of diplomats. Informal, wisecracking, cynical, uninterested in bureaucratic procedures, with an unquenchable passion for café society and racetracks, Hopkins, the son of an Iowa harness salesman, had first come to the attention of the Roosevelts while doing social work in the slums of New York City. He became a top relief administrator in the New Deal, and then Secretary of Commerce. Roosevelt may well have looked favorably on him as a possible successor, but Hopkins lost any presidential ambitions and a good deal of his stamina as the result of an operation for stomach cancer in 1937. Thereafter, he appeared, as Jonathan Daniels put it, like "Death on the way to a frolic." And, thereafter, he existed for only one purpose — to serve

Franklin Roosevelt. In May 1940, he moved into the White House, where he stayed for the next five years. He instinctively understood Roosevelt's moods and desires, and also knew how to shape both. His loyalty to FDR was unquestioned; and he acted as the President's agent, problem-solver, war-expediter, and troubleshooter, both in Washington's bureaucracies and in high diplomacy.

At the end of July 1941, wearing a homburg borrowed from Winston Churchill, he boarded a seaplane in Scotland, flew to Archangel, there changed planes and flew on to Moscow, where he presented Stalin with an introduction from Roosevelt: "I ask you to treat him with the identical confidence you would feel if you were talking directly to me." [19]

Hopkins, like the other wartime leaders coming from the West, was fascinated by the thought of meeting the isolated ruler of the Kremlin. They found not the Bolshevik Revolutionary nor the Bloody Tyrant, but rather a short, stocky, willful Georgian — with his stiff hair brushed back, he struck the permanent undersecretary of the British Foreign Office as looking like a porcupine — who, doodling wolves while he talked, would laconically and flatly get right to the point. Obsessive about security and secrecy, unconcerned about human life, he sought to master every threat in the most thorough way he could. The task was never-ending, for, as his daughter has written, "He saw enemies everywhere." In his last interview with a foreigner before his death, Stalin told a little parable about how to deal with enemies: the Russian peasant who sees a wolf knows what the wolf intends to do, and the peasant does not try to tame the wolf, nor does he delay, but rather kills the animal as quickly as he can. So Stalin had dealt with the Soviet peoples. "He has shut himself up within the innermost spheres of hell," Victor Serge wrote of him. "Though intrepid, he lives in fear. Crafty, he lives on suspicion. Today, he ordains assassination, tomorrow apotheosis."

It was Stalin's brutal and bloody rule — "the despotic regime of a dictatorship of industrial development" — that had pushed Russia at a forced pace into the industrial age. Yet Stalin himself knew less and less of what went on beyond the walls of the Kremlin and his holiday dachas. In the 1930s, in the midst of the nightmare of collectivization, he was shown faked motion pictures of the happy, contented life of peasants on collective farms. After the war, he would occasionally press money into his daughter's hand, although he had himself no idea of what the money was worth or how much anything cost. The only monetary values he knew were the old prerevolutionary ones. He himself never spent money; he had no place to spend it and nothing to spend it on.

Yet the Westerners also saw Stalin's qualities as organizer, administrator and commander that had recommended him to Lenin and finally brought him to undisputed leadership. "Stalin's greatest talent," one historian has written, was as a "master-builder of bureaucratic structures, and this it was that determined his conceptions and his methods . . . He reacted, as was to be expected, by using the lever whose use he best understood; he resorted to force, with the appropriate controls." Attending to specifics, be they boundaries, coal production, or railway tracks, Stalin seemed to have little time for great conceptions or grand designs, his own or anybody else's. "A declaration I regard as algebra," he once said to Eden during the war. "I prefer practical arithmetic."

Notions of world revolution were to him algebra. He preferred the practical arithmetic of realism in international politics; he aimed, and so this was the thrust of Soviet foreign policy, to play the game of nations. From time to time, foreigners understood this. "The Soviet authorities are extremely realistic, and it is most difficult to persuade them with abstract arguments," reported the Japanese ambassador to Moscow, in the closing days of World War II. At almost exactly the same time, the American ambassador to Moscow, Averell Harriman, made exactly the same point. "I am afraid Stalin does not and never will fully understand our interest in a free Poland as a matter of principle," he said. "He is a realist in his actions, and it is hard for him to appreciate our faith in abstract principles."

The Yugoslav partisans, who might have had reason to think otherwise, learned the same thing when they set up an Anti-Fascist Council at the end of 1943. The Boss — as Stalin was known to a small circle in Moscow — was furious. "He considers this," one of his deputies reported to the Yugoslavs, "a knife in the back of the Soviet Union and a blow to the Tehran decisions." Commenting on the bitter blasts from Moscow, Moša Pijade, a leading Yugoslavian communist, could only conclude in 1943, "Stalin's revolutionary days are over. He has become a statesman and is no longer sensitive to the needs of a revolution. He is worried about the boundaries of great states and agreements on spheres of influence." [20]

And what was Stalin's greatest achievement? That he presided over the industrialization that not merely modernized the Soviet Union, but transformed it into one of the world's superpowers? That he was the man of steel who led the Soviet Union through the Great Patriotic War, in which twenty million of its citizens perished? That he then built a new empire in an age when empires were supposed to fall, not rise? That as many died in the war he ceaselessly and brutally waged against his own people as in the Second World War? That, in one of the great hoaxes of the twentieth century, he so successfully duped what he called the "honest fools," both at home and abroad, into believing that Moscow was the font of tomorrow's better world, and he, the embodiment of the coming utopia? That, in the words of a Yugoslav, he "killed more good communists than the bourgeoisie of the whole world put together"? Or simply that, through it all, he survived, and ruled almost unchallenged for almost three decades, and then, in a dacha just outside Moscow, died a nonviolent death — though it was violent to see, for during a period of several days he slowly suffocated as a consequence of a stroke?

That was in 1953. Twelve years earlier, in June of 1941, in the first days of the German invasion, Stalin had suffered a nervous collapse. But he had recovered and reassumed control by the time of Hopkins' arrival, and he succeeded in presenting himself as a rough but beleaguered and courageous potential ally. Even as the German blitzkrieg was furiously pushing into Russia, Stalin talked with Hopkins far more directly, intimately, and honestly than he had ever before conversed with a Western politician. In a masterly but matter-of-fact way, he described Russia's dire problems and listed the weapons and materials needed. (Masterly though the presentation was, there is reason to think now that Stalin requested weapons and materials inappropriate to Russia's immediate problems.) Stalin, in these conversations, clearly regarded Hopkins as an extension of Roosevelt, as indeed by this time he was.

Hopkins left Moscow on August 1. His trip had set in motion not only lend-lease aid to the Soviet Union but the Grand Alliance itself. Stalin had impressed Hopkins, though in a tentative way. "The caviar and smoked salmon were almost too much!" Hopkins wrote a week after he left Moscow. "I would hardly call Uncle Joe a pleasant man, although he was interesting enough, and I think I got what I wanted, but you can never be sure about that."

Hopkins also came away convinced that the alliance could only be conducted through contact at the highest levels, outside the normal bureaucratic channels, certainly not through Laurence Steinhardt, then the American ambassador to Moscow. "It seemed to me after my conference in Russia with Stalin that the President should personally deal with Stalin," he noted in October 1941. "It was perfectly clear that Stalin had no confidence in our Ambassador or in any of our officials in Moscow. I gathered he would have felt the same way about the State Department if he had been asked."[21] The experience with other personal emissaries like Averell Harriman and Joseph Davies bore out this contention, although Roosevelt himself did not meet Stalin until the two gathered with Churchill at the Tehran Conference in late November and early December 1943.

The main questions to be decided at Tehran were military. Stalin, bitter toward the British and suspicious of them, insisted that his allies open a Second Front against the Germans in Western Europe. Roosevelt and Churchill promised that an invasion would take place in the late spring of 1944. The Russians for their part pledged a coordinated offensive in the East.

The three leaders agreed in a general way to dismember Germany after the war. They also concurred that there would be some undefined shifts in the borders between Russia and Poland (to the advantage of Russia) and between Poland and Germany (to the advantage of Poland). Roosevelt and Stalin discussed shearing France of its colonies in Indochina.

Roosevelt raised with Stalin the American plans for the United Nations. Stalin indicated considerable doubts about such an organization. Leaving no question about his own views, FDR reassured Stalin that he had not forgotten the fruitless debates in the League of Nations. The center of his design continued to be a Great Power consortium.

Stalin indicated during the conference that the "communization" of Europe was hardly his first concern. Replying to Churchill's confession that he had done everything in his power after World War I to contain Bolshevism, Stalin ironically said that the Russians had discovered "it was not so easy to set up Communist regimes."

Still, he left many questions unanswered. At one dinner, Churchill asked about the Soviet Union's postwar territorial goals.

"There is no need to speak at the present time about any Soviet desires," Stalin replied. "But when the time comes, we will speak." [22]

"I think that as a roving Ambassador for the first time I did not 'pull any boners,'" Roosevelt wrote to Sumner Welles after the conference. Tehran also provided Roosevelt with some confirmation of the soundness of his design for the postwar order.[23]

As already noted, Roosevelt believed the peace had to be based upon the realities of power, which meant that it would have to be grounded in a Great Power consortium. The British easily fit into this design. The key question concerned the role of the Soviet Union. Here Roosevelt operated on a series of axioms very different from those of the Soviet specialists in the State Department.

He believed that Russia could no longer be considered an outsider, beyond the pale of morality and international politics. What that meant in the context of the war was already obvious. The President recognized that the major land war in Europe was taking place on the Eastern Front; it was there that Germany could be defeated, with a consequent reduction in American casualties. A kind of comparative advantage set in. The Russians specialized in men, dead and wounded, while the United States pushed its industrial machine to new limits. A year after the German invasion of the Soviet Union, Roosevelt declared that "Russian endurance" was "still the main strength."

The war, which promised to bequeath a great power vacuum in Europe and at the same time erased all doubts about Russia's power and capabilities, made inevitable the emergence of the Soviet Union as a paramount and indispensable factor in the postwar international system, especially in Europe. Thus, the alternative to a broad understanding would be a postwar world of hostile coalitions, an arms race — and another war.[24]

Some such understanding was possible because the breach that had opened at the time of the Bolshevik Revolution had narrowed and could narrow further. Roosevelt thought of the Soviet Union less as a revolutionary vanguard than as a conventional imperialist power, with ambitions rather like those of the Czarist regime. In other words, Roosevelt emphasized the imperatives of statehood in Soviet policy, rather than the role of ideology. In contrast to the Riga axioms, he proceeded on the proposition that a totalitarian domestic system did *not* inevitably and necessarily give rise to a totalitarian foreign policy. As important, he assumed less coherence and purposefulness in the Kremlin's behavior in international politics than did those who operated on the Riga axioms. Since the Soviet Union was not so much a world revolutionary state, Roosevelt believed the Grand Alliance could be continued after the war in the form of "business-like relations." He also knew that the Soviet Union would be preoccupied after the war with its vast task of reconstruction, and would be desperately interested in stability, order, and peace.[25]

Successful collaboration among the Great Powers would necessitate the allaying of many years of Soviet hostility and suspicion. Roosevelt regarded the dissipation of distrust as one of his most important challenges. The United States could prove its good faith by sticking to its agreements. Even if the West could not deliver immediately on its promised Second Front, at least it could provide the aid it had pledged — and, in that way, also do itself a considerable favor. Again and again, Roosevelt ordered that the production and delivery of lend-lease goods be speeded up, that the quantities be increased. It was a battle down the line. "Frankly," the President sharply reminded a subordinate, "if I were a Russian, I would feel that I had been given the run-around in the United States."[26]

High-level personal contact was the most important method by which suspicion could be dispelled and some precedent established for postwar concert. This provided a major reason for the wartime summit meetings. As time went along, Roosevelt became increasingly confident of success.

The apparent progress in this task gave rise to another axiom — one could do business with Stalin. After Hopkins' trip to Moscow in July 1941, Stalin was increasingly seen in a fresh light — as a realistic, rational statesman. Tehran certainly gave strong support to this new image.

All of this put even more emphasis on high-level contacts. "I know you will not mind my being brutally frank when I tell you that I think I can personally handle Stalin better than either your Foreign Office or my State Department," Roosevelt had already written Churchill in March 1942. "Stalin hates the guts of all your top people. He thinks he likes me better, and I hope he will continue to do so."

This reliance on informal, personal channels fit in well with Roosevelt's own preferences, his confidence, perhaps even his overconfidence. Indeed, in 1943, Stimson tartly summed up the "Rooseveltian view" of "good administrative procedures" — "He wants to do it all himself." [27] Roosevelt always depended upon an immeasurable quality, his famous charm, to achieve measurable results, to move and hold people in order to attain his goals in both domestic and international politics. That charm, in turn, was a product of considerable self-confidence and a buoyant, though neither naïve nor untested, optimism.

There were two other important reasons for taking this tack. Roosevelt considered Secretary of State Cordell Hull "much in the stratosphere," and lacked confidence in the State Department bureaucracy. Thus, the State Department was excluded from most of the significant wartime diplomacy, and its officials passed the time either in making voluminous plans for a postwar Wilsonian world, or sulking in their tents. Those historians who confuse the State Department's concerns with those of FDR on such questions as the United Nations or economic planning can be seriously misled.[28]

Decisions on the Soviet side were obviously made only at the most senior levels. Those not at the top — that is, in some sense, everyone save Stalin — were held in check, fearing to depart from their instructions. Important business could only be done with the dictator.

One of Roosevelt's fundamental assumptions was that it was vitally important that the United States have a realistic estimate of Soviet power and the sphere of influence it was carving out, and that it pay close heed to Stalin's "security objectives." Spheres of influence were not a take-it-or-leave-it matter, but rather a basic datum of international relations.

But his very awareness of these needs created difficulties for Roosevelt. He had to speak in two languages. With the Russians, he talked of a Great Power consortium, based on the realities of international politics. At home, he continued to try to obscure this basic program in the idealistic Wilsonian language, which by then had become the lingua franca of postwar thinking. Lord Halifax pointed out the crux of the difficulty in Anglo-American relations with the Russians when he noted in 1942 "how important a place all those ideas of security are going to hold in Stalin's mind, and how much they are likely to influence his judgment in regard to cooperation with ourselves." Halifax hoped it would be possible to find a solution "to take account of both our moral obligations and the forces of *realpolitik*, which are going to be deciding forces in Europe for many years to come, with those eighty millions of sulky Germans in the middle of it." [29]

A resolution of the still-implicit tension between these two methods for organizing the peace — realpolitik and Wilsonianism — would demand all the improvisational talents of Franklin Roosevelt, the artful dodger.

Meanwhile, Roosevelt tried to finesse the problem with literal double-talk. Early on, he had realized that Soviet borders would include an eastern chunk of Poland, Bessarabia, the Baltic states, and some of Finland. He knew too that Russian influence would reach farther into Europe. Under such circumstances, it would be futile to oppose Stalin's immediate goals since he had the power to obtain them anyway, and better to try to temper the character of Soviet influence in the context of a larger understanding.

In January 1945, meeting with a group of senators, Roosevelt seemed to suggest that spheres of influence, the villain in Wilsonian ideology, had been granted a hearing at Tehran and then banished. What he said next, however, was just the opposite. "The occupying forces had the power in the areas where their arms were present and each knew that the others could not force things to an issue." The President added the obvious: "The Russians had the power in Eastern Europe." It was clearly impossible to have a break with them. *"The only practicable course was to use what influence we had to ameliorate the situation."* Roosevelt made the same kind of point when the question of a Great Power veto in the international organization came up. "Unanimity was as a practical matter inevitable and might as well be conceded in a formal matter." The world had to be faced as it was; Russia would define its own security interests around its rim. On some issues, it would be not merely futile but actually dangerous to try to force the Russians to bend to an American will.[30]

Churchill, acting on many of the same premises, made his own effort to find a practical solution when he journeyed to Moscow in October 1944 — this, the occasion of the famous percentage deal for the division of the Continent, with the Russians given hegemony in Eastern Europe. This approach certainly seems paradoxical, if not cynical, in the light of Churchill's bitter denunciation of exactly such a division in his Iron Curtain speech a year and a half later.

But Churchill was conflicted in his own mind, a problem obvious to his contemporaries. "I can't help being rather impressed by Winston's sharp change of front on Russia," Halifax noted in 1942, for having called Eden "every name from a dog to a pig for suggesting composition with Stalin, he now goes all out for it himself in a message to the President." Two weeks after the 1944 Moscow meeting, Churchill's doctor observed that the Prime Minister "seems torn between the two lines of action . . . At one moment he will plead with the President for a common front against Communism and the next he will make a bid for Stalin's friendship. Sometimes the two policies alternate with bewildering rapidity." [31]

It was "composition" that Churchill sought in Moscow, to put algebra aside and work out the arithmetic — mutually acceptable rules that would accord with the interests and powers of the major victor states. An explicit spheres-of-influence settlement would reduce the ambiguities that could give rise to conflicts among the members of the Grand Alliance. Indeed, the very recognition of spheres might reduce their ultimate exclusiveness, for neither side would feel the need to tighten its defensive grip in order to fend off a feared drive against its sphere from the other.

Churchill vividly described the scene in his memoirs. The first meeting with Stalin began in the Kremlin at ten in the evening of October 9. "The moment was apt for business." Churchill took a half sheet of paper and wrote out the percentages that were to reflect degrees of "predominance": Rumania, 90 percent for the Russians; Greece, 90 percent for the British (in cooperation with the United States); Bulgaria, 75 percent for the Russians; Hungary and Yugoslavia, 50–50.

He pushed the paper across to Stalin. The dictator paused, then made a large tick with a blue pencil and passed it back.

"Let us burn the paper," Churchill said.

"No, you keep it," replied Stalin.

No doubt embarrassed by the apparent cynicism of the moment and the difficulties that followed in the postwar years, Churchill attempted in his memoirs to play down the significance of the agreement. The division applied, he wrote, only to "immediate war-time arrangements . . . All larger questions were reserved on both sides for what we then hoped would be a peace table when the war was won." But the many historians who have uncritically accepted Churchill's after-the-fact rationale have been led astray.

The actual minutes of the conversation demonstrate that Churchill knew exactly what he was doing, that he was seeking a permanent understanding: "The time would come when they would meet at the armistice table, which might also be the place where the peace was settled," he said. "The Americans would find it easier to settle at an armistice table, because there the President could decide, whereas at a peace table the Senate would have to be consulted." In other words, such "temporary" settlements were meant to become faits accomplis.

Stalin "understood" Churchill. "It was a serious matter for Britain," said the Soviet dictator, "when the Mediterranean was not in her hands." Just as Russia was ceded "first say" in Rumania, so, Stalin agreed, Britain would have "first say" in Greece. Churchill won a further concession from Stalin regarding Italy. While claiming that it would be easier to "influence" the head of the Italian Communist Party were he in Moscow, Stalin nevertheless acceded to Churchill's wish that the Soviet Union "soft-pedal the Communists in Italy and not . . . stir them up."

Churchill did not hide what was on his mind. "The Prime Minister said it was better to express these things in diplomatic terms and not to use the phrase 'dividing into spheres' because the Americans might be shocked. But as long as he and Marshal Stalin understood each other, he could explain matters to the President." [32]

The Russians left no question that they preferred such practical arithmetic to the algebra of declarations. "At Moscow, we were given an even warmer welcome than we got when I went with Eden last year, and the visit was, on the whole, a great success," wrote General Hastings Ismay, Churchill's chief of staff. Stalin came to dinner at the British embassy ("having never previously had a meal at any foreign embassy"), attended the Bolshoi Ballet with the Prime Minister, and even went to the airport in a pouring rain to see the British delegation off. "I am no nearer understanding the Russian mentality than I was at the beginning of the war," added Ismay, "but I believe unless we and the Americans acquire and retain their friendship, there is little hope for the peace of the world." [33]

Churchill had assured Stalin that he could explain matters to Roosevelt, but considerable explication seemed called for. Both the good feeling and Churchill's position while in Moscow had been somewhat undermined by messages from Roosevelt. The President informed Stalin that the Moscow conversations could only be regarded as preliminary, pending another Big Three meeting. He included a fundamental statement of the new global vision that would shape American policy in the postwar era, a vision that seemed to reject spheres: "There is in this global war literally no question, either military or political, in which the United States is not interested. You will naturally understand this."

Roosevelt's disclaimer resulted from the intervention of Hopkins and Charles Bohlen. The latter had predicted two possible results of these bilateral conversations: "a first class British-Soviet row over European problems or . . . the division of Europe into spheres of influence on a power politics basis." Either, he warned, "would be disastrous."

It was not, however, that Roosevelt himself had suddenly embraced again the Wilsonian faith; his motivations were different. He had come to regard Britain as a junior member of the Grand Alliance, did not wish any of his own options foreclosed, and did not want (as Hopkins told Halifax) to "find himself pushed somewhat into a back seat." Moreover, especially in the weeks immediately before the 1944 presidential election, he had to be most careful to prevent the disclosure of any embarrassing "secret treaties" involving the domestically explosive Eastern European questions. (Of course, this percentage deal was not a treaty, rather an understanding, a modus vivendi.) Churchill was certainly right in his fear that "spheres of influence" would have shocked American public opinion. At the beginning of 1945, Halifax wrote to Churchill: "The trouble with these people is that they are so much the victims of labels: 'Power Politics, Spheres of Influence, Balance of Power, etc.' As if there was ever such a sphere of influence agreement as the Monroe Doctrine! And, as I can only tell them when they talk about being outsmarted . . . they evidently outsmarted somebody when they made the Louisiana Purchase!" [34]

"Roosevelt weather" was the term applied by FDR's political staff to the favorable weather that seemed to signal victory on each of those four November days that he had been elected President. The Russians adopted the same phrase to describe the unseasonably mild climate in the first two weeks of February 1945 over the Crimea, which juts down into the Black Sea from the underside of the Ukraine. At the seaside resort of Yalta, on the southern coast of the Crimea, the last Czar had maintained his summer palace. There the Big Three gathered for their final wartime conference, between February 4 and 11, under bright, clear skies that seemed a harbinger of victory, not only in the war but also over the unfamiliar terrain of postwar international politics. FDR brought his practicality to bear, in an effort to make firm the foundations of his Grand Design. The pleasant days and nights matched the climate of the conference itself — auguring victory for Roosevelt's foreign policy.[35]

Marking the high tide of Allied unity, the Yalta Conference was a point of separation, a time of endings and beginnings. The conclusion of the war was at last in sight; the remaining days of the Third Reich were clearly numbered. Stalin, to the relief of the Joint Chiefs, gave further assurances that Russia would enter the war against Japan some three months after fighting ended in Europe, in exchange for certain territorial concessions in the Far East.

Aside from that central question, the major issues at Yalta concerned the politics of a postwar world. The decisions waited upon the energies of three tired men. "I think Uncle Joe much the most impressive," Alexander Cadogan, permanent undersecretary of the British Foreign Office, wrote to his wife. "The President flapped about and the P.M. boomed, but Joe just sat taking it all in and being rather amused. When he did chip in, he never used a superfluous word, and spoke very much to the point." [36]

By and large, the Russians made more concessions than the West, and when they presented their own proposals, they were, in fact, sometimes simply returning proposals delivered to them at earlier dates by the Western powers.

The Russians, remembering their difficulties in the League of Nations, which culminated in their expulsion, were worried that they would find themselves isolated in a new international organization controlled by the United States and the United Kingdom through their allies, clients, dominions, and "Good Neighbors." The Russians accepted an American compromise, whereby the Great Powers retained a veto in the Security Council, and the Western leaders agreed to support the admission of two or three constituent Soviet republics. The British won assent to a modified Great Power role for France, including both a zone of occupation in Germany and participation on the German Control Commission.[37]

Roosevelt successfully pushed for a "Declaration on Liberated Europe," an ill-defined lever for Western intervention in Eastern Europe, but which mainly interested Roosevelt as a device to satisfy public opinion at home. He took it up only after he had turned down a more binding State Department proposal for a High Commission on Liberated Areas because "he preferred a more flexible arrangement." [38] Accord also followed on a number of less pressing points.

Two issues proved more difficult: the central question of Germany and the endless Polish imbroglio. Poland, the emblem of the early Cold War, took up more time than any other issue at the conference. The Allies did agree that the Russian-Polish border should be moved westward, to the Curzon Line, and, though not in very precise terms, further consented to compensation for Poland in the form of what had been German territory on its west.

More difficult was the nature of Poland's new government, that is, whether to install the Western-supported London exile government, bitterly anti-Soviet, or the Lublin government, little more than a Soviet puppet.

Britain went to war so "that Poland should be free and sovereign," said Churchill. Britain's only interest, he assured the other leaders, was "one of honor because we drew the sword for Poland against Hitler's brutal attack." Of course, he added, Polish independence could not be a cover for "hostile designs" against the Soviet Union.

Stalin, however, was still interested in practical arithmetic. "For Russia it is not only a question of honor but of security." As to honor — "We shall have to eliminate many things from the books." As to security — "Not only because we are on Poland's frontier but also because throughout history Poland has always been a corridor for attack on Russia." Twice in the last thirty years "our German enemy has passed through this corridor."

Churchill replied that he himself had little fondness for the London Poles, which was one element in the general weakness of the Western position on the Polish question. "Admittedly," a British diplomat commented, "Uncle Joe's masterly exposition of the Russian attitude over Poland sounded sincere, and as always was hyper-realistic."

At last, the Allies agreed to "reorganize" the Lublin government with some men from London and from the Polish underground, but details were left to Molotov and the two Allied ambassadors in Moscow to work out.[39]

For Germany, the Russians pushed for dismemberment; in substance, their proposal was the suggestion Roosevelt had made at Tehran. The two Western governments went along, reluctantly.

The Russians also insisted on receiving reparations from Germany. Postwar planning in the U.S. had generally rejected reparations. America certainly had no need for reparations; and reparations had been in bad repute in both Britain and the United States since J. M. Keynes' *Economic Consequences of the Peace*, published shortly after the First World War. "We are against reparations," Roosevelt had bluntly said before Yalta.

At Yalta, however, the Western countries met a Soviet Union urgently determined to exact reparations. As early as September 1941, in conversations with Averell Harriman and Lord Beaverbrook, Stalin had asked flatly: "What about getting the Germans to pay for the damage?" Stalin's "second revolution" had been an industrial revolution, an upheaval that had cost much in human life and in the manner in which the survivors lived. Stalin's interest in reparations was compensatory as well as punitive; he wanted help in the huge task of reconstruction that lay ahead. By 1945, the Germans had wrought enormous destruction. Twenty million people had been killed — though it was years before the Kremlin revealed the full magnitude. Seven million horses had been lost, as were 20 out of 23 million pigs. Destroyed were 4.7 million houses, 1710 towns, and 70,000 villages. Twenty-five million people were homeless. Sixty-five thousand kilometers of railway tracks had been ruined; 15,800 locomotives and 428,000 freight cars had been either demolished or damaged.

Here, however, the Soviet concern went beyond the simple arithmetic of devastation. Reading through the minutes of meeting upon meeting during the war and after, the historian must conclude that reparations were not only a central issue, but also a highly significant symbol in Moscow's postwar vision — although always only of peripheral interest to the Americans. Perhaps the Russians could never understand the nature of American concern for Eastern Europe; similarly, the Americans could never comprehend the emotional intensity the Russians attached to reparations. Reparations may well have been as much a "test case" for the Russians as Eastern Europe was to become for the Americans.[40]

At Yalta, Churchill adamantly opposed reparations, warning that England "would be chained to a dead body of Germany." Concerned about economic consequences and criticism at home, Roosevelt wavered until Hopkins shoved him a note: "The Russians have given in so much at this conference that I don't think we should let them down." The President finally agreed to set $20 billion, half for the Russians, as the basis for further discussions, though with the understanding that reparations were to be in goods, production, and equipment, and not in cash. The British declined to commit themselves to a figure. Their attitude was summed up by one of their delegates, who declared that the Russian figures were "fantastic arithmetic and quite outside the bonds of possibility."

Although Western policymakers later denied that the $20 billion represented a fundamental point of agreement and subsequently downplayed its importance, this was not the case. "The Russians had a very carefully worked out program," Secretary of State Edward Stettinius told Stimson and Navy Secretary James Forrestal in mid-March 1945. "The President backed up this program as a relatively moderate one, and one that would not create economic disruption in Europe."[41]

The overall British attitude was suggested by a letter from Cadogan on the last day: "I have never known the Russians so easy and accommodating. In particular Joe has been extremely good. He *is* a great man, and shows up impressively against the background of the other two aging statesmen." Churchill had been frustrated and despondent during the conference, in part because of his sense of Britain's declining power. Yet he too toward the end of the meeting told his doctor that he had been impressed by Stalin's humor, understanding, and moderation. He recovered more verve upon his return to London. "As long as Stalin lasted, Anglo-Russian friendship could be maintained," he told some Cabinet members. "Poor Neville Chamberlain believed he could trust Hitler. He was wrong. But I don't think I'm wrong about Stalin."[42]

Roosevelt was a realist; he knew that everything depended upon implementation of the accords, and that, in turn, would depend upon intentions and future alignments. He was gambling. He hinted at this caution in a note he scribbled to his wife the day he left Yalta: "We have wound up the conference — successfully I think." [43]

That said, there can be no question but that Roosevelt departed the Crimea optimistic and satisfied. Basing his conclusions on conversations with Roosevelt, Admiral Leahy decided that Roosevelt had "no regrets about what the Russians were to get. He thought they were valid claims." But FDR's satisfaction extended beyond the agreements themselves. He regarded the conference as a hopeful answer to the question about postwar cooperation with Russia that he had posed to Eden two years earlier, in the course of their after-dinner survey. This summit meeting in the Crimea had been a testing and, more important, a confirmation of what we might thus call Franklin Roosevelt's "Yalta axioms."

Stalin himself had gone out of his way to endorse the premise that underlay FDR's Grand Design. The dictator had pointed to "a more serious question" than an international organization. One should not worry too much about small nations. "The greatest danger was conflict between the three Great Powers." The main task was to prevent their quarreling and "secure their unity for the future." [44]

It is true that Roosevelt, once home, delivered a speech to Congress, pure in its Wilsonianism, in which he declared that Yalta spelled the end of unilateral action, exclusive alliances, spheres of influence, power blocs, and "all other expedients that had been tried for centuries — and have always failed."

But, out of public earshot, he continued to stress the realities of power and the basic structure of a Great Power consortium. Two days after his speech to Congress, talking privately about Germany, he said, "Obviously the Russians are going to do things their own way in the areas they occupy." But he hoped that a general framework of collaboration would prevent the Soviet sphere of influence from becoming a sphere of control.[45]

His optimism was shared down the line, even by some in the State Department, as well as among prominent foreign policy spokesmen outside the government. "The general atmosphere of the Conference was extremely good and it was clear throughout that the Russians genuinely wished to reach an agreement," reported H. Freeman Matthews, deputy director of the Office of European Affairs. John Foster Dulles had earlier criticized the Atlantic Charter for being "too much a static, rather than a dynamic concept of the world." But now he was quick to praise. Yalta opened "a new era ... The United States abandoned a form of aloofness which it has been practicing for many years and the Soviet Union permitted joint action on matters that it had the power to settle for itself." And James Byrnes, director of the Office of War Mobilization, flying home early from Yalta, passed the word to newsmen that Stalin had been lavish in praise of the United States and that "Joe was the life of the party." [46]

Yet the Roosevelt weather did not long survive the conference. The Moscow discussions about Poland became deadlocked over the question of whether a reorganization of the Lublin government meant that it would be the basis of the postwar government, or whether an entirely new coalition government was to be created. There were also difficulties involving the Balkans. The Russians insisted that they should have the same kind of "first say" there as the Western powers had claimed in Italy — and were forcefully asserting that say, especially in Rumania.[47]

The most acrimonious exchange was over the so-called secret surrender negotiations concerning German troops in northern Italy, which were conducted in Switzerland, principally in Berne, by Allen Dulles of the Office of Strategic Services and SS leader Karl Wolff. The West maintained that it was purely a local field matter, having nothing whatever to do with a separate peace in Western Europe. The Russians, alleging duplicity, charged that such an agreement would enable the Germans to transfer troops from Italy to the Eastern Front, the very thing that at Yalta the Russians had asked to have prevented. So intemperate did Stalin's accusations become that Roosevelt finally cabled him, "Frankly, I cannot avoid a feeling of bitter resentment toward your informers, whoever they are, for such vile misrepresentations of my actions or those of my trusted subordinates." [48]

Yet nothing came of the talks with the SS leader, and the bitterness at the top of the alliance did not persist. To Harriman, who insisted that a major break was at hand, the President replied, "It is my desire to consider the Berne misunderstanding a minor incident." And in his last telegram to Churchill on April 11, 1945, he declared: "I would minimize the general Soviet problem as much as possible because these problems, in one form or another, seem to arise every day and most of them straighten out as in the case of the Berne meeting. We must be firm, however, and our course thus far is correct."[49]

The very fact that the Berne incident could be resolved gave Roosevelt new hope that his foreign policy would work in the postwar period. But the problems were getting ever more complicated. The postwar world was at hand, questions could not be deferred, the unifying factor of the common enemy would soon be gone.

There remained, moreover , the considerable gap between Roosevelt's *foreign* foreign policy and his *domestic* foreign policy. It would take enormous skill to be the realist and the idealist at the same time; and Roosevelt, the self-styled realist, certainly knew that. When it was suggested by an aide that he could appear at the upcoming planning meeting for the United Nations Organization in San Francisco and dispel problems with a "wave of the magic wand," he wearily replied that he doubted whether he still had such a wand to wave.

And there were other considerations. The Yalta axioms were very much the personal possession of Roosevelt and a few powerful independent agents, whose only loyalty was to him. Those axioms had no institutional base in the government; in a sense, their very emphasis on high-level personal contacts, outside of bureaucratic channels, precluded that. Certainly they were not popular in the State Department.

What the State Department thought, however, was not very significant so long as Roosevelt was there to set boundaries, not merely through his prerogative to approve or reject, but also by his presidential powers to promote or exile, to set questions, to give attention or inattention. In September 1944, Cadogan had remarked of Roosevelt in his diary, "A lot turns on his health." In the note FDR himself had scribbled to his wife on February 12, his last day at Yalta, the President had added, "I'm a bit exhausted, but really all right."

Two months later, on April 12, 1945, several hours after drafting that last cable to Churchill — "I would minimize the general Soviet problem" — Roosevelt complained of a terrific headache and collapsed. Later in the day he was dead.[50]

> In every authoritarian state, political life too readily becomes a struggle for access to the ruler and for the control of his sources for information.
>
> — GEORGE KENNAN, September 1944 [1]

III

The World Bully

"WE SHALL NOT KNOW what he is really like until the pressure begins to be felt," General George C. Marshall said to Secretary of War Henry Stimson as the two rode back to the Pentagon after their first White House conference with the new President. Harry Truman was as shocked as anybody by the turn of fate. "I've really had a blow since this was dictated," he wrote on April 13 as a postscript to a letter he had begun a day earlier, while presiding over the Senate before the news of Roosevelt's death had reached him. "But I'll have to meet it." [2]

In those first days, the men who had served Roosevelt could do little more than speculate about the unknown Missourian who had succeeded the war leader.

"No one knows what the new President's views are — at least I don't," Stimson observed. "The threads of information were so multitudinous that only long previous familiarity could allow him to control them."

"The man has a lot of nervous energy, and seems to be inclined to make very quick decisions," noted Treasury Secretary Henry Morgenthau, Jr. "But, after all, he is a politician, and what is going on in his head only time will tell."

Commerce Secretary Henry A. Wallace, walking through Truman's car on the Roosevelt funeral train, caught sight of the new President sitting with Edwin Pauley, a California oil man and major contributor to the Democratic Party who, as director of the 1944 Democratic Convention, had helped devise the machinations that won the vice-presidential nomination for Truman. No doubt with some jealousy and resentment toward the man who had taken his place as Vice President, Wallace mused that "an era of experimental liberalism had come to an end" and wondered what Pauley and others of that ilk "would do to the putty which is Truman." [3]

But Wallace was underestimating Truman, who was a man of strong and defined character. "It did not take long to see through the mask of his self-deprecation," observed Jonathan Daniels, who worked as press secretary during the first days of transition. On subjects on which Truman was not informed, however, he could be molded; and on one subject above all — foreign affairs — he was woefully uninformed. He had not even been abroad since Army service in the First World War. Harry Hopkins, closer to the new President than any other member of Roosevelt's entourage, worried that Truman "knows absolutely nothing of world affairs."

Truman was the first to admit his own ignorance. "They didn't tell me anything about what was going on here," he complained forlornly, but with some justice, more than a month after the succession. He had been chosen as Vice President as a compromise, in order that Roosevelt would not have to choose between two more experienced men, James Byrnes and Henry Wallace. After the election, he was treated rather as a hired hand; he was to sit unobtrusively in the Senate and mind his own business. As Vice President, Truman apparently conferred with Roosevelt just twice.*

If FDR had acted differently, if he had admitted Truman into policy councils, he might have felt that he was making an unpleasant admission about his own sense of mortality. Of course, there was

* Some sense of the relationship between the two men is suggested by Roosevelt's instructions to Truman regarding communications during the Yalta Conference: "If you have any urgent messages which you wish to get to me, I suggest you send them through the White House Map Room [communications center]. However, only *absolutely urgent* messages should be sent via the Map Room. May I ask that you make them as brief as possible in order not to tie up communications. If you have very lengthy messages the Map Room officer will have to exercise his discretion as to whether it is physically possible to send them by radio or whether they will have to be sent by pouch." Two and a half months later, in what may have been his last contact with Roosevelt, Truman wrote to FDR at Warm Springs: "Hope you are having a good rest. Hate to bother you but I have a suggestion to make." It concerned appointments for federal loan administrator and postmaster general.

precious little time in which to bring Truman into the foreign policy process; Roosevelt spent less than a month in Washington during the eighty-two days that made up his last administration.[4]

Still, one of the strongest criticisms that the historian can make of Roosevelt's tenure in the presidency is the manner in which he left it, with his chosen successor a domestic politician, inexperienced and uninformed about foreign relations, facing one of the great turning points in modern history: the replacement of the European-dominated international system by a global system. To make matters more difficult, U.S. foreign policy at this time depended very much on Roosevelt himself, and on his complicated effort to pursue two contradictory lines at once — Wilsonianism for domestic opinion, and realism in Great Power relations.

Truman's difficult inheritance points up a problem of presidential transition. Candidates for the presidency often choose their running mates on grounds of political utility, not of experience and ability, and then, if their campaigns are successful, assign their Vice Presidents peripheral and routine tasks. An abrupt transition, like that which occurred in April 1945, leaves the new President with the urgent need to demonstrate continuity; re-establish public confidence and international credibility; convince senior officials appointed by and loyal to the former President (as well as members of Congress, the press, even himself) that he now is *the* President; gather together those "multitudinous threads of information"; make a judgment about whose opinion to accept and whose to reject so that he can understand what has actually been happening — and then make the required decisions. In other words, he must try to become President in fact as well as in name. So Truman struggled through much of 1945. That effort helped shape an incipient Soviet-American confrontation and gave increasing substance to the new idea of national security.

Harry Truman was born in 1884 into a devout Baptist family. They lived on a farm for a couple of years, and then in 1890 moved to Independence, Missouri, a few miles to the east of Kansas City. An unusual ailment, colloquially known as "flat eyeballs," forced Truman to start wearing thick glasses at the age of five, and so kept him out of boyhood games and turned him into a voracious reader. History became his lifelong love, in particular, the biographies of great men and military chronicles. Even as a practicing politician later in life, he would sometimes be reading five or six different books at once. Rejected by both West Point and Annapolis because of his vision, he worked for a time as a bank clerk, then returned to the physical rigors of the family farm. He only left it at the age of thirty-four to fight in France during World War I. The camaraderie of Army life and the pleasure he took in being Captain Truman changed his course. He came home determined to do something more with his life than farm. His first venture, a men's clothing store, failed in the postwar depression. He turned to politics. A fiercely loyal Democrat, he won election as a veterans' candidate to the administrative position of judge in Jackson County. He was more an ally of the political machine of Tom Pendergast than a member; but when he came to the United States Senate in 1935, at the age of fifty, he had to endure the humiliation of being thought merely an errand boy for the Kansas City boss. He wore off the label by hard work, and his conviviality won him membership in the Senate's inner club. National prominence came when he proved to be a very effective chairman of a Senate committee that investigated defense industries during World War II.

Unlike Roosevelt, Truman was no renegade, but very much a traditional Wilsonian. While still in the Senate, he played a key role in getting that body to endorse America's postwar participation in the United Nations.[5] The ideas of spheres of influence and a Big Power peace were abhorrent to him. Truman, himself part of the great public consensus, had no idea that Roosevelt had been speaking two languages, nor did he know that aspects of Russian behavior in Eastern Europe were in response to Roosevelt's Great Power diplomacy. Truman could not believe that Russia's quest for security had a rationality; he had to ask himself who could threaten the Soviet Union. Certainly he could not entertain doubts about American intentions. When he was finally confronted with foreign policy questions, all he had as background was his storybook view of history and a rousing Fourth of July patriotism. He tended to see clearly defined contests between right and wrong, black and white. Neither his personality nor his experience gave him the patience for subtleties and uncertainties. Truman admitted that he was "not up on all details" and was trying "to catch the intricacies of our foreign affairs," but he recognized that the nation and the world demanded reassurance, and he was determined to assert himself.[6]

The way in which he caught up on foreign affairs, the people he listened to, the circuits through which information reached him, which problems gained his attention — all these would have an immediate and, in part, a transforming effect on policy. By the time of his first meeting with a high Soviet official, Truman had caught up enough to deliver a blistering rebuke to Molotov. What was said in that meeting on April 23 signified a major shift in American attitudes toward the Russians, a change that the Russians, engaged in their own calculations, could not miss. Truman had rejected the Roosevelt axioms in favor of a cluster of other assumptions, transitional ones, between the Yalta and Riga axioms, which reflected a general confusion and uncertainty about the objectives of the Soviet Union in world affairs. The Russians were thought to have taken advantage of American generosity, especially lend-lease; further, they supposedly were breaking solemn agreements. But if the Russians were treated firmly, according to these new axioms, they could be brought around. In other words, the Soviet Union could be made to accept a subsidiary role in the postwar world. This view focused on the Soviet Union as a state power, albeit a "world bully," rather than as the revolutionary state. It was an "open image"; the Soviet Union was susceptible to pressure and could be bargained with; its behavior could be modified.[7] Truman had arrived at this assessment not by controlling the "threads of information" but by doing the only thing he could — accepting ideas formulated by those around him, then acting on them as his instinct, personality, and the situation dictated. Four sources were prominent.

Almost immediately on becoming President, Truman asked Admiral William Leahy to remain as Chief of Staff to the President and help him "pick up the strands of the business of war." An 1897 graduate of the Naval Academy, Leahy was a gruff, conservative, old-fashioned man, who was suspicious of all foreigners. Claiming expertise in the field of explosives, he was convinced, almost until it was dropped, that the atomic bomb would be a dud.

His distrust of the Soviet Union was total; communism was, for him, a dirty word, arousing "wrath and anger." At Yalta, he had been a dissenter, prophesying that the result of the agreements would be to "make Russia the dominant power in Europe, which in itself carries certainty of future international disagreements and prospects of another war." Leahy directed the preparation by the White House Map Room secretariat of the major briefing papers for the new President, with special emphasis on Poland and the secret surrender dispute involving German troops in northern Italy. In presenting them to Truman, on April 19, Leahy concentrated on Stalin's "insulting language" during the secret surrender, and was pleased to note that Stalin's cables affronted the President's "solid old-fashioned Americanism." Leahy left the meeting confident that his new pupil would take a "strong line" at the upcoming talks with "Molly." [8]

The second influential source was the embassy in Moscow, in particular, Ambassador W. Averell Harriman, who proved to be one of Truman's most admired mentors. While still a college senior, he was elected a director of the Union Pacific Railroad, which had been built up by his father, the tycoon E. H. Harriman. During the years between the two world wars, the younger Harriman occupied himself with international banking (including a brief investment in a vast manganese concession in the Soviet Union, which led to a fleeting acquaintance with Trotsky) and with becoming a polo player of some repute. In 1941, when Harriman was forty-nine, Franklin Roosevelt chose him as a special envoy, first to go to London to oversee the economic lifeline between the United States and Great Britain, later to Moscow as United States ambassador. In that latter post, he almost surely saw Stalin more often than any other American ever did, before or after. He puzzled the Russians a bit. "How can a man with a hundred million dollars look so sad?" Maxim Litvinov once asked one of Harriman's colleagues.

When he first undertook the Moscow assignment, Harriman believed that the Russians would collaborate in the postwar world despite behavior "crude and abhorrent to our standards." In March 1944, he wrote, "In spite of the conjectures to the contrary, there is no evidence that he [Stalin] is unwilling to allow an independent Poland to emerge." By the late summer of 1944, however, the ambassador had lost much of his optimism. Difficulties in the military aid program had always troubled him, but the real turning point came when Stalin refused to cooperate in delivering aid to the Polish underground during the Warsaw uprising that began in August. Harriman concluded that the Russians were cynically waiting for the Germans to kill off troublesome anti-Soviet, Western-oriented Poles before moving themselves. "I am for the first time since coming to Moscow gravely concerned by the attitude of the Soviet Government," he cabled Washington. "These men are bloated with power . . . They expect they can force acceptance of their decisions without question upon us and all countries." [9]

At this time the ambassador was much influenced by George Kennan, who had joined the embassy in 1944.* Harriman spent long periods talking to and learning from his new charge, "batting out flies," in his own phrase, sleeping on questions, then resuming the discussions the next day in an effort to find some explanations for the continually "perplexing developments" in Soviet policy.[10]

This is not to say that the two men saw eye to eye. Kennan, as he later recalled, already favored "a full-fledged and realistic showdown with the Soviet Union" over Eastern Europe.[11] If the West was not willing, he wrote to Bohlen at the time of Yalta, "to go whole hog" to frustrate the Soviet Union, then the only thing to do was partition Germany, divide the Continent into spheres, and determine "the line beyond which we cannot afford to permit the Russians to exercise unchallenged power or to take purely unilateral action." This point of view evolved into what became known as the containment doctrine. Kennan urged Ambassador Harriman to accept explicitly a division into spheres, and to do what he could to marshal American opinion against the new enemy. But, in December 1944, Kennan concluded a memorandum to Harriman, "I know you do not see these things as blackly as I do, and that you will probably not share these views." [12]

What Harriman saw was not a revolutionary state but a bully on the international scene; and, while Kennan thought Soviet goals were immutable, Harriman believed that the Russians could be made to play a different game. "I have been conscious since early in the year of a division among Stalin's advisers on the question of cooperation with us," he wrote Harry Hopkins in September 1944. "It is now my feeling that those who oppose the kind of cooperation we expect have recently been getting their way." His crucial point:

* Despite his identification with the George Kennan who was his namesake, cousin of his grandfather, and explorer of Russia, this George Frost Kennan misses in his memoirs a most curious connection — the elder George Kennan in 1922 published a two-volume biography of Averell Harriman's father.

"Unless we take issue with the present policy there is every indication the Soviet Union will become a world bully wherever their interests are involved." And the solution? "I am convinced that we can divert this trend but only if we materially change our policy toward the Government . . . I am not going to propose any drastic action but a firm and friendly *quid pro quo* attitude." He also indicated his own mood: "I am disappointed but not discouraged. The job of getting the Soviet Government to play a decent role in international affairs is, however, going to be more difficult than we had hoped." [13]

Yet Harriman continued to be of two minds; Soviet cooperation was possible, although he defined cooperation to include Russian subservience to the American system or, as he put it, "our concepts." For him, "spheres of influence" was "the unpopular term."

"Averell is a bit of a weather-cock," the British ambassador in Moscow had noted, and Harriman now swung closer to Kennan's views, agreeing that American leaders needed to be alerted to a crisis at hand. He intensified his warnings about the need for a tougher stand. "I do not believe that I have convinced the President of the importance of a vigilant, firm policy in dealing with the political aspects in various Eastern European countries," Harriman regretfully noted after seeing Roosevelt back in Washington in November 1944, though he found the State Department "fully alive to this necessity."

In the early months of 1945, especially after Yalta, during the difficulties over the Balkans and the formation of a new Polish government, he became almost frantic. "The war is going wonderfully well again now," Harriman's daughter Kathleen wrote from Moscow to her sister on March 8, 1945. "But the news is slightly dampened here by our gallant allies who at the moment are being most bastard-like. Averell is very busy — what with Poland, PWs and, I guess, the Balkans. That house is full of running feet, voices and phones ringing all night long — up until dawn." But Roosevelt continued to reject Harriman's interpretation, and refused his request that he be allowed to return home to report personally on deteriorating relations.[14]

The President's death and Stalin's consequent decision to send Molotov to the San Francisco Conference gave Harriman an occasion to return to Washington to argue his case, as well as an opportunity to establish his position with the new President. Flying west over the Atlantic, he managed to beat Molotov by two days; the latter took a safer route, by way of Siberia and Montana.

Harriman arrived on his Paul Revere mission, nervous, with a tic in his right eye, fearing that a break was at hand, but convinced that the alarm had to be sounded. "Russian plans for establishing satellite states are a threat to the world and us," he informed State Department officials, adding that the United States had "great leverage," especially in the form of economic aid. He warned Navy Secretary James Forrestal that "we might well have to face an ideological crusade just as vigorous and dangerous as Fascism or Nazism." He told the new President that the United States faced a "barbarian invasion of Europe." The theme caught on. "The Soviet Union's interpreting our attitude as a sign of weakness," warned Assistant Secretary of State Nelson Rockefeller, was being "mirrored in many Latin American countries, where governments were losing their respect for the United States for giving in to the Russians so frequently."

His trip home had accomplished Harriman's personal goal: to assure himself continued direct access to the White House and to strengthen his relations with the new President. But his success did not please everyone in the State Department. "I am burned up with the way in which Harriman has been acting," Secretary of State Stettinius complained on April 22. "He went to see the President without any of us knowing about it and has not reported to anyone yet what took place." [15]

Edward R. Stettinius, Jr., had become board chairman of United States Steel when he was thirty-eight. He was a bluff, handsome man with prematurely white hair, a big smile, and very white teeth. (Latin American diplomats often called him *Los Dientes*, "the Teeth.") He was regarded with some affection, but not with great respect, by many in the State Department, where he was known as Big Brother Ed. Roosevelt, in order further to concentrate power in his own hands, had deliberately chosen the weak Stettinius as successor to Hull at the end of 1944. The new Secretary could preside skillfully at meetings, and possessed a keen eye for public relations and cleanliness, but did not have much of a mind for diplomacy. How seriously could others take a Secretary who seemed more concerned that messages to the President be typed on the State Department's special large-character typewriter than with the content of the messages, who enthusiastically urged FDR to set aside an hour every Wednesday to take tea with "incoming and outgoing" foreign and American ambassadors?

Because Roosevelt's death put Stettinius first in the line of succession, his days as Secretary were numbered.[16] Nevertheless, at this point, Stettinius retained influence. As the principal channel between Truman and the State Department, he transmitted the Department's institutional concerns to the President. An initial briefing memorandum on April 13 informed Truman: "Since the Yalta Conference, the Soviet Government has taken a firm and uncompromising position on nearly every major question." But Stettinius had shared in the Yalta optimism, and still looked forward to the United Nations extravaganza he was producing, which was to open shortly in San Francisco. He moderated to some degree the attitude of the career officers. Stettinius and H. Freeman Matthews, director of the Office of European Affairs in the State Department, agreed on the following conclusion: "A spectacular change from the mood of the Conference to the more recent developments of an unfavorable nature can be explained on the basis of political leaders whom Stalin had to advise on his return to Moscow. These leaders may well have told Stalin that he had 'sold out' at Yalta. They are the equivalent of our isolationists." Both Stettinius and Matthews continued to hold a favorable image of Stalin himself. Matthews said that Stalin was the only dictator he had ever seen who had a sense of humor.[17]

As the war in Europe was coming to an end, the British argued that a more forceful line had to be taken toward the USSR. Poland was not only a question of "honor," as Churchill had said at Yalta; it was also his obsession. Whatever Churchill's optimism after Yalta, a combination of factors — the Soviet position, domestic political pressures, stubbornness on the part of the London Poles — quenched it.[18]

Roosevelt's death gave Churchill an opportunity to reassert his views; he wasted no time. Truman, susceptible to Churchill's great prestige, was more likely than the former President to accept the Prime Minister's interpretation. "It is important to strike a note of our unity of outlook and action at the earliest moment," Churchill wired immediately. Anthony Eden, on his way to San Francisco, stopped in Washington to size up the new President and share what

Churchill modestly described as "our impressions of what is actually happening in Moscow and Warsaw." Eden saw Truman twice, and they quickly came to an understanding on the Polish question. The Foreign Secretary declared that Anglo-American relations had never been closer; he had successfully conveyed to his receptive listener the British position that the Soviet Union had to be "brought up sharply against realities" and made to recognize "Anglo-American strength." [19]

Truman's attitude — and, finally, the attitude of the United States government — toward the Soviet Union was a compilation and extraction of the views urged on him from four sources: Leahy, Harriman, Stettinius, and Churchill. Yet their views were not the only ones being fed into the Oval Office. Truman also heard from individuals who had functioned as special agents for Roosevelt. The very fact that they were associated with no bureaucracy or organization had appealed to the late President, who appreciated that each of them, to one degree or another, shared his ideas on Soviet relations. Harry Hopkins told Truman that Stalin "is a forthright, rough, tough Russian . . . He can be talked to frankly." Hopkins, however, was desperately sick; he had left his bed in the Mayo Clinic only when he received the devastating news from Warm Springs. Although he talked with Truman about his observations, he was in no position to argue against the views of the others. Joseph Davies, too, was in the hospital and did not see Truman for some time after the accession.[20] Bernard Baruch — "that old Pooh-bah," as Roosevelt once called him [21] — sent Truman a memorandum in which historian D. F. Fleming, sketching briefly Russian-Western relations since the revolution, advised American leaders at least to try to understand the Soviet viewpoint. There is no indication that Truman took the time to read the paper. In any case, the advice would have been drowned out by what he was hearing in his immediate circle.[22]

The only serious dissenter who could make himself heard was War Secretary Henry Stimson. Unlike most others, he was not an advocate of either the United Nations or of America's global mission. Nor was he convinced of the unavoidable enmity of the United States and the USSR. He stood closest to Roosevelt's own concept of a Great Powers peace. In December 1944 and January 1945, he warned Roosevelt and Stettinius that it was unrealistic to proceed with an international organization before securing understanding among the Great Powers. Both Stimson and Roosevelt recognized that the interests of the USSR in its border regions would take precedence — inevitably, however unpalatably to the U.S. — over the interests of other states; the two men, unlike many other policymakers, could substitute what might be called a Mexican analogy for that of Munich. That is, they could understand how uncomfortable the U.S. would feel if Mexico were to become a potential ally for another Great Power. Not checked by domestic political considerations as Roosevelt was, Stimson could be explicit.[23]

In early May 1945, he talked over the telephone with Assistant Secretary of War John McCloy, then in San Francisco:

Stimson: I think that it's not asking too much to have our little region over here which never has bothered anybody
McCloy: Yes
Stimson: outside it, and retain — uh — less easily called upon right to intervene abroad
McCloy: Yes, yes
Stimson: I mean we don't go abroad unless there's a world war ... The thing should be pared out so that we are not immersed in what I used to call the local troubles of Europe
McCloy: Yes ...
Stimson: Well you don't think that Russia is going to give up her right to act unilaterally in those nations around her which she thinks so darned — are useful, like Romania and Poland and the other things — you don't think she's going to give that up do you?
McCloy: Uh, no, she will, no ...[24]

Stimson worried that "some Americans are anxious to hang on to exaggerated views of the Monroe Doctrine and at the same time bite into every question that comes up in Central Europe."[25] He had already noted in his diary on April 16: "Our respective orbits do not clash geographically and I think on the whole we can probably keep out of clashes in the future." At all costs, he wanted to avoid stepping into the "Balkan mess."[26]

Stimson had only one opportunity to convey such views to President Truman, and that was during the Molotov visit. Molotov had come to pay his respects at the American embassy in Moscow in the early morning hours of April 13, where a party had been stunned into silence by the news of Roosevelt's death. Stuttering from nervousness, Molotov spoke highly of the departed President, although, it seemed to some, with a certain economy, and then started asking questions about the unknown new President.[27] Now, just over a week later, he was in Washington for a crucial firsthand appraisal.

On his arrival, on Sunday, April 22, Molotov had a polite conversation with Truman. Another meeting was scheduled for late the next afternoon. Before the second meeting, on the morning of the twenty-third, Stettinius, equipped with "the essential paper" prepared by Elbridge Durbrow, assured the British that if no progress was made he would "mobilize the President to talk like a Dutch Uncle to Molotov." In the middle of the afternoon, Stimson found himself unexpectedly summoned to an emergency meeting at the White House with Truman and his other senior advisers to prepare for the next meeting with Molotov. "Without warning, I was plunged into one of the most difficult situations I have ever had since I have been here," Stimson noted in his diary.[28]

Right from the beginning, the President structured the discussion, making clear his own views and indicating the responses he expected: "Our agreements with the Soviet Union so far had been a one-way street and that could not continue; it was now or never." Truman said he intended to go on with the plans for San Francisco and "if the Russians did not wish to join us they could go to hell."

Only then did the President seek advice. Most of the men echoed his words. "We had better have a showdown with them now than later," said Navy Secretary Forrestal.

Although he was acutely embarrassed, Stimson did what he could to argue restraint. He thought it was State Department clumsiness and an American emphasis on "idealism" and "altruism," rather than on "stark realities," that had created the near crisis. Harriman and the American military representative, John Deane, had magnified small slights and irritations into major issues, and now Stimson saw the policymakers "rushing" headlong toward a break. In an effort to slow them down, if not bring them to a halt, he suggested several crucial points to be added to the calculations: Political democracy was not so easily grafted onto societies where no liberal tradition existed; only the United States and the United Kingdom "have a real idea of what an independent free ballot means." He pointed out that in the major military matters, the Russians had kept their word and the United States military authorities had come to count on it. In fact, "they had often been better than their promise." Poland was an unwise test case: "Without fully understanding how seriously the Russians took this Polish question we might be heading into very dangerous waters."

Then he pointed out one of the most important factors: "The Russians perhaps were being more realistic than we were in regard to their own security."

Stimson, however, was alone. Only Marshall agreed that the U.S. should avoid antagonizing the Russians, but his reasoning was more narrow: the Russians could delay entry into the Pacific war "until we had done all the dirty work." Admiral Leahy, though he argued against the Stimson position, did make a curious admission: "The Yalta agreement was susceptible to two interpretations."

Truman was obviously disappointed in Stimson's advice. He explained that he would make up his mind with Harriman, Leahy, and the State Department representative — and he said goodbye to Stimson, Forrestal, and the service chiefs.[29] But his mind was already cast by what he had heard in the previous eleven days. Passing lightly over the dissent of Stimson and Marshall, Admiral Leahy accurately summarized the prevailing sentiment: the United States should get tough. "It was the consensus of opinion of the conferees that the time had arrived to take a strong American attitude toward the Soviets, and that no particular harm can now be done to our war prospects even if Russia should slow down or even stop its war effort in Europe and Asia." The bully would be taught a lesson.

At about the same time, Molotov was seeing Joseph Davies. The Russian worried that "full information" might have died with Roosevelt and that "differences of interpretations and possible complications would arise which would not occur if Roosevelt lived." Davies, concerned that Truman "might rely on others" and make a "snap judgment," advised Molotov to ask for a chance to explain the Russian position.[30]

Molotov saw the President at five-thirty on April 23. Struggling to follow Davies' advice in an unexpectedly tense situation, he tried to outline the Russian case, especially on the Polish question.

The President, however, was in no mood for ambiguities. Three days before, having discussed matters with Harriman and Stettinius, he had declared: "We could not, of course, expect to get 100 percent of what we wanted," but he felt that "on important matters . . . we should be able to get 85 percent." Now, bent on obtaining that chunk, Truman brushed over Molotov's statement and instead lectured the Russian in what Leahy described as "plain American language." The Russians had to stick to their agreements, as interpreted in Washington. Relations could no longer be "on the basis of a one-way street."

Molotov turned white at the dressing down. "I have never been talked to like that in my life," he said.*

"Carry out your agreements and you won't get talked to like that," Truman replied curtly.[31]

Those who had urged their views on Truman were pleased by his performance. Leahy noted in his diary that the "President's strong American stand" left the Russians only two courses of action: "either to approach closely to our expressed policy in regard to Poland" or to drop out of the new international organization. He went on to add: "The President's attitude was more than pleasing to me, and I believe it will have a beneficial effect on the Soviet attitude toward the rest of the world. They have always known we have the power, and now they should know that we have the determination to insist upon the declared right of all people to choose their own form of government." On the same day, Eden had assured Churchill that "the new President is not to be bullied by the Soviets." [32]

A stern lecture by the President of the United States to the Foreign Minister of the Soviet Union was hardly the cause of the Cold War. Yet that exchange did symbolize the beginning of the postwar divergence that led to confrontation. And it signaled to the ever-suspicious Russians that Roosevelt's policy might well be finished, and that, with the war in Europe ending, the Americans no longer needed the Russians, and might challenge their dominance in Eastern Europe. It also flashed a message to top U.S. officials that Truman was setting out on a course different from that of his predecessor.

Why this verbal confrontation? Especially, why over Poland? The

* "Knowing who his boss was," Adam Ulam writes of Molotov, "one must assume that the Soviet statesman was exaggerating."

Soviets had their own lessons about Russian security, painfully learned and obsessively held, to guide their thinking. Their entire strategic overview was based on vast land armies moving between Germany and Russia. They were not going to give up those Polish "gates," won with so much blood, to a group that Molotov characterized as "secretly an enemy" — and the London Poles would have had to agree with his characterization. Admiral Leahy had concluded his diary account on April 23 with an odd statement: "I personally do not believe it is possible to exclude dominant Soviet influence from Poland, but that it is possible to give the Government of Poland an external appearance of independence."[33] Did this concern for appearances mean that the Senate and public opinion were Truman's primary concern? No, for public opinion at that time held many diverse, contradictory strains; indeed, if anything, policymakers felt that the public was naïve and uninformed about the Soviet Union.

A primary reason was the inclination toward global involvement that now governed the reactions of many American leaders. It was not merely that Americans were concerned about the fate of the peoples of Eastern Europe, although that concern was there. In 1937, it will be recalled, the American minister in Riga, Arthur Bliss Lane, had described Eastern Europe, with the possible exception of Russia, as "perhaps the least important of all the areas in the world with which the United States has to deal." The intervening years had transformed the American mind. The American leaders no longer simply found dictatorship abhorrent; they felt *responsible* for what happened all over the world. They were gripped again by messianic liberalism, the powerful urge to reform the world that has been called Wilsonianism. They wanted a world safe both for liberal democracy and liberal capitalism. Why else had they joined the war against totalitarianism and tyranny? It was for the best of reasons, then, that they would oppose the Soviet Union on its Eastern European sphere. They were liberators, not imperialists.[34]

There were those on both sides of the dispute in the policy councils who did not share this outlook, but for the most part it was very widely held. It was Harriman's view, and it was Truman's, and it was embodied in the great domestic Wilsonian consensus. Truman may well have thought he was carrying out Roosevelt's policies; he did not perceive that Roosevelt had bequeathed him a hand in a very tricky game, that of playing off the domestic consensus against the Great Power consortium. Truman could not have seen it, for he was part of that domestic consensus.

And this is why Poland had become a test case, a test of Russian intentions: would the Soviets subscribe to the universal system (which was really an American system) or would they pursue a distinct strategy of their own? But the Americans had structured the test in such a way as to ensure negative results; they had chosen a poor question. For Russia, Stalin had emphasized at Yalta, Poland was "not only a question of honor but of security." This was practical arithmetic; not merely Stalinist Russia, but any great power, its armies in the field, would seek to assure itself of the orientation of its neighbors. It was unfortunate that only one major policymaker, and one who temperamentally could not be a Truman intimate, Henry Stimson, had pointed out that geographic propinquity should be weighed at least as carefully as universal principle. Some months earlier, reporting on Poland, Averell Harriman had declared, "I don't see how we can afford to stand aside without registering the strongest objections." That statement, alas, characterized America's part in deciding the fate of Eastern Europe. Postponement, alarm, outrage, vocal protest, commitment to the Atlantic Charter, identification with the position of the London Polish government, but also an absence of American forces — all these elements defined that role.[35]

There was another aspect to this global stance. America's relation to the rest of the world was in the process of being reformulated. In place of the hoary terms "national interest" and "national defense," a new term that symbolized the reformulation was coming into use: "national security." Dangers did not have to be "clear and present" to be alarming. America's safety and security were also now measured by what took place far beyond its borders. World War II had been a close enough call. U.S. leaders dared not stand by and watch another dictator, another potential Hitler, step-by-step expand his realm and base of operations. The course of events in Poland, the Soviet sphere in Eastern Europe — these were seen to constitute immediate risks for the United States. "Russian plans for establishing satellite states are a threat to the world and to us," Harriman told State Department officials in April. "The Soviet Union, once it had control of bordering areas, would attempt to penetrate the next adjacent countries." And thus the United States had to make an issue out of Poland and try to push back the Soviet sphere. "The issue ought to be fought out in so far as we could with the Soviet Union in the present bordering areas," added Harriman.[36]

Truman might have responded differently, but was the victim of his own narrow references, and the needs cast upon him by his accession. "Whom would he rely on?" This was the question Joseph Davies had noted down on April 12; it was the question that inevitably occurred to every member of the old Roosevelt court. Truman, in his difficult situation, did the only thing he could — he listened to those whom he took to be Roosevelt's principal advisers, save for the obvious exception of the ailing Hopkins. In the middle of May, when he had begun to have second thoughts, he told Roosevelt's daughter, perhaps defensively, perhaps only plaintively, that all his advisers had urged him "to be hard with the Russians." [37]

Franklin Roosevelt, who had appeared a permanent fixture of the national life, had died suddenly at a critical time in world affairs. People, including the new President himself, required reassurance. Truman had to prove himself, and that meant showing that he was tough, that he could not be pushed around, that he was decisive and in charge. Roosevelt tended to defer problems, to wait, to slide over them and around them. Truman much preferred a crisp solution. During his first weeks as President, many senior officials commented on the quick and self-assured way in which he seemed to make up his mind. But Henry Wallace was more perceptive than many others: "Truman's decisiveness is admirable. The only question is as to whether he has information behind his decisiveness to enable his decisions to stand up." A few weeks later he noted that Truman had been "very incisive and hard-boiled" at a Cabinet meeting. "This tendency toward an incisive and hard-boiled attitude has its advantages but sooner or later it will result in obscuring the truth and then there will be trouble."

Even Truman's friend, House Speaker Sam Rayburn, worried. He remarked approvingly on Truman's alacrity in making decisions, but added, "I am afraid one of these days he will make a decision based on inadequate information." [38]

You don't know how difficult the thing has been for me. Everybody around here that should know anything about foreign affairs is out.

— HARRY TRUMAN, June 1945 [1]

IV

The Straight One-Two to the Jaw

ACROSS THE BOARD, policy reflected the new attitude — toward Indochina, Yugoslavia, and Japan, at the United Nations conference in San Francisco, and in the effort to use American economic power to discipline the errant Soviet state. Counterforce, however, brought not the desired effect but, instead, incipient confrontation; so Truman soon stepped back, toward the Yalta axioms and a composition of differences.

Many of the threads of information in these confusing weeks ran through the hands of one official, Undersecretary of State Joseph Grew, who oversaw day-to-day business in the Department during the long periods when Secretary Stettinius was attending conferences.

Acting Secretary for two thirds of the time from January into August of 1945, Grew had been in the Department forty-one years, ten of them as ambassador to Japan, including a half year of internment at the outbreak of World War II. The deeply conservative Grew suffered a hearing problem, which intensified the introversion that was part of his temperament. He had never forgiven the Bolsheviks for making their revolution, and retained an implacable hatred of the Soviet Union and communism. (One of his few consolations for having to mingle socially with the Russian ambassador while in Japan was being able to buy caviar at a little over two dollars a pound.)

Wartime service in Berlin and Vienna during the First World War and in Tokyo in the years leading up to the Second had left him with a deep conviction that aggression had to be resisted.[2]

For several decisive months, Grew channeled and structured the information and recommendations reaching the President's desk. As Acting Secretary in a hurried, confused time, he met with the President once, sometimes several times a day. In many cases presidential "decisions" were no more than pro forma approval of recommendations shaped by Grew and others. Truman knows "the score all along the line [and] certainly won't stand for any pussyfooting in our foreign relations and policy, all of which, of course, warms my heart," Grew wrote on May 2. "When I saw him today I had fourteen problems to take up with him and got through them in less than fifteen minutes with a clear directive on every one of them." He oversaw the preparation of reports on Soviet policy in Eastern Europe for Truman, and brought in visitors who repeated to the President what was in the reports. On May 19 Grew declared he had never known a President "so genuinely grateful for advice on any subject." A month later he wrote Stettinius, "The President has been magnificent in backing up nearly all my recommendations."[3]

The change in administrations and orientation was manifested almost immediately in American policy toward Indochina. Roosevelt had made unmistakably clear that he held, as Secretary Stettinius put it on January 3, 1945, "some very definite political views on this subject." FDR opposed the return of French rule, favoring instead some sort of international trusteeship until Indochina achieved independence. Roosevelt's plans had suffered setbacks by this time, particularly because they depended upon a Chinese Policeman in Asia — which was obviously already a chimera by the end of 1944. In addition, the British joined Charles de Gaulle in opposing the strategy, leading Roosevelt to complain at one point that he had tried to discuss the question with Churchill — "or perhaps discussed is the wrong word. I have spoken about it 25 times, but the Prime Minister has never said anything."[4]

After FDR's death, U.S. leaders began the steps, without realizing their significance, that led initially to U.S. support for France in the first Indochina war and then to America's deep involvement in the second Indochina war. The State Department officials who initiated the change viewed Indochina within the framework of a perceived world communist threat. Thus, they opposed a nationalist movement with a strong communist element, and at the same time wanted to solidify relations with France — in part so that France would be a European bulwark against Soviet influence on that continent. Expressing the view of the Office of European Affairs, James Dunn assured Harriman on April 21, "The Department is making every effort to improve relations with France . . . The main point of difficulty is Indo-China, a problem now being studied." The Office of European Affairs proposed "a return to the *status quo ante* without any commitments from France." In Dunn's view, it was "necessary to propitiate France." [5]

Sharp disagreement came from the Division of Far Eastern Affairs, whose members believed that the authority of the European colonial powers in Asia had been undermined by Japanese victories during the war, and that the nationalist forces could not be stifled any longer. But Truman, apparently, was not informed of the views held by both FDR and the Far Eastern Affairs Division, and the Office of European Affairs triumphed. "The record is entirely innocent of any official statement of this government questioning, even by implication, French sovereignty over Indo-China," Stettinius assured French Foreign Minister Bidault within a month of Roosevelt's death.[6]

In 1945, Southeast Asia was still of secondary interest, on the distant periphery of world affairs. Europe was the caldron of international politics, and it was there that a more obvious effect of this new attitude, as well as the most important instance of Grew's influence, became apparent. This was in the United States government's stand during the Trieste crisis in May, when fighting between the United States and Britain on one side, and Yugoslavia on the other, seemed imminent — at times only hours away. The crisis was a contest between Anglo-American forces and the well-organized Yugoslavian partisans for occupation rights and control of Trieste and the Venezia Giuilia hinterland, an area of mixed Italian and Slav populations that was a target of nationalist agitation from both sides. What was of crucial importance, though not known by U.S. policymakers, was that the Soviet Union opposed Yugoslavian actions as dangerous and provocative adventurism. The situation, although tense, was primarily a *local* problem.[7]

Once the dispute broke out, the State Department quickly adopted two premises: the Yugoslavian occupation of a substantial part of the region was a case of totalitarian aggression; and the Yugoslavs were acting as agents of the Russians.[8] Underlying these premises were the Riga axioms. Indeed, the political officer who was in the field, advising the Allied forces and shaping the reports and recommendations sent home, was Alexander Kirk, who had been in charge in Moscow before World War II.

The situation, as reported, simply confirmed what Grew and other officials believed about the Soviet Union. From the first, Grew felt the clash had to come. In this he was joined by Churchill, who also thought Trieste should be made into a major issue, and so informed Truman in several messages, including his first major "Iron Curtain" telegram, on May 12: "What will be the position in a year or two, when the British and American armies have melted . . ." [9] Grew declared to the President that Trieste was of great importance "to the future peace of Europe," and that the problem was one of deciding whether the United States would allow Russia to use satellites to establish "whatever states and boundaries look best for the future of the USSR." Truman had resisted an armed confrontation for fear of an outcry in the United States against taking on the popular partisans. But he changed his mind and accepted Grew's interpretation: "The only solution was to 'throw them out,' " he said.[10]

Yet though the President accepted the premises, policy implementation was curtailed because the chief military adviser, Henry Stimson, did not. He thought the State Department was "unrealistic" and that the British were trying to manipulate the Americans. This is just "one of the periods which come in every war," Stimson told the President on May 10. "It was not wise to get into the Balkan mess." Successful in urging restraint, Stimson was able to get the Americans and the British to limit themselves to a show of force; the Yugoslavs responded on May 18 with a conciliatory message. Tension receded, and Eden, upon his return to London, pronounced the situation "better." [11]

For Grew, the Trieste episode went beyond a diplomatic problem. It was dramatic corroboration of views already held. In the early morning hours of May 19, after a sleepless night, gripped by pervasive anxiety, Grew wandered downstairs in his home and set out his understanding of international problems and "Soviet Russian expansion" in a codified form. It was very much the view from Riga. World War II had resulted in "the transfer of totalitarian dictatorship and power from Germany and Japan to Soviet Russia which will constitute in future as grave a danger to us as did the Axis." Eastern Europe represented "the future world pattern [Russia] will aim to create" — step by step, through Europe. Then, he wrote, both the Near East and the Far East "will be brought into the same pattern." War with the Soviet Union "is as certain as anything in this world can be certain." The United States should respond by maintaining its military power and strengthening relations with Britain, France, and Latin America (though he noted skeptically, "These countries will do us in the eye whenever they can"). The "most fatal thing" would be "to place any confidence whatever in Russia's sincerity," for she regards "our ethical behavior as a weakness to us and an asset to her." His immediate conclusion: "As soon as the San Francisco Conference is over, our policy toward Soviet Russia should immediately stiffen, all along the line. It will be far better and safer to have the showdown before Russia can reconstruct herself and develop her tremendous potential military, economic and territorial power." [12] Grew was attempting to have the Trieste issue, a limited and local problem, treated as the first stage in what he saw as the major and inevitable conflict of the postwar years.

Grew had tried in two ways to stiffen American policy in connection with the war against Japan. He based this attempt on a premise in his early morning memorandum: once the Soviet Union entered the war in the Far East, "then Mongolia, Manchuria, and Korea will gradually slip into Russia's orbit, to be followed in due course by China and eventually Japan." Better, then, to bring the war to a speedy end before the Russians could move.

In the middle of May, in the atmosphere of growing tension with Russia and Yugoslavia, he initiated a canvass, with Averell Harriman's cooperation, to ascertain "whether we are going to support what has been done at Yalta" (that is, the concessions made to the Soviet Union in the Far East),* or whether those concessions would in some way be withdrawn. The inquiry was aimed primarily at the War Department and Stimson. The War Department successfully opposed reconsideration, arguing that Russia could almost certainly

* In the secret Yalta agreement, the Russians had guaranteed to join the war against Japan two or three months after the end of the European war in exchange for certain "concessions." These included the southern part of the island of Sakhalin; the internationalization of the port of Dairen with Soviet interests "preeminent"; the lease of Port Arthur as a naval base by the USSR; and joint Soviet-Chinese operation of two railways in Manchuria.

obtain most of these concessions by its own armed power, "regardless of United States military actions short of war." The War Department wanted to do nothing that might interfere with prompt Russian entry into the war against Japan, for Soviet assistance "almost certainly . . . will materially shorten the war and thus save American lives." Stimson also thought it foolish to raise so controversial a question with the Russians without a clearer notion of whether the atomic bomb would work and thus perhaps provide an alternative to Soviet participation.[13]

Late in May, Grew and John McCloy began arguing for acceptance of a formula that, by letting the Japanese know that they could retain the Emperor, might contribute to an early settlement. Such a declaration was not made, however, because of the avalanche of problems tumbling in on policymakers: the transition of responsibility in the Department of State; the conflicting signals from Tokyo; Stimson's desire to wait for more concrete information about the development of the atomic bomb; fear that the Japanese military would interpret such an offer as a sign of American weakness and weariness and thus take fresh heart for the last battle; and Roosevelt's demand for unconditional surrender. This policy not only had powerful public support but also the backing of senior U.S. military officers, who feared that a surrender less than unconditional might lead to an "inconclusive peace." [14]

Despite their common opposition to the Yalta concessions, there was an important difference between Averell Harriman and Joseph Grew, the same one that separated Harriman from George Kennan and other members of the Riga School. Those whose thinking had been shaped by the Riga axioms saw no way for the United States to affect the inevitable Soviet objectives; they wanted to throw up the necessary barricades as quickly as possible. The contrast was heightened at the end of May when Harriman suggested that the United States recognize the governments of Rumania, Bulgaria, and Finland. Elbridge Durbrow, now chief of the Eastern European Division, took strong exception. Recognition, he argued, would mean that "we were in reality dealing only with a branch of the Kremlin." He added, "We have made too much of a fuss about getting a Democratic Government in Poland to through [sic] it all down the drain by this move." [15]

Harriman and Truman, however, clung to the transitional image of Russia as "world bully." The Soviet Union was susceptible to pressure, especially economic pressure, which could be used to control, discipline, and punish it. Harriman told the Secretary's Staff Committee on April 21 that it was "important for the Department to get control of all the activities of agencies dealing with the Soviet Union so that pressure can be put on or taken off, as required."

This effort centered on the questions of postwar loans and credits, lend-lease, and reparations.

In January, both Foreign Minister Molotov, in Moscow, and Treasury Secretary Henry Morgenthau, in Washington, had raised the question of America's making multibillion-dollar postwar loans to Russia. Roosevelt, though expressing "keen interest," ordered the matter deferred.[16] Harriman and the State Department wanted to use deferral as a tactic, which would amortize its political worth. An immediate response, declared Will Clayton, Assistant Secretary for Economic Affairs, would mean to "lose what appears to be the only concrete bargaining lever for use in connection with the many political and economic problems which will arise between our two countries." Deferral was further emphasized in April. "Our experience," Harriman cabled, had "incontrovertibly proved that it is not possible to bank general goodwill in Moscow."[17]

A more limited counterproposal to Molotov was prepared, with the proviso that it depend upon "favorable" political conditions. For Grew, who believed in the revolutionary state, political conditions could never be favorable. He would, he said in May, "be very reluctant to sign any commitment for the future." Harriman, who believed in relations and negotiations, thought the loan could be useful. In May, after Molotov asked why he had never received a response to his January message, Harriman sent Washington an exasperated telegram: "I do feel that some reply or explanation is due the Soviet Government."

Grew, to whom Stettinius had delegated the matter, left no doubt that the loan was not under active consideration. Deferral was permanent. Though Treasury Secretary–designate Fred Vinson continued to believe as late as July that a loan was "our ace in the hole," he was one of a dwindling number. Donald Nelson, a prominent businessman who served as head of the War Production Board and had discussed trade prospects with Stalin in 1944, complained to Truman at the end of July that credits were stuck in the "State Department pigeon-hole."[18]

Meanwhile, Grew was a leader in the effort to bring pressure to bear on the Russians through lend-lease. This was a clear reversal, and one the Russians could not mistake, of FDR's policy.[19] Pulling in the reins on lend-lease, it was thought, could help discipline the Russians, and at the same time right the balance, so that the Russians would no longer get the better part of the bargain that was the Grand Alliance. The symbolic dressing-down of April 23 could be applied in practice. Domestic politics also played a role, for many congressmen feared that lend-lease would be used as a stratagem to float postwar reconstruction loans for foreign nations.[20] Nevertheless, the nature and methods of what turned out to be an abrupt termination, rather than a curtailment, leave little doubt that it was international politics rather than domestic considerations that provided the major stimulus.

Taking advantage of his pivotal position, Grew collaborated with Leo Crowley, head of the Foreign Economic Administration, to get the President to sign an order on May 11 choking off lend-lease. The State Department, observed an official from the War Department, apparently saw it as "a political weapon in connection with difficulties in Central Europe." All agencies agreed, Will Clayton said on May 11, that "the lend lease program for the U.S.S.R. should be so flexible that it could be cut off at any time." Joseph Grew replied, "Lend lease assistance is this government's only leverage against the Soviet Union." [21] While there was general agreement that the reins should be pulled back smartly, Crowley, with Grew's encouragement, interpreted the order so rigidly as to snap the neck. Even ships on the high seas were ordered to turn back.

Harriman and Stettinius, who had agreed that the restrictions should be handled with the skill required to preserve the leverage, were, along with Clayton, shocked at the method of execution. The British, who also suffered from the cut-off, complained bitterly. Stalin later described it as "brutal." The Russians left no doubt that they understood the matter as a form of pressure. The outcry forced some revision, so that goods already in the pipeline would be delivered. Nevertheless, the situation had become so acute that Harriman, reverting as if out of habit to methods he had used under Roosevelt to circumvent the State Department, telegraphed Harry Hopkins personally on June 21: "Am gravely concerned over delays in action on Russian Lend-Lease . . . Do what you can to get immediate action." [22]

Reparations provided the third tool with which to exert economic pressure on the Soviet Union.

The Russians were most anxious to begin the Moscow discussions provided for at Yalta; the British had expressed more willingness to accept the Yalta figure of $20 billion; and an American delegation, headed by Isador Lubin, was poised to leave in mid-April of 1945. However, Harriman, recognizing the Russians' urgency, suggested using reparations as a bargaining lever against "their little willingness to implement a number of the Crimea decisions." He asked that reparations be integrated into an "over-all policy." Yet, still showing that curious ambivalence, he also advised that Lubin "should show at all times a sympathetic approach to the Soviets' desire to obtain large reparations from Germany." [23]

After Roosevelt's death, the reparations question was re-evaluated and, as Harriman had recommended, was integrated into a larger policy. First, lend-lease, economic aid, and reparations all became part of the same bargaining lever. Second, policymakers decided to de-emphasize the $20 billion figure, in effect, discarding it. Third, Truman decided to remove the statistician Lubin as head of the delegation. "This is the most important job in the United States as of this moment," Truman explained to him. "It will determine the whole future of the economy of Europe, and I want somebody as head of the delegation who can throw his weight around." Truman chose instead the tough oil operator Edwin Pauley.[24]

The reparations guidelines were revised in early May, during the period of mounting tension with the Soviet Union and growing concern over the economic chaos in Western and Central Europe, which, Stimson warned Truman, could lead to "political revolution and Communistic infiltration." [25] Former President Herbert Hoover, who had administered relief on an anti-Bolshevik basis in Europe after World War I, was brought back from exile in the towers of the Waldorf-Astoria to join the policy councils, with the active support of Stimson, Forrestal, and Truman himself. By the middle of May, Hoover had seen both the President and Stimson. Hoover and Stimson agreed that the "non-military industry" of neither Germany nor Japan should be destroyed; their plants were vital to the world economy.

But Hoover went much further than Stimson on the question of Russia; and it is plausible that this voice, speaking with considerable experience, would have carried weight. His views were substantially those of the Riga School. The day before Grew wrote his apocalyptic memorandum, Hoover had communicated almost identical fears to Stimson. He also warned the Secretary that Stalin "will set up governments that are largely Communist and likely to become more so in Italy, Greece and Northwest Germany." [26]

In this atmosphere, the reparations guidelines were revised to become as restrictive as possible, and to ensure that the problems of Western Europe and Germany received precedence over those of the Soviet Union. There were two key points. Reparations from current production — that is, the output of German industry — were to be kept as low as possible. Second, all exports from this production would be used first to pay for goods imported from the West, and only after that for reparations deliveries to the East. This was the so-called First Charge Principle. Germany was to be integrated into a multilateral, but American-dominated, world economic order before reparations (in effect, aid) went to the Soviet ally. By this time the Americans were already deeply concerned about the wholesale removal of goods and machinery from Germany by the Russians. "They take everything they can," said Robert Lovett, who played a major role in revising the outlines.[27] What the Americans did not take into account was that German industrial capacity, even after wartime destruction, was probably greater in 1945 than it had been in 1939.[28] Visual evidence also led the Americans to exaggerate the extent of destruction in Germany.

A major factor in United States assessments of the Soviet reparations position was the assumption that the Russians had a well-worked-out plan, shaped by political considerations.* On the contrary, economic concerns were at least as important as the political, and the evidence (which was, of course, not necessarily obvious to American officials at the time) indicates not only great confusion but a bitter battle up to the highest levels of the Soviet government.[29] Georgi Malenkov, head of a "Special Committee for the Economic Disarmament of Germany," arguing that Germany might recover as quickly as it had after the last war, pushed for "economic disarmament," a pastoralization plan. Arrayed against him were the Soviet military, as well as interests represented by Andrei Zhdanov, the

* Again bearing out the general contention that countries tend to exaggerate the purposefulness and policy coherence of nations perceived as rivals.

ideological spokesman, and Anastas Mikoyan, Minister of Foreign Trade. Nicholai Voznesensky, the chief planner, allied with the latter group, in fact formulated the slogan "Reparations for Fulfillment of the Five Year Plan." Officials worked in the interests of their own ministries, competing, even battling with other ministries, and complicating the situation in the Eastern Zone of Germany.

This situation prevailed well into 1946. A former high official of the East German government, Wolfgang Leonhard, recalled driving through the Russian sector of Berlin with a political officer of the Red Army, who pointed to an apartment block and said, "That's where the enemy lives."

"Who — the Nazis?" Leonhard asked.

"No, worse still — our own reparations gang!" [30]

Nothing was settled when the Reparations Commission met in Moscow in the summer of 1945. The Americans insisted on the First Charge Principle; the Russians resisted. The U.S. delegation also felt that the Russians lacked either ability or interest in hard arithmetic.[31] Making matters more difficult was the fact that the Americans and the Russians were talking about different things. The U.S. delegation wanted to discuss commodities and goods — so many railway engines, so much steel, and so forth. The Russians would have none of that; they were prepared to talk primarily in terms of dollar value.

One day during the meeting, Isador Lubin, who had gone along as number two in the American delegation, went walking on the banks of the Moskva River with a senior economist from the Russian delegation.

"Tell me, you're an economist," said Lubin, "explain to me what is the logic of talking about billions of dollars — billions of dollars at what price level, before the war or the present? You can put any figure for any goods. We can say this railroad engine is worth 10 million dollars, and so we can arrive at 20 billion dollars' worth of reparations by manipulating the price level.

"You're interested in rebuilding the USSR," Lubin continued. "We're interested in helping you rebuild. What is it that you need? What is there in Germany that can help you do that, and at the same time not put Germany in a position that we will have to support her for the next generation or two?"

The Soviet economist looked at Lubin and smiled. "You know," he said, pointing up toward the Kremlin, "those people up there are just like you Americans — capitalists."

The Russian was certainly right about the Americans. Some members of the U.S. delegation could not conceal their antagonism and their belief that their directives were too soft; some could not control their entrepreneurial drives. Several of Pauley's colleagues, recruited from the oil business, sold their suits in Moscow at a going price of $250 each.[32]

The effort to "get tough" with Russia, to block what was perceived as Soviet aggressiveness and selfishness, to force Russia to live up to the American interpretation of major agreements — this had been done out of sight. Those in the State Department who urged in these months that the United States "go public" with its diplomatic difficulties were generally rebuffed. The only place where the clash did become visible was at the extravaganza that opened at the San Francisco Opera House on April 25, 1945, the conference to draft the charter for the new United Nations Organization.

"The Delegation was going into the San Francisco Conference under pretty favorable conditions," Secretary Stettinius had observed shortly before the meeting opened. "The only question was the Soviet Union."

"This had always been the only question," delegation member Representative Charles Eaton replied dryly.[33]

The conference represented the interpenetration of international and domestic politics. Senator Arthur Vandenberg, who was a member of the U.S. delegation, rightly remarked that he and his colleagues would have to answer not only to the Soviet Union but also "to the American people and the Senate."[34] Vandenberg, who emerged as the most powerful member of the delegation, rejected the Yalta concept of a Great Powers peace, but had only platitudes and international romanticism — the UNO as "the town meeting of the world" — to offer in its place. Poland was the lens through which he looked at the Soviet Union. Shortly before going to San Francisco, he had written that Poland mattered to him both "for her own precious sake and as a 'symbol.'" He could get "no greater personal satisfaction" than leading "a public denunciation of Yalta and all its works as respects Poland." There was also a question of political satisfaction; he had squeaked into office again in 1944 by only a few thousand votes, and Michigan had a large and vocal Polish population.

Despite popular enthusiasm — autograph hunters besieged delegates — the conference was often acrimonious. Alexander Cadogan, who only a few months before at Yalta had declared that Stalin "*is* a great man," now wondered of the Russians: "How can one work with these animals? And if one can't, what can one hope for in Europe?" The overwrought anti-Russianism of Senator Vandenberg is evident from some diary entries: "Russia may withdraw. If it does, the conference will proceed without Russia . . . The Conference opens today — with Russian clouds in every sky. I don't know if this is Frisco or Munich . . . We must 'stand by our guns' . . . This is the point at which to . . . *win* and *end this appeasement of the Reds before it is too late.*" [35]

The behavior of the American delegation, the tone of the conference, the briefings offered by the ubiquitous Harriman — such factors caused some observers to worry about a Truman "get tough" policy. On April 30, James Byrnes, already slated to become Secretary of State, wrote to Walter Lippmann that the peace "will depend upon what is in the hearts of the people of Russia, Britain and the United States. We cannot promote it by promoting distrust of the Soviets. We must have confidence in each other. And if we expect them to fulfill promises, we must scrupulously fulfill our pledges to them."

In a remark that was an indication of how he would act when he became Secretary, Byrnes said that events demonstrated the wisdom of Lippmann's published suggestion that the Big Three's representatives settle as many differences as possible prior to the conference.

Lippmann wrote back from San Francisco on May 10 that he was "more disturbed about the conduct of our own policy" than he dared say in print: "Though the issue here has apparently been drawn between the Soviets and ourselves, this alignment is not inherent in the nature of things but is due to inexperience and emotional instability in our own delegation. . . . This should never have happened. It would never have happened, I feel sure, if President Roosevelt were still alive, and it will lead to great trouble not only over such matters as the Polish question but throughout the Middle East if we do not recover our own sense of national interest about this fundamental relationship."

About the same time Byrnes was writing to Joseph Davies, "I share your regret as to the Russian situation . . . The feeling that has developed at San Francisco has not helped the Administration in its effort to amicably settle the serious problems." [36]

By the middle of May, Truman himself was beginning to have serious doubts about the "get tough" stand. The "slash-back" on lend-lease had made him somewhat wary of people like Crowley and Grew. He was also wondering if Churchill was manipulating him. "I was having as much difficulty with Prime Minister Churchill as I was having with Stalin," he observed in a memorandum on May 21. "Each of them was trying to make me the paw of the cat that pulled the chestnuts out of the fire." [37] Truman felt the need for other sources of information. "I am new at this thing," he had said to Morgenthau on May 4. A few weeks later, he added, "You don't know how difficult the thing has been for me. Everybody around here that should know anything about foreign affairs is out." It was a difficult time for Truman. "I'm one American who didn't expect to be President," he told his morning staff conference in May. But there was no escape from the exhausting responsibilities of the presidency. He tried to relax with a daily swim in the White House pool and rub-down before dinner, but the press of work was overwhelming, and he was often very tired. He was supposed to get new glasses in May, but he had been reading so many reports and documents, trying to get all the business of government into his head, that his eyes were not right for examination. He missed the conviviality of the Senate club. "I am the lonesomest man in Washington. I have nothing to do but walk around all by myself," he said. "If I hear there is any party going on, I go down and join the boys . . . I am going up to Joe Davies' Friday night to play poker with him." [38] *

Davies, the favorite villain of the Riga School, had several opportunities to hear Truman voice his doubts about the harder line. On April 30, telling Davies about the brittle exchange with Molotov a week earlier, Truman declared, "I gave it to him straight. I let him have it. It was the straight one-two to the jaw." He added that the

* Davies made a note on the evening: "It was a men's party and Marjorie retired. We had a pleasant evening swapping stories and having a typical men's good time. It seemed to do the President good . . . He undoubtedly rather chafes under the constant surveillance, which of course is necessary."

Soviets only understood "the tough method." But then Truman let down the bravado. "Did I do right?" he asked.

Davies' minutes of a conversation on May 13 that continued from four-thirty in the afternoon, with a break for dinner, until midnight indicates how "greatly worried" and even confused the President was. The books piled on the floor in the upstairs hall of the White House emphasized the fact of transition; indeed, the Truman family had actually moved in only a few days before. Sitting in a study on the second floor, Truman at once said how "very much disturbed over the Russian situation" he was, and complained that he was getting very little help. "These damn sheets," he said, pointing to newspapers on his desk, were "stirring things up, making it still more difficult." Exasperated, he suggested that Molotov had gone "out to San Francisco to make trouble," and also asserted that Tito would not have put pressure on Trieste "without the approval of the Kremlin or 'The Generals.' " To Davies' surprise, Truman speculated that Stalin was already "out of control and the Generals [are] dominating the situation."

The President listened attentively, however, as Davies summarized the aspects of wartime diplomacy on which Truman had been poorly informed. Davies said most State Department officials dealing with Russia and Europe were "conditioned in their hostility to the Soviets." Truman agreed that there was such hostility, but declared that there would be a change.

Davies also told Truman of his correspondence with Molotov about the worsening relations, in which the Soviet foreign minister had pointedly written: "I think that personal contact of the heads of our governments could play in this matter an extremely positive part." Truman indicated considerable interest in a high-level meeting, but said budget preparation would prevent his getting away until July. (A week later, Truman confided to Davies, "I have another reason which I have not told anybody" for postponing a meeting until July. The reason was the atomic bomb, about which he then told Davies in detail.) [39]

Even Harriman was now worrying that a break was imminent. On the plane returning from San Francisco, he and Charles Bohlen decided that had Roosevelt been alive he would have sent Harry Hopkins to Moscow to restore "amity" in Soviet-American relations. In Washington, Hopkins, thin, ill, and bedridden, expressed enthusiasm for the trip. Truman, already primed by his conversation with Davies, approved. It would be wrong, however, to assume that Truman had suddenly made a sharp turn. Like Harriman, his mentor, he was still of two minds. He ordered Hopkins to emphasize to Stalin that the United States would carry out its Yalta agreements, and that he expected the Soviets to do likewise. In his memorandum of the conversation, Truman noted, "I told Harry he could use diplomatic language or he could use a baseball bat if he thought that this was the proper approach to Mr. Stalin."

Objections to this mission came from those, like Grew, who saw a threat to their new-found hegemony over policy. For the time being, however, Truman was taking the advice of the late President's non–State Department intimates, returning to a Rooseveltian approach, trying to solve problems and restore mutual confidence at the highest and most direct level, through a trusted agent. Referring to the career diplomats, Truman told aides on June 5, "When you deal with the striped-pants boys, you have to be careful." [40]

With the Hopkins mission, the United States had traveled full circle in its relationship with the Soviet Union. Hopkins' 1941 Moscow trip had been the first step in collaboration, the beginning of the Grand Alliance. This journey (except for a pale reminder in December 1945) marked its end. Hopkins, who as head of the Protocol Committee had always strived to get more aid to the Soviet Union more quickly, was regarded with a special trust and affection by the Russians. Stalin once said Hopkins was the first American with whom he had spoken *po dushe*, "from the soul."

The range covered during Hopkins' two-week stay and the relative frankness of the talks make the meeting noteworthy as a landmark in the history of the Cold War. In their first talk, citing growing concern in American public opinion, Hopkins expressed his own fear that "the entire structure of world cooperation and relations" that Stalin and Roosevelt had "labored so hard to build would be destroyed." Stalin replied that he would not "use Soviet public opinion" as a screen, but rather would outline the "alarm" felt in "Soviet governmental circles" resulting from recent moves by the United States. "The American attitude towards the Soviet Union had perceptibly cooled once it became obvious that Germany was defeated," he said. It was "as though the Americans were now saying that the Russians were no longer needed." It became evident that the Soviets were touchy about agreements and sensitive about their Great Power status. At one point Stalin remarked tartly that the Soviet Union was no Albania.[41]

The Soviet dictator was very careful to raise the question of American economic pressure. If the termination of lend-lease was "designed as pressure on the Russians in order to soften them up then it was a fundamental mistake," said Stalin. If the Russians were "approached frankly on a friendly basis, much could be done . . . Reprisals in any form would bring about the exact opposite effect."

Other matters were dealt with more happily. Stalin quickly promised that Russia would enter the war in the Far East by August 8 if the Yalta agreements were kept. He assented to a Four-Power trusteeship for Korea. He also endorsed a stable China, united under Chiang Kai-shek, making clear both the limited interests of the USSR in the area and his skeptical attitude toward the Chinese communists. Responding to an urgent cable from Washington, Hopkins brought up the impasse at San Francisco on voting procedures in the UNO's Security Council. The Soviet delegation was demanding a veto on discussion as well as action. Hopkins outlined the American proposal: free discussion, a veto on action. Stalin listened carefully, then debated the Soviet Foreign Office position with Molotov in front of Hopkins. "Molotov, that's nonsense!" he finally said, and accepted the American proposal. He was letting Hopkins see how little attention he gave to the United Nations.[42]

As usual, the most difficult question was Poland.[43] The post-Yalta deadlock over the makeup of the new government had continued. Hopkins and Stalin took the dispute into their own hands. Their discussions were complicated by the Red Army's arrest of sixteen "underground" Poles inside Poland. After days of strenuous discussion, the two men produced a list of non-Lublin Poles who were to journey to Moscow for consultations — and so at last they broke the Polish stalemate.[44]

Stalin left no doubt of his own hard-headed respect for America; he recognized that its power far exceeded that of the Soviet Union and even accepted, to some extent, American global interests. Whether the United States wished it or not, he said, it was a world power and would have to accept worldwide interest. It was only American intervention that had defeated Germany in the First World War. "All the events and developments of the last thirty years had confirmed this." In fact, the United States "had more reason to be a world power than any other state. For this reason," Stalin said, he "fully recognized the right of the United States as a world power to participate in the Polish question and the Soviet interest in Poland does not in any way exclude those of England and the United States."

Hopkins' mission was a success. If it had not restored "amity," it was at least a candid exchange that had secured agreement on important questions and, equally important, substantially reduced both tension and suspicion. Harriman reported afterward to Truman that Stalin had also been "gravely concerned over the adverse developments during the past three months." The mission "has been more successful than I had hoped." Although "unsolved problems" would continue, the visit "produced a much better atmosphere for your meeting with Stalin." But Harriman, with a sigh of resignation, remained a Wilsonian, committed to algebra in international relations: "I am afraid Stalin does not and never will fully understand our interest in a free Poland as a matter of principle. He is a realist in his actions, and it is hard for him to appreciate our faith in abstract principles."

The improvement in Soviet-American relations was noted throughout the policy elite. In the middle of June, Henry Stimson observed, as if he were dismissing the entire problem, that he had been troubled "over the recent pinpricks and little explosions which [have] taken place in our relations with Russia." Even Joseph Grew wrote to Stettinius, "I think you are justified in your feeling that the overall picture of our foreign relations is encouraging." [45]

Yet the remission produced by the Hopkins mission was only partial. Truman had been pleased at the outcome, at Hopkins' "accomplishment," and now saw greater value in top-level meetings.[46] Its influence on his interpretation of foreign affairs was immediate and direct. He said, as the mission was drawing to a close, that Russia, "like any other totalitarian state," was dominated by cliques. "If you could sit down with Stalin and get him to focus on the problem, Stalin would take a reasonable attitude." But if the problem never reached Stalin, it might be handled by the "Molotov clique" or "the northern clique." Stalin, Truman felt, "didn't know half the things that were going on." It was almost as though Truman were projecting his own problems onto Stalin. Throughout his first months as

President, Truman had been, as Charles Bohlen recalled, "puzzled by conflicting advice." He had felt acutely the lack of sound counsel. Initially, Truman had heeded the opinions of those who wanted to "get tough" and force a showdown. He had not, however, accepted the Riga axioms and the image of the revolutionary state. In many instances, he said, the Russians did not know in their own minds "what they wanted to do." He had now seen some efficacy in the Yalta axioms, though he had not readily embraced them either. Rather, he had accepted the "world bully" image drawn by Harriman. He looked forward to the coming Big Three meeting at Potsdam. His aim was to roll back Soviet influence. The means included, in some undefined fashion, the atomic bomb, and, more clearly defined, economic pressure. He described the problem in terms of his favorite game, poker. "Russia was pretty much destroyed from Poland," he said. "Unless they did something to remedy that situation promptly, they would have extensive starvation." That was why, Truman explained, he felt he had "the cards in American hands" and he proposed "to play them as American cards." The President expressed succinctly what he saw as the relationship, but he showed little awareness of Stalin's capacity for patience or ability to bluff. "We didn't have to go to the Russians for anything and the Russians very definitely had to come to us for many things." [47]

Harry Hopkins was obviously not the conventional diplomat. In January 1941, shortly after he had come to live in the White House, Roosevelt had called him "that half man." Although ostensibly referring to Hopkins' extreme frailty, perhaps Roosevelt also thought of Hopkins as a complement, an extension, of his own crippled self. After Roosevelt's death, his agent for the Grand Alliance seemed more ghostly than ever. At a big Kremlin banquet during his last mission in June 1945, Hopkins, emaciated, exhausted from dancing, with sweat glistening on his forehead, murmured to Ivan Maisky, "You know, I've got a leave of absence from death."

He managed to survive for another half year, until the end of January 1946. The Yalta axioms lingered on for just about as long.[48]

PART TWO

Peacemaking

> The Soviet Creed has now become a dynamic force in the world. The supposed result of the operation of that creed has caught the imagination of masses everywhere . . . We can readily become jittery and, if so, incidents will occur which will strain our relations. That ought not be and it need not be.
> — JOHN FOSTER DULLES, January 1945

V

The Highest Common Denominator

IN LATE JUNE 1945, when senior officials left the old State Department building at the end of the day, they departed not for home and dinner but for the Shoreham Hotel. There, secretly, in James Byrnes' apartment, they briefed the soon-to-be Secretary of State on the major problems of American foreign relations.[1] On July 3, Byrnes was publicly sworn in. Three nights later, he set sail with Truman aboard the S.S. *Augusta* for Europe and the Potsdam Conference.

Not long after the meeting began, Henry Stimson complained that Byrnes was "hugging matters in this conference pretty close to his bosom."[2] The Secretary of War was hurt at the way Byrnes was shutting him out of policymaking. He might have added that Byrnes was running things out of his hat. But that was the new Secretary's way of operating, the methods developed in thirty-five years of public life.

As 1945 went on, U.S. officials expressed many contradictory opinions about Soviet objectives and the appropriate American foreign policy. Benjamin V. Cohen, one of Byrnes' closest confidants, later recalled: "There was considerable conflict not only between people involved, but also within each individual." In particular, the conflict was acted out in Byrnes' mind, made more complicated by his character. Compromise, negotiation, adjustment of conflicting viewpoints — these to him represented the pinnacle of politics. "Good government lies in seeking the highest common denominator," he wrote. "This is as true in international council as it is in the county court house." The search for a denominator that could satisfy East and West guided his efforts as Secretary.[3]

James Francis Byrnes was born of immigrant Irish stock in Charleston, South Carolina, in 1879. His father died shortly before his birth. He was brought up by his mother, a hard-working dressmaker. At fourteen, Byrnes quit school, learned shorthand, became a court stenographer, then a lawyer; in 1910 he was elected to the United States House of Representatives. A local newspaper approvingly described him during that campaign as a "live wire . . . hustler . . . self-made man." By this time, Byrnes had already spotted the central principle of his career. "Working as a court stenographer, I had begun to learn that in all relationships in life, success and happiness can be achieved only by a willingness to make concessions." In the House and later the Senate, glorying in the give-and-take of committee work, he developed his skill as a negotiator and composer of differences. Some called him a fixer. Although Roosevelt once referred to him as "my wandering boy," he was for the most part a loyal lieutenant of the President, an expediter of New Deal and then war-preparedness legislation. FDR rewarded him with an appointment to the Supreme Court in the summer of 1941. Fifteen months later the President drafted him into the White House as "assistant President," responsible for domestic problems, first as head of the Office of Economic Stabilization and then of the Office of War Mobilization.[4] Byrnes was the adept bureaucratic warrior, a master manipulator of people and the levers of government, easing his way with geniality, informality, and a certain amount of Harper and Old Taylor bourbon whiskey.[5]

In 1944, Byrnes understood Roosevelt as promising him support for the vice-presidential nomination. But Roosevelt concluded that Byrnes' lapsed Catholicism and his southern background would alienate Catholics and black voters in the big cities of the North. FDR turned instead to Truman who, when compared to either Byrnes or to Vice President Henry Wallace, seemed the candidate least likely to cost the ticket votes. Byrnes felt betrayed not only by Roosevelt but also by Truman, who had been a Byrnes protégé since coming to the Senate and, in fact, had indicated that he would nominate Byrnes at the Chicago convention. Byrnes nursed his wounded ambition and pride, and loyally served on — for a time. He accompanied Roosevelt to the Yalta Conference, practicing his old shorthand by taking notes during the sessions. His official resignation reached Roosevelt at Warm Springs, Georgia, on March 30. "Too bad some people are so primadonnaish," was the President's rather ungenerous comment. Finally, on April 8, 1945, Byrnes packed up and went home to Spartanburg, South Carolina, to what he assumed would be retirement.

Four days later Roosevelt died. Navy Secretary Forrestal immediately dispatched his plane to South Carolina to bring Byrnes back to Washington. The new President was eager for Byrnes' guidance, grateful for his familiar presence. Byrnes rode up to Hyde Park on the train with Truman, and sat in the third row with the Truman family during the late President's funeral, which was held in the little garden on the Roosevelt estate. For the next few weeks, Byrnes was the tutor, advising the President on how to handle people, using his shorthand notes ("my souvenirs," he called them) to brief Truman on the Yalta Conference, representing the President on the Interim Committee, which formally recommended at the end of May that the atomic bomb be used without warning on Japan.[6]

The day after they returned from Hyde Park, Truman proposed that Byrnes become Secretary of State, which would put him next in line for the presidency, now that there was no Vice President. Byrnes quickly accepted. Both men agreed that the appointment should be kept secret until after the United Nations conference, so as not to undercut Stettinius at San Francisco. The Byrnes-Truman relationship already held within it the grounds for discord. Byrnes could not put aside the thought that he might have been sitting in the Oval Office himself. He treated his former protégé with an easy familiarity not altogether distinguishable from condescension; Truman, acquiescent at this juncture, voiced unlimited confidence in Byrnes and deferred to his judgment. Byrnes had accepted the Secretaryship with a new vision of what could be the summit of his career — if not President, he could be peacemaker.

Byrnes began his efforts in the Berlin suburb of Potsdam, where in mid-July the Allied leaders assembled for the last of the great wartime conferences. Churchill, code-naming it Terminal, had insisted since early May that such a meeting be convened in "some unshattered town in Germany" before "the British and American armies have melted," which, he feared, would remove the dike against the red tide from the East. Many of Truman's own advisers likewise urged an early meeting. Truman put off the assemblage, partly because he did not like the idea, partly because of the many problems facing him in his new job, but also to await more definitive word on S-1, the atomic bomb.

The neighboring suburbs of Potsdam and Babelsberg, the latter the once favored haunt of the German film colony, had somehow survived the war mostly intact. "Here we are," Cadogan wrote, "in the midst of this devastated and denuded country, living in a little town of our own." Most of Berlin was a city of corpses, rubble, bombed-out buildings, and broken sewers, wandering women, children, and old men — a city of the dead, a monument to the Hitlerian dream.*

In their diplomatic enclave on the outskirts of this shattered capital of the defeated, the victors were to begin making the peace.[7]

Hovering above the many specific questions was, for the American and British, another problem — their long-standing effort to assay the international objectives of the Soviet Union. Stimson devoted much of his time in Berlin to thinking about how to manage Russian-American relations with the imminent advent of nuclear weapons. Disturbed and confused, he presented the President with a memorandum, "Reflections on the Basic Problems Which Confront Us," in which he argued that the best hope was to get Stalin to establish civil liberties.[8] A British diplomat described a luncheon conversation with his colleagues: "Debate on the perennial question whether Russia is peaceful and wants to join the Western Club but is suspicious of us, or whether she is out to dominate the world and is hoodwinking us." Their conclusion is a virtual rule of international relations: "It always seems safer to go on the worse assumption."

The Russians, for their part, were trying to get a better fix on the new President. The Soviets had known what to expect from Roosevelt, Deputy Foreign Minister Andrei Vyshinsky told Davies, but they knew next to nothing about Truman. The next day Vyshinsky clumsily asked if Truman and Byrnes were close.[9] The British de-

* The monuments were personal as well. While at Potsdam, Eden learned officially that his son, a Royal Air Force pilot, had been killed in the crash of his plane on a mountainside in Burma.

cided that Truman was "quick and businesslike." This was an image Truman deliberately fostered. "I took 'em on a ride when I got down to presiding," Truman wrote his mother after the first meeting. "It was a nerve-wracking experience but it had to be done." Stalin cooperated in expediting matters, unlike Churchill, who was distracted by the upcoming British general election, which, he said, "hovers over me like a vulture of uncertainty." The Prime Minister's long, rhetorical digressions annoyed not only Truman and Stalin but even the Englishman's own subordinates. "He butts in on every occasion and talks the most irrelevant rubbish, and risks giving away our case at every point," Cadogan wrote. "Every mention of a topic started Winston off on a wild rampage." [10]

Before the conference, three of Truman's top aides had advised him, "As a well known Missouri horse trader, the American people expect you to bring something home to them." But the give-and-take, the manipulation, the drawing and redrawing of the maps of the world — all this only made him restless and uncomfortable. He preferred draw poker to the wrangling of high diplomacy. What he wanted most, at the beginning, was a Soviet commitment to enter the war in the Far East; Stalin so promised the first day. "Could go home now," Truman said. Frustrated at the slowness of subsequent proceedings, he whispered to Byrnes during a plenary session, "Why, in ten days, you can decide anything!" He departed Potsdam with the vow, "I'll never have another." [11]

For the most part, Truman only approved and presented policies and positions worked out by others. He advanced only one desideratum that was really his own. Drawing on the lessons he had extracted from his reading of history, he insisted on the internationalization of European waterways, which, he said, had been "a hot bed for breeding wars during European history." The proposals got no serious attention from the other governments — Stalin pointedly noted the omission of the Panama and Suez canals — and caused some embarrassment in Truman's own delegation.[12]

Byrnes made most of the policy. He excluded both Stimson, who had headed several international delegations during his long career, and Harriman, who never forgave him. Byrnes seemed to be everywhere. "Jimmy B. is a bit too active," Cadogan noted dryly. But that was the way the President wanted it. As Truman said, he was "backing up Jim Byrnes to the limits." [13]

Encouraged by the success of the Hopkins Mission, apparent proof that one could do business with Stalin, Byrnes arrived in Potsdam with some optimism. But he foresaw difficulties. He feared that the President was "being continuously hammered" to be "tough with the so and so's." Byrnes himself had grown more disturbed about the violence Russia was doing to "democratic processes" in Eastern Europe.

Without too much difficulty, the conferees settled a number of questions: They created a Council of Foreign Ministers, in which France and China as well as the three Great Powers would be represented. Germany would be administered under a four-power control council composed of the Allied occupation commanders (with the French). The defeated nation was to be treated as a single unit for economic purposes (which in the next few years became the basis of great contention). The negotiations failed, however, to make any progress on three issues — reparations, the former German satellite states (Italy, and some of the Eastern European countries), and Poland's borders. These dominated the proceedings, leading to a fear that the conference would break down, without agreement.[14]

Neither side would budge on reparations. The Americans continued to insist on the First Charge Principle. That is, the German economy had to pay for its imports before it could be made to pay reparations. "This is like the receivership of a big corporation," Assistant Secretary of State Will Clayton tried to explain to the reparations subcommittee. "Otherwise, creditors would get nothing." The Russians replied that their people, after so many sacrifices, could not understand why "the Wall Street bankers" had to be paid first. "Your Reparations Commission and your Government will not even 'set a figure for discussion' as to reparations," Molotov said. On July 30 Joseph Davies noted, "Reparations had poisoned the situation."[15]

The second issue that made for days of fruitless discussion was that of the former satellites. When the Americans raised the question of normalizing relations with Italy, Stalin replied that it should be linked to the normalization of relations with Hungary, Rumania, and Bulgaria. Such a step ran counter to the thrust of America's Eastern Europe policy. Byrnes was emphatic; the United States would not recognize the three eastern countries with their present governments.

Finally, the conferees could not agree on how much former German territory should be included in Poland. The Americans believed that the Russians had, in effect, unilaterally handed the Poles an occupation zone and they were afraid the loss of territory would create grave economic and political problems in Germany.

In the midst of this stalemate, a new factor changed American thinking — now making U.S. leaders eager to wind up the conference as quickly as possible. Their reason was the atomic bomb. Truman had hoped that a test might be successfully completed before the conference ended. The "upper crust want it as soon as possible," General Groves, the head of the Manhattan Project, told the atomic scientists on July 14, pushing them to hurry the test. It took place at Alamogordo, New Mexico, on July 16, "brighter than a thousand suns," more powerful than most had imagined.[16]

Stimson brought first word from Alamogordo to the President on July 16. "I feel fine!" the President said, as he came down the stairs after hearing the report. He told a joke about a girl who swore to drown herself if pregnant, and her boyfriend's response — "It has taken a great load off my mind."

On July 21, Truman learned that the weapon was far more destructive than expected, and that the bomb would be ready for combat use very soon. "He was a changed man," Churchill noted of Truman after the July 21 plenary session. "He told the Russians just where they got on and off and generally bossed this whole meeting." S-1, as the bomb was known, made Truman more impatient. On July 22, he wrote out in longhand the order to use the bomb, though not before he had left Potsdam and the Russians. Late that afternoon, a savage windstorm sprang up in Berlin, lifting the dust and rubble of the ruined city, carrying it inside the perimeters of the enclave where men thought about the destruction about to come on Japan, and throwing it wildly about. The air was dark even though it was still daytime.[17]

The reassuring news about the bomb wrought a complete reversal of U.S. goals for the conference. Initially, the primary aim was to get the Russians to declare war as quickly as possible against Japan — the declaration in itself perhaps providing the blow leading to surrender. If not that, it certainly would increase the military pressure on Japan, distribute casualties more widely among the Allies, and shorten the war. Now, however, U.S. thinking had changed. Perhaps the bomb, rather than the Russians, would save the American lives. Moreover, the U.S. might now win the war before the Russians could (as Byrnes put it) "get in so much on the kill" — that is, press claims on China and share in the Japanese occupation. Byrnes' confidant Walter Brown had noted on July 18: "JFB had hoped Russian declaration of war against Japan would come out of this conference. Now he thinks the United States and United Kingdom will have to issue joint statements giving Japs two weeks to surrender or face destruction (secret weapon will be ready by that time)." On July 24, Truman and Byrnes knew that Stimson and Marshall (the latter, less wholeheartedly) felt that Russian participation against the Japanese was no longer necessary, though nothing could prevent them from moving into Manchuria. The bomb, rather than Russian intervention, might make unnecessary the 500,000 casualties Marshall had predicted. Truman and Byrnes were now eager to end the conference so that the bomb might be used quickly, and thus stave off, or at least slow, the Russian advance in East Asia.[18]

But the fundamental reason for using the bomb remained what it had always been — to end the war in the Pacific as quickly as possible, and so save American lives. It was a weapon of war to be used in war. The Americans were not sure that the bomb would have sufficient impact by itself to bring about an immediate Japanese surrender. The hope that the Russians might be contained in Asia was an additional reason for using the bomb. But it is difficult to link the decision to drop the atomic bomb to American concerns about a Soviet sphere in Eastern Europe. Such sentiment existed, but it was secondary and not thought out.[19]

The Americans had to control their impatience. The conference required an intermission — Prime Minister Churchill and Foreign Secretary Eden flew to London on July 25 to await the outcome of the British general election, the tally having been delayed by the counting of the overseas servicemen's vote. The night before leaving Potsdam, Churchill dreamed he saw himself lying under a white sheet, his feet sticking out, dead. "Perhaps this is the end," he said to his physician. Labourite Ernest Bevin was no more optimistic; certain that the Conservatives would win, he had taken a cottage in Cornwall for the whole month of August. But Bevin was wrong;

Churchill's premonition, right. The Tories lost in a landslide. "Anyway we've had a damned good gallop for five-and-a-half years," was the way Churchill bid official goodbye to Ismay, his chief of staff.

As a member of the coalition government, Attlee had been part of Churchill's delegation. He too had gone back to London. On July 28, he returned to Potsdam as Prime Minister. Some thought that the advent of the Labour government, especially with Hugh Dalton as Foreign Secretary, would mean a leftward movement in British foreign policy. Orme Sargent, soon to be permanent undersecretary of the British Foreign Office, voiced a common fear when he predicted "a Communist avalanche over Europe, a weak foreign policy, a private revolution at home, and the reduction of England to a second class power." However, the Labour Party was hardly composed of wild-eyed revolutionaries. French Foreign Minister Bidault later marveled, "Only the English, with their fantastic capacity for empiricism, could possibly have admitted a man like Attlee to the Socialist ranks." Too often, members of the Labour Party, like social democrats throughout Europe, had been the objects of communist attack. For many years, the reticent Attlee had regarded the Russians as "ideological imperialists." In addition, instead of Dalton, the new Foreign Secretary turned out to be the former leader of the Transport and General Workers Union, Ernest Bevin, whose antipathy toward communists had been repeatedly stoked through four decades of union battles. Bevin's appointment assured continuity in British policy, save that he brought to diplomacy a combative bluntness that was most unlike the almost limpid grace of Anthony Eden.[20]

Byrnes now began to push for a package deal. In the reparations subcommittee, Clayton and Ben Cohen had already begun to devise a reparations compromise that would allow each country to take reparations from its own zone. If the Russians would accept this, then the West would give ground on the Polish frontier. Byrnes decided to do what he called "a little horseback trading," adding the satellites to the package, and agreeing to the Neisse as the Polish boundary.[21] On July 31, the Big Three approved all three elements in quick succession, making it possible for the conference to end.

Under the final article on reparations, the Soviets would take their reparations from their own zone. In addition, the Russians and the Poles would get 15 percent of "unnecessary" capital equipment from the Western zone in exchange for food and raw materials, and another 10 percent with no exchange. Despite provisions for "common policies" for Germany, the thrust of this agreement ran against the American insistence on treating Germany as an economic unit, and was a significant step toward partition. This was recognized at the conference.

"If we fail to reach an agreement, the result will be the same?" Molotov asked Byrnes.

"Yes," Byrnes replied.[22]

As to the satellites, the Council of Foreign Ministers would prepare, as its first task, the peace treaty for Italy, and then treaties for the "recognized democratic governments" of Rumania, Bulgaria, and Hungary. It was an exercise in ambiguity. The real decision was a lack of common decision. The consequence was that, as one historian put it, "the determination of future events in Italy fell to the West, and in the other satellites to the Soviet Union." [23]

Finally, the de facto recognition of the Polish boundary as propounded by Stalin implied considerable discretion for the Russians in Eastern Europe. Thus, on each of the outstanding issues, the Great Powers had found that the best way to cooperate was to give each a freer hand in its own sphere. Because they could not agree on how to govern Europe, they would begin to divide it; this was how the Yalta system worked.

At Yalta, it was possible to accept Stalin's explanation that Russia was seeking security through territorial alterations. But at Potsdam, the Soviet arguments about marching the Polish frontiers westward were coupled with demands for joint control over the Dardanelles, for trusteeship over a former Italian colony on the Mediterranean (Libya), and for a share in the administration of Tangiers. All these were seen as part of a suddenly unmasked expansionist ambition. Byrnes feared the Russians wanted Libya as a base for action against the West and as an opening in Africa that might lead them to the Belgian Congo, the world's most important source of uranium.

"Somebody . . . made an awful mistake in bringing about a situation where Russia was permitted to come out of a war with the power she will have," Byrnes said on July 24. "England should never have permitted Hitler to rise . . . The German people under a democracy would have been a far superior ally than Russia . . . There is too much difference in the ideologies of the U.S. and Russia to work out a long term program of cooperation." [24]

But the day before, Stimson discussed the Russian claims with Truman: "He [the President] evidently thinks a good deal of the new claims of the Russians are bluff." [25] The acceptance of Byrnes' package improved the feelings of most of the policymakers, British and American. Bevin spoke for many of them when, on August 4, he pronounced the conference a "distinct success . . . The real results were achieved in the last four days." [26]

During the conference the Americans had found the Russians stiff, humorless, and completely bound by their instructions. Stalin himself, though apparently in ill health, perhaps having suffered a minor heart attack, was businesslike and made a more favorable impression. Will Clayton, who had been in the thick of the reparations negotiations, left Potsdam thinking that Stalin had been "pretty fair." Stalin again was playing the hard-nosed realist, uninterested in algebra. "In politics," he declared, "one should be guided by the calculation of forces."

The two most important Americans left moderately encouraged. Speaking for Byrnes, Walter Brown noted on the last day: "The conference ended on a high note of harmony . . . It was noticeable that Stalin was keeping his eyes on Byrnes as he concluded his talk, and then he launched into a praise of Byrnes for the fine work he had done. He stated that it was Byrnes who worked out the differences and brought the Big Three together in making so many important decisions. It was an unusual tribute coming from Stalin." Meanwhile Truman, on July 28, told Forrestal that he was being "very realistic with the Russians" and he "found Stalin not difficult to do business with." On the trip home, Truman told the officers of the *Augusta:* "Stalin was an SOB but of course he thinks I'm one, too."

This was the only time Stalin and Truman would ever meet, but even in later years Truman did not feel the need to disguise his favorable reaction to "the old guy," as he sometimes thereafter referred to Stalin. "I hoped in Potsdam that the Russians would keep their agreements," he told Jonathan Daniels in 1949. "They gave the impression that they would. I like Stalin. Stalin is as near like Tom Pendergast as any man I know. He is very fond of classical music. He can see right straight through a question quickly . . . I got the impression Stalin would stand by his agreements and also that he had a politburo on his hands like the 80th Congress." [27]

*

In sum, while the American policymakers were concerned about Soviet expansionism, as well as put off by Russian bad manners, they nevertheless departed Potsdam in a hopeful frame of mind. But it must be said that a complicating factor had entered into the calculations of senior officials — the atomic bomb. A whole host of wartime technological developments — involving mechanization, speed, fire power, air power — had upset conventional plans and patterns of defense and altered the geographic basis of war. But the atomic bomb stood out as qualitatively different, a quantum leap in the technology of warfare; it was a dismal promise to make geography meaningless. In a profound sense, this development could only result in a deep insecurity; with one stroke, it seemed to have wiped out all the rules of warfare. Military men stepped back, dazed. On August 1, when General Douglas MacArthur, then in Manila, was told of the new weapon and what it might do, he said simply: "Well, this changes warfare!"

What security could this "absolute weapon" bring? Shortly after the end of the war, strategist Bernard Brodie wrote: "The traditional concepts of military security which this country has developed over the last fifty years — in which the navy was quite correctly avowed to be our 'first line of defense' — seem due to revision . . . Concern with the efficiency of the national defense is obviously inadequate in itself as an approach to the problem of the atomic bomb." All that had become clear was that "our military authorities will have to bestir themselves to a wholly unprecedented degree in revising concepts inherited from the past." [28]

At first, Western leaders believed that the bomb provided them with a simple solution to complicated international problems. "The New Mexico situation had given us great power," said Byrnes at Potsdam on July 29, still despondent about the possibility of successfully concluding the conference. "In the last analysis it would control," he added. Alan Brooke, the commander-in-chief of British armed forces, wrote in his diary on July 23 that Churchill was "completely carried away" with the atomic news. "We now had something in our hands which would redress the balance with the Russians," Churchill said to him. "The secret of this explosive and the power to use it would completely alter the diplomatic equilibrium which was adrift since the defeat of Germany." Back in Washington on July 30, Stimson observed the same kind of feeling as the other two men when he alluded to the "differences of psychology which now exist since the successful test. I did not realize until I went over these papers now what a great change it has produced in my own psychology." Stimson rightly emphasized the psychological import. Certainly the acquisition of nuclear weapons meant a vast increase in military power. But it would be a clumsy instrument in international relations.[29]

Even the manner in which it was introduced was awkward. U.S. officials knew that the Soviets had been using espionage to try to obtain information about the Manhattan Project, and so probably were already aware that the U.S. had a weapon that was almost operational. Still, the Westerners were fearful that Stalin would demand information about it on the spot if he were officially informed. On the other hand, they did not want to be accused in the near future of bad faith with an ally. And so, in a deliberately offhand manner, Truman walked over to Stalin after the plenary session on July 24 and remarked that the United States had a big bomb. Good, replied Stalin. He hoped the United States would use it. Truman and Byrnes concluded that Stalin had missed the significance of what the President had said. On the contrary, Stalin apparently knew exactly of what Truman was speaking. Immediately after the conference, he discussed the matter with Molotov. "Let them," replied the foreign minister. "We'll have to . . . speed things up."

On the long flight home, Bohlen and another specialist on Russia, Llewellyn Thompson, discussed the bomb's possible influence on Soviet-American relations. What could be done with the bomb? Threaten the Russians? What if the Russians refused to budge? Go to war? That was unthinkable. What would happen then?[30] Perhaps the absolute weapon was only the ultimate sanction, a deterrent, a court of last resort for all-out war. Nevertheless, Truman had been "tremendously pepped up" when word first came of the successful New Mexico test. Indeed, the news induced euphoria, a feeling of omnipotence, magically relieving the frustrations of conventional diplomacy. Most of the Americans who knew about the bomb thought it could be put to work in diplomacy — but did not know how.[31]

There was little delay in using it in war. The Japanese response to the July 26 Potsdam Proclamation, calling for unconditional surrender, was indeterminate. On August 5, final assembly of the first bomb was completed. The next day, a B-29 dropped it over Hiroshima. It had the force of 13,000 tons of TNT. The city was totally destroyed; perhaps a hundred thousand people were killed immediately, and tens of thousands more would die of radiation poisoning. On August 9, the Red Army crossed into Manchuria, as the USSR at last went to war against Japan. The peace advocates by now had the momentum in the Japanese Cabinet, but they did not move swiftly enough. On the same day, the second atomic bomb was detonated over Nagasaki. Its effect was no less devastating than that of the first. The use of the second bomb can be explained not in terms of necessity, but only by the momentum of events. On August 10, Japan made clear its intentions to surrender, and did so on August 14, and so the Second World War was over.

The atomic age had begun.

Six weeks after Potsdam, the first Council of Foreign Ministers met in London. The war with Japan was over, and the focus of international relations now clearly centered on difficulties between East and West. As the United States led a renewed challenge against the Soviet sphere in Eastern Europe, problems deferred at Potsdam came out into the open.

Byrnes regarded the Council of Foreign Ministers as his own creation, and, pleased with the outcome at Potsdam, approached its first meeting with some optimism. Truman, eager to turn his attention back to the more familiar range of domestic problems, was happy to leave the foreign stage to Byrnes. London was to be his show.[32] *

Byrnes was optimistic for another reason. He thought the atomic bomb would strengthen his negotiating hand. Before Byrnes left for London, Stimson tried to get him to agree that some plan should be devised for approaching the Russians, but failed. "His mind," Stimson observed, "is full of his problems with the coming meeting of foreign ministers and he looks to have the presence of the bomb in his hip pocket, so to speak, as a great weapon to get through the thing." Stimson was not the only one to doubt the bomb's diplo-

* At the end of the first day's meeting, delegation member Theodore Achilles asked Byrnes to approve a telegram to the State Department reporting the day's developments. "God Almighty," said Byrnes, "I might tell the President sometime what happened, but I'm never going to tell those little bastards at the State Department anything about it." So Achilles recollected.

matic utility; in September, scientist Vannevar Bush warned Truman that the "gun on our hips" might not be so valuable diplomatically. "There is no powder in the gun, for it could not be drawn, and this is certainly known."

Byrnes paid little attention to such warnings. He did not, however, plan to brandish the weapon, but rather to depend upon what one historian has called "its understated presence" to influence the Russians. But the Soviets would not allow its presence to remain understated. At a reception in the House of Lords shortly after the conference began, Byrnes, in the words of Walter Brown, went "after Molotov in typical Senatorial fashion." The Secretary asked Molotov when his sightseeing would be finished so they could "get down to business." Molotov in turn asked Byrnes if he had an atomic bomb in his hip pocket.

"You don't know Southerners," Byrnes replied. "We carry our artillery in our hip pocket. If you don't cut out all this stalling and let us get down to work, I am going to pull an atomic bomb out of my hip pocket and let you have it."

Molotov and his interpreter laughed.

A cocktail party provided the scene for a strange charade. Molotov, who had been teasing Bevin about various matters and perhaps drinking more than usual, suddenly raised his glass and said, "Here's to the atom bomb — we've got it!" Another Russian abruptly put his hand on Molotov's shoulder and led him from the room, as if to indicate Molotov had said something that should not have been said. The whole scene was acted out in front of Byrnes. "Whether this incident was all prearranged, or whether it was a slip of the tongue was not known," Byrnes commented afterward, "but it is most likely just another attempt upon the part of the Russians to instill the impression upon the rest of the peoples of the world that they too have the bomb." More likely, with the bantering the Russians were signaling that the American monopoly would not frighten them into acquiescence on other issues.[33]

The conference never got down to real business. Discussions on the Italian treaty dragged on. Citing the Soviet Union's "considerable experience in bringing about friendly relations between nationals," Molotov put in an emphatic claim for trusteeship over part of the former Italian colony in Libya. The Western leaders rejected it, for they were convinced that the Russians really wanted a way station on the road to the Belgian Congo. (Molotov did kindly suggest that, if the Russians could not obtain an Italian colony, they would console themselves with the Belgian Congo.) Perhaps the Russians were serious. It is more probable that they were only throwing in the extra desiderata to trade them away at a later date — and perhaps to parody what they perceived as Western intervention in the Soviet sphere in Eastern Europe.[34] Byrnes also rejected Molotov's request that a control commission be discussed for Japan. The British, despite their own desire for some such organization, supported Byrnes.

The real problem at the conference was the Balkans. The Russians had submitted draft proposals for peace treaties that shocked the U.S. delegation's Eastern European specialists, including Maynard Barnes from Bulgaria, Burton Berry from Rumania, Leslie Squires from Hungary, and Cavendish Cannon, the former chief of the Division of Southern Europe and the delegation's political adviser. All subscribed to the Riga axioms, and to the universalist contention that Eastern Europe had to remain "open." They concluded that the Soviet proposals "would eliminate American participation in the reconstruction of the Balkans and would guarantee to the U.S.S.R. even more important roles than her physical position and power would insure." "Urgent steps" were necessary "to impress the Secretary and his advisers with the reality of the Soviet 'trap' and the necessity of preventing acceptance of the Soviet proposal." [35] Similar pressure came from State Department officials in Washington, and from the British. Byrnes spent all day, September 16, on this matter, and then went to see Molotov privately, "primed to lay the issues on the table." [36] The issue continued to be the Soviet sphere in Eastern Europe, although the Americans tended to forget they had their own new spheres in Italy and Japan, where the Soviets had agreed to give them a free hand.

Byrnes said that it was "essential for the future of the world that our nations continue to cooperate." He was not objecting to the situation in Hungary and Finland, where the Soviets were tolerating democratic procedures. During the conference the United States moved to recognize Hungary as a "carrot" to the Russians. But the United States, Byrnes told Molotov, would not conclude treaties with Rumania and Bulgaria because their governments were not representative. Byrnes said that he wanted governments both democratic and friendly to the Soviet Union — "these two considerations were not irreconcilable." Molotov replied that the Soviet Union was cooperating on the Italian peace treaty. Would not the United States do the same for the Russians on the Balkan, Hungarian, and Finnish treaties? If the United States did not, he warned, a very bad impression would be created in Soviet public opinion.[37] The threat was not convincing. After talking with Byrnes on the seventeenth, Walter Brown noted, "The outlook is very dark." [38]

Byrnes and Molotov had another go-around. The Soviet Union would never tolerate a government unfriendly to it within the border countries, said Molotov. The USSR, he added, had not protested the West's having its own way in Italy. But his arguments were futile. The United States would not recognize the Soviet sphere. The American draft treaties for Rumania, Bulgaria, and Hungary (the work of Squires, Barnes, and Berry) all began with the same preamble — that the United States would not negotiate a peace "until there has been established a government broadly representative of all democratic elements in the population and pledged to the earliest possible establishment through free elections of a government responsive to the will of the people, which can be recognized by the United States." [39]

The inventive Byrnes had another idea. Perhaps he could allay Soviet fears about security. He privately suggested to Molotov a Four Power treaty guaranteeing demilitarization of Germany for twenty-five years. "A very interesting idea," Molotov said, but he would have to refer it to Moscow. Meanwhile, there was something else he wanted to take up. He was furious about the preambles in the United States draft treaties; they were "a challenge directed to the Soviet Union." Why did they have to be in writing, Molotov asked; why could not the United States simply state its objections orally? Byrnes would not withdraw the preambles. Then, said Molotov, he would be "forced to answer."

After this exchange, Byrnes was "blue over the outlook.[40]

The question of the Balkan treaties first came up in official conference session on September 20 and 21. The same arguments and half-insults danced back and forth between Molotov and Byrnes. Molotov suddenly announced that he was being pushed on the defensive. He was also isolated. Britain had lined up with the United States. Before the meeting, France had been a question mark. This was its first Big Power function. Since its coalition government contained representatives of the large French Communist Party, there was some thought that it would act as a bridge between East and West. Prior to the meeting, Foreign Minister Bidault had candidly remarked that France's world position was weak; it lacked both economic and military power. "France," he said, "must rely upon justice, equity, and fair play." It also seemed to rely upon the United States and Britain, as it sided for the most part with them. And the Chinese delegates, though distinguished mainly by their politeness and silence, left no question as to with whom they stood.[41]

On September 22, Molotov took a new tack. An error, he said, had been made in the procedures of the conference at the opening. France and China, according to the Potsdam agreement, were not to participate in discussion on Eastern European treaties, and he would not do business until they were excluded.

The next day, Bevin met privately with Molotov. Their conversation had a bad start when Bevin expressed his fear that Soviet-British relations were "drifting into the same condition as that which we had found ourselves with Hitler." He meant, he later suggested, only "that absence of frankness led to situations which became irretrievable." Molotov had understood Bevin otherwise and quickly responded: "Hitler had looked on the USSR as an inferior country, as no more than a geographical conception. The Russians took a different view. They thought themselves as good as anyone else. They did not wish to be regarded as an inferior race." Bevin replied that neither the British government nor the Labour Party regarded the Russians as inferior. "But," he said, "in this country there was a growing feeling that the tables had been turned and that we were being treated as inferiors both by the Russians and the Americans." Molotov argued strenuously for an enlarged Soviet role in the Mediterranean, including Russian bases in the Dardanelles. France and Italy had ceased being Mediterranean powers. Britain, he warned, "could not go on holding a monopoly in the Mediterranean." Molotov also complained that the German reparations commission had not (as he was quoted in the British minutes) "done a damn thing."

The two never really discussed the impasse over French and Chinese participation. But on September 25, Bevin told the British Cabinet that while the actual terms of the (Potsdam) Protocol strictly interpreted lent some support to the Soviet view . . . the intention had been that all members of the Council would take part in all the deliberations. To Byrnes, he privately admitted that the Russian objection was "strictly legally right, although morally wrong." [42]

No one had any doubt of what was really on Molotov's mind. The arguments about France and China, Bevin explained to the British Cabinet on September 25, were "only the outward manifestations of the fundamental disagreements on principle which had arisen with the Soviet Delegation, who were obviously determined to oppose any proposals which might affect the territories within what they regarded as their zone of influence." He saw little hope of further progress and already believed that "the right course was to adjourn."

And Byrnes summarized the basis of Molotov's ploy in a teletype to the White House. "He is mad because the United States and Britain will not recognize Rumania."

Molotov continued to indicate that he wanted to do a little negotiation. "I do not understand your Secretary of State," one Russian official told Bohlen. "We have been told that he is a practical man, but he acts like a professor. When is he going to start trading?" [43] But trading did not begin. Tempers were growing short. Byrnes in private said that Molotov was "trying to do in a slick dip way what Hitler had tried to do in domineering smaller countries by force." After eight days of Soviet delay, Bevin finally exploded in conference session, saying that Molotov's objections were the "nearest thing to the Hitler theory I have ever heard." Molotov got up and started to walk out. But Bevin's apology, for which the Soviet foreign minister pointedly waited at the door, brought him back.

"After weeks of work, our nerves are on edge," said Byrnes, trying to bring some calm. "However, we must not lose our patience." [44] It was time to find the highest common denominator.

Byrnes may have been saved from a Soviet "trap" by his State Department subordinates; but, in evading that one, he fell into another. This was the one created by the conflicting roles Roosevelt had bequeathed to his successors — on the one hand, managing a Great Power consortium; on the other, responding to the universal principles of the domestic consensus. The trap was sprung by John Foster Dulles, senior Republican on the delegation, spokesman for the domestic consensus, and, with Vandenberg, the Republican foreign policy leader. Unlike Byrnes, who was temperamentally a compromiser, Dulles wanted to stand on absolute principles, muddled though they might be.

Ponderous and pious in manner, careful and slow in speech, Dulles was "shadow" Secretary of State. Born into a family of ministers, missionaries, and diplomats (his grandfather, John W. Foster, was Secretary of State under Harrison; his uncle, Robert Lansing, under Wilson), Dulles had in 1919 become chief American reparations counsel at the Versailles Conference. During the interwar years, he specialized in international law as senior partner in the Wall Street firm of Sullivan and Cromwell. Some thought him the highest priced lawyer in the country. Though he had been an agnostic much of his adult life, he returned to religion late in the 1930s, and faith seemed to reveal to him an ethical framework for international relations. It also provided a way back to the world of high politics for a man grown bored and restless in his legal work.[45]

He mixed piety with a "dynamic" theory of secular history, borrowed from Arnold Toynbee, who, Dulles said, proved that "all known civilizations" rise and fall "in terms of 'challenge' and 'response.'" Dulles relished every opportunity to sermonize. "I pull up a chair and we start discussing world politics," he noted in a 1938 diary of a China trip. "I develop my theories about 'dynamic' and 'peaceful' change." Before Pearl Harbor, taking a position that would later leave him open to charges of appeasement, Dulles criticized the "have" nations of France, Britain, and the United States for failing to treat equitably the "have-not" nations of Germany, Japan, and Italy. Not all regarded Dulles' mixture of piety and geopolitics as illuminating. In 1942, Alexander Cadogan of the British Foreign Office found Dulles "the wooliest type of useless pontificating American." By war's end, Dulles was a leading figure in the foreign policy elite, and chief foreign policy adviser to the once and future presidential candidate, Thomas Dewey.[46]

During World War II Dulles was hopeful about postwar relations with the Soviet Union. In January 1945, he noted that "the Soviet creed has now become a dynamic force in the world" and had "caught the imagination of masses everywhere." He warned his fellow Americans: "Under such circumstances we can readily become jittery and, if so, incidents will occur which will strain our relations. That ought not to be and it need not be." He thought "no dictatorship is wholly absolute," and that the Soviet system would become more like the American.[47] In February, Eugene Lyons, an editor of *Reader's Digest*, dismissed as "fantastic" Dulles' assertion that *both* the Americans and Soviets had reason to distrust each other. The shadow Secretary calmly replied: "The very fact that millions of Americans share your view that we should distrust the Russians is, I think, a reason why Russia should distrust us. Trust only thrives in an atmosphere of mutuality . . . A task of the future will be to clear up such mistrust. If either side makes that impossible, that bodes ill for the future peace of the world." [48]

Dulles thought that cooperation would occur within the framework of an international organization. He assumed that Russian trust would express itself in willingness to subordinate Soviet interests to a universal order prescribed by America. Early in 1945, he said that a spheres-of-influence settlement would be a major setback for mankind, and complained that the United States was not doing enough to prevent it.[49]

As senior adviser to the American delegation and Senator Vandenberg's "lawyer" at the San Francisco United Nations Conference in the spring of 1945, Dulles opposed a Great Power consortium because it would be "the arbiter of the world." The Soviet Union, however, was concerned only about its own interests, and feared any international system that might be used against it. At San Francisco Dulles decided that the Russians wanted a world organization "in order to get the maximum possible voice outside their own sphere of influence," and blamed them for the conference's problems.[50]

Now, in London, less than six months later, Dulles saw only malevolent purpose in Soviet behavior. He reinforced the sense of urgency about the Balkans impressed upon Byrnes by State Department officials. Byrnes was treating Dulles as a "law partner in conducting a case." By September 30, the time for final arguments was at hand. On Sunday morning, Dulles went to see the Secretary in his suite at Claridge's. "Well, pardner," said Byrnes, "I think we pushed these babies about as far as they will go and I think that we better start thinking about a compromise." Compromise was what Dulles opposed. The word "appeasement" would never again be attached to his name. With the end of the war, he believed, the claim of expediency was invalidated. "Principle and morality must be re-established in the world." He also insisted on applying the "lesson we have so painfully learned, that peace is indivisible." [51] Dulles replied that a compromise would be the first step on a dangerous road of appeasement. He threatened a public attack on

Byrnes as an appeaser, should the Secretary take the course of compromise.[52]

Byrnes was alarmed. Dulles achieved what he wanted, forcing Byrnes to choose between the domestic and the Great Power consensus. The Secretary did make one more half-hearted attempt to find a compromise. Later in the day he saw Molotov, who said that the basic problem was to find "common attitudes" toward Rumania and Bulgaria. The Soviet foreign minister suggested that United States recognition would be followed by quick elections. Byrnes rejected this offer, but then asked, would it not be possible for some changes in the governments to be made, just enough to "convince the world" that these governments were really representative?

It was not possible, said Molotov.[53]

The conference broke up without a protocol, which was an open admission of failure. For the time being, Byrnes' creation, the Council of Foreign Ministers, lay in public ruin.

Many had thought that the postwar configuration of international politics would be a face-off between Britain and the Soviet Union, with the United States somewhere in between, an uneasy mediator. But the London Council pointed toward a polarization of East and West in which the United States took one of the two leading roles.[54]

On the surface, Bevin reacted with some good humor to the failure of the conference: "Like the strike leader said, 'Thank God there is no danger of a settlement!' " Yet British anxiety ran very deep. Pierson Dixon noted a "slightly stunned atmosphere" in the Foreign Office. "We have been so used during the war to successful meetings of the Big Three, ending in a fanfare of triumphant proclamations to the world."

The British analysis of the conference's problems was more narrowly defined than the American, and linked to traditional concerns in their own diplomacy. Orme Sargent, Undersecretary responsible for Soviet affairs, concluded that the Russians wanted to cooperate with the West, but on their own terms, and from as strong a position as possible. The Foreign Office believed that the Soviets wanted to extend their influence into the Middle East and the Mediterranean basin. This drive, the British thought, was motivated by what Attlee called "an inferiority complex, very strong" and by what Dixon called the "intense jealousy of our position in the Mediterranean and the Middle East now that France and Italy have degenerated as world powers." They also saw at work in Russian policy a general drive for power and position. The threat posed by Russian expansionism was made more acute for the British by another problem. What has been called "the endless and endlessly boring tasks of empire" were now clearly coming to an end, the pace quickened by the strains and costs of the Second World War. British policymakers feared that the Russians would seek to capitalize on the weaknesses of the empire and the United Kingdom itself, both to weaken further the ties that held the empire together, and to increase their own power and influence.

To make matters more uncomfortable, the British felt that the Americans were also pushing them aside. During the conference, Bevin told the Cabinet that Britain was faced "with increasing hostility and distrust between the United States and Soviet delegations, each of whom sought to strengthen its own position without regard to our point of view." The Cabinet later agreed that "we should make clear to the United States government that it was impossible for us to work with them if they constantly took action in the international sphere, affecting our interests, without prior consultation with us." [55]

It may be surmised that the Russians left the conference with a growing sense of isolation. "The truth is peeping out," Dixon noted. Molotov "hates having us, the Americans *plus* the French always lined up against him." For his part, Molotov certainly grasped the British line of analysis. At Potsdam, he had complained, almost plaintively, to Joseph Davies that the British Foreign Office was convinced that "the Soviet Union had designs on their Empire. Nothing which the Soviet Union could do or say could persuade them that the Russians wanted nothing more than what they had, except security from outside." [56] The Russians must have been puzzled by the Western inconsistency on the question of spheres. What had happened to the Churchill-Stalin agreement of October 1944, by which the Russians had so faithfully abided in Greece? Moreover, the United States held tight rein, the Russians felt, on its own "little sphere," the Western Hemisphere. The day after the conference opened, Truman declared that he would "not permit interference by any non-American power in the affairs of the nations of North, Central and South America." The United States also claimed islands in the Pacific in the name of national security, and took exclusive responsibility for Japan. While the foreign ministers were meeting in

London, Truman released a statement reaffirming MacArthur's (and American) supremacy over Japan, a move which Byrnes admitted was "bad because it made Stalin think we were acting in Japan just as he was acting in the Balkans." [57] The Russians had willingly conceded Italy to the United States and the United Kingdom. Thus, Byrnes' and Bevin's principled stand on Rumania and Bulgaria must have struck the Russians as ominous and perverse, as well as an insult to their status as a Great Power.

Byrnes returned to Washington discouraged. He worried about his public role as peacemaker and wondered whether the Russians were preparing for peace or war. He was not at all sure how to deal with them. "Peacemaking is not a sensational process," he said during the conference. "It is a wearisome, tiring thing." [58]

The London Council had taught him and his fellow policymakers the limits of atomic diplomacy. Molotov, replying to a banquet toast during the conference, said, "Of course we all have to pay great attention to what Mr. Byrnes says, because the United States are the only people who are making the atomic bomb." Listen, the Russians might; budge, they would not; the bomb was far too awkward to be of much direct use in diplomatic negotiations.

For his final act in his many years of government service, Henry Stimson in September 1945 proposed a direct approach to the Russians on controlling the terrible new secret. To begin with, it would involve an exchange of scientific information, combined with Russian concessions. Stimson concluded that such a step was necessary because the bomb "constitutes merely a first step in a new control by man over the forces of nature too revolutionary and dangerous to fit into the old concepts." Byrnes' strategy of negotiating with "this weapon rather ostentatiously on our hip" disturbed him. He feared it would only embitter relations. The United States should go directly to the Soviet Union on this question, and not waste time and put off the Russians with "loose debates" in an international conference.

Stimson formally laid out his thoughts during a Cabinet luncheon of September 21.[59] Dean Acheson, sitting in for Byrnes, who was still in London, supported the Stimson proposal. Intelligent and informed support also came from Henry Wallace, one of the few high government officials who actually grasped the scientific basis of nuclear energy. He favored retaining the engineering know-how while sharing theoretical information, in exchange for access to Soviet laboratories.

The opposition to Stimson was fierce, with Forrestal taking the lead. The bomb and the knowledge that went into it, he asserted, were "the property of the American people . . . The Russians, like the Japanese, are essentially Oriental in their thinking, and until we have a longer record of experience with them on the validity of engagements . . . it seems doubtful that we should endeavor to buy their understanding and sympathy. We tried that once with Hitler . . . There are no returns on appeasement." Instead, Forrestal proposed that "we could exercise a trusteeship over the atomic bomb on behalf of the United Nations."

Each side failed to perceive what the other was talking about. One side was suggesting the exchange of scientific information and an approach to the Soviets. The others were criticizing what they thought were proposals to hand over the atomic bomb to the Russians, and set up a multilateral control system. Some sense of the intensity of the discussion is conveyed by the comments of two officials about each other. Forrestal recorded that Wallace was "completely, everlastingly and wholeheartedly in favor of giving it to the Russians." Wallace noted that "Secretary Forrestal took the most extreme attitude of all . . . a warlike, big-Navy, isolationist approach." [60]

Truman asked the Cabinet members to submit their views in writing. Acheson, as Acting Secretary, supported Stimson: "Overall disagreement with the Soviet Union seems to be increasing. Yet I cannot see why the basic interests of the two nations should conflict. Any long-range understanding based on firmness and frankness and mutual recognition of the other's basic interests seems to me impossible under a policy of Anglo-American exclusion of Russia from atomic development. If it is impossible, there will be no organized peace but only an armed truce." Undersecretary of War Robert Patterson, about to succeed Stimson, also supported the Stimson approach.

But Byrnes, returning from the London Council, added his voice to those calling for a hard line on the bomb. He changed the State Department position. The inability to use the bomb as a bargaining chip at the London Council had frustrated him. Now he wanted to "see whether we can work out a decent peace" before cooperating with the Russians on atomic policy. He had no confidence in inspections. If Americans could not get into Bulgaria and Rumania, he said, "it was childish to think that the Russians would let us see what they were doing." Citing the Nazi-Soviet Pact, and the Soviet repudiation of its nonaggression pact with Japan, he felt "It would not be wise for us to rely on their word today." [61]

The argument over Russia and the bomb hinged on another debate. How long could the monopoly last? How many years were there before the Soviet Union would develop an atomic device? The technical community — the scientists and engineers who had developed the bomb — gave the Russians three to five years. The scientists knew that the Russians possessed the requisite scientific capabilities. George Kistiakowsky was head of the explosives division at Los Alamos. He recalled: "Our work with high explosives was to a significant extent guided by a theoretical paper explaining the theory of detonation, which was written by John Von Neumann at our request. It so happened that there was an identical theory, completely independently published in the Soviet Union about the same time." Oddly, Von Neumann's paper was stamped secret; the Soviet paper remained unclassified. The bomb used at Nagasaki was an implosion device, related to a shaped charge. "The Russians had a very developed technique of shaped charges," observed Victor Weisskopf, deputy leader of the Theoretical Division at Los Alamos.

The key question was whether or not the bomb would work. "The real difficulty was not knowing whether it was possible at all," said Kistiakowsky, "so we had to spread our efforts over many directions so as to make sure we didn't miss anything." The basic secret — that a bomb was possible — was demonstrated to the Russians and the rest of the world in August 1945. Knowing that the bomb was feasible, they then would have learned a great deal about how to focus their efforts from unclassified sources — in particular, from the Smyth Report, published under the auspices of General Groves in August 1945, which outlined the developments leading to the bomb. And, finally, they would have learned more from espionage, although it is still a mystery how much more and how important the information through this source would have been.[62]

In sum, from August 1945 onward, for the Russians, the task of making an atomic bomb had narrowed to an engineering problem. As Vannevar Bush wrote to Truman in September 1945, the "secret resides principally in the details of construction of the bombs themselves, and in the manufacturing process." It was a matter of organization and resources. Bush told the Cabinet that the Russians could make the bomb in five years "provided they devote a very large part of their scientific and industrial effort to it." It was reasonable to assume that they would. Had the situation been reversed, the United States would have done whatever was necessary to catch up. As the dynamic of the arms race since has shown, hegemonic nations cannot easily accept inferiority, either real or felt. Industrial representatives from Union Carbide, DuPont, and Tennessee Eastman, the main private contractors for the Manhattan Project, supported the theoretical scientists' estimate of the likely Soviet timetable.

Those who favored a direct approach to the Russians — Stimson, Patterson, Acheson, Henry Wallace — did so because they accepted the evaluation of the scientists and engineers. Wallace, for instance, warned the Cabinet that the United States might create a false security behind "a scientific Maginot line type of mind." He pointed out that atomic research had, to a great extent, "originated in Europe . . . It was impossible to bottle the thing up no matter how much we tried."[63] The awareness of the political implications of science's tendency to ignore boundaries might make one gloomy. The best solution seemed to be a direct approach on this critical issue. There would be risks in such a move. But, since the Russians could build the bomb themselves in a relatively short time, there was unavoidable risk in any other course, as well.

According to the other point of view, mainly that of the military, the monopoly would last for decades. "To a certain type of mind, fortunately few, high command brings a conviction of omniscience," Vannevar Bush later wrote of Admiral Leahy. "His view was like the postwar attitude of some of the public and many in Congress: There was an atomic bomb 'secret,' written perhaps on a single sheet of paper, some sort of magic formula. If we guarded this, we alone could have atomic bombs indefinitely."

General Groves, the head of the Manhattan Project, suggested that the Russians would need at least twenty years. But his prediction was based on assumptions more sophisticated than those of Admiral Leahy. Groves' notion of the "breathing spell" was tied to a tripartite American monopoly — theoretical knowledge, engineering know-how, and industrial plant and raw materials. The last, in some ways, was the key in his view. The Manhattan Engineering District had engaged in an extensive secret survey to locate the necessary raw materials throughout the world, and, like oil men showing up before news of the wildcat strike is out, to quietly acquire control of them.

To believe in a raw materials monopoly, however, called for a highly selective reading of the surveys. Physicist Isidor Rabi told a Council on Foreign Relations meeting in November 1945 that, even using data "incomplete and rather old," deposits of high-grade uranium ores "are comparatively widespread, occurring in Canada, the United States, Russia, Africa, and Czechoslovakia." Prior to 1930, Bohemia had been a major source of uranium for the U.S. After the war, the Russians exploited the deposits in the East German–Czechoslovak border region at a fevered pace. Acutely aware of the error in Groves' assumptions, chemist Irving Langmuir dismissed as absurd the general's contention that it would be decades before the Russians could have an atomic capability. "But," he said, "some of the Senators to whom General Groves' statement was made were much impressed by it."

Those accepting Groves' argument included not just senators, but also senior policymakers — Byrnes, Forrestal, and, apparently, Truman. The notion of the raw materials monopoly seems to have been particularly convincing. "General Groves tells me there is no uranium in Russia," Byrnes had declared with confidence in May 1945.[64]

Why did senior policymakers prefer Groves' conclusions to those of the scientists? While the scientists "made" the bomb, the Army had administered the entire project. Groves was perceived in institutional terms as the source of responsible opinion. The scientists who disagreed tended to be seen as errant individuals. Officials like Byrnes and Forrestal regarded the scientists as a group as unstable, emotional, naïve, untrustworthy, and ill-equipped to determine high policy. Byrnes did not like them and resented their efforts to butt into senior governmental councils. Finally, Groves' advice was comforting. The bomb, Groves said in early September, means "complete victory in our hands until the time another nation has it." The world became simpler, more manageable. The United States held the trump card. Had Byrnes and Forrestal accepted the scientists' contention, international politics would have become ambiguous and contingent, and policy that much more difficult to make.

Groves had even more reassuring things to say. In a speech to IBM executives in September, he pledged that the monopoly "can be used also as a diplomatic bargaining point to lead to the opening up of the world so that there will be no opportunity for a nation to arm secretly."

But at London Byrnes had learned that the bomb was not quite the comfort he had hoped. Groves was wrong — the bomb could not be used as an offensive weapon in diplomacy. Certainly it provided unprecedented military power, but of a defensive kind — a deterrent. The United States could not credibly threaten to loose atomic bombs on the Soviet Union because of the composition of the Rumanian cabinet. The threat could not be graduated; it was all or nothing.

Two months earlier, the news of the Manhattan Project's great success had pepped up the President, but the effects of the tonic had worn off. "There are some people in the world who do not seem to understand anything except the number of divisions you have," Truman complained to Budget Director Harold Smith in early October. Realizing that the President was disturbed about the failure of the London Council, Smith tried to cheer him up. "Mr. President, you have an atomic bomb up your sleeve."

"Yes," replied Truman, "but I am not sure it can ever be used." [65]

> The problem of Russian capabilities and intentions is so complex, and the unknowns are so numerous, that it is impossible to grasp the situation fully and describe it in a set of coherent and well-established conclusions . . .
>
> — GEROID T. ROBINSON, Chief, Research and Intelligence, State Department, December 10, 1945 [1]

VI

The A-1 Priority Job

DURING THE AUTUMN of 1945, after the breakup of the London Council, American policymakers struggled to work out a coherent interpretation of Russian behavior. Returning from a round-the-world trip in early November, Assistant War Secretary John J. McCloy spoke of a universal fear of Russia. He told the diners at a banquet of the American Academy of Political Science that "everywhere you go, the topic is up — the concern over Russia's ambitions, how far she is going to go, how to deal with her — it is in every aspect and every corner of the world . . . That is the A-1 priority job for the statesmen of the world to work out." [2]

Certainly this was the priority job in Washington. The autumn of 1945 was a time of evidence-sifting, of testing of explanations, theories, and interpretations — all of which would result in a wider and wider acceptance of the Riga axioms. But why should an interpretive structure that posited unlimited Soviet ambitions become so generally adopted if, at least arguably, Stalin was pursuing a conservative, limited, even traditional foreign policy?

In an unfamiliar situation, with the international system still in the process of reconstitution, suspicion was at a high point. There were many undecided issues, the outcome of which could fundamentally affect the arrangement of power. The Riga, rather than the Yalta, axioms provided a clearer framework for perceiving and understanding what was unfolding on the world stage, especially given the character of the Soviet system. The Yalta axioms were more ambiguous, more difficult to apply, of less moral certitude, and clearly not the kind of approach that would win wide applause. The American commitment to Wilsonianism, reinforced by the war; the recent experience with Hitler's Germany, and of Stalin's terror — all these served to emphasize the most sinister aspects of Soviet foreign policy. The Rooseveltian duality — Wilsonianism at home, a Great Power consortium abroad — was easier to maintain so long as the war was still in progress. With the conclusion of the war, matters became more problematical — the rationale for alliance no longer automatically existed, and the difficult issues could no longer be deferred. Moreover, the perception of Soviet expansionism made the doctrine of national security more compelling. The political scientist Arnold Wolfers once speculated that "those nations tend to be most sensitive to threats that have either experienced attacks in the recent past or, having passed through a prolonged period of an exceptionally high degree of security, suddenly find themselves thrust into a situation of danger." He had postwar America much in mind. As we shall see, however, the configuration of personalities, bureaucracies, and domestic politics was also crucial.

The A-1 priority job of assessing Russian objectives took place in an atmosphere of confusion and mounting anxiety. Dean Acheson, the new Undersecretary of State, was more moderate than Grew and still known as something of a "liberal" toward the Soviet Union. Nevertheless, he worried that war might be inevitable. Harriman, backing off from some of his more frantic appeals of the preceding spring, now said, "We must recognize the fact that we occupy the same planet as the Russians and whether we like it or not, disagreeable as they may be, we have to find some method of getting along." [3] Reporting to the Commission on a Just and Durable Peace, John Foster Dulles declared, "To secure unity, it may be necessary to compromise ideals. On the other hand it may be possible to maintain ideals but only at the expense of the division of the world into spheres of influence. The choice between the two alternatives is not an easy one. I do not think we are yet face to face with that alternative because we have not yet given our principles their best chance to succeed." Dulles was not willing to allow that a spheres-of-influence settlement was inevitable. Yet he was somewhat restrained in his own analysis of what motivated Soviet policy. "Russia has a real fear of encirclement by the United States," he told a Council on Foreign Relations meeting at the end of October. "If we can persuade the Russians that we have no plans for their encirclement, they may be induced to make peace on a general basis." [4]

The President himself had reacted sharply to the failure at London and the conflict so implied over the Balkans. After the impasse developed during the London Council, he wired Byrnes: "Do everything you can to continue but in the final analysis do whatever you think is right and tell them to go to hell if you have to." Byrnes indicated in his reply from London that he at least wanted to conclude the meeting in such a way that it would be possible to meet again.

The London Council had quickly proved how limited was the diplomatic utility of the U.S. atomic monopoly. The tonic effects of July and August had worn off, leaving the Truman administration confronted by the now already-familiar problems associated with Soviet foreign policy. Throughout the month of October, the President repeatedly returned to the topic of American military power and the state of the nation's arsenal. On October 5, discussing with Harold Smith plans to reduce military manpower to two million by June 1946, Truman said he had begun to wonder "if we might be demobilizing too fast."

On October 8, Truman held an important press conference at Tiptonville, Tennessee, in which he translated his new concern with military power into declaratory policy. Drawing upon General Groves' version of the American monopoly, he outlined three aspects of the secret — scientific knowledge, engineering know-how, and the "resources and industrial plant." That last "secret," Truman felt, was the key element. If other nations, said the President, "catch up with us on that, they will have to do it on their own hook, just as we did." He did not really think they could.

The next day, October 11, an old Missouri friend named Fyke Farmer stopped in to see Truman at the White House. The two men talked about the headlines on the Tiptonville press conference: U.S. WILL NOT SHARE ATOM BOMB SECRET, PRESIDENT ASSERTS.

"Mr. President, what it amounts to then is this," said Farmer. "That the armaments race is on, is that right?"

"Yes," Truman replied, but he added that the U.S. would stay ahead. He thought world government might come in a thousand years, but it was "nothing more than a theory at the present time."

"His attitudes appeared to me," Farmer noted later, "to be that of a man who has made up his mind and was supremely confident of correctness of the decision which he made."

The President made an even more important public statement on October 27 in a Navy Day speech, clearly intended to be heard in Moscow. American foreign policy, he said, would be based on "fundamental principles of righteousness and justice." Those principles embraced self-determination and the Open Door. He turned to the question of the Balkans — the United States would not "recognize any government imposed upon any nation by the force of any foreign power." By standing firm against spheres, Truman spoke for the domestic consensus. But, in order to give force to such words, he affirmed a commitment to military superiority, putting more emphasis on conventional forces because of the lessons learned about the atomic bomb at the London Council. What he did say about the bomb, however, was of great significance — that the United States would hold it as "a sacred trust," and one of infinite duration. He thereby implicitly ruled out a direct approach to the Soviet Union.

Yet, in this same period, Truman also insisted that the two emerging superpowers suffered from a language barrier and that "Russia has been badly represented in this country." He told Stettinius that it was "inevitable that we should have real difficulties but we should not take them too seriously." A falling-out among allies was virtually inevitable at the end of a war. The problems could be solved "amicably if we gave ourselves time." Truman's preoccupation with what he called his own "bad enough" domestic problems was evident when he suggested that the Russians were having "very real problems at home . . . This might explain some of the things that they had been doing." Stalin, he added, was a "moderating influence" in the Kremlin. "It would be a real catastrophe if Stalin should die at the present time." [5]

At the center of the confusion and anxiety stood Byrnes. Not only did he have to find a common denominator with the Russians, but he had to cope with the pressures and forces buffeting him from many sides at home. In the State Department a growing Riga circle advised him to take a hard line with the Russians, and to give up attempts at accommodation. Loy Henderson had returned to Washington early in 1945 to head the Near Eastern Division. He made no secret of his view that the Secretary was "trying too much to depend on his ability as a compromiser," and pressed him strongly. "Active participation by the United States in foreign affairs involves risks," he wrote in one memorandum. "If we are to follow the line that we should not embark upon any undertakings in the international field which involve risks, our foreign policy is certain to be weak and vacillating."

Elbridge Durbrow recalled, "We all had somewhat different angles and different emphasis, but basically we all were very much concerned about what Stalin and Co. were doing and about the blind naiveté of much of the public and also quite a bit of official thinking." In a letter of December 8, 1945, Durbrow said, "My life has become one of complete HELL . . . the Soviets are slipping over in Manchuria, Korea, Iran as well as the usual eastern and southeastern Europe and other areas of Soviet machinations . . . I have had to do a lot of . . . hobnobbing with the boys on the second floor. In any event, we are trying to keep up the good fight." [6]

Byrnes was also hearing other points of view. Ben Cohen, a shy, skillful lawyer who had drafted much New Deal legislation, was State Department counselor. He was Byrnes' speechwriter, confidant, and private brain truster. He urged patience, contending that the United States should not force a break. He and certain others felt that the most significant thing was that the two countries were still talking to each other, trying to settle differences. Perhaps a common language might emerge from such a "process." [7]

Some sense of the Secretary's uncertainty and hunger for an interpretative framework can be obtained from a quick diary: On October 4, Kennan sent a cable predicting that the Russians would orchestrate "maximum trouble for Western Governments through groups in their own countries." On October 8, Byrnes responded with a personal letter, telling Kennan that his report contained "much food for thought." At about the same time, Byrnes went before the Senate Foreign Relations Committee, where he was criticized for not being tough enough with the Russians. On October 9, Joseph Davies came to see Byrnes. The former ambassador launched into another of his disquisitions on the need to see the Soviet point. Byrnes was now so much on the defensive over the apparent breakup of Allied unity under his stewardship that he exploded. Molotov was "insufferable," he told Davies. He said that he was "almost ashamed" of himself for having taken what he did from Molotov. If he ever told the Senate what Molotov told him, Byrnes continued, the situation would have been made very much worse.

On October 16, the Secretary pointed to a map to prove to Patterson and Forrestal that the Russians wanted Libya to "facilitate their access right down to the Belgian Congo . . . The Russians are really serious with regard to Libya." He said it was the cause of all his troubles. Yet, a few weeks later, Byrnes told the skeptical Patterson, McCloy, and Forrestal that Stalin's position on Japan was "sound," and that the Soviets believed "that the rest of the world is ganging up on them."

Byrnes' uncertainty was made clearly evident in a speech he delivered on October 31. It was obviously intended to moderate the uncompromising tones of the President's recent Navy Day speech. It was also an effort to reconcile the Yalta and Riga positions. Byrnes said that the United States comprehended the Soviet Union's "special security interests" in the Eastern European countries. It was understandable that Russia would never again tolerate politics in those countries "deliberately directed against the Soviet Union's security and way of life." The United States would "never join any groups in those countries in hostile intrigue against the Soviet Union." Yet he declared just as vehemently that the United States stood squarely for a "world system." In the atomic age, he said, "we live in one world . . . Regional isolationism is even more dangerous than is national isolationism. We cannot have the kind of cooperation necessary for peace in a world divided into spheres of exclusive influence and special privilege." [8]

Byrnes, by this time, was already seeking to resolve his contradictions. To do so, he took two steps that were in themselves contradictory. The first was the Ethridge mission to the Balkans.

"The story of the American-Soviet negotiations concerning the Balkans after World War II is the story of the first important lessons learned by the United States about the postwar trend of Soviet policy," wrote Mark Ethridge and Cyril Black.[9] The controversies over that corner of Europe helped to shape American perceptions about East-West relations. The report that Ethridge and Black brought back to Byrnes was an important instrument in the diffusion of the Riga axioms.

The London Council had been stalemated by the Balkan question. Byrnes worried that he was being poorly informed by U.S. representatives in the field. So, at least, Molotov had asserted. Byrnes, sharing some of Roosevelt's suspicion of the State Department, thought that its officials were too conservative and excessively anti-Soviet, and suspected that those stationed in the Balkans were too involved in the domestic politics of those countries. At the London Council even Dulles was surprised at the extent of such involvement. Byrnes had considered dispatching Dulles to make an independent investigation of conditions in the border countries. Instead, shortly after returning from London, Byrnes chose for the mission Mark Ethridge, who was publisher of the *Louisville Courier-Journal.* "With the breakdown of the London Conference, we're completely alienated, and I want to establish touch," the Secretary told Ethridge. He hoped that Ethridge would bring a fresh, unbiased viewpoint to this situation, and perhaps return with proof that the situation in the Balkans was not so bad after all.

Ethridge was impeccably qualified in other ways as well. He was a Southerner, a New Deal liberal, a shrewd and respected journalist, a "fighting optimist," and he had been a supporter of Henry Wallace for the vice-presidency in 1944. His wife had been chairman of Russian War Relief in Kentucky. Ethridge thought coexistence between Russia and America possible. Thus, on the other hand, if Ethridge did confirm the State Department position, it would be most helpful to Byrnes in dealing with liberal segments of public opinion.[10] Ethridge's colleague on the mission, Cyril Black, was a young member of the Princeton history faculty who was serving in the State Department during the war.

Ethridge and Black logged 13,000 miles, talked with about three hundred people in Rumania and Bulgaria and in Moscow (including Vyshinsky). The more extended reports showed the confusing mix of ideas present at the time, a confusion that mirrored the complexity of the situation. Ethridge emphasized the fact that he was not anti-Soviet or anticommunist. Russia did have real grievances against Rumania, he reported. Not only had Rumania prospered under German occupation, but Rumanian looting in Russia was considerable, including the entire Odessa streetcar line. "Even Maniu, the traditional democratic leader, had done very little overtly to show his displeasure with the [Nazi] occupation." The political balance was such, said Ethridge, that there was a real possibility of civil war.[11]

Nevertheless, the overall thrust of the report was that Russia was "behaving like an imperialistic power in the worst sense," utilizing local communist parties to establish economic and political domination over Rumania and Bulgaria.*

Ethridge wrote that it was "dangerous and unrealistic" to pursue a "Munich policy with regard to any of the countries now occupied by Russia." Yet his image of the Soviet Union still remained that of the world bully that could be disciplined. He thought Russia was concerned with prestige, and downplayed the significance of Soviet concerns about security. "If we could read the minds of Russian policy makers, I believe we would discover a serious doubt of the correctness of their own policy." If the United States pursued a strong policy with vigor, the Soviet Union would give way. His suggestions, Ethridge wrote, "are based on the feeling that there is no way to improve our relations with Russia except to deal with her in a way she understands. I am confident that the only result can be improvement of relations, even if they get much worse before they are improved."

Ethridge decided that State Department officials had been overly restrained in their reporting, for fear of antagonizing a Secretary they knew was already somewhat skeptical about them. He concluded with a comment that could only have pleased the State Department representatives in the Balkans: "I also believe that the American people ought to know much more of the truth than it does know."[12]

The reports from the Ethridge mission certainly pleased Department officials. They embraced the conclusions, and made sure that Byrnes was aware of them. John Hickerson, deputy director of the Office of European Affairs, said, "We feel we must voice our conviction, which is likewise shared by Mr. Ethridge, that no settlement of these specific problems seems possible if they are treated as isolated cases." The United States should stick to its "principles . . . Since

* In mid-November, while Ethridge was on his mission, elections were held in Bulgaria. There was considerable pressure against the noncommunist politicians, who appealed to their supporters to abstain. The result was an overwhelming majority for the "Fatherland Front" and the legitimation of communist (and Soviet) domination of the country.

to concede a limited Soviet sphere of influence even in this area of strategic importance to the U.S.S.R. might be to invite its extension to other areas, our continued reiteration of the principles that a firm and lasting peace can only be achieved if the people of the liberated areas can exercise the right of self-determination seems the only course open to us at this time." [13]

Such an analysis posed certain problems. The geographic position of the Soviet Union virtually dictated its foreign policy goals in Eastern Europe — to create from that region both a sphere and a shield. What else could be expected? The Russians could not put much stock in the United Nations, which in the best of circumstances was an organization of little meaning on issues of high policy. At this time, it was perceived by the Russians much more as an extension and instrument of American policy. Depend upon the United States? Franklin Roosevelt, a known quantity, was dead, and the new President proclaimed that the U.S. would keep its atomic monopoly as a "sacred trust." And so, the Russians pursued an autarkic security policy, which in turn could only strike the American Wilsonians as rapacious and ominous.

Even if the U.S. had decided that Soviet objectives were limited to Eastern Europe, and implicitly accepted the Churchill-Stalin percentage deal of 1944, it would not have meant that the U.S. condoned the entire range of Soviet action. But the Russians could hardly be expected to behave as Wilsonians, and they did have the power, presence, and proximity to achieve their own crucial goals. It was also clear that the U.S. could do much less than the Russians in Eastern Europe, short of risking major war, a cost too great for the peoples of Europe and America. In addition, although neither State Department officials in the Balkans nor members of the Ethridge Mission could see the full picture at the time, the United States was carving out its own more significant sphere at the same time. As Cyril Black recalled exactly three decades later, "In the larger arena of power politics, the U.S. in effect traded the substance of influence in Bulgaria (and also in Rumania and Hungary) for a predominant role in Italy and Japan."

Byrnes decided not to release the Ethridge Report. To do so would have publicly announced a stalemate, even a break with the Russians, which in turn might well have foreclosed Byrnes' chance to be what he wanted to be — a peacemaker. His next move was a counterstep. His instinct for compromise pushed "high principles" aside as he sought to restore amity in the Grand Alliance.

That tension was mounting was obvious. Sitting in an empty State Department on Thanksgiving Day, trying to catch up on unfinished business, Byrnes let his thoughts run over the faltering hopes for postwar collaboration. If the Soviet Union did not join the U.N.'s Atomic Energy Commission, then "we can just kiss off" the United Nations. Soviet abstention would turn the entire world organization into "a pretty stale chicken." Too much was at stake not to try to improve relations. At London, he had wanted to find a way to deal with Stalin directly. Byrnes recalled that the Yalta Conference had made provision for periodic meetings of the Big Three foreign ministers. The Five Power Council of Foreign Ministers, set up at Potsdam, had not abrogated this earlier procedure. Byrnes decided that the three should meet — this time, in Moscow. In the best Roosevelt tradition, he would try to rescue understanding from misunderstanding. He would go to Moscow with a small delegation, work away from publicity, get around Molotov and go right to Stalin — and he would go out of his way to disassociate himself from the British.[14]

Byrnes angered Bevin by taking up the matter with Molotov before telling London. Foreign Office officials feared "the Russians will gain, we shall gain nothing, and the Americans will give away our interests to the Russians for the sake of a settlement." On December 6, Bevin, worried about offending the French, told other members of the British Cabinet that he saw no use in such a meeting. But he was, he said, "in some difficulty, for the suggestion of a meeting had already been made to M. Molotov, and it now seemed that Mr. Byrnes was determined to go to Moscow, if necessary alone."

Lord Halifax summed it up when he told American officials in Washington, "You've got us in a bit of a hole." The British, though grumbling, went.

The Russians were not totally impressed by such dissension. After arriving (no easy matter in itself — Byrnes' pilot became lost in a treacherous blizzard coming into Moscow and ended up landing at the wrong airport), Byrnes jokingly told Stalin that although the U.S. was supposed to have a bloc with England, he had "even neglected to inform Mr. Bevin soon enough."

"This was obviously only a cloak to hide the reality of the bloc," the suspicious dictator replied.[15]

The growing Riga circle had also opposed the meeting, afraid of what Byrnes might give away. Some sense of the Riga group's attitude toward Byrnes may be surmised from diary entries Kennan made during the course of the conference. Attributing to Bevin what was clearly his own view, Kennan described the Secretary as "only another cocky and unreliable Irishman." Speaking now for himself, Kennan wrote that Byrnes' weakness in dealing with the Russians was that he wanted "to achieve some sort of an agreement, he doesn't much care what. The realities behind this agreement, since they concern only such peoples as Koreans, Rumanians and Iranians, about whom he knows nothing, do not concern him. He wants an agreement, for its political effect at home. The Russians know. They will see that for this superficial success he pays a heavy price in the things that are real." [16]

Kennan was wrong. Byrnes paid no heavy price, *except* in terms of his political position at home. In Russia, the Yalta strategy worked. The Moscow Conference was the one moment of accommodation and compromise in the otherwise bleak history of postwar polarization.

This is not to say that the conference was not without many frustrating, exasperating, bitter moments. Molotov kept asking Byrnes when the U.S. would withdraw its troops from China. The Secretary finally responded that Molotov was asking these questions merely because he liked the sound of Byrnes' voice. Molotov replied that while he found Byrnes' voice very pleasant, "even more pleasant would be an agreement for the simultaneous withdrawal of troops."

The reluctant Bevin was hardly in a mood to compromise. From the start, he planned to tell Molotov "how uneasy Soviet intentions" made him. As he explained to Byrnes, the Russians "were attempting to undermine the British position in the Middle East . . . Just as a British admiral, when he saw an island, instinctively wanted to grab it, so the Soviet government if they saw a piece of land wanted to acquire it . . . The world seemed to be drifting into the position of 'Three Monroes.' The United States already had their 'Monroe' on the American continent and were extending it to the Pacific." Byrnes took exception to that last assertion, but Bevin refused to retract it.

Byrnes, however, wanted to negotiate. As at Potsdam, he was the organizer of the Moscow agreements — with a little help from a "friend." The major agreements resulted from Byrnes' two private meetings with Stalin. The Russian dictator, rested after his first holiday in several years, was in (for him) a jovial mood. When Byrnes, making polite conversation, asked him what he had been doing on holiday, Stalin said, "Reading your speeches." Byrnes congratulated him on his good taste.

"That was *must* reading for me," Stalin replied.[17]

The conference resolved the London deadlock on the Balkans with an agreement on procedure for a peace conference to draft the postwar treaties. Meanwhile, Bulgaria, which had just held elections of a sort, would be "advised" by the Soviet government to include two noncommunists in its cabinet. Ambassadors Harriman and Clark-Kerr would join Vyshinsky on a commission that would go to Rumania to supervise the addition of two noncommunists to its cabinet and to guarantee the establishment of civil liberties.

Byrnes also brought up an American-British-Canadian proposal for a United Nations Atomic Energy Commission that would recommend a system of control. Truman, Attlee, and Prime Minister Mackenzie King of Canada had approved the proposal at a conference in Washington in mid-November. Their meeting had underscored the American monopoly by making postwar partnership with the British and Canadians dependent upon unilateral American decisions.

Save for the inevitable disagreement as to whether the proposed UNAEC be under the General Assembly (the U.S. position) or under the Security Council (the Soviet position), the Russians endorsed the proposal. "Much to everyone's surprise," scientist James Conant wrote at the end of December, "the Russians did not argue or talk back." Making a banquet toast, Molotov returned to one of his favorite forms of taunt — this time saying that Conant might have a piece of fissionable material in his waistcoat pocket. Stalin rose immediately and said quietly that nuclear energy was too serious a matter to be the subject of jokes.[18]

The Americans also introduced a plan for a Far Eastern Commission and an Allied Council for Japan. A senior War Department official had reported on October 10 that "heat [was] being put on the Secretary of State by the British, Russians, possibly the French, Chinese and others in the running of Japan." From Japan, however,

MacArthur had informed the War Department, there was no evidence of "any dissatisfaction on the part of other United Nations with what is going on." Then Stalin — no doubt, in reply to American protests about the Balkans — had unexpectedly stressed the question of Japanese control in late October when Harriman had come to see him at his holiday dacha in Sochi. In response, Byrnes introduced these Far Eastern plans. The Russians readily accepted them. Since, however, the proposal copied the Russian procedures in the Balkans, which in turn copied British and American procedures in Italy, it diluted MacArthur's proconsular powers virtually not at all.

The conferees also agreed that American troops could remain in China as long as necessary to disarm Japanese troops. In one of his conversations with Byrnes, Stalin explained, "The Soviet Government would have no objection if the United States wishes to leave its troops, but they would merely like to be told about it." Stalin also reaffirmed his tepid support for Chiang as unifier-to-be of China. China clearly remained an American client, which was the American goal. Before departing Byrnes had told reporters in an off-the-record session that he did not want to see the Japanese replaced by the Russians in China. "The interest of every Church in the U.S., the economic and strategic interests of the U.S. dictate the U.S. policy in China," he said.[19]

China was part of an aside which helped to explain the surprising Russian insistence on a trusteeship over Libya, as well as Stalin's ability to adjust his rhetoric to that appropriate to the different Western states.

"The United Kingdom had India and her possessions in the Indian Ocean in her sphere of influence; the United States had China and Japan, but the Soviets had nothing," Stalin privately told Bevin.

"The Russian sphere extended from Lubeck to Port Arthur," Bevin replied dryly.*

Finally, provision was made for the unification of Korea. The only issue on which there was no agreement was troop withdrawals from Iran. Although Byrnes predicted real trouble over that question, he did not push it. There would never be a time when all questions

*Stalin was certainly playing the role of *realpolitiker*. He also told Bevin that he was "anxious that the British should not leave Egypt" and spoke (as Bevin later reported to his colleagues) "with sympathy and understanding of our policy towards India."

could be settled, he said. He wanted "to conclude the good work which the conference had accomplished" and did not want to "jeopardize this by attempting to take up all questions at once." On that note, the conference ended.[20]

Byrnes had trouble adjusting to the Russian schedule of working nights and sleeping late into the day. By the end of the Moscow Conference, he was exhausted, but also pleased. He slept in the plane until it reached the Azores, and then, between there and Newfoundland, dictated a speech expressing his renewed optimism. He felt that substantial progress had been made in a generally amicable atmosphere. The teetering alliance had been rescued, and the success of the conference seemed to confirm the value of the Rooseveltian approach. He decided that there was no need to release the Ethridge Report.

On December 30, Byrnes delivered a speech over a nationwide radio hook-up. He said that "a successful peace" required both "justice and wisdom" and "the support of those nations whose unity is essential to preserve the peace." The achievement of these two conditions, maintaining both a domestic and a Great Power consensus, had been the goal of Franklin Roosevelt.

At Moscow Byrnes found "ample scope for the achievement of these essential results." The agreements would facilitate the completion of the peace treaties with the former German satellites, which in turn would permit withdrawal of troops from occupied territories. At the end of the speech, Byrnes returned to his own first principle — compromise. International conferences were not athletic stadiums in which individual statesmen might score points. "They are intended to be useful in the adjustment of delicate social and human relations between states with many common interests and many divergent interests. In international affairs, as in national affairs, conflicting interests can be reconciled only by frank discussion and by better understanding. The meeting in Moscow did serve to bring about better understanding." [21]

Unfortunately for Byrnes, while understanding may have been growing in international affairs, this was not the case at home. A broad front against Byrnes was developing in the councils of government, a front that included the President himself.

The Moscow agreements outraged many officials in the State Department. The American mission in Bucharest regarded them as a "sell-out" and considered resigning *en bloc*. Alexander Kirk, ambassador in Italy, a key figure in the Trieste crisis and former chargé d'affaires in Moscow, thought that Byrnes was "awful" and that "we have given far too much away to the Russians." Loy Henderson circulated to other high officials a memorandum, which he said was of "extremely tentative nature," entitled "The Present Situation in the Mideast — A Danger to World Peace." The key point was an analysis of Soviet goals as maximalist: "The Soviet Union seems to be determined to break down the structure which Great Britain has maintained so that Russian power and influence can sweep unimpeded across Turkey and through the Dardanelles into the Mediterranean, and across Iran and through the Persian Gulf into the Indian Ocean. During the last five years, two great barriers to Russian expansion had disappeared, namely, Germany in the West and Japan in the East . . . Judging from recent events in the Near East, Russia now appears to be concentrating upon the removal of a third barrier in the South." Henderson thought that American foreign policy was weak and naïve in the Middle East. He argued that the United States "should endeavor to find some means of alleviating the situation" and not to "allow the matter to drift." His immediate suggestion, a Four-Power settlement, did not really square with his analysis of the problem. Henderson's view was very different from the one Byrnes brought back from Moscow. So the two poles of Riga and Yalta stood again in sharp contrast. But aside from Byrnes and his small circle of advisers, the Riga axioms enjoyed wider and wider support in the State Department. By the end of 1945, Durbrow recalled, the Russians' "real intentions became more than clear to all who followed developments closely." [22]

More influential initially was opposition from other quarters. Senator Vandenberg's growing restiveness threatened the bipartisan coalition. When Byrnes first became Secretary, Vandenberg had snapped that the United States gets back "Byrnes and Yalta." Vandenberg felt that he was not being consulted as regularly and fully under the new regime as he should be. He objected to the American-British-Canadian agreement of mid-November to press for a system of atomic control under the United Nations. Even more incensed with Byrnes' Moscow proposals on atomic energy, he, with other senators, went to the White House several times in November and December to argue that the U.S. should not share anything with the Russians. After the publication of the Moscow communiqué, Vandenberg denounced the provisions on atomic energy as "one more typical American 'give-away.'" Truman, who always had one eye on the Senate, was disturbed by the cracks in the coalition. Yet he did not agree with Vandenberg's stand on the atomic question, and supported Byrnes'. Officials in the Executive branch, such as Navy Secretary Forrestal, also became more explicitly anti-Soviet in this period.[23]

The individual who had the most influence on Truman was in the White House. The staff in the White House was small, and in flux, and only a couple of people really concerned themselves with international politics. The chief adviser on foreign affairs was the somewhat xenophobic old admiral, William Leahy. He had been critical of Roosevelt in 1944 for bypassing Byrnes in choosing a vice-presidential running mate. In 1945 he had enthusiastically supported Truman's appointment of Byrnes as Secretary of State.[24]

But in this autumn of puzzlement and confusion, Leahy distrusted Byrnes' efforts to preserve the wartime alliance. There was, too, an element of personal resentment and antagonism, for the admiral's importance had declined now that there was a strong Secretary of State. In August, Byrnes had already indicated that he was "irked" with Leahy, who "still thought he was Secretary of State, just as he was under Roosevelt." Byrnes made clear that he would "show him differently."

In late October, Leahy set himself against U.S. plans for a Far Eastern Commission to oversee the occupation of Japan. Even though the proposals guaranteed complete American supremacy, Leahy feared that they would result "in a Soviet control of Japan, which would be highly detrimental to America's postwar interest in Asia."

A couple of days later, the admiral took comfort in Truman's Navy Day speech. He hoped, he noted in his diary, that it would "attract microscopic attention" abroad. The same diary entry indicates that he was beginning to take up the Munich theme that he would press upon the President. The Navy Day speech, he said, might force "our diplomatic appeasers to pay closer attention to the vital interests of America." [25]

At roughly the same time, senior U.S. officials learned the first details of what proved to be the postwar spy scandals. Near the end of September, Prime Minister Mackenzie King hurriedly journeyed to Washington to inform President Truman personally about the Gouzenko case, a Soviet atomic spy network, centered in Canada. He told the President that at least one U.S. State Department official was supposed to be involved. "It would not be surprising," Truman said. "There must be similar penetrations by Russians into the conditions in the United States." Dean Acheson said that he thought the reference was "to an assistant secretary." [26] *

Then, on November 27, Major General Patrick Hurley dramatically resigned as ambassador to China. Roosevelt had sent the flamboyant Hurley to China to help bring about a coalition government under Chiang that included communists.

While he was ambassador, Hurley had fought his own private war with the American China specialists, who thought he was ignorant of Chinese affairs and too committed to Chiang and to his own ego. Embittered by his failure to effect a coalition, Hurley returned to the United States in the autumn of 1945, threatened to resign, was dissuaded, but then decided that the State Department was conducting a press campaign against him, and did resign — launching in the process a broadside that would prove most useful to the right-wing China lobby in later years. He accused the professional diplomats who served on his staff of supporting both communism and traditional colonialism. But he also went out of his way to say they were

* Yet Truman was not overly alarmed about the significance of this disclosure. He subsequently told Stettinius that he was not as concerned about Soviet espionage as Mackenzie King, for, in fact, there was no "precious secret" of the atomic bomb. He was also fairly confident that no serious breach of security had occurred. After the Gouzenko affair broke in the press in mid-February 1946, Truman privately upbraided Secretary of War Patterson when Patterson suggested that there was a "dangerous trend toward breakdown in security of the Atomic Bomb Project." Said the President: "I am under the impression that careful investigation by the Department of Justice and other government agencies charged with responsibility in this field reveals no breach of security on the part of any official of the United States Government or any of the scientists engaged in the Manhattan District Project. On the contrary, it appears that there has been meticulous compliance with security provisions, and the record of both government officials and scientists constitutes a demonstration of patriotism and integrity in which the country can take pride. If there are any violations, unknown to me, which have come to your attention, I hope you will advise me and also take prompt, vigorous action."

not serving Soviet objectives. Stalin had personally assured Hurley that he did not regard Mao's forces as communists and would support Chiang as unifier.*

"The Foreign Service has been called a lot of things, but this is the first time anyone thought of labelling it Communist," mused John Melby, an American diplomat stationed in China. "And it seems we are imperialists at the same time." Hurley's charges also created some incredulity in the Department in Washington. "According to this morning's paper this may be the last letter I will be allowed to write you unless the boys on Alcatraz can send letters to the outside world," Elbridge Durbrow wrote to Arthur Lane. Durbrow added, "The Hurley blast is creating quite a stir and we are all going to be under investigation. Since he accused some of the FSO's of being pro-communist, I am sure someone will come out and say there are also a lot of fascists — so, I'm glad to have known you." [27]

Byrnes had paid little attention to the unfolding saga of General Hurley. "He has so many Russian problems," China specialist John Carter Vincent said in early November, "that he hasn't gotten around to getting a good understanding of this situation." Unfortunately, for Byrnes, Hurley's resignation complicated the Secretary's Russian problems.

A few days before quitting, Hurley called on Admiral Leahy to discuss State Department "interference" in his mission. Since Leahy believed that the State Department did harbor un-American elements, he could overlook the inconsistency of Hurley's charges and accept what fit his own prejudices. The day after Hurley resigned, Leahy described the general's public charges as "a very mild allegation of what he described to me as communistic leanings and actions of a number of the assistants in the State Department." Leahy had now found an explanation for Byrnes' "appeasement." On that same day, Leahy conferred with Truman and Byrnes, as well as General George Marshall, who was to be Hurley's successor in China. Leahy noted, "Today I sense for the first time the feeling that Secretary Byrnes is not immune to the communistically-inclined advisers in his department." [28]

Byrnes' revitalization of the Yalta axioms only confirmed the old

* Djilas quotes Stalin in February 1948: "When the war with Japan ended, we invited the Chinese comrades to agree on a means of reaching a *modus vivendi* with Chiang Kai-shek. They agreed with us in word, but in deed they did it their own way when they got home."

admiral's suspicions. On December 26, he angrily noted in his diary that Byrnes was making "concessions to expediency that are destructive of the President's announced intention to adhere strictly to policies that are righteous and in exact accord with his foreign policy" as expounded in the Navy Day speech. "Russia has been granted every demand that wrecked the London conference by the refusal of the UK and the U.S. to agree at that time." Two days later, he dismissed the Moscow communiqué as "an appeasement document." Leahy was already known as chief of "the get-tough-with-Russia crowd" around the President. [29]

These influences — from Leahy, Vandenberg, the State Department bureaucracy, others in the Executive branch — were pressing on a President who found himself beset by complex, unfamiliar, seemingly intractable problems. Coming back on the boat from Potsdam in August, he had complained to White House aide Samuel Rosenman that till then most of his time had been taken up with one foreign crisis after another, and that he wanted to give some attention to domestic affairs. He tried to stay away from foreign questions, but the Russian difficulties could not easily be avoided any longer. In mid-October, Truman confessed that he was "getting to that stage" of staying awake nights, worrying. When he had first become President, he had announced that he would leave the Cabinet members to do their own work, and would intervene only if they were not doing a good job. Now, Truman began to hold Byrnes personally accountable. The foreign headaches involving the Russians were the worst. "They confront us with an accomplished fact and there is little we can do," he told his staff conference in mid-December. "I don't know what we are going to do."

The disagreements on policy between Truman and Byrnes were becoming complicated by a personality clash developing between the two men. In the first months after his accession, Truman, lonely and awed by the position, would point to a portrait of Roosevelt in the Oval Office and say, "I'm trying to do what he would like." Truman had been willing, even eager, to defer to Byrnes, in whom he went out of his way to express confidence. As late as September, when advising Joseph Davies on a foreign affairs speech, Truman said, "But be sure to feature Jim Byrnes."

In the last months of 1945, however, Truman was growing accustomed to being President. But Byrnes, as if out of ingrained habit, continued to treat him in the way a senior senator might treat a freshman senator. Byrnes tended to dominate the Tuesday Cabinet luncheons, dispensing his opinions freely, but showing (at least so it seemed to some) little regard for the opinions of others and clearly condescending to the President. Byrnes was too ambitious a man for the wound he had suffered at the 1944 convention to have really healed. As hard as he tried, he could not repress the thought that he, not Truman, should have been sitting at the head of the Cabinet table. Meanwhile, Truman's reverence for the office of the presidency bordered on the religious. Thus it was becoming easier for him to believe those who told him that the Secretary's apparent condescension was an insult not only to him, but also to the office of President.[30]

By November, or early December at the latest, the frictions produced by politics and personality had ignited a smoldering anger in the President. Truman was losing confidence in his Secretary.

At this time, Truman remarked to Harold Smith, director of the Bureau of the Budget, that the country domestically was "out of trough of the slump, and that the situation was bettering." His attention was returning to foreign affairs. At the end of November, he told Smith that he was "pretty unhappy" with the State Department. A week later, he added, "I would have a pretty good government, don't you think, if I had a good Labor Department and a good State Department?" In singling out those departments for special blame, the President was really pointing to the Administration's two greatest problem areas — labor relations and Russian relations. But, of course, they would have been problem areas no matter who the secretaries might have been. "Unfortunately," he observed, "some of the things about which Pat Hurley is spouting off about are true." He complained that he had urged Byrnes to improve administration in State. But nothing had been done. "The State Department was probably worse off than it had ever been in this aspect."

At the end of the first week in December, a tired and pressured Truman, trying to relax on a weekend cruise, said to Davies that Byrnes "was a conniver." The President said that he had "to do some conniving himself to keep the boat steady." A few days later, Byrnes made an announcement about the U.S. position on Germany without reviewing it first with the President. After learning about it from his morning *New York Times*, Truman acidly observed to aides that he "should not have to read the newspapers to get the U.S. foreign policy." [31]

In such circumstances, Byrnes was not likely to return from Moscow to the cheers he had expected. Before departing for the conference, Byrnes had assured Truman that "if something comes up that seems like a decent trade," he would try to get the President on the telephone so they could come to a decision together. In fact, communications between Moscow and Independence, where Truman was spending the Christmas holidays, had been brief and incomplete, the result of bad telephone connections and the exigencies of decision making. It took Byrnes six hours merely to reach Foreign Minister Bidault in Paris by phone. In addition, of course, Byrnes believed that he operated with a wide mandate. Nevertheless, Truman had returned to Washington on December 28, angered that he had not been consulted on the communiqué. He became even more angry when he learned that Byrnes had already cleared radio time for a nationwide speech. Almost immediately the President set off on another Potomac cruise, leaving curt word that Byrnes was to follow.[32]

The next day the Secretary arrived in Washington. He was surprised to learn that Truman had not waited for him, and in turn was irritated, after his long travels, to find the message ordering him to report immediately. Nevertheless, some four hours after landing — just long enough to bathe, lunch, and glance at cables — Byrnes was airborne again, this time to Quantico, Virginia, where he boarded the President's yacht. That same day, Leahy, in his diary (and presumably to the President), complained again that the Moscow accords were "not in agreement with the President's previously expressed ideas." But Truman may well have been angered more by what he saw as the personal slight, the lack of communication, and the apparent disrespect. As soon as Byrnes boarded the *Williamsburg*, he and the President went to Truman's quarters where they stayed for well over an hour. When they came down for dinner (as recollected later by Clark Clifford, then an assistant naval aide), they were "just as friendly as they could be." Byrnes had apparently, in Leahy's words, "satisfied the President" by explaining the problems of coding and decoding, bad telephone connections, and time pressures at the end of the conference. Although the President's anger had waned, Leahy's suspicion had not. At the dinner that followed, Leahy commented in his diary, "I repeatedly asked Mr. Byrnes for information as to what benefits accrue to the United States and was unable to get a satisfactory reply." Clark Clifford recalled how it looked to others: "Leahy, in a really effective and gentle manner with which Byrnes could not take exception, had the needle in him." As the dinner table was being cleared for poker, Byrnes begged pressing duties and departed. Because of fog and ice, he could not fly, but rather spent several hours driving back to Washington. When he got back to his apartment at the Shoreham Hotel, with political difficulties perhaps as much in mind as road conditions, Byrnes remarked, "That trip was more dangerous than the one to Moscow." [33]

On December 31, Byrnes delivered a valedictory for the old year. "Last year I was Director of Mobilization. I thought I was having a bad time between horse racing and curfews, but I will now say that mobilizing a nation for war is a small job compared with the effort to mobilize the world for peace." He rejoined the party on the *Williamsburg.* Trying to court and disarm the opposition, he spent much time discussing the Moscow agreements with Leahy. Everyone seemed in better spirits at the New Year's Eve party, where they celebrated with renditions of favorite Navy songs — which especially pleased the old admiral. Byrnes, proud of his tenor, took the lead. The next day Byrnes had a New Year's dinner that included black-eyed peas — he was mindful of the southern adage that a man who eats black-eyed peas at New Year's will be lucky all year long. His luck, at best, would prove only mixed.[34]

"The New Year starts with no international war in progress anywhere in the world," Admiral Leahy began his diary on the first day of 1946. But his mind was on other things. "The American Department of State and the British Labour Government have adopted a policy of appeasement of the Soviet Government that is reminiscent of Mr. Chamberlain at Munich, and dangerous to the political interests of America and England." Leahy started to catalog probable civil wars in the coming year, but he could not keep his thoughts away from the State Department. "I start a New Year in the bad graces of the State Department."

The Department and its Secretary, however, were in the bad graces of the President — whose anger had only temporarily been assuaged.

In the first week of December, Mark Ethridge had written a summary of his report on the Balkans and a four-page single-spaced letter based on it, both on Byrnes' instructions before the latter's departure for Moscow. These compressions gave greater attention to Soviet violation of democratic traditions. "Peace will be secure only if based on truly representative governments in all countries with western political traditions," Ethridge wrote in the summary. "To concede a limited Soviet sphere of influence at the present time would be to invite its extension in the future." (The historian might find it difficult to locate the "western political traditions" in the authoritarian past of either Rumania or Bulgaria.) Both papers had been bottled up before the Moscow Conference, also on Byrnes' orders.[35]

Only on January 2 did Byrnes transmit the first of the two Ethridge papers, the letter, to the President, along with a casual covering note — "This is the letter from Mark Ethridge I promised to send you for your files."

Truman did not receive the letter until the morning of January 5, and, as it turned out, the letter was not something he casually ran his eyes over, and then put aside for filing. On the contrary, it rekindled Truman's anger, not only because of Ethridge's description of how communists were monopolizing political life in the Balkans, but also because Byrnes had postponed its delivery to him. Truman was so angry that he wrote out in longhand a stinging "My dear Jim" letter. Later in the day, when Byrnes came to the White House to see the President, Truman's own letter lay on the desk between them. Truman asserted, in a diary note he wrote shortly after, and subsequently in his memoirs, that he read the letter to Byrnes. If he had, the prideful Secretary almost certainly would have resigned. More likely, the President used it to guide an exchange conducted in more moderate tones.[36]

Nevertheless, Truman's agitated letter provides an excellent gauge of the President's outlook on the world and his attitude toward the Soviet Union in this period. The first half of the letter was devoted to complaints about Byrnes' independent habits. Truman was insistent that all major decisions be subject to his approval. "Now I have infinite confidence in you and your ability but there should be a complete understanding between us on procedure." The letter then went on to say that Truman had just read Ethridge's letter, and that he would not approve recognition of Rumania and Bulgaria, which he called "police states," until their governments were "radically changed." The changes made in Polish borders had been a "high-handed outrage" but unfortunately an "accomplished fact." He regretted now that the Americans had felt at Potsdam, at least initially, that they needed to assure early Soviet entry into the Pacific war. "The Russians have been a headache to us ever since." The presence now of Russian troops in Iran, and the fact that Russia "stirs up rebellions" constituted "another outrage if I ever saw one." Truman, in abrupt terms, made clear that he had resolved the question of Soviet intentions in his own mind — by settling hard on a maximalist interpretation: "There isn't a doubt in my mind that Russia intends an invasion of Turkey and the seizure of the Black Sea Straits to the Mediterranean. Unless Russia is faced with an iron fist and strong language another war is in the making. Only one language do they understand — 'how many divisions have you?' "

"I do not think we should play compromise any longer," said the President. He laid out a long agenda in equally blunt language — no recognizing of Rumania and Bulgaria "until they comply with our requirements"; making known the American position on Iran "in no uncertain terms"; insisting on the internationalization of the Kiel, Rhine-Danube waterways, and the Black Sea Straits; maintaining "complete control of Japan and the Pacific"; rehabilitating and creating strong central governments in China and Korea; insisting on the return of ships from Russia and lend-lease settlement. To prevent any misunderstanding, he laid down the law: "I'm tired of babying the Soviets."

And yet, Byrnes had not babied the Russians; he had negotiated with them. If anything, the Moscow Conference had demonstrated that force was not the only way to do business with the Soviet Union. To be sure, admitting as much would have involved a retreat from Wilsonian principles. Negotiation was what Roosevelt had attempted — quietly trying to put aside these principles in order to organize relations among the Great Powers for the postwar world. For most policymakers, on the contrary, the lessons of the interwar years and of the war itself had only reinforced a commitment to universalism, renewing their belief in American purity, and generating an expansive notion of national security. Truman later suggested that his remark about being tired of babying the Soviets "was the point of departure of our policy." The Rooseveltian legacy was virtually spent. As if to symbolize the change, the late President's most effective agent, Harry Hopkins, died in January 1946. Now, in the highest echelons of government, Yalta was no longer a symbol of realistic accommodation based upon "the factor of power." Increasingly, it would suggest naïveté, weakness, and appeasement. Byrnes at Moscow had proved that the Yalta axioms were still viable, but they were no longer acceptable in the American government. One President had insisted, despite much resistance in levels below him, that the Yalta axioms form the basis of American-Soviet relations; now, his successor was insisting that the axioms be abandoned.

Truman also now intended to make much clearer that he indeed was the President. At a press conference in mid-January, he was asked about the recognition of Rumania and Bulgaria.

"I still have the final say," Truman replied sharply.

Meanwhile, a somewhat chastened Secretary of State had begun to make a new compromise. Ben Cohen later recalled, "Byrnes was very sensitive to the forces about. He liked to find accommodation . . . Byrnes would go as far as he could to make a settlement, based on the highest common denominator of the forces above him. And so, as the forces began to stiffen, he began to stiffen." [37]

With the A-1 priority question about Soviet intentions almost settled, he had no choice but to seek a lower common denominator, and to strive to find it not in Great Power councils, but within the forum of domestic American politics.

I fear it will be difficult to induce our Secretary of State to tacitly admit fault in our present appeasement attitude.

— WILLIAM LEAHY, February 21, 1946

Naturally all of us who have been working on Russian affairs have been concentrated on trying to fathom the workings of the Soviet mind and to develop our knowledge of Russia to a point where we would be able to make a pretty good estimate of probable Soviet behavior in given states of circumstances.

— GEORGE KENNAN, June 1946

VII

The Right Attitude in Mind

TEN IN THE EVENING was the time when Joseph Stalin often chose to receive foreign diplomats. At that hour early in April 1946, Walter Bedell Smith, formerly chief of staff to General Eisenhower and now the new American ambassador to the Soviet Union, was led into a paneled conference room in the Kremlin for his first meeting with the Russian dictator. On the wall behind Stalin hung portraits of Suvorov and Kutuzov, the great Russian marshals of the Napoleonic Wars.

Smith began with a question: "What does the Soviet Union want, and how far is Russia going to go?"

"We're not going much farther," Stalin replied, with what might have been gruff humor.

Smith assumed the reply was a serious one, and he was not satisfied. He noted the fate of Latvia, Lithuania, and Estonia, as well as the situation in the Balkans and the Near East. "We ask ourselves," he said to Stalin, "if this were only the beginning." [1]

Smith in fact thought he already knew the answer — that it *was* only the beginning. For his question came at the end of a period of ideological formulation in Washington. During the early months of 1946, American officialdom for the most part had resolved the contradictory interpretations about Soviet behavior and intentions into a coherent view.

The ideological reformulation was ordered from the top. In February, President Truman had expressed what Admiral Leahy characterized as "sharp disapproval of the recent attitude of appeasement toward the Soviet Union." The United States, said the President, had to take "a strong attitude without delay." Such statements amounted to specific criticism of Truman's own Secretary of State, James Byrnes; and Byrnes, adept and seeing no alternative, began to adjust his position. By spring, no one could doubt that the President's desire was being carried out. "You will have noted a general toughening of the official attitude not only towards our Polish friends," a State Department officer wrote to the ambassador in Poland, "but, what is more important, toward the originator of many of our present difficulties and misunderstandings. We all hope that it will produce fruit." Of Ambassador Smith, Truman had no doubts; Smith was going to Russia, the President observed in March, "with the right attitude in mind." [2]

The hardening of attitude was part of a larger movement, the polarization into East and West. The Alliance was receding from sight, and the Cold War confrontation was beginning to emerge. Three other developments accelerated the trend. First, the disputes between the Great Powers, heretofore conducted in privacy, were now played out in public, on a world stage. Second, Western leaders began calling for increased military strength to meet what they perceived as a Russian threat. Third, the locus of controversy, which had been confined to Eastern Europe, was now shifting to other regions, beyond the sphere marked out by the forward march of the Red Army. In the spring of 1946, Iran became the scene of the first Cold War crisis.

Since 1945, a need had been felt throughout the policy elite for a coherent statement of Soviet postwar intentions, and the consequent implications for American policy. Navy Secretary James Forrestal, one of the most apprehensive, complained that he had "been unable to find one." So he commissioned Edward Willett, a Smith College professor, to provide it. A "solution to the enigma of Russia" was what the Secretary wanted. "Are we dealing with that nation solely as a national entity or are we dealing with such a national entity plus a philosophy which amounts to a fervent religion?" [3] In his paper,

Willett declared that Soviet leaders remained committed to a global, violent proletarian revolution, which in turn meant that "violence between Soviet Russia and the U.S. would seem to be inevitable." [4]

Forrestal was so pleased with Willett's analysis that he distributed copies to the President, members of the Cabinet, other prominent people in government, media, and industry, even to the Pope. "I realize it is easy to ridicule the need for such a study as I have asked Willett to make," Forrestal wrote to Henry Luce, "but I think in the middle of that laughter we always should remember that we also laughed at Hitler." [5]

Other officials also tried to make sense out of a confused picture. In February, Charles Bohlen circulated a series of more moderate memoranda that drew as much on the Yalta as the Riga tradition, and almost certainly reflected his close work with Secretary Byrnes. The central problem, he wrote, "is that of integrating the policies of a dictatorship, directed virtually exclusively towards the furtherance of the national interest of the Soviet state, with the principles of world cooperation and international morality essential to the development of a peaceful and stable world." He hoped that, through an evolution and improvement of conditions within Russia, "the Soviet attitude towards the outside world in its policies and methods in international affairs will undergo progressive modification." He set out a Wilsonian goal: "to induce the Soviet Union in its own interest and in the interests of the world" to act in the spirit of the United Nations charter. But he advocated Rooseveltian tactics: "In view of the peculiarities of the Soviet state and the mentality of the Soviet leaders, the United States should encourage preliminary tri-partite conversations between the British, Soviets, and Americans on any issue which is likely to come before the world organization." [6]

A study of Soviet intentions by the Joint Intelligence Committee of the Joint Chiefs of Staff in February came to similarly mixed conclusions. It did see security as the ultimate Soviet goal, a state goal, not that of a revolutionary movement. It explained that the Soviet conception meant a high degree of strategic security plus the attainment of a position that the Russian leaders considered sufficient for meeting "any challenge of the western powers in combination."

The problem posed by any question of Soviet intentions called for an understanding of Soviet psychology. The Joint Intelligence Committee had wrestled with the problem of comprehending the political and military interests of the USSR "as conceived by the small ruling group." Yet, said the report, "No precise definition can be given, nor are all of them susceptible of rational explanation, at least by non-Russians." [7] At virtually that moment, however, there would be one non-Russian who would provide such understanding — who could, it would seem, probe deeply into the very minds of the Stalinist leadership, and so formulate both the problem and the appropriate response.

The crucial reformulation was initiated by the practice of electoral politics of a sort — the campaign in January and February 1946 for seats in the Supreme Soviet. Most of the speeches by Stalin's associates concentrated on the vast problems of reconstruction. The year 1946 had already been dubbed the Year of Cement. As to international affairs, both Molotov and Malenkov declared that the Soviet Union would not be intimidated by other countries. Russia was now "a supremely important factor in international life," said Molotov, adding that Stalin's participation in international talks was the best guarantee of success. Molotov still spoke of the "Allies" and Russia's need for "a long period of peace and fully-assured stability." Only Andrei Zhdanov, the most explicitly anti-Western and xenophobic member of Stalin's entourage, was outspokenly hostile in his references to the former Allies. "We've got to be extremely vigilant," he told the war-weary residents of Leningrad.[8]

The most important speech, of course, was that delivered by Comrade Stalin in the Bolshoi Theater on February 9, the eve of polling. Although he began with an orthodox declaration that the Second World War had arisen out of capitalist contradictions, he nevertheless was cautious and friendly in his remarks about his Western Allies. Contrasting the two world wars, he said that the second had "assumed from the very beginning an anti-Fascist liberating character, having also as one of its aims the establishment of democratic liberties." The entry of the Soviet Union only strengthened the already existing "anti-Fascist and liberating character" of the Second World War. "On this basis was established the anti-Fascist coalition of the Soviet Union, the United States of America, Great Britain and other freedom-loving countries, which subsequently played a decisive part in the rout of the armed forces of the Axis powers." The war had been a victory for all the Allies.

More specifically, the Second World War had tested the Soviet system, and the ultimate victory was proof of the success of the forced march into industrialization, a vindication of Stalin's policies. It was *his* system that had survived. Without the Five-Year Plans, Stalin said, Russia would have collapsed like the Austro-Hungarian empire. He repudiated claims in the West that the industrial transformation was either a miracle or an invention of the Cheka (the secret police) — for "miracles do not exist in this world, and our Cheka is not so powerful that it could abolish the laws of social development." He made clear that the now-proven principle of emphasizing heavy industry would continue in the new Five-Year Plan. Reconstruction was his major preoccupation.[9]

Westerners, unable to see that Russia's options were few, interpreted Stalin's speech as signifying a return to isolation, a commitment to remilitarization — and worse. Supreme Court Justice William O. Douglas told Forrestal that it was a "Declaration of World War III." [10]

Stalin's speech set off a round of discussion in the State Department. Calling it "the most important and authoritative guide to postwar Soviet policy," H. Freeman Matthews, director of the Office of European Affairs, predicted that it would become "the Communist and fellow-traveller Bible throughout the world." [11] Elbridge Durbrow, chief of the Division of Eastern European Affairs, announced that the speech represented a reversion to Stalin's 1928 policy of isolation. While the speech seemed ominous to State Department officials, they also took a curious comfort in it, for they found in it apparent confirmation of what they already believed. It also received wide and concerned domestic attention. "The importance of Stalin's statement has been realized by our press and public to a degree not hitherto felt," Matthews approvingly observed.[12]

Yet officials also wondered why they had received no detailed comment from George Kennan, who had emerged as the chief commentator on Soviet affairs. Matthews ordered Durbrow to "goose him." Durbrow drafted a cable for Matthews' signature, saying that the "speeches in large part serve to confirm your various thoughtful telegrams" and asking him for "an interpretive analysis of what we may expect in the way of future implementation of these announced policies."[13]

Kennan had not been heard from because he was overburdened with duties as chief of mission with the end of Harriman's tenure as ambassador; moreover, he was laid up with a winter's collage of ailments — cold, fever, sinus, tooth trouble, another attack of ulcers. His mood was certainly ulcerous, aggravated by those still following the Yalta axioms. In January, he suggested to both Durbrow and Bohlen that he was considering resigning soon from the Foreign Service. He was, he indicated, dissatisfied with U.S. policy, felt his own talents were not being properly utilized, and wanted to put down "roots" back in the United States. In particular, Byrnes' Moscow diplomacy the month before had disgusted him. With it in mind, he later wrote: "It is axiomatic in the world of diplomacy that methodology and tactics assume an importance by no means inferior to concept and strategy." Shortly after Byrnes left Moscow, Kennan set to work on a rulebook for dealing with the Russians that was really a total rejection of the Rooseveltian approach. Some of the adages were:

Do not encourage high-level exchanges of views with the Russians unless the initiative comes at least 50 percent from their side.

Do not be afraid to use heavy weapons for what seem to us to be minor matters.

Do not be afraid of unpleasantness and public airing of differences.

The Matthews query that followed Stalin's speech offered him a different kind of forum in which to make the same point. He seized the opportunity and composed a cable that was almost certainly the longest telegram to that date in the history of the Foreign Service, and the most widely read and highly praised.[14]

The most important work that Kennan himself ever wrote, highly personal in its style, drawing upon themes he had developed in the 1930s, the Long Telegram (as it came to be known) was also a classic restatement of the Riga axioms, indeed the most important such statement of those attitudes ever made. The heart of the telegram was Kennan's analysis of the "Soviet outlook." He assumed the guise of a doctor who studies an "unruly and unreasonable individual." What Kennan attempted was an anatomy of the collective psychology of the "people who make up the apparatus of power." [15]

"Basic inner-Russian necessities" and not an "objective analysis of situation beyond Russia's borders" shaped their attitude toward the world, said Kennan. He explained, "At bottom of Kremlin's neurotic view of world affairs is traditional and instinctive Russian sense of insecurity." Soviet rulers could compensate only by going permanently on the attack "in patient but deadly struggle for total destruction of rival power, never in compacts and compromises with it." Coexistence was impossible in Moscow's view, he was saying.

While declaring that Marxism was the "fig leaf of their moral and intellectual respectability," Kennan also reminded his readers that the devotion was not merely one of lip service. "No one should underrate importance of dogma in Soviet affairs." [16] The "basic Soviet instinct" was "that there can be no compromise with rival power and the constructive work can start only when Communist power is dominant."

Kennan laid out a frightening picture of the postwar world before the policy elite in Washington: "We have here a political force committed fanatically to the belief that with US there can be no permanent *modus vivendi*, that it is desirable and necessary that the internal harmony of our society be disrupted, our traditional way of life destroyed, the international authority of our state be broken if Soviet power is to be secure." [17]

For its part, the United States, he all but said, was at war, and should adopt a wartime frame of mind. From *cordon* he was advancing toward the idea (and policy) of containment: "Impervious to logic of reason, [the Soviet Union] is highly sensitive to logic of force. For this reason it can easily withdraw — and usually does — when strong resistance is encountered at any point." The West, he suggested, should be drawn together in a tighter bloc by the United States.[18]

The Long Telegram was an extreme reading of both the 1946 election speeches and of the international situation. Kennan had placed so much emphasis on ideology, theology even, as to virtually ignore the role of realpolitik in shaping Soviet policy. Furthermore, he presented Stalin as a fanatic revolutionary, rather than a careful, calculating politician bent upon the consolidation of Soviet power and the reconstruction of the USSR — Stalin, after all, was a leader who had publicly conceded that the "calculation of forces" overwhelmingly favored the West, in particular, the United States.

Was the Soviet conception of "security" as open-ended as Kennan asserted, or was that partly a projection of the new American doctrine of "national security"? Kennan rejected out of hand the possibility that the Soviet Union had an interest in stability and compromise, and that it was pursuing limited goals. In so doing, the American observer was overlooking how great a trauma the war had been, the political consequences of the devastation, and Stalin's own behavior in international politics. The image of the revolutionary state so transfixed Kennan that he ignored the great constraints with which the Russian leaders had to contend. He had confused Marxist rhetoric and Soviet reality. The contradiction in his portrait of the Soviet Union and its leaders — the rational fanatic, the devastated aggressor — went unrecognized.

The Long Telegram, truly, was not a fresh evaluation of a complicated situation, but rather a restatement of the Riga axioms. The members of the Riga School, as much as the hard-line Marxist ideologue, believed that peaceful coexistence was impossible; compromise a delusion, and conflict inevitable. So Kennan, the diplomat, proclaimed the dangers of diplomacy and accommodation. Kennan was in part reacting to the frustrations of working under the system prescribed by Franklin Roosevelt for dealing with the Soviet Union, as well as to the danger he perceived. Thus, his stark message took on an extra intent — for the Long Telegram was meant to, and indeed did, mark a complete repudiation of the Yalta axioms.[19]

The reaction to the telegram in Truman's Washington was swift and extraordinary. It forcefully brought the chargé's name to the attention of many people, including those in the White House. As Matthews had predicted that Stalin's speech would become the bible for Communists, so the telegram became the bible for American policymakers. It formulated the issues in Soviet-American relations for much of the policymaking elite, although it expressed what many already believed. A "splendid analysis" was Byrnes' comment.[20] Matthews told Kennan that it was "magnificent," adding, "I cannot overestimate its importance to those of us here struggling with the problem."[21] L. C. Stevens, the naval attaché in Moscow, recommended it to his superiors: all the papers on American-Soviet relations that he had seen in two and a half years were based upon "wishful thinking," but the Long Telegram was a "remarkably clear and sound presentation of basic elements of problems of relations USSR and USA and to world." He urged his colleagues in the Navy

Department to study the telegram because "problem transcends diplomacy." [22] Copies were rushed to U.S. diplomatic missions around the world, to General Eisenhower, Secretary of War Robert Patterson, and the top War Department planners. Navy Secretary James Forrestal virtually adopted the Kennan analysis as his own. He had hundreds of copies made, and distributed them throughout the Navy Department and (in the recollection of White House aide George Elsey) "sent it all over town." [23]

All in all, the reception to his Long Telegram eased, at least for the time, Kennan's many dissatisfactions. His two years in Moscow had been hard and he was tired, Kennan wrote to a friend in mid-April, but he felt less discouraged than he had for some time. "I have a feeling," he explained, "that some of the most dangerous tendencies in American thought about Russia have been checked, if not overcome. If we can now only restrain the hot-heads, and panic-mongers and keep policy on a firm and even keel, I am not pessimistic." [24]

The Long Telegram, leaked to a number of journalists in an effort to shape public opinion, became the source for a full-page article in *Time* magazine, which was accompanied by a map labeled "Communist Contagion" that showed Iran and Turkey and Manchuria as "infected," with Saudi Arabia, Egypt, Afghanistan, and India "exposed." [25]

The news leak was part of a major, although not closely coordinated, effort by government leaders to carry out Kennan's suggestion; namely, to dramatize the disputes among the Great Powers and push public opinion toward a state of alert.[26] For the postwar anticommunist consensus existed first in the center, in the policy elite, before it spread out to the nation.

Immediately after World War II, public opinion was a tangled mat of contradictory strands. Spokesmen for certain Eastern European nationalities and for the hierarchy of the Catholic Church had been overtly critical and suspicious of the Soviet Union throughout the war, but there was also a significant pro-Soviet left. Other Americans still clung to a now-enervated isolationism. Robert Taft, the leading isolationist spokesman, opposed not only American involvement in "power politics," but also the continuing expansion in presidential power. But the Wilsonian temper dominated the country. Most

Americans believed in the new international organization and hoped that it would solve the problem of power in international relations. The continued existence of the broad wartime internationalist consensus muted partisan Republican criticism. "The President and Mr. Byrnes have some tough nuts to crack and I feel it is vitally important for them to have a united nation behind them," Senator H. Alexander Smith wrote to Robert Taft.[27]

Many in the middle of the political spectrum continued to be mildly sympathetic to the Soviet Union. A number of nonleftist politicians, in fact, spoke out against anti-Soviet sentiment. In February 1946, the respected Republican senator from Vermont, Charles Tobey, lashed out at the "attempt to arouse public opinion against the Soviet Union . . . I consider such to be *dangerous* and *ill-considered* . . . The principal national interests of these countries will not conflict. We have had our differences, we will have others, but they will *never* be as important as our *common* interests and *common* aims."

Indeed, great confusion clouded public opinion on foreign affairs. Many Americans were not thinking about international politics. They were preoccupied with other problems — inflation, scarcity, demobilization, and normalcy. A great many Americans had lost any interest in world leadership, Harriman warned his colleagues in the Moscow embassy, and wanted nothing more than to "go to the movies and drink Coke." Some indication of how long the confusion among those thinking about foreign policy lasted is suggested by a letter Dulles received as late as September 1946, inviting him to help clarify matters for members of the Committee on Foreign Relations in Detroit, an affiliate of the Council on Foreign Relations. "Frankly we are pretty much at sea," wrote an official of the group. "Two or three times after rather extended discussions with well-informed discussion leaders we have come to the conclusion that the United States and Russia can 'get along' and live in the same world, enjoying a reasonable amount of peace and harmony. We concluded also that Russia only wants to secure her borders, is internally unprepared for another war, and consequently doesn't want one, and has no intention of grabbing new territory, or trying to evangelize the world toward communism. These are the things our committee has believed but we are becoming disillusioned and would like to have someone who knows the answers to help us straighten our thinking."[28]

In early 1946, members of the inner policy circles, alarmed at what they considered public apathy toward the Soviet threat, began their effort to make up the national mind. Senator Vandenberg saw his role as twofold: to apply pressures on Byrnes to keep him from "loitering around Munich," and to speak to the nation at large. He gained wide attention with a speech on February 27 in which he suggested a very grim answer to the question "What is Russia up to now?" Hamilton Fish Armstrong, editor of *Foreign Affairs*, congratulated him for "precipitating some elements in the bottle containing the cloudy solution labelled 'American Public Opinion about Soviet Russia.' "[29]

John Foster Dulles labored effectively among the nongovernmental foreign policy community. Meeting with a group of New York bankers in March, he stressed Russia's "ideological" aggression. "The Russians have decided that their system isn't safe in the same world as ours," he declared. Banker Russell Leffingwell of J. P. Morgan noted afterward that "Foster was simply overwhelming at lunch and left me, and all who saw him, in a state of depression so much more extreme than that in which we sat down."[30]

Two weeks earlier, Dulles had spoken on the same subject at the Council on Foreign Relations. During dinner, he had pointedly raised with Leffingwell the case of Thomas Lamont, head of the Morgan bank and perhaps the foremost American capitalist to associate himself with the Soviet-American Friendship Society during the war.

"Foster wondered whether you still support Russia's policies, and if not, why you don't say so publicly," Leffingwell wrote.

"I do not see much point in my saying publicly 'I have never been in sympathy with the [Soviet] government's policies and am not in sympathy with them now,' " Lamont replied. "Do you?" Still worried, Lamont wrote again, two days later, "I don't know what I have to take back . . . Do you?"

"It doesn't seem possible that many people could, because of your defense of Russia's claims when she was so loyally fighting with us against fearful odds, assume that you were equally pleased with Russia's present policies," Leffingwell replied. He advised Lamont not to worry, but also suggested that Lamont lunch with Dulles so that the latter could "expand his ideas."[31]

Later in the spring, Dulles took his message to the public. "Until recently I have not felt clear enough in my own mind about Russian foreign policy to feel like giving leadership in any particular direction," he wrote to a friend. "As a result of the opportunities I have had over the last year and more, I now feel that I have a clear understanding of the fundamentals, at least, of Soviet foreign policy." So emboldened, he devoted several weeks in April and May to composing a long paper on Soviet foreign policy. "I think it will help to crystallize American public opinion at a critical time," he informed British Foreign Secretary Bevin.

The paper appeared as a two-part article in *Life*.[32] Dulles painted a picture as grisly as Kennan's. "Peace and security" in the Russian mind "depend upon eradicating the non-Soviet type of society." The Russian leaders were seeking to "create world harmony, a great political calm which will be the *Pax Sovietica*." Dulles advised Americans to "maintain a strong military establishment," stand up to the Russians at every point, provide foreign aid, "cure social ills," and go to church more often.

"I can think of no articles in my experience in journalism which so definitely accomplished a job," Henry Luce immediately wrote him. "For a great many people, directly and indirectly, your article ended all doubts as to the inescapable reality of the Russian-Communist problem." [33]

Most important of all such efforts to arouse public opinion was Winston Churchill's Iron Curtain speech. The war had been a period of exultation for him, the climax for which his entire life had been a preparation. But in the midst of victory, at the very moment that the arbiters of peace had gathered at Potsdam, the British electorate had rejected him.

After his defeat, exhausted and personally humiliated, Churchill slipped quickly into melancholia and self-pity. Although he was the Leader of the Opposition, he had no heart for party politics. Members of the Tory hierarchy whispered that he needed a long rest.

"Sir, why don't you go right away?" burst out a barber as he clipped the former Prime Minister's hair in the House of Commons barbershop, the walls of which had been stripped bare of a wartime multitude of Churchill photographs. "That would be much better than hanging about this place like you're doing." [34]

The cold comfort Churchill had first taken in the deterrent and admonitory powers of the atomic bomb had dissipated. By the autumn his fears and anxiety about Stalin and the Soviet Union were mounting again. Late in October, he talked out some of his themes with Prime Minister Mackenzie King of Canada: "Russia was grabbing one country after another — one Capital after another . . . They should have been stood up to more than they were." But communists were most difficult to deal with; they were like "Jesuits without Jesus in the relationship." Above all, he told King, the Anglo-American alliance "must not be written off, it must be understood." [35] Churchill had realized long before the war's end that the only way Britain in its weakened condition could maintain its Great Power status was as a junior partner of the United States.[36]

An opportunity to help sustain the existence of the alliance — and to climb out of his personal depression — came in the form of an invitation to speak at Westminster College in Fulton, Missouri. As an added inducement, Truman promised to present him. Churchill's doctor had been insisting he seek rest in the sun, and the former Prime Minister decided to combine his trip to Missouri with a winter holiday in Florida.

"The welcome that he will get there will do him even more good than the sunshine and the rest," his wartime chief of staff, Ismay, wrote with relief to Eisenhower. "I confess that I hate seeing him so deeply and continuously involved in party politics . . . I should like to see him reserve himself for the really great issues, and the really great occasions, and to leave 'village cricket' alone." [37]

The Labour government looked favorably on the trip, not only for its effects on Russian relations, but also because the United Kingdom might draw a measure of "reflected popularity" that could help win congressional approval for a $3.75 billion American loan to Great Britain, then under consideration. The Foreign Office helped Churchill by providing him with secret papers as he prepared his speech.[38]

Arriving in the United States in January 1946, Churchill went to Florida, where he rested and sunned himself. He told Walter Bedell Smith that he was "reconnoitering for things to paint," and, in fact, finished his first painting in three days. During the next month, he went over his proposed speech, both in Florida and in Washington, with senior American officials, including Truman, Byrnes, and Leahy. The approval was general. Further discussion followed on the train ride to Missouri. Churchill also played poker with the President, losing a total of seventy-five dollars. But, as he later told Lord Halifax, "It had been well worth it!" [39]

In the speech, delivered on March 5 at Fulton, Churchill for the first time publicly used the phrase "Iron Curtain": "From Stettin in the Baltic to Trieste in the Adriatic, an iron curtain has descended across the continent." Everywhere else, except in the United States and the British Commonwealth, communists and fifth columnists "constitute a growing challenge and peril to Christian civilization." The Russians did not want war: "What they desire is the fruits of war and the indefinite expansion of their power and doctrines." Since "there is nothing they admire so much as strength," the only recourse was "the fraternal association of the English-speaking peoples" — and, in particular, a permanent military alliance between the United States and the British Commonwealth, staked upon the possession of an atomic monopoly and interchangeability in the military forces of the countries.[40]

The speech created a storm. Referring both to that speech and Stalin's election address, Leffingwell wrote, "I consider the greatest service rendered to mankind postwar has been rendered by Stalin and Churchill recently by exposing as they did the gravity of the peril Russia is presenting to the world." Henry Luce told Churchill that he had "only put into words what was gravely in the minds of many Americans." Commerce Secretary Henry Wallace, however, denounced "any ideas of 'The American Century' or 'The Anglo-Saxon Century' . . . any recrudescence of imperialism even under enlightened Anglo-Saxon atomic bomb auspices." But Churchill had stepped too far in front of opinion, and many centrist figures, including a number of moderate congressmen, also criticized the speech.

At a dinner given by Henry Luce shortly before Churchill's departure from the United States, the former Prime Minister sampled some caviar, and regretfully mused, "You know, Uncle Joe used to send me a lot of this, but I don't suppose I'll ever be getting any more." [41]

He was right, for the speech created so much alarm in Eastern Europe and the Soviet Union that Stalin gave two interviews within ten days. He attacked the speech, denounced Churchill as an "inveterate Tory," and sought to calm fears. The Munich analogy was not the only way to bring Hitler into discussions of current international problems. Stalin posited a "race" analogy: Churchill's argument that "only English-speaking nations are superior nations" was reminiscent of Hitler's claims that the Germans were "the only superior nation." He assured both Russians and foreigners that he was convinced that "neither nations nor their armies are striving for a new war, they want peace and are striving for maintenance of peace," and urged "public and ruling circles" abroad to rebuff the "inciters of war."[42]

Since their countries were still formally allies of the Soviet Union, American and British leaders went through the ritual of publicly separating themselves from Churchill's ideas. In fact, Bevin agreed completely with what the former Prime Minister had said. Admiral Leahy described the speech as "a courageous statement of Mr. Churchill's belief in the inherent righteousness of power in the English-speaking world." He happily anticipated unfavorable reaction from the Soviet Union — and what he called local "pinkies." President Truman feared that the United Nations would be wrecked if he did not officially disassociate himself from Churchill's sentiments, and so at a press conference he said he had not read the speech beforehand. As he explained to his mother and sister, "I think it did some good, although I am not yet ready to endorse Mr. Churchill's speech."

A month after the speech, Lord Halifax, British ambassador to Washington, wrote to Churchill: "There has been a steady movement of understanding what your Fulton speech was about and appreciating it. Many people of a kind that I should hardly have expected to take that line, have said to me what an immense service you rendered by stating the stark realities and what an effect that had upon the thinking and the policy of the Administration. I have very little doubt that is true."[43]

The speech did assist in winning approval for the United Kingdom loan agreement. Negotiated the previous fall, it was intended to help Britain pay for necessary imports in the face of an immense, war-aggravated balance-of-payments crisis. Without such aid, John Maynard Keynes had lectured Cabinet ministers, "There was no hope of escaping a financial Dunkirk." For a $3.75 billion loan, the Americans exacted major concessions, the effect of which was to subordinate Britain to an American-dominated international economic order. These terms were much criticized in the U.K. But Halifax wrote to King George: "I do not think it is generally realized in England to what extent the Americans with whom we had been working were in fact waging a war on two fronts; negotiating with us, and at the same time feeling obliged to protect themselves against attacks from many sides on the home front." The loan certainly did confront many political hurdles within the United States. Opposition came from a heterogeneous coalition, which included Midwestern congressmen, Irish-Americans, pro-Zionists, some businessmen, in concert with those disturbed by the mild socialism of the British Labour Party. By the winter, a real danger existed that Congress would not approve the loan.

At that point, however, economics and politics began to merge. The loan was swept along by the rising tide of anticommunism. The emerging anticommunist consensus, not the ideology of a restored world economy, generated the support necessary to get the loan through Congress. In May, a group of Republican congressmen met to discuss the loan with Assistant Secretary of State Will Clayton.

"The economic arguments in favor of the loan," Representative Christian Herter wrote to Clayton shortly after, "are on the whole much less convincing to this group than the feeling that the loan may serve us in good stead in holding up a hand of a nation whom we may need badly as a friend because of impending Russian troubles."

"I am sure you are right," Clayton responded.

A beneficiary of anticommunism and international polarizations, the loan won final approval during the summer.[44]

While the Iron Curtain speech itself may initially have gotten mixed reviews, it clearly pointed the way for public opinion. Only a dwindling circle in Washington worried about the manner in which "the stark realities" were being presented. "All this anti-Russianism is bad," Senator Claude Pepper complained to Henry Wallace. The former Vice President himself had declared in his March speech, "The U.S. had nothing to gain but on the contrary, everything to lose by beating the tom-tom against Russia." [45]

In those early months of 1946, however, the tom-toms were growing unmistakably louder, and no one heard them more clearly than that artful master of Washington's tribal ways, Jimmy Byrnes. Pressure began mounting on Byrnes with the new year. After the sharp criticism that followed his Moscow trip, he had to prove anew his credentials both in Truman's Washington and abroad. He was home less than a week before setting off again for London and the first meeting of the United Nations General Assembly. It was in February that Byrnes made the decision to forsake private Great Power diplomacy in favor of "public diplomacy" — "increased publicity to the course and content of our negotiations." As Ben Cohen said at the time, "Statesmen must share their trials as well as their triumphs." Byrnes wanted to develop support for a firmer line with the Soviet Union; he hoped to use that elusive creature — "an aroused world public opinion" — in order both to scare the Russians back inside their own borders and to restore his own political position. But, as Cohen later remembered, public diplomacy was a two-edged sword: increased publicity helped to alert people to "the hard realities," but it also helped transform "the conference table from a forum of negotiation and agreement into a forum of propaganda."[46]

At the United Nations General Assembly in London in January 1946, the difficulties over Iran began to break into public view. The subsequent crisis of March 1946 was a landmark in the development of the Cold War. For it was the first time that the new, tougher American attitude took force as policy. It also represented a shift in the East-West contention from Eastern Europe to a new periphery of conflict that involved a collision in what had been traditionally Russian and British spheres. Finally, it became the first public breach among the superpowers. The United States also took the lead away from Britain and sought to make the Russians back down by playing to the gallery of world opinion. One further factor complicated the situation — oil. Anxieties about Russian expansionism coincided with fears about an imminent oil drought in the United States. Yet, removed from its place in the history of the Cold War, stripped of ideology and idealistic protestations, the Iranian crisis was primarily but a classic scramble by Great Powers — in an area in which Great Powers had been in the habit of scrambling — for influence, for strategic position, and for possession of that most valuable of all natural resources, oil.

By the end of the Second World War, there was already a general agreement in and out of the U.S. government that America's oil reserves were running out, that there was an urgent need to stake out major new foreign sources, and that the effort, for both economic and political-military reasons, should center on the vast, untapped reserves of the Middle East. Forrestal told Byrnes in September 1945 that Middle Eastern oil was not only of "substantial interest" to the Navy but also "one of the great interests of the whole country — people I have relied on most in private industry advise me that there can and probably will be a very substantial shortage in our own reserves if we continue to permit the offshore shipments of oil to the same degree as before."[47] In November 1945, Loy Henderson, now head of the Division of Near Eastern Affairs, succinctly set out the matter: "From the point of American national interests, it is hardly necessary to point out that the war has emphasized the strategic importance of the Near East, a region whose component countries are in a state of intense political, social and economic readjustment. There is a need for a stronger role for this Government in economics and political destinies of the Near and Middle East, especially in view of the oil reserves."

Oil, therefore, was very much at the heart of the Iranian crisis, although American officials almost routinely denied it. At the height of the crisis, Byrnes ordered the ambassador in Tehran not to discuss oil concessions: "It is important that no one should obtain a false impression that our determination to carry out our obligations under the Charter and the Iran Declaration has been influenced in the slightest by a selfish interest on our part in Iranian petroleum." Though such a statement was accurate in a narrow sense, it was in a larger sense an exercise in mystification, an effort to disguise the American interest in order to avoid legitimizing the Russian one.[48]

In 1941, the Russians and British had instituted a joint military occupation in Iran because of Reza Shah's close relationship with the Germans. They wanted to safeguard what was the most important supply route into the Soviet Union, and to protect the oil fields and refinery that were vital to the war effort. Reza Shah was forced to abdicate in favor of his son. In January 1942, the two powers signed a treaty with Iran, promising to evacuate the country six months after the end of the war.

Three factors appear to have shaped the postwar Soviet interest in Iran. First, Stalin wanted to ensure his Great Power prestige, and to recover all territory and influence that the Czarist empire had once held — and northern Iran had traditionally been a Russian sphere. Second, he was obsessed with a pursuit of security, and the border of northern Iran was little more than a hundred miles from the Baku oil fields.[49] But third, as much if not more than anything else, the Russians were mesmerized by the same potent force flowing up from beneath the ground — oil — that drew the Americans' attention. Although not a producing region, this part of northern Iran, lying close to the established fields at Baku, appeared tempting, all the more so when measured against the heavy devastation the war had laid on Russia's own production. Surely, the Russians, with real experience of drastic shortages, might have been at least as anxious about future reserves as the Americans.

In turn, the American position was determined by three concerns — to secure an Iranian oil concession; to block Russian expansionism; to prevent threats from developing to other American interests in the Middle East, particularly the even richer reserves of Saudi Arabia. The United States, as much as Russia, was an expansionist power on the scene. Meanwhile, the British were on the defensive, trying to hold on to their sphere, willing, if all else failed, to bargain off a northern sphere to the Russians, as they had in 1907, so long as they could hold on to their southern sphere. The conflict of purpose between the British and the Americans should not be underestimated, but it would also be a mistake, as some writers have suggested, to equate it with the Russian-American dispute.[50]

During World War II, American oil companies and the U.S. government worked in harness to gain concessions and extend American influence in Iran. The United States provided aggressive aid to companies seeking concessions, and also provided a host of advisers to the Iranian government, including its two chief petroleum experts. Late in 1942, Wallace Murray, then the head of the Division of Near Eastern Affairs in the State Department, suggested, "We shall soon be in the position of actually 'running' Iran through an impressive body of American advisers." [51]

The Russians indicated throughout the war that while they were "neutral" on British and American concessions in the south, they wanted their share in the form of exclusive concessions in the five northern provinces — the one area exempted from the original concession of 1901 because it lay within an area of Russian interest. As the heated competition among the Western companies moved toward a conclusion in 1944, the Russians jumped into the scramble, demanding in heavy-handed fashion a northern concession. To block the Russian move, seen by the government in Tehran as a threat to Iranian independence, and in an effort to tie troop withdrawal to petroleum rights, the Iranian government in the autumn of 1944 put off the granting of further concessions until after the war.

At Yalta, a few months later, Eden mentioned Iran in a private conversation with Stalin. "You should never talk to Molotov about Iran," the dictator said. "Didn't you realize that he had a resounding diplomatic defeat there? He is very sore with Iran." [52]

A few Western officials did suggest that the Russians were seeking what corresponded, in Moscow's books, to equal treatment. "After all," noted W. H. Young of the Eastern Division in the British Foreign Office in 1943, "to Russian eyes, our activities, and still more those of the Americans, can hardly fail to indicate an exaggerated interest in Persian affairs." But the Americans chose to cast the issue in idealistic, inflated terms. The State Department, in an internal May 1945 policy statement, pledged the United States to strengthen the Middle Eastern countries in order that they stand neither in a British nor a Russian sphere. It added, "As to the Russians, we should discourage any form of Soviet economic impact on Middle Eastern countries which is justifiably objectionable to them." [53]

By autumn 1945, the two elements that were to shape the crisis were in place — the continuing presence of Soviet occupation troops in Iran, and the existence of a separatist regime under Russian protection in the north, in Azerbaijan. This region, the breadbasket of Iran, contained a fifth of the country's entire population. Its people, speaking a Turkic dialect identical to that of Soviet Azerbaijan, had a long history of separatism. Moreover, in the years before World War II, their economic and political resentments toward the policies of the central government had mounted. In November and December 1945, a newly formed Democratic Party, led by Jafar Peshevari, and containing strong elements of the Tudeh (Communist) Party, seized control of the province, with a program calling for autonomy within the Iranian state, as well as country-wide reforms. It set out on its own reform course that won it a significant following. However, the continuing identification with the disliked Russian occupation troops, who were preventing the central government from reasserting its authority, cut into its popularity.

By the time Secretary Byrnes went to the Moscow Conference in late December, policymakers in Britain and America were afraid that Russian designs extended to all of Iran. They wanted to get the Soviet occupation troops out by the agreed deadline of March 2, 1946.[54] But the effort to solve the problem through Great Power diplomacy at Moscow failed.[55]

Byrnes pursued an equivocal, rather low-key policy on Iran through January 1946. Under pressure from the British, who did not want questions asked about their own sphere, the Iranian government developed second thoughts about challenging the Russians, but did finally bring the question to the Security Council in late January.[56]

Byrnes' equivocation resulted from the contradictory impulses within him and the conflicting pressures about him. His own instinct was still to seek a cloakroom compromise. He continued to be convinced that the general settlement at Moscow had been a wise one, and that such methods could help solve other problems, like that involving Iran. But he had been stung by the unexpected criticism when he returned from Moscow. Truman, in his "letter" of disapproval of January 5, had given Iran a central place in the bill of indictment. "Some of his best friends call him a fixer, a compromiser, an appeaser, and they worry that such a man should be the custodian of U.S. foreign policy," *Fortune* wrote of Byrnes at the beginning of 1946. "He is said to lay out three hats in the morning, so he can compromise on the one in the middle." The magazine pointedly added: "He is the present successor to the Presidency." He continued to feel pressure from beneath him in the Department. While in London, in the middle of January, he was alerted to the atmosphere in Washington by Donald Russell, his old law partner and then Assistant Secretary of State for Administration, who wrote, "I must confess, however, that there is apparently more anti-Russian spirit than I thought possible."[57]

The anti-Russian spirit was with him, in London, in the form of Arthur Vandenberg and John Foster Dulles, both members of the delegation, and both among the most bitter critics of the Moscow Conference. Writing to Dulles a few months later, Vandenberg complained that Stalin had learned during the war "that all he had to do was 'stay tough' " and the Americans would be "at Munich," appeasing him. "He has got to be 'unlearned' of that false lesson. We started teaching him at San Francisco. You added immensely to his knowledge at London last fall. Then Jimmy cancelled it all out upon the occasion of his humiliating pilgrimage to Moscow. But we retrieved some ground at London this winter." For the two Republicans, retrieving lost ground meant taking a hard line on any issue they could find.[58]

Averell Harriman, coming to London during the U.N. meeting, observed widespread sniping at Byrnes. One prominent Democrat told the ambassador how dissatisfied Truman was with "Byrnes' plowing ahead without consultation," and expressed his own doubts that Byrnes would last. "From almost everyone I talked to," Harriman noted, he heard about disgruntlement "with the inadequate information and treatment they had received from Byrnes . . . Byrnes is pursuing his policy of not consulting anybody and making up his own mind." John Foster Dulles told Harriman that the delegation's members "give Byrnes credit for capacity, but do not like the atmosphere of lack of frankness and opportunism which he is creating. All unanimously feel that the distinction of American foreign policy . . . is now being lowered by Byrnes. Byrnes is letting the British slip away from us, not because of any disagreement on policy but merely by offending them through his unwillingness to consult and what Bevin considers his somewhat overbearing attitude. It must be remembered that Bevin as a labor leader has a certain sensitivity which comes from his background."

With no excess of fondness himself for Byrnes, Harriman was not unsympathetic to all this criticism.

In late January, the U.N. took up the question of Iran by agreeing to postpone deliberations. The March 2 deadline for the withdrawal of troops was not yet at hand, and Russia and Iran agreed to the official United Nations suggestion that they undertake bilateral discussions. Meanwhile, Ahmad Qavam took over as premier from a conservative, pro-Western politician, which facilitated negotiations. For the cagey old Qavam, who owned considerable land in the north, intended to steer a middle course. He believed that oil, rather than a Russian grab for Iran, was the heart of the problem, although he also realized that Russian concessions could be an important opening wedge for a sphere of control.[59] The British, while critical of the American role, were pleased with the U.N. deferral.

At the end of January, Byrnes was back in Washington. He still thought composition was working. He wrote to Mark Ethridge on

January 29 that he was not yet satisfied with conditions in Bulgaria. But in Rumania, he said, "Vishinsky really endeavored to comply in full with the Moscow agreement." He told the Cabinet of his "difficulties" with Dulles and Vandenberg, explaining that their "activities from now on could be viewed as being conducted on a political and partisan basis." He also pointed out that the Russians "like to discuss stability and peace with the United States alone." But now Byrnes could sample the anti-Russian sentiment more fully. There was much talk in Washington of a rift between President and Secretary of State, and the opposition to Byrnes was much more in the open.[60]

Truman himself in this period was discouraged, harassed, confused, and overworked. At the beginning of February, a message from his mother was passed on by his cousin: "Tell Harry to be good, be honest, and behave himself, but I think it is now time for him to get tough with someone." Later in the month, Truman discussed his manifold problems with Budget Director Harold Smith. He lacked adequate staff support and, in Smith's judgment, was not effectively using the staff he had. He was staying up to read as much as thirty thousand words of memoranda a night. The President compared present conditions to those after the First World War, and then picked up a copy of *The New Republic* open to an article by George Soule on that subject. At the end of February, he complained, in what Smith described as "notes of despair," about the "avalanche of things that were piling up" on him. A few weeks later, meeting again with officials from the Bureau of the Budget, the President held up an issue of *Collier's*, with an article entitled "Truman's Unhappy Year." The assistant budget director replied that it could be entitled "The Country's Unhappy Year." [61]

Truman wanted sharp distinctions between right and wrong in foreign affairs. He felt that at least in this arena he should not have to exhaust himself balancing competing interests. But Byrnes was not delivering the certainty that the President thought the Secretary owed him, and that the President himself saw. The same voices that had been so influential at his accession reinforced his current state of mind. In February, Leahy recorded in his diary that Averell Harriman, returning home at the end of his Moscow ambassadorship, stopped in at the White House to criticize "our present policy of appeasement of the Soviet Union." Leahy added that Truman also thought the United States should "adopt a strong diplomatic opposition to the Soviet program of expansion, but I fear it will be difficult to induce the Secretary of State to tacitly admit fault in our present appeasement attitude." [62]

Yet by the end of February Byrnes was prepared to make exactly that tacit admission, to demonstrate that he too possessed the "right attitude." By this point, Byrnes could no longer play Roosevelt. He had to choose between a domestic consensus and a Great Power consensus. He chose what was the only real course open to him, to re-establish his position at home. Loy Henderson remembered a specific moment when State Department officials clearly saw a change in Byrnes. During a meeting of the senior officials in February, Undersecretary Acheson brought up the subject of Iran. Benjamin Cohen argued that the maintenance of good relations with the Soviet Union was the chief problem. Henderson disagreed sharply. "If the Russians get this, they'll try another," he said. The United States could not tolerate the Russian activity, for if it did, then the entire structure of peace would break down. The rising sound of discord in the office next to his own brought the Secretary in.

"What's all this loud talk?" Byrnes asked. "I want to get in on it."

They summarized the arguments for him — first Cohen, and then Henderson. The latter uttered only a few sentences, when Byrnes interrupted, "We're going to take a stand on that." [63]

Byrnes' shift came into public view with a major foreign policy speech to the Overseas Press Club on February 28, in which his attack on the Soviet Union and its policy in Iran was almost explicit. (Byrnes was now careful to submit the speech for advance approval to Truman, who also advised the Secretary "to stiffen up and try for the next three months not to make any compromises.") The speech signaled Byrnes' switch from cloakroom to public diplomacy. He put aside the reasoning that had led him to organize the Moscow meeting and said that clashes of interest "should be publicly revealed." And, if they were not taken to the United Nations, "these forums would be detached from reality and in the long run turn out to be purposeless and futile." He criticized the use of small adjustments that might be an "entering wedge for further and undisclosed penetrations of power." Calling for a strong military establishment, he said that the United States would use its influence to ensure that other powers "live up to this [U.N.] Covenant." He also said that the U.S. would actively seek to forestall aggression. He delivered a major statement of globalism, a call for the Open World, a rationale for American involvement at any point on the map: "We will do nothing to break the world into exclusive blocs or spheres of influence. In this atomic age we will not seek to divide a world which is one and indivisible."

Iran had in fact stimulated a wide agreement in the policy councils that Big Power arrangements were immoral. U.S. leaders thought that somehow power itself — except for the disinterested American power — could be banished, that a heterogeneous system of independent states, large and small, weak and powerful, could constitute a polity that would function on the principles of "one man, one vote." For example, in the middle of March, John Hickerson, of the Office of European Affairs, noted, "I think we are standing at the crossroads. There can be two types of world. The first one is a world built around the UNO conception, built on the principle of the sovereign equality of all states. The second is a big-power world with spheres of influence. I think the United States could probably get along pretty well in the second but for a thousand reasons I hope and pray that we shall have the privilege of living in a world built on the UNO conception. I feel so strongly about it that I am willing to go down the line for such a world — and right now." [64]

By this time Byrnes was ready to go down the line on the Iranian question. It was never clear that the Iranians would. Premier Qavam spent three weeks in Moscow in February and March. Though obviously subjected to intense pressure, Qavam moved toward a broad settlement that included the withdrawal of Soviet troops, a joint oil exploration agreement, some autonomy for Azerbaijan, and the dispatch of a new, less obnoxious Soviet ambassador to Tehran.[65] Qavam was, in fact, performing a difficult balancing act — trying to avoid alienating his would-be American sponsor, and yet not antagonize his truculent Soviet neighbor. He relied on two spokesmen — one Soviet-oriented and the other Western-oriented — to issue contradictory policy pronouncements, and then in turn repudiated them.[66]

As Qavam prepared to leave Moscow, the March 2 deadline came and went. The British withdrew their last soldiers, but the Russian troops remained, "pending," in Tass' words, "examination of the situation." Examination took an odd form, for an American consul in northern Iran reported large-scale and ominous Soviet troop movements in the region and then "full-scale combat deployment."[67]

For the first time in the postwar period, a crisis mentality gripped those in the policy elite. "There is a very dangerous situation developing in Iran," Truman told Harriman. "The Russians are refusing to take their troops out — as they agreed to do in their treaty with the British — and this may lead to war."

In the State Department, Loy Henderson ordered the preparation of a large, blown-up map of Azerbaijan, complete with arrows. The map was used to illustrate briefings hurriedly arranged for Byrnes and other top officials. They were told where each arrow was aimed — the Turkish border, the Iraqi border, the Iranian oil fields, Tehran.

The USSR was "adding military invasion to political subversion in Iran," exclaimed Byrnes. Beating a fist into the other hand, he added, "Now we'll give it to them with both barrels."

All the senior officials agreed that "only one conclusion could be drawn — the USSR seemed determined to face Iran and the rest of the world with a *fait accompli.*" Acheson, however, urged a certain amount of caution — "we ought to let the USSR *know that we were aware of its moves,* but 'leave a graceful way out' if it desired to avoid a showdown." The Department dispatched another note to Moscow demanding "information at once regarding the purposes" of the troop movements.[68]

It was not surprising that men whose memory of war was so fresh — who remembered Germany's step-by-step advance a decade earlier — should find cause for deep concern in any sudden flurry of military activity. Moreover, Truman in particular had come to believe that the U.S. had been disadvantaged in relations with the Soviet Union because it was always being confronted with *fait accomplis.* He did not want to face another accomplished fact in the form of a Sovietized Iran. However, the conclusions drawn in the State Department also reflected the consolidation of the Riga framework for interpreting Soviet behavior. The arrows on the map symbolized the belief that the Russians were working by some larger plan. Yet another hypothesis was also plausible — that the troop movements were a heavy-handed bluster and bluff, aimed not only at impressing the Iranians, but also to show the West that Russia — as a Great Power — could not be pushed around in its own backyard. The Russians did *not,* after all, follow the path of the arrows, but rather marched in the opposite direction, toward home. They did not need any fiery oratory in the United Nations to know that a move in any of those other directions would have been seen as a threat to interests vital to the West, and that a strong Western response would have been most likely.

During Qavam's Moscow discussions, Stalin and Molotov had exclaimed, "We don't care what the U.S. and Britain think, and we are not afraid of them." But, of course, they were afraid, and this was one region where they felt especially vulnerable. The United States, however, proceeded on the assumption that Russian aggression was imminent, and that the Russians had to be publicly exposed in order to bring the crisis to a proper settlement.[69]

The Iranian ambassador brought the question of Russian troops back to the Security Council on March 19, although it was never clear exactly what Qavam wanted him to do. On the same day, Gromyko asked that the subject be delayed until April 10, by which point he expected a settlement; and, a week later, the Soviets announced, in somewhat ambiguous terms, that the evacuation of some districts, which had begun on March 2, would shortly be completed, and that the overall evacuation would be finished in five or six weeks "if nothing unforeseen should take place." Meanwhile, negotiations between the Soviet and Iranian governments were continuing. U.N. Secretary-General Trygve Lie concluded that private discussion, away from the spotlight of the United Nations, would be the most effective way to bring about a Soviet withdrawal. "I thought that a debate in the Security Council now would probably intensify rather than ease the dispute."

However, neither the Iranian ambassador nor, as Lie later pointedly recalled, the State Department, especially its Near Eastern Division, would agree.[70] The United States applied pressure on Iran to refuse Soviet compromise offers and to keep the issue alive at the United Nations. Both Byrnes and Truman ruled out any delay in the Security Council debate. "I intend to insist on full disposition now," Byrnes informed Bevin. Byrnes himself went to New York to present the American case, declaring that if the United Nations did not immediately take up the Iranian question, "UN will die in its infancy of inefficiency and ineffectiveness." Gromyko — faced by a public display at a moment when the parties were close to a settlement — angrily staged the first of many Soviet walk-outs.[71]

Within a few days, by April 4, the Iranian crisis was abruptly over.

The Security Council debate did not force the Russians out of Iran; it publicized the problem, but did not solve it. It came to its end because Tehran and Moscow had agreed to a settlement framed when Qavam had been in Moscow. On April 5, Forrestal admitted to Byrnes that foreign oil "is a hot subject." [72]

The crisis never developed into a full-blown East-West confrontation, but it had fueled the larger, emerging polarization. The dispute had opened to Soviet-American competition a new arena — one that would later be called the Third World. As polarization increased, each side saw the other engaged in provocative action.

On April 4, the same day the crisis was settled in Tehran, the new American ambassador Walter Bedell Smith made his evening call at the Kremlin. Stalin quickly raised the issue of Iran, and spoke at length on the subject. He wanted a government in Tehran that, unlike that of Qavam's predecessor, was not overtly hostile to the Soviet Union. Such desires were not unknown in "British and American international relations." He spoke caustically about "the obstacles placed in the way of Soviet efforts to obtain oil concessions, particularly by Great Britain and later by the United States." He criticized the refusal of the United States to agree to a delay in the Security Council. "If such a request had been made by the U.S. in similar circumstances, the Soviet Union would willingly and gladly have conceded it." The troops would be out by May 5, as promised.* He assured Smith that the Soviet Union was not about to quit the United Nations. Stalin then passed on to the Iron Curtain speech — "an unfriendly act and an unwarranted attack on himself and the USSR which, if it had been directed against the United States, would never have been permitted in Russia."

Did he really believe that the United States and Britain were united in alliance against the USSR, Smith asked.

"Da," replied Stalin.[73]

For the Americans, "principles" had been at stake in Iran. They had acted on the basis of a globalist impulse. They denied to some

* Truman, as much as Stalin, regarded Iran as a kind of test in Soviet-American relations. On March 23, Ambassador Smith came to see Truman in preparation for leaving for Moscow. The President, as he recorded in a diary note, instructed Smith "to tell Stalin I held him to be a man to keep his word. Troops in Iran after March 2 upset that theory. Also told him to urge Stalin to come to U.S.A."

degree, even to themselves, their own real interest. The Iranian crisis arose at the moment when almost the entire American policy elite had assumed the "right attitude in mind."

The Riga framework ruled out alternative explanations for events, as well as evidence that did not accord with it, and it emphasized the existence of a larger Soviet plan. For example, in April, Robert Murphy, political adviser to General Lucius Clay, the American commander in Germany, conveyed General Clay's disagreement with Kennan's Long Telegram — it did not seem to accord with Clay's own reasonably successful working relations with the Russians in Germany. In reply, H. Freeman Matthews warned, "You get an entirely distorted picture if you attempt to draw general conclusions" from the Berlin experience. He went on to deliver a terse, codified summary of the Long Telegram worth quoting at length because it expressed the now dominant, virtually unchallenged outlook in high policy circles:

"When I said that the prospect was 'grim' I had, of course, in mind the longer term rather than the short range," Matthews wrote. "No one here thinks for a moment that the Soviets want war with us at this time. It is, however, basic doctrine in the Kremlin that the Soviet and non-Soviet systems cannot exist in this world side by side. This basic belief amounts to a religion to the true Communist and its implications make it impossible to visualize real peace in the world unless or until there is a fundamental change in Soviet thinking." He added that the Soviet leaders "want no peace, or stability or rehabilitation in Europe — or at least west of the Iron Curtain — for under such conditions their infiltration and communization methods do not prosper. And these methods are one of the two arms for Soviet expansion — the other of course being direct military pressure on neighboring states, as in Iran. There still is, of course, one real long-term hope, namely, that 'education' behind the Iron Curtain will eventually result in a change in basic Soviet policies." But there was no hope of present accommodation.

"Sorry I have no time to go into this at length," Matthews concluded, "but I am just swamped getting ready for our forthcoming meeting in Paris."

The meeting to which he referred was the first session of the Paris Peace Conference.[74]

Early in the proceedings in Paris, Byrnes told French Foreign

Minister Bidault that, if the conference did not go well, he would try to have the meetings "thrown open to the public so that world opinion can see just what the situation is and just where stumbling blocks lie." He had been much impressed with the way "opinion had rallied behind the American position" at the Security Council discussions on Iran. Newspapers and correspondents "who had previously misunderstood our position with regard to Russia had come around completely and had been greatly shocked at Russia's attitude toward a small country." A few months before, Byrnes explained, the American public was eager to cooperate with the Soviet Union, but the Russians had "completely dissipated" that feeling by their policies.

Byrnes introduced a telling personal note: "He, himself, had gone to the extreme where he had been subjected to considerable criticism for 'appeasing' Russia and yielding too much. This period, however, had passed, and American opinion was no longer disposed to make concessions on important questions."

The Secretary blurred the point, for the change in "American opinion" was, very specifically, a change in Jimmy Byrnes. As a result, his political position at home had become stronger. On the advance draft of Byrnes' February 28 speech, the one that advertised his public change of mind, Truman had written: "A good speech — I think." Two weeks later, in the middle of March, Admiral Leahy somewhat less charitably observed that Byrnes' "recently announced attitude towards American foreign policy is so correct as to have been of superlative value if it had been announced earlier." A few days later Leahy even felt the need to go to the State Department to assure the Secretary personally that he was not leading a dump-Byrnes cabal. He suggested that anti-Byrnes news leaks were probably coming from within the State Department. After Byrnes' performance at the Security Council session in March, Arthur Vandenberg was quick to praise. "Jimmy valiantly recaptured some moral ground at New York last week," the senator informed Dulles.

Yet Byrnes still wanted to be the Peacemaker. Despite his new suspicions and more uncompromising attitude, he continued to think a settlement was both possible and necessary. His image of the Soviet Union was not yet completely closed and set. He posed a question to Bidault — was Russian policy "based on a desire for security or expansion?" It would not be long before that last question would be answered to his satisfaction.[75]

A great deal of misapprehension arises from the popular use of maps on a small scale.
— LORD SALISBURY

Do not confuse *sécurité,* the feeling of having nothing to fear, and *sûreté,* the state of having nothing to fear.
— LAROUSSE [1]

VIII

The Gospel of National Security: Preparing for the War Just over the Horizon

IN LATE OCTOBER 1941, Secretary of War Henry Stimson summarized his reflections on the European war and the changing international scene in a letter to Franklin Roosevelt. "Our whole strategic possibilities of the past twenty years have been revolutionized by the events of the world in the past six months."

But vulnerabilities, not possibilities, became overwhelmingly evident shortly thereafter, on December 7, 1941, when Japan launched its surprise attack on Pearl Harbor. Ten days later, when Henry Stimson again tried to gather his thoughts, American leaders were still in a state of shock. Stimson wondered now "whether our basic theory of defense and reliance upon that fortress is not too static and whether the Japanese have not now by this fearful disaster revealed to us a situation which must be remedied." [2]

In the course of fighting the war and preparing for the peace, a new basic theory — a doctrine of national security — developed to explain America's relationship to the rest of the world.[3] It was born of technical and political transformations and out of men's experience and understanding of them. A political and bureaucratic struggle over the postwar military establishment gave the doctrine additional force. But it only gained its full meaning when it meshed with the Riga axioms in the minds of American policymakers. By the end of the war, U.S. leaders were already consciously using this theory to describe their vision of the new relationship. In the autumn of 1945, civilian and military heads of the different services trooped up to Capitol Hill to testify before a Senate committee on the question of unification of the military services. Whereas in an earlier round of such hearings, in spring 1944, "national security" barely came up at all, in these 1945 hearings, a year and a half later, the policymakers constantly invoked the idea as their starting point.

"Our national security can only be assured on a very broad and comprehensive front," argued the most forceful advocate of the concept, Navy Secretary James Forrestal. "I am using the word 'security' here consistently and continuously rather than 'defense.' "

"I like your words 'national security,' " Senator Edwin Johnson told him.[4]

The words themselves were not new. Their use went back at least to the eighteenth century. Madison, in *The Federalist,* listed "security against foreign danger" as the first reason for transferring powers from the states to the central government. But the term "national security" was not common in American political discourse until the middle 1940s.[5]

Just before World War II, some scholars had begun to adopt the phrase. Of particular importance was a seminar organized by Professor Edward Mead Earle for faculty members from Princeton University and the Institute for Advanced Study. A number of prominent (then or later) specialists on international relations took part. Their aim was to explore the relationship between military affairs and foreign policy, and "national security" became a unifying concept for analyzing the connections between the two. "The term played a certain role," recalled Felix Gilbert, who participated in the seminar. "It was considered highly desirable to emphasize that, if the United States would enter the war, this would not happen for Wilsonian idealistic reasons, but for reasons of *Realpolitik,* i.e. reasons of national security." [6]

Walter Lippmann provided the most prominent statement of the concept during the war in his best seller, *U.S. Foreign Policy: Shield of the Republic,* published in 1943. He argued that "the ideal of peace" and the "unearned security" of America's geographic position had "diverted our attention from the idea of national security."

At certain moments, unfamiliar phrases suddenly become common articles of political discourse, and the concepts they represent become so embedded in the national consciousness that they seem always to have been with us. So it was for the phrase "national security" in 1945, in the months just before and after the end of the war in the Pacific. "The abstract noun 'security' has acquired a very concrete significance for us," Joseph E. Johnson, chief of the Division of International Security Affairs in the State Department, observed in the summer of 1945, a few days before the atomic bomb was dropped on Hiroshima. "It is impossible to read a newspaper, or leaf through a magazine, or to go to a dinner party, without being made sharply aware by a story or an article, or a chance remark, of the widespread interest in the future security of the United States." The new concern, he explained, amounted to a revolutionary change in the national attitude toward security, a change linked directly to a "veritable revolution in international relationships." He was right — the phrase was everywhere. "We are in a different league now," *Life* informed its readers in September 1945. "How large the subject of security has grown, larger than a combined Army and Navy . . . The military problems ahead of us are all related to foreign policy and to each other."

The phrase expressed the new conventional wisdom of the postwar military establishment. In a speech at the Army Industrial College in the autumn of 1945, a War Department planner listed some of the basic requirements of national security — a much-expanded intelligence service, a "national realism that will permit us to start all-out preparations for war when we see aggressive intent in another nation," and the ability to speedily mobilize for war.

"I only wish that we had more apostles to carry the gospel of national security," one of the senior officers of the college told him at the conclusion of his talk.[7]

But we should not assume that "national security" had become merely a fashionable phrase with which a speaker might impress an audience or a congressional hearing. On the contrary, its sudden popularity resulted from the fact that it encapsulated an outlook on the world, a mentality. The doctrine both described a new relationship between the United States and the rest of the world and suggested policies to be followed in the light of this perceived condition. One can hypothesize that there is a desire among Americans, when it comes to foreign policy, to find a single concept, a Commanding Idea, that explains how America relates to the rest of the world, that integrates contradictory information, that suggests and rationalizes courses of action, and that, as a court of last resort for both policymakers and public, almost magically puts an end to disputes and debates. If such is the case, then "national security" has been a Commanding Idea for more than three decades of American history.[8]

We must remember that "national security" is not a given, not a fact, but a perception, a state of mind.

And what characterizes the concept of national security? It postulates the interrelatedness of so many different political, economic, and military factors that developments halfway around the globe are seen to have automatic and direct impact on America's core interests. Virtually every development in the world is perceived to be potentially crucial. An adverse turn of events anywhere endangers the United States. Problems in foreign relations are viewed as urgent and immediate threats. Thus, desirable foreign policy goals are translated into issues of national survival, and the range of threats becomes limitless. The doctrine is characterized by expansiveness, a tendency to push the subjective boundaries of security outward to more and more areas, to encompass more and more geography and more and more problems. It demands that the country assume a posture of military preparedness; the nation must be on permanent alert. There was a new emphasis on technology and armed force. Consequent institutional changes occurred. All of this leads to a paradox: the growth of American power did not lead to a greater sense of assuredness, but rather to an enlargement of the range of perceived threats that must urgently be confronted. Arnold Wolfers speculated correctly when he wrote: "Probably national efforts to achieve greater security would also prove, in part at least, to be a function of the power and opportunity that nations possess to reduce danger through their own efforts." [9]

The doctrine of national security drew upon perceptions of four changes. First, the creaking, Europe-centered international system was transformed into a global system dominated by two former outsiders, the United States and the Soviet Union. Before the war, the conventional wisdom held that a multiple system of defense assured

American safety and insulated it from the problems of the world: it was assumed that the country was geographically remote from the other Great Powers; that the superior American naval fleets protected the approaches; and that the United States could call upon great natural and industrial resources, greater than those of any potential enemy. It was also thought that the European balance of power itself would collapse slowly enough to give sufficient warning of any coming danger. So slight was the concern with foreign dangers that, in the middle 1930s, Hamilton Fish Armstrong, the influential editor of *Foreign Affairs*, felt constrained to point out that "some people in the United States were doubtful whether the United States security could be placed so high as 100 percent, particularly in the case of a conflict affecting the Philippines or the Caribbean."

These factors had provided an arguable basis for isolationism, but the Second World War, a global war, unlike the First, had made them meaningless. And now the United States had emerged as a hegemonic power with a new worldwide role to play. American leaders — moved by a traditional missionary impulse, convinced of their global responsibility, full of the self-confidence that comes of success, fundamentally unhurt by war in a wounded world — eagerly reached for their mandate of heaven. Indeed, it already seemed within their grasp. In 1939, senior American officials still traveled by ship to Europe. By 1945, a John McCloy or a James Forrestal could in a matter of weeks make a whirlwind tour by plane around the world. At each stop, he would be greeted by American generals and admirals, all of them commanding local U.S. forces. American proconsuls were running Germany and Japan, and the American industrial machine produced half the world's product. And so it was with some self-confidence that John McCloy could tell his colleagues in the War Council, upon returning from a round-the-world inspection trip in autumn 1945: "The world looks to the U.S. as the one stable country to insure the security of the world." [10]

A second source for the new doctrine was a response to experience — the lessons men had learned, the common understanding both of the condition that made for general war, and of the practice of global warfare. The series of events that began for Asia in Manchuria in 1931 and for Europe in the Rhineland in 1936 were seen as part of a pattern, part of the dynamic of dictatorial, expansionist, totalitarian states.[11] In retrospect, it seemed that each time there was a crisis, the nonaggressor states had passively stepped back, which only further whetted the aggressors' appetites. Nowhere, in retrospect, were the peace-minded states found more wanting than at Munich in September 1938. And surely there was a lesson in Munich. On the very day that Chamberlain flew to Munich, one unheeded American diplomat had warned Washington that the stronger Germany became, the more diplomats conceded to Hitler, the further Hitler would press his territorial expansion. Who in the mid-1940s could forget that recent past, and who would easily dare its repetition? But in the mental universe of the policy elite, "Munich" came to be not merely an analogy, but an iron law and a moral principle — never again. Matters that might have qualified the principle — the nature of the case at hand, historical circumstance, the configuration of international politics — were lost. The word *appeaser*, easily thrown about, became the most pungent of foreign policy expletives, the quickest way to silence a dissenter, forestall diplomacy. And, of course, appeasement connoted weakness, and so suggested blindness and stupidity or, worse, something approaching treason. Again and again, the lesson of Munich was explicitly summoned for interpreting events and shaping policies in the postwar years.

So it was that "Hitler's salami tactics" over the years became the "domino theory." The Munich lesson rested on the assumption that international events moved in simple chain reactions, that all points on a map were equally close, and that every event was of equal import. Such a view was the impetus behind Averell Harriman's telegram from Moscow on the Polish question in 1944: "What frightens me however is that when a country begins to extend its influence by strong arm methods beyond its borders under the guise of security it is difficult to see how a line can be drawn. If the policy is accepted that the Soviet Union has a right to penetrate her immediate neighbors for security, penetration of the next immediate neighbors becomes at a certain time equally logical." In other words, any step taken by Russia beyond its own borders in the name of Soviet "security" would by definition clash with what became known as American "national security." Kennan suggested exactly that point two years later. "We must make the Russians understand," he said, in 1946, that "they must confine their security demands to our concept of security demands." To proceed on the assumption of the inevitability of spheres of influence was impermissible. For such spheres, it was thought, could only pose a threat to the peace of the world.

A third source was the perception of a need to have the accouterments of armed force in place to make the American position credible. Roosevelt had regretfully discovered in 1938 that the United States did not have the military power to "overawe" potential adversaries. Its small air force and 185,000-man army were insufficient to frighten the dictators.[12] By 1946, however, Ferdinand Eberstadt, an important architect of the "national security state," could observe that most policymakers "feel that foreign policy, military and domestic economic resources should be closely tied together." Eberstadt happily added, "We now have in the departments concerned men who have learned those lessons and who are practicing those lessons." James Forrestal put the matter a bit more bluntly. "Either we make the UN work," he observed in March 1946 of an organization in which he had no confidence, "or we face a world in which we must maintain such overwhelming military power as to make it abundantly clear that future aggressors will eventually suffer the ruinous fate of Germany."[13]

The experience of managing a global war had also provided lessons. Mobilization was no easy task, but it had been done, and on an awesome scale. Between 1940 and 1945, the Navy alone had grown in personnel from 160,997 to 3,383,196; during those same years, the United States produced as much steel as the rest of the world — allies, enemies, and neutrals — put together.[14] Policymakers concluded that in the future there would be no time to mobilize, and so preparedness had to become something permanent.

Was this lesson any less vivid for any other wartime leaders? Stalin made the point during a luncheon for Churchill at the time of their October 1944 meeting. "As men drink, their tongues become looser," Stalin said. "I have an idea about the Allies not having been ready for the war, an idea which may sound like a paradox . . . We were all unprepared, but not through stupidity . . . The experience of the first and second world wars proves that the peace-loving nations — Britain, the United States, and the Soviet Union — owing to their policy of peace are always condemned to be unprepared for war . . . That is an advantage for the aggressors and a disadvantage for the peace-loving nations. It is a law . . . Who is to blame? The slowness had to be — it was a law."

A law? Was that as close as Stalin could come to admitting his own terrible mistakes in the late 1930s up through June 22, 1941? "What conclusions are we to draw?" asked Stalin. In the future, he said, a major role will be "played by the organization of security and of bodies to prevent war" — a small standing army, he predicted, drawn from the Great Powers.[15]

But that was not the system adopted. In a world where sovereignty remained the jealous prerogative of nations, the "organization of security," in terms of preparedness, would be a matter first for national action, not collective action.

Fourth, technological developments dramatized the felt need for preparedness. Mechanization, speed, fire power, air power — innovations here upset conventional plans and patterns of defense. Imagine that a war that began with Polish cavalry charging German tanks ended with the V-2 over London and the atomic bomb detonated in the air above Hiroshima. While the debate about air power's relation to other forms of military force went on, no one could deny that it had altered the very nature of war. The same was true of the single most important innovation — the atomic bomb. Technology had shrunk the dimensions of the world, and transformed the character of warfare — and in ways not altogether easy to understand. As the British General Hastings Ismay observed in 1947, "The pace of war has increased out of all recognition." [16] It was clear to postwar American leaders that research and development and the country's entire industrial machine, much more than ever before, had to be permanently integrated with the nation's arsenal.

Two additional factors gave the doctrine of national security its explicit shape and urgency. One was the unification debate, which pitted the Navy against the Air Force, with each attempting to stake out a new role that would justify a large establishment in the postwar era. Each tried to top the other with an expansive concept of its postwar mission. Yet, an acrimonious bureaucratic battle would have been insufficient in itself. The parties to the debate required a palpable enemy. As German fears before the First World War had focused on Russia, and as French anxieties in the interwar years had centered on Germany, so this doctrine of national security could gain meaning, substance, and focus only when directed against another country — an external threat, a foreign danger. Thus, in the immediate postwar years, the Soviet Union gave the doctrine its purpose and urgency.

Yet, we must remember that the doctrine of national security did not emerge apart from Soviet-American relations. It also helped to provide a framework for evaluating the problems of international politics and Soviet behavior. As we shall see, the distinctive ideology and institutions of the National Security State began to develop when the Riga axioms merged with the doctrine of national security.

The unification debate was a classic case of bureaucratic bloodletting, a bitter half-decade struggle over the question of how to organize America's postwar military establishment most effectively.[17] The debate shaped the definition of national security and its requirements. The postwar years would mean less money, and thus the great service empires of the war would, so it was feared, contract into impoverished principalities. The questions before the services then were several: how to survive on the reduced diet of appropriations? how to reduce without losing importance relative to the other services? how to justify their missions in the new era that opened with the defeat of the Axis?

The Army saw unification as the way to maintain its core structure in the postwar years, and to cope with a reduced budget that Marshall, remembering the interwar years, was sure would bring another "long period of agony." The Army also hoped to win budgetary and strategic independence from civilian overview, and to restrict the Navy's air arm and the competitive Marine Corps. Unification also offered a way to deal with a dangerous, rebellious, cocky child, the semiautonomous Army Air Force.

The Air Force supported unification because under this arrangement it could achieve complete co-equal independence, and, then, with its intense need for capital go on to win (so it was hoped) the major share of the budget. Air officers, convinced that the war had demonstrated the pre-eminence of air power, were sure that independence would result in their dominance. All three services, wrote an adviser to Air Force General Spaatz in September 1945, would "come under the new medium, the air. At first the tail will wag the dog, then become the whole dog . . . The baton of leadership in this Air Power–Atomic Bomb struggle is lying there for some institution or group to pick up."

In making great claims for the commanding role of air power and the atomic bomb, the Air Force partisans were pronouncing obsolete the Navy, their rival for capital investment. Thus is explained the vigor with which the Navy fought outright unification. Naval leaders were convinced the unification would mean not only merger, but also the loss of their prized air arm, in effect, the *submerging* and sinking of the Navy. The Air Force would capture both congressional appropriations and the popular imagination. They feared that their seagoing mission would be regarded as anachronistic, and that they would be relegated to third place, perhaps ultimately little more than a glorified Coast Guard.[18]

In November 1943, General Marshall endorsed unification, marking the real start of the struggle over the future shape of the military establishment. The Army and Navy had already found many issues about which to squabble — whether, for example, the Army would give the Navy a million square feet in the new Pentagon building, or only 800,000. But the unification issue truly set them off against each other. "There is developing, I fear, a cleavage between the Army and the Navy on the subject of a single Department of Defense," Stimson noted in his diary by May 1944. "I always feared this would be so. It's too good to be true to think that the Navy won't stick to their own particular little peculiarities and stick out for an independent Navy." The Navy saw the matter just as darkly from its side. "I have been telling King, Nimitz and Company," Navy Secretary James Forrestal wrote in September 1944, "it is my judgment that as of today the Navy has lost its case, and that either in Congress or in a public poll the Army's point of view would prevail." James Forrestal was not the sort of man to give up any ship, and, with him at the helm, the Navy began maneuvering for position in the postwar battle ahead.[19]

The Air Force claimed that it had inherited the Navy's role as the nation's primary guardian. The Air Force's goal was complete independence from the Army. Beyond that, it envisioned an imperial system of overseas bases encircling the earth. It initially justified this vision as part of the supervisory control of the defeated Axis powers and a contribution to the new United Nations. In fact, such planning was meant to ensure a commitment to hardware and thus larger appropriations.[20] In one version of the plan, for instance, bases would be located in Newfoundland, Labrador, Baffin Island, Greenland, Iceland, Bermuda, Azores, Puerto Rico, Trinidad, British and French Guiana, Brazil, Ascension Island, Liberia; at Dakar, Cape Verde Islands, Canary Islands, Casablanca; in the United Kingdom, France, Belgium, Holland, Western Germany, Switzerland, Italy, Denmark; and along the north and central Africa air routes.[21]

Air power lay at the core of the unification struggle, and thus was crucial to the definition of national security and America's global role. The airplane, of course, had ended America's geographic isolation from potential enemies. Air officers argued that their self-proclaimed mission — strategic bombing — had become the most important. The great waves of B-17s, B-24s, and B-29s, roaring in swarms of many hundreds or even a thousand or more over the industrial cities of Germany and Japan, provided the air advocates, in their own minds, with both vindication and proof of the rightness of their cause. The Navy had to reject such "proof," for acceptance would mean suicide for the proud service.

The energy with which the effectiveness of strategic bombing was debated testified to the ferocity of the unification struggle. The United States Strategic Bombing Survey, meant to help objectively resolve the questions, itself became caught up in what one historian has called "the war over who won the war [which] by the summer of 1945 had become a matter of more pressing interest than any other single factor of concern to those planning the future of the various services." Partisans on both sides searched for evidence with the fervor of advertising men. "We have a great opportunity right now if we act intelligently," Robert Lovett, Assistant Secretary of War for Air, wrote to General Spaatz in late April 1945. "We can photograph and measure bomb damage until we are blue in the face but nothing is as persuasive as the statement of the German leaders as to what did them the most harm . . . We need a lot of such statements from military leaders as well as plant managers to offset the inevitable claims that will be made by the proponents of other arms. Of equal importance with claims of Germans is, of course, the statements of our own leaders which you have been so successful in getting in the past."

The Air Force did succeed in capturing public and official imagination. In May 1945, War Secretary Robert Patterson flew down the Rhine Valley. Wherever he looked, he saw the effects of the bombing. "I have not seen a train moving on the railroads in Germany and no boats are moving on the rivers and canals," he observed.

"Boats on Rhine cannot operate until destroyed bridges are lifted." From his low-flying aircraft, Patterson saw all the proof for strategic bombing that he needed.[22]

Many, inside government and out, willingly, even eagerly, accepted the Air Force case. Strategic bombing seemed to offer a simple way to meet future unknowns, and to guarantee the upper hand to the United States. Still, with the war ending, the Air Force worried. "I have an uncomfortable feeling that everything we have accomplished to date may be put in jeopardy by a combination of circumstances," Lovett added in his April letter to Carl Spaatz. "What we need is stability at this time, not only to avoid giving the impression that we are suffering from mild hysteria but also, and even more important, making it evident that we are not acting from hand to mouth." Two months later, General Lauris Norstad was more specific in expressing Air Force fears: "The Navy, headed by one of our most competent financiers, who is also thoroughly familiar with fiscal policy, will align their objectives with those of the nation, and, if the Army policy is not astute, will assume the responsibility for national defense."

Norstad's apprehension was justified. The Air Force had a formidable opponent in Navy Secretary James Forrestal. Indeed, of all the apostles of national security in the years of our narrative, James Forrestal was the most important. "It has been a fetish of mine that the question of national security is not merely a question of the Army and Navy," he said, without overstating the matter, in the autumn of 1945. "We have to take into account our whole potential for war, our mines, industry, manpower, research, and all the activities that go into normal civilian life. I do not think you can deal with this only by the War and Navy Departments. This has to be a truly global effort.

"After all, somebody said war is merely an extension of policy," he added. "I do not know who said it." [23]

James Forrestal lived his entire life in combat, struggling to find personal security. He won both money and power, but the security always eluded him. He overcame the sickliness of childhood with a lifelong dedication to rugged sports, exercise, and physical strength. At Princeton, like Kennan a few years after him, Forrestal was something of an outsider, but he responded not with a voyage of exile, but by moving toward the center. Active in sports, voted most likely to succeed by his class, editor of the *Daily Princetonian*, he, curiously, dropped out shortly before graduation. It has been suggested that the reason was academic trouble, which might help to explain his intellectual yearnings in later years. He would seek out and sponsor experts who could provide him with the names and quotations and ideas that would make him seem profound.[24]

Forrestal began his career on Wall Street as a bond salesman for Dillon, Read. He also had a brief stint as a naval aviator during World War I. (His commander reported that he could make a good officer, but that he needed "toning down from a radical socialistic attitude with men, and worrying whether it is right to be a soldier.") Energetic, persuasive, pugnacious, a quick learner, eager to work longer and harder than anybody else — he had the qualities of a supersalesman, and they not only helped to make him a great deal of money, but also to become a vice president of Dillon, Read in 1926, its president twelve years later. During the 1920s, he spent many of his lunch hours boxing in a New York gymnasium. Once, sparring too eagerly with a professional there, he broke his nose, a source of pride to him in later years.

In 1940, Harry Hopkins brought him to the White House as one of the special presidential assistants with a "passion for anonymity."[25] But that was a passion Forrestal did not have, and he was much happier when he went to the Navy Department where, as Undersecretary, he directed the vast business of mobilization with extraordinary skill. In 1944 he became Secretary.

Forrestal was not only a talented, hard-driving administrator, but also the true bureaucratic empire builder; having become much richer than most other men, he now wanted to become more powerful. He was always reaching out to gather responsibility and power and attention, sending out newspaper and magazine clippings, giving unsolicited advice, cultivating the press while denying any interest in publicity, doing what he could to make his presence noticed and felt. Although uninvited, he went to the Potsdam Conference; he sent books explicating the dangers of communism to J. Edgar Hoover; he characteristically began a letter to Will Clayton with major foreign policy recommendations: "Dear Will: Two suggestions which are entirely out of my bailiwick, but anyway I'm going to make them."[26] At one point, George Marshall, after becoming Secretary of State, responded to a Forrestal suggestion with a forceful reminder that the purpose of the United States Navy was to uphold American foreign policy, and not vice versa.[27]

At what point Forrestal began to focus on the Soviet Union as the future enemy is unclear. In Algeria, in August 1944, he asked Charles de Gaulle about communist influence in France and told the general of the "widespread fears in America that a Russian menace would be substituted for a German menace." Yet a couple of months later he wrote to Averell Harriman: "There is general agreement that England, Russia and ourselves have got to play together; it will need patience and tolerance on the part of all hands to accomplish that — the strains and tensions will increase the farther we get from danger. These are obvious bromides, but I find it is a good thing to keep saying them to oneself because, as you and I found in the 20s, it is easy for success to pry the best friends apart."

However, there is little question that during the autumn of 1944, he was clearly assimilating the Riga view, a shift no doubt eased by his combative outlook on life. He was one of the first senior policymakers to be convinced that the United States had to maintain considerable military power and organize itself for a protracted confrontation with the Soviet Union. He was to be constantly upset that others had "difficulties in preparing for the war just over the horizon."

In September 1947, he became the first Secretary of Defense, a post tailored very much to his own specifications. He was then at the height of his power and influence. Jonathan Daniels gives us a picture of him in these years: "There is a quiet, animal quality about his apparent physical perfection. He has the carriage which movies gave dramatically to better gangsters, swift, easy, with the suggestion of possible violence and the surface of perfectly contained restraint."[28]

Even though the national security state was developing according to his own design, Forrestal found progressively less security in his personal life. "He lived his life as a conflicted man, walking a tightrope held taut by a concept of original sin at one end, the American dream of success and recognition at the other," recalled a friend of thirty years.[29] He could never work free of his driving ambitions, but, as time went on, he became less sure of what direction those ambitions should take. The dangers seemed real, of all kinds, and all around him — not just from the menacing Slav abroad and the secret communists at home, but also from a President who disliked him, Zionists and columnists and air advocates — all of which undermined his political standing. There were also a multitude of administrative strains and pressures on him, a failed marriage, and all the other tensions and emotions that he tried to squirrel out of sight.

Power began to slip away from him within a year after he became Secretary of Defense, and he found it harder to play the tough-guy role. The strain of working seventeen or eighteen hours a day, trying to manage a sprawling, contentious bureaucracy, took its toll. His lines of authority in the military establishment were not at all clear, and the armed services did not hesitate to challenge him publicly. He lacked that sense of humor which might have occasionally relieved the tension.

Those who worked with him saw the small signs of an approaching breakdown — or remembered them afterward. Aides observed that part of his scalp had become irritated and red from continued scratching, and then, in the autumn of 1948, they became aware that he was issuing contradictory orders. Cabinet members noticed that he often carried a newspaper in his pocket, which he took out to read at moments of pressure. Members of the Chevy Chase Country Club would remark that he held a course record — not for his score, but for the speed and silence with which he grimly pursued the weekly business of golf.

Finally, in March 1949, he was replaced as Secretary of Defense. He felt under such strain that he asked at the last minute that the swearing in of his successor, Louis Johnson, be advanced three days, to March 28. The next day he went to Capitol Hill for a farewell ceremony, and then back to the Pentagon, where he disappeared into a small office that had been set aside for his use. A former aide, Marx Leva, found him sitting there, with his hat on his head, staring into space. Leva had him driven home. Later in the day, Ferdinand Eberstadt telephoned the Forrestal house.

"He won't speak to anybody," said the butler.

"You tell James," Eberstadt replied, "he can get away with that with a lot of people but not with me."

Forrestal came to the telephone, only to talk incoherently about the Russians.

Very worried, Eberstadt arranged for him to fly to Hobe Sound, Florida, for a rest. On the way to the airport with Eberstadt and Marx Leva, Forrestal said nothing save to repeat three times, "You're a loyal fellow, Marx."

Greeted in Florida by Robert Lovett with talk of golf, Forrestal replied, "Bob, they're after me." Cabinet members back in Washington heard an even more dramatic story — that Forrestal ran through the streets shouting, "The Russians are coming. The Russians are coming. They're right around. I've seen Russian soldiers." [30]

He made at least one suicide attempt while in Florida. On April 2, he was flown back to Washington and admitted to the Bethesda Naval Hospital. He was visited by his successor, Louis Johnson, possibly the last person that Forrestal should have seen.

Some hours before sunrise on a Sunday morning in May, Forrestal was copying lines from Sophocles' chorus about the warrior Ajax, "Worn by the waste of time." He put down his pen, found a window that he could open, tied one end of his dressing-gown sash to a radiator and the other around his neck, perhaps hung for a moment in the dark, and then plunged sixteen stories to his death.[31]

In the years before this pitiful end, Forrestal was one of Washington's most attractive, forceful, and dynamic figures. Once during a Cabinet luncheon, when he was impatient with somebody's discourse on international affairs, Forrestal broke in, "The trouble with you is that you waste your time talking about the international scene and it's just intellectual masturbation — it may be a pleasant way to pass the time, but it gets you nowhere!" [32]

He took the lead in the unification debate even before World War II ended. As Navy Secretary, responding to the wide support for air power, he pushed the Navy to redefine its mission in terms of *sea-air power*, putting emphasis not on the much-denigrated battleship, but upon the aircraft carrier as the basis for the Navy of tomorrow. This meant that the Navy would no longer simply fight other navies, but would also become a potent force in attacking land armies. Countering the claims of the Air Force, Forrestal's energetic advocacy of sea-air power would give the Navy a major role in any war with the Soviet Union — a country hardly approachable by conventional sea forces, and one for whom naval power was not of much importance. The Navy thus had found a new justification — American security could be protected only if the Navy staked out a global mission, heavy in capital investment, and one that put it in the front line against the postwar threat, the Soviet Union.[33]

Forrestal's advocacy of sea-air power highlighted the emerging focus of postwar military planning. With virtually no competition, the Soviet Union had become the only candidate for "future enemy." What significance lay in so characterizing the Soviet Union? To begin with, it was a kind of technical exercise. War planning, if it is to be useful, needs a target, an enemy, an aggressor, and the Soviet Union provided a reasonable candidate for the purpose. Russia was a rational choice for another reason. After the Second World War, the Soviet Union had emerged as the only power that could possibly challenge the United States militarily, and the bonds of fraternal friendship to tie the two countries into amicability hardly existed. Planners appropriately took such considerations into account. But, as we have already seen, there was also a growing and genuine fear about Soviet intentions and capabilities, a concern that disputes between the two nations and the two systems might trigger armed conflict. Finally, presenting the Soviet Union as a threat did offer a rationale for an expanded mission for the services. The Soviet Union's new role in world politics was a blessing for all parties to the unification debate, for it provided the justification for each service's concept of its own mission and utility, as well as furnishing grounds to criticize proposed contributions claimed by rivals.

Real fears and bureaucratic interests made the positing of the Soviet Union of great importance and gave real force to military planning. It is difficult to determine when those who were party to the unification debate spoke sincerely and when they spoke cynically; no doubt, many themselves often did not know. The very fact that the two motivations so neatly fused together makes it impossible to identify that boundary line.[34]

For much of the war, partly because of the strategic bombing doctrine, the Air Force downplayed the Soviet Union as a future enemy. Yet how could the airmen justify a large budget and expensive technology in a world without genuine threats?[35] Although planners had talked of a future "Eurasian" enemy in 1944, not until early 1945 did they explicitly so identify the Soviet Union. This identification meshed with the doctrine of national security, budget battles with the Navy, and their desire for an independent air arm. "Land mass army and air force presently of equal predominance," read an Air Force intelligence estimate of the Soviet Union in July 1945. "With the advent of peace concerted efforts will be directed toward complete development of air power. Country poses threat to security of United States." [36]

The Air Force was making up for its slow start. As Forrestal and the Navy pushed America's "security borders" right up against regions vital to the Russians, so the Air Force counterattacked by discovering new vulnerabilities in the skies and thus new tasks for it to perform.* By autumn 1945, the Air Force was already using the Russian "enemy" as the main reason for maintaining the powerful air arm that was the prime organizational goal. In October 1945, General Spaatz complained that a report on Soviet intentions underplayed the threat: "The conclusions do not cover enough ground," he said. "With the rapid weakening of our forces in Europe and Asia, the USSR is able to project moves on the continent of Europe and Asia which will be just as hard for us to accept and just as much an incentive to war as were those occasioned by the German policies." He admitted that the likelihood of a Russian attack on the United States in the near future was small. "However, the next war will not necessarily be started by attacks against the U.S. proper. Until the interior of Russia is opened to us with the same freedom with which the U.S. has been opened to them I believe we should proceed rather slowly toward demobilizing our Armed Forces, particularly units of our Strategic Air Forces." [37]

Also, in the autumn, at the congressional hearings on unification, Air Force General James Doolittle found a way to redefine American security with a simple switch of a map. The normal Mercator projection had been responsible for "fallacious theories," he explained, and so he replaced it with a polar projection.

"Now look at the polar projections," said Doolittle, innocently indefinite. "We don't know who our next enemy may be. We hope we will never have another enemy, but we have to accept the possibility

* In late August, John Snyder, director of the Office of War Mobilization and Reconversion, told Truman that on one day he had seen "a Navy lay-out which provided for all of the world." On the next day he saw "an air force lay-out which also provided for all the world." He added that he had "inadvertently" asked about plans for coordination, but had been told there were none.

that we may have an enemy . . . However we can eliminate certain areas and certain people as never being potential enemies of America."

The polar projection did make the world suddenly look very different. Within easy flying distance, hovering over the United States, stretched the vast and ominous land mass of the Union of Soviet Socialist Republics. The conclusion drawn from this cartographical display was clear — America's new frontier was "an air frontier." That, of course, called for a commitment to a larger air force. Doolittle was advocating a "catch up" campaign.[38] What was odd about this campaign was that there was no one to catch up with. The Air Force's private intelligence estimates left no question that the Russians were many years behind the Americans in air power.[39]

The Army was the one service that continued to base its postwar outlook upon the Yalta axioms. Unlike its prodigal child, the Air Force, it had not acquired the same expansionist concept of security. Instead it defined American postwar interests in a more limited fashion, concerning itself with occupation policies, an orderly demobilization, unification, and universal military training. The Army did not perceive Russia as a threat, both because it did not believe the USSR was bent on a march of infinite expansion and because it did not see how Russia could endanger the United States. Moreover, the Army believed the suffering and destruction caused by the war in Russia would not merely preclude aggressive action, but also, by forcing a preoccupation with reconstruction, would push the USSR toward cooperation with the U.S.[40]

This is not to say that all Army officials shared the attitude. "We appear to be leaning over backwards to be nice to the descendants of Genghis Khan," General George Patton complained. "We're letting them dictate to us when patently we could and should dictate to them and do it now and in no uncertain terms." [41] A more important exponent of this view was John J. McCloy, Forrestal's friend, neighbor, and frequent tennis partner, and the top War Department civilian in charge of political-military affairs.[42]

The commanding view, however, was that of other senior officials — Stimson, Marshall, Eisenhower. "I am somewhat disturbed by some evidence that American soldiers are judging our Russian allies too much upon external appearances such as smartness, cleanliness, and, sometimes, personal habits," Eisenhower said on August 6, 1945. He wanted to do something "toward indoctrinating our own people" to understand what the Russians had experienced. "They have not had our great advantages in sanitation, education, and, of course, there is always the great language bar to any real social contact. But the Russians have contributed mightily to the winning of this war. They have produced good soldiers and brilliant generals, and, moreover, they are naturally a friendly race." Eisenhower aimed to "prevent our soldiers drawing false conclusions and later spreading these conclusions at home where they are certain to be harmful." The personal rapport he had established with General Zhukov amplified Eisenhower's own cordial feelings.[43]

On leaving Germany, Eisenhower delivered what one State Department official sarcastically described as "valedictory instructions to try to get along with the Russians." Back in Washington as commander-in-chief, Eisenhower told the War Council that Zhukov had assured him that "Russia was determined to make friends with the United States, to raise its standard of living, and to live up to every agreement made." [44] Others in the Army also continued to resist the Riga axioms.[45]

General Lucius Clay's sharp disagreement with Kennan's Long Telegram of February 1946 provides one of the most dramatic examples of the Army attitude. As part of its wide distribution, the Kennan cable was sent to senior military officers abroad. Clay's State Department adviser, Robert Murphy, reported in early April to H. Freeman Matthews of the Office of European Affairs that the general was "pretty violent" against it. Clay saw it as a kind of alarmist Pearl Harbor warning, meant to put the State Department on record to protect it from future recriminations. He also viewed the Long Telegram as an example of the "British line," and as an indication of success for "the British technique of needling our people over a period of months."

Murphy went on to explain that "an inventory of what has been accomplished in Germany he finds not too discouraging." Although some Americans held the Russians responsible for all problems in the Occupation, "an important part of whatever blame there is clearly attached to the French Government which thus far has done everything it could to sabotage many principles of the Berlin Conference agreement." While many British officials also advocated a divided Germany, the Soviet representatives "cannot be accused of violation of the Potsdam agreements." Indeed, said Murphy, "They have been meticulous in their observance." Murphy also asserted that the Soviets had grounds for their suspicion and distrust of the French and British. He also felt that "in all fairness" he had to point out that the Russians had gone out of their way to be friendly with the Americans. "Zhukov, Sokolovsky, and Sobelev had told me at different times and in different ways that they sincerely want the friendship of Americans, that there will never be a war between the two countries, that they are grateful for what the United States has done for the Soviet Union." (But Murphy did add, "I leave it to George Kennan, of course, to place the proper evaluation on a personal contact of this kind.")

Murphy concluded with what was both his and Clay's attitude at the beginning of April 1946: "I would like to make it quite clear that in our local innocence, we have never and still do not believe for a minute in imminent Soviet aggression. I am convinced that the most undesirable thing in the minds of whatever Russians I meet here is early and large-scale warfare."

General Clay, however, was manning an increasingly lonely outpost, for the Riga axioms had established themselves as the new conventional wisdom. Upon receiving Murphy's letter, Matthews replied speedily, saying that Clay was "100% wrong" when he presumed that the Army commanders had been sent Kennan's Long Telegram at the urging of the State Department. "The initiative came entirely from the top (and I mean the top — not G-2) in the War and Navy Departments, and it represents their thinking *entirely*."[46]

While the senior officials of the services may have arrived at a consensus in their thinking about Russia, such was hardly the case with unification. Indeed, the institutional fray had grown hotter. In 1945, Forrestal commissioned his friend Ferdinand Eberstadt, a mutual fund pioneer from Wall Street, to head a committee that would explore the entire defense establishment, in effect, to produce a case against out-and-out unification. The Eberstadt Report, which provided the outline for the 1947 unification act, stands out as a central document in the evolution of the national security state.[47]

Submitted in mid-September 1945, the report claimed that unification would promote administrative inefficiency and lead to "the subordination of civilian to military life." Instead it advocated something "far more drastic and far-reaching" than unification of the services — "a complete realignment of our governmental organizations to serve our national security in the light of our new world power and position, our new international commitments and risks and the epochal scientific discoveries." The United States should be permanently prepared, ready with "an alert, smoothly-working and efficient machine" so that all political, military, and economic means would be available to forestall any attack.[48]

Here, "national security" was self-consciously used to denote a much expanded vision. "The changing content and scope of the phrase 'national security' is apparent from a contrast of our international commitments and responsibilities after World War I and World War II." The new commitments "have greatly enlarged the sphere of our international obligations, reflecting present concepts of our national security in terms of world security." The report called for a strong postwar military establishment, as though the world were filled with predatory enemies like those that stalked it in the 1930s.[49]

The committee recommended major organizational changes designed to prepare the United States for "waging peace, as well as war." The key word in the report was *coordination*, rather than *unification*. A National Security Council, composed of top-level policymakers in the Executive, would assure continuous exchange of information and points of view, and provide for concerted action. The Joint Chiefs of Staff would be formally established. A National Security Resources Board would make for industrial readiness, a key element in military preparedness. In the most important plank, there would be no unification, but rather three coordinate services, each with civilians holding the top places. The Navy would continue to hold on to an air arm. A central intelligence agency would be established. The military would play a much larger role in directing and utilizing scientific research. Finally, the report emphasized that public opinion would have to be persuaded that an urgent crisis was at hand.[50]

The Eberstadt Report soothed no one; so bitter was Lovett in early November 1945 that he declared the Army should "fight fire with fire." One senior British military official in Washington reported to

London in December that, while there might be "chaos in Whitehall . . . believe me it is nothing compared with the state of chaos" in Washington. The unification debate, he said, was "quite beyond words." After visiting Washington, Hastings Ismay could only express astonishment, in a letter to Bedell Smith, at the "tremendous dog fight" taking place over the postwar U.S. military establishment.[51]

Truman put off intervening in the unification debate as long as he could. But, finally, on December 19, 1945, he sent to the Hill a message entitled "National Security," in which he called for complete unification along the Army's lines. "It does not appear that any member of the executive departments or the military services should disagree," War Secretary Patterson noted the day of the President's message.[52]

Patterson, however, underestimated the Navy, which continued to stall, resist, speak out, and delay decision. Also, on the day of his message, Truman complained privately that the Navy was especially "profligate and unrealistic" in its budget demands. The President became more and more angry. He told Forrestal personally that he had been seriously offended by the Navy's behavior. "The Navy people had a complex," Truman moaned at the end of February; they had "developed the attitude of step-children." [53]

Only one major institutional change was effected during this period, and that involved intelligence. Prior to World War II the United States possessed a minuscule and ineffective intelligence setup. Air Force General Hoyt Vandenberg, one of the postwar directors of Central Intelligence, pointed out in 1947 that America did not have a first-class service before the war "because the people of the United States would not accept it." He added, "The most important factor in making people intelligence conscious was the disaster at Pearl Harbor."

Pearl Harbor was an intelligence disaster on two levels. The first was simply failure of observation. One of the U.S. military attachés in Tokyo before World War II recalled in 1947 how he and his colleagues had conscientiously mapped out bombing plans for the largest Japanese cities and for heavy industry, and dispatched the information back to Washington, with target priorities indicated.

"However, I will have to admit the general mobilization went on in Japan right under our noses," he said. "Our best estimate was that if Japan did declare war on us suddenly, it would not be before July 1, 1942." The second was the failure of responsible officials to pick out clues pointing to the imminent Japanese attack from what has been called the background "noise."

The situation was remedied during World War II, not only with much enlarged military intelligence services, but also by the creation of the Office of Strategic Services, under William Donovan. By the end of the war, the OSS employed over 12,000 people. On October 1, 1945, Truman officially abolished Donovan's organization, dispersing its personnel among the military services and the State Department.

With the object lesson of Pearl Harbor behind them and the role of a superpower before them, officials throughout the U.S. government agreed that a return to the prewar intelligence setup would hardly do. Indeed, they looked back with disdain on their predecessors. "My opposite numbers here in the fall of 1941 didn't know the difference between Algeria and French Equatorial Africa," observed Sherman Kent, a senior intelligence official after the war. "If you went into one of the [intelligence] offices and said what do you know about the water supply in Libya, they would pull out the folder and the folder would have one cable, dated about 1927, one page out of the smut section of a Hearst Sunday supplement which was entitled 'Thirst in the Desert,' a travel folder with a picture of an oasis and two date palms, and that was the information in the file on the water supply of Libya." [54]

Although it was generally agreed that the United States would require a much larger intelligence operation, it was not at all clear who would control it. A number of agencies competed for dominance, or at least tried to prevent others from gaining control. There was considerable confusion and backbiting, so much so that at a White House meeting on January 9, 1946, Budget Director Harold Smith declared, "I am not so sure that we are not approaching the subject of intelligence in a most unintelligent fashion."

Finally, on January 22, 1946, Truman established a Central Intelligence Group (CIG) under the jurisdiction of a National Intelligence Authority. Two days later, the President celebrated its birth with a private ceremony at the White House. He presented black hats, black coats, and wooden daggers to Admiral Leahy, his representative on the National Intelligence Authority, and to Admiral Sidney Souers, first director of the CIG. Truman then produced a flowing fake black mustache which he affixed on Leahy. Others marked the occasion in their own ways; Sosthenes Behn, the versatile head of International Telephone and Telegraph, called in on Leahy at the White House to generously "offer for consideration the possibility of utilizing the service of the company's personnel in American intelligence activities." [55]

The CIG was a compromise among competing plans. It was meant to coordinate and reconcile information being produced by about twenty-five organizations in Washington. But the other agencies, jealous of their prerogatives, were not very cooperative. The CIG began to acquire more independence in June 1946, when Souers was succeeded as director by General Vandenberg, who had been head of Army intelligence during World War II, and was a nephew of Senator Arthur Vandenberg. Vandenberg worked aggressively to expand both staff and functions. In the spring of 1946, the National Intelligence Authority directed the CIG to carry out research and analysis "not being presently performed" by other departments; and, under Vandenberg, the CIG assumed the critical task of producing its own intelligence. Bureaucratically, it proved easier for the CIG to generate its own intelligence than to try to coordinate and reconcile that emanating from other organizations that were hardly eager to be coordinated. But it should also be noted that the CIG in this period remained very small by Washington standards.[56]

By winter and spring 1946, as we have seen, the "right attitude in mind" was held by most American leaders, including those in the military establishment. So the problem of Russia was linked to the future of the services in an expansive definition of national security. Forrestal continued to take the lead. In February, Budget Director Smith noted that, in a meeting with President Truman, the conversation turned "to the view of the Secretary of the Navy, who seemed to feel that in the face of the Russian situation — whatever that is — there should be no evidence of demobilization of the Navy below 500,000."

The Russian situation was not altogether a happy one, Truman said, although indicating that he did not quite share Forrestal's sense of urgency.

The Navy Secretary would not be stayed. He won John Foster Dulles' concurrence with his own worry "on the national drift toward the state of not only physical but also mental demobilization." Forrestal urged his academic expert, Edward Willett, to stress in the paper Willett was endlessly preparing on Soviet ambitions that the Russians aimed "to make their system global." Willett compared the powerful "crusading spirit" of the Soviet Union to the weak "driving force" of the U.S. — nothing more than "the somewhat passive concept of self-defense."

In late February, Forrestal, even while he was talking of Britain, saw Soviet threats all over the map: "We must look at the places on the map where Russian and British lines may cross — the Mediterranean, the Scandinavian Peninsula, India, Indonesia, China, the Middle East, the Suez Canal, Egypt, Tripolitania, the Straits of Gibraltar." Here certainly was demonstration of Lord Salisbury's dictum — "A great deal of misapprehension arises from the popular use of maps on a small scale." The threats suggested by Forrestal were considerably exaggerated. They could be taken seriously only if one in turn exaggerated Russia's military capabilities and considerably exceeded even the suspicion of the USSR that was already part of the new conventional wisdom. But in expressing such alarm, Forrestal was also suggesting a vigorous role for the postwar Navy. Indeed, unlike the "somewhat passive concept of self-defense," national security was a conception for activists and enthusiasts — calling for action across a broad range and all around the planet.[57]

Forrestal sought to demonstrate the far reach of American power in whatever ways he could. In late February 1946, he arranged for the flag to be shown in the eastern Mediterranean by having the battleship *Missouri* carry back to Turkey the body of its ambassador, recently deceased. Byrnes and Truman heartily approved. Forrestal almost immediately tried to push further; he sought to have a task force accompany the *Missouri* as a prelude to re-establishing an American fleet base in the Mediterranean. At this juncture, however, in the midst of the Iranian crisis, the Administration rejected the task force proposal as too provocative. At about the same time, despite Byrnes' fear that further U.S. atomic tests "might have a bad effect upon the already disturbed world situation," Forrestal won a go-ahead for the Navy's atomic tests scheduled for Bikini in July.[58]

The Air Force, although still trailing behind its maritime rival, also saw the utility of a more visible Russian threat. In late March, Robert Lovett wrote to General Spaatz that he had spent a few days in the sun at Hobe Sound, Florida, with Averell Harriman, recently retired as ambassador to the Soviet Union. Harriman assured Lovett that the only sector of the U.S. military that impressed Stalin was American air power. The Russians recognized, said Harriman, "that our position and influence in the world will, as far as she is concerned, be in some direct ratio with our supremacy, or lack of it, in the air." Harriman suggested that the Air Force make its case for new aircraft and the requisite budgets "coincide with the interests in the so-called Russian situation now filling the press." As in April 1945, Lovett was much concerned with timing. "The American public rarely listens to arguments unless it is worried," he explained to Spaatz. "Hence, the present time, while Iran, Manchuria, and Eastern Europe are daily causing concern, may be an appropriate occasion in which to indicate that we cannot delay much longer the necessary steps to place us in a position of strength in the air."

The unification controversy itself, which had done so much to stimulate the articulation of the concept of national security, continued to impede a more forceful assertion of America's very great power. "You and I both feel that it is extremely unfortunate to have the Services arrayed in opposition to one another over this issue," Robert Patterson wrote Forrestal on March 11, 1946. "I have tried to get together with Jim Forrestal on a compromise," Patterson wrote to Stimson more than a month later, "but thus far without success." [59]

By the spring of 1946, two lines of thought had intersected. Perceptions of Soviet intentions affected the way American leaders defined the issue of national security, which was what the new ambassador, Walter Bedell Smith, explained to an attentive Stalin during that late evening visit to the Kremlin in April 1946: "We are faced in America, as in the USSR, with the responsibility of making important long-range decisions on our future military policy, and these decisions will depend to a large extent on what our people believe to be the policies of the Soviet Union." [60]

The conceptual framework of national security also affected the interpretation of Soviet intentions and capabilities. Indeed, the doctrine of national security was a fundamental revision of America's perceived relation to the rest of the world, of what Stimson in 1941 had called "our basic theory of defense." The nation was to be permanently prepared. America's interests and responsibilities were unrestricted and global. National security became a guiding rule, a Commanding Idea. It lay at the heart of a new and sometimes intoxicating vision.

> The objectionable feature of their foreign policy is that they are attempting in foreign affairs to do precisely what they have been doing at home for nearly 30 years.
>
> — JOHN FOSTER DULLES, May 1946

> The observations of Molotov and Vyshinsky again reveal the Soviet thesis that the relations between the great powers were more important than the strict observance of the Charter.
>
> — CHARLES BOHLEN, April 1946

IX

Casting the Die: The Anticommunist Consensus

THE COUNCIL OF FOREIGN MINISTERS convened for a new session in Paris on April 25, 1946. Police lined the street for a block approaching the Luxembourg Palace; delegates, as they made their way up the stairs and through the corridors, were saluted by the drawn sabers of the Garde Républicaine; and newsmen scurried about the proceedings. This was a celebration for France — readmission to the Council meant a renewal of her prestige as a Great Power.

For the next half year, Paris was the center of world diplomatic activity. "So far as political matters are concerned, much will depend upon the outcome of the Paris Conference," Soviet specialist Llewellyn Thompson wrote to Ambassador Lane in Poland, "and we are therefore to some extent marking time before attempting to make any new major decisions of policy." [1] Yet the issues that touched the Paris meeting tangentially were to prove more important in shaping basic attitudes and policies than those at the center of the discussions. Moreover, even as certain progress was made both in the Council, and then in the larger Peace Conference that opened in late July, the process of polarization between East and West continued apace. In the months of February and March, the Iranian crisis had marked out a widening terrain of contention outside Eastern Europe. In the summer months, while the delegates talked and argued in

Paris, new areas were falling into controversy, in particular, the eastern Mediterranean and, the most important European question of all, Germany. In this context, the idea of national security took on greater meaning for American policymakers. The Riga outlook was integrated more fully both with an economic policy increasingly reoriented to containment, and with a reformulation of America's military position. By the time the last delegate had packed up and left Paris in October, the gospel of national security was well on its way to becoming dogma, and the most prominent heretic had already been expelled from the temple.

Byrnes went to Paris in a frame of mind different from that at preceding conferences, closer to the hard line of the Riga outlook. In consequence his domestic political position had improved markedly. "Byrnes has increased in stature," Averell Harriman said in April, adding with some satisfaction, "We are not going to yield at Paris." Yet Byrnes felt far from secure. Still unsteady were the Secretary's relations with Truman, who during this time complained to Budget Director Harold Smith that (as Smith noted) "he had a terrific number of things on his mind," and that Byrnes "had cried on his shoulder yesterday, and that he, the President, did not have any shoulder to cry on." Byrnes' effort at least to try to negotiate peace treaties with the German satellite nations had aroused considerable opposition within the State Department, where the image of the Soviet Union had virtually "closed." Elite opinion was generally running ahead of Byrnes.

In May 1946, John Foster Dulles wrote to a pacifist clergyman: "Resort by Soviet leaders to measures of forceful coercion has been characteristic for nearly 30 years within the Soviet Union, and long preceding the atomic bomb. The objectionable feature of their foreign policy is that they are attempting in foreign affairs to do precisely what they have been doing at home for nearly 30 years." Such was certainly becoming the new conventional wisdom — domestic Soviet totalitarianism inevitably meant a totalitarian foreign policy — that is, a foreign policy motivated primarily by ideology and geared to unlimited expansion and the complete domination of the international system. A basic argument of this history is that the connection was not inevitable — indeed that caution, rather than insatiable appetite, was probably a better characterization of Stalin's postwar foreign policy. But the distinction was difficult to make, had obvious risks of its own, and appeared amoral, at least in the short run, and many gave up on the effort. "We have already fallen to quarreling with Russia like two big dogs chewing on a bone," was the observation in late 1945 of J. William Fulbright, a freshman senator already known as something of a maverick. He had added, "To be tough or soft toward a nation is not a policy." But, by 1946, he too had subscribed to the anticommunist consensus. "Is it the purpose of Russia to dominate the world through a subtle combination of infiltration and force?" he asked in a speech in May. His answer — "Yes." [2]

In Paris, the "get tough" pressures on Byrnes were present and inescapable, in the persons of Arthur Vandenberg and, to a lesser degree, Tom Connally. These two "Senatorial heavyweights," as a British diplomat recalled, invariably flanked Byrnes but "never said anything and maintained a rather disapproving silence throughout which must have been rather discouraging, not to say embarrassing, for their leader." [3]

In private, however, Vandenberg was anything but silent. "Byrnes has 'stood up' 100%," Vandenberg wrote Dulles on May 13. "He only 'almost weakened' once — at which point I put on one of my well-known exhibitions. I am more than ever convinced that communism is on the march on a world-wide scale which only America can stop." On May 28, Vandenberg admitted (in a part of a letter to Henry Luce not published in the senator's *Private Papers*), "Much of our present trouble in the Council results from the fact that Molotov can *literally* quote the Potsdam Agreement and the Moscow Agreement to his own *technical* advantage." He noted further that Molotov was in "a trading mood," but that the United States refused to "compromise principles." And, with the customary comfort the senator took in rhetoric, Vandenberg announced, "Paris was Munich in reverse." [4]

The second session of the Council was split into two parts, the first meeting from April 25 through May 16, and the second from June 15 through July 12. It was a propaganda war, with Byrnes aided by Bevin and (though somewhat less) by Bidault, pitted against Molotov, each side seeking to score points off the other for the benefit of the galleries. But it must be said that the Russians had hardly mastered the art of public relations with the "bourgeois press." After trying for three weeks to see Andrei Vyshinsky, the *Time* correspondent was fobbed off with the advice that he could do no better than to read *Izvestia*.

The first part of this Paris session stalled on the issues of the Italian and Austrian peace treaties, in particular, the fate of Trieste and the Italian colonies, and the question of reparations from Italy. With strong British support Byrnes also pushed for the Open Door in Eastern Europe, and tried to set a date for the convening of a general peace conference. That last worried the Russians, who feared a retreat from a Great Power consortium.[5] "The Americans were far tougher than at London or Moscow," Pierson Dixon, private secretary to Bevin, noted in his diary on May 6. On May 14, he added: "Byrnes bent on a breakdown, presumably so as to teach the Russians international conduct. Byrnes is an admirable representative of the U.S., weak when the American public is weak, and tough when they are tough."

Perhaps because the participants realized that they were all playing to the galleries, there was at times a geniality that had been absent at the London meeting the preceding autumn.

"Gentlemen, I propose we go to the bar," said Byrnes, rising at the end of the last sitting in mid-May.

"It will be the only proposal of the Conference which was immediately and unanimously accepted," Molotov responded, whereupon the foreign ministers headed for the champagne.

The second part was equally unproductive until late in June, when, with discussions now removed from the sight and hearing of the press, the Russians began to give way. A general compromise was arranged. Trieste would be internationalized; Russia would get her reparations from Italy; the question of the colonies would be postponed; the peace conference would open at the end of July; the draft treaties were approved. The Russians emphasized that they wanted the Four-Power agreements to be the basis of the peace conference. They did not want to find themselves outvoted in a mini General Assembly.[6]

In spite of the compromises, Byrnes, in these two months, came to a turning point in his thinking, a firm conclusion that, in turn, pushed Germany onto center stage. As noted earlier, a few days after arriving in Paris for the beginning of the Council, Byrnes had asked Bidault whether Russian policy was "based on a desire for security or expansion."[7] But Byrnes already had in mind a device to test Russian intentions — a twenty-five-year Four-Power treaty guaranteeing German demilitarization. The idea's paternity could be traced back to a proposal in Vandenberg's January 1945 speech, in which the senator had proclaimed his conversion to internationalism. Both Molotov, at the London Conference in September, and Stalin, at the Moscow Conference in December, had expressed a certain tepid interest when Byrnes informally broached the idea.[8]

Byrnes was hopeful that the treaty would open the door to Soviet cooperation and allay Soviet fears and suspicions. It would guarantee a long-term American presence in Europe and at the same time, remove — at least in Byrnes' mind — the justification for Russian hegemony in Eastern Europe. As Truman said, "It was calling their bluff." When Byrnes returned from Moscow, he summoned James Riddleberger, head of the Central European Division. "The only way to alleviate Soviet distrust is to commit the United States to German disarmament," the Secretary said. He asked Riddleberger to draft the treaty in such secrecy that not even Riddleberger's immediate superiors would know of it. The Division chief stayed nights in his office to work up a draft. He went so far as to do his own typing, rather than risk a leak through a secretary. Byrnes' confidant, Ben Cohen, joined him in the efforts. A draft was dispatched to Molotov in mid-February, but only in April did Molotov acknowledge receipt, with the ominous comment that the treaty "arouses serious objections."[9]

On April 28, three days after the Council formally convened, Byrnes and Molotov discussed the treaty face-to-face at an intimate and unpleasant dinner hosted by the American in his suite at the Hôtel Meurice. Molotov complained that the U.S. position on Iran had not been that of a "friend."[10] But Byrnes steered the conversation toward Germany and his pet project. There were many people in the United States, he said, who were "unable to understand the exact aim of the Soviet Union" — whether it was "a search for security or expansionism." Such a treaty (and a similar one for Japan) would "effectively take care of the question of security." Byrnes left implicit, but clear, the interpretation that would be placed on a Soviet failure to embrace his proposal. Molotov again said the Soviet Union favored the treaty in principle, but insisted that it should wait on other matters: "The most important matter was to carry out the previous agreement for the immediate disarmament of Germany."[11] For the Soviets, as we shall shortly see, "disarmament" had a somewhat different meaning than it did for the Americans. Byrnes had just about made up his mind. A few days later he "confessed confidentially" to an American journalist "that he had almost given up hope for a united Germany." Instead, he had begun to think that the three western zones could become a viable and independent country.[12]

Byrnes' shift on the German question reflected not only the apparent Russian rejection of his favorite proposal, but also a widespread effort among senior U.S. officials to alter the course of America's German policy. Although it is a point befogged by the haze of recollections and the scrambling of chronologies, Germany, the most important of all European questions, did not become a subject of real contention until well into the spring of 1946. In the days after Potsdam, when American officials in Germany made lists of the problems confronting a successful occupation, not even so conservative a man as Robert Murphy put Soviet-American relations near the top. Even John McCloy, in the autumn of 1945, saw reason in the joint occupation of Germany for optimism about Russian-American cooperation. Well into 1946, many officials continued to regard France as the more important villain paralyzing Four-Power control — a point forgotten as the Cold War developed.[13] In March, the Four Powers arrived at what appeared to be a fundamental agreement on the level of steel production in Germany. This accord was attributed to the ability of the U.S. and the USSR to work together. "We have reached the situation where we can get mad and argue about one point," said Clay, "reach a compromise and not have it affect our personal relations or any subsequent points we might take up." His attitude, as we saw in the last chapter, certainly persisted into April when he stingingly rejected Kennan's Long Telegram.[14]

There were important countervailing pressures. Many State Department officials, moved by the Riga axioms, began to downplay French obstructionism and emphasized instead the conflict with the Soviet Union over Germany. They wanted to bring the War Department around to their view. Fearing collaboration between Russia and a new Reich, Matthews informed Acheson in early April, "It is high time we made some top level decisions with regard to Germany."[15] Kennan drew the matter more starkly. Just as he had assumed the year before that the Russians had a well-worked-out reparations plan meant to achieve political goals in Germany and Western Europe, so now he warned of a "Soviet political program" for taking over all Germany. Therefore, he advocated that partition be carried "to its logical conclusion" with the development of a West German state. Ambassador Smith supported Kennan's vew in April: "I have held for many months that our immediate objectives should be the integration of the western zones of Germany into a political unit oriented towards western Europe and western democracy."

Yet, at about the same time, Smith also complained, "We are so lacking in knowledge of the workings of the [Soviet] regime." [16] In fact, the available evidence indicates that the Americans misinterpreted the Soviet interest in Germany, partly because they could not know what was happening inside the Kremlin. In the Russian mind, the configuration of issues was different. The Churchill speech, the American emphasis on and expansion of its air power, among other things, gave the Russians some grounds to question Western intentions.[17]

More important, the Americans did not understand that when Molotov spoke of German "disarmament," he meant reparations, as well as the destruction of any residual German military capability. The Russians were so obsessed with the idea of reparations from Germany that well into 1946 they were removing much of the second set of tracks on the East German railway — hardly a wise strategic move if they considered that a military clash with the West was likely. Reparations from Germany were assigned a major role in Russian thinking about reconstruction. Indeed, the Soviet economic planner Voznesensky formulated the slogan "Reparations for Fulfillment of the Five-Year Plan."

But by the summer of 1946, the Soviet effort to extract reparations from Germans by removing capital equipment had failed.* The enterprise was beset by bitter internal antagonisms and was carried out in an ill-conceived, hasty, wasteful fashion. The bureaucratic wrangling, which involved even Stalin's immediate deputies, focused on two issues: first, whether to take reparations from current production or seek to pastoralize Germany by removals of equipment and whole

* In August 1946, Clay suggested that the Americans had acquired an "exaggerated impression of the scale of removals" by the Russians from the Eastern zone because "of the Russian desire to prepare for the arrival" of the Allied control agencies in Berlin.

factories and, second, under whose auspices in the Soviet bureaucracy policy would be executed. These problems placed considerable pressure on Molotov and other officials to press the Western states on reparations. For instance, in June 1946, Robert Murphy reported that Marshal Sokolovsky, the head of the Soviet occupation, had come to dinner at his house. Sokolovsky "was communicative only on economic subjects . . . Sokolovsky's position on reparations out of current production and the German export-import program is if anything hardened." The Soviets pressed harder on reparations in part to counteract a trend in Western policy (which the Russians correctly perceived) toward the division of Germany. But the rigid and blundering Soviet behavior, in turn, only strengthened that trend.[18]

The American officials were generally convinced (though with the partial exception of Clay himself) that not only were reparations part of a larger Soviet political program to extend Russian power into Western Europe but also that reparations were antithetical to German and Western European recovery.* Commenting further on his conversation with Sokolovsky, Murphy observed: "As far as we can make out, it seems to boil down to a proposition that the Soviets intend to squeeze the last drop from the orange." But the Americans probably erred when they assumed that reparations and recovery were incompatible. German industrial capacity had greatly expanded during the war. By 1943, Germany probably had more machine tools than the United States. Only the German transportation and liquid fuel systems were heavily damaged; aside from them, the economic infrastructure was mostly intact. Eighty percent of the heavy industry in the British and American zones had survived the war. Moreover, the total industrial capacity exceeded what would have been required to produce the output levels of the prewar years; not more than half of the Reich's 22-million-ton steel-making capacity was ever used for peaceful purposes.[19]

As the basic American outlook was reformulated, reparations became even more unacceptable. The diffusion of the Riga axioms and the new doctrine of national security were joined by a re-evaluation

* U.S. officials also worried that reparations would provide an infusion for the Soviet military establishment. In September 1945, State had informed the War Department that the Soviet Union continued to produce war materials at a high rate and that any assistance from the outside would only help "maintenance of the war-time production of arms" and "political-military aims which it is intended that production further."

of the problem of the world economy. War Department officials were increasingly receptive to the State Department view of the German problem, which emphasized Russian rather than French obstructionism.[20]

By early May, General Clay was acutely concerned by the lack of economic recovery, and was disturbed by the failure of an intense month-long American attempt in all control committees to break down zonal barriers. He hoped to force agreement for administering the four zones as a single economic unit. Acting more or less on his own authority, certainly astounding many U.S. officials, Clay thus took a most significant step: he ordered a halt in the U.S. Zone to the further dismantling of plants for reparations delivery. But, contrary to the interpretations of subsequent memoirs, this step was aimed at least as much at the French as at the Russians.[21]

In mid-May, Clay flew to Paris to put the case to Byrnes. As the staff memorandum he had with him said, "The whole edifice will come crashing down on our heads . . . if something is not done soon to break down the zonal barriers." Shortly thereafter, he proposed integrating the American and British zones. He was still more explicitly critical of the French than of the Russians, though he did add: "If agreement cannot be obtained along these broad lines in the immediate future, we face a deteriorating German economy which will create a political unrest favorable to the development of communism in Germany and a deterrent to democratization." [22] Those remarks pointed the direction in which Clay's own thoughts ran. But they also indicated Clay's sense of what would make the most effective selling point.*

In the second week of July, Molotov emphatically refused to advance Byrnes' proposal for a treaty. The Secretary no longer had any doubts. If the Russians were interested simply in security, then they would have embraced the treaty. How could they have questioned

* Having just returned from a consulting visit to Germany, Walt W. Rostow of the State Department's German-Austrian Economic Affairs Division wrote to the Division chief, Charles Kindleberger, on June 10, 1946, "Whether correct or not it is the Berlin view that Clay's hold-up of reparations is designed rather more to get the French obstruction cleared up than to show up Soviet intentions." He added that American officials in Berlin were cautiously optimistic about the Soviets. Their experience had shown them, Rostow said, that "hard-bargaining straight-forward Americans who know their objectives, and who have reasonable objectives, can do business with the Russians." They also thought that Soviet policy still "looked towards treating Germany as an economic unit."

U.S. intentions, American sincerity? The treaty's rejection convinced Byrnes that the Russians were bent on further westward expansion, and that for this reason they wanted to aggravate economic paralysis and political disintegration in Germany. After a July 10 speech by Molotov that was apparently aimed at German public opinion, Byrnes reviewed the American position on Germany with top officials. He gave Clay the go-ahead to begin fusing the American and British zones into one economic entity that became known by the comic opera name of Bizonia. The British, though worried about taking steps that would divide Europe, were so burdened by the costs of their occupation in the Ruhr that they were willing to proceed. Bizonia would come into official existence on January 1, 1947.

"There seems to be no doubt that the issue presented by the Byrnes invitation to proceed with economic unification on a partial basis has created much soul searching and tension," Charles Kindleberger wrote from Berlin on August 3, 1946, "and that the French and USSR delegations are worried by the prospects at the same time that they are unwilling to give in. The Soviet tactic appears to be to keep on talking; and since the US position is that the arrangements are open to all, there is a natural disposition to hold the matter open a little longer to see if the last Soviet remarks really mean that they will join.

"Coupled with this," Kindleberger added, "is a sense of tragic inevitability about the split."

Many of the Americans did not expect the Russians ever to go along. Ben Cohen, for instance, concluded that the best hope for maintaining amicable relations with the Soviet Union lay in disengaging from as many common problems and joint enterprises as possible. Too many differences separated the two sides for them to work together on a matter so centrally important as Germany; even when they used the same words, they could not understand each other. A division into two Germanys would be preferable to a struggle for the soul of a united Germany, a contest that might well end in a third world war. But it was just as hard to disengage amiably as to work together. "Working with the Russians is like a husband and wife that can't get along and can't agree to live together," Cohen would say. "But at the minute they agree to separation, they find they can't agree on the terms of the separation." [23]

Though the immediate economic worries should not be overlooked, this fusion of the British and American zones also represented a key step in the creation of a bulwark against the presumed menace from the East. "We have cast the die here in economic integration with the British zone," Clay wrote on the last day of July. "This is forcing the issue and while we hope it will expediate quadripartite action, it may just have the reverse effect. However, I could not continue longer in economic stagnation and this at least will help." Yet Clay continued to be of two minds. He was even willing to consider reparations from current production, so long as steps toward German economic recovery went ahead. Moreover, he still questioned the application of the Riga axioms to Germany, though less vigorously than he had when presented with Kennan's Long Telegram the preceding spring.

In late July, Eisenhower queried him about Soviet obstruction. "It is difficult to find major instances of Soviet failure to carry out agreements reached in quadripartite government of Germany," Clay replied. Either interpretations honestly differed, he explained, or the French were also to blame.[24]

At about the same time, Byrnes asked Cohen to begin drafting a speech to counter Soviet appeals to the German public. Byrnes explained his motives in a letter to Truman on September 2. Molotov's July 10 speech at the Council of Foreign Ministers "was intended to win German support and was successful," he said. "It is the opinion of the representatives of *New York Times, Washington Post* and others who have recently visited Germany that we should promptly offset the propaganda that we are so disgusted with European affairs that we will not remain in Germany."

Byrnes delivered his speech on September 6 in the Opera House in Stuttgart. He hoped to please the German people with strong backing for self-government and economic revival. Byrnes was critical of the failure to establish central administrative agencies, and he suggested that the cession of German territory to Poland would not be regarded as permanent. Byrnes also sent two important messages to the Russians. In a point developed by Cohen, the Secretary said that he did not want Germany to become a pawn or a prize in a struggle between East and West. Yet, responding to the earnest persuasion of General Clay, he promised that American occupation troops would stay in Germany so long as those of any other country

— i.e., the Soviet Union — did the same. The Secretary had a further point in mind — to reassure German officials who were throwing their lot in with the West that they would not later be abandoned. As Byrnes explained to Treasury Secretary Snyder three days after the speech, "The argument was daily made that while the Soviets would remain, the Americans would leave." [25]

Even as the die was being cast in Germany, Byrnes might have had reason for second thoughts. On the last evening of the Council of Foreign Ministers meeting in Paris, Byrnes joined Molotov at the Soviet embassy for what was, for once, a cordial dinner. Molotov, almost charming for a change, agreed with Byrnes that it would have been better if he had communicated in advance the Soviet stand on some issues, and so avoided bitter debates.

Byrnes decided to take advantage of the opening. "Why then don't you tell me what is really in your hearts and mind on the subject of Germany?"

The Soviet Union, Molotov replied, simply wanted what it had asked for at Yalta — ten billion dollars in reparations and participation in Four-Power control of the Ruhr.

As Byrnes mulled the matter over in the following year, he concluded that Molotov had spoken the truth — that those were "the real desires of the Soviet high command." [26]

The Council of Foreign Ministers gave way to a twenty-one nation Peace Conference in Paris at the end of July. It was not noteworthy for its accomplishments, but for what this parody of the Versailles Conference revealed of the developing confrontation. There was much idealistic but useless chatter about the rights of small nations, but precious few signs of businesslike relations among the Great Powers. "It is a public performance, not a serious discussion," said Harold Nicolson, a veteran of Versailles now in Paris for the British Broadcasting Company, and one of the shrewdest observers of the proceedings. More than anyone else, Byrnes, responding to the many political pressures on him, and out of his own personal frustrations, helped move the meetings in that direction.

The Secretary of State was just about ready to give up "fixing."

"The road ahead of us is a very difficult one," he wrote, a few days before the Conference opened. "We cannot hope to change the thinking of the people of the Soviet Union. That is our trouble. Ordinarily, when you can agree with one on a statement of facts you can expect to reach the same conclusion. That is not true when mental operations of people differ as widely as in the case of the gentlemen who represent the Soviet Union and ourselves."

Shortly after the Conference opened, Byrnes privately explained that his strategy was to stir up the small powers to "strengthen his arguments on disagreed issues" and then "get to work behind the scenes 'in the jury room.' " But the delegates never really did get to work in the jury room. Even Bevin was put out with Byrnes' insistence on publicity. "This means that one can never think aloud without being overheard, and that all real negotiation is impossible," he explained to Nicolson. "Believe me, 'arold, our trouble is that the Russians are frightened and the Yanks bomb-minded." [27]

In August, while Byrnes sat at the Paris Peace Conference, Washington managed a crisis. Early that month, the Soviet Union delivered a note to Turkey, which was also sent to Washington and London, calling in blunt terms for the revision of the Montreux Convention.* The Russians sought to have control of the Dardanelles vested solely in the Black Sea powers, and also wanted to share joint fortifications in the Straits with Turkey. The Straits and an assured warm-water port were of course historic obsessions of Czarist as well as Soviet policy. During the Second World War, with Turkey a neutral tilting toward Germany, such claims received a favorable hearing from the Western powers.

According to the minutes of the October 1944 Moscow meeting, Stalin had described the Montreux Convention as an anachronism. "If Britain were interested in the Mediterranean then Russia was equally interested in the Black Sea," he explained.

"It was no part of British policy to grudge Soviet Russia access to warm-water ports," replied Churchill. "They no longer followed the policy of Disraeli or Lord Curzon. They were not going to stop Russia. They wished to help."

"The spearhead was directed against Russia," said Stalin. "It

* The Montreux Convention gave Turkey considerable control over the right of passage (including denial of that right) through the Dardanelles of warships belonging to the other Black Sea powers. It was signed in July 1936 by Turkey, the Soviet Union, Britain, France, Japan, and four Balkan countries. The U.S. was not a party.

should be dropped." He compared the Russian interest in the Straits to Britain's at Suez and Gibraltar, and that of the United States in Panama. "Russia was in a worse situation."

Churchill said he wanted "to bring Turkey along by gentle steps," but added that Russia had a "right and moral claim." Later in their October conversations, Stalin returned to the Montreux Convention. He wanted the Prime Minister "to remember this subject."

Churchill asked Stalin "to state secretly what improvements" he had in mind.

Stalin replied that he only wanted Churchill "to bear the matter in mind as the Soviet Government would raise it." [28]

At Yalta, Roosevelt also agreed that revision was justified. At Potsdam the three Great Powers endorsed such a revision.

The Russians, however, were slow to remind the Turks of their claim. Although the ultimate Russian notification in August 1946 was in accord with the Potsdam understanding, American policymakers — their world outlook in the process of being reformulated — now saw this claim as dangerous and provocative, a prelude to Soviet seizure of the entire Middle East and a major threat to American national security.[29]

In August, a few days after the Soviets finally delivered the note, Forrestal and other top War and Navy Department officials anxiously gathered at the State Department to confer with Acheson and Loy Henderson. "It was agreed," Forrestal noted, "that it was desirable to canvass the United States policy and decide now whether this country proposed to take a firm attitude . . . or do as we have in the past — protest, but ultimately give in." The State-War-Navy Coordinating Committee formulated a position paper that contemplated military force.[30]

At a meeting in Truman's office the next day, the advocate Acheson used the paper to present one of the first clear and indeed vivid statements of the containment doctrine. "Appeasement" was being translated into what would later be called the domino theory. Joint fortifications on the Straits would lead to Soviet control of Turkey, which would lead to Soviet control of Greece and the entire Near and Middle East, which would leave the Soviet Union in "a much stronger position to obtain its objectives in India and China." The Russians would be deterred only by knowledge that the United States is "prepared, if necessary, to meet aggression with force of arms."

"We might as well find out whether the Russians were bent on world conquest now, as in five or ten years," the President declared. He added that he would see it through to the end. The President approved both the sending of a tough note to the Russians and the dispatch of a powerful American task force to the eastern Mediterranean, which Forrestal soon established as a permanent presence in the region.[31]

A few days later Yugoslavia shot down two American transport planes that had violated Yugoslavian air space. Outright conflict seemed that much closer. On August 21, Eisenhower surprised Forrestal and Admiral Chester Nimitz by saying that he did not think the Russians would go to war, and that neither the shooting down of the planes nor a Russian occupation of the Dardanelles constituted a *casus belli*. "This showed the Army's inability," Forrestal complained afterward, "to grasp the importance of control of the seas and their lack of appreciation of strategy in the broadest geographic terms."[32]

In fact, the Russians neither invaded Turkey nor did much else. Their real aim seemed to have been the registration of their claim before the prescribed deadline had passed. The language was harsh, but the procedure accorded with the decision reached at Potsdam.

Notwithstanding, the Turkish episode did lead to the expression of the anticommunist consensus among American policymakers. The image of the Soviet Union had, we might say, "closed." The official American view of Russia was no longer ambiguous. Excluded now were assessments keyed to the nature of a particular problem or suggesting that the Russians were confused or crudely reactive. Interpretations and assessments from this point on derived from the axiomatic construct that the Soviet Union was not a Great Power operating within the international system but rather a world revolutionary state bent on overturning that system. These axioms and the doctrine of national security coalesced to create a permanent crisis mentality among the Americans. Here, operating for the first time, was an interpretative framework that would govern American policy well into the 1970s.

As the Turkish question continued to lie in the crisis box, State Department officials began to advocate a policy of military and economic aid based on containment. The plea for such aid highlighted a major reordering of priorities in America's foreign economic program. The effort to restore a nineteenth-century liberal world economy would have to wait. The perception of an emerging postwar economic crisis, combined with the fears about the Soviet Union, now convinced policymakers that America's economic might and its planning for a stable economic environment had to be subordinated to its international political interests.[33]

The reorientation became clear in the spring and early summer of 1946. The case in point was a $650 million credit granted to France, in which the prime consideration was no longer multilateralism, but the strengthening of pro-Western forces. The aim was, as Byrnes told the Cabinet, to "combat this Russian influence."[34] Also, in early summer, the United States took the decisive steps of withdrawing support from the United Nations Relief and Rehabilitation Administration (for which it was providing most of the funds, but without commensurate control), beginning to develop an export control system for Soviet trade, and officially killing any plans to make a loan to Russia. Rather than use its economic power to build links with the Soviet Union, the U.S. would use that power to throw up walls against communism.[35]

But the crucial — and ultimately self-defeating — step was not taken until August and September. At the Paris Peace Conference, Byrnes caught sight of the Czechoslovakian delegates heartily applauding a diatribe by Vyshinsky, in which he charged the United States with trying to manipulate its economic power to dominate the world. This was an example of the Czech bargain. To protect their internal independence, they would trail along in the Soviet wake on foreign affairs. That was the only way the coalition of communists and noncommunists could stay together in power, permitting Czechoslovakia to remain a possible bridge between East and West. But Byrnes was enraged, for the United States was then negotiating a $50 million line of credit to Czechoslovakia for the purchase of U.S. Army surplus stores, of vital use for reconstruction. "It was amazing," Ben Cohen later recalled. "He really felt emotionally involved, not recognizing that they had no alternatives. He felt the delegates had shown their personal contempt for the United States." Byrnes ordered the credits canceled. The Czechs would be punished. Noncommunist politicians in Czechoslovakia regretted the action more than the communists, for Byrnes' decision was counter-productive — it undercut the position of the noncommunists. The matter of Czechoslovakian credits was the first instance of what became American policy.

"I feel," Byrnes wired Clayton in September, "that you should have a full realization within the Dept. of the importance of world developments in recent months." No longer could economic aid be based upon the specific economic situation. The relation of such assistance to America's overall multilateral goals would also have to become secondary. "The situation has so hardened that the time has now come, I am convinced, in the light of the attitude of the Soviet Govt. and the neighboring states which it dominates [that] we must help our friends in every way and refrain from assisting those who either through helplessness or for other reasons are opposing the principles for which we stand."

"Concur completely," Will Clayton wired back. He recognized the need to turn from the re-creation of a nineteenth-century world economy to more immediate tasks.[36]

Running parallel to the Paris meetings were negotiations to establish controls over atomic weapons at the United Nations in New York.

The first American step toward the creation of an international regime was a study carried out under the direction of Dean Acheson and David Lilienthal that was completed in March 1946. It proposed the establishment of an international agency, the Atomic Development Authority, which would control both raw materials and production plants. It did not put great emphasis on inspections, nor did it envision sanctions.

Seeking to win public and congressional support, Byrnes and Truman then appointed Bernard Baruch to head the negotiating at the United Nations. Acheson and Lilienthal were appalled by the choice. For his part, Baruch did not like the idea that the report already seemed quasi-policy. "You'd better get another messenger boy," Baruch snapped at Acheson. "Western Union don't take 'em at my age." Reassured by Truman and Byrnes, the old Pooh-bah (in Roosevelt's phrase) — extraordinarily vain, looking for a crown to his career, but never really too straight on his facts — took command of the negotiations with the declaration, "I am a tough baby." He was also an extremely self-confident old baby. "I concluded that I would drop the scientists because, as I told them, I knew all I wanted to know," he told Vannevar Bush. "It went boom and it killed millions of people and I thought it was an ethical and political problem and I would proceed on that theory." He recruited Ferdinand Eberstadt as chief tactician and strategist, banker John Hancock as chief of staff, and several other equally conservative men, who were alarmed at the thought that uranium mines might slip out of the hands of private enterprise. In an effort to place his imprimatur on the Acheson-Lilienthal Report, Baruch introduced a number of Wilsonian twists into the American proposal, including sanctions, no veto, and an insistence that this was a General Assembly, not a Great Power, matter. He and his associates, relying as they did on General Groves, had more confidence in the persistence of the atomic monopoly than did many of the scientists.[37]

In May, Eberstadt reminded Baruch that he really ought to consult top military leaders so that his proposal would be "in line with our military policy and the needs of our national security." Baruch immediately solicited such opinions. The Chiefs of Staff defined the problem in such a way as to make Baruch's task impossible: the bomb should continue to be at the heart of America's arsenal, and a system of controls should be established that would prevent the Russians from developing the weapon. Army Chief of Staff Dwight Eisenhower wrote that "we cannot at this time limit our capability to produce or use this weapon." He opposed any steps that might "further unbalance against U.S. world power relationships," and insisted that "free and complete inspection" had to be the first step.[38] Baruch and his associates put greater weight on the opinions of the military than on those of atomic scientists, and so made the crucial error of assuming that the Russians would not be able to develop a weapon — or even tap an adequate uranium supply — for many years.[39]

Baruch presented his plan to the United Nations in June. He proposed the establishment of an International Atomic Energy Authority. It would move through a series of stages to acquire complete control over raw materials and atomic plants throughout the world. Countries violating its mandate would be subject to punishment, and, unlike the Security Council, there would be no veto in the IAEA.

On the other hand, the United States would retain a hidden veto:

The international regime would begin with a complete survey of raw materials and inspection of facilities. No time limit was put on each stage, and all members had to agree that a stage was completed before moving on to the next stage. Thus, the Americans would still retain their arsenal of atomic weapons long after the Russians had surrendered the crucial information about their raw materials sources and the state of their research and development.

With some foresight, a Soviet journal pointed out, "No country which desires atomic energy and is independently capable of getting it by 1949 will consider an Atomic Energy Authority which, through its process of stages, would postpone the event for many years, as the Baruch proposal would require."[40]

Andrei Gromyko replied a few days later with a plan totally at variance with the Baruch approach. He called for a convention to ban the production and use of atomic weapons, to be followed by the destruction of all existing weapons. He offered no controls or sanctions. A system of control would only follow sometime in the future. In addition, each nation-state would retain sovereignty for itself; Gromyko was absolute in his insistence that the veto could not be abrogated in the IAEA.

The British ambassador in Moscow, Clark-Kerr, had pointed out late in 1945 that the dropping of the new bomb had shocked the Russians, much intensifying their sense of insecurity. Even Baruch was willing to acknowledge that fear was their dominating emotion. How could they then have accepted any general plan like the one put forward by Baruch? "Whatever the motives behind the offer," one scholar has observed, "its effect would have been to place the Soviet Union in a position of permanent inferiority."[41]

In the absence of parity, there was little basis for an agreement. American atomic tests were conducted at Bikini Atoll in the Pacific, in July 1946, just as debate was beginning in the United Nations, so underscoring the reality of an American monopoly. Baruch and his associates did have some difficulty in understanding why the Russians would not embrace the proposal. "Gromyko asks why the United States produces bombs if we have good intentions," observed John Hancock, one of Baruch's chief aides. "We believe we are firm in our good intentions." Yet, from the beginning, there was also the sense among American leaders that Baruch was merely going through the motions, waiting for public opinion to reach the point where it would sanction a break, preparing, in Byrnes' words, "a clear and adequate basis for such a breakdown." [42]

"There has been a tremendous change in public attitude toward Russia," Baruch stated on August 1. "We must do everything we can to reach an agreement; nevertheless, we must face facts. If we have made every effort to reach an agreement, we can then face a break with a clear conscience." The problem, he added, was "far too important to do any trading about." His colleagues shared his attitude. Finally, on September 17, Baruch wrote a memo to Truman, officially informing him that the negotiations were going nowhere.[43]

Could either side have pursued these negotiations very seriously? Perhaps an adequate control system was simply impossible to achieve. Two great unknowns confronted the United States and the USSR, and the resolution of either could have decisively shifted the balance of power between them. One was Germany; the other, nuclear weapons. Neither the Soviet Union nor the United States could willingly run the risk that the other would carry the day in either area. The most stable solution? That each would have its own Germany, and each, its own atomic arsenal. In that way a kind of stability would be introduced into their relationship. In the meantime, the interests of the Soviet Union and the United States on the question of atomic weapons were asymmetrical.

Thus, each introduced proposals in the U.N. that would have improved its own relative position. The Baruch Plan would have removed the Soviet "advantage," that is, the secrecy surrounding its raw materials and development program. The Gromyko Plan would have stripped the U.S. of its "advantage," its monopoly of an extant arsenal of the actual atomic weapons. The interests of the two countries would remain asymmetrical until parity, the danger of nuclear proliferation, and the journey to the brink over Cuba in 1962 finally began to create a basis for accord. So sensitive was the issue of the bomb that even the United States and the United Kingdom, closely aligned, having similar institutions and traditions, and having collaborated to produce the first bombs during the war, could not maintain their cooperation in the postwar years.

But, as with so many other international episodes, failure — here, the Soviet rejection of the Baruch Plan — contributed further credence to the Riga axioms. Most Americans decided that the Russians had rejected a spacious, generous American offer for malign purposes. The U.S. embassy in Moscow reported that the Soviet negotiating position "is based upon and directly derives from the Soviet world outlook." [44]

In the summer of 1946, President Truman instructed Clark Clifford, his special counsel, to prepare a comprehensive statement on Soviet-American relations. A successful young lawyer from St. Louis, Clifford had entered the White House as an assistant naval aide, but quickly distinguished himself. Personal relations also helped his rapid ascent, for Truman felt comfortable with Clifford. He was a Missourian who had never worked for Roosevelt, and so could not compare the two Presidents, even implicitly. He was probably the single most capable member of the White House staff during the Truman years, and the President came to trust him and depend on him across the range of domestic and foreign problems.

Unlike many of the other Missourians who came into the White House, Clifford was both an astute political strategist and a committed pragmatic liberal. Not long after joining Truman's staff, Clifford was called in by the President. Complaining that many of the people around Roosevelt had been "crackpots and the lunatic fringe," Truman said, "I want to keep my feet on the ground. . . . I don't want experiments. The American people have been through a lot of experiments and they want a rest from experiments." But Truman was less clear on the direction in which he did want to move. Clifford became leader of the liberals in Truman's immediate circle of advisers around the President. The special counsel took the lead in what proved to be a two-year struggle over the thrust of the President's domestic program. The liberals ultimately carried the day in the form of the Fair Deal, and a good deal of the credit belongs to Clifford.

Responding to the President's request for the report on Soviet-American relations, Clifford, working with George Elsey, another White House aide, began by soliciting the views of senior officials. People, even memoranda-writers, are generally more vaguely conscious than articulate, but the queries from the White House forced policymakers to formulate and express basic ideas. The replies, written during the summer months of 1946, revealed virtually unanimous acceptance of Kennan's argument in the Long Telegram that the

United States was, in effect, at war with the Soviet Union, and should therefore adopt perspectives and policies appropriate to war.

The exchange between the White House and the State Department indirectly provided some evidence of Byrnes' problems with Truman's staff. On July 18, Elsey noted that Admiral Leahy, aside from "surprise and a little pique" that "so large a project as an evaluation of our relations with Russia" could get going without his knowledge, was enthusiastic about the enterprise. Elsey continued, "Jimmy Byrnes was much more startled than Leahy when Clifford went to see him. However, he took it as a direct order from the President and promised to get to work at once. He rambled on with Clifford for several minutes, and said that perhaps he could not provide all the 'agreements,' as he thought Harry Hopkins had had some, and others were buried in the Roosevelt papers. When Clifford told me this, I promptly said that Byrnes, in my mind, already had the reputation of being a liar in this subject. He had publicly denied having had knowledge of the Roosevelt-Stalin agreement at Yalta on the Kuriles . . . whereas I, for a certain fact, had briefed him on this in April and May of 1945. Byrnes, I told Clifford, was trying to pass off some of the blame for his lack of success in dealing with the Russians on 'secret' agreements made by Roosevelt. Clifford then asked a great number of questions on various conferences — Cairo, Teheran, Yalta, Potsdam — who was there, what was decided, etc. He says Truman is awfully vague on all of these but Potsdam."[45]

In their formal replies to the Clifford-Elsey queries, the two military departments defined national security in the broadest sense. Soviet naval activity — actual or potential, whether it were in the Arctic or Pacific oceans, in the Baltic, Black, or Mediterranean seas — threatened U.S. security, according to Chester Nimitz, the chief of Naval Operations. The Russians, he said, were preparing for such ventures as attempting "to neutralize" Britain by blockade, bombardment, and invasion, and were aiming to launch submarine raids against American coastal cities. The way that he suggested to deter such threats happened to accord with the Navy's institutional interest — maintaining "our naval forces in strength, position and readiness." The Navy wanted to develop major presences in the Atlantic and Mediterranean.[46]

The Army, as well, contended that the United States should adopt an adversary stance. Secretary of War Robert Patterson and his War Department associates insisted that the Russians fully expected and even wanted a war, and held the Soviet Union responsible for most of the world's troubles — thereby ignoring domestic upheavals in many countries, general economic dislocation, the collapse of colonial empires, and the rising tides of nationalism throughout the world. They argued that the United States needed to be ready for imminent Russian "use of armed forces on a global scale. Security preparations in light of this estimate must be both political and military." As with the Navy, such an analysis provided the rationale for the Army to pursue its service interests.[47]

In addition to Kennan's Long Telegram, the State Department provided Clifford and Elsey with an extensive list of Soviet violations (in letter and "spirit") of many agreements, a number of other cables, and a thirty-four-page policy guide. This last argued that the extension of Soviet influence in Eastern Europe was just the beginning of a policy of aggrandizement that could only be "contained" by "armed resistance on the part of other major powers in areas where they feel their vital interests to be endangered." Thus, the United States had to develop a strong military establishment, and integrate its foreign, economic, and military policies. The local dimensions of any question were secondary or even tertiary in the grand scheme of the incipient East-West conflict: "We must conduct a global policy and not expect to advance our interests by treating each question on its apparent merits as it arises," the State Department asserted, despite its reluctant recognition that "the Soviets are operating in regions which might justifiably be considered as within a Soviet security zone."

All the State Department documents insisted that the Kremlin was a superbly functioning mastermind. "The Soviet Union operates on a world-wide basis," said the authors of the policy guide. "Each move in its foreign policy is carefully planned and integrated with moves on other fronts." This belief was related to what might be called "the paradox of the two tactics." For example, on June 15, Ambassador Smith had reported from Moscow a "different behavior" on the part of the Soviets in Asia — USSR efforts at mediation in China, a similar trend in Iran, settlement of border difficulties with Afghanistan. But Smith cautioned Washington not to be taken in by the apparent move toward "correct relationships." The Russians had not abandoned their "predatory aims" in Asia; they were simply following a different tactical approach. With such an enemy, diplomacy could only be dangerous.[48]

All the policymakers ruled out agreement with the Soviet Union on German reparations. Truman's reparations ambassador, Edwin Pauley, went even further. He said — incorrectly — that the 1945 reparations agreements were mainly meant to eliminate Germany's war-making capability and not to aid reconstruction in the USSR and elsewhere.[49]

In his covering letter to the President, Clifford commented on the "remarkable agreement among the officials with whom I have talked and whose reports I have studied" on the need to reorient American policy toward the Soviet Union. Top priority, said Clifford, was the need for "accurate knowledge of the motives and methods of the Soviet government." For such knowledge, Clifford fell back on the "bible," Kennan's Long Telegram, and quoted from it extensively.

Clifford's covering letter went on to say that a separate and time-honored "European Policy" or "Indian Policy" or "Near Eastern Policy" no longer had any basis. All had to be subordinated to a Soviet Policy, and all American actions had to be "considered in the light of over-all Soviet objectives." Moreover, American public opinion had to be aroused to the Soviet danger and to the need for "stern policies." The very existence of the Soviet Union threatened American security — a true mirror image of Kennan's view of the world set of the Soviet leaders. American security was endangered not only by Soviet military might, Clifford said, but also by the dominant position Soviet military officers enjoyed on Eastern European control commissions, by the activities of U.S. communists — and even by the tour that some visiting Soviet engineers were making at that time of water and sewage disposal systems in a few American cities.[50]

The Clifford Memorandum — much of it actually written by George Elsey — was a compendium of the new foreign policy wisdom. The Riga axioms and the new doctrine of national security had come together to form the distinctive postwar outlook of American foreign policy leaders. All questions of international relations had to be evaluated against the overriding issue of the Soviet threat. The question was not the nature of Stalin's terror. Ironically, in fact, very few in the West could even begin to grasp the extent of Stalin's terror within the Soviet Union; rather, the problem was to assess the role of the Soviet Union in international relations. American leaders might have seen themselves confronted by a cruel, clumsy, bureaucratized, fear-ridden despotism, preoccupied with reconstructing a vast war-torn land. Instead, the Americans were convinced that they faced a cunning, sure-footed enemy, engaged in a never-ending drive for world hegemony.

Top American officials also recognized that U.S. public opinion did not fully share their outlook.

Clark Clifford gave Truman his report at the end of a working day in September, and the President stayed up most of the night reading it. Early the next morning, he telephoned Clifford at home. Truman asked how many copies of the report existed. Ten, Clifford replied. Truman ordered Clifford to bring the other nine to him immediately.

"This has got to be put under lock and key," Truman explained later in the morning, after receiving the other copies from Clifford. "This is so hot, if this should come out now it could have an exceedingly unfortunate impact on our efforts to try to develop some relationship with the Soviet Union." [51]

This was a tactical judgment. Truman, like most other policymakers, certainly accepted the image presented in the Clifford Memorandum. Such an attitude left little room for dissenters in the high councils of government. By this time, in fact, only one prominent dissenter so remained to bedevil the men who were making policy.

Franklin Roosevelt once remarked that Henry Wallace was no mystic, only a liberal philosopher. But others, many Democrats as well as Republicans, regarded him not only as a mystic, but also an enthusiast, a wild spender, a naïve and woolly-minded idealist who wanted to give every Hottentot a pint of American milk every day. To a skeptical State Department official, he was one of the "Post-War Dream Boys." More than Roosevelt himself, Wallace came during World War II to symbolize for conservatives what they saw as the past and present excesses and future dangers of the New Deal.[52]

The rumpled Henry Wallace was an optimistic, intelligent, curious, prescient man, and a capable public administrator. With his roots in the farmland of the Midwest, he always had an abiding faith in "the healing qualities of mother earth." He was a first-rate plant geneticist, the author of perhaps the first realistic econometric study ever published in the United States, and one of the few high government officials in the 1940s who actually *understood* the scientific basis of atomic energy.[53]

After FDR's death, Wallace stayed on as Secretary of Commerce — he and Byrnes, the might-have-been Presidents standing uncomfortably close to Truman. But Wallace proved to be an increasingly anomalous figure in Truman's Cabinet. Shy and aloof, often ill-at-ease, Farmer Wallace (as Alice Roosevelt Longworth had dubbed him) had neither gift nor taste for practical politics. Endowed with little tactical judgment, he was inept at wheeling and dealing in Washington and within the Democratic Party — characteristics that helped to trap him at the extreme left of the political spectrum in the 1948 presidential election. His colleagues in the Truman Administration suspected him of such heresies as Keynesianism, and regarded him as an unrealistic, untrustworthy, and unconvivial crusader. While they played poker and swapped stories, he gave an hour a day to tending his thousand or so strawberry plants.[54]

Truman constantly implored Wallace to stay in the Cabinet, because of what the President presumed to be Wallace's crucial following on the Democratic Party left and in the industrial unions. There was some superficial cordiality between the two men. "The only regret I have, 'after burning my bridges behind me,' " Harry Truman wrote Wallace shortly after receiving the 1944 vice-presidential nomination, "is the fact that I had to beat you in order to be nominated." Truman often gave the impression that he agreed with many things Wallace said to him, and Wallace reminded him to take vitamin pills for his headaches.[55] In truth, however, while Truman respected Wallace's work as Secretary of Agriculture during Roosevelt's first two terms, he did not like him personally, and did not want to be lectured on what Roosevelt would have done in this or that situation. In June 1945, Truman told Henry Morgenthau, "Wallace is nothing but a cat bastard." Morgenthau was puzzled. He had never heard that epithet before. But, obviously, it was no compliment.

Perhaps Truman also transferred to Wallace some of the anger he felt toward organized labor, especially the CIO, which was generally regarded as part of the Wallace constituency. Some measure of Truman's feelings was apparent from notes that Chester Bowles, director of Economic Stabilization, made of a conversation with Truman in

June 1946, about labor relations: "The President again interrupted to say that labor's promises were not worth the paper they were written on . . . that labor people were generally unreliable; and that he was President of the United States, and was going to exercise all his powers as President of the United States . . . The President's interruptions were continuous, violent, and highly emotional, and it was very difficult to carry out a coherent presentation of the problem and its possible solution . . . The entire half hour which I spent with him was punctuated by extraordinary profanity. And the discussion was far more emotional than any I have ever had with any public official in my memory."[56]

And Wallace could only be, like Byrnes, but perhaps less obviously so, resentful of Truman's elevation, as well as wary of what he suspected was a misappropriation of Roosevelt's legacy both domestic and international. "Apparently these are days when you look one way, and go another," he complained in October 1945. Two months later, Wallace noted that Truman "does *so* like to agree with whoever is with him at the moment."[57] He felt that Truman and his top advisers were behaving in a bellicose fashion and were moving to force a confrontation with the Soviet Union. By the winter of 1945–46, Wallace was a dissenter, who clearly had the *wrong* attitude in mind. After the resignation of Harold Ickes, he hung on, the last New Dealer in the Cabinet.[58]

Although publicly an unabashed universalist during the war, Wallace had concluded that a spheres-of-influence settlement was inevitable. He also believed that the Soviet position might well be affected by Russian interpretations of American policy, and that even a nation that was not a totalitarian dictatorship might grow uneasy if it found itself ringed by military bases. Wallace was afraid of a new world conflagration and worried about the consequences of what he called, in April 1946, "a spirit of competitive rearmament." While he thought the problems of settling on a peace were almost overwhelming, he also saw a "complete absence of direct conflicts in national interest" between Russia and the United States.[59]

The man, however, suffered three blind spots. He tended to believe that those who took greatest alarm at the Soviet Union were at least fellow-travelers of fascism, and from time to time was even willing to entertain the absurd idea that American military officers were moving toward a coup. Second and more central, Wallace was quicker to put forward reasons why U.S. actions appeared threatening to the Russians than why U.S. leaders might be disturbed by Soviet behavior. This emphasis is clear from a letter he wrote Eisenhower at the end of the war. "I have no fear about our being able to get along with Britain," Wallace said, "but with regard to Russia there is danger of our taking an attitude which will cause trouble in the future." Of course, Wallace was casting himself in the role of critic, trying to influence U.S. policy to avoid an international polarization. But the credibility of his critique was undermined by this approach, and, by 1948, the critic of U.S. foreign policy would sound to many like an apologist for Soviet policy.

Third, Wallace was somewhat Anglophobic and incorrectly believed that the British, whose interests did appear to conflict directly with Russia's, was pushing the United States toward an adversary posture. "The British are very likeable people," he noted after dining with Attlee and Halifax in November 1945, "but it seems to me their whole attitude inevitably leads to causing the other peoples of the world to feel inferior and fearful and therefore willing and anxious to strike out in a violent way." [60]

If Churchill's Iron Curtain speech signaled the "right attitude" in the minds of most American policymakers, then it also brought into clear public view the obvious fact of Wallace's dissent. "We should hold out our [Democratic] party as a place of refuge for the progressives," he told Senator Claude Pepper in March, "but at the same time make clear that the cause of progress is not furthered by them remaining as a minority in a party which can never become progressive." [61] Also, toward the end of March, in what he assumed was an off-the-record interview with a Scandinavian journalist, Wallace suggested "it would be better for the world" if the United States did not establish an air base in Iceland, because the Russians would regard such an installation as a direct threat. His remarks on Iceland, published in distorted form, attracted acrimonious criticism. Joseph Alsop, something of a spokesman for the Riga School in the State Department, told Wallace personally that he was behaving like Chamberlain at Munich in 1938, and warned Wallace that his foreign policy was "diametrically opposed to that of the President and Jimmy Byrnes."

"Joe was on the verge of hysterics and I couldn't help feeling sorry for him," Wallace noted later. "He thinks the whole world is going to be ruined because we don't get sufficiently tough with Russia. I think it is going to be ruined because of our trying to put Russia in an impossible position by ganging up with Britain against her. I am sure that Joe and the hard-boiled elements in the State Department are wrong and Joe is sure that I and the liberals are wrong."[62]

Wallace, however, was also concerned about the domestic consequences of the virulent anticommunism he saw developing and of a large and permanent military establishment that would inevitably follow. Wallace was not an admirer of Stalin's system, but, rather, disagreed with other American leaders over the appropriate strategy for dealing with the Soviet Union. He thought a bellicose America would only ensure a bellicose Russia.[63]

In July, Wallace laid out his formal dissent to Truman in a five-thousand-word letter. Citing rising war fears in the United States, he urged a re-evaluation of American policy on two grounds. First, Soviet intentions were not immutable but, at least in part, were a response to Soviet perceptions of Western policy. Unlike Kennan, he thought the Russians did have some real present-day, as well as historic, reasons for their insecurity. U.S. military expenditures and policies "make it appear either (1) that we are preparing ourselves to win the war which we regard as inevitable or (2) that we are trying to build up a predominance of force to intimidate the rest of mankind." He pointed out the futility of the Baruch Plan; the Russians were being asked to show their two high cards — information about the state of their atomic energy program, and data about raw materials — before getting anything in return. He thought that economic aid and trade "might well help to clear away the fog of political misunderstanding."

As for the second line of criticism, he attacked the new idea of national security. There was "no lasting security in armaments" but only greater insecurity, he said. He expressed concern about the effects on the economy of the 1947 projected budget, in which 80 percent went for war and war-related expenditures. He wanted "a shift in some of our thinking about international matters," though he failed to perceive the precarious security that would be afforded by a nuclear balance of terror. Nevertheless, he argued that " 'security' on the basis of armaments" offered the United States nothing but "security against invasion after all our cities and perhaps 40 million of our city population have been destroyed by atomic weapons."

Wallace could hardly have expected a favorable reception from the White House, for the letter amounted to a clear critique of the recent Truman-Byrnes leadership in international affairs, and a call for a change in the course of American foreign policy. Moreover, it did show the Commerce Secretary's tendency to downplay the disturbing and ominous aspects of Soviet behavior. A few days before Wallace sent his message to the White House, one of his aides had pointed to this weakness in the letter. "It devotes too much space to the means for allaying Soviet distrust while slighting the grounds for American distrust of the Soviets," commented Richard Hippelhauser. "Insufficient space is devoted to the cause of our basic distrust of the Russians. The fear, upon which the war-mongering press and radio commentators have seized, is not only that the Soviet system will succeed in Russia; it is also that we are sincerely afraid that other countries upon the borderline area of Soviet influence will also become totalitarian along the Russian Communist lines and that we in the United States have become the last stronghold of political freedom and free enterprise."

Wallace, in his final draft, did not acknowledge that second and more pertinent source of fear.

Truman, already suspicious of Wallace, measured the letter in terms of personal loyalty and domestic politics. He handed it to Clark Clifford on July 24. "Take this and read it carefully," the President said. "It looks as though Henry is going to pull an 'Ickes.' " *

Clifford took the letter back to his own office where he went over it with George Elsey. Clifford thought it had been prepared with a view to publication. "It looks," he said, "as though Wallace is paving the way for an eventual break — and a wide open break — with Truman on the subject of U.S. policy toward Russia."

Elsey disagreed. "I do *not* believe that the letter in any way means Wallace is thinking of 'taking a walk' . . . It is a serious, sober

* Early in 1946, Interior Secretary Harold Ickes, along with Wallace the last of the New Dealers in the Truman Cabinet, had opposed the President's nomination of Edwin Pauley as Navy Undersecretary. Ickes worried that Pauley, an oil man, would gain control over the Navy's petroleum reserves; he feared another Teapot Dome scandal. Truman, loyal to the man who had helped engineer his 1944 vice-presidential nomination, stood by the appointment. Indeed, he looked on Pauley as a possible first Secretary of Defense in a merged military department. Ickes scathingly denounced Pauley before a Senate committee, then resigned, launching a number of broadsides against Truman, including the charge that the President suffered from a "lack of adherence to the strict truth."

and very earnest plea by an intellectual for a program in which he ardently believes."

Truman wrote a perfunctory note to Wallace acknowledging the letter. "I have been giving this entire subject a great deal of thought," the President said, "and I shall continue to do so." [64] But Truman gave little consideration to the substance of the letter. Time was running out on Wallace's public career. With the polarization proceeding between East and West, the dissent of those trying to slow that process was losing its place.

Wallace planned to give a speech on September 12, 1946, that would express his views on foreign policy. It would be the high point of a Madison Square Garden rally meant to help kick off the 1946 congressional campaign. On September 10, Wallace went over the speech page by page with Truman, and the President gave what seemed to be his hearty approval — and in fact so told reporters. Wallace was puzzled that Truman could see no inconsistency between his speech and the outlook of Byrnes. But, then again, Wallace had already noted, "I suspect there had never been a President who could move in two different directions with less time intervening than Truman." Wallace himself did not doubt the speech would be controversial. "This speech will probably make everyone sore," he said earlier on the day of delivery, "but it is the way I think and perhaps it will help clear the air."

Late on the evening of the preceding day, September 11, a newspaper columnist mentioned the speech over a game of bridge to James Riddleberger, who apparently was the first State Department official to learn that Wallace was planning to give a major foreign policy address. The next day he alerted his colleagues in the Department. Will Clayton and John L. Sullivan, Navy Undersecretary, having found out what was in the Wallace text, tried to reach the President to get him to halt the address. They were unsuccessful. Truman would not intervene.[65]

The Wallace who spoke in Madison Square Garden was the Henry Wallace of 1946, trying, in his bold and balanced address, to find a middle ground, a way out of confrontation — and not yet the Progressive Party candidate of 1948. The middle ground, however, had caved in. As he delivered the speech, Wallace found himself frequently hissed and booed by extreme left-wing partisans in the audience. He criticized repression and the denial of civil liberties in the USSR, as well as "namby-pamby pacifism" in the U.S. At the same time he said that the West should accept the fact that there would be a Soviet sphere in Eastern Europe, and added, "The tougher we get, the tougher the Russians will get." The true point of difficulty was not the adjustment of minor territorial disputes, but rather American-Soviet relations. "The real peace treaty we now need is between the United States and Russia." He blamed what he suggested were excesses in American policy on the influence of Republicans and of Great Britain.[66]

The speech was widely and correctly interpreted as a critique of American policy. Not only was "everyone sore," but many were also most vocal in their outrage. Truman, worried about losing Wallace before the 1946 congressional elections, tried to find a way out of what he described to his mother as "Wallace trouble." The President attempted to backtrack on his public approval of the speech, placate a furious Byrnes and Baruch, and at the same time get Wallace to muffle future comments on foreign affairs.

Then, however, someone, probably in the State Department, leaked to columnist Drew Pearson the long letter Wallace had addressed to Truman in July. The White House thought Wallace was the source.

The situation was now even worse. Forrestal and Patterson were in the position of denying that they were warmongers, and Baruch and Byrnes were threatening to resign.

Pointedly declaring that he himself was not an imperialist, the President met Wallace on September 18 to try to gag him at least until the end of the Paris Peace Conference. Truman told Wallace that Byrnes was giving him hell. On the same frustrating day, Truman wrote his daughter that a President "can't be his own mentor" or "live the Sermon on the Mount," but rather must be a Machiavelli, Louis XI, Caesar, Borgia, Talleyrand, "a liar, double-crosser and an unctious religio, a hero and a whatnot to be successful."

The next day, September 19, H. Freeman Matthews, in Paris with Byrnes, wrote to Robert Murphy: "As of this afternoon, things in general just could not be worse — I refer of course to the Wallace business — and the gloom around the Meurice is far thicker than any London fog. Personally, I have not felt so depressed since the end of the war. To see everything that Mr. Byrnes has been working for with such patience and foresight kicked out from under at one fell swoop is pretty tough. But to have all this happen for no better reason and because some people — mistakenly, I believe — feel they can collect a few more votes from the extreme Left without losing them elsewhere in November is just too tragic, both for the country and the world. The only consolation is the surprising degree of unanimity with which the press of the United States has rallied to the support of Secretary Byrnes and his policies.

"This is a crucial day," Matthews added, "and the atmosphere may possibly clear up one way or another in the next 48 hours."

Byrnes, pushed hard by Vandenberg and the press, his position at the Peace Conference called into question, would have none of a Truman-Wallace compromise that would permit Wallace to speak out again in the future on foreign affairs. If Wallace were not permanently silenced, Byrnes bluntly said, he would resign.

In a teletype conversation with Truman on September 19, Byrnes continued, "Representatives of the other delegations keep our delegation busy asking whether the Administration will permit Wallace to make another speech attacking us. These governments would never permit a member of the Cabinet to do such a thing and they cannot understand how we would permit it unless his views were shared or there was such a serious division of sentiment among the people that the government was afraid to stop . . . You and I spent fifteen months building a bi-partisan policy . . . Wallace destroyed it in a day."

"The foreign policy will stand as it is," Truman responded. "The situation will be made perfectly clear tomorrow."

Byrnes said that Truman's expression of support "makes me feel good."

"Keep on feeling good," the President replied. He added that Byrnes ought to relax and have a drink.

Truman now knew that he could not finesse the problem. He was very angry to find himself in such a position, and Wallace became the unqualified target for his anger. On September 19, he made a diary note about his meeting with Wallace the day before. While not a fair representation of their conversation, it certainly reflected Truman's fury. "I am not sure [Wallace] is as fundamentally sound intellectually as I had thought . . . Wallace is a pacifist 100 percent.

He wants us to disband our armed forces, give Russia our atomic secrets and trust a bunch of adventurers in the Kremlin Politburo. I do not understand a 'dreamer' like that. The German-American Bund under Fritz Kuhn was not half so dangerous. The Reds, phonies and the 'parlor pinks' seem to be banded together and are becoming a national danger. I am afraid they are a sabotage front for Uncle Joe Stalin."

On September 20, Truman sent Wallace a letter, apparently as hotheaded as the diary note, demanding the Commerce Secretary's resignation. Wallace had the courtesy to return the letter to Truman to save the President future embarrassment. Later in the day, in a more amiable manner, Truman made the request over the telephone. Truman announced the resignation to a news conference packed with reporters. There were gasps and low whistles. After the last of the reporters had left the room, Truman sat down in a chair, and, as he did so, turned to his press secretary and said, "Well, the die is cast."

Once the deed was done, and Wallace had left the Administration, Truman relaxed. "There is too much talk about the Russian situation," he wrote on September 21 to John Nance Garner, who had been Roosevelt's first Vice President. "The situation, I think, is cleared up since yesterday and from now on we will have smoother sailing. I am sure that I will."

The anger Truman had felt toward Wallace had turned to puzzlement. "Henry is the most peculiar fellow I ever came into contact with," he wrote to his mother and sister.[67]

Byrnes meanwhile felt vindicated and received the many congratulations that go to a victor.

John Foster Dulles, in reviewing the affair, sketched out the basic Wilsonian impulses — in particular the rejection of spheres of influence — that helped to shape the anticommunist consensus. Dulles thought Wallace's aspirations worthy but "unrealist in application." The July 23 letter "reflects the attitude towards the Soviet Union which we all had when we began negotiations" at the U.N. conference in San Francisco. But, citing his own experience since, Dulles continued, "It is a good initial approach to say that if you pat the dog and he still nips you, then it is necessary to think of another approach. Wallace has been sitting behind the scenes and has not had to go through the experience of having his hand nipped." And, said Dulles, the division of the world into spheres "just will not work and, in my opinion, ought not to work."[68]

The day in September it became known that Wallace's July 23 letter was in the hands of Drew Pearson, White House aide George Elsey was at the State Department, arranging for the printing and binding of the Clifford Memorandum on Soviet-American relations. In his covering letter, Clifford had pointed to the "remarkable agreement" among American officials about the need to reorient policy toward the Russians. Wallace's departure removed the one glaring exception to that agreement.[69]

Even after that, the discussions would continue (as they have ever since) over issues of specific policy implementation. What ceased, however, was the debate over the basic ideological outlook. It was settled. The alternatives suggested by the Yalta axioms were to be ignored for a generation.

George Kennan, hurrying around the country to conferences and military installations in order to dispense the new wisdom, was already becoming something of a celebrity in certain circles. On September 17, he delivered a post-mortem on why the United States had been unable to deny the Soviets their sphere in Eastern Europe. "Sorry," he said in reply to a question after a lecture, "but the fact of the matter is that we do not have power in Eastern Europe really to do anything but talk. You see what I mean. It seems to me this issue is a rather theoretical one. There is no real action we can take there except to state our case." That, of course, was always the weakness of an American strategy that sought to challenge the Soviet sphere *directly*. But now, because of its inability to do anything else, the United States had virtually conceded the sphere, and Kennan's mind was filled with the new threats he saw posed by the very existence of the world revolutionary state.

Two weeks later, on October 1, traveling to New Haven to talk to the Yale Institute of International Studies, he took it upon himself to comment on what he saw as the error in much thinking about the Soviet Union. He defined his subject as "Trust as a Factor in International Relations." He cited Wallace and Anthony Eden as the naïve optimists who thought that signs of trust could "dispell Russian suspicions" and "bring the Russians into collaboration with us." In truth, however, what he was really criticizing were the Yalta axioms and now-defunct Roosevelt approach toward the Soviet Union. "Some of you have been maintaining for years, as I myself have, that the occupants of the Kremlin are strong and ruthless men who cannot be placated or influenced by gestures of appeasement from any quarter and whose challenge demands something more from this country than a few propitiatory offerings fearfully and hastily tossed in the path of the advancing apparition." Such gestures "serve only to strengthen the hands of the most arrogant and impossible elements in Russian psychology and in Russian society, and they lead us on a path to which there is no end short of the capitulation of the U.S. as a great power in the world and as a guardian of its own security.

"Some of you may feel that this places too great stress on the factors of ideology," he continued. "I could not go along with this. I think it would be a great mistake to underrate the importance of ideology in the official Soviet psychology." Kennan called for a long-term policy of "firmness, patience and understanding, designed to keep the Russians confronted with superior strength at every juncture where they might otherwise be inclined to encroach upon the vital interests of a stable and peaceful world." But he warned his audience that the policy must be carried out in an unprovocative manner "not subject to misinterpretation." It was ambiguity such as this that made it George Kennan's fate down through the years to claim that his words were always being misinterpreted.

Other men, however, had neither the time nor Kennan's inclination for nuance. Truman bluntly stated the essence of the new outlook. On the morning of September 10, a few minutes before Henry Wallace walked in to go over the draft of the troublesome speech, the President expressed his own fear that Russia was "going to run hog wild." [70]

Actions of the Soviet Government in the field of Foreign Affairs leave us no alternative other than to assume that the USSR has aggressive intentions. It seems clear that there can be no question of "deals or arrangements" with the USSR. That method was tried once with Hitler and the lessons of that effort are fresh in our minds.

— JOHN HICKERSON, February 1947

X

The End of Diplomacy

EARLY IN THE NEW YEAR, in the course of a speech reviewing U.S. foreign policy in 1946, John Foster Dulles declared, "In 1947 we shall need the ability to say no but we shall need more than that."[1] During 1946, American leaders had come to share in a great apprehension about Soviet intentions. The new doctrine of national security was becoming a common currency of the political process as well. Institutional changes were taking place. Still, while U.S. officials felt the need, they had not yet devised coherent policies to embody their beliefs. James Byrnes was continuing his search for a settlement with the Russians, in an effort to bring the Second World War to a close on mutually acceptable terms.

International politics continued to focus on diplomacy, though the American interest in this process was noticeably diminished at the 21-nation Paris Peace Conference, which went on for almost a month after the Wallace incident. "The most encouraging thing here is to know what a very strong line we are taking," Arthur Bliss Lane, the American ambassador to Poland, wrote on October 14 during a visit to the American delegation in Paris. "This should pay dividends." The Americans played to the noncommunist majority. But Bevin, changing his tactics, withdrew from the public fray. He wanted to work "things from behind the scenes," rather than charge into constant public debate with the Russians. "Both the Russians and the

Americans were too bomb-minded," he said. "Both were afraid of the other. Some Americans said that, since they had the bomb now and the Russians hadn't, they had better have a show-down at once." Bevin had staked out a different, if not altogether clear, position: "I won't have the bomb in the Foreign Office." But he found the Russians no less difficult to work with than in the past. "Molotov was just like a Communist in a local Labour Party," he told Hugh Dalton. "If you treated him badly, he made the most of the grievances and, if you treated him well, he only put his price up and abused you next day." The cumbersome conference was a tiresome affair, sometimes in session from 10:00 A.M. one day until 2:30 P.M. the next day, with breaks for meals, but not for sleep. But it somehow managed to get through all the paperwork involved in the satellite treaties, including 300 amendments. It adjourned on October 15, leaving final agreement for the Council of Foreign Ministers.[2]

In early November the Council of Foreign Ministers reconvened in New York to consider the recommendations from the Paris Peace Conference and to draw up the treaties for the five satellite states. Just prior to the meeting, Elbridge Durbrow, now chargé d'affaires in Moscow, had sent an analysis that again outlined the dangers of conducting diplomacy with the Russians. "Their continuing diplomatic offensive coupled with seemingly contradictory attitude," Durbrow explained, "are designed to confuse and disrupt west, prevent rest of world forming solid front which would oppose consolidation of their present gains and future Soviet expansion." The Russians aimed to prolong negotiations with the West so that they "will tire and lose interest in situation in Soviet periphery." The Soviets were banking, added Durbrow, on an economic crisis in the West.

Durbrow encapsulated the general view held by U.S. policymakers. Those who did not subscribe were subjected to criticism and pressure. State Department officer Donald Heath, for example, complained to James Riddleberger, chief of the Division of Central European Affairs, that the handling of the Russians at the highest level in Germany was "far below the incisiveness, realism, and aggressiveness that has marked Secretary Byrnes' actions in recent months." Robert Murphy "tries to inject a healthy pessimism, but, unless at long last he has just seen the light, General Clay still apparently has some belief in fairies, viz., that by cordial personal relations and an occasional firm stand we can bring the Russians to a sincere cooperation in Germany." Heath added a P.S.: "Don't call me a red baiter for I am not. Just sadder and wiser." [3]

Byrnes himself, in New York, was, if not sadder and wiser, at least more frustrated. He quickly lost patience with the pettiness of the Council proceedings — what he described as the "haggling over minutiae, the meaning of phrases, changing of unimportant language." On November 29, he telephoned Charles Bohlen. "Come on, Chip, we'll go to see Molotov. I have an idea." They went to the Russian's suite at the Ritz Hotel.

"In thinking the whole matter over, I really believe the wisest thing for us all to do is admit failure and to disband this meeting," Byrnes told the startled Soviet foreign minister. The Council was deadlocked, the Secretary added, and it would be better to explain their disagreements to the world.

Molotov began stuttering. "No, no, Mr. Byrnes, don't take hasty actions. Just wait until this afternoon's meeting and you will see developments."

As the two Americans went down in the hotel elevator, Byrnes said, "Well, I hope that works."

It did. Molotov came back almost immediately with specific proposals and concessions. And, on December 6, the Council officially approved the treaties for Italy, Rumania, Bulgaria, Hungary, and Finland.[4]

Byrnes' work was done. The preceding April, after hearing from his doctors that he had a heart condition, Byrnes had filed a resignation letter, to become effective upon completion of the satellite treaties. Later medical consultation indicated that the first tests were wrong. But that letter stayed on file. Certainly the mutual loss of confidence between Byrnes and Truman, as well as policy differences, played some role in the Secretary's plans and the President's easy acceptance. When the satellite treaties were finally finished, Truman took him up on his resignation. Byrnes' last major official act was to place his signature on the five peace treaties in a ceremony held on January 20, 1947, in the old State Department building. It must have been a disappointing moment for Byrnes. He had fallen short of his great hopes. Not only not President, he had also failed to become the Great Peacemaker. The most important and difficult treaty question — Germany — was still unresolved. But Byrnes had deliberately chosen such a strategy, to deal with the easier questions first, and to save for later the more difficult or even impossible task.[5]

These satellite treaties usually rate little more than a footnote in most histories of the Cold War, which is misleading. For their completion marked the outer limits and the end of the effort to make a peace after the Second World War.

Byrnes' decision to pursue the satellite treaties first was, in its own way, a kind of compromise — between those who thought any type of real settlement was impossible, and those who thought the first eighteen months after the war would have been better spent on the central question, Germany. The former group was much the larger, but in the latter was one of the most perceptive, Walter Lippmann. In December 1946, he delivered a eulogy for the efforts of the peacemakers. "Contrary to all precedents in settling wars, they chose to begin their peacemaking with the satellites of their principal enemy. This meant that they would attempt to govern the moon in order to regulate the sun . . . The Big Three chose to begin the settlement of the world war in the eastern half of Europe. This was a gigantic blunder . . . For it narrowed the issue between Russia and the West to the very region where the conflict was sharpest and a settlement the most difficult . . . In this region the Russians were in possession and could act; Mr. Byrnes and Mr. Bevin could only argue and protest. In any other region they had power, influence, and possessions with which to bargain. They had two thirds of Germany, much the best part of Germany. They had Japan . . .

"The one thing they did not have," Lippmann continued, "was ground armies to match the Red Army in the region which the Red Army had just conquered and triumphantly and at a terrible cost of blood and treasure. Yet that was the region where they elected to put to the test their relations with the Soviet Union and the whole great business of a world settlement. Was it not certain that here they must fail, as in fact they have failed, and in the failure to reach a settlement where it was most difficult to reach it, that they must make it infinitely difficult to make any general settlement? Let no one seek to explain away the failure by pointing out how brutal, how stubborn, how faithless, how aggressive the Russians have proved themselves to be. The worse one thinks of the Russians, the greater must be deemed the error of having elected to challenge the Russians first of all on the ground where they were most able to be, and were most certain to be, brutal, stubborn, faithless and aggressive.

"For the effective answer to the Soviet domination of Eastern Europe was to lay the foundations in Western Europe of a general settlement in which the whole of Europe could eventually be included . . .

"My contention is that we have fought the battle of freedom, nobly, perhaps, but that we have not fought it well."

While there were many who were eager to criticize Byrnes, very few would have done so from Lippmann's perspective. But then Lippmann was one of the declining number interested less in the theology of confrontation than in the diplomacy of Great Powers.[5]

With Byrnes' departure, whatever remained of American interest in negotiation and settlement ran out very quickly. Certainly Byrnes himself had stiffened during his often-frustrating one and a half years as Secretary; still he had remained a relentless negotiator, always hoping to find a compromise, a shared interest, a common denominator. He could renounce diplomacy no more easily than he could renounce his own character. That was not true of his successor, the former Army chief of staff, General George C. Marshall.

Little was known of the private Marshall — his sins seemed to run no farther than an endless taste for maple candy and for pulp fiction. The contrast between the old Secretary and the new Secretary could not have been more striking. Marshall was remote and austere; Byrnes, convivial and informal. Byrnes was an independent operator, a fixer. For him bureaucracies existed mainly to be ignored or outwitted. Marshall had no talent for, nor did he take joy in, negotiation, the process of give and take. He was not a compromiser, but rather a commander, interested in duty, order, and sound administration. Just a year before, at the end of 1945, as the chief of staff prepared for retirement, President Truman had phoned him — in the aftermath of General Patrick Hurley's flamboyant resignation — to request that he go to China to patch up the American effort to mediate the civil war. Marshall's first response was no. He had promised his wife to retire and, as he told Ismay, his patience was exhausted. But duty was duty, and he soon accepted the mission.

The frustrations in China certainly did exhaust whatever patience he might have had left. His year-long effort, through all of 1946, to construct a compromise and coalition ended a complete failure. By November 1946, Marshall had concluded that it was a mistake to ever think that a compromise was either possible or desirable. He correctly blamed the Nationalists (whose corruption, inefficiency, and reactionary politics appalled him) as much as the communists for the failure of his mission. He also observed that the Chinese communists operated somewhat independently of Moscow. From time to time while in China, Marshall would meet Russians at social functions, and he kept hearing from them what he once described as "little lectures on the true meaning of democracy." Such, he said, he found impudent.

In early January 1947, he was once again preparing for a departure, this time back to the United States. "It is a tired, angry and frustrated man who is packing up tonight," Foreign Service officer John Melby wrote in his diary. Two days later, Melby added, "It was typical of him that he took off almost unnoticed and that his new job was kept completely secret until he was in the air and beyond reach of supplication." [6]

Marshall carried great prestige with him into the office of Secretary of State. During the war, Roosevelt had even considered, despite the obvious semantic problem, appointing Marshall to a new post of Field Marshal. Marshall also brought with him a good measure of exhaustion. Prestige and exhaustion did not necessarily make for a happy combination. "Marshall is a four-engine bomber going only on one engine," said Dean Acheson later in the year, during the course of one of his morning walks with Felix Frankfurter. "I don't know what is the matter with him. He doesn't seem to bring his full force into action." Acheson felt that Truman held Marshall in such high regard that the President would not allow himself to voice to Marshall anything that might sound like criticism.[7]

The new Secretary was hardly well acquainted with the range of foreign issues, and needed to prepare himself quickly for the upcoming Moscow Council of Foreign Ministers. So top State Department officials filed in for an hour or so a day, beginning in late January 1947, going over the problem areas with him. Of special interest was the discussion on the Soviet Union, based upon a briefing paper infused with the Riga axioms and summarizing the State Department bureaucracy's own explanation of why the peace was failing.

The paper began by pointing out that the major problems confronting U.S. policy since the war had centered on the Soviet Union. The communists proclaimed the inevitability of a collision between capitalism and their form of socialism, while the United States operated on a different premise — "toward drawing the Soviets into participation on as broad a scale as possible in the political, economic and cultural life of the world with a view to breaking down by degrees the deeply rooted Russian distrust of the outside world and demonstrating to the Soviet leaders both the advantages of international cooperation and the fallacy of their theory of the inevitability of conflict." The Soviets had shown little interest in this approach, the paper continued, instead establishing control over Eastern Europe as a prelude to further expansion. In other words, the briefing document presented as clear proof of aggressive intentions what could also have been indicative of more limited and traditional Russian aims.

Here followed some self-criticism: "It was at this point that American policy, which had been benevolently disposed toward immediate Soviet aims in the early post-war period and had not clearly recognized the nature of long-range Soviet objectives, began to harden."

The paper's authors claimed that American firmness, plus internal Soviet problems, had led to a relaxation of Russian pressure beyond its own borders. Picking up, however, on the analysis Durbrow made in the preceding autumn, the authors advised against seeing any genuine signs of conciliation in such behavior. There was no possibility that contradictory moves indicated contrary pressures or even uncertainty in Moscow: "Lenin's slogan, 'One step back, two steps forward' is still gospel for the men of the Kremlin.* With the pressure off, the adversary is expected to lower his guard and be an easy target for the next blow. It is imperative that we not be misled by this tactic — one to which American public opinion has repeatedly shown itself to be vulnerable."

The paper called for two responses. The first was to formulate U.S. policy toward the Soviet Union "on a global, not a piecemeal basis." Because the United States was thought to be facing a monolithic, implacable opponent in international communism, discussion and agreement on individual issues were not really important, indeed even diversionary. The second requisite response was a commitment to a program of visible military strength. "We cannot effectively counter Soviet expansionist tendencies unless we maintain our armed forces at a level where they will command respect."

American leaders would soon become convinced that the Soviet

* Actually, the title of Lenin's 1904 pamphlet was "One Step Forward, Two Steps Back." It was a polemical attack on rivals in the Russian revolutionary movement.

commitment to a crusade for world communism was as immutable and as basic as the flow of a great and undammed river.[8]

The need to reassert American military power had become a litany in policy councils.[9] The great stumbling block continued to be the divisive struggle over the organization of the military establishment. In April 1946, Truman informed aides, "I am very much interested in Unification of the Armed Forces because I think it will help the budget to a large extent; it will make for efficiency in a Military Policy and it will put us in a position where we can immediately meet any emergency which may arise." He added that he had had "long sessions" with senior military officers, "and I think we are nearing a complete understanding of what is wanted."

The President was much too optimistic. Through most of 1946, compromise on unification appeared beyond reach. "The single department is not aimed at the Navy," Patterson wearily said in April. "Russia, France and China have integrated their three services into a single department, and even old conservative Britain says that something of the kind seems to be necessary. They all seem to think that this integration is the prime lesson of the war, so far as organization is concerned. I agree with them." So did most Army and Air Force officials. But the Navy would not agree. "Forrestal just will not face up to the issue," Patterson complained in May 1946.

Forrestal, of course, continued to see Soviet threats everywhere, and he did everything he could to make certain that others saw the same dangers. Just to be safe, he sent Byrnes a copy of an article entitled "Spiritual Revival Is Held Vital to Stem Communism." Forrestal and the Navy also remained firmly opposed to unification. Departmental status for the Air Force, said Admiral Arthur Radford, was nothing more than "a first step in much larger and more ambitious plans for the Air Force to take over the whole business of national defense."

Then, on January 3, 1947, Robert Patterson shared a car with Forrestal after a Cabinet meeting. The tone had changed. The two men agreed on the damage that the unification battle was doing both to national defense and to military morale. Patterson was willing to compromise. Here was the beginning of the end of the unification struggle. On January 16, their compromise was made public. In essence, the Army accepted the plan championed by Forrestal in the Eberstadt Report — a single Secretary of Defense with coordinating powers, a National Security Council and a smaller War Council, a National Security Resources Board, a Central Intelligence Agency, and a command structure headed by the Joint Chiefs of Staff. "The ideal (from my point of view) was unattainable," Patterson explained shortly thereafter. "A compromise solution, raising air to a position of parity with the ground forces and sea forces and creating a single responsible head of the entire establishment, would go far toward solving our present difficulties and would be a distinct step forward." [10]

The struggle, however, had not interfered with the increasing emphasis placed on military power as a major "solution" to the Russian problem. And the solution came to center upon the atomic bomb. The Bikini tests in July 1946 at first had been disappointing; they had seemed to show that the bomb, while a weapon of mass and unprecedented destructive power, nevertheless did have finite limits. Subsequent reports erased some of the disappointment. By August 1, Secretary of War Patterson, having received the report from the Joint Chiefs of Staff's evaluation board, had become more enthusiastic. "The conclusions as to the effect of the atomic bomb are clearly revolutionary and affect things up and down the line," he told his colleagues.[11]

American leaders no longer hoped that the bomb would in some vague way make the Russians more tractable. Instead, they thought of it, more narrowly, as a counterbalance to the specter of Soviet force. As Eisenhower had informed Baruch in June 1946: "The existence of the atomic bomb in our hands is a deterrent, in fact, to aggression in the world." General Carl Spaatz elaborated: "Possible causes of war appear on every hand and no effective control has yet been devised. The conventional military strength of the United States has been reduced drastically by the hysterical pace of demobilization. The atomic bomb because of its decisive nature is now an essential part of our military strength. Our monopoly of the bomb, even though it is transitory, may well prove to be a critical factor in our efforts to achieve first a stabilized condition and eventually a lasting peace. Any step in the near future to prohibit atomic explosives would have a grave and adverse military effect on the United States." [12]

Here, like the troops and airplanes that Roosevelt wished he had in 1938, was a tool with which to "overawe" potential adversaries. The faith in the lasting power of the American monopoly gained wider acceptance. But officials also worried about the atomic inventory. Patterson and Groves successfully opposed a third test at Bikini because they did not want to use up another of the limited number of weapons. At about this time new effort went into speeding up production; according to scientist James Conant, speaking in October 1946, the United States was manufacturing five bombs a year.[13]

On December 31, Baruch successfully forced a showdown in the U.N. Security Council on his proposals for the control of atomic energy. The Baruch Plan passed by a vote of 10 to 2. Russia and Poland cast the opposing votes — which meant, of course, that the Baruch Plan was not really approved at all. And so, on the last day of 1946, any genuine effort to head off a nuclear arms race came to an end. In the same month, as already noted, the satellite treaties were completed. With that, the effort to make a peace also ran out.

In the summer of 1946, Robert Patterson was not yet sure whether American security planning should depend mainly on the atomic bomb and air power. But by the end of the year, he was coming around to the view that it would, in the context of what was being called the "striking force."

"It is generally understood today," Vannevar Bush wrote Patterson on January 3, 1947, "that we cannot prepare for defense only and be secure against attack, that we must be ready for the instant counterattack in overwhelming force, if some aggressor is not at some time to descend upon us. Certainly when it comes to that sort of striking force it should be in being, furnished with the latest possible weapons, and trained to the minute, and this means atomic bombs and airplanes to carry them, and it also means the provision for seizing bases where necessary, communications, and all the rest." This orientation was reflected in the overall military budget, where 58 percent was allocated to the Air Force.

In the course of a War Council meeting on January 15, Patterson made clear that he had accepted this strategic vision. Of all the aspects of defense, he began, "the budget defense is the critical War Department problem at the present time." Kenneth Royall, the Undersecretary of War, argued that not enough of the Army's budget was earmarked for the Army's traditional needs.

Patterson dismissed the concern. "A striking force — the Air Force — and the occupational problems are irrefutable arguments and every item of the budget can be defended by using them," he insisted. "The Navy can't shoot at this." *

Two months later, Patterson left no doubt of the reliance upon the bomb when he wrote Eisenhower that the War Department was "already following a policy that assumes the unrestricted employment of atomic energy as a weapon." [14]

The military was taking to heart Vannevar Bush's dictum: "The whole practice of warfare was being revised by the laboratories." As a memorandum Forrestal passed to Truman declared: "We are on the threshold of a new era of applied science." This meant an increasing attention to research and development, as well as a conscious effort to tie sectors of industry and the university community to the armed forces. By the spring of 1946, Secretary of War Patterson had determined that R&D had to be reorganized and given greater prestige. "The importance of this work in the future cannot be doubted," he explained. The Navy and Army shortly thereafter agreed to establish a Joint Research and Development Board that would coordinate and guide the development process. The new emphasis took other forms. The Office of Naval Research, established in 1945, assumed responsibility for funding long-term basic research; and the Navy's Bureau of Aeronautics spent 50 percent more in fiscal 1946 than in 1944. The Army's 1946 research program amounted to $281.5 million, compared to $277.5 million in 1944, when the nation was still at war. In 1947, military R&D had risen to about $500 million.

So rapid was this development that, at a War Council meeting in December 1946, Undersecretary Kenneth Royall asked whether too much money and effort was going to R&D. Eisenhower replied that he himself had carefully gone over the Army's project list, and only two items looked doubtful — a 150-ton floating bridge and a 100-ton tank.

Still not satisfied, Royall suggested that military R&D programs would destroy industry's incentive to undertake its own research.

"Research was getting more and more difficult," replied Stuart Symington, Assistant Secretary for Air. "Much of it was beyond the

* The budgetary attractiveness of the atomic striking force had been suggested the year before by some calculations done by William Shockley of Bell Telephone Laboratories "indicating that atomic bombing was ten to 100 times less expensive" than conventional strategic bombing, "which means that the loss to the enemy will be 40 to 600 times greater than the cost of inflicting the loss."

capacity of individual business to undertake. Therefore, we have to have the government itself sponsor or undertake much of the development, placing research in various institutions."

Technological development, of course, had come to occupy a larger part of the arsenal, and attention to it was a sensible response. At the same time, however, this trend helped lay the foundation for the development of a major political constituency — composed of the armed forces, and sectors of industry and the academy — all with a vested interest in the development of new weapons. Planned obsolescence, in other words, became a large factor in strategic thinking; and R&D was quickly becoming a method of rivalry for position and budgets among the services.[15]

The aircraft industry was developing a significant peacetime dependence upon the military budget. Conversion to civilian production was proving far less extensive than had been hoped, and thus industry leaders came to realize that even in peacetime their firms would remain in business primarily on the basis of military orders. In February 1947, the dollar value of all industry shipments totaled $52 million — of which the military accounted for $42 million. This dependence, according to the industry journal *Aviation News,* constituted "both the strength and weakness of the industry." Half a year later, the magazine more insistently pointed to the "urgent necessity for more and larger Army and Navy production contracts to keep alive aircraft companies with the greatest war production potential."[16]

Senior government officials shared this concern. In June 1947, Patterson urgently asked Truman to restore funds for two planes — a long-range photo reconnaissance aircraft and an all-weather fighter — that had been dropped "because of considerations of economy."

"These two planes will meet a strategical requirement of the Air Force," said Patterson, "and at the same time they will provide additional orders to the aircraft industry essential for maintaining a minimum production potential."

"The Budget Director was called," Truman replied to Patterson, "and directed to carry out the suggestions of the Secretary of War."

Obviously, it would have been unwise for U.S. leaders to allow this high technology industry, which after all produced the key element in the American arsenal, to disintegrate. On the other hand, the dependence created a deep and permanent stake in a large and growing defense budget and thus in an arms race, which in turn meant that alarms were sounded for threats that did not exist. The superiority of the American air forces over the Soviet in the late 1940s was very considerable. Yet an editorial in *Aviation News* in April 1947 would have led any reader to think that the Soviets were far in the lead. It announced that there was "an operational air force" in the Soviet Union "more than twice that of the U.S. . . . While the U.S. has let her postwar heavy aircraft output go to pot, or 2 percent of our war rate . . . the Russians have doubled their wartime production capacity . . . Congress, wake up!" [17]

Another aspect of the emerging national security state was the development of military assistance programs — to Turkey, Iran, and then to Latin America. Of special note was the October 1946 proposal by the Joint Chiefs to institute a program of military assistance to Iran. The stated reasons were to establish a presence, to create "a feeling of good will toward the United States," to help the central government to maintain internal order, and to encourage it to wipe out the last vestiges of Azerbaijanian separatism. The real reasons, of course, were Iranian oil, protection of approaches to Saudi Arabian oil, and provision for bases and staging areas near the Soviet Union. "As to counterdefensive operations," explained one document, "the proximity of important Soviet industries makes the importance of holding the Eastern Mediterranean–Middle Eastern area obvious. This is one of the few favorable areas for counteroffensive action." [18] This last was exactly what Stalin's preclusive sphere in Eastern Europe was intended to prevent (and now did so) elsewhere on the Russian rim.

Here we encounter another twist to the game of nations, a further dimension to Arnold Wolfers' contention that nations live dangerously. The inclusion of Iran and Turkey into what was now defined as American national security and the resultant policy — in this instance, military assistance — were intended to reduce danger. These steps were based on the assumption that Soviet intentions were fixed and unswerving. For instance, in autumn 1946, the Joint Staff Planners had circulated a long paper on probable developments in world politics up to 1956. The Soviet Union, they announced, posed a threat to the fundamental interests of the West: "The basic objective of the USSR appears to be a limitless expansion of Soviet Communism accompanied by a considerable territorial expansion of Russian imperialism. She will pursue this policy with persistence and flexibility, recognizing no neutral ground, and hence no neutrals, and using any means which fit her purpose." However, the extension of American power around the Soviet rim could only increase the Soviet sense of danger, leading the Russians to respond in such a way as to increase, rather than decrease, the very range of dangers the United States had sought to forestall.[19]

The common conclusion among American leaders was reinforced by another assessment, also mistaken, about the size and strength of the Red Army. "Certainly we should not underrate Soviet military power but it is equally important not to overrate it, and I believe there has been a tendency to do so," General John R. Deane, former chief of the American military mission in Moscow, warned in October 1946. The estimates could run wild. Senator Warren Austin (soon to be the U.S. ambassador to the U.N.), in April 1946, declared that the Soviet leaders were maintaining an army of ten million men, and training new recruits at the rate of one and a half million a year. But even Deane's own calculations were still off. He, along with other informed observers, both inside and outside the U.S. military, assumed that the size of the Red Army would stabilize at somewhere between 3.5 and 4 to 4.5 million men, and that the total Russian military establishment would number 4.5 to 5.3 million men.[20]

In fact, in May 1945, the Red Army had reached its maximum size of 11,365,000. On June 23, 1945, demobilization began, and proceeded rapidly. By early 1948, the Red Army (including, apparently, the air force) would be down to 2,874,000 men. Bearing in mind that a significant part of the Russian forces were, like the American Army, engaged in occupation and police functions in conquered territory, the number does not seem so large. The Russian figure of early 1948 can be roughly compared to the ceilings for the American military for July 1, 1947 — 1,070,000 in the Army; 558,000 in the Navy; 108,000 in the Marines. The British armed services contained well over a million men. In addition, the United States held sole claim both to the atomic bomb and to an effective striking force in its strategic bombing units. One can understand, then, why the Soviets might well have seen a vocal commitment to a reassertion of American military power as puzzling or disturbing or both.

The Americans had overawed themselves. Nevertheless, they believed that they had to respond to the specter of Russian strength.[21]

Of course, there was a third reason. The services were battling against each other for shares of the budget, and threats were required to defend their claims. Yet, even if there had been a thoroughgoing unification, and not that which resulted from the Patterson-Forrestal compromise, one might still suppose that military officers would have discovered Soviet threats to justify programs to develop and produce weapons they would need in years ahead, or believed they would need in years ahead — or thought would be nice to have. Bureaucracies often work that way.

So alarmed by the exaggeration was Hanson Baldwin, the distinguished military affairs correspondent of the *New York Times*, that he felt the need to deliver a semiprivate warning to the officers corps in the July 1947 issue of *Armed Force* magazine. "The sad fate of the shepherd who cried 'Wolf, Wolf!' when there was no wolf, and whose cries went unheeded when there was a wolf, carries a moral of considerable significance to the armed forces in the summer of 1947," Baldwin wrote. Too many military men and too many of their civilian spokesmen, he continued, "have been belittling the military strength of the United States. The warnings have assumed a shrill vehemence out of all accord with the facts and are resulting in 'selling the United States short' in the forum of international opinion . . . We are still potentially the strongest military power on earth, and actually we have tremendous elements of military superiority, as well as some definite weaknesses."

But, too concerned about American weakness, or at least too eager to stress it, U.S. policymakers thus moved to assert American power by again expanding the American arsenal.[22]

With this emphasis upon military power, with its implication of fundamental confrontation, the world set of American policymakers was virtually in place. Diplomacy with the Soviet Union had no role in their vision of international politics. "Actions of the Soviet Government in the field of Foreign Affairs leave us no alternative other than to assume that the USSR has aggressive intentions," wrote John Hickerson, number two in the Office of European Affairs, in mid-February 1947. "It seems clear that there can be no question of 'deals or arrangements' with the USSR. That method was tried once with Hitler and the lessons of that effort are fresh in our minds. One cannot appease a powerful country intent on aggression. If the lessons we learned from dealing with Hitler mean anything, concessions to the Soviet Union would simply whet their appetite for more." Hickerson went on to point out accurately that the American people were committed to the Wilsonian premises of the United Nations. They would revolt against Big Power politics, of the type Roosevelt covertly practiced with Stalin during the war and which Byrnes unsuccessfully tried to follow in the spotlight of postwar peacemaking. The alternative to diplomacy was permanent preparedness. The Russians could not be stayed by political deals, said Hickerson, only by a "vigilant determination on the part of peoples and governments of the U.S.A. and the U.K. to resist Soviet aggression, by force of arms if necessary." [23]

A few days after Hickerson wrote his memorandum, the United States was suddenly confronted by a grave crisis that was also an opportunity, and American leaders speedily began to find their way to the requisite policies — the "right" attitude in mind at last becoming the right policy in action.

PART THREE

The Great Divide

> I think it is a mistake to believe that you can, at any time, sit down with the Russians and solve questions. I do not think that is the way that our problems are going to be worked out with the Russians.
>
> — DEAN ACHESON, April 1, 1947

XI

The All-Out Speech

IN MID-FEBRUARY 1947, Harry Truman said with a laugh that he hadn't faced a crisis for four weeks, and he couldn't get used to it.

Within a few days, Truman was face to face with one of the most dramatic crises of his entire career. The response to it, the Truman Doctrine, publicly proclaimed on March 12, marked a major turning point in America's postwar foreign policy. With it, policy began to catch up with ideology.[1]

By the end of 1946, as we have already seen, the debate in policy councils about how to characterize the Soviet Union's postwar aims had come to a clear conclusion: these aims were thought to be aggressive, expansionist, devious, and unlimited. In January 1947, the Central Intelligence Group reported eight examples of seemingly moderate and conciliatory Soviet behavior — from concessions on Trieste and substantial reductions in occupation forces in Eastern Europe, to a relaxation of its position on the veto in the United Nations and an agreement to begin drafting peace treaties for Austria and Germany.

All of these developments, however, said the CIG, simply underlined the Kremlin's ability to alternate between its two tactics of "international collaboration and unilateral aggression." Nothing of significance was to be read into the apparent signs of moderation: "New tactics of compromise and conciliation have been adopted merely as a matter of expediency." The CIG emphasized that "the Kremlin has not abandoned any of its long-run objectives."[2] In other words, any signs of Soviet concessions or willingness to compromise were suspect and to be rejected.

By this point, policymakers were also coming to realize that the passage through what had casually been called the postwar economic "transition" would not be easy, that the wounds of war ran far deeper than optimistic planners had assumed. American leaders began, with the Truman Doctrine, to devise policies deemed appropriate to the world as they now understood it — policies based upon containment, intervention, military buildup, and economic reconstruction. They thought they were taking defensive actions, but the effect would be otherwise — a great expansion of America's political, economic, and military role in the world. Such steps reversed the trend toward retrenchment, which had begun in August 1945, and instead pointed the United States toward a new confrontation not only with Moscow-directed communists, but also with other leftists, nationalists, and various kinds of progressives, some of whom, had they operated at home rather than abroad, might have fit comfortably into Truman's Fair Deal. The change happened quickly, facilitated by a pent-up demand for action that finally found expression in the bureaucracy.

On becoming Secretary of State, George Marshall established a new orderliness and clearer lines of authority within the State Department. Marshall's own appointment also brought to the fore Dean Acheson, an impressive, elegant presence and a most persuasive advocate. Acheson carried to his practice of international relations what one historian has called an "extraordinarily articulate" ideology of foreign affairs. For nothing was he so nostalgic as for the Pax Britannica of the nineteenth century, with its blessings of peace, prosperity, and good order. He saw himself laboring to reconstruct a new hegemonic system, a Pax Anglo-Americana, but really a Pax Americana. What mattered in such a system was power, not negotiations.[3]

The son of the Episcopal bishop for Connecticut, Acheson spent his childhood in the comfortable and secure turn-of-the-century world of Middletown, Connecticut. Through life he clung to what he saw as the values, manners, and outlook of his upper-middle-class culture, which linked England to the eastern United States and Canada in the late Victorian and Edwardian eras. In the summer of

1911, in the months between Groton and Yale, while he was working on a railway construction crew in Canada, he first began to cultivate a bushy mustache. It was turned up at the edges, as though it might have belonged to a mid-nineteenth century British colonial military officer. It would become his anachronistic trademark in mid-twentieth century America. At Yale he was an easy member of society and a good athlete; his rowing coach as a freshman was Averell Harriman, who was two years ahead of him. At Harvard Law School, he was a protégé of Felix Frankfurter. In 1919, he went to Washington, D.C., to clerk for Supreme Court Justice Louis Brandeis.

"He isn't more than wistfully moved by the possibility of applying intelligence to life on a large scale because he knows that there isn't much intelligence to apply," Acheson wrote at the time of Brandeis. "I don't think the Justice puts the slightest faith in mass salvation through universal Plumb Plans."[4] Acheson might as well have been describing his own attitudes in later life, though, of course, he always retained faith in his own intelligence.

In the years between the two world wars, Acheson established himself as a prominent and powerful Washington attorney, his career interrupted only by a brief and unhappy stint as Undersecretary of the Treasury in the first Roosevelt Administration. The outbreak of war in Europe brought him onto the public scene as a leading interventionist, arguing that Britain stood as the first line of defense for American civilization.

In two speeches, made before the U.S. entry into World War II, Acheson outlined views on foreign policy that he would reassert throughout the rest of his career, save that Soviet Russia would be substituted for Nazi Germany. The collapse of the Pax Britannica, he argued in November 1939, had given rise to the "appearance of the totalitarian military state." To respond, he said, the United States had to move swiftly — toward a reconstruction of the world economy and greater military preparedness. "With a nation, as with a boxer, one of the greatest assurances of safety is to add reach to power." In June 1940, he added: "We are faced with elemental, immoral and ruthless power. In dealing with it, you can be wrong only once. Remember, I beseech you, that the judgment of nature upon error is death." The United States had to organize itself for war. To doubt, to debate too long, to question — all of this was to give aid and advantage to the enemy.[5]

During World War II, Acheson joined the State Department as

Assistant Secretary of State for Economic Affairs. In late 1944, when Edward Stettinius (dubbed "Snow White" by the press) became Secretary, Acheson (known as one of the Secretary's "seven dwarfs") was shifted to congressional relations. Acheson had some difficulty in the job, for he had a hard time keeping his wit, barbed tongue, and considerable self-confidence in check. As Dean Rusk, one of Acheson's later assistants, remembered, "When you go up to Congress, you should have a little hay behind your ears. Acheson wouldn't do that." [6]

Byrnes succeeded Stettinius; and Acheson, as he later put it, "signed on as mate of the good ship 'Jimmy Byrnes' " — as Undersecretary. With his discipline and administrative abilities and with his capacity for hard work, Acheson maintained the continuity and organization of the Department while Byrnes toured abroad (350 out of 562 days as Secretary). In effect, Acheson was the liaison between Byrnes and the small circle of advisers around Byrnes, on the one side, and the rest of the Department, on the other. Acheson was not particularly happy on this "voyage." He developed a distaste both for Byrnes' style and for the Secretary's pursuit of negotiations with the USSR. Acheson came to regard the Council of Foreign Ministers rather as a waste of time. He did develop a warm relationship with Truman, facilitated by his curiously patronizing loyalty to the President. Truman placed high value on personal loyalty as well as on respect for the presidency, and Acheson exhibited both. Members of Roosevelt's Cabinet had customarily met FDR's train when he returned to Washington after an election and then escorted him back to the White House. Remembering this, Acheson — the morning after the disastrous November 1946 elections, when the Democrats lost control of the Congress for the first time in sixteen years — went down to meet Truman's train at the station. He found himself all alone on the platform, save for the stationmaster and a couple of reporters. Truman asked Acheson to come back to the White House to help draft a statement on the election, and he never forgot Acheson's show of respect.[7]

Immediately after the war, Acheson had some hope of finding accords with the Russians. "Over-all disagreements with the Soviet Union seem to be increasing," he observed in September 1945, in supporting Stimson's plan for making a direct approach to the Russians on atomic energy. "Yet I cannot see why the basic interests of the two nations should conflict." He lost any such optimism over the next several months. "We have got to understand that all our lives the danger, the uncertainty, the need for alertness, for effort, for discipline will be upon us," he said in June 1946. "This is new to us. It will be hard for us." The following year, he criticized the Byrnes interlude as Secretary: "We kept the idealism and destroyed the power."[8]

Marshall's appointment certainly helped strengthen Acheson's own position. "Dean is full 'Deputy Chief of Staff' and most things now channel through him," wrote John Hickerson of the Office of European Affairs in February 1947. "So far it has all gone smoothly." At last Acheson would be able to do what he believed needed doing — to translate thought into action.[9]

By winter 1947, Acheson and other policymakers were no longer trying to find ways to roll back the Soviet sphere, but rather to prevent that sphere from expanding. They felt that economic disarray and devastation were set against them. Attention centered on the Near East. Turkey was suffering from the strain of keeping its armed forces mobilized. Even more worrying, Greece was wracked by civil war and economic collapse.[10]

Alarming reports had been coming in from Lincoln MacVeagh, the American ambassador in Athens. In late 1946 and early 1947, MacVeagh was joined by two U.S. special representatives with impeccable New Deal credentials. One was the newspaper editor Mark Ethridge, who had visited the Balkans for Byrnes in 1945 and was now a member of a United Nations commission investigating border violations. The other was Paul Porter, a lawyer, head of an economic survey mission. From these three men there now flowed a stream of despairing reports. By mid-February 1947, they concurred that there was an emergency. The Greek government was perilously near the breaking point. Its position was undermined by a resurgence in leftist guerrilla activities and its popular support was eroded by corruption, inefficiency, and economic chaos. According to the three American observers, Russia bore significant responsibility and would be the major beneficiary of the situation: "Soviets feel that Greece is ripe plum to fall into their hands in a few weeks," warned Ethridge. Drawing upon the Munich analogy, he presented the domino theory:

"If Greece falls to communism the whole Near East and part of North Africa as well is certain to pass under Soviet influence." [11]

This type of analysis — channeled through Loy Henderson, chief of the Division of Near Eastern Affairs — found a receptive hearing throughout the State Department. Early in February, economic officers in State tried to make up a list of six potential economic crises. "We got eight," explained one official in March. "We couldn't cut it down to six. Greece was the first on the list. Everybody named it first." Using a memorandum prepared by Loy Henderson (dated February 20), Dean Acheson warned Marshall that "a totalitarian regime of the extreme left will come to power" in Greece unless the United States began an immediate program of expanded military and economic assistance.[12] But such an expanded program might have taken months to develop had the British not precipitated swift action the very next day.

For many months the Americans had known of a debate between the British Treasury and Foreign Office regarding major cutbacks in military expenditures abroad, especially in Greece. "Nor, even if we *had* the money, am I satisfied that we *ought* to spend it this way," Chancellor of the Exchequer Hugh Dalton wrote to the Prime Minister in November 1946. "I am very doubtful indeed about this policy of propping up, even with American aid, weak states in the Eastern Mediterranean against Russia. I am sure that we should run into a tremendous political storm if we ever avowed such a policy in public." Two months later, Dalton warned that the Labour Government faced a first-class economic and political disaster at home. "We are, I am afraid, drifting in a state of semi-animation, towards the rapids." Aided by unforgettably bad weather and a fuel crisis, Dalton finally carried the day against the Foreign Office and persuaded his colleagues to "put an end to our endless dribble of British taxpayers money to the Greeks" — and to present the matter in Washington in such a manner as to incite the Americans to assume that responsibility.[13]

But the British message of February 21, announcing that London's aid program to Greece would terminate at the end of March, succeeded in galvanizing American officials even beyond any Englishman's expectation. "The Americans took fright lest Russia should overrun the whole of the Balkans and the Eastern Mediterranean," Dalton noted in March. "The Treasury officials told me afterwards that they never thought that the effect would be so quick and so volcanic."

But the Americans were primed for crisis. When Loy Henderson brought word of the British decision to Dean Acheson, the Undersecretary declared, "We're right up against it now." [14] Iran and Turkey in 1946 had already provided the dress rehearsals for this, the first real Cold War crisis. Participants were struck by the unanimity of opinion within the U.S. government about the urgency of the matter, its global implications, the necessity for forceful response, and the sense of standing at an historic turning point. In Loy Henderson's Office of Near Eastern Affairs, the mood was one of elation.[15] No one doubted that anything less than American security and the nation's survival were at stake. "From a military point of view," said War Secretary Robert Patterson, "the independence of Greece and Turkey were of vital importance to the US strategic position." Navy Secretary Forrestal put the dangers of a leftist victory in Greece more pithily — "You have the world cut in half." A few days later Forrestal told the President that the civil war in Greece "was simply the manifestation of what had been in the process of development for the last four years." He added, "If we were going to have a chance of winning, we should have to recognize it as a fundamental struggle between our kind of society and the Russians' and that the Russians would not respond to anything except power." [16]

When congressional leaders met President Truman and other senior Administration officials on February 27, Marshall sketched a Cold War stretching far out into the future. "It is not alarmist," he stated, "to say that we are faced with the first crisis of a series which might extend Soviet domination to Europe, the Middle East and Asia."

And yet, even General Marshall was too sober for Acheson. "My distinguished chief," Acheson later wrote, "most unusually and unhappily, flubbed his opening statement. In desperation I whispered to him a request to speak. This was my crisis. For a week I had nurtured it."

Acheson now took the floor. He dramatically declared that "a highly possible Soviet breakthrough [in the Near East] might open three continents to Soviet penetration. Like apples in a barrel infected by the corruption of one rotten one, the corruption of Greece would infect Iran and all to the East . . . Africa . . . Italy and France.

. . . Not since Rome and Carthage had there been such a polarization of power on this earth."

Acheson was at his most persuasive. The congressmen were convinced. Vandenberg urged the President to make his public case no less dramatic. On March 7, Truman informed his Cabinet that he "had no choice but to go forward." On March 11, Acheson was able to cable the American embassy in Athens that "highest level decision, *provided necessary Congressional action taken,* is to abandon stopgap measures and embark on program of substantial aid to maintain Greek independence which may require several years. *This of course represents major decision in US policy.*" [17]

The caveat pointed to what was regarded as the major stumbling block — the need to find a way to communicate the Executive's urgency to a budget-conscious Republican Congress and an apathetic public. Assistant Secretary of State John Hilldring had said in December 1946 that the Department's greatest fear was "the reluctance of our people to remain on the international scene" and their apparent unwillingness to make "political and financial and personal sacrifices." On February 24, 1947, John Hickerson urged that the new program be presented to Congress "in such a fashion as to electrify the *American people.*" [18]

Insofar as there was debate within the Executive, it was neither on the facts of the matter nor on the appropriateness of the response, but only on the tone of the speech. George Kennan, it appears, had some trouble accepting the conventional wisdom of the moment. His own anticommunism was of a far more sophisticated variety, and he found the language of what was to become known as the Truman Doctrine speech too universal in its claims, too evangelical. George Marshall and Charles Bohlen, en route to Moscow for a Council of Foreign Ministers meeting, also wired back that there was "a little too much flamboyant anti-Communism in the speech," but it was explained to them in reply that the Senate would not go along "without the emphasis on the Communist danger."

White House aide George Elsey doubted that this was the moment for what he called the "All-out speech." There had been, he said, "insufficient time to prepare what would be the most significant speech" of the Truman Administration. "There has been no overt action in the immediate past by the U.S.S.R. which serves as an adequate pretext." The situation in Greece was "relatively abstract" and the American public was not ready. He also worried that delivery of the All-out speech as the Foreign Ministers meeting opened in Moscow would "destroy the Conference which gives promise of producing an acceptable Treaty of Peace for Austria, if not for Germany." He argued, instead, for a speech limited in scope, focusing on American responsibility for general European reconstruction.[19]

But on March 12, before a joint session of Congress, Truman delivered the All-out speech, with its appeal for $300 million for Greece and $100 million for Turkey. Truman drew the picture starkly — that the existence of the Greek nation was threatened by several thousand communist guerrillas, that this clash was only part of a global struggle "between alternative ways of life," that the "fall" of Greece would lead to tumbling dominoes right across the map. "It must be the policy of the United States," the President declared, "to support free peoples who are resisting attempted subjugation by armed minorities or by outside pressure." [20]

Truman's speech did express the anticommunist consensus that had emerged within the Executive branch; its language also accurately reflected the lines of discussion inside the Administration during the preceding month. In other words, the Doctrine was not a cynical maneuver, as some writers have since argued. But it was deliberately written as a "sales job." The British abdication of responsibility in Greece had provided the Americans with an opportunity to announce and act on what were now strongly held beliefs, and the All-out speech represented a deliberate effort to create a public consensus for the private beliefs within the Administration.[21] The public's own attitudes were still confused and inchoate, as a State Department report found in February: 60 percent of the people were generally critical of the Soviet Union, and only 20 percent, conciliatory. On the other hand, more than 70 percent opposed a "get tough with Russia" policy.

The Administration now wanted support for toughness. This marked a significant change. Two years earlier, in June 1945, at a time when Harry Hopkins was privately patching up relations with the Soviet Union, Arthur Bliss Lane, then ambassador-designate to Poland, had unhappily observed that "there is no intention to give publicity at the present time to the facts underlying our differences with the Soviet Union." In March 1946, Lane was still urging his superiors in the State Department to spotlight Soviet actions in Eastern Europe. "Education of the public cannot take place overnight," he reminded them. "It will perhaps take a year or two." He failed to get the response he wanted so long as James Byrnes was Secretary. By March 1947, circumstances had changed. A few days after the All-out speech, Lane came to the White House to congratulate the President on it — "the Polish people were dancing with joy" — and to explain that he was going to resign in order "to acquaint the American people with Soviet policies of dominating European countries."

"This is very fine," Truman told him. "You will help me a great deal if you will do what you propose." [22]

But the Administration was attempting to do in a matter of weeks what Lane had thought would take a year or two. The program encountered doubt and resistance right across the political spectrum. The conservative Republican Robert Taft worried about the expense of the program and the confirmation it might give to spheres of influence. Representative Christian Herter, a moderate Republican, wondered if U.S. officials had the "extraordinary skill" to intervene successfully. Eleanor Roosevelt wanted "a high level effort to settle matters directly with Stalin." Members of the Americans for Democratic Action (Arthur Schlesinger, Jr., informed the State Department) "unhappily supported" the program in the half-hearted belief that its objectives "were liberal."

Yet, in the last analysis, the Administration's bracing, apocalyptic appeal could not be resisted. The Senate approved the program, 67 to 23; the House, 287 to 107. Harry Truman signed it into law in a Kansas City hotel on May 22.

Members of the polity elite could by this time begin to cease worrying that the public was indifferent or insufficiently alert to the Soviet threat as perceived in Washington. In fact, by the spring of 1947, anticommunism was becoming a powerful force in American politics. Some were already beginning to worry that the public was going too far. "I look personally with some dismay and concern at many of the things that we are now experiencing in our public life," George Kennan had observed the day before Britain announced its decision to quit Greece. "In particular, I deplore the hysterical sort of anticommunism which, it seems to me, is gaining currency in our country."

In the spring of 1947, the socialist leader Norman Thomas, himself a veteran battler on the left against communists, made a trip to California. He noticed a dramatic change since his previous visit fourteen months earlier. "Then the tendency was too much complacency about Russia and too much appeasement," he wrote. "Now there is a high degree of rather hysterical anti-Communism, which is being exploited by the reactionaries."

Between 1945 and 1947, the percentage of the public perceiving Russia as "aggressive" rose from 38 to 66 percent. For Truman and many of his advisers, anticommunism meant primarily anti-Sovietism. This was not true, however, for a major part of the public, for which anticommunism was more broadly defined to include subversives and "enemies within" — mostly imaginary — and even New Dealers and supporters of what would soon be called the Fair Deal. This wider definition, pushed by the conservative wing of the Republican Party as an electoral device, became first a major constraint on the Truman Administration, and then a significant factor for many decades in the national life.

The Republicans' victory in the 1946 congressional election was widely attributed, in part, to their exploitation of charges of disloyalty and subversion in the federal government. In November 1946, shortly after the election, trying to pre-empt the field before the new Congress could move, Truman named a Temporary Commission on Employee Loyalty. In late March 1947, a week and a half after the Truman Doctrine speech, the President acted on the commission's recommendations. With Executive Order 9835, he established a federal loyalty program, which authorized investigations by boards into the political beliefs and associations of all federal employees, whatever their jobs. Also introduced in 1947 was the Attorney-General's list of "subversive organizations." Both the loyalty boards' investigations and the list constituted an intrusion into civil liberties and gave legal force to smear and innuendo. They helped to make internal security into a potent political issue, and to legitimize the more far-reaching attacks on civil liberties that followed.

Yet we must recognize that these steps were not part of a campaign to whip up domestic fervor, but rather, at least as viewed from the White House, efforts to contain such passions and to forestall possible efforts by the Eightieth Congress to manipulate them for partisan purposes. And, surprisingly, the strategy worked — for two years. This domestic anticommunism was an inevitable reaction, if also to become a contributing factor, to the polarization of the Cold War. And we should keep in mind that a search for traitors was also occurring in the Soviet Union, but in a much crueler and more brutal manner, afflicting many who had contact with the West, and many who had not — intellectuals, returning Soviet soldiers who had been German prisoners of war, and even entire ethnic groups. Multitudes were deemed disloyal, and suffered horrendously.[23]

Washington's hopes and plans for a liberal world order had to be set aside, for the episode involving the Truman Doctrine forced the merger of politics and economics. The Near Eastern crisis had created a precedent for further crisis thinking and for a significant extension of presidential power in peacetime. This last development was rather reluctantly accepted by members of the crucial congressional body — the Senate Foreign Relations Committee.[24]

The commitment to Greece and Turkey was seen, on the one hand, as a defensive response. As Tom Connally, the senior Democrat on Foreign Relations, remarked during the executive hearings, "They are after us now all they can be." On the other hand, the commitment signified an assertion of a global mode of thinking and responsibility in the context of a worldwide struggle with Soviet Russia and communism. "It happens that we are having a little trouble with Greece and Turkey at the present time," General George Lincoln, of the War Department's Plans and Operations Division, said to the senators on April 2, "but they are just one of the keys on the keyboard of this world piano that is being played at the present time."[25] All senior officials subscribed to the imagery that featured the masterminds in the Kremlin. "They look around them and see what the world looks like and what sort of break they may get on that day, and they try to take advantage of the breaks," Kennan explained. "They are fast operators. They play a very delicate and dangerous game."[26]

It is unwise, of course, to underestimate a potential adversary in the international system; but it is equally unwise to overestimate him. Here, the Americans surely overestimated, giving the Soviets more credit than they deserved. Rigidity, fear, and caution certainly characterized the Soviet system; Stalin's court was at war within itself; its members feared to give the dictator information he would not like; only a few tired and overworked men could make decisions. Conservatism, not adventurism, more aptly characterized Stalin's postwar foreign policy.

We should not assume, however, that opinion in American policy circles was monolithic about the degree of Soviet responsibility. The situation was "clear-cut." So the Foreign Relations Committee was told by Ambassador MacVeagh, who had lived in Greece for many years, and who maintained close relations with the leading families of the old order. A social revolution afflicted Greece, he complained, "and not one of those nice old revolutions we used to have in the old days." More important, as MacVeagh saw it, *the social revolution was imported from abroad:* * "The fellow to blame was the fellow who controls the little countries to the north of Greece, the fellow who is backing them, right square back to the Moscow Government." [27]

New Deal liberals found the situation less clear-cut, for they saw themselves in an uneasy alliance with the kind of "economic royalists" that Roosevelt had so vigorously denounced. These Americans did put some blame on Greece's old order. They were critical of the politicians who could not rise above petty rivalries and corruption, the security forces who could not resist instituting a white terror, the rich families who skillfully evaded taxation and made profits out of relief assistance.

The case of Paul Porter, a New Deal liberal who had been head of the Office of Price Administration, exemplifies the difficult and painful dilemmas other liberals would face as intervention abroad became part of American foreign policy. While conducting his economic survey in the winter of 1947, he reported, "There is really no State here in the Western concept. Rather we have a loose hierarchy

* MacVeagh may have been exaggerating for the benefit of congressmen, or his own viewpoint had changed, for in October 1946 he wrote a letter in which he said, "Lack of leadership is certainly what principally ails this country [Greece] at the present time — leadership which can see beyond political problems which are not only local in character but also completely out of date. The five-year Metaxas dictatorship seems to have effectively prevented the rise of a new generation of politicians to take the place of the oldsters, who have now come back into the saddle, for lack of other leaders, and who still think in terms of the old struggle between Royalists and Venizelists, entirely missing the meaning of the developments in Europe and the world which World War II and the rise of Russia have brought about. Small men, old men, and men entirely lacking in the sense of realism which the situation requires, are what we are having to deal with now."

of individualistic politicians, some worse than others, who are so preoccupied with their own struggle for power that they have no time, even assuming capacity, to develop economic policy." Later in the year, at a private dinner with Forrestal and journalists James Reston and Joseph Alsop, Porter said that Greece was in shambles. He told them how Prime Minister Maximos owned the American embassy building, leasing it to the United States, but insisting on payment in gold at the Federal Reserve Bank in New York City, and how less than 2 percent of the hard currency income generated by a hundred ships made available to Greeks by the U.S. was being remitted to Greece. Most was kept abroad, where it did the Greek economy no good. The political repression repelled him.

"I told Maximos one day, 'The stories that are coming out of here, about sending the political prisoners to the islands, are creating a very unfortunate climate of opinion in the United States,'" Porter recalled. "Two days later, he very proudly told me that he had ordered no more raids be made after midnight. This was a great concession."[28]

Porter and Ethridge talked over the tangled situation many times while in Greece together. "He never did get to the point where he said to hell with them, but he got to one point where he almost said it," remembered Ethridge. But Ethridge convinced Porter otherwise, arguing, "We have to try to save the Greek government and then throw the rascals out."[29] Porter finally concluded that the repression and corruption were secondary, and that "a foreign power" was financing and directing the communist rebels. He agreed with Ethridge that if the Iron Curtain slid down to the Mediterranean, then the Russians would gain control of the Suez Canal, and then . . . "The seeds of another war were there," was the way Porter remembered it. "Oh, hell, we had to take over running Greece. There was no choice."[30]

The Greek rebels did indeed obtain assistance from Yugoslavia, Bulgaria, perhaps Albania. Yet the civil war in Greece — for that is what it was — arose primarily from local sources. As John Iatrides, one of the keenest students of these events, has pointed out, "The Greek crisis was basically a domestic affair of long standing, compounded by Balkan tensions and rivalries. The Soviet Union not only did not cause or aggravate the Greek situation but apparently disapproved of the communist rebellion and instructed the Greek Communist Party to refrain from resorting to violent tactics. By 1948, and very probably from the outset, this fact was known to the Greek Government (as its archives made clear), which for obvious reasons chose not to publicize it, promoting instead the view that Greece was fighting the very forces which threatened all Western and democratic nations." The Americans were highly receptive to that latter view by 1947. But it must be understood that their interpretation of events in Greece was distorted by the wide acceptance of the Riga axioms, which assumed a Russian mastermind behind the scenes in every local crisis.

EAM * (and its military arm, ELAS **) was a broadly based, left-oriented resistance movement, under loose communist leadership. It controlled most of continental Greece by the time of the German withdrawal in the autumn of 1944. EAM had an active membership of upward of 700,000 people, and had won the support of large segments of the working class and peasantry, portions of the population that had traditionally been deprived of political influence. It had proved itself by far the most successful of the wartime guerrilla groups, and had managed during the war — at least in the countryside that was under the military control of ELAS — to carry out a program of reform and modernization, mixing popular justice with terror. Already established during the war, however, was a vendetta culture — revenge and counterrevenge — that would set band against band, family against family, and would provide the soil in which civil war would flourish. EAM demanded a share in political power on the basis of its popular support and the strength of ELAS. During the autumn of 1944, EAM acted in a generally moderate, although also confused fashion. In part, this was because the regular Greek Communist Party (KKE) was undecided whether to attempt to seize power or to participate in the political process. The communists had no support from Moscow. Indeed, they were abandoned by Stalin, who kept to his October 1944 deal with Churchill. Greece was left to the British sphere, and Moscow's attitude toward the Greek left throughout this period varied between indifference and outright hostility.

* National Liberation Front.
** National Popular Liberation Army.

The political structure of the country was delicately balanced as the end of the war approached. It fell apart when police opened fire on an EAM demonstration in Athens in December 1944. The result was the "second round" of the civil war. Stalin had ceded Churchill the first say in Greece, and British troops intervened — the only occasion when a wartime resistance movement did battle with Western forces. The opposing parties finally arranged a truce in January 1945, when the nationalist (right-wing) forces — with the British help — won the battle of Athens against EAM/ELAS.[31]

Churchill was determined to isolate EAM, rather than involve it in the Greek political process. Here, at least, Britain still held the lease, and Churchill was going to play out the imperial role. Greece became a thoroughgoing British client.

The British did not necessarily want to strengthen the conservative forces, but they did want to neutralize or defeat the Greek left, hoping that moderate, liberal, and pro-British elements would gain power. Unfortunately, the state apparatus, particularly the army and the police, had been controlled by the right since the days of the dictatorship of General Metaxas in the late 1930s. The British did not wish to purge it for fear that the leftists would benefit, and the authority of the state be thus weakened. They may also have been unable to exert any veto over promotions in the security forces. The result was the suppression of the left and the retention of control by the right. There had also been a considerable swing in public opinion toward the right as the result of the atrocities of the 1944–45 crisis, which were generally attributed to the left.

The right seized the opportunity to initiate a white terror, with which they tried to drive even moderate leftists from political life. As in the days of General Metaxas, real political and economic power remained concentrated in the hands of a small group of wealthy merchants and industrialists.[32]

The left made a major error in March 1946 when it decided to abstain from the parliamentary elections. The extent of this abstention is a matter of contention, but the figure probably lies between 30 and 40 percent. True enough, electoral fraud practiced on behalf of conservative candidates would have been extensive in any event under the circumstances, but the parliament so returned need not have been so heavily weighted to the right. Corruption was now endemic, and the ascendant right used its monopoly of power to wage a destructive campaign against communists, a category defined with the widest latitude. This program ignited the "third round" of the Greek Civil War of 1946–49.

The white terror was soon in full swing. Vendetta, practiced by both left and right, became a way of life. "Honest resistance men," remembered David Balfour, the British chargé, "were not getting a square deal." Right across the country, people suspected of leftist sympathies were being fired from their jobs, refused new employment, harassed, beaten up, arrested, deported, and often killed. To make matters worse, the government provided weapons to "nationalist" gangs, which operated without the restraint of conventional discipline. In this atmosphere, former EAM members, as well as younger men now confronted by official lawlessness and a life of poverty, took to the mountains once more. By the summer of 1946, leftist guerrilla bands had again begun to operate on a large scale.

Political passions were increased by the British insistence that a referendum on the single most emotional issue, the question of the return of the king, be held in September 1946. The referendum brought King George back. Bevin had pleaded with George to behave like a constitutional monarch — "Kings are pretty cheap these days," the Foreign Secretary reminded him. But George's return only increased divisions in the country. In October, Ambassador MacVeagh wrote that "the king, who has been brought back as a 'solution' for the problems which the politicians will not tackle, is the same old muddled indecisive figure that he always was."

The other Balkan states, particularly Yugoslavia, provided prodding and encouragement, as well as supplies, training, and a sanctuary, for the guerrillas across their borders.[33] The Greek communist leaders were divided into rival factions and disagreed on such issues as the timing of the civil war and urban uprising versus peasant war. But they took the initiative in organizing the left in the civil war, and, after 1946, held firm control over it. They were not merely responding to the white terror; they wanted to lead an armed revolution to victory.[34]

By early 1947, the country was indeed in shambles. Subhi Sadi, the Chase Bank's Middle Eastern representative, and hardly a person to be accused of leftist bias, reported to New York: "The country is in a complete state of chaos, and outside the cities, in a state of absolute anarchy. Actually there are two Greeces: cities such as Athens, Piraeus, and Salonica where the Government is in control but with the help of strong security forces — especially in the working people's quarters; and the countryside where the Government is not in control except where the Armed Forces operate." Sadi thought the schism between right and left was so wide that only intervention by an outside power could bring some resolution. "Whereas immediately after the civil war of 1944 the Communists (Andartes) had lost favor and become a small and hated minority, today the situation is different. The Greek Government having moved further right the past three years has become fully as extreme as the Communists, and has lost the public support of the masses which compose the Liberals. These masses having lost faith in the Government on account of its excesses and lack of action in improving the economic situation are beginning to look to the Guerrillas as their sole hope of deliverance. Corruption, lack of administration, suppression of most civil liberties, economic and financial chaos and black markets are the order of the day in Greece."

An informed Western observer, William Hardy McNeill, previously assistant U.S. military attaché in Athens, returned to Greece for a three-month survey in the spring of 1947. He concluded that around a communist hard core there had collected "a far wider penumbra of sympathizers, organized into a 'popular front' known as EAM. Many poverty-stricken peasants, and a majority of the working class of the towns belongs or are strongly sympathetic to EAM, though in the nation as a whole the movement commands the loyalty of only a minority of the population, perhaps 30 percent." [35]

And how did the Truman Doctrine fare in this harsh environment? "It was necessary to interfere in their internal affairs in order to get them straightened out," said Acheson at the end of 1947. But the affairs were still far from sorted out. American intervention and penetration had taken the form of a large mission that assumed control over major economic and political decisions. So great was its power that the Chase Bank's Middle Eastern representative reported in the autumn that the mission had "literally taken over the direction of the country." The stronger the American role became, the weaker the authority of the Greek government became, the more estranged it was from the nation as a whole. "We are in the awkward position at the moment of really having no Greek Government to deal with," Undersecretary Robert Lovett, who had succeeded Acheson, complained in August 1947 to the Greek ambassador.[36]

Some U.S. officials recognized that the Greek oligarchy continued to be corrupt and incompetent. They knew for instance that the Minister of Public Order, Napoleon Zervas, was tainted by Nazi collaboration, and indeed, as the head of the American mission put it, that he was "making more Communists than he is eliminating." They continually hoped to find or create a Third Force, composed of moderate progressives, between reaction and revolution; but they little understood that the more they intervened, the less this was possible, that as they became committed, so also they became hostages to the right. Perhaps, as has been argued, the very act of intervention weakens the authority and morale of the government so supported, polarizes the situation, and motivates a nationalist opposition.[37]

In Greece at least, despite the growing American involvement, the situation, as seen by U.S. policymakers, steadily worsened. By August 1947, John Foster Dulles was worrying about talk within the Administration of introducing U.S. troops into Greece. By the end of the year, planning had begun for that eventuality.[38]

In fact, American combat troops were not introduced, but the role of the American military mission was expanded, and the techniques of intervention and penetration had their first major postwar application.* American military advisers played a major role in planning and overseeing Greek army operations. Hundreds of thousands of people became refugees. Napalm was used for the first time. Dwight Griswold and General James Van Fleet, heads of the American economic and military missions respectively, were included in Greece's Supreme Defense Council, which really ruled the country during the civil war. And then there was the ludricrous case of the senior American assigned to the Ministry of National Economy. He insisted on signing not only the originals of all documents leaving the Ministry but also the carbon copies because, according to a report to the American embassy, he "just does not trust any of the Greek officials that the copies made from the signed original draft will be true copies."

By the summer of 1949, the American-backed government forces finally won their victory. There were several reasons. Once the guerrillas had committed themselves to a strategy of conventional

* But the reader is advised to remember that, as thoroughgoing as the American penetration of Greece was, it was much less than that of the Soviet Union in Eastern Europe. In addition, the Americans observed restraints on violence that the Russians ignored.

warfare, they became more vulnerable. The organization, firepower, and morale of the government forces were steadily improving. The guerrillas had increasing difficulty after 1948 in making up their losses because the areas in which they could recruit were constantly shrinking. American power over the Greek army command was also important, for it reduced political influence over promotions and the conduct of the war.

Yet it has been argued that, in a guerrilla war, the guerrillas do not have to win, only to avoid losing, and thus ultimately wear down the political will of the interventionist. At a critical moment for Greece, however, there were splits within the communist ranks — between Tito and Stalin, and within the Greek Communist Party. When Titoism became a heresy, the Greek communists joined in the denunciation. The Yugoslavs retaliated by closing their border, thus shutting off supplies and eliminating a safe haven. The Soviets did nothing to provide any assistance. In addition, by some accounts, the Stalinist leadership of the Greek Communist Party had difficulty in coping with a popular movement, and was more concerned with its own authority and purging opponents within the left than in providing effective leadership for the entire movement.[39]

The Truman Doctrine committed the United States to a global struggle with the Soviets. American leaders now saw a Russian mastermind at work in every local crisis. Still, most policymakers did recognize that there were limits to what the United States could do. Admiral Leahy fulminated in late February 1947, "I am unable to understand General Marshall's apparent willingness to become involved in saving the Greek and Turkish governments in view of his present attitude toward the Government of China. The two situations seem to be identical, and it appears to me that a stable non-Soviet Government in China is of much more importance to America than the Mediterranean States." But, unlike Leahy, most policymakers did recognize that intervention in China would have required a massive effort. As Kennan remarked at the National War College: "China is not small, definitely."[40] And so the United States avoided direct military intervention in the Chinese civil war.

But another point must also be made. Even if the Greek civil war was primarily a local affair, the international consequence of victory for one side or the other would have been very significant. It was uncertainty — the rules of international relations not established, no kind of modus vivendi understood — that could produce another war. A spheres-of-influence arrangement was meant to reduce the uncertainty, to help nations live less dangerously. That Greece was part of the Western sphere was something Stalin had recognized in the October 1944 understanding. Looking back, Churchill said in May 1946 that the agreement had permitted him to become "busy getting peace restored in Greece. This involved the killing of large numbers of Communists in Greece. Stalin knew that. It went on for a month. Never once said a word. He held to the understanding he had given." In effect, Stalin reiterated the agreement in early 1948, when he criticized Yugoslavian assistance to the Greek guerrillas. The venture, he angrily told Edvard Kardelj and Milovan Djilas, has "no prospect of success at all. What, do you think that Great Britain and the United States — the United States, the most powerful state in the world — will permit you to break their line of communication in the Mediterranean? Nonsense."[41]

The situation was more complicated than many writers have suggested. The Greek Communist Party was in the Stalinist mode. Had EAM won, a broad leftist government might well have given way to one not on the model of an independent Yugoslavia, but, instead, of the same pattern as in Rumania and Bulgaria. A red terror might then have supplanted the white terror. The resulting opportunity for the Soviets might have been too attractive to pass up, and Greece could well have slipped into Moscow's grip. This, in turn, would have dangerously upset the precarious international balance that might have existed. Also, it is hard to see how the people of Greece would have been better off, either politically or in material life, under that kind of system than was the actual case.

Top American officials themselves saw the Truman Doctrine as a belated retreat from efforts to influence events in the Soviet sphere. Instead, it was a major step toward consolidating a Western sphere. "It would be silly to believe that we can do anything effective in Rumania, Bulgaria, or Poland," said Dean Acheson. "You cannot do that. That is within the Russian area of physical force. We are excluded from that. There are other places where we can be effective." That is why the Truman Doctrine was a turning point in the history of the Cold War. One State Department official explained to Mrs. Roosevelt that the United States "had been retreating" ever since Yalta. (This, of course, was not exactly true; rather, efforts to expand American interests into Eastern Europe, into the Soviet sphere, had been unsuccessful.) Nothing could be done with the Russians, the official continued, until the United States indicated "very clearly that we did not intend to retreat any further."

Such was the message Americans gave to the Russians.

Shortly after Truman's speech, Mark Ethridge received a visit in Athens from his Soviet counterpart on the U.N. border commission, Alexander Lavrishev.

"What does it mean, Mr. Ethridge?" asked Lavrishev.

"Means you can't do it, Lavrishev," replied Ethridge.[42]

The year before, American leaders had shifted from private to public diplomacy. Now, with the Truman Doctrine, these men — frustrated, impatient, always troubled by the necessity of trying to do business with the Stalinist tyranny — renounced altogether the utility of diplomacy with the USSR.

"I think it is a mistake to believe that you can, at any time, sit down with the Russians and solve questions," Acheson said in executive hearings of the Senate Foreign Relations Committee on April 1, 1947. "I do not think that is the way that our problems are going to be worked out with the Russians. I think they will have to be worked out over a long period of time and by always indicating to the Russians that we are quite aware of what our own interests are and that we are quite firm about them and quite prepared to take necessary action. Then I think solutions will become possible."

"You are not planning any early participation for the settlement of these issues?" asked Senator H. Alexander Smith.

"You cannot sit down with them," reiterated Acheson.

What was odd about Acheson's statement was that the Americans were right then sitting down with the Russians at the Council of Foreign Ministers meeting that had opened in Moscow on March 10, 1947. But there was no sign of a settlement. "It looks to me as if we are getting perilously near a position in which a line-up is taking place," Bevin observed of the Council in a letter he wrote Attlee from Moscow. "There is courtesy, there are no high words being used, no tempers, but all of it is cool and calculated and between the two big boys looks to me to be pretty determined." French Foreign Minister Bidault later rightly said that the Council, with its parties, banquets, toasts, and other "frozen amusements," marked the end of an era.[43]

The American delegates, sharing Acheson's skepticism about negotiations, were certainly uninterested in compromise. A get-tough attitude had become an end in itself. In late February, a senior State Department official — possibly Bohlen — said to a *Time* correspondent that the U.S. delegation had little interest in negotiating with the Soviets. "Marshall," the briefer explained, "is going to Moscow knowing in advance that nothing would be decided there for the peace of the world . . . Our experience with them has proved by now that it is impossible to negotiate with them. It is either to yield to them or to tell them 'no' . . . Our own policy changes. Their policy cannot change. Neither Molotov nor Stalin nor the Politburo can change it. It is a dogma. If you read what the *Red Star* was writing about the capitalist world last week, you will see that it is exactly the same stuff as was written in 1924." But the briefer did have some advice for the readers of *Time* — "to gather all our strength and resources for whatever is in store for us."

The American delegation was led by George Marshall. The general was tired and not prepared for the difficult problems, and he did not provide strong or well-informed leadership. John Foster Dulles wielded considerable influence.[44]

The purpose of the Council was to make progress on the German and Austrian peace settlements. When it was over, William Draper, Clay's chief economic adviser, advised Herbert Hoover that it was "anything but a howling success." He said that the key stumbling block was reparations. "The Russian demands for reparations from current production were made just as expected and are the real issue preventing a German settlement. The other issues could, I believe, be settled without too great difficulty if this were out of the way." [45] That may have been an exaggeration. Germany presented an infinitely complex problem, which was, at the same time, a very simple one — neither side could take the risk that a reunited Germany might become an ally of the other.

Nevertheless, the Russians left no doubt that reparations were their first concern. "The Soviet Government does not conceal the fact that it wants reparations from Germany," said Molotov, "nor does it conceal the amount which it wants." Nor did it conceal the extent of destruction in Soviet Russia. Yet again, Molotov plaintively ran through the statistics — the numbers of people left homeless; villages, railway stations, and collective farms destroyed; cows, pigs, and goats that had disappeared. "Things are in very bad shape in Europe as a whole," Stalin remarked to one American visitor during the conference. He did not add that, as bad as they were in Western Europe, they were worse in Soviet Russia. There was famine in the Ukraine, where party officials were alarmed by reports of cannibalism. The Soviet effort to remove entire factories from Germany had led to great waste, and the pressure must have mounted on Russian diplomats to obtain reparations from current German production. The Russians did not for a moment doubt either the justice or the urgency of their claim. They also knew, as Stalin put it, that "things are not bad in the United States." [46]

From time to time, some Americans did recognize the importance of reconstruction to the Russian position on Germany. "One only has to visit Russia to realize how much of its policy is affected by dire need," Clay noted during the conference. In fact, Clay argued in Moscow, as one delegation member put it, "that we should give the Russians some current reparation to buy economic unity" in Germany.

But the American position continued to remain "no reparations from current production." Most of the Americans never really comprehended the problems that shaped Russian demands. In part, the Russian style of presentation seemed almost calculated to stiffen Western resistance. The Americans assumed that the reiteration of claims for reparations by Molotov and his colleagues was merely part of what Dulles called the Soviet "process of exhaustion." [47]

The American, British, and French foreign ministers were also thinking of the problems of Western Europe, especially the need for coal and an increase in industrial production. They feared that, in Bevin's words, the Russians would "loot Germany at our expense." The Westerners would not compromise on the First Charge Principle for reparations. They did not want to pour resources into Germany only to have the Russians siphon them off from the other side. The matter as seen by most members of the American delegation was summed up by economist Charles Kindleberger: "The Molotov economics are of course fantastic . . . Germany shall be able to pay Russia its reparations, pay reparations in coal to France, balance its export and import trade so that no occupying power has to bear any cost, increase its standard of living and particularly food level, bear internal and external occupation costs, all simultaneously."

Moreover, the Americans and British were beginning to place more emphasis on merging the three Western zones in Germany, and partition was already very much in the minds of senior Americans.*

There were still other reasons to oppose reparations. The Americans feared that such resources would be used to build up Soviet military strength. They also believed that the Russians regarded reparations as a tool for disordering the West and gaining, as Ambassador Smith had warned, "eventual control of continental Europe." [48]

For all these reasons, the United States would not budge on current reparations. Clay did not hide his disagreement. He complained, said Kindleberger, that "the Secretary and [Ben] Cohen don't know what they want, are disorganized and ultimately are going to throw away Germany." Clay's response, Kindleberger continued, was "violent and a little insubordinate. He says that it will lose the chance of unifying Germany, that it shows how badly this whole matter is now being run and he managed to hint to the Russians that he has nothing to do with it."

On March 31, Clay told Marshall that he could serve no further use in the delegation, and, with the Secretary's permission, he left Moscow immediately.

Others in the American delegation were happy to assume a stance of firmness and determination, knowing that it would not advance matters in Moscow, but hoping to affect public opinion elsewhere. As Dulles wrote to Vandenberg, "There is increasing evidence that our strengthened position is rallying support throughout much of Europe."

After seeing Stalin on April 15, Marshall came to a crucial conclusion — that the Soviet Union wanted to promote economic and political disintegration in Western Europe. The meeting with Stalin commenced, as usual, at 10:00 P.M. in the Kremlin. Marshall was

* At Moscow, John Foster Dulles helped persuade Marshall to see the Soviet Union as the root of all problems in Germany and to overlook French obstacles to treating Germany as a unit. Supporting the French view that the Ruhr should be separated from Germany, Dulles clashed sharply there with Clay. "Clay and Draper claim that Germany will go communist shortly after any proposal to infringe on its sovereignty over the Ruhr is carried out," Kindleberger wrote. "Dulles claims that France will go communist if the demands of the French for coal and the Ruhr are not met."

surprised by Stalin's appearance; the generalissimo did not look well, he seemed to have somehow shrunk into his clothes. "You look just the same as when I saw you last time," Stalin said, "but I am just an old man." With such pleasantries out of the way, the two men got down to business. Marshall complained about Soviet failure to settle lend-lease, and Stalin countered with a complaint about the failure of the United States to respond to the Soviet loan proposal. The dictator returned to his central concern. At Yalta, he said, the United States had agreed to ten billion dollars in reparations for the Soviet Union.

Now there was apparently a different point of view, Stalin said — "to take no more reparations than had already been taken." This the Soviet Union could not accept, he continued. Its "people had been told the figure of ten billions. Over 20 years this would not be hard for the Germans. The United States and England might be willing to give up reparations; the Soviet Union could not."

Stalin added, however, that the impasse in the conference was not "so tragic." These were only "the first skirmishes and brushes of reconnaissance" on difficult questions. "Differences had occurred before on other questions, and as a rule after people had exhausted themselves in dispute they then recognized the necessity of compromise." Stalin gave Marshall some advice — "to have patience and not become depressed."

The Russians apparently meant that advice seriously, for that was the line adopted at the end of the Council, despite the Truman Doctrine speech. "We can say without hesitation," declared *Pravda*, "that the Conference marked the beginning of the solution of the German problem." Bevin left Moscow in an exuberant mood, relieved simply to be leaving Moscow. When Vyshinsky came to see him off at the railway station, the British Foreign Secretary broke into song:

> The more we are together, together, together
> The more we are together,
> The merrier we shall be . . .

"What a jolly man!" Vyshinsky commented sarcastically.[49]

Marshall and his colleagues departed in anything but a jolly mood. "Many were the hours we listened to the same old records, the same technique, the same fruitless arguments about minor matters, the same distortions and the same blaring propaganda," Hickerson wrote to James Dunn. "There was perhaps a little less bitterness at the table but that was probably due to the seriousness of the issues and the width of the gaps that separated us. The French were particularly disillusioned with the Comrades and came out, I believe, much closer to us than they have been for years, thanks largely to Molotov's rudeness and his unwillingness to go along with them on the Saar."

Marshall himself interpreted Stalin's advice about patience as a sinister invitation to wait for European conditions to worsen so that the entire continent might fall into Soviet hands. He fully accepted the assessment of Soviet intentions made by virtually all policymakers. He had become quickly convinced of the wisdom of the strictures against sitting down to negotiate with the Russians, of the dangers of diplomacy. All the way back to Washington, he talked of the need to find some way to prevent the complete collapse of Western Europe.[50]

The Moscow Council marked for the Americans the final rejection of Franklin Roosevelt's tentatively optimistic approach to postwar Soviet-American relations. A few months after the meeting, Edward Mason, who had been Marshall's chief economic adviser at the conference, observed that "Moscow represents, in a sense, the culmination of a trend away from Yalta, away from the position held, at least by American representatives at Yalta, that a sufficient community of interest existed between east and west to permit agreement on certain basic principles of international organization, and toward the position that such a community of interest is lacking . . . toward quite a different conception."

It fell to John Foster Dulles to make explicit the "lessons" of the meeting, as perceived by U.S. officials. "Still another asset we bring back is a better understanding of how Soviet foreign policy works," he said immediately upon his return. "It depends little on getting results by diplomatic negotiation. It depends much on getting results by penetrating into the political parties and organizations of other countries."

A few weeks later, having further collected his thoughts, he spoke at the Council on Foreign Relations. "Until our ideas and ideals have shown their holding power, Russia will continue to push," he said. While noting "strange fluctuations" in Soviet policy on Germany, he did not stop to consider that such fluctuations might indicate improvisation and confusion among Soviet leaders. "Probably the Soviets genuinely feel that the two forms of society are incompatible. Stalin, for foreign consumption, states that the two can exist together, but that is not what is taught in Soviet publications and in Soviet schools."

Russia, he said, was on the offensive. His central point and conclusion came in the form of a warning: "The Soviets have a world plan to overthrow capitalism wherever it may be and to substitute police states." [51]

JAMES RESTON: The only weakness in what was otherwise a magnificent statement of the President — namely, that he gave the impression, rightly or wrongly, that the people who were going to get help were the people who were in desperate straits and who had an armed minority at their border; whereas I would like to have seen him indicate that you can fight Communism in other ways — in economic ways.

JAMES FORRESTAL: The core of the thing is are you going to try to keep Germany a running boil with the pus exuding over the rest of Europe?

Telephone conversation, March 13, 1947 [1]

XII

The Margin of Safety

EVEN AS U.S. POLICYMAKERS were formulating the Truman Doctrine, they saw before them in Western Europe an economic crisis with momentous political ramifications. Their response took the form of a policy that answered several questions at once — what to do about Germany? what to do about Western Europe? what to do about the Soviet Union? The goals were several as well — the economic revival of Western Europe, the creation of an environment hospitable to democracy and capitalism in Western Europe, the maintenance of the balance of power on the European continent, and the "containment" of the Soviet Union and communism. The industrial might of western Germany was presented as essential for the recovery of its noncommunist neighbors. In this way, with its firm entrenchment in a Europe-wide framework, a reconstituted West Germany would become politically acceptable throughout the rest of Western Europe.

The chosen instrument for achieving these various goals was American economic power. "It is necessary," Harry Truman reminded members of the Associated Press in April 1947, "that we develop a new realization of the size and strength of our economy." [2] The realization involved a subordination of international economics to international politics, an essential feature in the rise of the national security state. Prior to 1947, economic matters (involving trade as well as reconstruction) and political questions were usually dropped into different boxes, although that separation had eroded somewhat by 1946.

Official thought on international economic matters, coming out of the Second World War, had been obsessed with preparing for a multilateral world — that is, an open international trading system, free of tariffs and other restrictions, and unhindered by bilateral trade agreements. Despite disagreement about the importance of foreign trade to the postwar American economy, many assumed that the trade barriers of the 1930s had helped pave the way to the Second World War, and they wanted to avoid a rerun. Dominating the planning was a curious kind of optimism about how easy it was going to be to pass through what was loosely referred to as the "post-war transition" and get on to the main business of constructing the new multilateral trading world.

This is not to say that American officials ignored the damage done by war. In his diary, for instance, Henry Stimson recorded his shock at the "powerful picture of the tough situation" that John McCloy brought back from a trip to Germany in April 1945 — a scene of devastation that suggested itself as "worse than anything probably that ever happened in the world."

In general, however, the officials in Washington who managed policy at the conclusion of the war and immediately afterward tended to discount the pressing problems symbolized by the urban rubble, which, like graveyards, dotted the Continent. Those who worked abroad, in public and private capacities, took more seriously the effects of the wartime trauma and the depths of the postwar problems. In February 1946, Colonel Sosthenes Behn, founder of International Telephone and Telegraph, wandered into the offices of his New York bank, J. P. Morgan, "very blue about the foreign outlook." Behn said that he "liquidated every foreign property that he could as fast as he could." His hope — "to build up a big domestic company." [3] A couple of months later, E. F. Penrose, an American economics official based in London, was struck on returning to Washington by "the attitude of rather casual and easy optimism about European revival in many Washington circles." In 1946, the State Department put more attention and more staff to work on an international trade charter and tariff reduction than on relief and reconstruction. The Administration was relieved to be done with UNRRA, the United

Nations relief organization, which was too independent of Washington and too controversial with many congressmen. Also, perhaps, a strong element of wishful thinking influenced the tendency to underestimate the task of reconstruction; for even before the war was over, officials had already concluded that postwar assistance programs would arouse considerable domestic opposition.[4]

At the end of 1945, an unexpectedly grave food crisis gave the first major signal that the "post-war transition" might prove much more treacherous than the blueprints had allowed. By early 1946, more than 125 million Europeans were subsisting on no more than 2000 calories a day; many of those millions, on no more than 1000 — in grim contrast to the 3300 calories a day that was the average in the United States.[5]

In response, Truman, in the spring of 1946, sent Herbert Hoover on another of the former President's regular spring forays into foreign policy, this time to survey famine conditions abroad. After World War I, Hoover had proved himself not only an expert famine relief administrator in Europe, but also an excellent strategist in using food to contain communism, and he was welcomed back into policy councils with something like religious awe. Foreshadowing what was to become a common theme in the next year, he argued, both publicly and privately, not only in Washington but also as he toured abroad, that economic distress should be evaluated in terms of conflict with the Soviet Union. Like Forrestal, he even felt the need to warn the Pope that "Catholicism in Europe was in the gravest danger from the Communist invasion, the gates of which would be wide open from starvation." Hoover sketched a similar scene for Attlee, but was somewhat disappointed when the only response from the British Prime Minister was, "This has been very interesting" and "I shall be seeing you at lunch."[6]

The food crisis eased later in 1946, temporarily at least, and optimism quickly returned to American leaders. Industrial production picked up in Europe — for instance, by 1947, Holland had exceeded prewar averages — and officials on both sides of the Atlantic were sure that the worst was past. On October 5, 1946, Hugh Dalton noted that he and Will Clayton "are agreed that UNRRA must definitely stop, as arranged, in the next year, and that, apart from the Germans, only Italy, Austria and Greece should rank for further doles from either the U.S. or U.K."[7] Then came a crisis so serious that, in itself, it pushed the polarization between East and West to the point of virtual partition of Europe.

The crisis had been pending, brought on not only by the visible destruction — the dead and injured, the apartments burned out, the factories flattened, the railway bridges destroyed — but also by invisible devastation. Capital equipment was obsolete and worn out. The labor forces in Europe were exhausted, undernourished, and disorganized. Technical skills had been lost. Such reconstruction as had taken place created a great hunger for American goods, and so aggravated the problems. And then the weather — droughts in the summers of 1946 and 1947 and what has been called a Siberian winter in between — brought conditions to a crisis point. The weather, to be sure, was not the cause of this crisis, but rather, the precipitant.

For clarity's sake, we might see the picture in three panels. The first was the food and raw materials crisis that had been mounting through 1946. Western Europe was no longer able to obtain food stores from traditional sources in Eastern Europe and the Far East. In Western Europe, soil fertility had declined markedly, and the traditional market links between town and country had been sundered. European wheat production in 1947 fell to less than half of what it had been in 1938. British coal production in 1946 was 20 percent lower than it had been in 1938; in the western parts of Germany, the output of coal was only two fifths of what it had been in 1938.

Second, the war had broken established habits and patterns of economic activity within Europe and between Europe and the rest of the world. The Europeans were not able to sell to former customers abroad. American efforts to penetrate the sterling bloc of the British Empire aggravated Britain's economic problems. The successful insistence by the U.S. that the British make the pound convertible in the summer of 1947 created an immediate, massive, and worldwide rush from pounds to dollars, and so made matters much worse. The most important of all the economic dislocations involved the collapse of Germany, which had formerly played a central role in Europe as both importer and exporter. Before the war, the three Western zones alone had been the source of one fifth of all industrial production in Europe; in the immediate postwar years, production there barely reached a third of those prewar levels.[8]

But, in 1947, the heart of the problem was a financial crisis. Part of the problem was inflation — wholesale prices had risen 80 percent in

France during 1946. Such inflation led to strikes and promoted instability. Even more important was the need to find a way to finance both the equipment necessary for reconstruction and the food and other raw materials that Europe needed to obtain from the United States. The trade balance between the United States and Europe was not at all in balance. In 1947, the United States exported to Europe almost seven times as much as it imported from Europe. This seemed to indicate a worsening trend, for U.S. imports from Europe had actually declined between 1946 and 1947, while the demand for U.S. exports — both manufactures and commodities — was increasing.

Meanwhile, inflation in the United States, which Washington started to see as a serious problem in March 1947, widened the gap. Wholesale prices in the United States rose 40 percent between June 1946 and September 1947. By the second quarter of 1947, the U.S. export surplus was running at a staggering annual rate of $12.5 billion.

How could Europe finance its vital purchases from the United States? Lend-lease had long since ended; UNRRA would cease in mid-1947; other credits were being drawn down. The foreign assets of the European countries were disappearing; and they had lost a very substantial part of the invisible earnings that had formerly flowed in from overseas investments, shipping, insurance, and so forth. They were unable to sell goods to traditional markets elsewhere in the world, and indeed these former markets themselves were now lining up in competition with the Europeans for the product of the American machine.

The result became known as the "dollar shortage" or the "dollar gap." The only way the Europeans could continue to buy was if the U.S. financed the purchases in some fashion.[9]

"The dollar shortage is developing everywhere in the world," British Chancellor Hugh Dalton complained in the spring of 1947. "The Americans have half the total income of the world, but won't either spend it in buying other people's goods or lending it or giving it away on a sufficient scale. The Fund and the Bank still do nothing. How soon will this dollar shortage bring a general crisis?"[10]

When the Americans finally perceived the crisis, they responded with alacrity, driven at times by something akin to panic, especially as they measured the problem against what they perceived as Soviet intentions. "I am deeply disturbed by the present world picture, and its implications for our country," Will Clayton noted, a week before the Truman Doctrine speech. "The reins of world leadership are fast slipping from Britain's competent but now very weak hands. These reins will be picked up either by the United States or Russia." But the United States could not assume this leadership "unless the people of the United States are shocked into doing so." He was not suggesting that they be deceived, but only that they be led to see the "truth" as seen by Administration officials and as reported "in the cables which daily arrive at the State Department from all over the world. In every country in the Eastern Hemisphere and most of the countries of the Western Hemisphere, Russia is boring from within." The key lay in providing the dollars necessary to finance recovery and thus underwrite political stability.[11]

By this point, the Americans were consciously turning away from trying to make the Great Power consortium work. Dean Acheson made this point on April 18 (while Marshall was still in Moscow) when he explained that diplomacy and negotiations, what he called the first of the country's instruments for carrying out its foreign policy, had not succeeded in building "with the Soviet Union that mutual trust and confidence and cessation of expansionism which must be the foundation of political stability. We have concluded, therefore, that we must use to an increasing extent our *second* instrument of foreign policy, namely, economic power, in order to call an effective halt to the Soviet Union's expansionism and political infiltration, and to create a basis for political stability and economic well-being." [12] In other words, Acheson was saying that the Rooseveltian approach had failed; containment, economic to begin with, was the appropriate course.

George Marshall arrived at a similar conclusion three days before Acheson's speech. As a result of his April 15 meeting with Stalin, the Secretary became convinced that the Russians were stalling, waiting for an easy victory in Europe. On his way home from Moscow, Marshall stopped for two hours at Tempelhof Airport in Berlin. There he instructed Clay to push economic revival in Bizonia. Back in Washington, the Secretary met a few journalists in an off-the-record session. "Marshall kept talking about Western Europe, especially France and Germany," James Reston noted.

Marshall ordered that more effort in the State Department be put into the staffwork for a new kind of aid program that would become known as the Marshall Plan. It was to be continental in scope (or at least half-continental), a point he had emphasized as early as February. And it was to cover the entire range of European economic problems. "We can no longer nibble at the problem and then nag the American people on the basis of recurring crises," observed Robert Lovett, who succeeded Acheson as Undersecretary in early summer. He added, "It is equally apparent that the Congress will not make funds available unless there is some reasonable expectation that the expenditure of these funds will produce more visible results; or alternatively, unless it can be shown that the failure to expend these funds will produce calamitous circumstances affecting our national security and our economic and social welfare." [13]

The Marshall Plan had two basic aims, which commingled and cannot really be separated — to halt a feared communist advance into Western Europe, and to stabilize an international economic environment favorable to capitalism. It was not much tied to any concerns about an impending American depression, which was what the Russians claimed at the time, and as some recent writers have argued. Such a case exaggerates both the importance and the general need that was felt for overseas markets. For instance, the export surplus of the United States with Europe in 1946 and 1947 accounted for just 2 percent of the U.S. gross national product. In fact, influential leaders like Harriman and Hoover explicitly supported increasing the output of the German steel industry so that the American steel industry would not become too dependent on the export market. The Council of Economic Advisers reported to President Truman in October that foreign aid, insofar as it financed exports, provided both "a temporary prop to the domestic market" and "an additional strain." [14]

As should be clear, the anticommunist consensus was, by this time, so wide that there was little resistance or debate about fundamental assumptions. One State Department official, for instance, described the "departmental frame of mind" as follows: "The failure to reach agreement on Germany at Moscow was due primarily to Soviet anticipation of continued deterioration in France, Italy and Western Germany plus hope for a U.S. depression. It was essential to improve the Western European situation in order to prevent further weakening in our bargaining power."

Here was a focus for the expansive doctrine of national security. Under George Kennan, the new Policy Planning Staff came to general agreement on May 15 "that the main problem in United States security today is to bring into acceptable relationship the economic distress abroad with the capacity and willingness of the United States to meet it effectively and speedily." American officials worked in an atmosphere of increasing tension. Ambassador Walter Bedell Smith, home on leave, told senior military intelligence officers in the War Department on May 16: "There are no limits to the Soviet objectives. Statements made by Lenin to the effect that a great struggle between Communism and capitalism will take place and that one or the other must go down are still being reiterated by Stalin." He added, "They have no inhibitions." Officials were more and more worried.[15]

Similar fears were becoming increasingly common outside government. Unless something were done soon to arrest the decline in confidence, businessmen would clearly make individual decisions that, in sum, would only speed Europe toward a collapse. "Everything I heard and read — and I hear and read a lot — points to the gravity of food, fuel, finance and communism impending in France," wrote Russell Leffingwell of the Morgan Bank in May. "It is a matter of great practical business importance to this bank. We cannot afford to have the Paris officers and directors living in an unreal Pollyanna dream, and we think it most important they should understand the gravity of the risks, and conduct their business accordingly."

No encouraging signs appeared in May. So short was the food supply in Germany and Austria that rations had fallen below the official level of 1550 calories — down to 1220 in some regions, even to 900 in others. "We do not see why you have to read the *New York Times* to know the Germans are close to starving," General Clay angrily cabled the War Department in May from Berlin. "The crisis is now, not in July."

The Americans feared that the Soviet Union would exploit the economic crisis to extend its political control over the rest of Europe.[16] But was this truly Moscow's goal? It seems unlikely. Certainly, the Truman Doctrine had been read and annotated very carefully in Moscow. Yet, despite its evangelical tone, its clear promise to use American economic power for explicit American political goals, and its establishment of American military power close to the Soviet periphery in Turkey, it was obviously understood by the Russians to be confined in operation chiefly to Greece, which was an area Stalin had deeded to the West. Stalin still seemed interested in maintaining the consortium, and his public statements represented that interest. If he could have at low cost pushed communism — or, to be more precise, extended *his* power — into Western Europe, no doubt he would have done exactly that. But he always had a tendency to exaggerate the strength of his enemies. Within the Soviet Union, where the balance of forces was in his favor, he had destroyed them; in international politics, where the balance was at best uncertain, he respected their power and tried to bluff and do business with them, and consolidate his own position, all at the same time. Perhaps he was more impressed by American power in the immediate postwar years than were the anxious American policymakers. Not only did the United States wield enormous economic strength, but its air power and the atomic bomb made up at least in the short term for the absence of a large American land army in Europe. He no doubt recognized that a major communist military or political assault in Western Europe would have generated an all-too-strong and unpredictable reaction in the United States. After all, the Americans had just intervened in Europe for the second time in less than three decades over the question of the balance of power on the Continent. Stalin presumably did not take too seriously the talk in the United States of preventive war, though no doubt he did take note of it. He also knew that, if circumstances changed, it could become a more immediate topic. In ordering the Yugoslavs to end their assistance in the Greek civil war, Stalin declared, as already noted, that Britain and the United States — "the United States, the most powerful state in the world" — would never permit their lines of communication in the Mediterranean to be broken. What he said about the American reaction to a communist victory in Greece could have been multiplied by ten for communist moves in France or Italy.[17]

Similarly, Stalin was not going to relinquish his sphere. The wartime Grand Alliance had been an international popular front. As its legacy and mirror, it had left behind national popular fronts, coalitions of communists and noncommunists. This was the case in Western Europe, in France and Italy, and also the case, although in far more difficult circumstances, in Eastern Europe, to varying degrees in Czechoslovakia, Hungary, even Poland. As the Grand Alliance fissured, such coalitions became anomalies, and coalition members on one side of the dividing line in Europe who were allied to forces on the other were regarded as fifth columnists, traitors-in-place. So strong was the memory of the Comintern that the Americans could not see clearly the advantages of dealing with national communist parties, of recognizing them as entities independent of Moscow, of using U.S. economic power to build a bridge across the chasm.

The worsening economic situation made the coalitions in Western Europe increasingly unstable.* Washington explained to the French and the Italians that economic aid was much more likely if (as the American ambassador in Italy put it), they "would find the means of correcting the present situation." Correction followed. The communists, though fighting hard to remain in the French and Italian governments, were pushed out of both in May 1947. A couple of days after the exclusion of the communists in France, John McCloy, the new president of the World Bank, announced a major loan to France.[18]

Stalin's answer came at the end of May — though it is still unclear whether this was a genuine response, a coincidence, or whether the Russians cynically used the changes in France and Italy as a pretext for their own purposes. In late 1945, under Soviet tutelage, the Hungarians had elected a noncommunist majority, with the leading role played by the Smallholders party. The country was governed by what the State Department privately called "a moderate coalition cabinet." The situation did not last. In February 1947, the former secretary-general of the Smallholders was arrested, allegedly confessed to espionage, and disappeared. Many in Hungary took as a very important signal the fact that his arrest had been carried out not by local security forces, but by the Red Army itself. In May, Premier Ferenc Nagy was implicated in the "confession," chose exile, and the communists very much tightened their control over the Hungarian government. This was only the most obvious example of how the Soviets were now consolidating their hold over Eastern Europe in the context of international polarization. Poland, for instance, had been the first issue to seriously divide the members of the Grand

* Of course, having communists in the Western European coalition governments did create problems. "We can't carry on a discussion between two Great Powers," Bevin had complained to Bidault, "with a third Great Power in the cupboard with a listening device."

Alliance, long before the war's end. In January 1947, it was resolved, in a fashion. That country had remained in a very unsettled domestic condition since the German defeat. As election day approached, the communists became ruthless against their opponents, the elections themselves were fraudulent, and the communist-dominated "Democratic Bloc" won an overwhelming majority in the parliament.

Polarization was having its influence in the West, as well, but there the now-excluded communist parties continued to function, protected by law. In Hungary, as elsewhere in Eastern Europe, terror was added to expulsion, with the consequent destruction not only of the noncommunist parties, but also of noncommunist politicians.

Most American officials saw the takeover in Hungary as further proof of Soviet expansionism. "You no doubt realize the extent to which this issue has rocked the Department," Harold Vedeler of the Central European Division wrote in August 1947 to Ambassador Steinhardt in Prague. "At the time the coup occurred many meetings and extended discussions were required before the Department was able to come to a conclusion on sending a note of protest rather than to take the matter to the Security Council at once." One of the reasons for not going to the Security Council was a desire to "concentrate on our Greek policy." Another was that if the Americans sought to have the Russians censured "for unilateral actions" in the Allied Control Council in Hungary, then "the Soviets might level counter charges against us concerning MacArthur's actions in Japan."

One could have viewed the events in Hungary in a less alarmist fashion — while not minimizing the internal consequences, still seeing it as a defensive, even conservative move on Stalin's part. Within the State Department some tried with no success to make that argument. "The Communist coup in Hungary is not 'a critical act of the struggle of Communism and Western Democracy for the control of Europe' but is rather a routine and anticipated move on the part of the USSR to plug an obvious gap in its security system," suggested H. Stuart Hughes, head of the Division of Research on Europe in the State Department. "It was not the democratic character of the Hungarian government that brought down upon it the wrath of the Soviet Union. It was its foreign policy of cultivating the favor of the Western democracies, particularly the United States. The Hungarian statesmen of the Smallholders Party simply refused to do as the

Czech leaders had done and to recognize the geographic and strategic realities that had placed their country within the Soviet sphere of influence and the consequent suicidal character of a pro-Western foreign policy." Hughes added that, if nothing more, "the Truman doctrine accelerated the process" of communization, for "the removal of the Communist ministers from the governments of France and Italy indicated that this doctrine was receiving a practical political interpretation in the West." [19]

As they devised this ambitious program of economic assistance for a prostrate polarized Europe, the Americans saw four challenges: first, to get the Europeans to create a cooperative plan that would move beyond relief to revitalization; second, to avoid the kind of criticism that had accumulated around the Truman Doctrine, of being too negative and too nakedly anticommunist; third, to keep the Russians out of the program; and, fourth, to get the Congress into the plan by winning its approval.

Marshall unveiled the concept in a speech at the Harvard Commencement on June 5, 1947. With his remarks, the State Department forestalled some of the sort of criticism that had hurt the Greek-Turkish program. Marshall sketched the picture of European collapse; called for a program of reconstruction, not relief; asked the Europeans to take the initiative; and invited all nations to participate, which meant that the Soviet Union was implicitly included in the invitation.[20]

The open invitation, however, was a ploy. The prospect that Russia might actually accept greatly alarmed the Americans, who had already written off the Economic Commission for Europe because of Soviet participation. But they had not wanted to bear the onus of excluding Russia from the proposed program. That would have created political problems in Western Europe. The U.S. might have been viewed as the power that had partitioned Europe. (Onus-shifting was one of the main goals of diplomacy and propaganda in these years, with each side trying to convince the international galleries that all blame for dividing the Continent lay with the other.) On the other hand, the Americans were hardly disposed to grant any aid to Russia for fear that it would try to immobilize any program it did join, and they were also convinced that Soviet participation would be the quickest way to assure congressional rejection. As Bohlen put it a few years later, they had taken "a hell of a big gamble" in not explicitly excluding Russia.

Their concern mounted when Molotov arrived in Paris at the end of June with upward of a hundred advisers, to join Bevin and Bidault in preliminary discussions on a European program. "I am deeply concerned about the next six months," Forrestal said on July 2, "and I've got one eye on what's going on in Paris and what I think will be the alternative if the result I hope eventuates from that — namely — that the Russians don't come in. I think the most disastrous thing would be if they did." [21] But the Americans could have been more confident then they were. The odds were in their favor. "In the discussion of any concrete proposals touching on American aid to Europe," read the internal instructions for the Russian group, "the Soviet delegation shall object in terms of aid that might prejudice the sovereignty of the European countries or infringe upon their economic independence." What that meant became evident when Molotov offered his own plan in the preliminary discussions: each country to draw up a list of its needs, and then ask the United States to come up with the requisite money. But it was clear to all the delegates in Paris that in exchange for aid the United States would insist on inspection, considerable disclosure, and cooperation, and that both the British and the French would agree to that approach, and that the Russians would not. As we shall see, the Russians were also concerned about the effect of such a program on their hold over Eastern Europe, and they realized that it would almost certainly deny them reparations from the Western zones of Germany. Moreover, in the American scheme the Russians might actually have been required to provide raw materials to Western Europe.

Molotov, according to Djilas, considered accepting an invitation to the follow-up planning conference, so that he could then stage a walk-out, but was overruled by Moscow; and so, on July 2, Molotov and his delegation packed up and speedily departed Paris and the preliminary meeting, blasting American imperialism on the way out.[22]

The Americans had hoped, however, that some of the Eastern European countries would participate in the program. In this regard, the Marshall Plan was the last great effort, using the powerful and attractive magnetism of the American economy, to draw these countries out of the Soviet orbit. The effort represented a reversal. In

1946, Washington had very consciously restricted and tightened aid and refused to give credits in an ill-conceived attempt to force those countries to break formally with the Soviet Union on foreign policy issues.[23]

Responding to Marshall's speech, Poland indicated that it might attend the Europe-wide conference that was to open in Paris on July 12. Certainly Poland's needs were great. UNRRA had estimated that, after termination of its own program, Poland would require almost $300 million in relief in 1947 just to satisfy such basic needs as "the health and growth requirements of her children and mothers." In the middle of 1947, 80 percent of Warsaw remained in rubble; up to 30,000 corpses still lay buried beneath the ruins of the Warsaw Ghetto. Polish officials made clear that they wanted to trade with the West. And in fact Poland was still trying, under its communist leaders, to pursue a path somewhat independent of Moscow. Wladyslaw Gomulka, secretary-general of the Polish party, was not following the Soviet model. He even went so far, in May 1947, as to declare that Marxism "does not give us any ready, universal indication or recipe which can be made use of with an identifiable result, without regard to time, place, and the existing conditions." [24] More obviously than Poland, Czechoslovakia was trying to maintain an independent course. Foreign Minister Jan Masaryk was a guest on the yacht of the Norwegian foreign minister when word came through that Molotov had agreed to go to Paris. "Never in my life have I seen a man so happy as Masaryk," remembered the Norwegian minister.[25]

After their Paris walk-out, the Russians would hardly allow the nations of Eastern Europe to participate in the American scheme. The Poles abruptly announced on July 9 that they would not attend the follow-up conference that was to open three days later. For the Czechs, matters were more complicated. They had already said that they would attend the second meeting. Masaryk and the communist premier Klement Gottwald, in Moscow on other business, were suddenly summoned to the Kremlin. Stalin and Molotov, expressing "surprise" at the Czech intention, indicated that they understood at least part of the purpose of the Marshall Plan; for they reportedly "emphasized their conviction that the real aim of the Marshall Plan and the Paris Conference is to create a western bloc and isolate the Soviet Union . . . Even if the loans should be granted sometime in the future by America they would not be without decisive limitations on the political and economic independence of the recipients." Thus, said the Soviet leaders, Czech participation would be interpreted "as an act specifically aimed against the USSR."

The Czechs renounced their acceptance.[26]

The most important reason for the Soviets' rejection of the plan would seem to have been their fear that it would disrupt their sphere in Eastern Europe. Second, they saw the Marshall Plan as an alternative to reparations — but an alternative that might be of no benefit to them. It was less important that American economists would poke around in Soviet production statistics. And because the Russians rejected the plan, so did the Eastern Europeans.

"Perhaps in view of the manner in which the incident dramatically revealed the real position of Czechoslovakia in international affairs, there could be detected a certain sympathy in the Department for this country, or at least the moderates, which had not been apparent since the summer of 1946," commented Harold Vedeler of Central European Affairs. But the Czech "trip to Canossa," as Vedeler called it, also created an odd kind of pleasure in American policy councils, in effect, further proof of malignant Soviet intentions. "Russians smoked out in their relations with satellite countries," Kennan noted to Marshall. "Maximum strain placed on those relations." The Americans did not see the Soviet reaction to the Marshall Plan as a defensive move by a country that could hardly compete with the United States economically, but rather as a further indication of aggressive designs. "The Czechoslovak reversal on the Paris Conference, on Soviet orders, is nothing less than a declaration of war by the Soviet Union on the immediate issue of the control of Europe," commented Ambassador Smith in Moscow. "The lines are drawn."[27]

The most important line on the European map had been drawn two years before, in 1945. It divided Germany between East and West. This line was supposed to be temporary, in pencil, as it were. But now, in 1947, it was about to be permanently inked in. For the Marshall Plan also provided a solution to the vexing problem of what to do about Germany. The basic question had remained unanswered. Were the Four Powers (but principally the United States and the Soviet Union) to cooperate in policing and punishing the former Reich, or were the occupation zones in the former Reich to become potential allies for one side or the other in the developing confrontation? For many months, American opinion on Germany had been shifting steadily away from favoring cooperation with the Russians. The failure to agree on common policies with the Russians and the expenses and difficulties of the occupation encouraged the trend. Moreover, as Europe failed to revive economically, the conviction grew in the West that Germany would have to play a central role in Western European reconstruction.[28]

In the autumn of 1946, Americans had taken a step toward partition when they amalgamated the British and American zones to form Bizonia. The initial emphasis was on economic problems alone. The Americans studiously avoided giving Bizonia a political coloration, because, explained General Clay in September 1946, "We believe it would widen the gap between west and east." [29] But by the end of 1946, Americans, at least those within policy councils, were tending to see Germany as a battleground between East and West. In December, former general John Hilldring, now Assistant Secretary of State for Occupied Territories, provided the double rationale for Bizonia: "It will serve the purpose of getting the United States government out of the red in three years in Germany, and it will give us a climate in which to plant our political ideas in Germany." He added, "We are fighting all totalitarian concepts in Germany, Nazism and Communism."

The break-up in April 1947 of the Moscow Council of Foreign Ministers meeting with no progress on Germany provided the impetus for the Americans to take the next steps. As Clay noted in early April, "My three weeks at Moscow convinced me that nothing of import will come from this conference other than to bring the issues squarely on the table." [30]

We must recognize, however, that "success" at Moscow might well have disturbed the Americans more than failure, for many feared that any compromise that maintained Four-Power unity would open the door to Soviet domination of Germany and the rest of Europe. "The present zonal basis will continue, which, I think, is good," Dulles wrote to Vandenberg during the Moscow Council. "It is useful to have more time to consolidate the Western zones and not expose them yet to Communist penetration." [31] Upon Marshall's return from Moscow, the reorientation of U.S. policy speeded up. The

Americans put more emphasis on raising the level of industry and restoring production in Germany, and thought more about the possibilities of a West German state.[32]

But the efforts to push economic recovery in Germany continued to encounter already familiar obstacles. While the overall thrust was clear, implementation created conflict and confusion between the State and War Departments. Clay frequently became so riled that he almost habitually announced his imminent resignation. An ongoing controversy between the British and Americans over the "level of industry" and socialism in the Ruhr coal mines hindered the development of Bizonia. Moreover, the very idea of economic recovery generated much resistance, for the future of Germany remained a volatile issue. The Russians, of course, remained adamant on the subject of reparations and obsessively fearful of a revivified Germany. But U.S. encouragement of German recovery also stirred much opposition in Western Europe, especially France. In addition, the Western Europeans wanted their reparations from Germany. "We have had a stop order in effect on reparations from our zone since May 1946," John Steelman, a senior White House adviser, informed the President in the spring of 1947. "As a result, we are getting a great deal of the blame for the inability of many western European nations to restore their capital goods structure. Moreover, much of the German plant is standing idle and some is rusting away."

The apprehension about German recovery was also widespread in the United States, and reached some who were close to the President, such as Edwin Pauley, Truman's reparations adviser. In March 1947, Herbert Hoover, returning from a survey of Europe for the Administration in one of his annual forays into foreign policy, wrote a report urging that German recovery be given the highest priority. Hoover's proposals outraged Pauley, who warned the President that they "would restore Germany to the same dominant position of industrial power which it held before the war . . . I cannot avoid looking into the future and contemplating the Germany which this plan would produce — a Germany not merely as powerful industrially as the Germany of Hitler, but *more* powerful because of the incredible advances of science." No one doubted, of course, that *something* had to be done about Germany — and quickly. "We are reaching a point," John Steelman told the President, "where almost any action would be an improvement." But he added, "There must be other approaches to these problems than the revival of a German colossus along the lines suggested by Mr. Hoover." [33]

The Marshall Plan was that other approach, an alternative solution to the German problem. It reduced the tension over German recovery by placing that nation at the center of a Continent-wide effort. Without Germany, it was argued, Europe could never recover, and the Americans made clear to jittery Europeans that success in the Marshall Plan depended upon an economically vital Germany. Aid from the United States would compensate the Western Europeans for the reparations they would not be getting from Germany. Meanwhile, economic recovery would keep most of Germany looking to the West, and so integrated into a Western system. Here, then, were the central and double aims of the Marshall Plan — economic recovery and economic containment. Here, also, was a solution to the German Question. But, while the American occupation authorities had a plan for the political fusion of Bizonia that they had informally discussed with the British by August 1947, they were reluctant to go the whole distance and commit themselves to the establishment of a separate government in Western Germany, at least until after the next Council of Foreign Ministers meeting.[34]

By the terms of Marshall's offer, the Europeans (albeit abetted by American "friendly aid in the drafting") were to draw up the actual plan themselves. This they did, though not without difficulty. There was a certain degree of suspicion of American intentions. The British believed that the U.S. was trying to interfere with the Labour Party's welfare state program, and they also thought Washington had aggravated England's financial problems. Galloping inflation in the U.S. had certainly compounded the dollar shortage. Britain was "being rooked" by the Americans, Dalton complained at the end of July. "We should tell them that we were going to *stop buying* and keep them guessing for how long . . . The result of this would be to bring prices down." The French opposed a concentration on German recovery for powerful emotional, as well as strategic, reasons. It was feared that this issue, highly explosive in French domestic politics, could topple the government. In addition, France had hopes of replacing German steel production with its own.

There was a good deal of conflict within the American government, as well. The State Department needed to convince the War

Department to integrate Bizonia formally into the planning for the Marshall Plan. At the end of August, Charles Bonesteel, who had moved over from War to State, provided Undersecretary Lovett with a script for a conference meant to persuade top-level War Department officials that Bizonia should become part of the Marshall Plan. In Bonesteel's dialogue and stage directions, we again see how officials polished their own beliefs, rather than fabricating fake ones, to sell policies: "Our approach should be more educational, with a slight dictatorial flavor . . . Chip and yourself present the broad global picture, bringing out the two-world assumption and the need to work on a tighter organization of the Soviet world. The importance of treating Europe west of the Iron Curtain on a regional basis should then be emphasized." After advising that "the budgetary nettle" be firmly grasped, Bonesteel moved to his climax. "We should then put forward the requirement that the German economic matters be discussed at Paris . . . Emphasis should be laid on the security aspect of drawing more closely to us the nations of Western Europe now wavering between communism and us. Throughout the presentation the strategic and security aspects should be underlined and emphasized at every opportunity."

As the Marshall Plan discussions proceeded, there was also disagreement within the State Department. Washington became unhappy with the excessive zeal applied to tariff reductions by one of the American officials who was helping to provide "friendly aid" by sitting in on the negotiations among the Europeans. Will Clayton — "Doctrinaire Willie," as Dalton had taken to calling him — was, in Washington's view, giving rather too much attention to reducing trade barriers, and U.S. officials exerted pressure "to bring Mr. Clayton fully in line with the departmental position." [35]

In mid-September, the sixteen Western European nations completed a proposal — with provisions to increase production and exports, create financial stability, and provide for increased economic cooperation. They forwarded it to the United States, and asked for twenty billion dollars over the next four years to pay for imports from America.

Despite efforts to deflect possible criticism of the proposal in Europe and the United States, American policymakers thought of the Marshall Plan as "a Truman Doctrine in Action" (in George Elsey's words). That is, it was a countermove to Soviet expansionism. "The problem is Russia," War Secretary Robert Patterson wrote to a newspaper publisher in June 1947. The "real menace," he said, was "the basic belief of the ruling group in the USSR that a communist state cannot exist in the company of democratic states." He also noted how he had shifted from the Yalta to the Riga outlook: "I thought during the war that the belief had been abandoned, but apparently it is still part of the creed. It means aggression, of course." [36]

What Patterson was expressing, of course, was the shared view of the men within the Executive who were making U.S. foreign policy. But now their common outlook was given formal, public, and even elegant statement. The prestigious journal *Foreign Affairs* published in its July issue an article entitled "The Sources of Soviet Conduct." Its author was a certain Mr. X. Appearing just as Molotov was sitting down in Paris with Bevin and Bidault to discuss Marshall's offer, the article undoubtedly strengthened the Kremlin's conviction that the Marshall Plan was primarily an anti-Soviet device. This Mr. X, author of what is arguably the single most famous magazine article in American history, was soon revealed to be none other than George Kennan — at this point head of the State Department's Policy Planning Staff and one of the major authors of the Marshall Plan. The article would forever link Kennan's name to the policy of containment.

The godfather of the article was James Forrestal, who for many, many months had been asking in one form or another that same question — whether the United States was facing a traditional nation-state or a militant religion. Forrestal personally had few doubts but that it was the latter. It will be recalled that he had commissioned an analysis on the subject by a Smith College professor, Edward Willett, who had explained Soviet foreign policy almost entirely in terms of ideology. Forrestal had been distributing Willett's various drafts to a decidedly mixed reaction. "I question the adequacy of an analysis of Russian foreign policy based mainly upon deductions from dogma," Robert Strausz-Hupe of the University of Pennsylvania informed Forrestal. Philip Mosely of Columbia University commented, "I cannot agree in drawing the conclusion that the Soviet government operates blindly on the basis of philosophical assumptions. It is only one element which enters into an immediate and concrete decision or into a program of, say, ten years of policy as sketched out for the future when they envision it." [37]

And, of course, Forrestal had sought the opinion of George Kennan, who, instead of commenting, presented at the end of January his own paper on "The Psychological Background of Soviet Foreign Policy." Virtually unchanged, it found its way as the Mr. X article into the July issue of *Foreign Affairs*.[38] Kennan had been asked to comment on a paper stressing the role of Soviet ideology, and this, as he himself said afterward, undoubtedly affected the thrust of his own piece. But Kennan was also continuing the line of argument of the Long Telegram as he here made the case that the United States was dealing not with a Great Power pursuing imperial goals, but principally with a messianic religion, an ideological force, for which coexistence was always a threat.

"Its political action," Kennan wrote, "is a fluid stream which moves constantly, wherever it is permitted to move, toward a given goal. Its main concern is to make sure that it has filled every nook and cranny available to it in the basin of world power. But if it finds unassailable barriers in its path, it accepts these philosophically and accommodates itself to them." The appropriate response, Kennan called "containment" — "the adroit and vigilant application of counterforce at a series of constantly shifting geographical and political points, corresponding to the shifts and maneuvers of Soviet Policy." He expressed some exultation over the challenge and "a certain gratitude to a Providence which, by providing the American people with this implacable challenge, has made their entire security as a nation dependent on their pulling themselves together and accepting the responsibilities of moral and political leadership that history plainly intended them to bear."

The article, reiterating the Riga outlook in a bipolar world, did express the outlook of the Truman Administration. It provided a name — "containment" — to describe this thrust in American foreign policy. But it should be noted that Kennan meant to admonish not only those whom he considered still blind to the inevitable challenge, but also those whose alarm had run wild. To that latter group, he was saying that the confrontation should not be seen in military terms, that hostilities need not be imminent, and that preventive war was unnecessary.

"The Sources of Soviet Conduct," by Mr. X, received wide attention. The article was quoted and cited, it seemed, almost everywhere in the American press. Both *Life* and *Reader's Digest* excerpted it. "I thought you might be interested in having a copy of the article by 'X' in the July issue of *Foreign Affairs* and have therefore arranged to get some reprints, one of which I enclose," a State Department official wrote to the American ambassador in Czechoslovakia. "I give you one guess on whom the author is . . . We leave it to you to make such distribution on a personal basis in your area as you may consider appropriate." [39]

By the summer of 1947, the "two-world assumption" had completely displaced any notions of cooperation. From Moscow, Ambassador Smith described the Czech reversal on the Marshall Plan as a Soviet declaration of war for the control of Europe. It is probable in turn that the Russians saw the Marshall Plan as a declaration of war by the United States for control of Europe. Although clothed in generous language, it capped a process of reorientation for Washington, away from relief and reconstruction per se to relief, reconstruction, *and* anticommunism. American aid would no longer be used to create links and bridges, but rather to isolate communists. The Russians now assumed that the United States would use its great economic power for the specific goal of isolating the Soviet Union, and that American leaders had lost all interest in the Great Power consortium. The Marshall Plan precipitated a dramatic shift in Soviet foreign policy. That the Czechs and even the Poles would consider participating in the Marshall Plan despite Soviet displeasures indicated to Stalin that a dangerous diversity existed within his sphere. This he would no longer tolerate in a changing international environment. For Stalin, spheres of influence would no longer mean a process of mutual accommodation but rather one of hostile confrontation.

In December 1947, Laurence Steinhardt, the American ambassador to Czechoslovakia, gave his own testimony as to the change that followed the Czech acceptance and then renunciation of the invitation to discuss the Marshall Plan: "It is no mere coincidence that the rather benign attitude of Moscow toward the Czech government suddenly hardened after the acceptance. By benign I mean that up to that time the Russians had not exercised much pressure on them. They had made a few suggestions here and there in connection with their political and commercial decisions, but not much more than other governments make to one another, and they had not, as far as we could see, directly interfered or given any orders." [40] Perhaps by

December of 1947, U.S. policymakers were feeling some nostalgia for the ambiguity that had characterized the Czech position in 1946 and into 1947.

The first public reaction to the Marshall Plan by the Russians was a hastily improvised series of trade treaties with Eastern Europe, called, with some exaggeration, the Molotov Plan. This, however, was only the beginning of the Russian efforts to consolidate a new empire.

If there was any turning point in Soviet policy toward Eastern Europe and the West, it was the organizing conference of the Cominform — the Communist Information Bureau — held in September 1947 in a manor house that was now a sanitorium belonging to the Polish State Security Service. Not a lineal descendant of the Comintern, and of considerably more exclusive membership, the Cominform advertised itself as a coordinating body for national communist parties in the Soviet Union and Eastern Europe, along with those of France and Italy. It was totally dominated by the Soviets, and was to be used to tighten the Soviet hold on Eastern Europe. It was also the mechanism for directing the Italian and French Communist parties to begin those disruptive activities in which, Washington thought, they were already engaged.

The Cominform was a device for restoring ideological unity to the communist parties, but this was ideology not in the service of Marx, but of the Soviet state. At the meeting in Poland, Andrei Zhdanov, already identified as a keeper of ideological purity in the USSR, proclaimed the division of the international system into two camps — that of "imperialist and anti-democratic forces" and that of "democratic and anti-imperialist forces." Curiously, he said that Soviet foreign policy continued to be based on the possibility of coexistence between capitalism and communism, but now the United States was creating a hostile bloc against the socialist states — that is, against the Soviet Union. The United States, he said, was an expansionist power, as evidenced by the network of military bases it was establishing around the world, and by the use of its economic power to create a sphere of influence over Western Europe and over Britain and its empire. There was some degree of truth in what Zhdanov said, although the Americans hardly saw it. Nor could the Russians admit that American policy was in part in response to a perceived threat of Soviet power and influence. Zhdanov was obviously deeply concerned about the revitalization of the Western zones in

Germany and their integration into a Western political and economic system.

The Soviets were responding in kind, and with a vengeance, to the drawing together of such a Western bloc. The cynical Russians, joined by the enthusiastic Yugoslavs, denounced the French and Italian parties for their parliamentary reformist course, their popular-frontism — the very line approved in the last meeting of the Comintern in 1943, and, more important, mandated by Stalin himself during and immediately after the war. "While you are fighting to stay in the Government," Zhdanov now taunted the French communists, "they throw you out." He ridiculed the Italians: "You Italian comrades are bigger parliamentarians than de Gasperi himself. You are the biggest political party, and yet they throw you out of the Government." Jacques Duclos, the representative of the French Communist Party, went into shock; he sat by himself in the park swinging his legs, talking to no one. He literally cried in rage. The Italian and French parties left the meeting in Poland with their marching orders: to intensify the class struggle, to go over — as they did with disruptive strikes — into opposition against the Marshall Plan and American influence.

In Eastern Europe, political diversity was to come to a quick end. Zhdanov criticized "national communism." This was an attack on Gomulka, who had defended a "Polish way to socialism," which was wide enough to accommodate the small entrepreneur and farmer. In fact, Gomulka had resisted the whole idea of a Cominform, but he was forced to accede to the Russian demand that the Cominform endorse collectivization (on the Soviet model) as the only appropriate path to socialism. In Berlin at the same time, East German communists were instructed that there was no longer a separate German road to socialism. The Cominform meeting marked the beginning of the Stalinist reign of terror in Eastern Europe, although the worst was yet to come. In the autumn of 1947, there was still a coalition in Czechoslovakia, although it seemed more and more like an archeological remnant, a relic of another time and spirit.[41]

Meanwhile, in Washington, the Truman Administration was very worried that Congress would not approve the Marshall Plan, even though the $20 billion proposed by the Europeans had been pared to $17 billion. Policymakers were sure that a congressional rejection would lead to the collapse of Europe. Budget-conscious Republicans, now in the majority on Capitol Hill, and highly suspicious of liberal "give-aways," were vocally resistant to the idea of further aid. They complained, as they added up the host of programs approved or pending, that (in the words of Representative John Taber) "there seem to be no grasp of any business principles in connection with this situation." There was also resistance on procedural grounds, a continuing resentment of the dramatic manner in which the Truman Doctrine was introduced, which had seemed to preclude any real debate.[42]

To deflect such criticism, the State Department drew Vandenberg deeply into the development of the Marshall Plan. A few years later Marshall would recall that he and the Michigan senator "couldn't have gotten much closer together unless I sat in Vandenberg's lap or he sat in mine." The Administration put considerable effort into selling the plan to Congress and the public. Hosts of special committees — some presidentially appointed, some congressional, some composed of leading laity like the now-retired Henry Stimson — studied the matter. All of them reported that the Marshall Plan was essential to the national security, and that it would help, not hurt, the United States economically. Even so, the winning of congressional approval was difficult.

An important point must be made here. As with the Truman Doctrine, the Executive was consciously trying to "educate," even manipulate, public opinion. But, again as with the Greek-Turkish aid, it was doing this in order to bring the public around to accepting its own worried world view. The arguments that the Administration used to present the issue to the public were congruent with the concerns expressed privately within policy councils. In their attempt to educate public opinion American leaders may have confused two things — the Soviet Union as the alleged perpetrator of economic distress in Europe, and the Soviet Union as likely beneficiary of that distress. But, then, that distinction was blurred in their own minds. When Marshall left Moscow in April 1947, he was convinced that the Soviet Union was deliberately retarding European recovery to achieve its own political goals.[43]

The sense of urgency among U.S. policymakers, high from the beginning, kept increasing, as it became more and more apparent that they had continued to underestimate the depth of the crisis. "At no time in my recollection have I ever seen a world situation which was moving so rapidly toward real trouble," wrote Undersecretary Lovett at the end of July, "and I have the feeling that this is the last clear shot that we will have in finding a solution." A few weeks later, Henry Ford II, as a member of a presidential air policy commission, went to see Lovett. "He was even more pessimistic than were the Joint Chiefs of Staff," Ford reported, "and felt that war could come at any time and that there were at least two crises a day in the State Department." The President himself was feeling the same way. "The British have turned out to be our problem children now," Truman wrote to his sister in August. "They've decided to go bankrupt and if they do that, it will end our prosperity and probably all the world's too. Then Uncle Joe Stalin can have his way. Looks like he may get it anyway." [44]

Bad news followed bad news in August and into September. The smallest wheat crop in France in 132 years. Extra rations distributed to Ruhr coal miners in a desperate bid to encourage higher production. Near-exhaustion of dollar reserves in France and Italy, while U.S. prices kept rising. Many European countries cutting back on the purchases of essential U.S. goods. And massive strikes — the communist parties in the West now clearly bent on a policy of opposition and disruption.[45]

The State Department's Policy Planning Staff summed up the situation: "The margin of safety in Europe, both from an economic and political viewpoint, is extremely thin." U.S. leaders concluded in early autumn 1947 that a Marshall Plan approved and appropriated by Congress in mid-1948 would be too late unless stopgap aid were provided immediately.[46]

At the end of September, Truman hosted a small group of congressmen in the Cabinet Room at the White House.

"I do hope that we can reach some decision on this and get things started," Truman said. "General Marshall has reviewed the trouble he is having with Russia in the United States, and Bob Lovett has given you the detailed picture. We'll either have to provide a program of interim aid relief until the Marshall program gets going, or the governments of France and Italy will fall, Austria too, and for all practical purposes Europe will be Communist. The Marshall Plan goes out of the window, and it's a question of how long we could stand up in such a situation. This is serious. I can't overemphasize how serious."

"I had hoped very much, Mr. President, there would be no special session of Congress," said Sam Rayburn. "Can't something be worked out?"

"It doesn't seem we can get the money any other way, Sam," replied Truman. "Congress has got to act."

"That is just the situation," added Lovett.

"Then the plan had better be well worked out, right down to the details, and everything ready so that we can get right to it the minute Congress meets," said Rayburn.

"Communism has started its campaign of aggression," said Charles Eaton, the Republican who was chairman of the House Foreign Affairs Committee. "We have already met the challenge in Greece and Turkey. We've got to stop Communism, and I'm ready to work with Senator Vandenberg."

But Majority Leader Charles Halleck had a word of caution: "Mr. President, you must realize there is a growing resistance to these programs. I have been out in the hustings, and I know. The people don't like it."

On October 15, Clark Clifford summarized the reasons for calling a special session of Congress: "Two most important issues today are high prices and aid to Europe. They are inevitably bound together. The situation in each instance is getting worse . . . In France the subway and bus strike is spreading and we can expect serious trouble. The President must have a plan. It must be thought through now so it can be quietly set in motion."[47] On October 23, Truman announced that he was calling the special session. The campaign for foreign aid continued. "The people can never understand why the President does not use his supposedly great power to make 'em behave," Truman wrote to his sister on November 14. "Well all the President is, is a glorified public relations man who spends his time flattering, kissing and kicking people to get them to do what they are supposed to do anyway." Three days later, he presented to a joint session of Congress his proposal for almost $600 million in interim aid for France, Italy, and Austria. A month later, after more debate and more flattering, kissing, and kicking, he was able to sign the bills providing the emergency assistance.[48]

Between Truman's message and the approval of interim aid, there occurred the last act, the anticlimax, of the Yalta approach — the London Council of Foreign Ministers meeting. As in Moscow the preceding spring, the issue again was how to proceed on a German peace settlement and what to do — or not do — about reparations. No optimism remained; polarization had gone too far. The Americans, British, and French all thought in advance that this Council would almost certainly fail, that they would not be able to work out a German settlement with the Russians, and that therefore they should go ahead and consolidate the Western zones. The Russians, for their part, expected to face a united Western front, which was planning to establish a Trizonia, and they were extremely bitter about the steps toward fusion that had already taken place.[49]

In October, looking ahead to the Council, Robert Murphy laid out Administration thinking on Germany. "We have maintained the position until there is either a break-down of the Four-Power relationship in Germany, or a solution of it, that we would not admit having established a political structure." However, if the London meeting did not lead to a resolution, "shortly thereafter we would be obliged to develop a political organization in Western Germany." He added, "Naturally, this is a serious step." The United States would be accused of splitting Germany, but Murphy was not too much concerned about this. "We will have to meet that charge when we get to it and we are prepared to do so."

He did foresee one danger — Berlin — "an island in the heart of the Soviet zone." The Russians, he explained, "could easily make our lives unbearable and we would eventually have to leave Berlin. But we have no intention of doing so."

There was something paradoxical in the American stance. Expecting failure in London, the Americans, along with the British, were at work on the foundations of a new West German state as an alternative to a Four-Power occupation. But such preparations in themselves were sure to increase Soviet suspicion and obstructionism and thus would guarantee the very failure that the Americans and British were convinced was at hand. On balance, however, it must also be said that the deterioration of the Four-Power occupation had proceeded apace, day by day, over many months. By the time of the London meeting, the Americans had had just about enough of any effort toward a Four-Power German settlement. Indeed, they feared it.* [50]

* On November 6, Marshall told the Cabinet that all he expected from the Russians at the next Council of Foreign Ministers meeting were "various ruses . . . to try to get us

So, there were charges and countercharges at the London meeting, which opened on November 25, 1947, but little of substance — save for what happened when the meeting ended. France left no doubt that it now belonged to the Western bloc; indeed, the French even encouraged secret meetings during the London Council among the three Western foreign ministers to discuss other possible solutions to the German question.

Knowing that he was isolated, Molotov responded with unyielding intransigence and acid propaganda. In 1933, it may be recalled, William Bullitt had marveled at what he called Molotov's "magnificent forehead" and was reminded of a "first-rate French scientist, great poise, kindliness and intelligence." But now all that Westerners noticed on Molotov's forehead was a bump that swelled when he felt pressured.[51] He was certainly under such stress in London, as he tried to find some way to stop the movement toward unification in the Western zone. But his violent language only strengthened the determination of the Western powers to proceed.

The two sides debated back and forth on reparations. The Russians still sought reparations valued at ten billion dollars, to be delivered by 1965. To this, the British were somewhat more responsive than the Americans, perhaps because they were more sensitive to the war ravages of the Nazis. But both nations rejected any compromise with the Russians on this issue. The State Department believed that Congress would not vote aid for Europe were the Soviet Union to receive German reparations.

On December 3, Bevin told Harold Nicolson about his strenuous efforts, the day before, to have a real heart-to-heart talk in his own flat with Molotov.

"You cannot look on me as an enemy of Russia," Bevin had said to the Soviet foreign minister. "Why, when our Government was trying to stamp out your Revolution, who was it that stopped it? It was I, Ernest Bevin. I called out the transport workers and they refused to load the ships. I wanted you to have your Revolution in your own

---

out of western Germany under arrangements which would leave that country defenseless against communist penetration." He explained, "The world situation is still dominated by the Russian effort in the post-hostilities period to extend their virtual domination over all, or as much as possible, of the European land mass." He said that the Americans would resist the Soviet moves at the foreign ministers meeting and instead "see that [Germany] is better integrated into Western Europe" and press the other Western European countries to so accept Western Germany.

way and without interference. Now again I am speaking as a friend. You are playing a very dangerous game. And I can't make out why. You don't really believe that any American wants to go to war with you — or, at least, no responsible American. We most certainly do not want to. But you are playing with fire, Mr. Molotov . . . If war comes between you and America in the East, then we may be able to remain neutral. But if war comes between you and America in the West, then we shall be on America's side. Make no mistake about that. That would be the end of Russia and of your Revolution. So please stop sticking out your neck in this way and tell me what you are after. What do you want?"

"I want a unified Germany," replied Molotov.

That was virtually all Bevin could get out of him.[52]

But a bit of explication is needed. A "unified" Germany meant treating Germany as an economic unit so that the Russians could obtain reparations from the Western zones. It also meant preventing the birth of a strong, Western-oriented West Germany.

Meanwhile, strikes, in part led by the communists to protest the Marshall Plan, were spreading in France. With Marshall's permission, John Foster Dulles left London on December 4 for a firsthand survey of the French situation. He brought back an alarming report — utilities running only intermittently in Paris, his own train rerouted because tracks had been blown up, industry at a standstill. The impression was widespread that Europe was rolling toward the precipice while the conference dragged on. *New York Times* correspondent C. L. Sulzberger wrote in his diary that he had come to Brussels "mainly to organize an emergency system in case the strike wave shuts off communications with New York; or even worse, in case it becomes a real political menace and a Communist bid to take over in Europe . . . am also distributing large chunks of money to correspondents in France, Belgium, Italy, Spain so they can get out their families if necessary, amid chaos." [53]

By December 6, Bevin and Marshall were privately planning how to bring about a breakdown in the Council.

"We ought," said Bevin, "to force the debate on the main outstanding economic questions and also possibly indicate our requirements for the political organization of Germany in a way to bring out that the Soviet objective was a Communist-controlled Germany."

"Quite frankly," replied Marshall, "what would be popular in the

U.S. would be that I should break off and tell the Russians to go to the devil." But he feared that such popular approval would not last. "It might be wise to indicate the differences on matters of real substance and to suggest that unless agreement could be had on them we would have to proceed — always making it clear, however, that we were not permanently breaking. It was important, of course, to choose our ground carefully and to time it to the best possible advantage."

Marshall, who had no intention of sitting through a long conference, concluded that the meeting could serve no further use. On December 11, he reported to Washington: "It is plainly evident that Molotov is not only playing for time but is consistently, almost desperately, endeavoring to reach agreements which really would be an embarrassment to us in the next four to six months rather than true evidence of getting together."

"We are all with you," Truman wired Marshall.[54]

During the weekend of December 13 and 14, the American delegation reached the decision to end the session. And so at the seventeenth session on Monday, December 15, after a last debate on reparations, Marshall called for adjournment. "No real progress could be made because of Soviet obstructionism," he said.

Denying responsibility for the impasse, Molotov accused Marshall of seeking adjournment "in order to give the U.S. a free hand to do as it pleased in its zone of Germany."

The Council, said Bidault, "should adjourn rather than further aggravate relations between the Four Powers." On that, at least, the foreign ministers could agree, and adjourn they did, without fixing a date for another meeting.

There was a certain relief in the break-up. "The Russians had at last run against a solid front," said Marshall three days later, with some satisfaction. But the ministers also recognized the gravity of the situation. Bidault privately worried that there might be a rupture in French-Soviet diplomatic relations, and that a coup was imminent in Czechoslovakia.[55]

The Council led to two specific outcomes. First, the Western powers agreed among themselves to move further toward the creation of a new West German political state, although trying to avoid, as Robert Murphy put it, "unseemly haste." There would be one more try at a united Germany, and if that did not work, then Bizonia would become the basis of this new state, along with, it was hoped, the French zone. They committed themselves to a German currency reform, an economic move to counter inflation, but also of great political significance if done without the Russians. The Western countries would carry it out by themselves if necessary, although Clay believed that it was not "absolutely impossible" to get the Russians to go along on a new currency.

Second, Bevin and Marshall decided that some kind of Western alliance was required. "The issue," Bevin said, "was where power was going to rest." He elaborated: "We must devise some western democratic system comprising the Americans, ourselves, France, Italy, etc. and of course the Dominions. This would not be a formal alliance, but an understanding backed by power, money and resolute action. It would be a sort of spiritual federation of the west."

There was no choice, Marshall replied. Events had to be taken "at the flood stream." [56]

Just before the Council session had opened, Edwin Pauley, occupying what was by then the largely ceremonial post of special adviser on reparations, had written to Marshall: "The forthcoming CFM meeting will be one of transcendental significance. It will constitute one of the Great Divides of American policy in this era."

Pauley was right. The London Council marked the end of the approach to postwar relations with the Soviet Union that Roosevelt had so optimistically, yet tentatively, outlined in the midst of the war. Such an approach had failed, ending in a dismal parody of diplomacy. We might be more precise and say that the Yalta axioms had died some months earlier, at Moscow in the spring of 1947. At London, they were buried. The Americans now looked in other directions.

Nations try to live less dangerously, to find some security, and so the Americans responded in kind to what they feared — to the threat of war by preparing themselves for war. The aging Admiral Leahy expressed the consensus among U.S. leaders when he wrote, the day after the break-up — in the course of noting in his diary that the impasse on Germany had resulted from Soviet insistence on reparations — that the consortium was finished. "No proposal was made by any of the Foreign Ministers for another meeting and it appears now that some other method of arranging a peace in Europe must be found." One step, he said, was a separate treaty with a Western-oriented West Germany, although "the Soviet Government would offer violent objection to such, even to the extent of using military power if necessary." Indeed, he feared that Russia would decide "to start its 'inevitable' war without delay." There was no choice in Leahy's mind — American foreign policy had to be militarized.

"In view of the very menacing situation that confronts western civilization," wrote the admiral, "I believe that the United States should begin a partial mobilization of forces of defense without any delay." [57]

> The U.S. aircraft industry turns out to have only one effective customer — the armed services of the national government.
>
> — *Fortune*, March 1948

> The only way to avoid having American policy dominated by crisis is to live in crisis — prepared for war.
>
> — *Fortune*, December 1948 [1]

XIII

Rebuilding the Arsenal

IN THE LATTER HALF of 1947 and the first half of 1948, the United States did move toward the "partial mobilization of forces of defense," that condition of permanent preparedness Admiral Leahy had advocated: a major expansion of the military establishment, the integration of significant industrial and intellectual sectors into this establishment, and the promotion of an anticommunist alliance.

These hallmarks in the rise of the national security state were wrought by the Spring Crisis of 1948. But historians and memoirists tend to overlook that crisis, losing it in the shadow of events the preceding spring, the Truman Doctrine and the Marshall Plan.

Broadly speaking, the year 1946 saw the victory of the Riga axioms in the policy elite, and the intersection of those beliefs with the doctrine of national security to form the distinctive Commanding Ideas of American Cold War foreign policy. The following year, 1947, witnessed two things: the abandonment of diplomacy with its "politics of composition," and the translation of the new outlook into policies of intervention and containment. In 1948, we shall see, military force became a central concern, as policymakers rebuilt an important part of the wartime arsenal, including the establishment of a permanent war economy. The Spring Crisis was the forge in which these changes were shaped.

*

In the autumn and winter of 1947 and 1948, the civilian leaders of the Truman Administration were opposed to any increase in the military budget. They did not want to drain money away from ambitious foreign aid programs, nor to divert congressional attention from those aid appropriations. There was also a real fear about the strains that a growing federal budget would place on the national economy. Instead, Truman and his advisers wanted the military services to settle conflicts over roles and missions, and so bring about presumed economies by eliminating duplication.

But the services seized upon the diplomatic difficulties with the Soviet Union to intensify the portrait of Russia as Enemy, and thus they bolstered their expansive doctrine of national security and their case for remobilization. They took the Marshall Plan as a signal for an enlarged military role in foreign policy and insisted, as Budget Director James Webb recalled, "that they had to start immediately a substantial build-up."

"I want to emphasize that I feel that there is grave danger of war with USSR within a few months," the commander of U.S. Air Forces in the Far East wrote to Air Force Chief of Staff General Spaatz in December 1947. "The world situation continues to deteriorate as is evidenced by the stalemate in London; by the increasing internal chaos in France and Italy; and by the decline in the strength of the central government of China. USSR has moved so far along the aggression road that she must continue to move along the same way. American public opinion will eventually demand that USSR be halted whether or not American military power is adequate. We must be ready out here in the Far East." [2]

The quest for enlargement was a continuation of the unification struggle by other means. Despite the truce declared by Robert Patterson and James Forrestal at the beginning of 1947, the battle between the services had continued for another six months, with no cooling of passions. "We can learn plenty from the Navy with respect to their public relations," W. Stuart Symington, Assistant Secretary of War for Air, wrote to General George Kenney, commander of the Strategic Air Command, at the end of May 1947. "We may well now be in the final round of the unification fight, a fight close to the heart of the Air Forces, because if we don't win it and the war is officially declared over, the Air Force reverts to its previous impossible position as a minor addendum to the War Department." [3]

Finally, in the last week of July, Congress passed a compromise National Security Act, which gave the Air Force independence. On July 26, Harry Truman signed it into law.

The President had wanted Robert Patterson for the new post of Secretary of Defense, but Patterson declined, saying that he wanted to return to New York City to make money. Truman turned to James Forrestal, who quickly accepted.[4]

This "unification" legislation did not result in real unification, but rather coordination, along the lines recommended by the Eberstadt Report. The authority of the position of Secretary of Defense was circumscribed.

The Air Force and Navy's basic struggle over roles and missions now moved from the arena of organization to that of appropriations. As General Ira Eaker suggested to an audience at the National War College, the military budget became "the controlling factor" and the "all-important topic." [5]

The budgetary contest centered on the competition between the Air Force's new long-distance B-36 bomber and a Navy "super" aircraft carrier. The carrier construction program would assure the Navy a role in air power. The Air Force, committed to a doctrine of strategic bombing, was convinced that the B-36 would guarantee its monopoly. It sought to establish a "70-Group" strength, which, one student of the period has observed, "symbolized the expansive aspirations of the Air Force." The Air Force also wanted bases in such regions as the Mediterranean to provide an alternative to the Navy's carrier fleet.[6]

The rivalry between the Navy and the Air Force emphasized the projection of the Soviet menace. In order to justify budget requests, each service continually sought out the appropriate threats, which only it could muster, while, at the same time, seeking to minimize the threats dramatized by the other service. In December 1947, Navy Secretary John Sullivan spoke gravely of the Soviet submarine fleet. "The Germans had less than 50 operating submarines and nearly won the Battle of the Atlantic," he told a presidential commission. "The Russians have five times that many operating submarines. They are capable of producing on short notice a large number of submarines of the latest design, vastly superior to any operated by the German Navy during World War II." Later in the month, the Air Force's director of intelligence assured General Spaatz that the Russian submarine threat was illusory: "The present great Soviet bugaboo which is being promoted is entirely over-magnified and completely out of perspective." [7]

Forrestal's shift of emphasis in 1944 in the Navy's postwar planning to a sea-air approach had become the heart of the Navy's strategy. In other words, not only the Air Force but also the Navy was now committed to air power. In this, they were part of an overall movement, a general commitment among American policymakers to the belief that air power was, in the words of Robert Patterson, "the most effective instrument of national policy that we have."

Air power was attractive for a number of reasons. It was capital rather than labor intensive, and thus provided a practical alternative to what was always unpopular — a large standing army. The approach suited America's geographic position in two ways: it made up for the obstacles in getting an army to Europe quickly, while the United States' own real vulnerability — if it had any at all — was almost exclusively along its "air frontier." Submarines hardly posed a real danger. Many had come to believe that air power would be the decisive factor in the next war. Air power took advantage of America's innovative talents and would encourage the nation's industries to develop and mobilize technology. A new and important industrial sector lobbied for it. Finally, air power — whether Navy or Air Force — had deep-rooted popular support.[8]

In 1947 and 1948, the commitment to air power was expressed in many forums. None was more important than the President's Air Policy Commission. President Truman established the Commission in July 1947, with five members under the chairmanship of lawyer Thomas Finletter, to formulate an integrated national aviation strategy. It held over 200 meetings and heard more than 150 witnesses before making its widely publicized report, *Survival in the Air Age*, on January 1, 1948.

The Commission clearly established itself as pro–Air Force with its outright endorsement of the basic Air Force goal of a 70-Group Air Force.[9]

What is important for us, however, is the manner in which it crystallized the national commitment to air power through the expansive doctrine of national security. Many of the witnesses expressed exactly such an outlook.

"Before these last two wars our concepts of security were the integrity of our own domain, and the freedom from either attack or danger of invasion or attack," James Forrestal told the Commission on December 3, 1947. "In my own view — and I think it is shared by most people — our security is now far broader than that . . . You cannot talk about American security without talking Europe, the Middle East, the freedom and security of the sea-lanes, and the hundreds of millions of underfed, frustrated human beings throughout the world . . . It would do us no good to be a Sparta in this particular hemisphere and have chaos prevailing elsewhere in the world. We could survive for some time, but I do not think we could continue what we call our way of life."

"It would have helped Athens a little if she had been stronger, would it not?" asked Chairman Finletter.

"Had Athens . . . a little less philosophy, and Athens had a few more shields, it might have been a good combination," Forrestal replied.[10]

The report itself developed these themes: "Our national security must be redefined in relation to the facts of modern war . . . Not being able to count on the creation, within the future for which it now has to prepare, of a world settlement which would give it absolute security under the law, it must seek the next best thing — that is, relative security under the protection of its own arms."

The Finletter Commission called for a military establishment "built around the air arm" and "based on air power," as the centerpiece of a state organized around the doctrine of national security. The Commission wanted a "degree of preparedness — new in American life."

"The creation of a strong Military Establishment capable of defending the country," it continued, "will put a disproportionate share of the power of the Government in the hands of the military, and at the same time will place new and heavy burdens on the civilian agencies of Government in matters contributing to the national security . . . Our policy of relative security will compel us to maintain a force in being in peacetime greater than any self-governing state has ever kept."[11]

The report reflected two different conceptions of air power. One was what might be called "war-fighting," which argued that air power provided the most expeditious form of military force for the United States. Such was the basic Air Force attitude, and that of the other services. "The low grade terror of Russia which paralyzes Italy, France, England, and Scandinavia can be kept from our own country by an ability on our part to deliver air atomic destruction," General Spaatz told the Commission. "If Russia does strike the U.S., as she will if her present frame of mind continues, only a powerful air force in being can strike back fast enough, and hard enough to prevent the utter destruction of our nation." [12]

More sophisticated was the idea of "deterrence." Bernard Brodie was probably the first postwar strategist to postulate a concept of deterrence based upon nuclear weapons.[13] But some, in testifying before the Finletter Commission, emphasized American air power as the key element in deterrence. "I place as one of the essentials in the avoidance of war with the Soviet Union, the maintenance of a strong, adequate air force capable of retaliation in the event of an aggressive move on their part," Averell Harriman testified. "There is no other way by which we can make an aggressive move on the part of the Soviet Union costly to them except by air attack ... Based upon my observations and discussions with the important leaders in the Soviet Union ... it has been quite obvious to me — that there is only one thing which the leaders of the Soviet Union fear, and that is the American air force." [14]

The Finletter Commission adopted both views: "Relative security is to be found only in a policy of arming the United States so strongly (1) that other nations will hesitate to attack us or our vital interests because of the violence of the counterattack they would have to face, and (2) that if we are attacked we will be able to smash the assault at the earliest possible moment."

The Finletter Commission feared that "our gravest danger" was a possible reluctance of the nation "to carry the financial burden" of an expanded military establishment.[15] It argued that the federal government should, through military procurements, underwrite a permanently enlarged aviation industry — that this industry, in effect, should become integrated into the military establishment.

In this, as in its commitment to air power, the Finletter Commission was only the most prominent of many voices.[16]

Two things about the aviation industry had become clear: it was economically weak, and its future depended upon military procurements.

The industry — comprised essentially of thirteen airframe manufacturers and two engine makers — was in trouble. The value of airframes produced annually dropped from a wartime high of $16.7 billion in 1944 to $671.5 million in 1947. From 96,000 military planes produced in 1944, output fell to 1800 military planes in 1947. Number one in terms of value of production during the war, the industry slipped to sixteenth by 1947. The industry lost $80 million in 1946 — and $115 million in 1947.

The expected and hoped-for postwar civilian demand for aircraft had turned out to be a mirage, and the companies found that they no longer possessed the wartime economies of large-scale production. The industry was learning that it depended much more upon military procurement than had been predicted. *Aviation Week* estimated in February 1948 that 90 percent of the aircraft business was either directly or indirectly military in nature.[17]

Through 1947 and into 1948, the industry conducted a vigorous public relations campaign that had two aims — one, to get the federal government to underwrite the existence of an industry far larger than civilian demand would justify — two, to increase substantially military appropriations for aircraft.[18] The military services and the press joined in. "Since we are living in a world of peril, it is not too much to say that the present state of the aircraft industry represents as grave an industrio-economic problem as exists in the U.S. today," warned *Fortune*. "The U.S. aircraft industry turns out to have only one effective customer — the armed services of the national government." This meant, *Fortune* explained, that while the industry's leaders intoned their faith in "free enterprise," they had in fact concluded that they could not remain in business without a large "guaranteed market" provided by the government.[19]

It was not simply a question of maintaining the industry, but rather of increasing its size once again, a problem communicated in the language of national security. "While air power of the United States may be adequate to meet present national security requirements," declared *Aviation Week* in February 1948, "there is a growing opinion that dramatic increases both in quantity and quality are necessary to meet requirements of the immediate future." [20]

It was not at all clear that air power would receive the budgetary support deemed necessary by industry and military leaders. In January 1948, President Truman asked Congress for a 35-percent increase in the budget for naval aviation for fiscal year 1949 (1948–49). Altogether, 54 percent of the total military budget in fiscal year 1949 was related to aviation, while 15 percent of the entire budget was so related. In February, the Air Coordinating Committee recommended to Truman that military aircraft production be trebled both because of the "international situation" and because civilian demand was not great enough to maintain the capacity necessary for expansion in an "emergency."

But *Aviation Week* reported that the prospects for an expanded program were dim: "Although the President's Air Policy Commission, and now the joint Congressional Board have mobilized support for increased military expenditures, the political pressure for other expenditures of the pork-barrel type remains stronger. With the Republican Congress striving to lower the ceiling on Federal expenditures and cuts in pork-barrel outlays unlikely in a presidential election year, the outlook for greatly increased aviation budgets is not bright." [21]

The ensuing Spring Crisis changed the budgetary accounts.

The Spring Crisis began in Czechoslovakia in the winter of 1947–48. The coalition of communists and noncommunists that governed the country was a remnant of the Grand Alliance, the last bridge between the two blocs. The coalition was based on a notion, held both by President Eduard Benes and Foreign Minister Jan Masaryk, that Czechoslovakia should and could look both east and west. But they recognized that the success of their experiment depended on events outside Czechoslovakia, namely a modus vivendi between the Soviet Union and the United States. The tension that had been growing since the preceding summer — reflected in the Marshall Plan, the Cominform, the consolidation of the blocs, the end of diplomacy — made the coalition increasingly unstable. An internal rivalry began to mirror the Soviet-American conflict.

Yet, to a surprising degree, the West, particularly the United States, had already consigned Czechoslovakia to the Eastern bloc. Benes and Masaryk had concluded that a reasonable degree of internal independence could be preserved only by acknowledging that the country lay within the Soviet sphere, that is, by acceding to the Soviet foreign policy line. On a trip to Washington in the autumn of

1947, Masaryk explained: "They were separated by a great distance from the western nations which could give them help directly and they were forced to make the best of a difficult situation caused by their contiguity to the Soviet sphere." He added that he was "not always free to adopt the kind of position he would like to take and that Czechoslovakian policy had to cut across that of the US." * (Masaryk had resigned himself to the precariousness of Benes' and his position, and — while sometimes optimistic and ebullient, sometimes melancholic — he could always be counted upon to be ironic. A Western friend once asked him if he found it difficult to have a communist serving as his chief deputy in the foreign ministry. On the contrary, Masaryk replied, it expedited things enormously and saved on telephone calls to and from Moscow.)

Such explanations as that which he gave in Washington were to little avail. American officials refused to acknowledge the significance of the country's geographic location, nor did they note the distinction between Czech domestic and foreign policies. James Riddleberger wrote of Masaryk to Ambassador Steinhardt: "I share your feelings of disappointment in this man who might well have utilized his background and name to stand up to the Communist extremists in behalf of the pro-Western elements and seriously attempted to influence the Government toward a course that would not alienate the Soviet Union yet at the same time preserve the friendly regard of the United States. I judge that he has been weak or blind." [22]

The communists enjoyed greater popular support in Czechoslovakia than anywhere else in Eastern Europe. In the elections in May 1946, they won 37 percent of the vote. Without that popularity, the communists would not have achieved power with the ease they did two years later. Unhappily, American policy toward Czechoslovakia helped contribute to public backing for the communists. U.S. lead-

* Masaryk might have added, but did not, that the Soviets had a very special interest in Czechoslovakia — the country was probably their most important source of uranium. That must have provided a powerful motivation for the Russian drive to keep Czechoslovakia securely inside its sphere. Eugen Loebl, a deputy minister of foreign trade until the end of 1949, estimates that if the Russians had bought the Czech uranium at world market prices in the course of the five-year agreement, Czechoslovakia would have received two billion dollars more. After 1949, the most notorious of all the forced labor camps in Czechoslovakia were those attached to the uranium mines. For some years thereafter, it was the practice to draft sons of "capitalist and middle-class families" to this forced labor, usually in the mines, in place of military service.

ers thought they could use American economic power to affect the Czech political situation — not by offering but by refusing to offer aid. "You may have no cause for concern that the Department will yield to any smiling persuasions of Masaryk," Riddleberger assured Steinhardt in December 1946. Steinhardt came back to the same point in June 1947: "It is my experience over the last 25 years that the hope of obtaining credits accomplished much more for us than once the credits had been extended . . . If we are going to extend credits to Czechoslovakia, our objective, in my opinion, should be far less as a reward for proper behavior in settling various outstanding matters than it should be with an eye to strengthening anti-communist forces in the government." Steinhardt was afraid that a premature granting would weaken those forces.[23]

On the contrary, the refusal to grant aid hurt those forces by eroding their popular support. It created the impression that the West was abandoning Czechoslovakia at a time when the Soviet Union seemed to be providing aid. The pro-Western politicians appeared unable to deliver, while the communists did. Czechoslovakia's lack of economic ties to the West also meant that the communists had less need to worry about the consequences of taking complete power; there was little to lose. Certainly, further aid would have encountered some congressional opposition, especially after Czechoslovakia's withdrawal from the Marshall Plan. But the failure to grant assistance marooned the noncommunists.

The summer harvest in 1947 had been very bad — grain reached only 63 percent of the target set; potatoes, only 48 percent. By the autumn, Czechoslovakia desperately needed to get food from the outside, and swiftly. The government appealed to the United States. Masaryk tried to make clear to Washington that Czechoslovakia's foreign policy was forced upon it, but failed. The United States stood firm on a policy of no food and no loans without major revisions in the Czech political stance.

With great fanfare, however, the Russians promised 600,000 tons of grain — enough to make up almost 40 percent of the country's shortfall. "Those goddamn Americans," Foreign Trade Minister Ripka is quoted as saying in Moscow in December 1947. "It's because of them that I've had to come here to sign on the dotted line. We told the Americans, and asked for 200,000 or 300,000 tons of wheat. And these idiots started the usual blackmail . . . At this point Gottwald got in touch with Stalin, who promised us the required wheat . . . And now these idiots in Washington have driven us straight into the Stalinist camp . . . The fact that not America but Russia had saved us from starvation will have a tremendous effect inside Czechoslovakia — even among the people whose sympathies are with the West rather than Moscow." [24]

The U.S. also undercut the Western-oriented politicians in Prague in an unavoidable side effect of its determination to restore the economy of the Western zones in Germany. "Of course the Czechs do not like the Germans," Steinhardt told an audience at the National War College in December 1947. "That is one of the principal difficulties that I have to contend with there . . . The one thing I sense strongly, and that is among the non-communists as much as among the Communists — is their resentment that we are building up Germany too fast . . . They feel they must look to the Russians for protection against Germany. With that feeling you can take it pretty much for granted anything we do to build up Germany will not be popular in Czechoslovakia." [25] This American effort in Germany contributed to the support for the Czech communists.

In the summer of 1947, and then even more so after the Cominform meeting, the political struggle within the country intensified. Bitter charges about spies, subversion, and coups flew back and forth. The Czech chess grand master Ludek Pachman, then an active communist, writes in his memoirs that the party informed members in the autumn of 1947 that "it is necessary to be prepared for a decisive encounter with the reactionaries before the elections," and that considerable energies went into organizing a "people's militia." Steinhardt, who rather respected Prime Minister Gottwald as a nationalist as well as a communist, observed that the Prime Minister had lost his affability and assurance, and acted instead as "uncomfortable and nervous as a cat."

While it was not understood at the time, many senior American officials, unlike the Western Europeans, had apparently written off Czechoslovakia by this time. On November 6, 1947, Secretary Marshall, in the course of a top-secret briefing, told the Cabinet, "The halt in the communist advance is forcing Moscow to consolidate its hold on Eastern Europe. It will probably have to clamp down completely on Czechoslovakia, for a relatively free Czechoslovakia could become a threatening salient in Moscow's political position . . . As long as communist political power was advancing in Europe, it was advantageous to the Russians to allow to the Czechs the outer appearances of freedom. In this way, Czechoslovakia was able to serve as a bait for nations further west. Now that there is a danger of the political movement proceeding in the other direction, the Russians can no longer afford this luxury. Czechoslovakia could too easily become a means of entry of really democratic forces into Eastern Europe in general. The sweeping away of democratic institutions and the consolidation of communist power in Czechoslovakia will add a formidable new element to the underground anti-communist political forces in the Soviet satellite area. For this reason, the Russians proceed to this step reluctantly. It is a purely defensive move."

Yet Washington was being much too quick in its write-off. The position of the noncommunist parties seemingly improved in the autumn, despite the grain, with a change of leadership in the Social Democratic Party. Indeed, the communists "have lost the ball," Steinhardt observed in December. "Whether the anticommunists can hold the ball I do not know. But certainly their prospects are far better than a few months ago." [26]

Very shortly thereafter, the pro-Western politicians lost their advantage. The conventional wisdom portrays the February events in Czechoslovakia as growing out of a conscious communist plan. Certainly tensions had been increasing, and the Czech communists were surely following the aggressive Cominform line. But events came to a crisis in a happenstance way. The communists took power by pushing hard against a door that was already half open.

In a very difficult situation, working under intense pressure, inadequately supported by the West, the noncommunist politicians in Prague gambled — and they lost. On February 19, whether as part of a Soviet plan or merely to capitalize on the publicity for their wheat deliveries, Soviet Deputy Foreign Minister V. A. Zorin, formerly ambassador to Czechoslovakia, arrived in Prague. The next day, February 20, twelve noncommunist Cabinet members, a minority of the coalition, submitted their resignations. They thought they had a clear understanding with President Benes — that he would not accept their resignations, and would either force a reconstruction of the Cabinet on more favorable lines or call for elections more quickly than the scheduled May date. Five days of crisis followed.

The communists used the police to search, arrest, and intimidate political opponents. While both sides tried to whip up visible public support, the communists were far more successful. Rumors rapidly spread throughout the country — the imminence of Soviet military intervention, the threat of a general strike. The communists won back the support of the Social Democratic leadership.

Ultimately, the target of all this activity was Eduard Benes. That was the weakness of the noncommunist strategy. The President, who had suffered a major stroke the preceding summer, was physically tired and still seriously ill. Indeed, he had difficulty in speaking. He feared a civil war. The Munich deal, a decade earlier, had permanently scarred him; he was afraid that the Western nations would once again abandon Czechoslovakia if it stood up in this time of crisis. He felt that he had no choice. On the morning of February 25, he allowed Gottwald to form a new communist-dominated government, without the pro-Western politicians.[27]

Masaryk agreed to remain as foreign minister. A few days later, he described Benes as a broken man; it was obvious that the President's attempt to be a bridge between East and West had failed. Masaryk added that he was staying as foreign minister to try to blunt communist ruthlessness and, in particular, to help people flee from the country.[28]

Immediately after the events in February, with encouragement and specific direction from Moscow, there began the process of arrests, purges, and executions that culminated in the great show trial of November 1952, which, with its fantastic accusations and fake confessions, replicated the Moscow trials and which sent eleven leading communists, including the party secretary, Rudolf Slansky, to death.[29] The goal was to create a system of tight control through a party and government that had no legitimacy and no roots in Czechoslovakian nationalism. The entire system would depend upon the Soviet Union.

Could the West have done nothing prior to February 1948 to help prevent the communists from taking complete power? Certainly Czechoslovakia did lie within the glacis that had been carved out by the advance of the Red Army. Yet were the Russians really in so dominant a position? At the end of 1946, British intelligence had placed the number of Russian troops in Czechoslovakia at just 5000; in June 1948, the Joint Intelligence Committee of the U.S. Joint

Chiefs estimated a mere 500. Could not the West have flexed its military muscle in Germany as events were unfolding in such a way as to bolster Benes and to make the Soviet Union and the Czech communists think twice?

As well as can be reconstructed, the truth seems to be that American leaders had already written off Czechoslovakia and its noncommunist politicians; U.S. officials thought the country was *already* a communist state, prior to February 1948. During those tense days, Marshall indicated that he was concerned not so much about what was happening in Czechoslovakia as in the impact elsewhere in Europe. "In so far as international affairs are concerned, a seizure of power by the Communist Party in Czechoslovakia would not materially alter in this respect the situation which has existed in the last three years," the Secretary said on February 24. "Czechoslovakia has faithfully followed the Soviet line in the United Nations and elsewhere and the establishment of a Communist regime would merely crystallize and confirm for the future previous Czech policy. However, we are concerned about the probable repercussions in Western European countries of a successful Communist coup."

All of this is not to say that the Americans deliberately willed what did happen in Czechoslovakia. Nor are we in any position to say how critical a factor the American disinterest was. But it should not be ignored, as has traditionally been the case, for U.S. policy did help to isolate the noncommunists.

There are those who in later years read the records of meetings of the communist leadership immediately after the assumption of power. The minutes, they say, show the communists almost comical in their confusion and surprise at what had happened and at the ease with which it happened. The communists had taken advantage of an accidental situation, a tactical mistake by the noncommunists, to turn it into a strategic victory. Had the democratic parties held on for another three months, the communists might well have lost ground, leaving the Soviet Union little pretext for intervention. Stalin was too cautious to risk a direct intervention, knowing that it might invite Western counteraction.

"As to the extent of Soviet interference and intimidation, it is now clear that President Benes was greatly frightened by the Soviet specter," Ambassador Steinhardt observed at the end of April 1948. "There was no evidence of any Soviet troop concentrations on the borders of Czechoslovakia. It also appears that the extent of the Soviet threats was probably less than on similar recent occasions in Finland and in Iran, both of which countries successfully resisted such threats whereas the Czechs succumbed to them." Steinhardt added that the resignations of the noncommunist ministers had "created a vacuum and the Communists moved in. Although the Communists did not precipitate the crisis (although they doubtlessly planned to do so), they took full advantage of it." [30]

George Kennan interpreted the communist victory in Czechoslovakia as a predictable defensive move, a consolidation of the Soviet sphere in the face of the initial success of the Marshall Plan and the impending construction of a new West German state.

But most policymakers also took the events — after the fact — to confirm what they already believed, proving the aggressiveness of Soviet intentions. The events in Czechoslovakia provided impetus to move to a new level of military preparedness.[31] Do not misunderstand. Washington did not create the developments in Prague. It did, however, capitalize on them.

Though genuinely apprehensive about Soviet objectives, the Administration exaggerated the extent of its apprehensions and outrage in order to win congressional support for four key programs: the Marshall Plan, universal military training, a restoration of selective service, and an expanded budget for aviation. Spokesmen dwelt on the possibility of immediate conflict to prepare for what they saw as a long-term struggle. But also, the military services wanted money from Congress to promote their separate interests. The President was acting, as well, to assert his own leadership in an election year. It would make for a neat argument were the historian able to point to one or the other of these factors as central, but that is not possible, for the aims were very much intertwined, even within individuals. What is incontestable is that the atmosphere of crisis was very real, even if its substance was more open to question.

"We are faced with exactly the same situation with which Britain and France were faced in 1938–9 with Hitler," Truman wrote from Key West, Florida, to his daughter Margaret on March 3, 1948. "Things look black," he said. "A decision will have to be made. I am going to make it."

Two days later, on March 5, a cable arrived in Washington from General Lucius Clay in Berlin, addressed to Lt. General Stephen J. Chamberlain, director of intelligence for the Army General Staff. Clay reported that, whereas he had previously thought war with the Russians was unlikely for at least ten years, he had recently "felt a subtle change" in Soviet attitudes and now feared that war could come with "dramatic suddenness." He added: "I am unable to submit any official report in the absence of supporting data but my feeling is real."

The cable, quickly disseminated through the policy elite, had no less impact than the Czech events themselves in shaping a crisis in Washington. "A real war scare ensued," Kennan recalled. Clay's terse message from Berlin has since been regarded as a prescient forecast of the Berlin Blockade and a landmark on the road to permanent polarization. In truth, the telegram had much more to do with getting budgets through Congress than with anticipating changes in Soviet behavior. General Chamberlain, visiting Berlin in the last week of February, had informed Clay that American forces around the world were in a poor state of readiness and that major military appropriations might not win congressional approval. American public opinion, he said, had to be galvanized into support for increased expenditures.

"Clay's cable, sent directly to Chamberlain, and not through normal command channels, was to be used as Chamberlain saw fit," Clay's biographer writes. "Its primary purpose was to assist the military chiefs in their congressional testimony; it was not, in Clay's opinion, related to any change in Soviet strategy." [32]

The Clay message certainly galvanized official opinion; policymakers took it as a most serious warning.

The crisis quickly intensified.

On March 6, the President talked with Marshall. The Secretary, George Elsey noted, "is nervous — world keg of dynamite — HST shouldn't start it." On the same day, Army Secretary Royall asked David Lilienthal, chairman of the Atomic Energy Commission, how long it would take to move "eggs" (atomic bombs) to the Mediterranean. The Chief of Naval Operations on March 9 proposed steps "to prepare the American people for war." Clark Clifford meanwhile had returned from Key West in agreement with the President that Truman should make a major foreign policy speech to Congress. Elsey noted the reasons: "Pres. *must* for his prestige, come up with a strong foreign speech — to demonstrate his leadership — which country needs and wants. Pres's prestige in foreign matters low now (Palestine, China) — Vandenberg and Marshall getting all credit on Marshall Plan." In a memorandum to Clifford, Elsey continued: "During the President's absence in the South, and especially since the fall of Czechoslovakia, demands for a stronger U.S. foreign policy have come from many sources . . . The strongest possible speech for the President would be one on Russian relations . . . The President could deliver a Russian speech better than a speech on any subject. His best delivery has been on occasions when he has been 'mad' . . . His poorest deliveries have been when he is merely *for* 'good things.' "[33]

Shocking news reached Washington on March 10 — it had been announced in Prague that Czechoslovakian Foreign Minister Jan Masaryk had committed suicide by jumping from a window. He had visited his father's grave a few days before, and had seen Benes for the last time on March 9. Perhaps Masaryk realized that Benes had no plans, that his own efforts would lead nowhere, and that he had in truth lost his future.

Yet he left no last testament, and numerous other mysteries surround his death. An official Czech investigation into his death in 1968 was abrogated by the Soviet invasion in August of that year, and the relevant documents, including the Masaryk archives, were apparently removed to Moscow. The most thorough investigation to date, carried out by a Western journalist in 1968 and 1969, lends strong credence to what has always been the opposing theory of Masaryk's death: The foreign minister was about to flee the country, as was known by both the Soviets and some local communists. This would have been so embarrassing to both that Masaryk was murdered, probably suffocated, and then shoved out a small bathroom window to make his death look like a suicide.

The fact and manner of Masaryk's death, as Kennan recalled, "dramatized, as few other things could have, the significance of what had just occurred" in Czechoslovakia — and also underlined the new depths of the division between East and West.[34]

On March 12, U.S. military commanders abroad were ordered to review emergency plans and "insure that such implementing instructions as might be required to expedite these plans into effect are prepared." The next day, the Joint Chiefs of Staff presented Forrestal with an emergency war plan to meet a feared Soviet invasion of Western Europe and the Middle East. Forrestal and the Chiefs agreed to seek a resumption of the draft, supplemental appropriations, and acquisition by the military of custody over atomic weapons.[35]

The President had planned a major address for a Saint Patrick's Day dinner in New York on March 17. It was to be, as Elsey recorded, "a trial balloon for a modified 'get tough' policy; trial balloon for Congress." But at a noon meeting at the White House on March 15, a new plan was discussed — that the President address Congress during the day on March 17, and then fly to New York to give his Saint Patrick's Day speech that night. Truman and his advisers considered the circumstances so urgent that they agreed that he should take this unprecedented and dramatic step.

On the same day, Charles Bohlen transmitted Marshall's concern about the speech: "he wants a weak message, drop intemperate language . . . simple, businesslike, no 'ringing phrases' — nothing warlike, or belligerent. Don't denounce, just state the facts."

"It has to be blunt, to justify the message!" Clifford replied. "He asks for legislation — how does he explain it?"

At 6 P.M. Army Secretary Royall came to the White House. "No troops for Alaska and Greenland now to seize airbases there," he reported. "If we got into trouble, we would lose all our troops in Japan and Europe."

The speech was drafted on March 15 and 16. "Quite a shock to read it," Elsey observed. "It seems to make sense."[36]

"Papers this morning full of rumors and portents of war," Forrestal wrote in his diary on March 16. That same day, the CIA presented Truman with an alarming estimate — that war was not probable only through the next sixty days. Beyond this, the agency would not commit itself.

Truman told that day's staff conference that if Congress did not act, "the country is sunk." He added that Marshall had advised him that he might "pull the trigger" with his speech. But Truman had made up his mind: "It was better to do that than to be caught, as we were in the last war, without having warned the Congress and the people."

Shortly after noon on March 17, the President went before a joint session of Congress. "The situation in the world today is not primarily the result of natural difficulties which follow a great war," he said. "It is chiefly due to the fact that one nation has not only refused to cooperate in the establishment of a just and honorable peace, but — even worse — has actively sought to prevent it . . . Since the close of hostilities, the Soviet Union and its agents have destroyed the independence and democratic character of a whole series of nations in Eastern and Central Europe. It is this ruthless course of action, and the clear design to extend it to the remaining free nations of Europe, that have brought about the critical situation in Europe today. The tragic death of the Republic of Czechoslovakia has sent a shock-wave through the civilized world . . . We have reached a point at which the position of the United States should be made unmistakably clear . . . There are times in world history when it is far wiser to act than to hesitate. There is some risk involved in action — there always is. But there is far more risk in failure to act."

The President expressed American interest in a Western military alliance — the first stage of which had been completed by the signing of the Brussels Pact earlier that day. But Truman made only three specific requests: passage of the Marshall Plan, enactment of universal military training, and restoration of selective service.

The speech was meant for an international as much as a national audience. Prime Minister Mackenzie King of Canada sat with his party caucus in Ottawa, listening to Truman's voice over the radio, virtually expecting the President to threaten war. "This was a day that had its place in history," the Prime Minister noted shortly after in his diary. "It really is the line of demarcation between the past and efforts to adjudicate difficulties with the USSR by conciliation and beginning of settlement by force, should the USSR not back down immediately." One may assume that other world leaders heard the same message, if not in English broadcast, then by translation.

Truman reiterated the message that evening at the Saint Patrick's Day dinner, and so underlined the gravity of the crisis. "Anti-communist addresses made by Cardinal Spellman and by President Truman were received with great enthusiasm," Admiral Leahy observed with satisfaction, "particularly a statement by the President renouncing association with Mr. Henry Wallace and his Communist friends." [37]

*

The March crisis took care of Henry Wallace, who had declared his third party candidacy for the presidency at the end of 1947. In the first months of 1948, polls indicated that he was a major threat to Truman's re-election chances. In the words of the campaign master plan that Clark Clifford and James Rowe had drawn up in the autumn of 1947, the requisite strategy was "to identify [Wallace] and isolate him in the public mind with the Communists."

Wallace had been so identified for some time in the Administration's mind. J. Edgar Hoover, director of the Federal Bureau of Investigation, was in the habit of sending "personal and confidential by special messenger" letters to Truman, via the President's aides, which contained a potpourri of sensational and not-so-sensational information passed on by informers. Many of these reports Truman obviously discounted, to say the least.* In fact, Truman was concerned about the extent of the FBI's own powers. The President, according to notes Clark Clifford made after one conversation in May 1947, was "very strongly anti-FBI . . . Wants to be sure to hold FBI down, afraid of 'Gestapo.'" At about the same time, Truman wrote to Clifford, "J. Edgar will in all probability get this backward-looking Congress to give him what he wants. It's dangerous." Truman feared that a strong, crusading, independent, investigating body might become capable of terrorizing government officials and private citizens alike.

Yet it is likely that one of Hoover's private messages — warning in January 1948 that the Communist Party was going all out for Wallace, trying to defeat Truman in order to pave the way for a "progressive president in 1952" — found a most receptive audience in the White House. For Truman had for some time regarded Wallace as disloyal, advertently or inadvertently, to the United States, and had not forgiven him for what the President viewed as personal disloyalty. Almost a year earlier, in April 1947, Truman had expressed his true feelings about the former Vice President. "I have known Mr. Wallace for fifteen or twenty years and I thought he was the best Secretary of Agriculture the country ever had," Truman wrote to Congress-

* A cross section of Hoover's information: that Stalin had "been deposed as leader of Soviet Russia" (1945); that Russia conducted its first experiments in atomic energy in 1940 aboard a submarine (1945); that U.N. Assistant Secretary-General Arkady Sobolov was spying on Soviet U.N. delegate Andrei Gromyko for the NKVD (1946); that David Lilienthal was a tool of the communists (1947); that Soviet officials thought the Truman Administration was pursuing "a policy of appeasement" toward the Soviet Union (1948).

man John Folger. "I am not so sure about his competence in the other positions which he filled. My experience with him as Secretary of Commerce was a very sad one. He would never have been Secretary of Commerce had I not been presiding over the Senate the day his nomination came up for confirmation. Things of that sort, however, do not seem to appeal to him. His political education began too late in life I fear. He seems to have obtained his ideas of loyalty, both personal and political, from his friends in Moscow and, of course, they have no definition for that word."

And so it was with some great pleasure that, after his harsh words about Wallace in his March 17, 1948, New York speech, Truman wrote in his diary: "I make a speech to the Friendly Sons of Saint Patrick, enlarging on my Congressional message and reading Henry Wallace out of the Democratic Party."

But Wallace himself had made the task much easier by his indifferent public reaction to the events in Czechoslovakia. In his first statement, he portrayed the communist acquisition of power as part of the consolidation of spheres going on in both halves of Europe — a view not so dramatically different from that of Marshall and Kennan, although Wallace did reveal an absence of sympathy for the noncommunists in Czechoslovakia, who after all were in the majority. Wallace then followed up by charging that Ambassador Steinhardt had been involved in plotting a right-wing coup, which supposedly had precipitated the communist takeover. He also suggested that Masaryk had committed suicide because of cancer or emotional depression. Wallace now appeared as a man too quick to criticize his own country and even quicker to excuse the Soviet Union. In so doing, he proved to be out of step with political sentiment in the U.S., and only succeeded in isolating himself at the extreme left of the political spectrum, which is exactly what Truman's political strategists regarded as vital for the upcoming campaign. Thereafter, Wallace, that most hapless politician, helpless with the press, fell increasingly under the sway of his communist supporters, and so neutralized himself as a threat to Truman in the 1948 elections.*

* Lillian Hellman, who was active in Wallace's 1948 presidential drive, remembered how Wallace asked her to go for a walk one day during the autumn campaign. "When we had walked for a while, he asked me if it was true that many of the people, the important people, in the Progressive Party were communists. It was such a surprising question that I laughed and said most certainly it was true. He said, 'Then it is true,

Indeed, as one historian has written, "Truman had transformed Wallace into a lightning rod to ward off Republican charges of softness toward Communism." [38]

On March 19, David Lilienthal saw Truman. "He looked tired, as I have hardly ever seen him, and under strain," commented Lilienthal. "He has been through a *week*. He decided to make the far-reaching statement of policy about Russia . . . The Southern states have been pounding him like all get-out, and even such friends as Sparkman had been saying he should not run for re-election to keep the Democratic Party from being 'cut to ribbons.' "

The crisis atmosphere persisted. On March 30, Forrestal requested that the National Security Council urgently prepare a report "on the problems of our internal security, including the probable scope of the dangers, the strategy and strength of the subversive elements in the event of an emergency, and the proposed countermeasures." The next day, he asked the Air Force "how soon and at what rate can we get B-29's out of storage?" Lilienthal observed on April 10: "The war feeling, the anxiety about the future, continues unabated." Later in April, *Business Week* published a special section on "Economic Consequences of a Third World War." [39]

Yet, within the Administration, the tension of the Spring Crisis was already beginning to run down. As early as March 24, the Council of Economic Advisers had queried the President whether the economy should be shifted from "free market practices" to the comprehensive price and wage controls required for war. His March 17 speech, the President replied, "should not be interpreted as taking us off a peace basis." On April 2, the CIA allowed that it could now extend its no-war estimate beyond sixty days — although the Air Force refused to concur.[40]

The Administration did nevertheless achieve most of its goals. Congress approved the legislation for the Marshall Plan in April, and the necessary appropriations in June. In the same month, Truman signed the draft back into law. Universal military training failed to get through Congress, but other important funding did. On April 1, Truman asked for a three-billion-dollar supplement to the fiscal year

---

what they're saying?' 'Yes,' I said. 'I thought you must have known that. The hard, dirty work in the office is done by them and a good deal of the bad advice you're getting is given by the higher-ups. I don't think they mean any harm; they're stubborn men.' 'I see,' he said, and that was that."

1949 (1948–49) defense bill. Initially, he had wanted only half that much, primarily in order to bolster ground forces, but the Joint Chiefs had convinced him that the larger sum was necessary — including $775 million for aircraft. The supplemental figure was raised to $3.46 billion later in the month.[41]

The Spring Crisis provided the occasion for a budget free-for-all among the services. "The Congress has been reacting in an extremely violent way to the President's March 17 speech under the spur of the military departments, and particularly Symington of the Air Force," observed Edwin Nourse, chairman of the Council of Economic Advisers, on May 10. "But besides the rivalry among all three branches of the military services to get the utmost expansion they can out of the war scare, the Maritime Commission and some other agencies are trying to make the most of it. Of course in a Presidential year, many members of Congress are eager to promise new or revived war plants, air fields, or other government expenditures in their respective districts." James Webb, director of the Bureau of the Budget, estimated that the services were seeking appropriations totaling $25 billion a year, using speeches and pressure "to scare the country into believing that anyone who wouldn't go along with these plans would be responsible for a catastrophe."[42]

Webb singled out Air Force Secretary Symington and General Kenney, commander of the Strategic Air Command, as the most extreme of the propagandists. The Air Force had in fact launched an aggressive campaign to increase funding for its aircraft procurement and a 70-Group force. It won considerable congressional and popular support. Symington and other Air Force officials disclosed intelligence "reports" about Soviet aircraft developments that suggested not merely considerable Soviet activity in aviation but also that the Russians had already overtaken the Americans in such areas as jet fighters.[43]

Truman was losing all patience with the squabbling of the military services. He said he was "getting damn sore" with Forrestal, and referred to Forrestal, Symington, and Army Secretary Royall as the "three muttonheads" in the Department of Defense.

Forrestal was caught in the middle. He could not restrain Symington and the Air Force officers. Yet also the Administration failed to give the Defense Secretary complete backing. He wanted to increase defense spending more than the Administration, but less than the Air Force and Navy. At a budget meeting at the White House on May 7, Marshall warned that "the policy of this country was based upon the assumption that there would not be a war and that we should not plunge into these war preparations which would bring about the very thing which we are taking steps to prevent." Truman clearly indicated that he wanted the budget to be kept down and that he was unhappy with the services, the Defense Department — and with Forrestal. After the meeting, Truman wrote in his diary, "Marshall is a tower of strength and common sense. So are Snyder and Webb. Forrestal wants to compromise with the opposition."

"Forrestal has lost control completely," said James Webb on May 25, reflecting Truman's own views. "The President gave directions to the services, but it turns out that Forrestal is so bulldozed that he wouldn't even distribute the President's directions to the services. Instead of Forrestal calling the Chiefs in and demanding that they indoctrinate the lower echelons, the President today had to deal directly with them, and gave them letters which contain the severest reprimand I have ever seen delivered, and in writing. It is a sad situation, and very disturbing . . . The idea of turning over custody of atomic bombs to these competing, jealous, insubordinate services, fighting for position with each other, is a terrible prospect."

Forrestal was worried that the momentum from the Spring Crisis was dissipating. The slackening tension, he complained to Marshall on May 29, together "with the political stresses of the election year, have combined, I believe, to produce a dangerous complacency on the part of certain elements in the country."

Forrestal himself was feeling the pressures. Aides noticed that he had developed a nervous habit at the dinner table of repeatedly dipping his finger into a water glass, then wetting his lips, completely unaware that he was doing it. From this spring, probably, dated the immediate circumstances that contributed to his final breakdown.[44]

A sudden increase in activity at Boeing plants in Kansas was "the only tangible reflection of the international situation in the aircraft manufacturing industry," *Aviation Week* reported at the end of March, two weeks after the Truman speeches. To assist the aviation industry and reduce the interservice controversy, Forrestal separated the aircraft procurement funds from the regular budget in order to rush the former through Congress — making two billion dollars scheduled for aviation in fiscal year 1949 available before the end of fiscal year 1948. By early summer, with funds already flowing for new bombers and jet-powered aircraft, the industry tooled up for a permanent war boom. "The aircraft manufacturing industry is on its way out of the red ink for the first time since the end of the war," *Business Week* stated in June. "Reason: big military orders placed last week by the Navy and the Air Force." [45]

The change in the condition of the industry was dramatic. The Air Force's fiscal year 1949 budget, rewritten in the course of the Spring Crisis, was more than twice what it had been in 1948, while that for naval aviation had increased in almost as great a proportion. Military airframe production was 11.4 million pounds in 1947—25 million pounds in 1948—with, at the end of 1948, 35 million pounds planned for 1949. "The Federal government is spending $4,895,000,000 on aviation in the current fiscal year," said *Aviation Week* in September 1948. "This is more than twice the $1,760,000,000 expended in the 1948 fiscal period. This is no temporary, short-term buying spree. It is the beginning of a five-year plan for military air rearmament and civil aviation development deemed essential by Congress. It is an unprecedented peacetime aviation program. Actually, military aviation budgets for the next five years may run as high as $31 billion." The goals of the Finletter Commission, seemingly so difficult to achieve at the beginning of 1948, were being met by the end of 1948; and, at the beginning of 1949, Forrestal could confidently declare that American air power "soon could exert the dominant influence in the world once wielded by the British Navy." [46]

The Air Force, using its budget to expand in other directions, proved the most aggressive of the services in developing, under the rubric of "research and development," what might be called a "national security community" of physical and social scientists. Early in 1948, *Aviation Week* described the Air Force as "the largest research contractor in the world with about $20 million worth of contracts currently in force." [47] Through the placing of these contracts under the patronage of universities and other organizations, it integrated a crucial group of academics and intellectuals into the military establishment. As with the aviation industry, this development marked a return to a wartime pattern.

The most influential such effort was "Project RAND," later known as the RAND Corporation (RAND standing for "research and development"), based in Santa Monica, California. Established as an adjunct to Douglas Aircraft in 1945, it had been mandated to conduct a broad program of "study and research to determine preferred methods and techniques in the conduct of international warfare." The mandate was interpreted most broadly.

RAND and similar programs embodied a major shift in attitudes among both military men and political and social scientists. Edward Bowles, an Air Force scientific consultant and one of the "fathers" of RAND, observed in 1946: "We cannot do intelligent, long-range strategic planning without taking into consideration our scientific and technological resources, nor can we give proper direction to research and technological development without its leadership having some concept of our strategic plans." The next year, Warren Weaver, vice president of the Rockefeller Foundation, explained to a RAND conference that military leaders "were quite willing to accept civilians on a certain service level in the past. They used to say 'We like to have you around, and if you are awfully smart we will ask you questions and you will answer them as well as you can; but then we will go into another room and shut the door and make our decision' . . . Now, however, they want us in the backroom with them. They want to talk over really fundamental questions, and they are actually admitting civilians at the planning level. That, I think is very significant." [48]

Problems with Douglas Aircraft and concern about conflict of interest when evaluating weapons systems proposed by other companies led to RAND's separation from Douglas in the spring of 1946 and its rebirth as an independent, nonprofit corporation. Its subsequent growth signified the development of the permanent relationship between the military services and the intellectual community in the name of national security.[49]

The development of the contractual community was part of an ever-growing emphasis on research and development. In 1948, the United States government sponsored 99 percent of the nation's aeronautical research — most of it military. The government's entire aeronautical research budget in fiscal 1948 was $303 million; $311 million was budgeted for fiscal 1949. The actual figure, after the Spring Crisis, rose to $486 million. Another way to demonstrate the change is by comparison to the past. The total military R&D budget in fiscal 1949 was almost as much as the *entire* military budget of 1924 — and 50 percent of the *total* military appropriations of 1937. Military expenditures in their entirety amounted to 10 percent of the total gross national product in 1948, and increased an average of 22 percent per year between 1948 and 1956, although, of course, so did the gross national product.[50]

The pursuit of security did not end with institutional changes within the United States. The American presence on European battlefields in two world wars could leave no doubt of a continuing American interest in denying hegemony in Europe to any one power, as well as an identification with liberal democratic systems in Western Europe. The indefinitely prolonged American occupation in Germany only underlined what was already clear, and what was certainly obvious to the Kremlin. Still, American leaders created a formal military pact, the North Atlantic Treaty Organization, to make this same point. NATO was certainly seen, as Robert Lovett explained in July of 1948, as "a substantial departure from the former foreign policy of this country . . . The United States had sought peace through weakness . . . After many heartbreaks it had reversed its policy and was seeking to deter aggression by proof of determination. The only question was how its determination should be implemented." It was never clear whether this show of determination was meant to deter a genuine military threat from the Soviet Union or to reassure a jittery Western Europe.

In December 1947, at the conclusion of the London Council of Foreign Ministers meeting, Bevin had broached the idea of establishing some sort of Western defense system. British officials immediately began preparing a more detailed proposal with which to counter what Orme Sargent, permanent undersecretary of the Foreign Office, described as "the Communist offensive." On January 2, 1948, Sargent forwarded a Cabinet paper to Attlee. "Progress in the economic field will not in itself suffice to call a halt to the Russian threat," it said. "Political and indeed spiritual forces must be mobilized in our defense. I believe therefore we should seek to form backed by the Americas and the Dominions a Western democratic system . . . As soon as circumstances permit we should of course wish also to include Spain and Germany without whom no Western system can be complete. This may seem a somewhat fanciful conception, but events are moving." The paper predicted that the Russians would react as savagely against such a proposal as they had against the Marshall Plan; they would seek to portray it as "an offensive alliance" against the Soviet Union. "On this point I can only say that in the situation in which we have been placed by Russian policy half measures are useless." [51]

The Americans in mid-January indicated approval of the British effort with one caveat: the Europeans would have to take the first step themselves, and the United States would associate itself with the enterprise in its "second stage." They wanted to be sure, in addition, that that new alliance was directed against a Soviet, and not a German, threat. But, as a memorandum Marshall passed to Truman said, "There will be no real question as [to] the long-range relationship of the US to it." [52]

The events in Czechoslovakia increased the sense of urgency among Western European leaders. "I know that you must have been disgusted and personally distressed by what has happened," Bevin wrote to the British ambassador in Prague after the Communists took power. "Living through a Communist revolution, as you have done, is unequalled as an education in the utter ruthlessness and perfidy of Communism, which is difficult, if not impossible, to grasp fully until one has seen it at work."

"A general stiffening of morale in Free Europe is needed," John Hickerson, director of the Office of European Affairs, urged Marshall on March 8, "and it can come only from action by this country." [53]

On March 17 (the day of Truman's two speeches) the Brussels Pact was signed by Britain, France, Belgium, the Netherlands, and Luxembourg. It provided for a joint defense system; if one nation were attacked, the others would come to its aid. The only potential aggressor identified by name, however, was Germany. Now the question was what the United States would do.[54]

Between March 22 and April 1, U.S., British, and Canadian officials met in the Pentagon to discuss the form a North Atlantic alliance might take. These conversations were highly secret, with elaborate security precautions — as a "deception measure," the British delegate Gladwyn Jebb traveled to New York City from time to time to attend U.N. Security Council meetings. While such measures may have deceived the American press, they surely did not deceive the Russians, for one of the members of the small British working group was Donald Maclean, the Soviet spy who defected in 1951. The significance of such agents in the British Foreign Office remains difficult to evaluate. Whether it will ever be clarified is not at all certain. These spies were well placed. Until February 1947, Guy Burgess, who defected with Maclean, had been secretary and personal assistant to Hector McNeil, minister of state in the Foreign Office. It is unlikely that the Soviets would have disregarded intelligence coming from agents so positioned, and one can assume that Maclean passed confidential information to the Soviets, who thus would have been knowledgeable about initiatives like the formation of NATO.[55]

Meanwhile, the Europeans themselves increasingly saw the solution to their security problems in dependence, as Bidault put it, "on the intentions and degree of preparedness of the United States." But the Europeans were not yet convinced of those intentions. In May, responding to an expression of doubt by the French, Lovett snapped: "We are not in any sense 'growing cold' on general security problems." Indeed, participating in a North Atlantic pact was viewed as the best way to demonstrate U.S. determination.[56]

But the determination could not be taken seriously without evidence of broad domestic support within the United States. Lovett and Senator Vandenberg, meeting frequently during the spring, hammered out the language for a resolution that would sanctify U.S. participation in a regional security pact under the rubric of Article 51 of the United Nations Charter. The Senate approved the so-called Vandenberg Resolution as "the sense of the Senate" on June 11, 1948. The way was clear for NATO.[57]

Great changes in the organization of American security had occurred in the months from the break-up of the London Council of Foreign Ministers in December 1947 to June of 1948. For the first time since 1778, the United States was entering a formal military alliance that committed it to go to war in defense of other nations outside the Western Hemisphere. The United States had explicitly committed itself to maintaining the balance of power in Europe. In a few months it had also gone a long way to give lasting shape to the new bipolar international system. The country had begun a major rearmament effort as the leader of a coalition in permanent confrontation with the Soviet bloc. An arms race would become the measure of the political struggle. At the end of 1948, *Fortune* summarized the change: "The only way to avoid having American policy dominated by crisis is to live in crisis — prepared for war."

Generally unremarked went the admonition of Walter Lippmann. Commenting on the assumptions underlying the Finletter Report, and indeed the whole rearmament drive, he observed, "We shall be repeating the supreme error of powerful states — which is to think that power is a substitute for diplomacy, and that absolute power gives absolute security."

The Spring Crisis was the engine responsible for putting rearmament into high gear. Hanson Baldwin, military affairs editor of the *New York Times* and chairman of a Council on Foreign Relations study group on "national power," had suggested to David Lilienthal in May of 1948 that the Spring Crisis had been a "wholly Washington crisis." [58]

But, toward the end of June, after rearmament had begun in earnest, after the military draft had been reinstituted, and after Congress had approved both the Vandenberg Resolution and the appropriation for the Marshall Plan, there came a real crisis that confirmed the deep division of Europe and shattered whatever remained of a postwar peace based upon the Grand Alliance. This was a confrontation, perilously balanced on the edge of outright military conflict, over the most important of all European questions — the future of Germany.

ROYALL: But I do feel strongly that the limited question of Berlin currency is not a good question to go to war on.

CLAY: If Soviets go to war, it will not be because of Berlin currency issue but only because they believe this the right time.

— Teletype exchange between Army Secretary Royall and General Clay
June 25, 1948 [1]

XIV

The End of the Peace

EARLY IN JANUARY 1948, General Clay and General Robertson, the heads respectively of the American and British occupation forces, met with West German leaders to discuss how to move Bizonia closer to statehood. "It is not possible to sit here with hands folded," Robertson told the assembled politicians. With the London Council of Foreign Ministers behind them, the Americans and British decided to seek a solution to the German question outside the framework of Four-Power cooperation. Their efforts, the Soviet reaction, and the crisis that ensued — these constitute the "great divide" in the history of the Cold War, after which there was no turning back to a Great Power peace. The problem of Germany, which in 1941 had created the Grand Alliance, now shattered what remained of that alliance.[2] The ensuing Berlin crisis was a "great divide" in another sense, not merely as symbol, but in literal fact — the partition of Germany and the division of Europe, the latter not into the spheres of the 1944 Churchill-Stalin agreement, but into hostile blocs.

Germany was the last and greatest of the unanswered questions between the United States and the Soviet Union. It became the most serious postwar crisis in Europe. Both sides responded to what they saw as provocations by the other. Yet, on balance, it must be said that the Americans took the initiative. The Soviets had no initiatives to take.

By the winter of 1947–48, U.S. policymakers had concluded that Germany could not play an independent role in the international system for many years to come. Inevitably, it would be aligned — all or in part — to one side or the other. A reunited Germany swinging back into the Soviet orbit, Secretary Marshall observed in February, would constitute the "greatest threat to security of all Western nations, including U.S." The American policymakers wanted to stabilize the economy of the Western zones, principally through a currency reform; shape a government in those zones; and fit a new West Germany into the Marshall Plan and the larger Western European economy — altogether a conscious repudiation of a Four-Power solution and thus a key step toward partition.

The Americans correctly assumed that a Four-Power agreement would be difficult to achieve. But they were almost surely wrong in their belief that the Russians were working by plan to gain control of all of Germany. "Although I attended most of the meetings of the Council of Foreign Ministers after the war," Charles Bohlen recalled, "it was never clear to me what Soviet objectives were."[3] It is entirely plausible that the only clear Russian objective was the extraction of reparations. Beyond that, the Soviets had no well-defined idea of a satisfactory and achievable German solution. Meanwhile, their pursuit of reparations ran counter to whatever political goals they might have devised. The Russians knew much better what they feared and did not want — a revivified and Western-oriented Germany — than what they did want. In addition, the Russians might without much difficulty have thought that the Americans were working by some master plan — even as the Americans imagined that they were acting in response to a Soviet master plan.[4]

After the adjournment of the Council of Foreign Ministers in December, the Russians made a number of conciliatory moves — the inauguration of reciprocal reparations deliveries from the East, negotiations on a lend-lease settlement, a reduction in their reparations claims on Austria, and agreement to an Austrian currency reform. But they were too late. American policy was already in place. "The failure of the CFM at its London meeting to make or give promise of progress toward agreement on the economic and political unity of Germany marks a turning point in the political evolution of post-war

Germany," concluded a memorandum prepared for Marshall in mid-January 1948. The Western zones, it added, would take on "increasingly a quasi-political character." [5]

Whereas one meeting in London, the Council of Foreign Ministers, had not brought an end to the German stalemate, another shortly thereafter did. A new London Conference convened on February 23 with representatives of the United States, Britain, France, Belgium, the Netherlands, and Luxembourg. "To my mind," Clay observed, "it is the most important conference of all yet held to the future of Germany." The meeting adjourned temporarily on March 6, having reached tentative agreements on how to proceed toward the establishment of a West German state. A weak caveat was added: "Ultimate Four Power agreement is in no way precluded." [6]

The currency reform was meant to end rampant inflation and widespread hoarding and to stabilize the Western zones for effective participation in the Marshall Plan. The mark had lost most of its standing as money, declining in some cases, with so few goods available, to one five-hundredth of its official value. Americans had agreed for some time that a reform was necessary. "*Monetary reform is overdue,*" Harriman had informed Truman the preceding August after a survey of Germany. "It is hard to understand how business is now being transacted with worthless currency . . . I, frankly, have grave doubts that a currency system could be successful including the Soviet zone, as the Soviet economic methods are so completely different from ours." [7]

A currency reform would be much more than a technical exercise. Currency is both a symbol of sovereignty and a mechanism for exercising sovereignty. Therefore, a new currency in the three Western zones plus West Berlin would signify some new political organization. It would also indicate breakdown in quadripartite control, exclusion of the Soviet Union from any say over the fate of Germany outside of its own zone, and so would amount to a major step toward partition, even before the establishment of a West German government. As the Council of Foreign Ministers meeting in London adjourned in December, U.S. and British officials had decided to try one more time for an all-Germany currency reform and, if not successful, then to go it alone. The effort was half-hearted.

Both the United States and the Soviet Union introduced monetary proposals in the Control Council. "If my colleagues would have enough patience," Marshal Sokolovsky said on February 1, "I would go through the U.S. proposal point by point and it would be evident that U.S. proposal is acceptable with exceptions but we must insist that the Soviet proposal be studied."

The Soviet proposal was not clear, Clay replied. "Currency reform has now been debated for the past two years," he added, and the United States was "unwilling to continue with financial conditions existing in U.S. zone."

Sokolovsky ended the session by declaring that the money was already in Clay's pockets — not incorrect, since the Americans had printed and stored new marks before the end of 1947.[8]

On March 10, a State Department official, Frank Wisner, asked whether quadripartite agreement was even "desirable from the U.S. standpoint, since quadripartite currency reform might enable the Soviets to frustrate further the economic recovery of western Germany." A bizonal currency reform "would represent a very definite move toward recognition of the East-West partition of Germany," he said. But, he added, it would also be "an important move toward much needed economic stability in Germany." He recommended that Clay be told that it was no longer U.S. policy to aim for Four-Power agreement.

"Better act fast," Lovett scribbled on the memorandum, and the next day so informed Clay, who replied that he had been thinking the same for some time.

In addition to currency reform and the establishment of a West German state, the Russians were also aware of both the American rearmament drive and the movement toward the creation of a North Atlantic military alliance.

They responded in a variety of ways. On March 3, Murphy reported that a "relatively harmonious period" in the Control Council following the London Council of Foreign Ministers had, late in January, given way to Soviet denunciation of Western plans to break up the Four-Power Council and the Four-Power administration of Berlin. Murphy ingenuously suggested that such "tactics" indicated "a Soviet intention to break up the quadripartite administration of Berlin."

"I personally feel that Control Council is defunct organization," Murphy reported a month later. Another American official at the Deputy Commandants for Berlin noted that the chief Soviet representative, who had formerly taken extensive notes of proceedings, now only doodled.[9]

In late winter and early spring, the United States and the Soviet Union exchanged a series of messages, a verbal duel in which each tried to make its record — onus-shifting again — to place the blame for the obviously imminent division of Europe upon the other. The Russians declared that they had sought to meet "halfway the proposals of the other powers" in the two Council of Foreign Ministers meetings in 1947. "Both the American plan of economic 'aid' and the British political plan of 'Western Europe' set up a Western Europe as against an Eastern Europe and, consequently, lead to a political cleavage of Europe." The State Department countered that "prior actions" of the Soviet Union were the source of the problems and attacked "an effort to shift the responsibility incurred by the Soviet Government itself for the present division of Germany." [10]

On March 20, Sokolovsky asked for information on the February London meeting of the United States and the five Western European states. He was not given any. He walked out of the Control Council. "I believe we have or are reaching a crisis in our relations," Clay reported to Washington. For a week and a half, at the end of March and beginning of April, the Russians tightened control over Allied rail traffic into Berlin — this was the "mini-blockade" — and the Western countries responded with what became known as "the little airlift." [11]

Toward the end of April, the London Conference reconvened, with the United States and Britain united in their goals. "We want a provisional German government soon," said William Strang, the Foreign Office official in charge of German affairs.

France, however, was the major obstacle to currency reform and to a West German state. The French government still feared domestic anti-German sentiment, politically more significant and powerful than in Britain or the United States. "Don't make it too hard for me," Bidault pleaded with the American ambassador in Paris. "I'll have to face the Assembly and given the attitude of the Communists, the Gaullists, and the Socialists, I don't know how we will come out . . . Tell your government I am on your side and in the long run I am sure we will work something satisfactory out, but at the same time I must think about public opinion here." The French also worried about provoking the Soviets into counteraction and, much more than the U.S. and Britain, about Berlin's isolated position, 110 miles inside the Soviet zone.

Moreover, the French had a different conception of security. They harked back to the Second World War and their ancient rivalry with Germany. The Americans had put World War II behind them, and, we already well know, now centered their security concerns almost exclusively on the Soviet Union. "French preoccupation with Germany as major threat at this time seems to us outmoded and unrealistic," complained General Marshall.

"Security in its limited sense as related specifically to Germany, it seems to us, still governs French public opinion," observed Ambassador Douglas, the American representative at the London Conference. "The French at times find it difficult to look over their next door neighbor and at the larger problem." [12]

To reassure the French, the Americans suggested that U.S. troops might remain in Europe indefinitely to guarantee France against both a revanchist Germany and a rapacious Soviet Union. "As long as European Communism threatens U.S. vital interests and national security we could ill afford to abandon our military position in Germany," Marshall informed Douglas on February 28. "We have not yet thoroughly thought through all the implications." He suggested that Douglas raise the matter as "your own personal views" with the French and the British. Douglas did so over lunch with Strang and René Massigli, French ambassador in London. "This was seized upon with alacrity and enthusiasm by all present," Douglas reported.

This strong hint was not enough to overcome French doubts. In April, Couve de Murville, Director-General for Political Affairs in the French Foreign Ministry and close to de Gaulle, interrupted a Riviera vacation to fly to Berlin in Clay's plane. Murphy happily noted that Couve's thinking had "progressed" considerably. "War with the Soviet Union within the next two or three years is inevitable — and that may mean this year," Couve said. He suggested that the problems with French public opinion had been exaggerated. Jean Chauvel, Secretary-General of the French Foreign Ministry, who was keen for agreement with the other Western powers, regarded Couve's change of heart as "a godsend."

The Kremlin was obviously alarmed by the evident progress toward the creation of a West German state. In April and May, after lifting their mini-blockade on Berlin, the Russians launched what *Business Week* called "a full-fledged Russian peace offensive," culminating in bids from Molotov, then Stalin himself, for high-level, bilateral U.S.-USSR negotiations to settle differences between the two countries. The Western Europeans were deeply concerned about such a prospect, and American officials quickly decided that acceptance of the Russian proposal would endanger their efforts to consolidate Western Europe. It was unclear, of course, whether the Soviet offer was genuine or merely a propaganda effort aimed at splintering the emerging Western unity. Washington did not want to take any chances, and so the United States did not investigate. Instead, it ignored the overture.

By the beginning of June, the French had come around sufficiently so that the London Conference could end with agreement on five related points: a German assembly would convene by September 1 to begin writing a constitution for a West German state; the new nation would be economically integrated into Western Europe; an international authority, with German representation, would oversee the Ruhr industrial base, but the area would remain part of Germany; U.S. forces would stay indefinitely in Germany; and the Americans, British, and French would seek to better coordinate economic policies in their respective zones.[13]

The stage was set for the first Berlin crisis.

Before proceeding, however, there is a most interesting question about the surprisingly low level of American concern about, and preparation for, a confrontation over Berlin. So unprepared were the Americans that, on March 31, when the Russians began the mini-blockade, Army Secretary Royall had to direct a hurried question to Clay: "Do you know of any documentation of agreement with Russians as to our rights to occupy and have access to Berlin? The State Department has not yet located any such information." Clay replied that the occupation agreement had been worked out in World War II, but that the access rights were only in the form of "oral agreement . . . They are implied in almost three years of application."

This is not to say that there was no concern at all. At the end of December 1947, the acting chief of the Division of Central European Affairs had predicted "a determined Soviet effort to get the Western allies out of Berlin," and advocated preparing for the development and possible retaliation. More than three months later, the Assistant Secretary of State for Occupied Areas urged Lovett that the State Department begin planning how to counter Soviet moves in Germany.

In late April, Army Secretary Royall wrote to former War Secretary

Stimson: "It appears to be the clear intention of the Soviet Union to force us out of Berlin on the basis of quadripartite control of the city and in fact quadripartite control of Germany is no longer a matter of fact. The Soviets have some basis for their argument, in view of the tripartite actions we have been forced to take regarding Germany, as a result of the breakdown of the Council of Foreign Ministers last December. They can argue with some logic that the Three Power Talks on Germany, initiated in London in February and to be resumed the 20th of this month, are proof of our intentions to abandon four-power control. They can also use our establishment of an economic council in Germany as an argument to the same end. We have tried to maintain an 'open door' to the Soviets in all of our actions in Germany but we cannot permit continued stagnation in that country and still hope to revive Western European economy in keeping with the objective of the European Recovery Program. So, as we have expected for months, the Soviets are now putting on pressure to force us out of Berlin. They have most of the trump cards in this situation since they control rail and road access to the city and certain of the most important public utilities such as electric power. General Clay has acted very firmly in the situation and has been backed up strongly by the government in Washington. We have the capability of supplying ourselves by air and intend to do so whenever necessary. We will hold out in Berlin as long as it is feasible, that is, until the Soviets make life unbearable for even a small group." [14]

A very significant reason for the lack of preparation was the manner in which General Lucius D. Clay, U.S. Military Governor in Germany, and his State Department adviser, Robert Murphy, defined the problem.

Born in Georgia, the son of a U.S. senator, a Senate page as a youth, Clay graduated from West Point in 1918, ranked first in English and history but at the bottom in conduct and discipline. He distinguished himself as an engineer and administrator as he rose through Army ranks. During the war, he had directed industrial production for the Army, becoming Byrnes' deputy in the Office of War Mobilization. The unusually strong backing he had received from Hopkins, Byrnes, and Morgenthau facilitated his appointment as Deputy Military Governor, and then Military Governor, in Germany. With an endless capacity for work, he fought with passionate intensity for whatever he believed at any given time. "Clay is a fine fellow when he relaxes," so the Army saying went, "the only problem being that he never relaxes."

During the first year in Germany, he was convinced that he was making progress in cooperating with the Russians. He blamed the French for the major difficulties, and denounced Kennan's Long Telegram. Economic problems and the buildup in East-West tensions greatly complicated the life of the Four-Power occupation, and the never-ending problems ground down Clay's early optimism, though he was still willing to consider reparations out of current production long after most of his colleagues had put this out of their minds. But, certainly by the latter part of 1947, Clay had become passionate in his conviction that the Soviet thrashing about concealed aggressive designs.

"Do you think this is a prelude to a declaration of war?" he asked James Riddleberger at one point, after listening to a Soviet attack on American policy in the Control Council. "No, Lucius," Riddleberger replied. "Sometimes it sounds like it, but I don't think so at this particular moment." [15]

Being number one in Germany only strengthened his almost self-righteous assurance. "Military governor was a pretty heady job," John McCloy recalled. "It was the nearest thing to a Roman proconsulship the modern world afforded. You could turn to your secretary and say, 'Take a law.' The law was there, and you could see its effect in two or three weeks. It was a challenging job to an ambitious man. Benevolent despotism."

While on a trip to Germany, Charles Kindleberger, director of the Division of German-Austrian Economic Affairs in the State Department, wrote back to his colleagues, "I find talking to Clay very difficult. He is personally very cordial, and frequently after a sweeping denunciation of the Department says with a smile that he doesn't mean me." Clay's deputy economic adviser told Kindleberger that all of the general's opinions "are either black or white because he knows that when decisions are put into operation down the line the chiaroscuro will develop in sufficient quantities anyhow. He has great knowledge of detail, as well as strong and frequently unexpected opinions. But he doesn't handle staff, delegate authority, build a working team which knows where it is going and why."

Threatening to resign to get his way (often through a maze of contradictory directives) became more a habit than a tactic with Clay —

indeed, he submitted his resignation at least eleven times over policy issues while military governor. Each time it was rejected. In 1947, George Kennan noted that he had never observed a "yearning for guidance" on Clay's part. On the contrary, the general sought to control the flow of information from Germany back to Washington. "The guy is really jealous on lines of authority," Kindleberger noted. In January 1948, Robert Murphy took strong exception to Clay's charge that State's representatives in Germany were functioning as "political commissars." Murphy explained that "Clay has never taken kindly to the matter of direct reporting by State Department personnel here," but, he said, he had made clear to Clay that the State Department would never "renounce its separate channel in an area as important as Germany." However, relations between Clay and Murphy were generally very good, and they saw eye to eye on most of the major political questions.[16]

Clay, with Murphy's firm backing, structured the problem of Berlin for the policy elite in three ways. Fervently wanting to proceed with economic recovery and the creation of a West German state, the two men downplayed the possible adverse consequences. Discussing Germany with Marshall and Bevin after the break-up of the London Council of Foreign Ministers in December 1947, Clay raised an additional question "concerning the future of the Western Allies in Berlin." Difficulties would obviously arise there, he said, but the Allies would put up with minor annoyances and hold on for as long as possible. "If things became too tough," he added, "they would have to refer to their Governments, but they would not bring the question up until it developed." [17]

Second, they convinced other policymakers that the price of not going ahead in Germany would be greater than whatever costs were encountered in proceeding. Thus, in late May 1948, when the French expressed concern about possible Soviet retaliation over Berlin, Ambassador Douglas dismissed the worry as based "on certain erroneous assumptions and conclusions." As Lovett replied to Douglas: "Assume Clay has taken into account that announcement concerning provisional govt may give Soviets excuse to intensify pressure in Berlin, also that U.S. and British delegations feel danger of delay in Germany is greater than risks involved in Soviet reaction."

Behind all this, however, Clay and Murphy were willing to accept a challenge they perceived as inevitable. Perhaps they even welcomed it as a way to draw the line. Yet, at the same time, they did not want to undertake any planning or preparations that would call attention to the real dangers, thereby possibly alarming not only the French and the British, but also policymakers in Washington, who might then put a brake on what they regarded as the urgent process of consolidation in Western Germany. Clay laid out at least some aspects of such thinking in a teletype conversation on April 10 with General Bradley, Army Chief of Staff. We may conclude that the communication, conducted in private, for the benefit neither of Congress nor of public opinion, represented Clay's real outlook on the eve of the confrontation.

"You will understand, of course, that our separate currency reform in near future followed by partial German government in Frankfurt will develop the real crisis . . . Why are we in Europe? We have lost Czechoslovakia. We have lost Finland. Norway is threatened. We retreat from Berlin . . . After Berlin will come Western Germany and our strength there relatively is no greater and our position no more tenable than Berlin. If we mean that we are to hold Europe against communism, we must not budge . . . If America does not know this, does not believe the issue is cast now, then it never will and communism will run rampant. I believe the future of democracy requires us to stay here until forced out. God knows this is not a heroic pose because there will be nothing heroic in having to take humiliation without retaliation."[18]

With the conclusion of the London Conference at the beginning of June, the Western powers prepared to introduce the currency reform in their zones. The French Assembly approved the London agreements on June 17. The next day the three Western allies announced imminent currency reforms in Western Germany, but purposely excluding West Berlin. The Russians had begun to restrict ground traffic again. Declaring that the West was dividing Germany, they announced that the whole of Berlin would be included in an East German currency reform. To permit this to take place would be to acquiesce both in a Soviet assertion of sovereignty over the city as well as in a practical assumption of new power by the Russians. Having anticipated the Soviet action, the West announced on June 23 that its new marks would circulate in the western sectors of Berlin. The next day the Soviets cut the overland routes between West Germany and West Berlin. They shut off electricity. The blockade had begun.

Supply was the key. There were over two million people in the western sectors of Berlin. On hand was enough food to last them 36 days, enough coal for 45 days.

On June 24 Clay called Air Force General LeMay in Wiesbaden and asked him to put his entire fleet of C-47s on the Berlin run. Meanwhile, Undersecretary of the Army William Draper and General Albert Wedemeyer were flying from Washington to London for a European inspection trip. Only after they had breakfasted over the Atlantic did they read their cables and realize that a blockade was on. Draper knew how many planes were available in Europe, and also had some idea of the supplies Berlin would require, since he had negotiated on this subject with the Russians in 1945. Wedemeyer had helped to direct the airlift over the "hump" in India during the war. Together, as they flew, they did their calculations, and concluded that an airlift for Berlin might work. It was not a sure thing. When they arrived in London, they talked to Clay, who had come to a similar conclusion. Draper flew on to Berlin, where he went over the details with Clay and his staff. And so the airlift was launched.*

There were certain elements of extra security in an airlift. The air corridors were the only avenue of access into Berlin guaranteed by written agreements; moreover, Russian interference with air traffic would be much closer to an act of war than blocking a highway.

Senior American and British officials speedily confirmed the decision to remain in Berlin and depend upon the airlift. "We were going to stay, period," Truman declared. Bevin was no less categorical — "The abandonment of Berlin would mean the loss of western Europe." [19]

By July 22, the airlift involved 52 C-54s and 80 C-47s, each making two round trips a day, altogether bringing in about 2500 pounds of supplies a day. The Western powers also responded with a counter-blockade against East Berlin and the Eastern Zone, denying the Soviet-controlled regions important industrial goods. The counter-blockade took other forms. Members of the Soviet military

* Draper, worrying about war, flew from Berlin on to Vienna, arriving in time for the American commanding general's Fourth of July garden party. He was surprised to see senior Russians toasting America's birthday as enthusiastically as their hosts, as if no crisis were anywhere in sight.

government habitually ignored legal speed limits as they sped from their villas in Potsdam through West Berlin to their East Berlin headquarters. But now Western military police began to enforce the regulations strictly, and an irate Marshal Sokolovsky found himself arrested and held for an hour, charged with speeding.[20]

The Berlin crisis brought relations between the Soviet Union, on the one side, and Britain and the United States, on the other, to a new level of tension — not war, but the edge of war. Bevin said he now realized "what agony Neville Chamberlain must have endured in September 1938."

"The situation in Europe is very tense, as you may imagine," Lord Ismay wrote to Eisenhower on July 8. "We are all standing on the edge of a precipice, and although all parties concerned are determined not to slip over the edge, there may be a puff of wind or someone may get dizzy and trip up; or again, someone may be deliberately malicious."[21]

In late July, when Clay returned to confer with officials in Washington, the commitment to remain in Berlin was reinforced — despite grumbling from the Air Force, worried that with too many of its planes in Germany, its strength elsewhere would be weakened. The airlift also involved an uncomfortable change of emphasis for senior Air Force officers, who had always regarded their prime mission as strategic bombing, not cargo-ferrying.[22]

On June 28, Ambassador Douglas, on instructions from Washington, asked Bevin whether the U.S. might send three groups of heavy bombers to Britain as a political gesture and to signal American interest in Europe's defense. Bevin hurriedly met with Attlee and other colleagues later the same day, and the British agreed. On July 15, the National Security Council formally ordered 60 B-29s — pointedly known as the "atomic bombers" — to England. Their arrival, after highly publicized flights from Kansas and Florida, led to the establishment of the first Strategic Air Command bases in the U.K. Other B-29 groups had already begun to simulate bombing missions over "targets" like the North Sea and the Suez Canal. More B-29s arrived in England in August; air strength was also beefed up on Okinawa; and jet aircraft, dispatched to Germany, began to make "familiarization flights" over the local countryside.

The forward basing of the atomic bombers in England was in itself a significant event — the heretofore implicit threat of nuclear retaliation was now made explicit.* By "bringing the nuclear weapons for the first time directly into the system of diplomacy and violence," one historian has written, deterrence ceased being just a theory and became a vital part of U.S. military strategy.[23] The atomic arsenal had become an appropriate instrument of policy.

Clay successfully defined the American commitment to Berlin.[24] But Washington did not accept his corollary argument that the United States should challenge the blockade directly. The Russians asserted that "technical difficulties" had forced them to shut the ground routes. Clay proposed several times that U.S. engineers in armed convoy be sent through to repair the roads: "to use the equivalent of a constabulary regiment reinforced with a recoilless rifle troop and engineer battalion attached as an escort for a convoy of about two hundred trucks . . . Troops would be ordered to escort the convoy to Berlin. It would be directed to clear all obstacles and to avoid shooting unless resisted by force. However, they would be ordered to clear obstacles even if such an action brought on an attack." [25]

Why did Washington not accept Clay's recommendations? On June 30, Forrestal and the Joint Chiefs of Staff discussed the matter. They concluded that diplomatic channels had to be exhausted first.

There was also confusion and uncertainty about the relative strength of the United States and the Soviet Union. Military leaders had complained so much about the dismantling of U.S. power that they had come to believe it, at least some of the time. Two letters to Chester Bowles from Colonel Frank Howley, American commandant for Berlin, illustrate this confusion.

"I still think we can put some sense into their heads but it won't be done by diplomacy or polite words," Howley said of the Russians in the tense days of early April 1948. "It'll be done by the cool fact that militarily we have the power and they don't, that economically we have the goods and they don't, that morally we have the convictions and they don't."

Yet in the even more tense days of late June, Howley again wrote: "I don't believe that we would be in this situation if we had not thrown away our might at the end of the war. I think we could then

* Curiously, it appears that these first groups of B-29s had not actually been modified to carry atomic bombs, and the American bombers based in Britain would not be so modified until 1949.

have sat down at a conference table and shown our hands frankly and arrived at those compromises so essential to peace. We are, however, so weak now physically that it is an invitation for the Russians to destroy us, to walk all over us, to humiliate us and to do what they want to do without consultation." [26]

The latter perception was uppermost in the minds of those who rejected Clay's summons to break the blockade. "For your information only," Forrestal informed Marshall in late July, "the Joint Chiefs of Staff do not recommend supply to Berlin by armed convoy in view of the risk of war involved and the inadequacy of United States preparation for global conflict." [27] Forrestal elaborated in a report to the National Security Council that the Chiefs thought the airlift would work for a "considerable" time, and they did not want to initiate action that "would shift the stage from one of local friction to that of major war." The risks appeared much greater to those in Washington than to American officials in Germany. "Strangely enough," one of Truman's military aides reported to the President after a trip to Germany, "those nearest to the hot-spot in Berlin are less apprehensive about a sudden outbreak of hostilities than those more removed from the Berlin scene itself." [27]

Yet the historian cannot avoid the conclusion that the Russians would either have backed down or been at a disadvantage in a larger confrontation. The United States was militarily stronger, and did have sole possession of nuclear weapons. Whether or not they believed them, senior U.S. officials possessed relatively accurate estimates of Soviet military manpower — estimates much lower than those publicly bruited about. At the beginning of June 1948, the Joint Intelligence Committee of the Joint Chiefs reported that the Red Army had stabilized at 2,500,000 men, with an additional 400,000 men in security forces. Furthermore, at that very moment, the Russians faced a separate crisis within their own new empire, which could only have heightened their anxiety about their ability to maintain order in the Eastern Zone and Eastern Europe.

The new constraint on the Soviet position, far from fully recognized in the West, was the Stalin-Tito split, which not only affected Soviet calculations in the tense summer months of 1948 but also shaped the political geography of postwar Europe.

Through 1947, Soviet foreign economic policy had produced tensions in Yugoslavia. The Russians used joint stock companies to dominate and exploit the Yugoslavian economy, reducing Belgrade's authority over Soviet activities within the country to a minimum. The system paralleled that in East Germany, save that in Yugoslavia the Russians were more interested in raw materials than industrial goods.[28] Relations were exacerbated by the Yugoslavian self-confidence in the face of overbearing Soviet officials and by the obvious Russian effort to establish intelligence networks in the Balkan country.

At the beginning of 1948, the conflict became more overtly political. The Yugoslavs were increasingly vocal in their unwillingness to subordinate themselves to the Russians. Stalin concluded that they were moving toward an independent foreign policy at the very time he wanted their policy to conform to Soviet interests to an even greater extent. He was convinced that Tito was striving for regional dominance in the Balkans. "The issue," Stalin told delegations from Yugoslavia and Bulgaria in February, "is concepts different from our own." But his concerns went beyond foreign policy. Unlike all the other Eastern European regimes, which depended almost completely on Soviet power, the Belgrade government clearly had strong national roots. Moreover, Tito in manner and thought was too independent, too sure of himself, and enjoyed too much prestige within his own country and in the rest of the world, including the other new socialist countries. In other words, Stalin saw in him what was intolerable — a rival.

The Russian dictator forced a Yugoslavian delegation in Moscow to sign an agreement promising mutual consultations — without even allowing them to consult Belgrade before signing! He then applied pressure through a variety of tactics. A bitter exchange of correspondence began in March. Stalin and Molotov set the tone with the first letter: "We think the political career of Trotsky is sufficiently instructive." The Soviets went on in the letters that followed to accuse the Yugoslavs of misbehavior, ingratitude, and ideological deviations — all of which the Yugoslavs denied.[29]

Initially, the Yugoslavs had great difficulty in comprehending the nature of Moscow's challenge. They were among the most honest of Stalin's "honest fools." Their commitment to communism had been like a religious faith; thousands of Partisans had died shouting "Long live Stalin." They had endured German bombing with the thought that every bomb that fell on them was one less on Soviet Russia. Without quite realizing what was happening, although now recalling the Moscow purges more clearly, they refused to give way. "We are not a pawn on a chessboard," Tito said in March. Their self-righteousness saved them.

Meanwhile the vituperative allegations from Moscow rose to a flood — including the charge that Tito, whom the Russians would have willingly sacrificed in the war, was an imperialist spy. The Russians also mobilized other communist parties to isolate and terrify the Yugoslavs. On June 28, 1948, *four days after the Russians began to blockade Berlin,* the Cominform expelled Yugoslavia and called for a coup against Tito. The Soviets organized an economic blockade that caused great hardship, and orchestrated a vicious propaganda campaign to bring the Yugoslavs to heel. Stalin failed. The Belgrade leadership held together; the Partisan ethic sustained party and country. Stalin dared not risk a direct military intervention, in part because he knew Russian forces would meet direct, strong, and committed resistance. Ironically enough, the Churchill-Stalin percentage deal of 1944 may also have helped to guarantee Yugoslavian independence, for the Russians could not anticipate how the West would respond to an invasion.[30]

The split caught the West unawares. U.S. officials at first doubted its reality. Then they were confused about what to do. They did not want to embrace Tito, both because of distaste for the Belgrade regime and so as not to embarrass him. A vigorous debate ensued. Washington overruled U.S. officials in Yugoslavia and elsewhere who wanted to be more forthcoming, especially on trade relations.

One might suppose that those summer months in 1948 were a time of considerable nervousness in the Kremlin. Stalin and his comrades needed all the bluff and nerve they could muster. The Russians saw an immediate threat in the creation of a West German state, especially as it paralleled U.S. rearmament and NATO. "To use Lenin's phrase, Stalin responded by prodding the capitalist world with the tip of a bayonet," Khrushchev later said of the blockade. But Khrushchev also noted that the "plan was badly thought out," and claimed that Stalin had discussed it with none of the other Politburo members, save perhaps for Molotov.[31] If the West had acted along the lines suggested by Clay, the Russians might well have given way.

Basically, politics in the West was a major, almost certainly the decisive, check on military action to break the blockade. Truman would have found it dangerous in the presidential election year of 1948 to have taken risks that appeared provocative enough to precipitate war. Clark Clifford and James Rowe had made this point very clearly in their autumn 1947 memorandum that outlined Truman's 1948 campaign strategy. "There is considerable political advantage to the Administration in its battle with the Kremlin." But only, they emphasized, "up to a certain point — real danger of imminent war." In the summer of 1948, Truman needed to find a middle ground. On the one hand, he did not want to provide any substance for the charges of bellicosity from the third party candidate on his left, Henry Wallace. On the other, he needed to deflect possible criticism from the Republican candidate, Thomas Dewey, that he was soft in dealing with the Soviet Union.[32]

More generally, in Great Britain and the United States, there would have been popular unwillingness to risk war over Berlin, an attitude mirrored in the British Foreign Office. "I know all of you Americans want a war," Bevin had said only partly joking to Bohlen in June, "but I'm not going to let you 'ave it." In Western Europe, such sentiment was much stronger, not only among members of the Communist Party, but across the political spectrum. Memories of the Nazi occupation were much too fresh, and there was already much anxiety about the creation of a new West German state. The United States would have found itself isolated had it appeared to champion a revived Germany at the risk of war. Even some senior American officials shared the disquiet. "From the political point of view, Berlin has become the important symbol it now is largely because we ourselves had made it so," Walter Bedell Smith told the State Department Policy Planning Staff in September. "To leave Berlin would indeed, as I am told, throw a pall over Western European hopes for security . . . Our present hysterical outburst of humanitarian feelings about the latter [Germans] keeps reminding me that just 3½ years ago, I would have been considered a hero if I had succeeded in exterminating those same Germans with bombs."

Moreover, the American case was not completely persuasive. In his June letter, Commandant Howley had expressed his hope that "the Russians will not irrevocably slam the door upon German unity and allied accord." [33] But the Western powers, for what they saw as very good reasons, closed the door upon the Four-Power cooperation. The Russians responded by shutting the one door available to them — the ground routes into Berlin. For Clay, the issue was clear;

the head-on collision between East and West was already at hand. But, as long as the airlift provided a middle way between withdrawal and collision, Washington would be satisfied. Very early on, senior policymakers made the point to Clay. On June 25, Army Secretary Royall held a teletype conversation with him.

"It seems important now to decide just how far we will go short of war to stay in Berlin," Clay said.

Royall assured the general that his currency decisions enjoyed complete support. "But I do feel strongly that the limited question of Berlin currency is not a good question to go to war on."

"If Soviets go to war," Clay replied, "it will not be because of Berlin currency issue but only because they believe this the right time. In such case, they would use currency issue as an excuse."

Royall changed the subject.[34]

The United States did use diplomatic channels. On July 26, Ambassador Smith was ordered "to probe Soviet intentions and to test their willingness to find a peaceful issue from the present situation." Smith, accompanied by the British and French ambassadors, first saw Molotov, then Stalin.

If there were now two German states, Stalin argued, then Berlin could not be regarded as the capital of one Germany, and so the Allies would lose the "juridical" basis for their presence in Berlin. This point the Western ambassadors strenuously disputed.

Stalin left no doubt that the blockade was meant to forestall a West German constitution. The Soviet maneuver had already failed; the Western military governors and ministers from the provincial states in the Western zones had met on July 1 to plan for the Constituent Assembly.

Stalin declared that he was very interested in one question. He understood, he said, "that a sort of parliamentary council was to be formed soon, and that this would set up a German Government. If this went ahead, the Soviet Government would be faced with a *fait accompli* and there would be nothing left to discuss."

Smith made a most important and perceptive point in reply. "Without wishing to go into the details of two years of frustrations and disagreements, the steps taken in the western zone seem to us defensive, just as the Soviet Government maintained the steps they were taking were defensive."

In truth, both governments had their "plans," though formed more out of accident, confusion, fear, increments, and constraints than from fervently desired and articulated goals. Each was also responding to an exaggerated vision of the extent of "plan" that supposedly motivated actions on the other side.

Stalin reiterated his complaint: "The only real issue he had in mind was the formation in the western zones of a German Government . . . That was the issue." He added that he did not want to embarrass the Western governments by forcing them to backtrack publicly on the London agreements, but the Soviet government would certainly be "embarrassed" were a government set up in the Western zones.

Smith said he found this very interesting and "had not previously considered the problem in this light." The ambassador, at least, had not realized that the blockade had one crucial purpose: to prevent the creation of a new West German state. (Apparently such Soviet experts as Bohlen had also failed to comprehend how important this objective was to the Russians.)

Stalin repeated what he had said almost a year and a half earlier at the Moscow Council of Foreign Ministers, that he "had always been confident that after much skirmishing they could return to a basis for agreement." [35]

Smith summed up the first round of talks both for Washington and for Clay in Berlin: "Doubt if I have ever seen Molotov so cordial and if one did not know real Soviet objectives in Germany would have been completely deceived by their attitude as both literally dripping with sweet reasonableness and desire not to embarrass." If it were possible to put off the implementation of the London agreements "without undue complications or loss of prestige," he continued, "it would give us a good club as with finalization of West German government we will have fired one of the last shots in our political locker."

"The question of what to do about the decisions of the London Conference present great difficulty," Bohlen wrote, in analyzing the matter for Marshall. He predicted strong pressure from some domestic groups and from France to put off the measures for a West German government in favor of Four-Power talks. France, he thought, might even line up on the German question with the Soviet Union in such a Council of Foreign Ministers meeting. "On the other hand, to halt these measures because of Soviet insistence would have a very serious effect in Germany, would certainly be violently opposed by General Clay and Ambassador Murphy, and might make their resumption in the event of a probable breakdown of the four power talks difficult if not impossible."

Bohlen correctly predicted Clay's reaction. The general argued vigorously that suspension would be a political disaster of the first order — it would signal American weakness and demoralize the Germans. "It is," he said, "the one thing I can think of which to abandon would be worse than to abandon Berlin." [36]

A few important policymakers disagreed. Smith wanted to put aside the juridical issue in order to find a modus vivendi; he put less stock in the commitment to Berlin. (It should be noted that in 1945 he had very badly wanted the job in Germany that went to Clay.) George Kennan struggled to work out a formula in the Policy Planning Staff that might prevent a divided Germany and a partitioned Europe.

But Clay's views carried the day. For Smith's benefit, Marshall, on August 26, outlined our "basic requirements for agreement": insistence on coequal Four-Power rights in Berlin; no abandonment of "our position" on Western Germany; "unequivocal lifting of blockade"; and quadripartite control of the circulation of Soviet marks in Berlin. In another telegram to Smith on the same day, Marshall made what was the central point: "We see no reason for haste in view of the very vital issues concerned." [37]

The Western ambassadors had continued to meet in the Kremlin. By the end of August, the conversations had produced a series of directives to govern the Allied Commanders in Germany in working out a Berlin compromise. The negotiations immediately moved to the Control Council in Berlin. Despite some conciliatory meetings and signs of Soviet concessions, the military commanders failed to agree on the key issues: Four-Power control of Berlin's currency, trade, and air traffic. After some days, the matter was referred back to Moscow. There was no success.[38]

Clay, for one, had assumed that agreement was out of the question in any event. "As you know," he wrote to former Secretary Byrnes on September 19, "an agreement with the Soviet Union at this time will prove impossible except under terms which would lead to our departure from Europe and I am convinced that a strong western

German government reoriented toward western Europe would do much to restore the political and economic balances in Europe in our favor. If this does happen it would of course put us in better shape for the final negotiations."

But it was not abstract "impossibility" that had prevented agreement. On September 1, two days after the Moscow conversations produced a directive, the Constituent Assembly began its work in Bonn, with Konrad Adenauer as president. The Americans and British left no doubt that they wanted the formation of a West German government to proceed quickly. The convening of the meeting reduced considerably the Soviet interest in a compromise, since the Russians had resorted to blockade to halt this very step. As Smith had pointed out, once the Constituent Assembly actually met, the West put aside one of its most useful bargaining levers.[39]

The Americans themselves lost interest in a compromise for a variety of factors. Land routes were not really necessary; the airlift had proved far more successful than was imagined in June. "The airlift has proved to me that we can stay here even if we have to make separate city of three Western sectors and can be moved out only by Soviet aggression without taking aggressive action ourselves," Clay declared in a teletype message to Royall on September 19. "It will cost considerable money but relatively only a fraction of what we are now spending to aid Europe and to rearm to stop Soviet expansion." [40]

The airlift was proving a technical achievement of the first order. By December, it supplied 4500 tons a day, 500 tons above what had been calculated as Berlin's minimum requirements. The winter weather was no deterrent; a plane still landed or took off every ninety seconds. By spring, the daily shipment had increased to 8000 tons a day, as much as had been carried by road and rail before the blockade.

The airlift was also of considerable military and political significance. It worked to Soviet disadvantage by strengthening the U.S. reliance on air power and broadening the concept. "The lift has been a stunning lesson for strategic airmen," *Fortune* observed in November. "It is now possible to move by air en masse from the continental U.S. to any part of the world. The anomaly of a 300-mile-an-hour global strategic air force tied to a ten-knot convoy is on the verge of disappearance. Air power is capable of providing its own logistical system." By transforming the logistics of supply, the airlift made the United States that much more of a global as well as specifically "European" power.

The blockade was a major propaganda blunder for the Soviet Union insofar as its standing in international opinion was concerned. "In terms of propaganda," one scholar has observed, "the situation cast the West in the position of using its strength in a humanitarian cause, while the Soviet Union was seen as a power which used starvation as an instrument of policy." [41]

The Americans also found new confidence in the economic recovery that had begun in Germany. "The Russians are retreating," Marshall said to Schuman and Bevin on September 21. "From now on, Berlin is the only foothold which they have against us; everywhere else, and particularly in Germany, they are losing ground. We have put Western Germany on its feet and we are engaged in bringing about its recovery in such a way that we can really say that we are on the road to victory."

Signs of recovery were unmistakable by the end of the summer of 1948. Production increased in the Western zones from 50 percent of 1936 levels in June to 60 percent in July, and output continued to grow rapidly. By providing incentives not only to work but also to buy and sell, the currency reform and related removal of price controls are credited with setting off the *Wirtschaftswunder*, the "economic miracle." [42]

The establishment of a new West German state was proceeding at a satisfactory rate. Meanwhile, rearmament at home was matched by further movement toward the North Atlantic Pact. A new round of conversations had begun in Washington in July on the major questions of the nature of U.S. affiliation, the extent of membership, and whether and when the United States would rearm Western Europe. As always, however, the question of Soviet intentions was much at the heart of all the discussions. It is striking that the Soviet experts, Kennan and to a lesser degree Bohlen, were more restrained in analyzing Russian objectives than most other policymakers, European as well as American. The two men downplayed the Soviet military threat and emphasized Soviet weakness and caution. The Soviet Union, Kennan explained, did not have a plan to take over Europe. He was unhappy with the whole North Atlantic enterprise. He thought it a diversion from economic problems, feared the final division of Europe and Germany, and was afraid that a preoccupation with a military threat that did not exist might help to create that very threat. Later in the talks, perhaps in response to criticism from other officials, Kennan backtracked, saying that he and Bohlen "had not meant to imply that there was no danger of war nor threat of war. What they had meant was they did not consider that the Soviet Union had deliberately drawn up a program of aggression."

In mid-July, Bohlen elaborated: "The most dangerous period had been in the immediate postwar years, 1945–47, when the U.S. military establishment was rapidly disintegrating and the American public had not yet been alerted to the Russian peril; yet it was significant that the Soviet Army did not move during that period. Furthermore, it should be remembered that the Russian Army had not moved beyond the line which we now refer to as the 'iron curtain.'" Referring to the recent Yugoslavian development, he thought that this indicated Russia, as a country, was "dangerously over extended . . . The Soviet troops in Germany, while numerous, were not generally regarded as being capable of a sustained move westward through Europe.

"Despite what the Russians may or may not do we still must not be deflected from our purpose to do all that is required by the present conditions in Europe," Bohlen continued. "The first benefit which should derive from any measures which we may take here would probably be a psychological one, a certain confidence in the future."

The discussions concluded on September 9 with agreement on a report for submission to the respective governments. Its analysis of Soviet goals and of the international situation expressed confusion about whether Russia did or did not constitute a military threat. That confusion, in turn, reflected doubt over the purpose of the pact — was it to deter a Soviet attack or to reassure the peoples of Western Europe? Perhaps the real significance of what became NATO was the latter. So it seemed to the Canadian ambassador to the U.S., Hume Wrong, who told the Washington Group: "One of the greatest advantages which the creation of such a system would bring would be the attainment of certainty, and particularly of continuing certainty about the long-term position of the United States." [43]

Certainty was much to be desired in the uncertain postwar world.

At the end of October, the five Brussels Treaty countries invited the United States and Canada to enter formal negotiations for a North

Atlantic Pact. Kennan, for one, still dissented. He complained that "intensive rearmament" constituted "an uneconomic and regrettable diversion of effort" that would promote a militarization of the confrontation with the Soviet Union. But most U.S. policymakers were firmly committed to the Pact. They pushed rearmament as a matter of the highest urgency, for Western Europe as well as for the United States.[44]

For George Kennan, this was a difficult period. Power to influence U.S. policy was slipping from him; events passing him by. Kennan, who had elegantly codified the Riga axioms, was now concerned at the rigidity with which they were applied, at the insistence upon portraying the Soviet "threat" in military terms. Perhaps he now saw more of the brutal but cautious imperialist power, bedeviled with its own problems, and less of the world revolutionary state. In other ways, he had surely moved. It was Kennan, after all, who had written in the winter of 1945 to a surprised Charles Bohlen, then at the Yalta Conference, that the U.S. and the USSR should "divide Europe frankly into spheres of influence." Now, in the latter half of 1948, he wanted to go to greater lengths than any of his colleagues to prevent a militarized partition. Kennan's own role within the State Department was changing, from that of savant and seer to grumbler and irritant. At last, in 1948, the American public saw the Soviet danger in the way Kennan had wanted them to see it in 1944 and 1945. But, as the anticommunist consensus became the intellectual law of the land, Kennan once again took exception to the conventional wisdom, setting off on yet another self-imposed exile.[45]

There could be no question that the anticommunist consensus had become firmly established in the country. Henry Wallace's dismal showing in the November 1948 presidential election, running on the third party Progressive ticket, was sufficient proof.[46] But it had been clear earlier, in the first months of the Berlin crisis. This was the final reason why the American policymakers were content and confident enough not to seek a quick resolution of the blockade. Indeed, the Berlin airlift was the dramatic occasion in which the anticommunist consensus became fixed in public opinion. "There has been a definite crystallization of American public and Congressional opinion over the Berlin issue," Marshall informed Smith in August, "and any agreement we make which appears to have sold out any of our basic rights in Berlin or Western Germany in exchange for lifting the blockade will be received with violent indignation here. From all reports the country is more unified in its determination not to weaken in the face of pressure of an illegal blockade than on any other issue we can recall in time of peace."[47]

Later in September, the Berlin crisis was referred to the United Nations Security Council. This constituted the final break over Germany, the end of the Four-Power control that had been meant to embody the Grand Alliance after World War II, and the acceptance of the division of the Continent. The United States, along with its Western allies, asserted itself through military power and a ceaseless pursuit of national security. Composition with the Soviet Union was impossible, for it was, as it always was in the Riga view, the world revolutionary state.

"Soviet long-run objectives are perfectly clear," Walter Bedell Smith told a group of officials in Washington in October 1948. "Their ultimate objective is the destruction of the capitalist system . . . They believe that can only be accomplished by violence and as the result of fearful conflicts during which one or the other system must go down."

The previous spring, Smith said, a committee in the Moscow embassy, under the chairmanship of Elbridge Durbrow, had prepared an estimate of Soviet capabilities for war and attitudes on war and peace. "At that time," Smith continued, "we reached the conclusion that the Soviet Union did not want to precipitate a war; that the Soviet Union would pursue its present policies by all means short of war; but that they had set their hand to a line of action which might produce hostilities, and they had taken that fact into account. Consequently, we felt the question of war versus peace was one which was under constant revision in the Kremlin . . .

"Nothing has happened since that time to modify our basic premise," Smith said, "except we now believe that the events which have taken place in Berlin and which are now taking place in the United Nations have moved us a little closer to the possibility of war."

Such fears were not restricted to the personnel in the American embassy in Moscow. "A terrific day," Truman commented ironically in a diary entry for September 13. "Berlin is a mess." He added that Forrestal, Symington, and Generals Vandenberg and Bradley "brief me on bases, bombs, Moscow, Leningrad, etc. I have a terrible feeling afterward that we are very close to war. I hope not."

For decades thereafter, both the United States and the Soviet Union would live with such a "terrible feeling," the daily fear of general war. And the two nations would prepare themselves accordingly.

Yet there was a most important additional element to this confrontation, and that was the "rule" that governed it. The rule had been confirmed during the Berlin crisis, for both sides clearly perceived that whatever could be achieved by war was less than the likely costs of war. Thus, there was an explicit agreement that crises would be contained. Ambassador Smith on September 16, 1948, summarized the rule, appropriately enough in the context of the Berlin crisis: "My opinion is Kremlin discounted completely the possibility that we might actually force the issue to the point of hostilities, just as we estimated no similar intention on their part." [48]

And so the end of the Second World War brought not peace, but rather an armed truce, a precarious balance, a crisis always short of catastrophe — always, that is, at least through this writing.

EPILOGUE

The National Security State from Blockade to New Era

The history of diplomacy is the history of relations among rival powers, which did not enjoy political intimacy, and did not respond to appeals to common purposes. Nevertheless, there have been settlements. Some of them did not last very long. Some of them did. For a diplomat to think that rival and unfriendly powers cannot be brought to a settlement is to forget what diplomacy is about. There would be little for diplomats to do if the world consisted of partners, enjoying political intimacy, and responding to common appeals.

— WALTER LIPPMANN, summer 1947

Epilogue: The National Security State from Blockade to New Era

THE RUSSIANS maintained the Berlin blockade into 1949, and the Western planes continued to fly into Templehof Airport. But the blockade's political consequences ran precisely counter to the Russian aim, for it promoted the cohesion of an anti-Soviet bloc. Western leaders sought with additional haste to create a West German state. The writing of the Basic Law, the constitution of the Federal Republic, was completed by February 1949, and adopted in May, bringing into existence the very political reality the blockade was meant to block. The Americans now energetically pushed economic recovery in Japan as well as Germany. France's participation in the airlift signaled a reluctant shift — to viewing Russia, not Germany, as its most likely potential enemy. And, to understate the matter, the blockade also dealt a stunning blow to Soviet efforts to court public opinion in the three Western zones, and, indeed, constituted a propaganda blunder of worldwide proportions. In January 1949, Truman announced his intention to provide military aid to Western Europe; in April, the North Atlantic Treaty was signed in Washington. The airlift itself became an ever more dramatic exhibition of American air power; in one twenty-four-hour period in April, Western pilots set a new record with 1398 flights into Berlin. Meanwhile, the Air Force's Strategic Air Command was in the midst of a major buildup, and, in February 1949, demonstrating true global reach, dispatched a new bomber on the first round-the-world journey. As General Clay said later that year, the blockade was "the stupidest move the Russians could make." [1]

With increasing urgency, the Russians wanted to liquidate the whole ill-conceived affair. An interview Stalin gave to an American journalist in January provided the first hint. (When Truman learned of Stalin's mode of communication, he jokingly suggested that the appropriate way for him to reply would be by giving an interview to Tass, the Soviet press agency.) Finally, in May, the Russians lifted the blockade in exchange for minimum concessions on the part of the West — a cessation of the counterblockade and a reconvening of the Council of Foreign Ministers.

The tone of the foreign ministers' meeting that opened in Paris in May showed a surprising shift from what had been the character of East-West exchanges over the last two years. "One thing is certain," said a State Department memorandum that went to Truman in late May, "the Russians are being unnaturally polite, restrained and non-provocative. Their proposals are unacceptable, and they must have known they would be. But their behavior has thus far been irreproachable. We are asking ourselves whether it could be that the fortunes of the cold war have shifted so dramatically in the past two years that it is now the Russians who are trying to follow, with regard to us, a policy of firmness and patience and unprovocative containment."

The Russians were trying to return to the *status quo ante*, that is, to reconstitute a Four-Power consortium to contain German "militarism." But it was much too late. The West would not agree to go back in time to halt steps toward a West German state, and the meeting adjourned on June 20, 1949, almost a year to the day after the Russians instituted their blockade.[2]

Yet the blockade did have to its credit one major accomplishment — of a sort. The confrontation, along with its demonstration of an implicit Soviet-American understanding that the crisis itself would be contained, effectively divided Germany, and a divided Germany was, after all, one solution to the German question.

The crisis did more — it also certified the division of the entire European continent.

Two years earlier, on March 13, 1947, the day after the Truman Doctrine speech, H. Alexander Smith, a Republican senator from New Jersey and also a good Wilsonian, recorded his reaction. "The

United States has to face the issue of accepting responsibility of leadership in world affairs or of letting the world drift into civil war and chaos," he said. "We must help the world help itself back to security and God . . . but it must be one world under the United Nations and not two spheres of influence. There must not be any balancing of power."

But such a division and balancing is what happened in Europe. The effort to deny spheres, to deny the Rooseveltian approach, had not only helped to make the division sharper than it might otherwise have been, but also made the Soviet-American confrontation more highly militarized, and much more costly and dangerous. Yet this result also provided, by the absurd but real logic of international relations, a certain stability.

There was, of course, a difference between the two spheres. The Americans held sway over a region in which diversity, including the participation of large communist parties, was tolerated. The Soviet Union, even before the defection of Tito, was transforming its sphere into one of tight control, with a Stalinist suppression of diversity. In the late 1940s, the brutal campaign was no longer merely aimed at "class enemies," but now hit just as hard at Stalin's "honest fools" — "nationalists," Jews, and those with some background of or connections with the West. The "teachers," as the Soviet secret police officials were called, moved in to direct the various Eastern European purges and make sure the quotas of "traitors" were met. The culmination was a series of show trials throughout Eastern Europe. Inside the Soviet Union, a reborn terror furiously pursued intellectuals, Red Army veterans, Jews, and "cosmopolitans," making the last years of Stalin's rule one of the ugliest periods in Soviet history.[3]

Yet, while the Cold War was hardly over in Europe, the worst of the international danger was. The uncertainties between the superpowers had been resolved, and after the Berlin blockade, the Cold War took on a new character; what had been primarily a European antagonism now became a global one. The area of competition moved to new peripheries, to Asia, and beyond, as it became a worldwide struggle over the orientation and allegiance of the new nation-states that succeeded the old colonial empires. The Cold War also created and constantly intensified a dynamic and dangerous arms race.

*

After the recognition of the USSR in 1933, Elbridge Durbrow had been among the first group of American diplomats to go into the Soviet Union with William Bullitt. One of the original State Department specialists on the Soviet Union, Durbrow returned to Moscow in 1946 to be Kennan's successor as chargé. In October 1948, back in Washington, he spoke to a group of American officials about "the objectives of Soviet policy."

"These people never have to worry about any changes in policy," he said of the Russians. "I was in Russia from 1934 to 1938, and they were calling Hitler every kind of a such and such, and in 1939 they were friends."

Events since 1939 had transformed the world. The United States and the Soviet Union had gone from tangential contacts to a Grand Alliance to a full confrontation. By 1948, each was the other's major foreign policy problem. The elapsed years had, for Durbrow, served to confirm the Riga axioms as the framework for assessing Soviet intentions. "The basic objective of Soviet policies is to extend Soviet domination and control over as many countries as possible, with the announced goal of eventual domination by all means, fair or foul," he said.

Was Soviet policy motivated by a quest for power or ideological zeal? "It is very difficult to determine when dialectic materialism ends and Dynamism Joe begins," said Durbrow. "They are all mixed together in their quest for their goal — world revolution." [4]

This talk came four months after the Berlin crisis had begun, and Durbrow was preaching to the converted. The blockade had certified not only the division of Germany and of Europe, but also the world set of American leaders.

Yet it was a world view living beyond its means. It lacked the requisite budget. So James Forrestal, one of the major architects of the national security state, had unhappily discovered. Through 1948, Forrestal was the man in the middle. Truman was insisting that the military budget for fiscal year 1950 not exceed a $15 billion ceiling. The Bureau of the Budget and the Council of Economic Advisers had convinced the President that anything higher would spell economic ruin for the nation. The budget did not *need* to be any higher, Truman thought, because of the American monopoly of the atomic bomb. Yet Forrestal had neither the prestige, nor the statutory authority, nor the power that comes from having a President's trust to resolve the service rivalries. He did not hide the fact that he himself thought the budget should be closer to $18 billion. By the spring of 1948, Forrestal's inability to control the interservice rivalry and his own emotional strains and conflicts were becoming obvious to those around him.[5]

In July 1948, a little more than two weeks after the blockade began, Forrestal tried to promote an indirect solution to the ongoing budget impasse. "Since the entire reason for the maintenance of military forces in this country is the safeguarding of our national security," he said in a memorandum he sent Truman, "their size, character, and composition should turn upon a careful analysis of existing and potential dangers to our security." He recommended the writing of a comprehensive statement of America's "national policy . . . particularly as it relates to the Russians." Such a description of threats, he was sure, would make the case for a larger budget.

Truman would not buy. The idea was interesting, he replied, but he curtly commanded: "The proper thing for you to do is to get the Army, Navy, and Air people together, and establish a program within the budget limits which have been allowed. It seems to me that is your responsibility."[6]

So Forrestal tried. In August 1948, he warned a meeting in the Pentagon that "the great arms program and the expansion of the armed forces themselves are sufficient to provide demagogic material for those who want to believe and want to imply and so state that the military seeks domination." He pleaded with the assembled officials to live quietly beneath the budget ceiling, and stop fighting among themselves. He told the Joint Chiefs that he wanted them to divide the moneys available and not press for their own uncoordinated requests. He failed. In November, he complained to Truman that he had been trying to get the Joint Chiefs "to agree upon a concept of strategy in the event of trouble. In doing so, the vulgarities of money always come up, because no strategic concept can be unrelated to cash." He also attempted to get Secretary Marshall to say that the international situation required a larger defense budget, but with no success.

"I am up to my ears here," he wrote to a friend in the same month. "Budget trouble." In March 1949, Truman in effect fired Forrestal as Secretary of Defense. He was a broken man. Two months later, he killed himself.[7]

His successor at the Pentagon was Louis Johnson, who had been Assistant Secretary of War just before World War II, a past president of the American Legion, Truman's last-minute fund-raiser in the 1948 campaign, and — following Truman's lead — a man committed to economy in the defense establishment. In the spring of 1949, the President told the National Security Council and the Joint Chiefs that he had established a "restrictive ceiling" on the military budget, and he meant to hold it, not only in the next budget, but in subsequent ones as well. The Marshall Plan and other programs of economic assistance took precedence over any further enlargement in the military budget.[8]

Then, in September 1949, the sense of danger was dramatically expanded. There was no longer any doubt whatever about the impending success of the communist revolution in China. But another kind of dramatic change was also at hand. On September 3, an American B-29, on patrol at 18,000 feet over the North Pacific, picked up a radioactive count slightly higher than normal. There was some tendency to discount that first report. During the next week, however, as the high-level winds blew over North America, over the Atlantic, and on over Europe, more radiation was detected. The Russians had indeed tested an atomic device, sometime in the last couple of days of August.[9]

The news cracked the illusory confidence of most U.S. policymakers that the American atomic monopoly would last several more years. The dissenting scientists had been right. Even if the Soviets did not have a delivery system immediately at hand, the strategic calculations had to be rewritten. The balance of power would now become a balance of terror.

The atomic bomb had been Truman's ace, the principal reason that he felt he could keep the lid on the military budget. But the ace was no longer pre-eminent. It was a time when the Americans might have thought about negotiations. But most policymakers believed that negotiation with the Russians was dangerous and that a diplomatic settlement was impossible.

So, instead, American leaders turned to the awesome question of whether to embark on the development of an even more terrifying instrument of annihilation. Should work begin on the hydrogen bomb? At the end of January 1950, after a tumultuous, emotional debate within the Executive, Truman gave the order to start developing the "super" and the required delivery systems. At the same time, he formally retrieved Forrestal's proposal of a year and a half earlier for an overall assessment of America's foreign and defense policies.[10]

The paper was drafted in February and March by State and Defense Department officials, under the leadership of Paul Nitze, an investment banker who had succeeded George Kennan as head of the Policy Planning Staff. The document, which became known as NSC-68, is as important as Kennan's Long Telegram and the Truman Doctrine in postwar history. It was the first formal statement of American policy. It expressed the fully formed Cold War world set of American leaders, and provided the rationalization not only for the hydrogen bomb but also for a much expanded military establishment. Dean Acheson was the project's patron, and his concerns were reflected in its description of the breakdown of the old international system. But, in its analysis of Soviet intentions and capabilities, its description of the threats to and requirements of "national security," and in its call for a much larger military establishment, NSC-68 was a true and fitting memorial to James Forrestal.[11]

In developing the "fundamental design of the Kremlin," NSC-68 gave dramatic and unambiguous answers to those two basic questions about the Soviet Union — What relation between ideology and foreign policy? What relation between Russian domestic practices and Russian behavior in the international system?

"The Soviet Union, unlike previous aspirants to hegemony, is animated by a new fanatic faith, antithetical to our own, and seeks to impose its absolute authority over the rest of the world," said NSC-68. The paper depicted what it described as "the institutionalized crimes" of the secret police and the terror in Stalinist society. "Being a totalitarian dictatorship, the Kremlin's objectives in these policies is the total subjective submission of the peoples now under its control. The concentration camp is the prototype of the society which these policies are designed to achieve, a society in which the personality of the individual is so broken and perverted that he participates affirmatively in his own degradation."

But the paper then jumped to the conclusion that there was a necessary connection between domestic and foreign practice, that the Soviet goals were unlimited, that they were dictated by ideology, and that coexistence with the USSR was impossible. "The Kremlin is inescapably militant," said NSC-68. "It is inescapably militant because it possesses and is possessed by a world-wide revolutionary movement, because it is the inheritor of Russian imperialism, and because it is a totalitarian dictatorship . . . It is quite clear from Soviet theory and practice that the Kremlin seeks to bring the free world under its dominion by the methods of the cold war." The Soviet Union's "fundamental design" necessitated the destruction of the United States, said the paper, and thus, the USSR "mortally challenged" the United States.

The paper argued that the Soviet Union devoted a far larger share of its gross national product to the military budget — 13.8 percent as opposed to 6 or 7 percent for the United States. Therefore, NSC-68 advocated that a rapid military buildup of the Western world begin at its center — that is, with the United States defense budget. It called for a drastic increase, suggesting that the United States could afford up to 20 percent of its GNP for security purposes, even in peacetime. State Department officials, in fact, wanted the military budget increased from under $15 billion to somewhere between $35 and $50 billion a year.[12]

Dissent on the major conclusions was limited. At a meeting in Paul Nitze's office at the State Department, Defense Secretary Johnson flew into a rage. The terms he used to denounce the document were so blustering that the chief Defense Department drafter was reduced to tears. But Johnson's outburst reflected more an erratic personality than substantive objections, and he assented to the paper when it was clear that Truman supported it.[13]

The only significant disagreement came from the two experts on the Soviet Union, Kennan and Bohlen, neither of whom at this point believed the Soviets had a world design. Both thought that caution guided Kremlin calculations and that the Soviets were sometimes only responding to Western actions.

Although NSC-68 was a lineal descendant of the Long Telegram (through an earlier document, NSC-20), Kennan, by 1950, was more concerned about the consequences of such thinking than about the need to generate any more anxiety about Soviet intentions. In 1946, he had discounted the utility of diplomacy. In 1950, he was on the other side, afraid that NSC-68 would sanctify the rejection of diplomatic opportunities. He also feared a vast growth in the military establishment and the militarization of foreign policy, for both of which NSC-68 provided the rationalization. And Kennan simply did not believe that the Soviet Union posed a military threat to Western Europe.

By 1950, Kennan was a critic, rather than a promulgator, of the Riga axioms. "It is safer and easier to cease the attempt to analyze the probabilities involved in your enemy's processes or to calculate his weaknesses," Kennan wrote in his diary. "It seems safer to give him the credit of every doubt in matters of strength, and to credit him indiscriminately with *all* aggressive designs, even when some of them are mutually contradictory."

But Kennan had little influence left, and declining patience for trying to exert that influence, especially after Dean Acheson succeeded George Marshall as Secretary of State in 1949. "By such views as I had to voice in our oral discussions [Acheson] was, I suspect, sometimes amused, sometimes appalled, usually interested," Kennan recalled. "But there were times when I felt like a court jester, expected to enliven discussion, privileged to say the shocking things, valued as an intellectual gadfly on hides of slower colleagues, but not to be taken fully seriously when it came to the final, responsible decisions of policy." [14]

For the most part, the acceptance of the premises of NSC-68 was as instantaneous and complete as had been the case with the Long Telegram four years earlier. The National Security Council officially approved the document in April 1950. Its effect on many was overwhelming. The President handed a copy to Charles Murphy, who had succeeded Clark Clifford as special counsel and who was one of Truman's principal advisers. Murphy was very busy, and, because he did not get to the paper during the day, he took it home. "What I read scared me so much that the next day I didn't go to the office at all," he later recalled. "I sat at home and read this memorandum over and over, wondering what in the world to do about it. The gist of it was that we were in pretty bad shape and we damn well better do something about it . . . It seemed to me to establish an altogether convincing case that we *had* to spend more on defense, that we had to straighten out our defense posture very markedly."

A change in economic thinking helped to win quick acceptance of such premises. James Webb, now Undersecretary of State, was no longer the effective advocate he had previously been against increased military spending. Indeed, he was now a strong supporter of such spending. Meanwhile, Leon Keyserling, who was in the process of becoming chairman of the Council of Economic Advisers, disdained the old ceilings on military expenditures. Instead, he emphasized the growth potential of the American economy, and suggested that the country could absorb considerably larger expenditures on defense.

But would Congress and the public support more spending? The President (as Webb put the matter in a memorandum to Truman in March) faced "the problem of how to get up enough public steam to support you in starting to build up our strength, and at the same time . . . not get up so much as to look provocative." [15]

While the Administration sought to find a way in the spring of 1950 to greatly enlarge the defense budget, events were pushing it toward another portentous decision — the first step in the U.S. intervention in Vietnam.

Since the spring of 1945, there had been a general, although uneven, movement in American policy, away from Roosevelt's idea of separating Indochina from France. In December 1946, war broke out between the French and the Viet Minh, the popular nationalist movement with a strong communist component under the leadership of the Ho Chi Minh. Shortly after the fighting began, Acheson wired the American consul in Saigon, "Keep in mind Ho's clear record as agent international communism, absence [of] evidence recantation Moscow affiliation, confused political situation France, and support Ho receiving from French communist party."

In the main, though, between 1946 and 1948, Washington's view of Vietnam was shaped by European politics and a desire not to alienate the French government. But U.S. officials did not conceal their belief that the French were trying to hold on to an outmoded and unworkable colonial system. Secretary Marshall asked the American embassy in Paris in February 1947 to remind the French government that there were two sides to the conflict in Vietnam. "Frankly we have no solution of problem to suggest," he added. The U.S. government did refuse to sell to France military weapons for use in Indochina.

By 1949, the impending victory of the communists in China had led to a hardening of policy on Vietnam — a conviction that developments in Indochina should be judged not by the requirements of European politics but by the need to halt what was seen as a Moscow-directed advance of communism in Asia. This concern became more and more dominant as Washington helplessly watched Mao Tse-tung's forces move toward victory. At the end of 1949, Truman approved a National Security Council report, NSC 48/2, which extended containment and the Truman Doctrine to Asia: "Now and for the foreseeable future it is the USSR which threatens to dominate Asia through the complementary instruments of communist conspiracy and diplomatic pressure supported by military strength. For the foreseeable future, therefore, our immediate objective must be to contain and where feasible to reduce the power and influence of the USSR in Asia to such a degree that the Soviet Union is not capable of threatening the security of the United States from that area." It further enunciated a general commitment to "support the non-communist forces in taking the initiative in Asia." Yet the document gave more emphasis to other parts of Asia, and was still somewhat ambiguous about Indochina, still sounding hopeful that a progressive "third force" could be found. It warned of the need "to satisfy the fundamental demands of the nationalist movement while at the same time minimizing the strain on the colonial powers who are our Western allies." It urged particular effort to "bring home to the French the urgency of removing the barriers to the obtaining by . . . non-communist nationalist leaders of the support of a substantial proportion of the Vietnamese."

In January 1950, both Moscow and Peking extended diplomatic recognition to Ho's government, a rival to the protectorate that the French were trying to establish under Emperor Bao Dai. Thereafter, the expansion of the definition of American national security to include Vietnam became more explicit, and the U.S. began to reach for the available instruments. Deputy Undersecretary of State Dean Rusk informed the Defense Department in March that "the Department of State believes that within the limitations imposed by existing commitments and strategic priorities, the resources of the United States should be deployed to reserve Indochina and Southeast Asia from further Communist encroachment." The preceding autumn, Congress had passed the Mutual Defense Assistance Program, which enabled the U.S. to provide arms, military equipment, and training on a worldwide basis. On May 1, 1950, in part hoping to bolster the resolve of the former colonial power, and so spare the United States a more direct form of intervention, President Truman approved ten million dollars in military assistance for the French and noncommunist local forces in Vietnam.

It was a small step, but it was the beginning. The Cold War had come to Asia. By 1954, the United States would have provided almost three billion dollars in military assistance for Indochina.

The decision on Vietnam reflected the firm belief among American leaders that they were engaged in a worldwide struggle with Soviet-directed communism. In assessing a situation, the global antagonism was always to be given priority over the nature of the local conflict and the appeal of nationalism.

Though there is no reason to doubt that this was the way they viewed matters, we must also observe that strong pressures in public opinion would have prevented them from acting on any other belief — and indeed would have made it most difficult to countenance, after Mao's victory in China, any further "loss" of real estate to the communists. A fervent, broadly-based anticommunism was becoming a powerful and bitterly divisive force in American national life. The Administration was put so much on the defensive that Clark Clifford observed in a memo to Truman in April 1949 that there was "an ominous trend in the United States toward the increasing curtailment of freedom of expression . . . With the possible exception of the days of John Adams and those of A. Mitchell Palmer, the situation is becoming more dangerous today than at any other period in American history. This situation of course plays into Soviet and Communist hands . . . It furnishes effective weapons to the opponents of the President's liberal program."

With Thomas Dewey's defeat in 1948 and the onset of the terminal illness of Arthur Vandenberg, the internationalists lost their grip on the foreign policy of the Republican Party. The communist victory in China energized the Republican right wing, which charged that the "loss of China" resulted not from the character of the two sides in the civil war, but from the fact that the Administration had abandoned Chiang Kai-shek and handed the country over to Mao. For several years, the Truman Administration had been warning of the dangers of communist subversion in other countries. Now a number of congressional committees made daily headlines with explosive allegations of widespread subversion within the United States —

from coast to coast, from Hollywood to the State Department. This was one of the major themes and points of attack against Acheson during his confirmation hearings for Secretary of State at the beginning of 1949. The Soviet atomic test in the late summer of 1949 heightened the widely felt sense of insecurity.

By the beginning of 1950, "the attack of the primitives," as Acheson acidly dubbed the fervent anticommunists, was reaching new heights — and finding new ammunition. On January 21, the former State Department official Alger Hiss was convicted of perjury for denying his alleged involvement in Soviet espionage. Four days later, Acheson handed the Republicans a ready-made issue when he told a press conference, "I do not intend to turn my back on Alger Hiss." On February 3, Klaus Fuchs, a physicist, confessed in London to spying on the Manhattan Project for the Soviet Union. The day before, when an aide brought news of Fuchs' confession, Truman advised him, "Tie on your hat." The President was prescient, for now anticommunist hysteria reached new heights. On February 9, Senator Joseph McCarthy told an audience in West Virginia that he had a list of 205 communist spies in the State Department — "names," he said, "made known to the Secretary of State." Although McCarthy never produced the names, he soon enough gave a name, his own, to describe the anticommunist passions. The senator found a receptive audience in a large segment of public opinion. Already that spring, the Gallup Poll reported that 39 percent of the respondents thought that McCarthy's charges were "a good thing." Thus the Administration found itself attacked more and more from the right, accused of being "soft" on communism.

Yet in the spring of 1950, Truman and his advisers continued to fear that Congress would not approve the money required for the substantial military buildup outlined in NSC-68. As far as the Administration was concerned, one of the many problems with the McCarthyites was that they were much keener to hunt witches and ferret out alleged domestic subversives than to appropriate money for foreign aid and military strength.

The Administration was still wrestling with the question of how to get the funding for the NSC-68 program when, in the early morning hours of June 25, East Asian time, North Korea threw its troops across the border to the south.

Thus began the Korean War.[16]

The Administration certainly did not want that war, but once embroiled in the conflict, it did not hesitate to use it to promote the general buildup of American military strength. What had been viewed as a four-year program was telescoped into two. Expenditures for major national security programs rose to $22.3 billion in fiscal year 1951, to $44 billion in fiscal year 1952, to $50.4 billion in fiscal year 1953. Obviously, some of this money went to fight the Korean War, but a very substantial part supported the general buildup of American strength.

Aviation Week made the consequences clear. "U.S. aircraft production lines are undergoing a tremendous and costly reorganization to meet the huge armament program set rolling by the world's worsening political situation," it declared in December 1950. Two months later, headlines in the magazine announced: "With Money No Problem, Strength Grows" and "Big Year Behind and Bigger Year Ahead." It declared that "U.S. air power, the most formidable weapon of World War II, is on its way back to hugely expanded status," and explained that the aircraft industry was returning to the production levels of 1944, the peak level of all-out world war.[17]

With the Korean conflict, a new phase had opened in the Cold War.

With the expanded funding, the architecture of the national security state was complete.

Today, more than four decades after its inception, the international order wrought by the Cold War has gone through major transmutation. The bipolar world has become multipolar. Economic issues have become matters of high politics, cutting across political alignments. In the 1990s, some of the most significant issues and tensions will involve the relationship among the economic superpowers—the United States, a more unified Europe, and Japan—and, in particular, what kind of role Japan will play in the future. The Pacific Rim has become a vital new center of world activity. In the communist world, the schism with Yugoslavia was followed by the much more significant and long-lasting split with China. The future course of relations within the Warsaw Bloc, between the Soviet Union and the various states of Eastern Europe—which was the starting point for the Cold War—is uncertain. The impact of the Gorbachev Revolution on the Soviet

Union itself is one of the most critical overarching issues for the entire world. Will the Soviet Union emerge fundamentally changed, or not? An additional question must also be asked: will it be stable? The developing world has emerged as a major force in world politics. The monopoly over military force by the two superpowers has been reduced by the proliferation of nuclear capabilities and conventional weapons, including "the poor man's nuclear bomb," chemical weapons.

It has been a long road. For the United States, the War in Vietnam proved to be a decisive turn. The American commitment to Vietnam resulted in part from the postwar world set of U.S. leaders. The Riga axioms and the doctrine of national security made Indochina appear a crucial arena in what was perceived as a struggle to frustrate the "fundamental design" of communism. The consequences of that intervention led to the conclusion that "fundamental designs" may sometimes be illusory and the global implications, secondary to local issues. The Vietnam experience created new checks on both intervention and the imperial presidency, and also reshaped worldviews. The war's outcome also left the Vietnamese people living under a regime incapable of delivering a civil government, in both senses of the word "civil." Yet a final irony of the Vietnam War is that a unified, communist Vietnam—one of the poorest nations in the world, though one of the most militarized—has found itself almost completely passed over by the extraordinary capitalist boom in the Pacific Rim. The Soviet Union of Mikhail Gorbachev is signaling that it is no longer willing to bankroll inefficient economies of ideological allies; and Vietnam is now trying to find a way to rejoin the world economy, including the seeking of investment from the classic bugaboos of imperialist theories, Western oil companies.[18]

The marked weakening of the anticommunist consensus in the United States in the late 1960s and early 1970s, on the American side, helped to make possible a new kind of relationship with the Soviet Union—tentative détente. This did not mean an end to the competition between the two superpowers. But it did mean a somewhat more explicit agreement on the rules of competition; a certain number of cooperative projects, of which arms control, based upon the purported acceptance of parity, was the most important; increasing communication and contacts on many levels; and a reduction in the state of permanent alarm on both sides. In practice, it meant a return to the Yalta axioms as the basic mode of dealing with the Soviet world, and perhaps a vindication for Franklin Roosevelt and his aims and methods in those fateful negotiations with Stalin and Churchill during the winter of 1945 in the ballroom of the Czar's summer palace. Détente was not possible with a world revolutionary state, but it was with a more conventional imperialistic and somewhat cautious nation, interested as much in protecting what it has as in extending its influence—and with its own worries about new tensions on its Chinese flank. With such a country, the United States could search out an uneasy, but more regulated coexistence—a reasonable objective in a world of nuclear weapons.

The process of détente was rocky from the beginning. In the midst of the Arab-Israeli "Yom Kippur War" of October 1973, the two superpowers went on nuclear alert against each other. That was something that had not happened since the Cuban Missile Crisis of 1962. Détente broke down for many reasons. The military buildup under Leonid Brezhnev and Soviet activities in the Third World reinforced suspicions in the United States. The Watergate scandal undermined the credibility of President Richard Nixon and his policies, including détente, and finally destroyed his administration. Although the scandal had thrown up Secretary of State Henry Kissinger as the repository of legitimacy during the last phases of the Nixon administration and into the Ford years, support for détente had been seriously eroded.

Jimmy Carter began his administration in 1977 with a great flurry of diplomatic activity whose stated objective was to pursue a comprehensive arms settlement with the Soviet Union. The haste with which the effort was launched, however, led some to believe that a second objective was also at work—to prove that Henry Kissinger, the architect of détente under Presidents Nixon and Ford, was no longer there, and to establish that the new administration could produce a new, improved version of détente. The initial initiative, which included an early trip to Moscow by Cyrus Vance, the new secretary of state, ended in disarray and discord. But, within two years, the Carter administration did succeed in carving out a new Strategic Arms Limitation Agreement with Moscow. In June 1979, Carter and Soviet President Leonid Brezhnev met in Vienna, signed the new treaty, and exchanged busses on the cheek. But implementation required approval by the Senate, and this was not forthcoming. Then, on Christmas Day 1979, the Soviet Union invaded Afghanistan, and

Carter shelved the treaty. "This action of the Soviets has made a more dramatic change in my own opinion of what the Soviets' ultimate goals are than anything they've done in the previous time I've been in office," said Carter. So President Carter went from Yalta to Riga.[19]

Ronald Reagan succeeded Carter as president. Campaigning as an implacable foe of diplomacy with the Soviet Union, Reagan had captured the anti-détente sentiment of the late 1970s. From deepest belief, Reagan seemed to argue that any agreement with the Kremlin had to be a trick and dangerous to the interests of the United States. His views about communism and the Soviet Union were shaped when, as president of the Screen Actors Guild in the late 1940s, he had battled the communists in Hollywood. Now, as president of the United States in the 1980s, he proclaimed that he would take them on in a global struggle. To engage in summitry with the Russians was to sup with the devil; for, he told a group of evangelists in 1982, the Soviet Union was nothing less than "the Evil Empire."

Yet, by 1985, Ronald Reagan had held his first meeting with the new Soviet leader, Mikhail Gorbachev, and, by 1988, had made far-reaching arms control agreements with him. "There seems to be an entirely different relationship" between the United States and the Soviet Union, said Reagan, the formerly irreconcilable critic of détente. By the end of the Reagan Administration in 1989, a decade after both the invasion of Afghanistan and his own election had seemed to seal the fate of détente, some former supporters were complaining that Ronald Reagan had become too concerned about public opinion and his own place in history and had gone soft on the Russians. From Riga to Yalta.[20]

These presidential odysseys illuminate the continuing struggle to define U.S. policies and interests towards the Soviet Union and the difficulties in constructing and maintaining a sufficiently wide and durable domestic consensus to allow consistency in U.S. policy. Not that the job would ever be easy. Moreover, as the decade of the 1980s gave way to the 1990s, the landscape of the Cold War had become so jumbled, even in Europe where it had begun, that even the most self-confident could become easily confused. Margaret Thatcher, the resolutely conservative and no-nonsense prime minister of Britain, was declaring not only that Gorbachev was a man with whom she could do business, but also even went so far as to announce, "We're not in the Cold War anymore." In West Germany, which was at the very center of contention between East and West in the late 1940s, Gorbachev was far ahead of the American president in the public opinion polls. Meanwhile, in some of the countries of Eastern Europe, capitalism and opposition parties, snuffed out in the late 1940s at the height of the Cold War, were returning to view. Poland held an election in which the communists were humiliated, and the recently illegal Solidarity union, triumphant. In the aftermath of the election, there was, as in the years of Stalin, a long telephone call between the top leadership of the Polish Communist Party and the "voshd"—or leader—in Moscow. But this time, the message was quite the opposite of that when Stalin was building his empire—do not try to fight or overturn the popular will. The Hungarians even staged a public barbed-wire cutting ceremony on the border with Austria. That proved to be symbolic of more far-reaching change. For, not long after, the Communist Party of Hungary turned itself into a socialist party that would compete in a multiparty system. But even these changes paled in November 1989, when The Berlin Wall came down. The very symbol of the Iron Curtain, divided Europe, and the Cold War itself, was no more. Not only was capitalism coming to Eastern Europe; so, it seemed, was democracy. It were as though a film of the critical years of 1945–1948 were being run backwards, and not in grim and gritty black and white, but rather in a more attractive color.

So perplexing were the changes that practically the first act of the administration of George Bush was to turn to that time-tested remedy called upon at different times by different presidents over the years of the Cold War, beginning with the Clifford Memorandum of 1946. Bush asked for a full-scale review of the Soviet Union, its intentions and capabilities, and the implications and requirements thereof for U.S. policy. "Wise men—Truman and Eisenhower, Vandenberg and Rayburn, Marshall, Acheson and Kennan—crafted the strategy of containment," President Bush said at the conclusion of his review. "Forty years of perseverance have brought us a precious opportunity. And now it is time to move beyond containment to a new policy for the 1990s, one that recognizes the full scope of change taking place around the world, and in the Soviet Union itself. In sum, the United States has as its goal much more than simply containing Soviet expansionism. We seek the integration of the Soviet Union into the community of nations.[21]

At the end of 1989, George Bush and Mikhail Gorbachev met for their first summit on ships off the island of Malta. It was at Malta, in early 1945, that Franklin Roosevelt and Winston Churchill had rendezvoused on their way to Yalta, in anticipation of which Churchill had composed an immortal piece of doggerel: "No more let us falter! From Malta to Yalta! Let nobody alter!" For his own private amusement, he added a little more: "From Malta to Yalta, and Yalta to Malta." And indeed, at the storm-wracked summit four and a half decades later, it was, at least in metaphorical terms, from Yalta to Malta. For the first time since the 1940s, the fundamental political organization of Europe itself was open to question. The summit schedule at Malta was interrupted by a huge gale, which prevented Bush from crossing over from an American destroyer to the Soviet liner, *Maxim Gorky*, inadvertently standing up Gorbachev for dinner. But, when they did meet, Gorbachev declared Soviet willingness to let history, rather than Soviet power, take its course in Europe, and Bush pledged not to seek advantage in the unfolding process.

The basic fact was the Soviet Union itself had pulled the plug on the order it had imposed on Eastern Europe. "The world leaves one epoch of cold war, and enters another epoch," said Gorbachev at the Malta summit. "It's a central part of contemporary history." After the summit, President Bush was asked for his personal reaction. "The emotional part of it," he replied, "is hard for me to describe because I'm not the most articulate emotionalist." But, said the president, "With reform underway in the Soviet Union, we stand at the threshold of a brand new era of U.S.-Soviet relations."

It was not that the end of ideology, or even the end of history, was at hand. But, very possibly, the political journey that began at Yalta in 1945 was coming to an end in 1989 at Malta; and the Malta Summit, following immediately on the toppling of the Berlin Wall and the political earthquake in Eastern Europe, could mark as well as anything else the end of the Cold War as it had been known since the end of the Second World War.[21]

What had changed? What provoked the move into the "new epoch"? The weapons of mass destruction were still in all their variety and gruesome incomprehensibility. So what had brought forth this "precious opportunity" and "this brand new era"? First and foremost was the change within the Soviet Union itself. After a series of false starts and geriatric successions, the new postwar and post-Stalin generation finally came to the fore. Dissatisfied with the poor performance of the economy, it called the whole system of central planning into question. Militarily, the Soviet Union was, of course, a superpower; economically, it showed many of the characteristics of a developing country. Food and consumer goods were in chronic short supply, as were services. Why should people work hard when there was little to buy with their rubles? People grumbled that everything seemed "broken." Industrial production appeared to exist to satisfy its own cycle—production to feed further production—irrespective of the consumer economy. In earlier years, the Soviet Union could compare itself economically to the United States and explain the differences in terms of the devastation wrought by the Second World War. But such an explanation could not work when the Soviet Union was measured against the astonishing success of Japan, which had also been devastated. That nation of crowded islands, whose only real natural resources were its people and their values and skills, had emerged as an economic superpower. Other Pacific Rim countries were following suit, and China, with economic liberalization, was making rapid progress. By comparison, the Soviet system was found stagnant and fault-ridden. In addition, a better-educated, less fearful public in the Soviet Union contained within itself a pent up desire for political openness.

One of the great political turning points for the Soviet Union was the nuclear accident at Chernobyl in the Ukraine in April 1986. For the first two weeks or so after the accident, the Soviet-system responded in its characteristic way—with denial and counterattack on the Western media. Then, abruptly, Gorbachev went on national television to deliver a somber, informed, and candid explanation of what had happened. The contrast to the traditional was stunning. Gorbachev's speech and the openness that followed ran so counter to the familiar mode of communication that some Muscovites speculated that the accident must have been even worse than acknowledged, to have occasioned such uncharacteristic forthrightness. The traditional Brezhnev system that Gorbachev had just inherited was shaken by Chernobyl and the response to it, and the pace of change was accelerated in its aftermath.

Over the next few years, political change moved at a disjointed speed that would not have been conceivable before the fact. Soviet newspapers and magazines were jammed with political and historical debates. Every aspect of Stalin's rule was examined and dissected; executed and murdered non-people were posthumously returned to life and rehabilitated. Questions were even beginning to be raised about the sacred figure of Lenin. Television talk shows delved into heretofore secret sides of Soviet life. Protest candidates ran against establishment party figures in unprecedented multicandidate elections—and won. Even officials without actual opponents on the ballot were turned out when a majority of voters crossed off their names.

This was not the Soviet Union that had been the familiar focus of Western foreign policy. Such developments would have been almost unthinkable half a decade earlier. The expectation had been, at best, for more Brezhnev. Yet change was, indeed, at hand; and it brought, to varying degrees, change and debate in the West—and a sense that new opportunities might be emerging. The old questions were asked about the USSR in a new light. What were its objectives and its capabilities? Was this, indeed, a new Soviet Union? What was the nature of the Soviet "threat" in this new context, and what were the opportunities for more stable, constructive relations? Perhaps containment had, after all, proved its point. Was this what George Kennan had prophesied in his Mr. X article more than four decades earlier? "The palsied decrepitude of the capitalist world is the keystone of Communist philosophy," he wrote in 1947 in his landmark essay. A policy of "firm containment" by the United States and the West would, if combined with economic robustness, eventually prevail. For "the United States has it in its power," through containment, "to promote tendencies which must eventually find their outlet in either the breakup or the gradual mellowing of Soviet power."[22] Stalin had mellowed into Khrushchev, and hardened again into Brezhnev. Gorbachev was giving "mellowing" a wholly new meaning.

One of the main forces driving change in the Soviet Union and in Soviet policies towards the West was dissatisfaction with the weight of military expenditure. For the Soviet Union, this was a truly lopsided burden. Any hope of revivifying the Soviet economy would require some relief from the crushing weight of the unproductive military spending. Redirecting resources away from the military sector was seen in Moscow as crucial to the success of Gorbachev's domestic reconstruction; and such redirection, in turn, required a new détente with the West. The years of failure in Afghanistan had soured the Soviet Union on force of arms alone. Such détente was welcome, at least in part, to the Bush administration. A flattening out or reduction in defense expenditures was necessary in Washington in order to make progress on the budget deficit, and pruning could much more easily be carried out in an atmosphere of détente than in one of confrontation.

Yet the outcome of the Gorbachev Revolution is far from clear. The initial enthusiasm for *perestroika*—restructuring—has given way to disappointment. It is no easy thing to remake the Soviet economy. It means lifting the dead hand of central planning, introducing accountability and autonomy, changing attitudes and values—and tolerating the strains, uncertainties, and excesses that go with competition and consumption. All of this is not accomplished overnight; and all this is not to the liking of many. Moreover, the effort to make the shift involves distortions, disruptions, logistical bottlenecks—and new shortages.

But is there an alternative? One Soviet official, asked about the alternatives to *perestroika*, replied, "Yes—catastrophe." He had in mind the political aspects as much as the economic aspects. The Soviet Union began a Third Revolution in 1985. Almost everything was opened to criticism—in a society with no tradition of legitimate debate and open discussion. Many of the underpinnings of legitimacy have been called into question. History provides the intellectual ligaments that ties together a society. So does ideology. The history is being critically examined; and the ideology of Marxism-Leninism, vigorously debated as well. Some years ago, one Soviet official described Marxism-Leninism as "dry bread."[23] Still, it was the bread upon which the society daily supped. It provided the rationale for power and authority. Remove it, and the ethnic tensions, particularly among the non-Slavic minorities, come to the fore in the multinational state. Remove it, and the rationale for tight Soviet control over Eastern Europe loses its force. Remove it, and the place of the military becomes less clear. Is the alternative to "dry bread" some form of democracy and tolerance in a society that has little history of either, or is it a retreat variously into tradition, Slavic nationalism, ethnic conflict, instability—or back toward authoritarianism and repression? These questions point to a fundamental issue facing Western policy toward the Soviet Union. For many years, especially in debates about East-West trade, there has been a chronic debate on the subject of the "hungry Bear" versus the "contented Bear." Are Western interests better served with a Soviet Union that is relatively well-off economically or one that is strained and troubled at home by poor economic performance? But there is now a new variation on which to reflect—what dangers might arise from an "unhinged Bear," an unstable and disordered Soviet Union? Should the Western countries cooperate economically with the Soviet Union in order to help forestall the unhinged Bear and the risks that might follow? That could well be one of the prime questions for the 1990s. In short, the outcome of the Gorbachev Revolution is far from clear; so is the degree to which Soviet-American relations will change course. Domestic developments inside the USSR will affect the second as much as the first.

As Soviet-American relations move into a new phase, and as Vietnam recedes into the past, the polemics of the great debates between traditionalists and revisionists on the origins of the Cold War have faded, and writing and discourse on the subject have taken on a more dispassionate tone, even civility. It is even argued that a new synthesis is now dominant, and one that tilts away from the revisionists. For some of the historical writing was so American-focused that it seemed to forget Stalin and what he was about, and to treat that cunning and cynical conspirator as little more than a passive walk-on. In addition, there was a tendency, perhaps predispositional in a profession given to reflection, to impute grander strategic visions to people who were in fact preoccupied with immediate battles and struggles, and more prone to improvisation—and to understate the political constraints that buffeted and checked these people. Events moved very rapidly in the years immediately after World War II, and each work day of those near the center of events had hardly seemed to begin before it was over.* In those circumstances, in the grim shadows of the

---

* This pressing factor of time can be overlooked by those whose rhythms are determined not by the cascading pressures of the daily crisis. Information comes in fragmentary pieces, and, of course, participants do not have the luxury of knowing how the story will come out. This is the point that George Elsey, a White House adviser in both the Roosevelt and Truman administrations, conveyed to the assembled members of the Society of Historians of American Foreign Relations: "You have access to more information than even the presidents had, and you have the time to ponder the meaning of events: a priceless advantage denied most of the time to a president and his staff."[24]

horror of World II and amidst global upheaval and disorder, there were hardly established policies—or indeed verities—on which to base actions.

Of course, Western analyses of Soviet policy leading up to, and during the Cold War are based upon fragmentary sources. At best, Western scholars have only the published Soviet documents, the Soviet press, some sanitized Soviet memoirs, and reporting by American and British diplomats. The same holds true for Soviet scholars working in the field. At this point, by far the most interesting archives of all are to be found, presumably, in the Stalinist "wedding cake" that houses the Foreign Ministry in Moscow (assuming that those archives were not destroyed) and the most interesting question is whether *glasnost*—openness—will extend to the archives. To Soviet scholars who ask, the reply is that the lack of access is no longer political, but organizational; the Foreign Ministry in Moscow does not, at this time, have the trained archivists to organize and review papers. At least so I was told in Moscow. What was also brought home was the degree to which, in the current turmoil in the Soviet Union, history is no mere "academic" subject. Indeed, what is striking is how central the history of the past is to the shaping of the future in today's Russia. The focus and weight of interpretation about the Cold War origins may have changed every five or six years in the United States. By contrast, until very recently, there has really been only one orthodoxy in the Soviet Union. Change—and illumination—could be at hand in Soviet writing on this subject, at least insofar as the larger transformation of the Soviet Union continues to proceed. Signs of what is possible are already evident in Moscow.

On one bright, still sharply cold spring day in the course of a visit to Moscow, I made my way across a wide boulevard streaked with ice and frozen mud and rivulets of muddy water. My companion, a Soviet historian, explained that one reason so many Muscovites had voted against the local Communist party establishment in recent elections was because of their despair at the decline in the city's services and maintenance, as evidenced in the condition of the streets. We made our way to his apartment where we spent many hours talking, the time marked only by the lengthening shadows across the wall of his study.

"History has become a real *idée fixe* of society as a whole," he said. "There is a new historical consciousness among the people, a general movement to rethink our own history. History has become central to all political discussion. The political impact of discussion of historical problems is very great. Sometimes, the public says, 'Don't discuss history all the time. Let's talk about the economy, the present day.' But history continues to be the core of public discussions."

Much of the discussion is, of course, specifically about Soviet history. There is some scholarly work on the Cold War, as well as polemical exchanges in the Soviet press, and Soviet scholars have held a few joint conferences with American scholars on the subject.

In analyzing the Cold War, this particular historian starts with a view of Stalin not as paranoid, but as very suspicious and revengeful. The settlement at Munich in 1938 convinced Stalin that Western countries were out to turn Germany against him, and the Nazi-Soviet Pact was his way to try to buy time. Also, by this interpretation, Western historians ignore the impact on Stalin of Russia's mini-war with Japan in 1939, which was not so mini, and the Soviet fear of a two-front war. Further according to his interpretation, the emerging U.S.-British partnership after World War II, combined with the secrecy about the atomic bomb (on which Stalin was nevertheless well informed by his spies), renewed his belief in encirclement, and he responded by seeking his enlarged "zone of security." Yet, be it noted that this Soviet historian, for the most part, must depend for his primary sources on Western archives.

Yet the basic questions about the Cold War, as indeed about the entire seven decades of Soviet power, are being asked with increasing vigor. In case I was to be in Moscow the following Monday, I was given a photocopied invitation addressed to various Soviet scholars asking them to gather at the main historical institute:

> You are invited to take part in the first of a series of round tables dealing with the problems of the Cold War. The first of these round tables will be considering in part the following questions:
>
> 1. What was the Cold War—a phenomenon of the policies of one country (or group of countries), or was it a result of the international system in operation at that time?

2. When did the Cold War begin, and which events initiated it?
3. What were the basic reasons for the Cold War?
4. Was there an alternative to the Cold War, and to what extent was it inevitable?

Such questions may sound very familiar to scholars of the Cold War in the West. But these are questions that would not have been asked openly in the Soviet Union even half a decade ago. If pursued, they will clearly have impact in Soviet writing on this subject. Still, the answers will be much illuminated when the moment arrives that, finally and now imaginably, the Soviet archives see the light of day.

In the meantime, the West will continue to puzzle over the question of Soviet actions and objectives, future and past. Much has changed since Gorbachev launched his revolution. Yet much more is unclear about how it will come out, and what Gorbachev's own political fate will be. But, whatever the course, the fundamental question about the Soviet Union's foreign policy and its meaning for the West remains endlessly fascinating and ceaselessly urgent. "Yalta" and "Riga" remain relevant and useful tools for thinking about East-West relations, even as the Yalta system in Europe has the possibility, finally, to become a thing of the past.

A reduction in tension between East and West, a rise in communication between them, and greater pluralism within the East—all these do not mean that the worthy Wilsonian vision of a harmonious international order is at hand. In dealing with the Soviet Union, in trying to analyze its objectives and capabilities, we continue to tread, as George Kennan wrote in his diary in 1950, "in the unfirm substance of the imponderables.[25] The global rivalry between the Soviet Union and the United States does remain the single most important and dangerous element in international politics. The balance of terror is measured in megatons so large that no human being can truly comprehend the horrors that nuclear war would bring. It continues to be a balance between the United States and the Soviet Union—each one's missiles remain targeted on the other. Whether George Bush's "precious opportunity" is seized or not will depend upon developments within both the Soviet Union and the United States, whether these two political systems prove to be "in phase" with each other—and on developments and surprises that occur elsewhere in the world.

So, even if the Cold War in its classic form has passed, the ever-perplexing questions about the Soviet Union's role in international politics are still very much with us, as are the questions about the means, meaning, and measure of American and Western security in a world of nuclear weapons. There are no final answers, only the spectacle of men and women moved by ambitions and opportunities, beset by fears and dangers, struggling to find transient certainties midst the onrush of events. We cannot therefore regard the story of the shattered peace as merely a fascinating and tragic history. It is, in truth, still the story of the origins of our own time.

NOTES
BIBLIOGRAPHY
INDEX

Notes

Prologue: The New Lore

1. Maynard Barnes, Lecture, Washington, D.C., October 1947.
2. *Foreign Relations of the United States: Yalta*, pp. 459–62, 549–56, 476, 665; Churchill, *Triumph and Tragedy*, pp. 344–45, 388–90; Lord Moran, *Churchill*, pp. 234–36. Hereafter the *Foreign Relations of the United States* series will be identified as *FR*.
3. Claude Pepper interview with Stalin, September 14, 1945, Box 46, Pepper papers. One historian has observed, "The life history of the Alliance conformed exactly to the pattern set by hundreds if not thousands of earlier coalitions which had been formed and passed away in the long course of history, beginning in the days of the Mesopotamian city states" (William H. McNeill, *America, Britain & Russia: Their Cooperation and Conflict*, p. 748).
4. Michael Vyvyan has observed that "no one questioned in 1914 that general mobilization by a great power must be followed by hostilities." In "The Approach of the War of 1914," *The New Cambridge Modern History*, 2nd ed., vol. 12, p. 165.
5. Dean Acheson, "Formulation of National Policy in the US," Lecture, Washington, D.C., December 1947.
6. Charles Bohlen, "US-Soviet Relations Today," Lecture, Washington, D.C., February 20, 1948.
7. F. H. Hinsley, *Nationalism and the International System*, p. 146.
8. See Arno Mayer's *Wilson versus Lenin: Political Origins of the New Diplomacy 1917–18*, especially pp. 368–93, for how the rivalry began.
9. Arnold Wolfers makes the point that all nations must to some extent live dangerously. See his *Discord and Collaboration*, p. 158.
10. Adam Ulam is one of the few writers to emphasize the possible utility of diplomacy in the postwar years. See *The Rivals*, pp. 96–101.
11. Hinsley observes that the international system has always been what "the outlook of governments and their publics upon the international system" have made it, "even if it has also been shaped by forces beyond men's control" (*Power and the Pursuit of Peace*, p. 9).
12. For analyses of Wilsonianism, see N. Gordon Levin, *Woodrow Wilson and World Politics* (especially pp. vii, 2, 5), and Arthur Link, *Wilson the Diplomatist*, pp. 11–22, 131–33. Louis Hartz in *The Liberal Tradition in America* argues that a Lockean consensus knits American society together. The "Wilsonian" program was of course not Wilson's *invention*. Nor was it uniquely American. The notion of a League, for instance, went back to the early Renaissance.

13. Cordell Hull in *U.S. Department of State Bulletin*, November 20, 1943, pp. 341–45; Byrnes to Daniels, December 8, 1945, Box 264, Byrnes papers.
14. Hans Morgenthau so argues in Lloyd Gardner, ed., *Origins of the Cold War*, p. 90.
15. The "policy elite" refers to government officials, mostly of higher rank, and mostly in the White House, State Department, military services, and intelligence agencies, but also elsewhere in the Executive branch and in the Congress, who have an impact on the U.S. foreign policy process — through the interpretation of events and issues in international politics that affect the United States, the establishment of the agenda of important problems, the shaping of policies, and through the direction and staffing of the institutions and bureaucracies meant to meet the problems in American foreign relations.
16. Stalin cited by George Kennan in "Contemporary Soviet Diplomacy," Lecture, National War College, October 22, 1946.
17. Bohlen to Stettinius, March 26, 1949, Stettinius papers.
18. For the contemporary debate, see Theodore Draper, "Appeasement and Detente," *Commentary*, February 1976, pp. 27–38; Paul Nitze, "Assuring Strategic Stability in an Era of Détente," *Foreign Affairs*, January 1976, pp. 207–30; Daniel Yergin, "Poor Detente," *The New Republic*, May 29, 1976, pp. 17–21.
19. Nadezhda Mandelstam, *Hope Abandoned*, pp. 611, 614, 617. And, of course, Alexander Solzhenitsyn, *The Gulag Archipelago*, and Roy Medvedev, *Let History Judge*. Robert Conquest arrives at twenty million dead through the following estimates — twelve million died in camps 1936–50 (an average of eight million inhabitants a year in camps, with a death rate of 10 percent); one million executions; seven million dead as a result of collectivization. *The Great Terror*, p. 710. M. Lewin estimates that ten million or more peasants were deported in collectivization "of whom a great many must have perished" (*Russian Peasants and Soviet Power*, p. 508). Although Solzhenitsyn introduced the "gulag" into the world's vocabulary, it had been noted in English much earlier. The magazine *Plain Talk* ran an article "Gulag — Slavery, Inc." in its May 1947 issue, with a map showing the major camps. Solzhenitsyn may even have seen the map in Russia. See Isaac Don Levine, ed., *Plain Talk*, pp. xi–xii, 235–39.
20. Few writers have recognized that "security" is not a given but rather depends upon a definition, indeed, that so basic a foreign policy concern can be conceived of in a variety of ways, in (as Arnold Wolfers has observed) "more or less moderate and in more or less ambitious and exacting terms." *Discord and Collaboration*, pp. 72–73, 91–94. Robert W. Tucker points out, "Nearer the truth, it would seem, is that our postwar policy expressed both a conventional security interest and an interest that went well beyond a conventional notion of security" and that this expansive interpretation of security was put to expansionist purposes. *The Radical Left and American Foreign Policy*, pp. 105–7.
21. In his still highly relevant book, William H. McNeill suggests, "A 'spheres of influence' deal with the Russians might have been possible" (*America, Britain and Russia*, p. 723).
22. Piers Dixon, *Double Diploma*, p. 165.

I. The Breach: The Riga Axioms

1. DeWitt Clinton Poole oral history, pp. 463–65; Maynard Barnes, "Current Situation in Bulgaria," Lecture, Washington, D.C., June 1947, p. 7.
2. For the October Revolution, Adam Ulam, *The Bolsheviks*, pp. 341–75; and E. H. Carr, *The Bolshevik Revolution*, vol. 1, pp. 100–113. For Trotsky and Chicherin, ibid., vol. 3, pp. 28–29, 370–80.
3. Joseph Grew, *Turbulent Era*, vol. 1, pp. 44–58; Waldo Heinrichs, *American Ambassador*, p. 49, photo facing p. 216.
4. "It is self-delusion on the part of the decision-maker to believe that he can get along without theoretical propositions," Arnold Wolfers reminds us. "If one looks more closely, one discovers that rather than emerging out of an intellectual vacuum, his hunches rest, in fact, on generalizations of some sort" (*Discord and Collaboration*, p. xiv). It is with this injunction in mind that I introduce the notion of "axioms" — by which I mean a series of related rules and principles used by policymakers for explaining, interpreting, and predicting the behavior of states — both one's own and foreign — in the international system. These axioms are not only evaluative, but also suggest courses of action. They are generated from experience, study, personal situation, and group association. The notion of axioms in this context is developed by Ernest May in "The Nature of Foreign Policy: The Calculated Versus the Axiomatic," *Daedalus* 91 (Fall 1962): 653–67. An "axiomatic policy," he suggests, is founded in "*a posteriori* reasoning." More recently, he has elaborated on the relationship between historical "learning" and foreign policy in *Lessons of the Past: Use and Misuse of History in American Foreign Policy*. Hadley Arkes, with his concept of "operating presumptions," is trying from a somewhat different angle to deal with the same problem — the relationship between how people think about international politics and the development of policy. *Bureaucracy, the Marshall Plan, and the National Interest*, pp. 14–15, 177–79, 199–200. Psychologist Irving Janis has suggested how cohesive foreign-policy decision-making groups tend to develop stereotyped group images, in *Victims of Groupthink*.
5. Robert P. Browder, *The Origins of Soviet-American Diplomacy*, pp. 3–4, 16–17; DeWitt Clinton Poole oral history, pp. 436, 441, 446–47, 463, 465.
6. Samuel Harper, *The Russia I Believe In*, pp. 126–28; Poole to Harper, March 29, 1923, Harper papers; Daniel Yergin, "Riga," *Atlantic Monthly*, April 1975, pp. 15–22. Poole oral history, p. 480, for Harper as the first expert.
7. Charles Bohlen, *Witness to History*, pp. 39–40; George Kennan, *Memoirs*, pp. 47–48; Harper, *Russia I Believe*, pp. 128, 135–37, 162. Kennan quote from Kennan, "Formulation of Policy in the USSR," Lecture, September. 18, 1947, Kennan papers.
8. Lane to Moore, June 18, 1937, Lane papers; Kelley to Harper, March 15, 1926, Harper papers.
9. *FR: USSR*, p. 6; Kelley to Harper, March 10, 1925, January 11, 1927, Harper papers.
10. Kelley to Steinhardt, December 6, 1947, Steinhardt papers. Critics tended to share Kelley's vision of his paternity. Spencer Williams, a

representative of the American-Russian Chamber of Commerce in Moscow, complained in 1934 about a "definite clique of 'Riga boys' among the officers of the embassy who share the Kelley viewpoint on Russia" (Thomas R. Maddux, "American Relations with the Soviet Union 1933–41," Ph.D. Dissertation, University of Michigan, 1969, p. 138).

11. Kennan, *Memoirs*, pp. 33–34, 47–49, 68–70; Bohlen, *Witness*, pp. 8–11, 28. The effects of such contacts were not limited to those who went through the formal training program. Elbridge Durbrow recalled that in almost three years of schooling in Paris he had met "a lot of White Russians, talked to them about the Revolution and about what had happened. I got interested and studied a great deal. From all that, I developed my own feelings that the Soviet Union was anything but a workers' paradise of any sort" (interview with Elbridge Durbrow).
12. Kennan, *Memoirs*, p. 59.
13. Browder, *Soviet-American Diplomacy*, pp. 99–112, 49–51, 79; *FR: USSR*, pp. 28–37; Kennan, *Memoirs*, pp. 56–59; Christopher Thorne, *The Limits of Foreign Policy*, pp. 215, 276–77. For business pressure on Roosevelt, see Edgar B. Nixon, ed., *Franklin Roosevelt and Foreign Affairs*, vol. 1, pp. 55, 324–25, 403–4.
14. Orville Bullitt, ed., *For the President: Personal and Secret*, pp. 3–15; Louis Fischer, *Men and Politics*, pp. 299–303 (includes Harpo). For the Bullitt Mission, see Arno Mayer, *Politics and Diplomacy of Peacemaking*, pp. 449, 464–71, 800–801.
15. Adam Ulam, *Stalin*, pp. 332, 353, 374; Alec Nove, *Economic History of the USSR*, ch. 7. Alexander Solzhenitsyn, *Gulag Archipelago*, p. 54.
16. Bullitt, *For the President*, p. 65; *FR: USSR*, pp. 57–60; Maddux, "American Relations with the Soviet Union," p. 85.
17. Bohlen, *Witness*, pp. 14–15, 24–35; Bullitt, *For the President*, pp. xv, 69, 86, 93; Charles Thayer, *Bears in the Caviar*, pp. 115–29; Joseph Davies, *Mission to Moscow*, p. 66; Elbridge Durbrow, "Contemporary Russia," Lecture, Washington, D.C., February 7, 1947; Kennan, *Memoirs*, pp. 60–63.
18. Henderson to Harper, December 27, 1934.
19. *FR: USSR*, pp. 172–73; Moore to Bullitt, May 8, July 9, 1934, Bullitt to Moore, May 4, 1934, Moore papers.
20. A. I. Sobolev, et al., *Outline History of the Communist International*, pp. 274, 371–400; Bullitt to Moore, July 15, 1935. Assistant Secretary of State R. Walton Moore, in forwarding Bullitt's letter about the Comintern meeting to Roosevelt, declared that the violation of "Litvinov's pledge . . . has been very complete" (Moore to Miss LeHand, August 1, 1935, Moore papers).
21. Bullitt to Moore, October 6, 1934, Moore papers; *FR: USSR*, pp. 143–47, 221–22.
22. Lloyd Gardner, *Architects of Illusion*, p. 17; Fischer, *Men and Politics*, pp. 303–8.
23. Bullitt to Moore, June 2, 1935, February 22, March 30, 1936, Moore papers.
24. *FR: USSR*, pp. 224–25, 244–49, 294; Bullitt, *For the President*, p. 160; Bullitt to Moore, June 2, 1935, Moore papers; Lane to Moore, November 17, 1936, Lane papers; Kennan, *Memoirs*, 80–82.

25. Interviews with Loy Henderson and Elbridge Durbrow; Bohlen, *Witness*, p. 17; Lane to Moore, November 17, 1936, Lane papers.
26. Kennan, *Memoirs*, pp. 6–7, 11–13, 20–21, 48–50, 76–77; Bohlen, *Witness*, p. 17; interviews with Loy Henderson, Foy Kohler, and Elbridge Durbrow: Bullitt to Moore, May 11, 1935, Moore papers, Kennan to Harper, January 4, 1933, Harper papers. The "Presbyterian elder" is from Gardner, *Architects*, p. 285. The fitness report is cited in Maddux, "American Relations with the Soviet Union," p. 137. Kennan's reference to "mysterious affinity" and "conservative person" are from Kennan, *Memoirs 1950–63*, pp. 116, 264–65.
27. Bohlen, *Witness*, pp. 3–5, 35. Kennan, *Memoirs*, pp. 62–63; Hazard to Harper, March 2, 1935, Harper papers.
28. Interviews with Elbridge Durbrow and Loy Henderson; Bohlen, *Witness*, pp. 18, 45; Kennan, *Memoirs*, pp. 61, 66–67, 80–81.
29. Kennan, *Memoirs*, pp. 81–82; Bohlen, *Witness*, pp. 20–24, 30–36; Thayer, *Bears*, pp. 95–96; Bishop, *The Roosevelt-Litvinov Agreements*, pp. 222, 281 (footnote 50); interviews with Loy Henderson and Elbridge Durbrow.
30. Kennan 1938 memoir, pp. 51, 71, Kennan papers; Henderson to Kelley, April 29, 1937, Lane papers; Bohlen, *Witness*, pp. 51–53. Medvedev, *Let History Judge*, p. 239.
31. Thayer, *Bears*, pp. 165–66; Bohlen, *Witness*, pp. 42–55; Henderson to Kelley, April 29, 1937, Lane papers; Joseph Davies, *Mission to Moscow*, pp. 72, 229; Kennan 1938 memoirs, pp. 59–60, Kennan papers; Kennan, *Memoirs*, p. 69.
32. For the conventional view, see Richard Ullman, "The Davies Mission and United States–Soviet Relations 1937–41," *World Politics* 9 (January 1957): 220–39, and Bohlen, *Witness*, pp. 44–45, 52. Davies' reputation has been lanced on his wartime book, *Mission to Moscow*, jokingly called "Submission to Moscow" by the Riga School. John Gaddis in *The United States and the Origins of the Cold War*, p. 35, calls it "an astonishing mixture of the ephemeral and the significant," but it is difficult to see how much more so than many other diaries. And, of course, it was written at the bequest of the White House during World War II to help out with public opinion problems.
33. Davies, *Mission to Moscow*, pp. 40–41; *FR: USSR*, p. 546; Maddux, "American Relations with the Soviet Union," pp. 148–49. Maddux's short and intelligent discussion of Davies' career as ambassador continues in ibid., pp. 254–61. For the servants and iceboxes, Hazard to Harper, December 7, 1936, Harper papers. Loy Henderson recalled that Davies had told him during the ambassador's last few days in Moscow that Roosevelt had instructed Davies that his mission was "not to report back to the government accurate information but to win the confidence of Stalin. He knew Stalin would get wind of what was being reported, and thus was always so lavish in his praise" (interview with Loy Henderson). Kennan in his *Memoirs*, pp. 82–83, recalls a meeting in Henderson's rooms at the end of Davies' first day in Moscow, where mass resignation was mooted. Henderson remembers it differently: irritated by the disrespect and signs of a cabal, and "determined to do all that is in my power to assist in making his term here a success," he forcefully

instructed Kennan that any such action was absolutely out of the question, and that the purpose of the Foreign Service was to support the ambassador. Interview with Loy Henderson; Henderson to Lane, January 23, 1937, Lane papers.

34. Henderson to Harper, March 2, 1942, Harper papers; Henderson to Lane, March 22, 1938, Lane papers; Maddux, "American Relations with the Soviet Union," pp. 148–49; Davies, *Mission to Moscow*, pp. 276, 368, 307.
35. Kennan, *Memoirs*, pp. 83–85; Bohlen, *Witness*, pp. 39–41; interview with Elbridge Durbrow; Kelley to Harper, June 22, 1937, Harper papers.
36. Nixon, ed., *FDR and Foreign Affairs*, vol. 3, p. 229; Moore to Bullitt, June 26, 1937, Bullitt to Moore, July 15, 1937, Moore papers; Henderson to Lane, June 7, 1937, Lane papers; Poole to Harper, June 27, 1937, Harper papers.
37. Henderson to Lane, June 7, 1937, Lane to Moore, September 7, November 17, 1936, Lane to Kelley, October 20, December 9, 1936, Lane papers. The quotes are from Lane to Dunn, June 18, 1937, and Dunn to Lane, July 8, 1937, Lane papers.
38. Henderson to Harper, July 20, 1940, Harper papers. The fact that these axioms were deeply held should not lead one to think they composed an absolute dogma, screening out all other perceptions. See for instance Henderson to Kelley, April 29, 1937, Lane papers; Kennan 1938 memoir, p. 21, Kennan papers; Kennan to Harper, June 7, 1938, Harper papers. Nor should one assume that all of those specializing in the Soviet Union had by this time passed through the program created by Robert Kelley. Foy Kohler recalled: "As the war came on, the Russian language and area training programs . . . were discontinued because of the shortage of officers. I, for example, belonged to what I have sometimes called 'the lost generation' in this respect; since in the late war years and the immediate post-war years those of us who went to Moscow had to be satisfied with intensive Russian language training and then to continue our studies after arriving at the post. However, at the same time, during World War II we took into the Department of State, as well as into such government agencies as Lend-Lease, many, if not all, of the academic experts on Russia from the outside" (letter to author, February 3, 1976).
39. *FR: USSR*, pp. 224–25, 310–11, 773–75.
40. *FR: 1940*, III, p. 407; *FR: USSR*, p. 310, 593–94; Henderson to Kelley, April 29, 1937, Lane papers; Kennan 1938 memoir, pp. 60, 72, Kennan papers; Bullitt, *For the President*, p. 200.
41. *FR: USSR*, p. 773; George Kennan, Lecture, Foreign Service School, May 20, 1938, Kennan papers.
42. Bohlen, *Witness*, pp. 26–29; *FR: USSR*, pp. 638, 775; *FR: 1940*, III, pp. 406–8.
43. Bohlen, *Witness*, pp. 67–86; Henderson to Lane, May 19, 1937, Lane papers.
44. Maddux, "American Relations with the Soviet Union," pp. 129–35; interview with James Riddleberger.
45. *FR: 1940*, I, p. 390; *FDR: Public Papers*, 1940, pp. 87–94; *FR: 1941*, I, pp. 757–58. For an excellent study of American thinking about "totalitarianism" and United States foreign policy, see Thomas Lifka, "The

Concept of Totalitarianism and American Foreign Policy 1933–1949" (Ph.D. dissertation, 1973, Harvard University).

46. *FR: 1941*, I, pp. 766–67; Maddux, "American Relations with the Soviet Union," pp. 326–41. American officials had engaged in a fitful, frosty series of talks with the Soviet ambassador in Washington for many months prior to the German invasion. Henderson expressed his "grave doubts that our policy of so-called appeasement will get us any place" (ibid., p. 335). The talks proved unproductive.
47. Robert Sherwood, *Roosevelt and Hopkins*, vol. 1, pp. 387–423; Ulam, *Stalin*, pp. 539–42, 560–61.
48. For Henderson: Henderson to Harper, March 16, March 23, 1942, Harper papers; interview with Loy Henderson. For Bohlen: *FR: Tehran*, p. 846; Bohlen, *Witness*, pp. 175–77. In March 1944, Bohlen speculated that the Soviet Union would probably content itself with "the minimum Soviet program" — alliances with Eastern European states on the model of the Soviet-Czech treaty. This would "constitute no threat to American interests in Europe" (cited in Lynn Davis, *The Cold War Begins*, pp. 135–36). It is said that others in the State Department, jealous and critical of Bohlen's relationship with FDR, would say jokingly that Bohlen walked up and down the corridors of the Department loudly praising Roosevelt's judgment — in order that his remarks should get back to the President.
49. Kennan, *Memoirs*, pp. 137–41; "Report on the Techniques of German Imperialism in Europe," April 1941, pp. 26–27, Kennan papers. The Germans, he continued in the latter paper, "are extremely anxious that their rule should not appear to be one of sheer oppression by force of arms. Uncertain and oversensitive to world opinion, they are eager to prove to the world that they have the political finesse to rule other countries, to get what they want of them, and yet 'to make them like it' . . . But whether they can make their rule popular is another question. Either they must develop their own dogma into something more satisfying for the aspirations of Europe as a whole, or they must become more modest in their aims and must allow more scope for the spontaneous national aspirations of other peoples. If they fail to do either of these things, their rule in Europe may be long and materially effective; but it will not be, even from their own standpoint, successful." (Ibid., pp. 26–27, 37.)
50. *FR: 1944*, IV, pp. 813–19, 839–42, 935; interview with Elbridge Durbrow.

II. The Yalta Axioms: Roosevelt's Grand Design

1. E. H. Carr, *The Twenty-Years Crisis*, vi; *FR: 1941*, I, p. 363.
2. Anthony Eden, *The Reckoning*, pp. 372–74; Robert Sherwood, *Roosevelt and Hopkins*, vol. 2, pp. 315–20; *FR: 1943*, III, p. 22; Orville Bullitt, ed., *For the President: Personal and Secret*, pp. 583–84.
3. Stimson diary, April 6, 1943.
4. Forrest Davis, "Roosevelt's World Blueprint," *Saturday Evening Post*, April 10, 1943, pp. 20–21, 109–10; File memo, December 2, 1942, Official file 4287, Roosevelt papers; Robert Divine, *Second Chance*, pp.

114–15. "Old Man's Grand Design" from interview with Elbridge Durbrow.

5. Rexford Tugwell, *In Search of Roosevelt*, p. 287; Rexford Tugwell, *The Brains Trust*, p. 444; *FR: Tehran*, p. 585; Max Freeman, ed., *Frankfurter-Roosevelt Correspondence*, p. 186. In describing Roosevelt as a "renegade Wilsonian," I am in disagreement with the traditional interpretation, which portrays Roosevelt as a believing Wilsonian, and also, at least in some authors, as rather naïve. See, for instance, Louis Halle, *The Cold War as History*, pp. 33–34; William H. McNeill, *America, Britain & Russia*, pp. 761–63, and to some degree, Franz Schurmann, *The Logic of World Power*, pp. 1–28.
6. *FR: 1941*, I, pp. 363–66. After America entered the war, when Secretary Hull proposed some kind of international organization at least to plan conferences, Roosevelt laughed and said, " 'I'll give you the Pentagon or the Empire State Building. You can put the world secretariat there' " (Cordell Hull, *Memoirs*, p. 1643).
7. Roosevelt quoted in Thomas Lamont memo, February 5, 1942, 127–37, Lamont papers.
8. *FR: 1942*, III, pp. 568–80; *FR: 1943*, III, pp. 35–39; Eden, *Reckoning*, pp. 372–79. By the spring of 1944, the political and military incompetence of Chiang's government forced Roosevelt to retreat from his idea that China could be the fourth policeman. In May, FDR told his Cabinet that "he was apprehensive for the first time as to China holding together for the duration of the war." Thereafter, Walter LaFeber writes, "From the Wallace mission through the Yalta agreements, FDR's major objective in China was no longer to make her a Policeman, but to separate the Russians from the Chinese Communists, and then use the Communists as a lever to force Chiang to make reforms so that his regime could survive." Walter LaFeber, "Roosevelt, Churchill, and Indochina: 1942–45," *American Historical Review* 80 (December 1975): 1288–89.
9. Halifax to Churchill, October 11, 1941, Halifax papers. For the methods by which FDR kept track of public opinion, see Richard W. Steele, "The Pulse of the People: Franklin D. Roosevelt and the Gauging of American Public Opinion," *Journal of Contemporary History* 9 (October 1974): 195–216.
10. The historian is Robert Divine, *Second Chance*, p. 151. Also ibid., pp. 68–69, 103–13, 141–55. *Second Chance* is the major work on the transformation of public attitudes during World War II. For the potent force of reborn Wilsonianism, see David Lawrence to Thomas Lamont, July 3, 1944, 103–204, Walter Lippmann to Lamont, April 29, 1944, 105–4, Lamont papers. On Fulbright, see Daniel Yergin, "Fulbright's Last Frustration," *New York Times Magazine*, November 24, 1974.
11. James Patterson, *Mr. Republican*, p. 201; Aldrich to Glender, April 10, 1944, Box 29, Aldrich papers. For Dulles and Hull, see Fred Israel, ed., *War Diaries of Breckinridge Long*, pp. 332–33; Hull, *Memoirs*, pp. 1690–91. Dulles represented what Vandenberg called "the Eastern internationalist school of thought" (Vandenberg to Dewey, May 10, 1944, Vandenberg papers).
12. Arthur Vandenberg, Jr., ed., *The Private Papers of Senator Vandenberg*, pp. xviii–xix, 4, 15, 126–45; Patterson, *Mr. Republican*, p. 341.

13. *FR: Tehran*, 530–32, 622; Divine, *Second Chance*, pp. 184–85; Sumner Welles, *Seven Decisions*, pp. 185–90. For a detailed study of the never-ending stages of State Department planning, see Harley Notter, *Postwar Foreign Policy Preparation.*
14. *FR: 1943*, III, pp. 36–39.
15. Lippmann to Lamont, July 7, 1944, 105–4, Lamont papers. For similarity of goals, see Eden to Halifax, April 27, 1942, Halifax papers; Eden, *Reckoning*, pp. 366, 445–56. Eden observed in 1944 that the British in part sought a world organization for the same reason as Roosevelt — to "induce the Americans, and this means the American Senate" to guarantee help in restraining "a hostile Germany or . . . any other European breaker of the peace." (Ibid., p. 445.) Ernest May describes the background of elite connections in *American Imperialism: A Speculative Essay.* For other aspects of Anglo-American relations, see Welles, *Seven Decisions*, pp. 72, 172; Eden, *Reckoning*, pp. 344, 405, 513; David Dilks, ed., *The Diaries of Sir Alexander Cadogan*, pp. 537, 542, 558–59, 577–78.
16. Stimson diary, October 22, 1943. For references to Anglo-American cooperation, see, for instance, Stimson diary, December 18, 1942, May 11, May 22, September 7, September 8, 1943.
17. Roosevelt to Lamont, February 9, 1940, 127–34, Lamont papers; *FDR: Public Papers*, 1940, pp. 92–93; Maddux, "American Relations with the Soviet Union," pp. 29–30, 321–41.
18. *FDR: Letters, 1928–45*, p. 1177; William Hassett, *Off the Record with FDR*, pp. 71, 147–49; Halifax diary, June 23, 1941.
19. Halifax diary, May 20, 1942; Sherwood, *Roosevelt and Hopkins*, vol. 1, pp. 4–5, 394–99, 419–20; Jonathan Daniels, *White House Witness*, p. 14.
20. For the porcupine, Dilks, *Cadogan Diaries*, p. 422. The historian is M. Lewin, *Russian Peasants and Soviet Power*, p. 517. Eden, *Reckoning*, p. 291; Ulam, *Stalin*, pp. 778–79 (for the parable); E. H. Carr, *Socialism in One Country*, vol. 1, pp. 189–205; Victor Serge, *From Stalin to Lenin*, p. 83; for the "dictatorship of industrial development," Heinz Brandt, *The Search for a Third Way*, p. 155; Svetlana Alliluyeva, *Twenty Letters to a Friend*, pp. 196, 209–10 (for the money). On Stalin's realism: Sato to Tojo, July 12, 1945, Box 571, Byrnes papers; Harriman in *FR: Berlin*, I, pp. 61–62; the Yugoslavs in Vladimir Dedijer, *The Battle Stalin Lost*, pp. 52–54. And then there is Stalin's understatement to an American during the war — "I am a careful old man."
21. The Yugoslav in Dedijer, *Battle Stalin Lost*, p. 223; for the death, Svetlana Alliluyeva, *Twenty Letters*, pp. 6–14. Ulam, *Stalin*, pp. 739–41, reflects masterfully on the preposterousness of the Stalin cult. For the Hopkins mission, John Erickson, *Road to Stalingrad*, p. 181 (Stalin's placing the wrong orders with Hopkins); Ulam, *Stalin*, pp. 539–42, 560–61; for the caviar, Hopkins to Ismay, August 7, 1941, Ismay papers; Hopkins memorandum, October 31, 1941, Box 126, Hopkins papers.
22. *FR: Tehran*, pp. 108, 530–33, 622, 489–502, 558–65, 485, 837, 555.
23. Ibid., pp. 584–85; Welles, *Seven Decisions*, pp. 190–91; Hassett, *Off the Record*, p. 226; Lubin memorandum to White House, December 10, 1943, Box 27, Lubin papers.
24. *FDR: Letters, 1928–45*, p. 1177; Hassett, *Off the Record with FDR*, pp. 71, 147–49; Halifax diary, June 23, 1941.

25. Eleanor Roosevelt, *This I Remember*, pp. 253–54; Averell Harriman, *America and Russia in a Changing World*, pp. 165–66; *FDR: Letters, 1928–45*, pp. 1365–66.
26. *FDR: Letters, 1928–45*, p. 1195; George Herring, *Aid to Russia*, pp. 53–61, 85–86; Edwin Locke oral history, p. 19.
27. Roosevelt quoted in Davis, *Cold War Begins*, p. 29; Stimson diary, February 1, 1943. In 1933, as negotiations preceding recognition bogged down, Roosevelt had remarked, in what foreshadowed his wartime approach, "Gosh, if I could only, myself, talk to some one man representing the Russians, I could straighten out the whole question" (John Morton Blum, *From the Morgenthau Diaries: Years of Crisis, 1928–38*, p. 55). "I found the President very sticky today when I talked to him about Russia on Winston's telegram," Halifax wrote in his diary for March 8, 1942. "His own public opinion, the general morality, effect on Poles, and all the rest of it. He continues to remain quite confident that if he could see Stalin he could settle in five minutes."
28. For Roosevelt and the State Department and Hull, see Byrnes letter, May 5, 1945, Box 191, Byrnes papers; Bohlen, *Witness*, pp. 122, 129, 165–66; Rosenman, *Working with Roosevelt*, pp. 9, 202–6; Harold Smith diary, January 1, 1945; Welles, *Seven Decisions*, pp. 61–62; Israel, *Breckinridge Long*, pp. 322–25; Halifax diary, November 29, 1941. Some recent writers have attributed much greater importance, both political and ideological, to Hull than the historical record accords. See Gabriel Kolko, *Politics of War*, p. 244. Stimson's diary is a good source for Hull's role — or lack thereof: "Hull repeated his frequent complaint that he had heard nothing from the President about the diplomatic movements in Europe" (November 3, 1942). Stimson noted that he was cutting short his attendance at regular meetings with Hull "because they are rather degenerating into a mourners' meeting, Hull leading off with his wails about his troubles" (May 25, 1943). And, sardonically, Stimson commented on Hull's passion for "his beloved trade treaties" (May 11, 1943). Also see Arthur Krock, *Memoirs*, p. 208.
29. Halifax to Churchill, January 11, 1942, Halifax papers.
30. Memorandum of conversation with Roosevelt, November 20, 1944, Lane papers; Harriman, *Special Envoy*, pp. 369–71; memorandum of President's meeting with senators, January 11, 1945 (italics added), Stettinius papers. Lynn Etheridge Davis makes a somewhat similar point when she writes, in the context of the Polish imbroglio earlier in 1944, the State Department's policy — postponement and "diplomacy of principle" — "continued to be the *public* policy of the United States government toward Poland. President Roosevelt's intimations of United States support for a reorganization of the London Polish government and acceptance of the Curzon Line were not publicized. No one informed the Russians that President Roosevelt now no longer opposed their frontier demands with Poland" (*Cold War Begins*, pp. 21, 43, 102–3).
31. Halifax diary, March 8, 1942; Lord Moran, *Churchill*, p. 221.
32. Winston Churchill, *Triumph and Tragedy*, pp. 227–28; Anglo-Soviet Political Conversations, October 9–17, 1944, VI/10, Ismay papers. Among the many historians misled are John Wheeler-Bennett and Anthony Nicolls: "Stress was laid on the temporary nature of such arrangements,

which were in any case only to last until the surrender of Germany and the creation of a final peace settlement" (*Semblance of Peace*, p. 198).

33. Ismay to Casey, December 11, 1944, Ismay papers; Harriman, *Special Envoy*, p. 362.

34. Sherwood, *Roosevelt and Hopkins*, vol. 2, pp. 469–72; Bohlen, *Witness*, pp. 161–63; Halifax diary, October 9, 1944; Halifax to Churchill, January 27, 1945, Halifax papers. Bohlen quoted in Davis, *Cold War Begins*, p. 157. Allen Dulles, as head of the OSS in Switzerland, was suspected of providing his brother John Foster Dulles and Republican presidential candidate Thomas Dewey with material for charging Roosevelt in the course of the 1944 campaign with engaging in "secret diplomacy" (Daniels, *White House Witness*, pp. 245–46).

35. Rosenman, *Working with Roosevelt*, p. 482; *FR: Yalta*, pp. 558–59.

36. *FR: Yalta*, pp. 396–400, 894–97; Bohlen to Rosenman, August 23, 1949, Rosenman papers; Dilks, *Cadogan Diaries*, p. 706.

37. *FR: Yalta*, pp. 660–67, 611–19. On Soviet concessions, see Diana Shaver Clemens, *Yalta*, pp. 42, 287–88.

38. Secretary's staff committee minutes, p. 5, Matthews' "Report on the Crimea Conference," February 27, 1945, Calendar Notes, January 19, 1945, Stettinius papers; *FR: Yalta*, pp. 848–49.

39. *FR: Yalta*, pp. 677–81, 718–20, 776–81; Edward Stettinius, *Roosevelt and the Russians*, p. 113. The British diplomat is Pierson Dixon in *Double Diploma*, p. 140.

40. FDR on reparations before Yalta, *FR: 1944*, I, p. 474; Stalin quoted in Sherwood, *Roosevelt and Hopkins*, vol. 1, p. 470; also see Eden, *Reckoning*, p. 290; for the destruction, Alec Nove, *Economic History of the USSR*, pp. 285–88. Although there is some overlap, the question of reparations should not be confused with that famous bureaucratic battle in Washington during World War II about "pastoralizing" Germany. For the lines of that battle, see *FR: 1944*, I, pp. 352, 358–59; John Morton Blum, ed., *From the Morgenthau Diaries: Years of War*, pp. 328–48, 362–63, 373; Stimson diary, September 6, 1944; Paul Hammond, "Directives for the Occupation of Germany," in Harold Stein, ed., *American Civil-Military Decisions;* Morgenthau's motto was, "Let them stew in their own juice" (Senate Judiciary Committee, *Morgenthau Diary: Germany*, p. 1082). Opposing pastoralization, Stimson feared transforming "the center of one of the most industrialized continents" into a "nonproductive ghost territory" (Stimson diary, September 5, 1944).

41. *FR: Yalta*, pp. 622, 134, 571, 901–3, 920. For the British official, Dalton diary, March 3, 1945. Stettinius, quoted in "Committee of Three," March 13, 1945, Stettinius papers. A paragraph omitted from the published *Forrestal Diaries* (pp. 35–36) bears out the Stettinius understanding: "German reparations set at $20 billion of which the Russians said their fair share they thought was $10 billion, to consist of capital goods . . . labor, machine tools and other items which they will enumerate." Forrestal diary, March 13, 1945, p. 227.

42. Diana Shaver Clemens, *Yalta*, p. 287; Moran, *Churchill*, pp. 259, 249–50; Dilks, *Cadogan Diaries*, pp. 708–9; Churchill on his return, quoted in Dalton diary, February 23, 1945. General Ismay wrote: "The Conference was a great success, not so much because of the formal conclusions

that were reached, but because of the spirit of frank cooperation which characterized all the discussions, both formal and informal . . . In the political field, there were a lot of tough fences, some of which the Conference failed to jump. But, at least, we got the course without any crashing falls" (Ismay to Casey, February 26, 1945, Ismay papers).

43. *FDR: Letters, 1928–45*, p. 1570; Bohlen to Rosenman, August 23, 1949, Rosenman papers.
44. On Leahy, see Elsey memorandum, June 27, 1951, Yalta file, Elsey papers; Sherwood, *Roosevelt and Hopkins*, vol. 2, p. 516; Stalin, in *FR: Yalta*, pp. 655–66. Also see Pickersgill, *Mackenzie King*, vol. 2, pp. 325–26.
45. *FDR: Public Papers*, 1944–45, pp. 585–86; for FDR's private thoughts, Edgar Snow, "Fragments," *Monthly Review* (March 1957): 402.
46. Secretary's staff committee minutes, p. 4, Matthews' "Report on the Crimea Conference," February 27, 1945, Stettinius papers; Dulles statement, February 27, 1945, Box 103, Dulles papers; for Byrnes, see Arthur Krock's Black Book, February 1945, Krock papers.
47. Churchill, *Triumph and Tragedy*, pp. 421, 426; Millis, *Forrestal Diaries*, p. 36; *FDR: Letters, 1928–45*, p. 1575; memorandum of Grew and Dunn phone conversation with Stettinius, March 23, 1945, Grew papers.
48. Churchill, *Triumph and Tragedy*, pp. 447–48. Clemens, *Yalta*, p. 132, describes the Russian position at Yalta regarding transfers from the Italian front. For Dulles' own account, see Allen Dulles, *The Secret Surrender.* A tightly argued critical interpretation is to be found in Gar Alperovitz, "Dickering with the Nazis," *Cold War Essays.* Of course, confusion, misunderstanding and cross purposes would seem inevitable when SS leaders scrambled for safety out of the rubble of Hitler's crumbling empire.
49. *FR: 1945*, III, p. 757, V, p. 210.
50. Dilks, *Cadogan Diaries*, p. 668; *FDR: Personal Letters, 1928–45*, p. 1570; James MacGregor Burns, *Soldier of Freedom*, pp. 599–600. For the magic wand, Daniels, *White House Witness*, p. 276.

III. THE WORLD BULLY

1. George Kennan, *Memoirs*, p. 524.
2. Stimson diary, April 13, 1945; Margaret Truman, *Harry S. Truman*, p. 216.
3. Stimson diary, April 12, April 13, 1945; Morgenthau presidential diary, April 14, 1945, p. 1549; Wallace recollections of funeral train, April 14–15, 1945, Wallace papers.
4. Hopkins in Eden, *The Reckoning*, p. 529; John Morton Blum, ed., *The Price of Vision: The Diary of Henry A. Wallace*, p. 452; Charles Mee, *Meeting at Potsdam*, p. 13; Jonathan Daniels, *White House Witness*, p. 287. For Truman's contact with FDR, Martin Sherwin, *A World Destroyed*, p. 146; Roosevelt to Truman, January 22, 1945, Truman to Roosevelt, April 5, 1945, Box 238, President's secretary's file, Truman papers.
5. Much of this biographical information is found in Margaret Truman's

account, *Harry S. Truman.* "He had read widely in history and government and in many respects was more learned and perceptive than even his admirers understood," Alonzo Hamby observes in the best study of the Truman Administration, *Beyond the New Deal*, p. 508.

6. Harry Truman, *Year of Decisions*, p. 72; *FR: 1945*, V, p. 223.
7. Many writers of both orthodox and revisionist tendencies attempt to deny a distinctive change of policy and approach in the transition from Roosevelt to Truman. A variation involves the assertion that Roosevelt had already changed, had retreated from what I have called the Yalta axioms. For this general line of argument, see, for instance, Kolko, *Politics of War*, pp. 315, 382; Robert Maddox, *The New Left and the Origins of the Cold War*, p. 78; Herbert Feis, *Churchill-Roosevelt-Stalin*, pp. 599–600; Arthur Schlesinger, Jr., "The Origins of the Cold War," *Foreign Affairs* 46 (October 1967): 24; Davis, *Cold War Begins*, p. 213. For a survey of this debate, see Michael Leigh, "Is There a Revisionist Thesis on the Origins of the Cold War?" *Political Science Quarterly* 89 (March 1974): 106–8. The evidence in this and the previous chapter clearly indicates a difference in outlook and implementation between Roosevelt and Truman. Note, for instance, Roosevelt's rejection of Harriman's April strictures and Truman's acceptance. Also note how Stimson, expressing a Rooseveltian view, found himself a dissenter later in April. Of course the international situation was changing swiftly. What Roosevelt would have done had he lived makes for interesting speculation but cannot be argued in any sound historical way. Which is the same problem as discussing what John Kennedy would have done about Vietnam after the 1964 presidential election.
8. Leahy diary, June 15, September 19, October 2, December 15, 1944, February 11, May 20, 1945; memorandum for Admiral Brown, April 16, 1945, Box 3, Elsey notes on Leahy, Box 103, Elsey papers; William Leahy, *I Was There*, pp. 347–49. The attitude in the Map Room mirrored Leahy's own. As a Map Room aide recalled, the Polish Question was already confirming "the darker fears and suspicions as to what the postwar posture of the Soviet Union would be . . . It was just that living day by day with the knowledge of events, reading, being a part of this flow of messages back and forth, being conscious of the pattern of military events — there was always the feeling that the Soviets expected everything from us but wouldn't even help us to help them" (interview with George Elsey).
9. Averell Harriman, *America and Russia in a Changing World*, pp. 2–8; *FR: 1944*, IV, pp. 802–3, 944, 993, 1009; Kennan, *Memoirs*, pp. 210–11. Averell Harriman, *Special Envoy*, pp. 327, 340–44, 363.
10. Kennan to Meiklejohn, October 5, 1944, Box 105–A, Hopkins papers; Kennan to Harriman, September 18, 1944, Kennan papers; *FR: 1944*, IV, p. 989; Harriman, *America and Russia*, pp. 33–34. A contrary view, however, should be noted. It was reported in 1946, "During Harriman's tenure . . . as Ambassador, Kennan's attempts to formulate and recommend a firm policy were very definitely discouraged by Harriman, who derived considerable amusement from Kennan's earnestness in the matter. It is worth remembering that an equally capable man, Mr. Loy Henderson, now Chief of the Division of Middle Eastern Affairs, was

completely removed from the sphere of Russian affairs during the war period, for advocating a strong line vis-à-vis the Soviets. This was during the White House era of wooing the Kremlin at any price. Henderson was . . . on ice" (memorandum from Tolley in Office of Chief of Naval Operations to Smedberg, February 26, 1946, Box 24, Forrestal papers).

11. Kennan, *Memoirs*, pp. 222–23, 578–82.
12. Bohlen, *Witness*, pp. 175–76; memorandum, September 18, 1944, Kennan to Harriman, September 18, 1944, December 18, 1944, Kennan papers.
13. *FR: 1945*, IV, pp. 988–90.
14. *FR: 1944*, IV, pp. 951, 993–94, 1001, 1009; *FR: 1945*, V, pp. 813, 832; Clark-Kerr to Eden, July 16, 1944, Ismay Papers; Harriman on Roosevelt and Kathleen Harriman in Harriman, *Special Envoy*, pp. 370, 419. Clark-Kerr did not share Harriman's upset. On March 27, 1945, he declared that Britain need not "allow recent events to lead us to fear the worst," and that the Anglo-Soviet alliance would "serve us well, and pay a steady, though not spectacular dividend" (Llewellyn Woodward, *British Foreign Policy in the Second World War*, vol. 3, pp. 561–63).
15. C. L. Sulzberger, *A Long Row of Candles*, p. 253; Millis, *Forrestal Diaries*, p. 47; *FR: 1945*, V, pp. 232, 840–43; Stettinius memorandum, April 22, 1945, Box 244, Stettinius papers.
16. Interviews with Elbridge Durbrow and Joseph Johnson; Will Clayton oral history; Harold Smith diary, January 1, 1945; ERS to WJ, October 10, 1948, calendar notes, February 2, 1945, Box 278, December 21, 1944, note, Box 220, Stettinius papers; Lane-Stettinius conversation, March 14, 1945, Lane papers. For an unflattering portrait of Stettinius, see Dean Acheson, *Present at the Creation*, pp. 130–34.
17. Truman, *Year of Decisions*, p. 15; memorandum of Yalta trip discussion with H. Freeman Matthews, April 19, 1945, Box 279, Stettinius papers. As late as May 15, Bohlen told Truman, "We all had felt that the Soviet failure to carry out" the Yalta agreements "had been due in large part to opposition inside the Soviet Government which Stalin had encountered on his return" (memorandum of conversation with President, May 15, 1945, Grew papers).
18. Moran, *Churchill*, p. 236; Churchill, *Triumph and Tragedy*, pp. 424, 401–2; *FR: 1945*, V, p. 148.
19. Churchill, *Triumph and Tragedy*, pp. 488, 491–92; Truman, *Year of Decisions*, pp. 34, 38.
20. Truman, *Year of Decisions*, p. 31; Davies to Truman, April 15, 1945, Box 16, Davies papers.
21. Interview with Paul Porter.
22. D. F. Fleming, "Why Are the Russians Slow to Trust the Western Powers?" April 21, 1945, Box 15, Baruch papers; D. F. Fleming to author, June 18, 1973. "Dr. Fleming, you will remember," Baruch reminded Truman, "is the man I told you about who knows more about international relations than anyone else I know" (Baruch to Truman, April 21, 1945, Box 71, Baruch papers).
23. Memorandum for Stettinius, January 23, 1945, Stimson diary. Also Stimson diary, December 31, 1944, January 22, 1945; McCloy memorandum of telephone conversation with Stimson, May 19, 1945, Stimson papers.

24. Stimson-McCloy telephone transcript, May 9, 1945, pp. 6, 9, Stimson papers.
25. Stimson diary, April 26, May 10, 1945.
26. Stimson diary, April 16, 1945.
27. Interview with Elbridge Durbrow.
28. Dilks, *Cadogan Diaries*, p. 732; Stimson diary, April 23, 1945; Stettinius memorandum, April 22, 1945, Box 244, Stettinius papers.
29. *FR: 1945*, V, pp. 253–54; Millis, *Forrestal Diaries*, p. 49; Stimson diary, April 23, 1945.
30. Leahy diary, April 23, 1945; Davies journal, April 23, 1945, Box 11, Davies papers.
31. *FR: 1945*, V, p. 233, 256–59; Leahy diary, April 23, 1945; Truman, *Year of Decisions*, pp. 81–82; Ulam, *The Rivals*, p. 64.
32. Leahy diary, April 23, 1945; Churchill, *Triumph and Tragedy*, p. 492.
33. Leahy diary, April 23, 1945.
34. Lane to Dunn, June 18, 1937, Lane papers; *FR: 1945*, V, p. 841.
35. *FR: 1944*, IV, p. 955; *FR: Yalta*, pp. 669–71. See Davis, *Cold War Begins.*
36. *FR: 1945*, V, pp. 841, 843; Blum, *Wallace Diary*, pp. 462–63.
37. Davies diary, April 12, 1945, Box 16, Davies papers; Blum, *Wallace Diary*, pp. 441, 448, 451.
38. Blum, *Wallace Diary*, pp. 440–41, 458–59.

IV. The Straight One-Two to the Jaw

1. Morgenthau presidential diary, June 1, 1945, p. 1638.
2. December 14, 1944, speech; Grew to Cabot, January 6, 1945, Grew papers; Heinrichs, *American Ambassador*, pp. 9–10, 48–49, 155–60, 231. Throughout the 1930s, Grew regarded Japanese expansion into Manchuria as a useful bulwark against communism, and had in fact opposed recognition of the Soviet Union in 1933 as a "serious sacrifice of principle and letting down of ethical standards" (ibid., pp. 212, 286–87, 159).
3. Grew to Lyon, May 2, 1945, Grew to Stettinius, June 18, 1945, memoranda of May 4 and May 19, 1945, Grew papers; Joseph Grew, *Turbulent Era*, p. 1455; Truman, *Year of Decisions*, pp. 228–31.
4. Stettinius to Dunn, January 3, 1945, Box 220, Secretary's staff committee, January 12, 1945, Box 235, Stettinius papers; Chester Cooper, *The Lost Crusade*, pp. 49–55. FDR on Churchill, in Walter LaFeber, "Roosevelt, Churchill, and Indochina: 1942–45," *American Historical Review* 80 (December 1975): 1286.
5. *FR: 1945*, V, p. 843; Secretary's staff committee, April 24, 1945, Box 236, Stettinius papers.
6. U.S. Congress, House, Committee on Armed Services, *United States–Vietnam Relations*, by Department of Defense, Series Print, vol. 1, pp. 15, 20–21. The commitment, of course, was not complete, as an October 1945 statement indicated: "US has no thought of opposing the reestablishment of French control in Indochina and no official statement by US GOVT has questioned even by implication French sovereignty over Indochina. However, it is not the policy of this GOVT to assist the French to reestablish their control over Indochina and the willingness of the US

to see French control reestablished assumes that French claim to have the support of the population of Indochina is borne out by future events" (ibid., pp. 22–23). For the conflict between the Office of European Affairs and the Division of Southeast Asian Affairs, see the statement by Abbot Low Moffat, chief of that division (1945–1947), in U.S. Congress, Senate, Committee on Foreign Relations, *Hearings on Causes, Origins, and Lessons of the Vietnam War*, 92nd Cong., 2nd sess., 1972, pp. 161–86, 186–87. In his insightful and important essay, Walter LaFeber argues that FDR's hopes had been undercut by the obvious weakness of China, his own inability to control the diplomatic and military bureaucracies, and by the concerted counterattack of the British and French. But his contention — that "Roosevelt, not Truman, discarded the trusteeship plan and allowed the French to return to Indochina" — is not clearly established. Walter LaFeber, "Roosevelt, Churchill and Indochina," *American Historical Review* 80 (December 1975): 1277.

7. Earl Alexander, *The Alexander Memoirs*, pp. 150–51; Adam B. Ulam, *Titoism and the Cominform*, pp. 85–86; Vladimir Dedijer, *Tito Speaks*, p. 243; *FR: 1945*, IV, p. 1166; *FR: 1945*, V, p. 1225.
8. *FR: 1945*, IV, pp. 1132–37; *FR: 1945*, V, pp. 1222–25.
9. Churchill, *Triumph and Tragedy*, pp. 572–74; Dilks, *Cadogan Diaries*, p. 741; Moran, *Churchill*, p. 268.
10. *FR: 1945*, IV, pp. 1132–34, 1138, 1146–48, 1152–58; Churchill, *Triumph and Tragedy*, p. 556; Dedijer, *Tito Speaks*, p. 204.
11. Eden, *Reckoning*, p. 537; Stimson diary, April 30, May 2, May 7, May 10, May 12, May 15, 1945. On May 15, Stimson observed that the President had decided "to push Tito hard and yet to withhold the threat of force. That makes a pretty stiff proposition because I imagine Tito is a pretty good gambler."
12. The full text of the memorandum, dated May 19, 1945, is to be found with a covering letter to Arthur Bliss Lane, April 7, 1947, Box 16, Lane papers. In publishing parts of the memorandum, Grew chose to omit the caustic remarks about Britain, France, and Latin America. See *Turbulent Era*, pp. 1445–46.
13. Grew to Forrestal and Grew to Stimson, May 12, 1945, memorandum of phone call, May 12, 1945, Stimson to Grew, May 21, 1945, Grew papers; Stimson diary, May 13, 15, 1945; minutes of Committee of Three, May 15, 1945, Stettinius papers. My own interpretation of Stimson's hesitation accords with that of Barton Bernstein, "Roosevelt, Truman, and the Atomic Bomb," *Political Science Quarterly* 90 (Spring 1975): 41–43. Martin Sherwin puts more emphasis on Stimson's overview of Soviet-American difficulties: "Stimson did not intend to threaten the Soviet Union with the new weapon, but certainly he expected that once its power was demonstrated, the Soviets would be more accommodating to the American point of view" (*A World Destroyed*, p. 190). Gar Alperovitz declares: "Contrary to a commonly held opinion, the "War Department did not object to raising the political questions because it feared it might jeopardize Soviet assistance in the war against Japan" (*Atomic Diplomacy*, p. 98). Alperovitz' conclusion depends upon a rather selective use of evidence, chosen in order to prove that Stimson au-

thored a strategy of the delayed showdown (ibid., pp. 57–58), a strategy in fact that never existed.

14. Memorandum of meeting with the President, May 28, 1945, memorandum of conversation with Stimson, Forrestal, and Marshall, May 29, 1945, Grew to Stimson, February 12, 1947, Eugene Dooman to Grew, April 12, 1948, Grew papers; Stimson diary, May 29, 1945; John McCloy oral history; State-War-Navy Coordinating Committee Report, June 12, 1945, Committee of Three, June 19, 1945, Stettinius papers; Grew, *Turbulent Era*, pp. 1424, 1437, 1445–46.
15. Davis, *Cold War Begins*, pp. 282–84.
16. Richard Gardner, *Sterling-Dollar Diplomacy*, pp. 10–11; *FR: 1945*, V, pp. 844, 948–49, 942–44. Molotov had suggested that Soviet-American relations must have "certain vistas" before them and rest on a "solid economic basis." Russia's economic needs were enormous — as Stalin remarked to a United States senator in September, "Our internal market is bottomless and we can swallow God knows how much" (Thomas Paterson, *Soviet-American Confrontation*, p. 48).
17. *FR: 1944*, IV, pp. 951, 997; *FR: 1945*, V, pp. 946, 966, 968, 994–98.
18. *FR: 1945*, V, pp. 1009, 1011; Truman, *Year of Decisions*, p. 80; Secretary's staff committee, May 11, 1945, Box 236, Stettinius papers. Vinson and Nelson quoted in Paterson, *Soviet-American Confrontation*, p. 47. In December 1944, Kennan had warned Harriman against "lopsided" American dependence on Soviet orders: The Russians will "not hesitate, if it suits their books, to exploit this dependence, together with their influence over organized labor groups, to gain political and economic objectives which have nothing to do with the interests of our people" (Kennan to Harriman, December 3, 1944, Kennan papers).
19. In January, when Senator Vandenberg suggested using American economic power to pressure the Russians on Eastern Europe, Roosevelt had replied: "Our economic position did not constitute a bargaining weapon of any strength because its only present impact was on lend-lease, which to cut down would hurt us as much as it would hurt the Russians" (January 11, 1945, memorandum of Roosevelt meeting with senators, Stettinius papers). Roosevelt, of course, also saw lend-lease as a device to allay Russian suspicions and set some precedent for postwar collaboration. George Herring in *Aid to Russia*, pp. 177–78, points out that Roosevelt's attitude at the time of his death was obscure.
20. Herring, *Aid to Russia*, pp. 185–90.
21. George Herring, "Lend Lease to Russia," *Journal of American History* 56 (June 1969): 105; Secretary's staff committee, May 11, 1945, Box 236, Stettinius papers.
22. Herring, *Aid to Russia*, pp. 204–8; *FR: 1945*, V, p. 1026. Herring in his illuminating and informed account suggests that the termination was the result of bureaucratic blunder, and a confluence of domestic pressures and international politics. See pp. 200, 209–11. On the contrary, the evidence leads to the conclusion that international politics was the leading factor. Much of the pressure from conservative senators was also from anti-Russian senators. In his memoirs, Truman claimed he had not read the cutback order, but simply signed the papers that Grew and Crowley presented him. Beforehand, however, Crowley had told Grew

that "he wanted to be sure that the President thoroughly understands the situation and that he will back us up and will keep everyone else out of it" because the Russians would be "running all over town looking for help" (Truman, *Year of Decisions*, pp. 228–31; Grew memorandum of telephone conversation with Crowley, May 11, 1945, Grew papers). See Paterson, *Soviet-American Confrontation*, pp. 43–46; Blum, *Price of Vision*, p. 447.

23. *FR: 1945*, III, pp. 1186, 1189.
24. Isador Lubin oral history (Columbia), pp. 84–86; Truman, *Year of Decisions*, pp. 308–12; Bruce Kuklick, *American Policy and the Division of Germany*, p. 132.
25. Stimson diary, April 19, May 16, 1945. See also Rosenman, *Working With Roosevelt*, pp. 545–46; Matthews to McCloy, June 15, 1945, Box 1, Matthews file, State Department papers; *Morgenthau Diary: Germany*, pp. 1490–91.
26. Stimson diary, May 1, 2, 3, 1945, Memorandum of Hoover-Stimson conversation, May 13, 1945, Stimson papers; Hoover to Stimson, May 15, 1945, Hoover papers.
27. For Lovett, see *Morgenthau Diary: Germany*, pp. 1438; Digest of State-War-Navy Coordinating Committee, May 4, 1945, Stettinius papers; Stimson diary, May 4, 1945; *FR: 1945*, III, pp. 1222–29. This discussion on the First Charge Principle derives from Kuklick, *American Policy*, pp. 135–37. He points out the United States would have had to finance the German economy in any event until it could be integrated into a new multilateral order. Other factors affecting German payments, aside from reparations, included war damage, sundering of export connections, and disruption of the international economy.
28. An American delegation subgroup that visited Germany in late May and early June found that "German capacity for war production was still largely intact" and that "extensive removal of plants and machinery were both possible and desirable" (*FR: 1945*, III, p. 1228).
29. *FR: 1945*, III, pp. 1211–13.
30. Wolfgang Leonhard, *Child of the Revolution*, p. 345; Robert Slusser, ed., *Soviet Economic Policy in Postwar Germany*, pp. x, 18–59. Even after the confusion was resolved in late 1946, Mikoyan still instructed officials going to work in Germany, "Remember that economics determines politics" (ibid., p. 55).
31. *FR: Berlin*, I, pp. 547–48. For Harriman's view, *FR: 1945*, III, p. 1213. "We went armed with a lot of information on what was in Germany, and we expected the Russians to enter the spirit of things, but they never did," recalled Abram Bergson, a key economist on the delegation. "We had no systematic elaboration of what their proposals meant for Germany. The problem was how to reconcile Russian large-scale removals to the East with our responsibilities to the West" (interview with Abram Bergson).
32. Isador Lubin oral history (Columbia), pp. 88–91; *FR: Berlin*, I, p. 521; Richard Scandrett, Jr., a prominent New York attorney and member of the delegation, put much responsibility for failure on Pauley: "His initial moves clearly indicated to the Soviets that what he really proposed was to renegotiate the Yalta agreements." See his oral history and Sum-

mary of Procedures of Allied Commission on Reparations, August 1945, p. 8, Scandrett papers. Lubin and the Soviet economist in Lubin oral history (Truman Library), pp. 28–29.

33. Secretary's staff committee, May 9, 1945, Box 236, Stettinius papers; Lane to Durbrow, June 4, 1945, Lane papers. Exchange with Eaton in *FR: 1945*, I, p. 297.
34. Vandenberg, *Private Papers*, p. 178.
35. Vandenberg, *Private Papers*, pp. 155, 176–80; Dilks, *Cadogan Diaries*, p. 739.
36. Byrnes to Lippmann, April 30, Lippmann to Byrnes, May 10, 1945, Box 199, Byrnes to Davies, May 21, 1945, Box 191, Byrnes papers.
37. Margaret Truman, *Harry S. Truman*, pp. 243, 253–55.
38. Morgenthau presidential diary, May 4, June 1, June 6, 1945, pp. 1579, 1638, 1652; Davies diary, June 8, 1945. For Truman's swimming, eyes, and not wanting to be President, Eban Ayers' diary, May 17, 26, 1945.
39. Davies journal and diary, April 30, May 13, May 21, 1945. Truman's diary entries on his conversations with Davies are in Hillman, *Mr. President*, pp. 115–16.
40. Bohlen, *Witness*, p. 215; Margaret Truman, *Truman*, pp. 252–53; Arthur Bliss Lane, *I Saw Poland Betrayed*, pp. 72–73.
41. Bohlen, *Witness*, p. 244; Sherwood, *Roosevelt and Hopkins*, vol. 2, pp. 539, 544–45; *FR: Berlin*, I, p. 61; *FR: 1945*, V, p. 313.
42. Sherwood, *Roosevelt and Hopkins*, vol. 2, pp. 544–51; Bohlen, *Witness*, p. 220; *FR: Berlin*, I, pp. 45–47; Morgenthau presidential diary, June 20, 1945, p. 1669.
43. "Again the Poles?" Stalin had said to Harriman in 1944. "Is that the most important question?" He added that he had been so occupied with the Poles that he had had "no time for military matters" (Harriman, *Special Envoy*, p. 315).
44. Harriman, *America and Russia*, p. 33; *FR: 1945*, V, pp. 303–5, 308, 314, 317–19, 328–29, 335; Sherwood, *Roosevelt and Hopkins*, vol. 2, pp. 544, 561.
45. Sherwood, *Roosevelt and Hopkins*, vol. 2, p. 551; *FR: Berlin*, I, pp. 61–62; Stimson diary, June 19, 1945; Grew to Stettinius, June 18, 1945, Grew papers.
46. Memorandum of conversation with President, June 6, 1945, Stimson papers.
47. *Morgenthau Diary: Germany*, pp. 1554–55; Bohlen, *Witness*, p. 216.
48. Sherwood, *Roosevelt and Hopkins*, vol. 1, p. 3; Maisky, *Soviet Ambassador*, p. 183.

V. The Highest Common Denominator

1. Speech, January 17, 1945, Box 50, Dulles papers; interview with James Riddleberger.
2. Stimson diary, July 19, 1945; Feis-McCloy conversation, December 8, 1952, Box 13, Feis papers.
3. Interview with Benjamin V. Cohen; Byrnes, *Speaking Frankly*, pp. 91–92.

4. Byrnes, *All in One Lifetime*, pp. 12, 5, 107, 87.
5. Donald Russell to Byrnes, August 1946, Box 552, Byrnes papers.
6. Wallace notes on Roosevelt funeral, April 14–15, 1945, Wallace papers; Curry, *James Byrnes*, p. 340; "primadonna," in Daniels, *White House Witness*, p. 279.
7. *FR: Berlin*, I, pp. 5–14; Dilks, *Cadogan Diaries*, p. 761; for Berlin, Charles Mee, *Meeting at Potsdam*, pp. 81–85; *The New Yorker*, July 28, 1945, pp. 48–51, August 4, 1945, pp. 42–47; *Life*, July 23, 1945; Eden, *The Reckoning*, p. 541.
8. Churchill, *Triumph and Tragedy*, p. 443; *FR: Berlin*, I, p. 257; Dixon, *Double Diploma*, p. 165; *FR: Berlin*, II, pp. 1155–57; Stimson diary, July 19, 20, 21, 1945.
9. Davies diary-journal, July 15, Davies diary, July 16, 1945. The Russians quickly concluded that they were up against a much more united British-American front (Zhukov, *Memoirs*, pp. 670–73). Indeed they were. As Dixon noted in his diary: "There has been much closer liaison this time between our delegation and the Americans . . . Here we are much closer to them and every night we have discussed procedure for the following day. There has been a satisfactory air of reality about the meeting" (*Double Diploma*, p. 161).
10. Dilks, *Cadogan Diaries*, p. 765; Truman, *Truman*, p. 269; Moran, *Churchill*, p. 297.
11. *FR: Berlin*, I, p. 228; Memorandum of talk with Truman, November 26, 1952, Box 13, Feis papers; Truman, *Year of Decisions*, pp. 312, 294; Robert Murphy, *Diplomat Among Warriors*, p. 312; Truman's going "home" in Davies diary, July 18, 1945; Truman's vow in Samuel Lubell, "Untold Tragedy of Potsdam," *Saturday Evening Post*, December 8, 1945.
12. *FR: Berlin*, II, pp. 303–4, 527. See Bohlen, *Witness*, pp. 228, 235; Murphy, *Diplomat*, pp. 310–12. Some writers treat Truman's waterway proposals more seriously than they deserve. See Lloyd Gardner, *Architects of Illusion*, pp. 78–82.
13. Davies diary, July 17, July 30, 1945; Dilks, *Cadogan Diaries*, p. 777; Byrnes, *Speaking Frankly*, p. 70; Feis, *Between War and Peace*, pp. 317–20. Byrnes excluded Harriman from the conference table (Byrnes and Truman were joined by Bohlen, Davies, and Leahy), ignored his expertise, and used Davies as liaison with the Russians. Harriman's lack of forgiveness is clear in his memoirs, *Special Envoy*.
14. Byrnes, *Speaking Frankly*, pp. 60–68; Davies diary-journal, July 15, diary, July 16, 1945; Lewis Strauss, *Men and Decisions*, p. 436; Secretary's Staff Committee, July 25, 1945, Box 235, Stettinius papers; *FR: Berlin*, I, pp. 239–41, 226–27, 357–63, 681, 715, 826–27.
15. Davies diary, July 28, July 30, 1945; Marshall Plan interview with Will Clayton; Clayton oral history.
16. For problems over former satellites and Poland, *FR: Berlin*, II, pp. 209–15. For delay of meeting, see memorandum of conversation with President, June 6, 1945, Stimson papers; Davies journal, May 21, 1945. For Groves quote and test, Martin Sherwin, *World Destroyed*, pp. 222–24.
17. Stimson diary, July 16, 21–23, 1945; pregnancy in Davies diary, July 16, 1945. For the windstorm, Dilks, *Cadogan Diaries*, p. 769; David Mac-

Isaac, "Strategic Bombing Survey" (Ph.D. dissertation, Duke University, 1970), p. 241.

18. Walter Brown diary, July 18, 20, 24, 1945; Margaret Truman, *Truman*, p. 274; Ehrman, *Grand Strategy*, p. 292; Stimson diary, July 23–24, 1945; Feis-Byrnes conversation, February 27, 1958, Byrnes papers; Millis, *Forrestal Diaries*, p. 78; Daniels, *Man of Independence*, p. 281.

19. My own research brings me into agreement with the careful, persuasive work of two historians, Martin Sherwin in *A World Destroyed* and Barton Bernstein in "Roosevelt, Truman and the Atomic Bomb," *Political Science Quarterly* 90 (Spring 1975): 23–69. Both establish that the few months of the Truman presidency, insofar as the bomb was concerned, amounted to a continuation of the basic themes and approaches of almost four years of Roosevelt policies, including the unquestioned overriding commitment that the bomb was a weapon of war to be used as quickly as possible in war, and the decision to exclude the Soviet Union as much as possible from knowledge of the project. Bernstein stresses how unsure were policymakers that a speedy surrender would follow the first atomic attack (pp. 52–53). The arresting argument of Gar Alperovitz in *Atomic Diplomacy* — that problems with the Soviet Union governed the actual decision to use the bomb, and that the bomb in turn governed "strategies" toward the Soviet Union from April on — rests on inadequate evidence. Much of the crucial documentation was closed to research when Alperovitz wrote. He certainly overinterprets what evidence he does have, and assumes that policymakers knew in the spring and summer of 1945 what they only knew after the fact, in autumn 1945 and later. Alperovitz mistakenly assumes that there was a coherent, assured policy "mind," pursuing such sophisticated plans as "the Strategy of Delayed Showdown." Rather, policy was confused and fragmentary, responding at one point to difficulties in American-Soviet relations, a few weeks later to the bloody, fanatical resistance on Okinawa. Always, the overriding aim was to end the war as quickly as possible. Too many questions about the bomb — would it work, when, what would its effects be? — existed to allow anything more than a most imperfect integration of it into overall strategic and diplomatic considerations. Alperovitz also makes certain strategic misinterpretations. He maintains (pp. 98–100) that by middle May Henry Stimson was arguing for a policy of delay regarding Russian entry in order to get the war over before the Russians came in. On the contrary, the Secretary was still looking for Russian entry at that time to help end the war. The Japanese campaign, he noted, involves "*two* great uncertainties: first, whether Russia will come in though we think that will be all right; and second, when and how S-1 will resolve itself." (Stimson diary, May 14–15, 1945; also hand-written memorandum, May 19, 1945, Stimson papers; Stimson to Truman, May 16, 1945, Box 157, President's secretary's file, Truman papers.) In mid-June, Truman approved the *first stage* of the Japanese home-islands invasion, to begin in November, with an assurance from Marshall that casualties would be *no more* than 63,000 (Leahy diary, June 18, 1945). What American official, taking Okinawa as a guide, could dare be complacent about the much larger casualties that they could expect from the final battle for the home islands? They could not

sit back and assume that strategic bombing or naval blockade would do the trick. (Subsequent claims about the adequacy of either without an invasion were not unconnected to the struggle over unification of the military services, a point overlooked by many writers.) On June 14, Truman told the Chinese foreign minister that his "chief interest now was to see the Soviet Union participate in the Far Eastern war in sufficient time to be of help in shortening the war and thus saving American and Chinese lives" (conversation with President, June 14, 1945, Grew papers). The atomic bomb would be used for much the same reason.

20. How little was the regard for Attlee! In describing arrangements upon first arriving in Potsdam, Cadogan wrote: "Several houses further on, is a drab and dreary little building destined to house Attlee! Very suitable — it's just like Attlee himself!" (Dilks, *Cadogan Diaries*, p. 761.) Churchill's dream in Moran, *Churchill*, p. 305; his gallop and Bevin's cottage, Ismay to Burrows, August 17, 1945, Ismay papers; Attlee, in Pickersgill, *Mackenzie King*, vol. 3, p. 71; Bidault, *Resistance*, p. 128; Sargent in Dixon, *Double Diploma*, p. 166. For Attlee's social democratic antipathy toward communism and his criticism of Harold Laski, Attlee to J. Chamberlain, December 27, 1941, Box 8, Attlee papers.
21. Davies journal, July 28, 1945.
22. *FR: Berlin*, II, pp. 439–40; Kuklick, *American Policy*, pp. 155–66.
23. Feis, *Between War and Peace*, pp. 194–95.
24. Byrnes-Feis conversation, January 28, 1958, Byrnes papers; Walter Brown diary, July 24, 1945; Feis, *Between War and Peace*, pp. 307–9.
25. Stimson diary, July 23, 1945; Harriman, *America and Russia*, p. 44; Davies diary, July 17, 1945.
26. Stimson diary, July 23, 1945; Davies journal, August 4, 1945.
27. Stimson diary, July 19, 1945; Will Clayton oral history, pp. 154–57; Millis, *Forrestal Diaries*, p. 78; Stalin's quote in Woodward, *British Foreign Policy*, vol. 4, pp. 568–69; the SOB quote in Knebel and Bailey, *No High Ground*, pp. 1–2; Walter Brown diary, August 1, 1945; research notes for *Man of Independence*, pp. 4–5, Daniels papers. When Truman returned to the White House, he immediately went upstairs to his study, played a few songs on the piano, called his wife who was in Independence, ordered drinks for himself and a few members of his staff, and then started talking about Potsdam. "Stalin was one," he commented, "who, if he said something one time, would say the same things the next time. In other words, he could be depended upon." Truman had no particular opinion of Attlee, but certainly did of Bevin, who reminded him of the U.S. union leader, John L. Lewis. "Stalin and Molotov," Truman said, "might be rough men but they knew the common courtesies." Bevin was "entirely lacking in all of them, a boor" (Eben Ayers diary, August 7, 1945). "Old guy" in Ayers diary, October 18, 1947.
28. MacArthur in David MacIsaac, "Strategic Bombing Survey" (Ph.D. dissertation, Duke University, 1969), p. 241; Bernard Brodie, "The Atomic Bomb and American Security," November 1, 1945, Yale Institute of International Affairs, Memo 18, pp. 11–12. It is interesting to note that Brodie, who became one of America's foremost strategists throughout the Cold War era, had become involved with military questions before the war because, in his youth, the only way in which he could afford the

pleasure of riding horses was by joining the Illinois National Guard. Interview with Bernard Brodie.

29. Byrnes in Davies diary, July 29, 1945; Churchill in Arthur Bryant, *Triumph in the West*, pp. 363–64; Stimson diary, July 30, 1945.
30. Churchill, *Triumph and Tragedy*, pp. 272–75, 300–361; Davies diary, July 29, 1945; Zhukov, *Memoirs*, pp. 674–75; Bohlen, *Witness*, pp. 237–38; Walter Brown, July 24, 1945, Byrnes papers. Truman's dissimulation was pointless because the Russians were known to be spying on the Manhattan Project, as Henry Stimson told Roosevelt (Stimson diary, September 9, 1943, December 31, 1944). Also it was known that French scientists associated with the project had probably told Frederic Joliot, a scientist and member of the French Communist Party, about it. Sherwin, *World Destroyed*, pp. 132–35.
31. Stimson diary, July 21, 1945; Feis, *Between War and Peace*, pp. 178–80.
32. Byrnes, *Lifetime*, p. 313; Theodore Achillés oral history.
33. Stimson diary, September 4, 1945; Walter Brown diary, September 13, 1945; Byrnes' determination to understate the bomb, Bush quote, and Molotov "misstatement" in Gregg Herken, "American Diplomacy and the Atomic Bomb" (Ph.D. dissertation, Princeton University, 1973), pp. 75, 100–102, 120–21. Herken's work is an excellent analysis of the relationship between the bomb and postwar diplomacy. Molotov's "mistake" is also cited in the Dalton diary, October 5, 1945.
34. *FR: 1945*, II, p. 164; Walter Brown diary, September 24, 1945; Davies diary, October 9, 1945; Herbert Feis, *From Trust to Terror*, p. 98; Dalton diary, October 5, 1945. According to Dalton, Jan Smuts of South Africa warned the British that the Soviets should not be given a trusteeship in Africa because he feared they would use it to "stir up the tribes."
35. *FR: 1945*, II, pp. 182–84; *FR: 1945*, IV, pp. 872, 329.
36. Walter Brown diary, September 16, 1945; *FR: 1945*, II, pp. 243–47, 263.
37. *FR: 1945*, II, pp. 194–202; *New York Times*, September 26, 1945, p. 6.
38. Walter Brown diary, September 16, 17, 1945.
39. *FR: 1945*, II, pp. 243–47, 263.
40. *FR: 1945*, II, pp. 267–68, 306–7; Walter Brown diary, September 20, 1945.
41. *FR: 1945*, II, pp. 206–7, 109.
42. *FR: 1945*, II, p. 516; Walter Brown diary, September 17, 20, 21, 1945; Leahy diary, September 22, 1945; Molotov-Bevin talk in CAB 129/3, pp. 53–56, Bevin to Cabinet, CAB 128/3, pp. 15–16, CM(45), Cabinet papers.
43. Bevin in CAB 128/3, pp. 15–16, CM(45), Cabinet papers; Byrnes-Leahy teletype, September 22, 1945, Leahy diary; Byrnes, *Lifetime*, p. 314.
44. Walter Brown diary, September 21, 1945; *FR: 1945*, II, pp. 485–86.
45. Allen Dulles, Carl McCardle, Thomas Dewey interviews, Dulles oral history. "It is too much to hope that the whole world will turn immediately to God," John Foster Dulles wrote during World War II, when chairman of the Federal Council of Churches Commission on a Just and Durable Peace, "but something can be done in this direction and part of the postwar plan should certainly include emphasis on religious philosophy." (Memo, November 1944, Box 144, Dulles papers.)
46. Dilks, *Cadogan Diaries*, p. 462; speech, February 8, 1944, Box 10; China

trip diary, March 6–9, 1938, Dulles to Conway, December 15, 1943, Box 139, Dulles papers. Also see John Foster Dulles, *War, Peace and Change*, and Townsend Hoopes, *The Devil and John Foster Dulles*, pp. 53–61.

47. Dulles speeches, March 18, 1943, February 5, 1945, Box 10, speech, January 17, 1945, Box 50, radio interview, November 5, 1943, Box 129, Dulles papers.
48. Dulles speech, February 5, 1945, Box 10, Lyons to Dulles, February 7, 1945, Dulles to Lyons, February 14, 1945, Box 140, Dulles papers.
49. Dulles speech, January 16, 1945, Box 10, Dulles papers. Also see speech of March 18, 1943.
50. February 26, 1945, statement, Box 103, Dulles papers; *FR: 1945*, I, pp. 577, 644, 997.
51. Interviews with Byrnes and McCardle, Dulles oral history; notes on Dulles talk, Box 1, Warburg papers; radio report, October 6, 1945, Box 80, Dulles papers.
52. Interviews with McCardle, Dewey, and Achilles, Dulles oral history; Dulles, *War or Peace*, pp. 29–30; Curry, *Byrnes*, p. 351; Townsend Hoopes, *Devil and John Foster Dulles*, p. 63.
53. *FR: 1945*, II, pp. 488–89.
54. Walter Brown diary, September 17, 20, 1945.
55. Dalton diary, October 5, 1945; Dixon, *Double Diploma*, pp. 189–95; Eden, *The Reckoning*, pp. 545–47; Pickersgill, *The Mackenzie King Record*, vol. 3, pp. 54, 59; *FR: 1945*, II, pp. 558–59; empire quotation from Quentin Bell, *Virginia Woolf*, p. 178.
56. Dixon, *Double Diploma*, p. 191; Davies diary, July 28, 1945.
57. Leahy diary, September 12, 1945; *New York Times*, September 25, 1945; Walter Brown diary, September 27, 1945.
58. Dalton diary, October 5, 1945; Sulzberger, *Long Row of Candles*, p. 268; Byrnes, *Lifetime*, p. 314. See Bohlen, *Witness*, p. 247, and Walter Brown diary, September 17, 21, 1945.
59. Stimson and Bundy, *On Active Service*, pp. 642–46; Stimson diary, August 12–September 3, 1945, September 4, 12, 17, 21, 1945.
60. Stimson diary, September 21, 1945; Forrestal diary, September 21, 1945, pp. 493–95; Millis, *Forrestal Diaries*, pp. 94–96; Blum, *Wallace Diary*, pp. 482–84; Norman Markowitz, *Rise and Fall of People's Century*, pp. 174–76. For the misunderstanding, see Herken, "American Diplomacy and the Atomic Bomb," p. 77.
61. *FR: 1945*, II, pp. 48–50, 54–56, 60. The Cabinet members' replies to Truman are in Boxes 112, 199, President's secretary's file, Truman papers. Agriculture Secretary Clinton Anderson's response was close to Truman's own thinking. "I listened carefully to the testimony that the Russians might be able to make an atomic bomb in five years," said Anderson. "I have my doubts . . . We know that in the production of the atomic bomb there was a certain element of American mathematical and mechanical genius which has given us the automobile industry, the great development of the telephone industry, and countless other inventive processes . . . which seem to be peculiarly the result of long years of mechanization of industry within the United States. I quoted to you those lines from Kipling which suggested that they had copied all they

could copy, but they couldn't copy our minds." He went on to say that, while the Russians knew the "trade secrets" for making autos and planes, they had depended upon American "machine tools, the equipment, the 'know-how' " to see them through the war. He added that he had spoken at a "splendid banquet" in Decatur, Illinois, sponsored by the Chamber of Commerce and the Farm Bureau, with "some 675 people drawn from every section of Illinois . . . I made it my point to ask every person I could get to what his opinion was on the question of how far we should go toward releasing the bomb, or the secret of atomic energy, to Russia. The answer was completely unanimous. I did not meet a single person who thought that Russia should be given any part of this secret" (Anderson to Truman, September 25, 1945). For Truman's similar views, see Ayers' diary, September 24, 1945.

62. Interviews with George Kistiakowsky and Victor Weisskopf. For a survey of the major issues in the Rosenberg spy case, see Daniel Yergin, "Victims of a Desperate Age," *New Times* (New York), May 16, 1975, pp. 21–27. Princeton University physicist Henry Smyth was chief author of *Atomic Energy for Military Purposes*, officially issued on August 12, 1945. Its publication actually surprised some scientists because of its detailed discussion of methods for producing refined uranium and plutonium, which many considered the most difficult part of building a bomb. The British opposed publication, as did some American officials. Other U.S. officials, however, argued that such a report was necessary for several reasons: to ensure the continuing cooperation of the scientific community, to help stimulate future advances in atomic research, to prevent wild speculation, and to anticipate possible political pressures for release of technical information. Margaret Gowing, *Independence and Deterrence*, vol. 2, pp. 118–21, 124; Vannevar Bush, *Pieces of the Action*, pp. 294–95; Hewlett and Anderson, *The New World*, pp. 368, 372–73, 400–401, 406.

63. Bush and companies quoted in Herken, "American Diplomacy and the Atomic Bomb," pp. 75, 66, 124; Blum, *Wallace Diary*, p. 483.

64. Bush, *Pieces of the Action*, p. 295; Clinton Anderson, *Outsider in the Senate*, p. 68; Herken, "American Diplomacy and the Atomic Bomb," pp. 23–25, 83–86, 94 (Byrnes quote, p. 25); Council on Foreign Relations Study Group, "National Power and Foreign Policy," second meeting, November 30, 1945, pp. 3–4, 12; Weed to McCone, October 30, 1947, with attachment on "World's Uranium Deposits," Air Policy Commission papers. In November 1946, Groves was notified by the War Department that the Russians had discovered a hitherto-unsuspected uranium source in eastern Germany, and that they had also "requested" the Czech government to provide uranium ore from known sources in that country. The reference for this is an unpublished paper by Gregg Herken, "Under a Most Deadly Illusion: Politics and Diplomacy of US Atomic-Energy Policy, 1942–49," p. 39. His sources include Patterson to Groves, November 1, 1946, Patterson file; Steinhardt to Byrnes, November 19, 1946, Harrison-Bundy file, Manhattan Engineering Division Records.

65. Herken, "American Diplomacy and the Atomic Bomb," pp. 113, 47–48 (Groves), 23 (Byrnes); Harold Smith diary, October 5, 1945.

VI. The A-1 Priority Job

1. Robinson to Bohlen, December 10, 1945, Box 3432, State Department papers.
2. John J. McCloy, "Personal Impression of World Conditions," in James Kroat, ed., *European Recovery: American Academy of Political Science Proceedings* 21 (1944–46, No. 4): 559–60; *New York Times*, November 9, 1945, p. 1; Millis, *Forrestal Diaries*, p. 106.
3. Arnold Wolfers, *Discord and Collaboration*, p. 151; Pickersgill, *The Mackenzie King Record*, vol. 3, p. 42; Hickerson to Matthews, October 2, 1945, 711.61/10–24, State Department papers; Sulzberger, *Long Row of Candles*, p. 269.
4. Notes from November 8, 1945, meeting, Box 115, Dulles papers; Dulles talk, October 30, 1945, Council on Foreign Relations papers. Dulles identified in the Council meeting three reasons that the Russians had frustrated the work of the London Conference: The Russians had harbored "suspicion of the West," based not only on past history, but on present events. Some of their present suspicion was justified, he said, citing an Office of Strategic Services report that remnants of a London Polish group was running an underground radio station in the American sector of Germany, beamed at Poland. Secondly, the Russians were "tough traders," and they may have gotten the idea at San Francisco that the United States "could be pushed around." He suggested finally that the Soviet leaders might not "really want a close relationship with the West," for fear it would create discontent and dissatisfaction among their own people (notes on Dulles talk, Box 1, Warburg papers).
5. Fyke Farmer in Herken, "Atomic Bomb," p. 93; Harold Smith diary, October 5, 1945; Stettinius-Truman meeting, October 22, 1945, Box 237, Stettinius papers; *Truman Public Papers: 1945*, pp. 381–88, 431–38. Tiptonville and Navy Day speech discussed by Herken, "Atomic Bomb," pp. 82–89. Truman-Byrnes wires in Byrnes folder, Box 159, President's secretary's file, Truman papers.
6. Interview with Loy Henderson; Henderson to Matthews, November 13, 1945, Box 1, Matthews file, State Department papers; Durbrow to author, January 12, 1973; Durbrow to Lane, December 8, 1945, Box 23, Lane papers.
7. Interview with Benjamin Cohen. Also see *New York Times*, September 30, 1945, IV, p. 5, October 14, 1945, IV, p. 3.
8. *FR: 1945*, V, pp. 888–91; *FR: 1945*, II, p. 61; Davies journal, October 9, 1945; Millis, *Forrestal Diaries*, p. 107. Byrnes speech in *New York Times*, November 1, 1945, p. 4.
9. Mark Ethridge and C. E. Black, "Negotiating on the Balkans," in *Negotiating with the Russians*, Dennett and Johnson, eds., p. 171.
10. For Dulles' surprise see both the digest of his talk on October 30, 1945, p. 7, Council on Foreign Relations papers, and notes on that talk, Box 1, Warburg papers; *New York Times*, September 26, 1945, p. 6; Ethridge to Wallace, February 6, 1945, Wallace papers; interview with Mark Ethridge.
11. Ethridge, "Report on Rumania: Background and Conclusions," Decem-

ber 6, 1945, and attachments, pp. 1, 11–13, FW 871.00/12–745, State Department papers. Ethridge recollected the intransigence, bluster, and cynicism of local and Soviet communists. Even when communists were trying to be agreeable, they put him off: "The chief of police in Bucharest telephoned the American Embassy in Moscow before we left and said, 'Please give us the exact time of Mr. Ethridge's arrival, as we want to arrange one of the largest spontaneous demonstrations in Rumanian history' " (interview with Mark Ethridge).

12. Ibid., pp. 10–15. Ethridge explained his premises: "Our moral strength in the world is at the present moment our greatest asset as a nation . . . we have held out to the hope of all countries, whether defeated or not, they can be guaranteed the opportunity to select their governments free from coercion and fear . . . Some of the satellite nations, such as Rumania, may deserve to stew in their own juices; some of them have behaved in such a way as to have no moral claim on us. But it is we who cannot afford the bad faith of reneging on our promises." In a subtle paper that observes the 'thirty years rule' — (that the passage of time obviates the need to place blame and derive policy prescriptions), Herbert Dinerstein suggests that Stalin may have counted on the continuation of the Grand Alliance and had much to gain from its maintenance. "Coalitions" in Eastern Europe were one necessary element. But the coalitions were organized by the survivors of the purges. (This applied to local communists as much as to the occupying Soviets). Their experience, practices and political culture left them ill-prepared for dealing with people not completely under their control. After all, they had survived (and continued to survive) only by being completely obedient. Thus, the Soviets and their local allies, while trying to make coalitions, ended up creating conflicts and confrontations throughout Eastern Europe. "What was conceived as a scheme for the continuation of wartime cooperation soon became a process of the ruthless elimination of any opposition," Dinerstein writes in his paper, "The Cold War from the Soviet Point of View: the Soviet Union and the Reordering of the International System After World War II."

13. *FR: 1945*, IV, pp. 407–8. Also see Matthews to Byrnes, November 16, 1945, 874.00/11–1645, State Department papers. Ernest May suggests that the American representative in Rumania "coached" Ethridge into some distortions of Rumanian politics. May is critical of the State Department reporting from that Balkan crucible. In dispatches likely to be passed to the Secretary of State or President, Barnes in Bulgaria "painted a monochromatic background. He characterized Bulgaria's notoriously corrupt Agrarian party as enthusiastically supported by 60 percent of the peasantry. His cables implied that the only period of authoritarian rule in Bulgaria had been that of wartime collaboration with the Nazis." In fact, a tight police dictatorship commanded the country before the war. "Whether designedly or not, Barnes conveyed the misleading impression that Soviet-backed communists had imposed a dictatorship on a country which had been and otherwise would be democratic." The representative in Rumania also "much overstated the historic power of democratic forces in the Balkans" (May, *"Lessons" of the Past*, pp. 28–29).

14. Cyril E. Black, "Witnesses to the Start of the Cold War in Eastern Europe: The View from Bulgaria," paper presented to the Conference on Slavic and East European Studies, October 1975, p. 24. For Byrnes' concern about faltering relations, Visson file, December 10, 1945, McNaughton file, December 13, 1945, McNaughton papers; Byrnes; *Speaking Frankly*, p. 109; press conference, December 11, 1945, Box 555, Byrnes papers.
15. Dixon, *Double Diploma*, p. 199; Davies diary, December 8, 1945; *FR: 1945*, II, pp. 591, 756; Byrnes, *Lifetime*, p. 332. Bevin in CAB 128/4, pp. 32–33, Cabinet Minutes 1945, Cabinet papers.
16. Byrnes, *Speaking Frankly*, p. 109; *FR: 1945*, IV, pp. 410–12; Kennan, *Memoirs*, pp. 286–88.
17. *FR: 1945*, II, p. 749, 629–31, 753.
18. Conant quote in Herken, "Atomic Bomb," p. 182; Bohlen, *Witness*, p. 249; *FR: 1945*, II, p. 736, 740–41. For the Truman-Attlee-King meeting, see Herken, "Atomic Bomb," chapter 6.
19. *FR: 1945*, II, p. 757, Visson file, December 10, 1945, McNaughton papers; Advisory Commission for Japan, October 14, 1945, Hull memo, October 10, 1945, OPD 366 S.6, RG 165, Modern Military records. H. Freeman Matthews reported to Byrnes, "If we operate a control council in Japan the way the Russians have operated in the Balkans we need have no fears with regard to MacArthur's ultimate authority . . . The Russians would probably expect MacArthur to run the show . . . Under the Russian system the president runs the show, as we know all too well, just about as he pleases. Such an arrangement would take care of Russian prestige, an aspect which is all important under their system" (Matthews to Byrnes, October 18, 1945, Box 3, Hickerson files, State Department papers).
20. *FR: 1945*, II, pp. 776, 805–6; Bohlen, *Witness*, p. 250; Stalin on Egypt and India in CAB, p. 2, Cabinet papers.
21. McNaughton file, January 4, 1946, McNaughton papers; *New York Times*, December 31, 1945, p. 4; press conferences, December 11, December 31, 1945, Box 555, Byrnes papers. Byrnes told Joseph Davies, "Substantial progress has been made" and the conference had resulted "in resumption of friendly discussions" (Davies diary, January 4, 1946).
22. Sulzberger, *Long Row of Candles*, pp. 292–93; *FR: 1946*, VII, pp. 1–6; Durbrow to author, January 12, 1973.
23. Vandenberg, *Private Papers*, pp. 225–33. Acheson, in his memoirs, suggests "Vandenberg, misreading one section, was up in arms" (*Present at the Creation*, p. 191). According to Leahy, "Mr. Acheson seems to have convinced the President that the agreement in regard to the atomic bomb is right" (Leahy diary, December 28, 1945). For Truman's reassurance to Byrnes during the conference, and the downplaying of sniping from Vandenberg and other senators, see *FR: 1945*, II, pp. 610, 709–10. For Forrestal, see Millis, *Forrestal Diaries*, p. 111.
24. George Elsey to author, November 30, 1972; Ben Cohen to James Byrnes, March 21, 1958, Box 992, Byrnes papers; Leahy diary, August 21, October 19, 1944, June 30, October 17, 1945.
25. Leahy diary, October 24, 27, 1945; Walter Brown diary, August 10, 1945.
26. Pickersgill, *Mackenzie King*, vol. 3, pp. 37–41; for Stettinius, Gaddis,

Origins of the Cold War, pp. 252–53; Patterson to Truman, February 27, 1946, Truman to Patterson, n.d., Box 112, President's secretary's file, Truman papers.

27. Herbert Feis, *China Tangle*, pp. 406–12; Acheson memo, October 11, 1945, Official File 20–1945, Truman papers; Feis interview with Truman, November 26, 1952, Box 13, Feis papers; John Melby, *Mandate of Heaven*, p. 49; Durbrow to Lane, November 29, 1945, Lane papers; Djilas, *Conversations*, p. 141.
28. Wallace-Carter phone conversation, November 1, 1945, Wallace papers; Leahy diary, November 28, December 11, 1945. Earlier in the year, Leahy had described a general who had told him that the State Department was "dangerously un-American" as "an officer of wide experience in international affairs, a high ability, and superlative integrity" (Leahy diary, March 29, 1945). After meeting Hurley and General Albert Wedemeyer on October 19, 1945, Truman noted, "I told them my policy is to support Chiang Kai-Shek" (Box 269, President's secretary's file, Truman papers).
29. Leahy diary, December 26, 28, 1945; Leahy, *I Was There*, pp. 347–48; Cohen to Byrnes, March 21, 1958, Box 992, Byrnes papers.
30. Harold Smith diary, October 16, 1945; Samuel Rosenman oral history; interview with Benjamin Cohen; Davies diary, May 21, 1945, Davies journal, September 18, 1945; Anderson, *Outsider in the Senate*, pp. 77–78. For "little we can do," Ayers diary, December 17, 1945.
31. Harold Smith diary, November 28, December 5, 1945; Davies diary, December 8, 1945; Leahy diary, December 12, 1945. For Byrnes' lack of consultation on Germany, Ayers diary, December 12, 1945.
32. McNaughton file, December 13, 1945, McNaughton papers; Acheson, *Present at the Creation*, p. 191.
33. Acheson, *Present at the Creation*, p. 191; McNaughton file, January 4, 1946, McNaughton papers; Leahy diary, December 29, 1945; Byrnes, *Lifetime*, pp. 342–43; Truman, *Year of Decisions*, pp. 549–50; Clark Clifford interview, research notes for *Man of Independence*, Daniels papers.
34. Leahy diary, December 31, 1945; McNaughton file, January 4, 1946, McNaughton papers; press conference, December 31, 1945, Box 555, Byrnes papers.
35. Leahy diary, January 1, 4, 1946; *FR: 1945*, V, pp. 633–41; interview with Mark Ethridge. The Ethridge letter, dated December 8, and Ethridge summary, dated December 7, can also be found in Box 172, President's secretary's file, Truman papers, with covering letters to Truman from Byrnes (dated January 2) and Acheson (dated January 11). For the authoritarian history of Rumania and Bulgaria in the interwar years, see Joseph Rothchild, *East Central Europe Between the Two World Wars*, pp. 293–322, 333–55; Ernest May, *"Lessons,"* pp. 27–29.
36. George Curry reconciles the conflicting accounts in a similar fashion in *James Byrnes*, pp. 189–90. For the different sides and Truman's letters, see Byrnes, *Lifetime*, pp. 400–404, and Truman, *Year of Decisions*, pp. 550–52. Truman made a longhand note on January 5: "Today I wrote this memo and read it to my Secretary of State. So urgent was its contents that I neither had it typed nor mailed but not only had to read it from manuscript but preferred to do it that way in order to give more

emphasis to the points I wish to make" (Box 269, President's secretary's file, Truman papers). In *Mr. President,* William Hillman noted, "One day the President said that sometimes he wrote letters which he never sent but wished he had sent" (p. 4). Also relevant is Clark Clifford's comment on Truman's almost-certainly faulty recollection of his meeting with Byrnes on the *Williamsburg* a few days before: "Clifford suggests that HST puts some of his later bitterness into his memory of this meeting" (Clark Clifford interview, research notes for *Man of Independence,* Daniels papers).

37. *Truman Public Papers,* 1946, p. 10; interview with Benjamin Cohen. Also in middle January, Truman informed the State Department that he now wanted to see the daily unclassified summary and the daily classified summary coming in from the London session of the United Nations, where Byrnes was representing the United States. Acheson to Truman, January 14, 1946, Box 159, President's secretary's file, Truman papers.

VII. The Right Attitude in Mind

1. Leahy diary, February 21, 1946; Kennan to Hickerson, June 20, 1946, 711.61/6–2046, State Department papers; *FR: 1946,* VI, pp. 732–36; W. B. Smith, *My Three Years in Moscow,* p. 53.
2. Truman to Wallace, March 20, 1946, Wallace papers (for the "right attitude"); Adolph Berle, *Navigating the Rapids,* p. 573; Leahy diary, February 20, 1946; Elbrick to Lane, March 11, 1946, Box 24, Lane papers. "I am so happy that you feel that General Smith has the right attitude," Wallace wrote to Truman. The Secretary of Commerce did not quite understand, however, what the "right attitude" meant to Truman. Wallace to Truman, March 21, 1946, Box 156, President's secretary's file, Truman papers.
3. Forrestal to Willett, December 19, 1945, Box 17, Forrestal to Walsh, January 15, 1946, Box 71, draft of Commerce and Industry speech, February 26, 1946, Box 19, Forrestal papers; Millis, *Forrestal Diaries,* pp. 57, 72, 128.
4. Edward F. Willett, "Dialectical Materialism and Russian Objectives," January 14, 1946, Box 17, Forrestal papers.
5. Robert Albion and Robert Connery, *Forrestal and the Navy,* pp. 184–85; Millis, *Forrestal Diaries,* pp. 127–28.
6. Bohlen memoranda, 711.61/2–1446, with covering memorandum from Maxwell Hamilton, State Department papers; Charles Bohlen to author, November 15, 1973.
7. "Capabilities and Intentions of the USSR in the Post-War Period" by the Joint Intelligence Committee of the Joint Chiefs of Staff, Washington, D.C., February 1946.
8. For the elections and speeches, see Alexander Werth, *Postwar Russia,* pp. 78–92. For the preoccupation with reconstruction, see Robert Slusser, ed., *Soviet Economic Policy in Postwar Germany,* and Alec Nove, *An Economic History of the USSR.*
9. *New York Times,* February 10, 1946, p. 30.
10. Millis, *Forrestal Diaries,* p. 134; Forrestal to Roy Howard, February 13, 1946, Box 69, Forrestal papers. Nuclear strategist Bernard Brodie re-

called, "Stalin's speech was a shocking thing to those of us who were not close enough to the top to know that some concern was already settling in at the top" (interview with Bernard Brodie).

11. Matthews to Byrnes and Acheson, February 11, 1946, Box 2, Matthews file, State Department papers.
12. Matthews to Kennan, February 13, 1946, 861.00/2–1346, Durbrow to Matthews, February 12, 1946, 861.00/2–1246, State Department papers.
13. Interview with Elbridge Durbrow; Matthews to Kennan, February 13, 1946, 861.00/2–1346, State Department papers.
14. Interview with Elbridge Durbrow; Kennan, *Memoirs*, pp. 290–93. For Kennan's thoughts on resignation, C. Ben Wright, "Mr. 'X' and Containment," *Slavic Review* 35 (March 1976): 12. Kennan, incorrectly on the basis of the documentation, attributes the Long Telegram to his pique at "the anguished cry of bewilderment" from the Treasury Department to Soviet lack of interest in the World Bank and International Monetary Fund.
15. *FR: 1946*, VI, pp. 697–98, 708. Of curiosity, at least to nit-pickers and pedants, Kennan insists in his *Memoirs* that the Long Telegram was 8000 words, whereas, printed in *FR: 1946*, VI, p. 696–709, it is rather in the neighborhood of 5500 words.
16. *FR: 1946*, VI, pp. 699–700.
17. *FR: 1946*, VI, pp. 697, 702–3, 706.
18. Ibid., p. 707.
19. Kennan, *Memoirs*, pp. 292–94.
20. Byrnes to Kennan, February 27, 1944, 861.00/2–2746; State Department papers.
21. Matthews to Kennan, February 25, 1946, 861.00/2–2546, State Department papers. "May I tell you how impressed I am with your cable," Assistant Secretary of State William Benton cabled Kennan. "I have heard much about you from Loy Henderson and others" (March 7, 1946, 861.00/3–746, State Department papers).
22. ALUSNA Moscow to CNO, March 4, 1946, Forrestal diary, pp. 906–7. A year and a half later, the naval attaché reminded Forrestal that the Long Telegram "can be read over and over with profit." Stevens to Forrestal, September 30, 1947, Box 72, Forrestal papers. Also see David Lilienthal, *Atomic Energy Years*, p. 26.
23. Vitthup to Craig, February 26, 1946, ASW 091 Russia, Modern Military records; Kennan, *Memoirs*, p. 310; interview with George Elsey; Wright, "Mr. 'X' and Containment," p. 14.
24. Wright, "Mr. 'X' and Containment," p. 12.
25. Robert Elson, *The World of Time Inc.*, vol. II, pp. 161–62. How sad to see Kennan's elegant periods transformed into pungent "Timese": "Russia wants power. Russia wants prestige. Russia wants security. Russia regards the peace as an opportunity better than any the Czars ever had, better than the Bolsheviks are likely to have even in a decade or two . . . By the ideological nature of the disease, Communism feels safe only when it is the doctor" (*Time*, April 1, 1946, p. 27).
26. There is an extensive debate about the relationship between foreign policy and public opinion, but much of that debate seems to be shaped in assumptions by the memory of prewar isolationism. See Gabriel Al-

mond, *The American People and Foreign Policy;* James Rosenau, ed., *Domestic Sources of Foreign Policy;* William Caspary, "The Mood Theory," *American Political Science Review* 64 (June 1970); Sidney Verba, et al., "Public Opinion and War in Vietnam," ibid., 61 (June 1967). In truth, however, the President with his aura of majesty, his access to so many levers, his ability to appeal to chauvinism and patriotism at key moments, has wide latitude. This was true even before World War II. "The public opinion of the United States depended so entirely on the President for its foreign relations," Henry Stimson said to pollster George Gallup six months before Pearl Harbor. Gallup agreed, saying that his polls "showed the public opinion was influenced every time the President spoke" (Stimson diary, June 4, 1941).

27. John Lewis Gaddis, *The United States and the Origins of the Cold War*, pp. 52–55, 138, 146; Taft to Nielsen, January 30, 1946, Box 784, Smith to Taft, October 1, 1945, Box 1264, Taft papers. Also see draft statement from Brownell, December 3, 1946, Box 146, Aldrich papers.
28. Speech, February 8, 1946, Box 39, Tobey papers; H. Robbins to Dulles, September 11, 1946, Box 140, Dulles papers; Harriman, *Special Envoy*, p. 531. Also see Hadley Cantril, *Public Opinion 1935–46*, vol. 1, p. 371.
29. Interview with James Riddleberger; Ben Cohen to Byrnes, March 21, 1958, Box 922, Byrnes papers; Vandenberg to Armstrong, April 2, 1946, Armstrong to Vandenberg, March 12, 1946, Arthur Vandenberg papers; Vandenberg, *Private Papers*, pp. 247–49.
30. Leffingwell to Lamont, March 14, 1946, Box 104–6, Lamont papers. Dulles must have overwhelmed his luncheon companions with his prediction that all Europe would fall easy prey to the advance of Russian communism, leaving England "a little helpless pocket on the edge of a Communist world," and that America "may be left unconquered if we don't show too much resistance to the Communist ideal."
31. Leffingwell to Lamont, March 4, 11, 1946, Lamont to Leffingwell, March 8, 1946, Box 104–6, Lamont to Leffingwell, March 11, 1946, 128–15, Lamont papers.
32. Dulles to Roswell Barnes, May 8, 1946, Dulles to Ernest Bevin, May 28, 1946, Box 140, Dulles papers; Dulles, "Thoughts on Soviet Foreign Policy and What To Do About It," *Life*, June 3, 1946, pp. 112–26, June 10, 1946, pp. 118–30.
33. Luce to Dulles, June 16, 1946, Box 140, Dulles papers. Byrnes told Dulles the article was a "splendid analysis of the situation" (Byrnes to Dulles, June 8, 1946, Box 140, Dulles papers). Luce later recalled: "We chose him to express . . . Well, I won't put it quite that way. He had ideas that he wanted to give expression to and they were much coincident with the general ideas that we had here" (Dulles oral history). The Luce publications were in the forefront of trying to reshape public opinion. For instance, in the May 20, 1946, *Life* (pp. 68–76), the Alsop brothers wrote a 4500-word article on the "Tragedy of Liberalism" — to wit, its failure to face up to "the challenge of Soviet imperialism." The columnists depicted Henry Wallace as the Neville Chamberlain of the 1940s. See Elson, *Time Inc.*, vol. II, pp. 60–66.
34. Moran, *Churchill*, pp. 312, 315, 322, 330–34; for the barber, Dalton diary, November 1, 1945.

35. Moran, *Churchill*, pp. 316, 322–23, 332; Pickersgill, *Mackenzie King*, vol. 3, pp. 85–87.
36. Leahy diary, September 19, 1944. For instance, on December 29, 1945, Ismay wrote Eisenhower: "If your armed forces and ours had more or less the same equipment, more or less the same doctrine, more or less the same organization — AND NO SECRETS of any kind between them — they would at once constitute a hard core of resistance to any breach of the peace. Thereafter, any other nation that was worthy and willing could join 'The Club' " (Ismay papers).
37. Harry Vaughan oral history; Moran, *Churchill*, p. 328; Truman to Churchill, November 17, 1945, Churchill to Halifax, December 12, 1945, Box 4, Attlee papers; Ismay to Eisenhower, December 29, 1945, Ismay papers.
38. Attlee to Halifax, October 30, 1945, Halifax to Foreign Office, October 31, 1945, TLR to Churchill, November 2, 1945, papers of February 16, 1946, Box 4, Attlee papers.
39. Smith to Ismay, January 23, 1946, Ismay papers; Leahy diary, February 10, March 3, 1946; notes on Truman manuscript, Box 573, Byrnes papers; Williams, *Twilight of Empire*, pp. 162–63. For some reason, Margaret Truman insists her father knew nothing of the contents of the speech until just before boarding the train. Margaret Truman, *Truman*, p. 312. On the contrary, early in February, Churchill spent an hour and a half with Truman at the White House. The President, Churchill reported, "welcomed the outline I gave him of my message" (Wright to Dixon, February 16, 1946, Box 14, Attlee papers). For the poker, Earl of Birkenhead, *Halifax*, p. 559.
40. *Congressional Record*, 79th Congress, 2nd Session, A1145–47.
41. Leffingwell to Lamont, March 28, 1946, 128–15, Lamont papers; Wallace speech, "In Honor of W. Averell Harriman," March 19, 1946, Schindler papers; Elson, *Time Inc.*, vol. 2, p. 159. Wallace also said: "I think we can make it clear to the Soviet Government that no country however powerful in a military or economic way can dominate by mere force even the smallest countries for very long. Russia can't ride roughshod over Eastern Europe and get away with it any more than we could in Latin America or England in India and Africa." For Churchill's stepping somewhat in front of popular sentiment, see *Public Opinion Quarterly* 10 (Summer 1946): 263–65.
42. *Pravda*, March 13, 23, 1946. One high Soviet official who said he had been with Stalin and Molotov when word of the speech arrived in Moscow reported that they had become agitated, seeing in the speech proof of hostility on the part of the "Anglo-Saxons," and of the desire to recreate a cordon sanitaire around the Soviet Union. Lord Gladwyn, *Memoirs*, p. 185. An official of the Soviet embassy in Washington complained, "He could scarcely believe his eyes when he read Churchill's speech . . . An alliance of this kind by two allies as a coalition against a third ally meant the liquidation of the coalition of the three powers" (Davies diary, March 15, 1946).
43. Charles Bohlen, *The Transformation of American Foreign Policy*, pp. 76–77; Truman, *Public Papers 1946*, p. 145; Leahy diary, March 5, 1946; Margaret Truman, *Truman*, p. 312; Halifax to Churchill, April 14, 1946,

Halifax papers. Churchill was, according to a British diplomat, even more successful in conveying his message in an off-the-record talk to an audience of 600 influential men in New York City on March 18. He was "very free in his reference to Russia and the Russian system." Its leaders "would enter the house by every open door and every open window, but when they found a door firmly shut in their faces, they would not seek to break it in, but would pass. They knew how far they could go, but they would try to go farther if not met with a firmly-drawn line of resistance" (Evans to Mackenzie, March 21, 1946, Box 4, Attlee papers).

44. Halifax to George VI, December 28, 1945, Halifax papers; Vandenberg, *Vandenberg Papers*, p. 231; Herter in Richard Gardner, *Sterling-Dollar Diplomacy*, p. 250. For the political problems, see Gardner's classic study, especially chapters 12 and 13. For Keynes, Dilks, *Cadogan Diaries*, p. 786.

45. Memorandum, Pepper-Wallace phone conversation, March 25, 1946, Wallace papers; Wallace speech, March 19, 1946, Schindler papers.

46. Davies diary, January 4, 1946, Box 17, Davies papers; Cohen to Byrnes, March 21, 1958, Box 922, Byrnes papers. For "persuasion" from within the State Department, see, for example, Henderson to Byrnes, January 3, 1946, Box 548, Byrnes papers.

47. United States Senate Special Committee Investigating Petroleum Resources, "American Petroleum Interests in Foreign Countries," p. 2. Also see ibid., pp. 23–25, 320, 438; the same committee's report on "Wartime Petroleum Policy," p. 11; Mark Lytle, "American-Iranian Relations 1941–47 and the Redefinition of National Security" (Ph.D. dissertation, Yale University, 1972); Stimson diary, June 11, 1943; Voskuil and Meyers, "Can United States Oil Reserves Meet the Postwar Demand?" in *American Interest in the War and the Peace;* Herbert Feis, *Petroleum and American Foreign Policy;* Feis, "The View from EA." For Forrestal, see "Oil in the Middle East," memorandum to the Secretary of State, September 3, 1945, Box 28, Byrnes-Forrestal telephone conversation, December 22, 1943, Box 28, Forrestal papers.

48. Henderson to Matthews, November 13, 1945, Box 1, Matthews file, State Department papers; *FR: 1946*, VII, p. 378; Lytle, "American-Iranian Relations," p. 29. In a paper advocating the construction of a U.S. military airfield in Saudi Arabia, the State-War-Navy Coordinating Committee declared in autumn 1945 that "U.S. reserves are rapidly diminishing; that at the present rate of exploitation and consumption our reserves are adequate for perhaps 12 to 15 years. Thus the world oil center of gravity is shifting to the Middle East where American enterprise has been entrusted with the exploitation of one of the greatest oil fields [in Saudi Arabia]. It is in our national interest to see that this vital resource remains in American hands, where it is most likely to be developed on a scale which will cause a considerable lessening of the drain upon the Western Hemisphere reserves." The report added: "Saudi Arabia possesses proved oil reserves that petroleum experts estimate at 5 billion barrels, or one fourth the reserves in the U.S." (SWNCC 19/20, September 20, 1945, CCS 381 Saudi-Arabia [2–7–45], Section 2, RG 218, Modern Military records.) It is interesting to note in the context of the "energy crisis" of the middle 1970s that Saudi reserves were conservatively estimated at around 180 billion barrels in 1977.

49. *FR: Yalta*, pp. 336–37; Lytle, "American-Iranian Relations," p. 5; Smith, *Three Years in Moscow*, p. 52.
50. Kolko, *Limits of Power*, p. 236; Lytle, "American-Iranian Relations", pp. 25, 55–56. It is instructive that in Senate hearings on petroleum, Senator Owen Brewster won an admission from General H. L. Peckham, liaison officer for petroleum in the War Department, that an American "hand" in Middle Eastern oil on a large scale would mean that "our whole military problem [is] radically transformed" and "our whole defense set-up will have to undergo pretty serious reorganization." Peckham, in turn, provided the military rationale for a "pre-emptive" move to gain concessions: "If we should lose our oil reserves in the Middle East, presumably they would then belong to someone else . . . if we had to depend on synthetics in this country while our enemies had access to the easy volume of oils that obviously are available in the Middle East, it would be to our great disadvantage" (Senate Special Committee, "American Petroleum Interests in Foreign Countries," pp. 45–46).
51. *FR: 1942*, IV, p. 242; Lytle, "American-Iranian Relations," pp. 51, 128, 132, 138–39.
52. Lytle, "American-Iranian Relations," pp.. 25, 124–45, 151; Jerrold L. Walden, "The International Petroleum Cartel in Iran," *Journal of Public Law* 2 (1962): 65; Elswell-Sutton, *Persian Oil*, pp. 108–11; Eden, *The Reckoning*, p. 515.
53. Young quoted in Lytle, "American-Iranian Relations," p. 84; digest of Coordinating Committee Report on American economic policy in the Middle East, May 10, 1945, Stettinius papers.
54. Richard Cottam, *Nationalism in Iran*, pp. 118–29. Writing from a traditional Cold War perspective, Cottam nevertheless points out: "Even strongly anti-Peshevari residents of Tabriz admitted that more improvements were made in the city of Tabriz in one year of Democratic rule than in the twenty years under Reza Shah. Because of these accomplishments, the regime attracted significant support from the populace. But the elements of the population that gave support were the very groups that understood politics the least — the peasants and illiterate laborers" (pp. 126–27). It might be added that they were also the ones who had the least stake in, and suffered the most from, the status quo. As regards Soviet interest, the remarks to State Department officials by Iran's ambassador to Washington after the crisis are illuminating. He underscored "the insistence of the Russians that they be accorded equal treatment in obtaining oil concession rights in Iran. He stated that the Russians repeatedly referred to the concession rights of the British in the South granted with full approval of the Majlis. The Russians complained bitterly of discrimination and that they had not been granted equal concession rights in the North." Memorandum of conversation with Hussein Ala, August 21, 1946, Box 3, Hickerson file, State Department papers.
55. *FR: 1945*, II, pp. 684–90, 750–52, 760, 774, 805–8; Byrnes, *Speaking Frankly*, pp. 117–21.
56. *FR: 1946*, VII, pp. 292–301, 304, 314–15.
57. Truman, *Year of Decisions*, pp. 551–52. For the State Department, see Lytle, "American-Iranian Relations," p. 248; *FR: 1946*, VII, pp. 289–90, 294; Russell to Miss Connor, Box 569, Byrnes papers; *Fortune*, January

1946, pp. 104, 235. In December, Dean Acheson had said that a long memorandum had been submitted to him advocating the sending "of a lot of missions" to Iran. "Some talk of oil, but one had to be careful about that." Acheson thought "the sending of missions would be bad business — the traditional instrument of imperialism, and other governments would be suspicious" (Acheson-Wallace telephone conversation, December 10, 1945, Wallace papers).

58. Vandenberg to Dulles, undated, Box 140, Dulles papers; Harriman, *Special Envoy*, p. 30. Dulles and Vandenberg tried to force the delegation to an open break with the Russians because of the latter's rejection of the American candidate for secretary-general, Lester Pearson of Canada — despite the fact that the Russians had already conceded on locating the United Nations in the United States and the further fact that Canada was politically very close to Britain and militarily tied to the United States. *FR: 1946*, I, pp. 175–79, 182. It should also be noted that both men were attuned to the oil issue. Dulles was representing American oil companies trying to get compensation in Eastern Europe, while Vandenberg was sitting on the Special Senate Subcommittee investigating oil resources. Allen Dulles to Steinhardt, January 11, 1946, Box 50, Steinhardt to J. F. Dulles, December 26, 1945, Box 83, Steinhardt papers.
59. *FR: 1946*, VII, pp. 315–16.
60. Harold Nicolson, *Diaries and Letters* 1945–62, pp. 48–49; Byrnes to Ethridge, January 29, 1946, Box 232, Byrnes papers; Millis, *Forrestal Diaries*, p. 132; Curry, *James Byrnes*, footnote 6 on pp. 365–66.
61. Harold Smith diary, conferences with the President, February 18, 28, March 20 (Appleby notes), 1946. Truman's mother in daily sheets, February 5, 1946, Box 83, President's secretary's file, Truman papers.
62. Joseph Jones, *The Fifteen Weeks*, p. 48; Leahy diary, February 21, 1946.
63. Davies diary, March 25, 1946; interview with Loy Henderson.
64. *Department of State Bulletin*, March 10, 1946, pp. 355–58; Hickerson to La Guardia, March 19, 1946, Box 5, Hickerson file, State Department papers. For another statement, see the Forrestal diary, April 5, 1946, p. 965.
65. Qavam continued to regard oil as the key point. On his return from Moscow he said "that from the viewpoint of practical politics understanding with the USSR on northern Iranian oil is long overdue" and admitted that it was hard to deny Soviet complaints that they were being discriminated against. Notwithstanding Byrnes' aforementioned command that concessions were not to be mentioned during the crisis, that topic kept bubbling to the surface both in the form of promises by Qavam and queries from the American embassy as to when the Iranian government would like to receive American company officials. Once again, Byrnes ordered the talks halted to avoid the appearance "that we have been influenced in our recent actions before the Security Council by selfish interest in Iranian petroleum" (*FR: 1946*, VII, pp. 371–74, 413).
66. Russian and American officials, as well as United Nations Secretary-General Trygve Lie, all noticed this peculiar, if useful, Iranian practice of using contradictory spokesmen. See Lytle, "American-Iranian Relations," pp. 284–89; Lie, *Cause of Peace*, pp. 76–78; *FR: 1946*, VII, pp. 356, 407. Other examples are in ibid., pp. 353, 377, 379, 389, 401.

67. *FR: 1946*, VII, pp. 335, 344; Truman, *Trial and Hope*, p. 94.
68. *FR: 1946*, VII, pp. 346–58; Harriman, *Special Envoy*, p. 350. The British analysis of the Iranian crisis narrowed to the question of oil. "The Cabinet should also consider the intentions of the Soviet Union," Bevin had told his colleagues on February 11, 1946. "Their attitude towards Turkey and Persia, their claims to former Italian Colonies in North Africa, and their attempt to secure the intervention of the Security Council in Greece all pointed to a desire to reduce British influence in the Mediterranean." However, on March 18, he said he had "some reason to believe that the explanation of recent Soviet activities in Persia was to be sought in their oil interests, rather than in a desire to acquire fresh territory or an outlet to warm-water ports." CAB 128/7, pp. 5–6, CAB, 128/5, pp. 121, Cabinet papers.
69. *FR: 1946*, VII, p. 352; Lytle, "American-Iranian Relations," pp. 290–91, 297. In late January 1946, Truman said that he thought Potsdam would go down in history as a "bad conference." Yet, he continued, "nothing more could have been done because [we] were confronted with so many accomplished facts before [we] started" (Ayers diary, January 24, 1946).
70. *FR: 1946*, VII, p. 365–67, 371, 378–79; Lie, *Cause of Peace*, pp. 30, 75.
71. *Truman Public Papers 1946*, pp. 163–64; *FR: 1946*, VII, pp. 369, 389; see ibid., pp. 390, 397, for examples of United States pressure. On March 28, Byrnes virtually insisted that the private Soviet-Iranian conversations should not proceed satisfactorily, for if they did, it would appear "that the United States is pressing the case of Iran for its own purposes."
72. Forrestal to Byrnes, April 5, 1946, Box 28, Forrestal papers. As it turned out, the Iranians delivered a further diplomatic defeat to the Russians. The Majlis never ratified the oil agreement, and the assurances given about Azerbaijan's autonomy were so vague as to amount to a Russian plea to be gentle — which Tehran was not when it invaded the province in the autumn, massacred "autonomists," and publicly hung their leaders. Werth, *Postwar Russia*, pp. 125–27. The American ambassador in Tehran realized at the end of the crisis that the United States might well have been used by Qavam, and might even have overreacted to the crisis. For on April 1, Murray cabled, "I realize that in broad picture mere presence Soviet troops in Iran constitutes form of duress. However, it may also be argued with some force that course of Qavam's negotiations to date in Moscow and Tehran demonstrates pressure on him is not overwhelming and that agreements which may be reached will have been result of give-and-take discussion by both sides" (*FR: 1946*, VII, p. 40). At one point, according to an official of the National Iranian Oil Company, oil was found in an area of Azerbaijan "but due to low permeability of the reservoir rocks and low recovery rate of the wells and considering the technical and economic conditions of that time this discovery was not considered of commercial nature and further exploratory activities were postponed for further study of the reservoir and other technical factors" (Abbas Ghaffari to author, January 22, 1974).
73. *FR: 1946*, VI, pp. 734–35; Smith, *Three Years in Moscow*, pp. 52–53. For Truman and Smith, Truman calendar notes, March 23, 1946, Box 269, President's secretary's file, Truman papers.
74. Murphy to Matthews, April 3, 1946, 861.00/4–346, Matthews to Murphy,

April 18, 1946, Matthews file, State Department papers; McNaughton file, April 20, 1946, McNaughton papers.

75. Byrnes at Paris in *FR: 1946*, II, p. 204; Leahy diary, March 13, 18, 1946; Vandenberg to Dulles, undated, Box 140, Dulles papers; Truman notation on February 28 speech, Box 626, Byrnes papers.

VIII. The Gospel of National Security

1. Salisbury, cited in Bernard Brodie, *War and Politics*, p. 356; *Larousse Modern Dictionary*.
2. Stimson to Roosevelt, October 21, 1941, Stimson papers; Stimson diary, December 17, 1941.
3. The amount of literature that invokes "national security" is vast; the amount that critically explores the concept is in short supply. For three discussions, see Bernard Brodie, *War and Politics*, pp. 341–64; Arnold Wolfers, "National Security as an Ambiguous Symbol," *Discord and Collaboration*, pp. 147–65; and (briefly) Adam Yarmolinsky, *The Military Establishment*, pp. 93–95.
4. U.S. Congress, Senate, Committee on Military Affairs, *Department of Armed Forces, Department of Military Security, Hearings on S.84 and S.1482*, 79th Cong., 1st sess. 1945, pp. 98–99, 117, 755. Compare U.S. Congress, House of Representatives, Select Committee on Post-War Military Policy, *Proposal to Establish a Single Department of Armed Forces*, 78th Cong., 2nd sess., 1944.
5. John Hamilton, ed., *The Federalist* (number 41), pp. 62–69, 319. See Joseph Johnson, "American Security and World Security," in Willcox and Hall, eds., *The United States in the Postwar World*, p. 281; Richard Current, "The United States and Collective Security," in DeConde, ed., *Isolation and Security*, pp. 33–35. In the late 18th century, Yale undergraduates debated the question, "Does the National Security Depend on Fostering Domestic Industries?" (W. W. Rostow, *How It All Began*, pp. 191–92). In the early 1930s, Charles Beard decided to explore the meaning of "national interest" because of what he saw as the increasing, even overwhelming, use of that term. Examining it from a Marxian perspective, he concluded that it was, in one form or another, a conception for promoting territorial American expansion and exports and that it signified not general interests but "particular" interests. His is an interesting though inadequate interpretation. Charles Beard, *The Idea of National Interest*, vol. 4, 21–23, 29, 141–44, 167, 310, 331–45. Still, Beard shows national interest playing the role of Commanding Idea, similar to that which I suggest for "national security" after 1945: "Since the foundation of the Republic, statesmen and publicists have written and spoken of national interest as if it were a kind of transcendent unity . . . They have treated it as a postulate which automatically provides rules for controlling policies and actions in foreign affairs, in general and in particular. Judging from their assertions and usages, the advancement of national interest is a binding obligation on American statesmen — the supreme obligation, with other considerations employed occasionally as features of policy" (ibid., p. 548).
6. Felix Gilbert to author, March 15, 1976; Harold Sprout to author, No-

vember 29, 1973. For Edward Mead Earle, "national security" in 1940 still summoned up the old "fortress" — "isolation, neutrality, the Monroe Doctrine, sea power, supremacy in the Caribbean, and interdiction of transfers of American territory in favor of a European or Asiatic power." Earle, "National Security and Foreign Policy," *Yale Review* 29 (March 1940): 458. A year later, in March 1941, Earle had concluded, along with many others, that the independence of Great Britain and the maintenance of its sea power and empire had also become stakes in American national security. He stressed that "without reference to moral considerations," national security called for "a vital concern in the existence of an ordered world." Earle, "The Threat to American Security," *Yale Review* 30 (March 1941): 473–76. Also see Earle, "American Security: Its Changing Condition," in *Annals of American Academy of Political and Social Science* 218 (November 1941): 193. Also influential were another group of scholars, these around the Yale Institute of International Studies. The most important were Arnold Wolfers, especially his *Britain and France between the World Wars*, and Nicholas Spykman, customarily known as a "geopolitician," and author of *America's Strategy in World Politics*.

7. Walter Lippmann, *U.S. Foreign Policy: Shield of the Republic*, pp. 35–36, 106; Joseph E. Johnson, "American Security and World Security," in Willcox and Hall, *The United States in the Postwar World*, p. 281; *Life*, September 17, 1945, p. 10; Allan W. Betts, "Industrial Demobilization Problems in the Army Air Force," Lecture, Army Industrial College, October 22, 1945, Baldwin papers.
8. For a preliminary discussion of the role of the "Commanding Idea" in American foreign policy, see Michael Mandelbaum and Daniel Yergin, "Balancing the Power," *Yale Review* 62 (Spring 1973): 321–31.
9. Arnold Wolfers, *Discord and Collaboration*, pp. 151–52. In an important and insightful article that questions the legal utility of "national security," Robert Post argues that the term is a matter of subjective determination: "Although political rhetoric often invokes national security as if it were a 'fact' beyond the control of policymakers, national security is dictated by policy rather than the reverse. It is not possible to supply national security with a content, military or otherwise, that is distinct from a political determination of foreign policy goals." Robert C. Post, "National Security and the Amended Freedom of Information Act," *Yale Law Journal* 85 (January 1976): 412–13. National security, however, can be specified as a "fact" insofar as it relates to core values that obviously and directly are threatened.
10. For the prewar conventions, see Samuel Huntington, *The Common Defense*, pp. 13–14, 26, 427; Armstrong, in Eighth International Study Conference on Collective Security, Meeting 4/4a, Liddell Hart papers; McCloy, War Council minutes, November 7, 1945, Box 23, Patterson papers.
11. Junior officials also regarded the 1930s as a central education in international affairs. As a young professor at Mills College in California, Dean Rusk devoted much effort in those years to a study of the Manchurian incident, motivated by "the instinctive feeling that it was much more significant than most people realized" (interview with Dean Rusk). "I

did not publish on the Manchurian incident even though I spent an enormous amount of time in informing myself about it. I have always taken the view that one does not have to cut down trees in order to publish an article on every subject in which one is interested" (Dean Rusk to author, December 5, 1973). In an article he did publish, Rusk suggested that the advent of dictatorships made cooperation in international affairs more likely. Dean Rusk, "Some Effects of Dictatorship on the Prospects for International Cooperation," *Proceedings of the Institute of World Affairs* 12 (December 1934): 188–93.

12. Harriman, in *FR: 1944*, IV, p. 993; Kennan in Wright, "Mr. 'X' and Containment," *Slavic Review* 35 (March 1976): 22; Roosevelt, in Forrest Pogue, *Education of a General*, pp. 335, 344. The unheeded US diplomat George Messersmith cited by Arnold Offner, in *American Appeasement*, p. 272.
13. Ferdinand Eberstadt, "Mobilization of War Potential," Lecture, Washington, D.C., October 8, 1946; Forrestal speech, March 23, 1946, Box 30, Forrestal papers.
14. Albion and Connery, *Forrestal and the Navy*, p. 287; Harold and Margaret Sprout, eds., *Foundations of National Power*, p. 668.
15. Anglo-Soviet political conversations, October 9–17, 1944, pp. 44–45, VI/10, Ismay papers. Stalin's "objective law" later became a subject of contention during the destalinization debates. See Thomas Wolfe, *Soviet Power and Europe*, pp. 60–61.
16. Ismay in III/7/12/4, Ismay papers.
17. Indeed, so classic a bureaucratic battle that the literature on it is large. Some important sources: Lawrence J. Legere, Jr., "Unification of the Armed Forces" (Ph.D. dissertation, Harvard University, 1951); Demetrios Caraley, *The Politics of Military Unifications;* Vincent Davis, *Postwar Defense Policy and the U.S. Navy, 1943–46*. In part: Paul Y. Hammond, *Organizing for Defense*, and Samuel P. Huntington, *The Common Defense*.
18. Caraley, *Military Unification*, chapters 3 and 4; Smith, *Air Force Plans*, p. 15. The adviser is Bruce Hopper to Spaatz, September 24, 1945, Box 20, Spaatz papers.
19. Legere, "Unification of the Armed Forces," pp. 235–53; Smith, *Air Force Plans*, p. 2; Davis, *Postwar Defense Policy*, pp. 37, 84–86, 99; Stimson diary, May 2, 1944; Millis, *Forrestal Diaries*, p. 60. For the Pentagon's floor plan, see Stimson diary, November 22, 1942.
20. Smith, *Air Force Plans*, pp. 35–38, 75–83, 105–7.
21. "US Post-War Aviation Aims in Europe," December 22, 1944, Box 58, Spaatz papers. The reasons proffered for the bases included military reasons, "important psychological advantages in encircling Germany" to impress upon the Germans that the United Nations "still united in contributing to the enforcement of peace in Europe," and as part of an American contribution to an international air police force.
22. Lovett to Spaatz, April 22, 1945, Spaatz papers; notes on European trip, May 10, 1945, vol. 5, Box 26, Patterson papers. The historian is David MacIsaac, "The United States Strategic Bombing Survey, 1944–47," (Ph.D. dissertation, Duke University, 1969), p. 182. MacIsaac points out that the press generally accepted the Air Force interpretation of the effectiveness of strategic bombing. Ibid., pp. 210–11. Strategic bombing

meant bombing operations conducted independently of other operations against the sustaining resources (primarily industrial) of an enemy's war capability. For an Air Force statement on strategic bombing, see Carl Spaatz, "Strategic Air Power," *Foreign Affairs*, April 1946, p. 388. The ideas of Guilio Douhet, the first coherent theorist of strategic bombing, were incorporated into the training of American air officers in the early 1920s. By the mid-1930s, the necessary technology existed, in the form of the experimental B-17, and by the end of the decade, the theory was well worked out, with an emphasis on target selection. MacIsaacs, "Strategic Bombing Survey," pp. 9–15; Smith, *Air Force Plans*, pp. 8, 28–29.

23. Lovett to Spaatz, April 22, 1945, Spaatz papers; Norstad, in Smith, *Air Force Plans*, p. 70; Forrestal, in Senate Military Affairs Committee, *Department of the Armed Forces*, p. 108.
24. Arnold Rogow, *Victim of Duty*, pp. 52, 57, 230–31. Rogow's work is a psychoanalytically oriented biography, rich in the recollections of Forrestal friends, at times penetrating in its insights, at other times simply overdrawn.
25. Rogow, *Victim of Duty*, pp. 60, 49, 79–80.
26. Ibid., p. 117; Forrestal diary, April 19, 1946, p. 1013.
27. Interview with Dean Rusk.
28. De Gaulle in Rogow, *Victim of Duty*, pp. 139–40; Harriman, *Special Envoy*, p. 293; Jonathan Daniels, *Frontier on the Potomac*, p. 223; war "over the horizon," Forrestal diary, May 15, 1946, p. 1063.
29. Rogow, *Victim of Duty*, p. 289.
30. Ibid., p. 228; Hanson Baldwin, "Big Boss of the Pentagon," *New York Times Magazine*, August 29, 1948; John L. Sullivan oral history, pp. 54–55. For the Cabinet, Anderson, *Outsider*, p. 80. For the events of March 29, Marx Leva oral history, pp. 42–47.
31. Rogow, *Victim of Duty*, p. 228; Millis, *Forrestal Diaries*, pp. 554–55. For Louis Johnson, Marx Leva oral history, pp. 47–48.
32. Anderson, *Outsider*, pp. 79–80.
33. Vincent Davis, *Postwar Defense Policy*, pp. 114–16, 149–50.
34. Two generally provocative studies, Vincent Davis' *Postwar Defense Policy and the U.S. Navy* and Perry McCoy Smith's *Air Force Plans for Peace*, suggest — incorrectly in my view — that the internal political imperative was a stronger factor than genuine perception of danger. The reason for that might be that the former factor seems more "rational" than the latter, given what we know today about the postwar condition of the Soviet Union. Smith, however, does point out that there may have been a considerable divergence between the views of Air Force planners and those of their senior officials (*Air Force Plans*, p. 110).
35. Smith, *Air Force Plans*, pp. 37, 44–45, 48, 105. The strategic bombing doctrine tended to make air officers discount the Soviet Union as a threat because technically it seemed far from possessing a strategic capability, and to discount it as a target because its large land mass and dispersed industry did not provide convenient targets. Ibid., pp. 52–53.
36. Ibid., pp. 69, 81.
37. Spaatz memorandum, October 11, 1945, Box 22, Spaatz papers. Snyder in Ayers diary, August 24, 1945.
38. Weil, "American Military and the Cold War," pp. 269–70; Senate Com-

mittee on Military Affairs, *Department of Armed Services*, pp. 291–92. Doolittle explained why the traditional notion of "defense" had to be retired. The lesson "comes from the late sage of South Bend, Ind.—'The only defense is a sound attack.' Much thinking about that word 'defense' has been foggy . . . Politically we are a defensive nation, but militarily we can never be."

39. Intelligence analysis, to General George McDonald, November 12, 1946, Box 21, Spaatz papers: "The USSR will remain predominantly a land power. The traditional conception of the [Red] Army as the only sure shield in defense and the only fully effective weapon in the attack will persist in the future." The Soviet Air Force "will remain essentially 'tactical' in design."
40. Smith, *Air Force Plans*, p. 94; Joint Chiefs memorandum attached to Hickerson letter to Johnson, October 9, 1944, Box 5, Hickerson file, State Department papers; *FR: Potsdam*, II, pp. 1420–22.
41. Patton to Stimson, September 1, 1945, Stimson papers. Patton boasted that his tanks could be in Moscow in thirty days — better than "waiting for the Russians to attack the United States when we were weak and reduced to two divisions" (Murphy, *Diplomat*, pp. 329–30).
42. Stimson diary, September 7, 1944; Weil, "American Military and the Cold War," pp. 300–303.
43. Interview with Averell Harriman, Dulles oral history; Weil, "American Military and the Cold War," pp. 290–91. For Eisenhower's concern, Eisenhower to Thompson, August 8, 1945, Box 107, Eisenhower papers.
44. "Valedictory" mentioned in Heath to Riddleberger, November 25, 1946, 861.5048/11–2546, State Department papers; War Council minutes, December 3, 1945, Box 23, Patterson papers; also see Eisenhower to Zhukov, December 6, 1945, Box 118, Eisenhower papers; and Mark Clark to Eisenhower, December 6, 1945, Box 6, Clark papers.
45. Wedemeyer reported his conclusion in November 1945, that the Russian leaders were more concerned with national development and security than "campaigning for Communization" (Forrestal diary, November 23, 1945, p. 656).
46. Murphy to Matthews, April 3, 1946, 861.00/4–346, Matthews to Murphy, April 18, 1946, Matthews file, State Department papers.
47. Interviews with Myron Gilmore and Elting Morison; Eberstadt to Forrestal, April 18, 1945, Box 62, Forrestal papers. In his letters to such prominent people as Baruch and Dulles, soliciting their opinions, Eberstadt singled out Russia as the key consideration in shaping the postwar military establishment. Eberstadt to Baruch, August 20, 1945, Box 69, Baruch papers.
48. U.S. Congress, Senate, Committee on Naval Affairs, *Unification of the War and Navy Departments and Postwar Organization for National Security, Report to Hon. James Forrestal, Secretary of the Navy*, 79th Cong., 1st sess., 1945, pp. 1, 3–6 (Eberstadt Report).
49. Ibid., p. 42. A member of the Eberstadt Report Staff recollected that Lippmann's book and the writings of Edward Mead Earle were among the more important influences. Interview with Myron Gilmore.
50. Eberstadt Report, pp. 6–14, 16–18, 37, 21, 150–52, 163, 181.
51. Lovett, in War Council minutes, November 7, 1945, Box 23, Patterson papers; Cornwall Jones to Ismay, December 3, 1945, Ismay to Smith,

December 18, 1945, Ismay papers. "The Eberstadt proposals were bound to be unsuitable," Budget Director Harold Smith wrote to Truman on May 22, 1946. "They would bring about the most drastic changes in the top structure of the Government — affecting the President personally — that have occurred in many years. Yet they were developed not from the President's viewpoint but by and for the Secretary of one of the military departments." In particular, he warned against a Council of Common Defense that would divest "the President of authority and responsibility which he cannot lose and still be President under our form of Government. Beyond that, it gives the military an undue control, in effect a veto power, over foreign policy" (Box 145, President's secretary's file, Truman papers).

52. *Vital Speeches*, 12 (1945–46): 169; War Council minutes, December 19, 1945, Box 23, Patterson papers.
53. Harold Smith diary, December 19, 1945, February 28, March 20, 1946. "It looks to me as if the suggestions for the navy are large," Truman observed, after reviewing the Navy's proposed budget for fiscal year 1947. "If my estimates are correct this would require an almost impossible budget" (Truman to Harold Smith, November 27, 1945, Box 145, President's secretary's file, Truman papers).
54. Hoyt Vandenberg, "Central Intelligence Group and Its Mission," Lecture, Washington, D.C., April 1947; Sherman Kent, "Strategic Intelligence," Lecture, Washington, D.C., January 1947 (also for military attaché). Roberta Wohlstetter, in *Pearl Harbor: Warning and Decision*, analyzes the failure to extract the correct "signals" or clues from the background "noise" prior to Pearl Harbor. For the OSS, Arnold to Secretary, Joint Chiefs, September 5, 1945, CCS 385, Sec. 2, Pt. 10, RG 218, Modern Military records; R. Harris Smith, *OSS:* Harry Howe Ransom, *The Intelligence Establishment*, pp. 56–76.
55. Harold Smith diary, January 9, 1946. For the White House ceremony and ITT, Leahy diary, January 24, February 7, 1946; Ayers diary, January, 24, 1946. For the bureaucratic struggle to control postwar intelligence, see Acheson, *Present at the Creation*, and U.S. Congress, Senate, Select Committee to Study Governmental Operations with Respect to Intelligence Activities, *Final Report: Supplementary Detailed Staff Reports on Foreign and Military Intelligence, Book IV*, 94th Cong., 2nd sess., 1975, pp. 6–9, 13–14.
56. Ibid., pp. 9–11, 13–15. General Vandenberg stated in 1947 that 26 different U.S. government organizations furnished intelligence information in Washington, D.C. "Central Intelligence Group," Lecture, Washington, D.C., April 1947.
57. Harold Smith diary, February 28, 1946; Forrestal comments on Willett's December 21, 1945, outline, Edward F. Willett, "Dialectical Materialism and Russian Objectives," January 14, 1946, pp. 37–38, Box 17, notecards for Commerce and Industry Association speech, February 25, 1946, Box 19, Forrestal papers; Salisbury, in Brodie, *War and Politics*, p. 356; Forrestal to Truman, November 3, 1945, Box 45, Forrestal papers.
58. Millis, *Forrestal Diaries*, pp. 141, 149–50; Forrestal diary, March 21, 22, 1944, pp. 941–44; Rogow, *Victim of Duty*, p. 159; Davis, *Postwar Defense Policy*, p. 224.
59. Lovett, in Weil, "American Military," p. 227; Patterson to Forrestal,

March 11, 1946, vol. 6, Box 27, Patterson papers; Patterson to Stimson, April 22, 1946, Stimson papers.

60. *FR: 1946*, VI, p. 733; Smith, *Three Years in Moscow*, p. 51.

IX. Casting the Die: The Anticommunist Consensus

1. Dulles quoted in Herken, "Atomic Bomb," p. ii; Bohlen, *FR: 1946*, II, pp. 146–47; Thompson to Lane, June 26, 1946, Box 25, Lane papers.
2. Harriman quoted in Sulzberger, *Long Row of Candles*, p. 311; Dulles, in Herken, "Atomic Bomb," p. ii; Fulbright, in Yergin, "Fulbright's Last Frustration," *New York Times Magazine*, November 24, 1974, p. 14; Harold Smith diary, May 2, 1946. On May 30, 1946, Robert Kelley, the "father" of the Riga School, wrote to Laurence Steinhardt, "Byrnes, despite his work in Paris, has not apparently won the confidence of the powers-that-be" (Box 50, Steinhardt papers). Interview with Benjamin Cohen, for State Department opposition to negotiating satellite treaties. One can almost concretely see the closing of the image of the Soviet Union held in the mind of State Department officials in the words of an internal State Department policy memorandum: "To prove definitely whether the Soviets have already decided on a policy of aggrandizement is not simple, for they have evolved many methods of disguised penetration and control . . . Within the past few months, Soviet influence or control has expanded to many areas . . . It is not entirely clear whether these are the limits of Soviet ambitions, based in large part on Soviet estimates of USSR's alleged security requirements, or whether, as unfortunately seems more likely, the Soviets have embarked on a policy of aggrandizement which will be contained only by the limitations of Soviet power or eventually by armed resistance on the part of other major power . . . The interests of the United States do not permit of a policy of uncertainty toward the Soviet Union in the face of such tactics." (Department of State, "USSR: Policy and Information Statement," May 15, 1946, Box 15, Clifford papers).
3. Lord Gladwyn, *Memoirs*, p. 193; Byrnes was embarrassed. See Blum, *Wallace Diary*, p. 585. "We can't plot permanent peace," Ben Cohen said on May 12. "What we would like to do is try and insure a sort of armistice or temporary peace for twenty-five years in the hopes the situation would ease during that time and a new generation would continue the peace with a new plan" (Sulzberger, *Long Row*, p. 313). While Byrnes respected and relied upon Cohen, he realized that Cohen had no political influence in such crucial chambers as that of the United States Senate.
4. Vandenberg to Dulles, May 13, 1946, Box 140, Dulles papers; Vandenberg to Luce, May 28, 1946, Vandenberg papers.
5. Bevin to Byrnes, May 16, 1946, Box 2, Matthews file, State Department papers; Vandenberg, *Private Papers*, p. 293; Curry, *James Byrnes*, pp. 210–24; for *Time*, Laguerre file, May 18, 1946, McNaughton papers.
6. Dixon, *Double Diploma*, pp. 212–13; Vandenberg, *Private Papers*, pp. 292–98; Curry, *James Byrnes*, pp. 225–32. For the bar, Laguerre file, May 18, 1946, McNaughton papers.

7. *FR: 1946*, II, p. 204.
8. *FR: 1945*, II, pp. 267–68; Byrnes to Childs, June 12, 1946, Box 249, Byrnes papers; interview with Benjamin Cohen.
9. Interview with James Riddleberger; Davies diary, September 13, 1946; *FR: 1946*, II, pp. 62, 83.
10. On Iran, Molotov criticized the American refusal to postpone consideration until April 10. The Americans could only shake their heads in amazement. "The observations of Molotov and Vyshinsky again reveal the Soviet thesis that the relations between the great powers were more important than the strict observation of the Charter," commented Bohlen in the dinner notes, "and that their actions and policies in effect were outside the jurisdiction of the Security Council" (*FR: 1946*, VII, p. 442).
11. *FR: 1946*, II, pp. 146–47, 173, 432; Curry, *James Byrnes*, p. 224.
12. Mowrer to Pollock, June 4, 1946, Pollock papers.
13. Murphy, *Diplomat*, p. 317; McCloy to Hilldring et al., October 10, 1945, Eisenhower papers; James Pollock diary, August 15, September 20, October 6, October 13, November 26, December 14, 1945, January 1, 1946. That Soviet-American relations *within* Germany were good in the first year of occupation is recalled in William Draper oral history, pp. 37–38, 47.
14. Pollock diary, March 8, 1946. At the Control Council meeting on that date, Pollock observed, "General Sokolovsky turned to Clay whenever he got into a hole."
15. *FR: 1946*, V, pp. 506–8; Matthews to Acheson, April 3, 1946, Box 2, Matthews file, State Department papers; for the differences between War and State, John Gimbel, "On the Implementation of the Potsdam Agreement," *Political Science Quarterly* 87 (June 1972): 250–58.
16. *FR: 1946*, V, pp. 517–19, 536; W. B. Smith to Secretary of State, May 25, 1946, 861.00/5–2546, State Department papers.
17. In April and May, American efforts to obtain a base in Iceland had been frustrated when the issue broke on front pages and stirred a political storm in Iceland. When Molotov brought up the issue in Paris, Byrnes ingenuously claimed that little more than a petrol station was contemplated. (*FR: 1946*, II, p. 248). However, Budget Director Harold Smith noted in his diary on May 2, 1946, that the President had angrily stated that Senator Claude Pepper "had made a speech which bitched up the agreements in connection with bases in Iceland."
18. Nove, *An Economic History of the USSR*, p. 296; J. P. Nettl, *The Eastern Zone and Soviet Policy*, pp. 185, 201, 205, 231, 295, 304, 310; Murphy to Matthews, June 17, 1946, Matthews file, State Department papers. Clay in Kindleberger to de Wilde, August 3, 1946, Kindleberger papers. The rivalries among Soviet bureaucracies and within Stalin's court are suggested, though not in detail, by Vladimir Rudolph, "The Execution of Policy 1945–47," in *Soviet Economic Policy in Postwar Germany*, Robert Slusser, ed., pp. 41–56. For the Soviet view of reparations as a major part of the "disarmament" of Germany, see, for instance, I. Faingar, "Economic Disarmament of Germany and the Reparations Question," *Mirovoe Khoziaistvo i Mirovaia Politika* (1946, Numbers 7–8): 12–29.
19. Manuel Gottlieb, *The German Peace Settlement and the Berlin Crisis*, pp. 148–55; Murphy to Matthews, June 17, 1946, Matthews file, State

Department papers; Gimbel, *American Occupation of Germany*, p. 26. For the figures on German industry, see J. K. Galbraith, "Is There a German Policy?" *Fortune*, January 1947. Galbraith was director of the Overall Economic Effects Division of the United States Strategic Bombing Survey. Also see United States Strategic Bombing Survey, *The Effects of Strategic Bombing on the German War Economy* (Report 3), pp. 51, 230 (table 37). For the fear of assisting the Soviet military establishment, see Murphy to Eisenhower, Clay, Smith, September 3, 1945, Eisenhower papers.

20. Millis, *Forrestal Diaries*, p. 172; *FR: 1946*, II, pp. 486–88. For State Department efforts to bring the War Department around to its point of view, see Smith, *Clay Papers*, vol. 1, pp. 110–11; John Gimbel, "On the Implementation of the Potsdam Agreement," *Political Science Quarterly* 87 (June 1972): 251–54, 262–63.

21. Lucius Clay, *Decision in Germany*, pp. 122, 132; B. U. Ratchford and W. D. Ross, *Berlin Reparations Assignment*, pp. 193–94. Charles Kindleberger recalls his own astonishment at Clay's move on reparations in letter to author, August 31, 1976. For the French orientation, see Gimbel, *American Occupation*, pp. 57–61. Writing long before archives were opened, William Hardy McNeill, like many other writers, mistakenly described Clay's move as primarily aimed at the Soviet Union. *America, Britain, and Russia*, pp. 652, 725–26. Subsequent evidence has supported Gimbel's position, as opposed to that of such critics as Thomas Paterson (*Soviet-American Confrontation*, p. 254), who have attributed State Department views to Clay at a time when he was clearly something of a dissenter, or at least a hold-out. Kindleberger, then director of the Division of German-Austrian Affairs in the State Department, made clear the differences between Clay and State in a letter from Berlin to J. K. Galbraith and Edward Mason: "Clay is running a German show; the State Dept tries to tell him from time to time to pay attention to the consequences on third countries. Especially has this been true in France where our policy has been to baby the government along, because of fear of Communist capitalizing on our toughness, while the French have stabbed our German policy in the back. Our failure to resolve the Ruhr-Rhineland last fall is still bitterly resented here (and in the War Department). When we applied the pressure, it was too late, and we failed to carry through on our threats to link the French policy on Germany to the loan, because the loan went to buy elections. On a number of things — restitution, reparation, international waterways, DPs, division of scarce goods between German consumption and export, German policy is also third country policy. Clay would be willing to agree wholly, however, with the proposition that German policy is Russian policy, though he might not be willing to go as far as Joseph Alsop who says that the only foreign policy is Russian foreign policy, and it must be dealt with simultaneously now in Germany, the Middle East, and China and ultimately, if we lose any of these, in Latin America, Africa, and the Far East as a whole. I sent a telegram shortly after my arrival here urging the necessity of distinguishing between US foreign policy on Germany as such, and US foreign policy through Germany elsewhere. I am more than ever convinced of the necessity to make the

distinction; I am still at a loss as to how to do it" (August 13, 1946, Kindleberger papers).

22. Pollock diary, May 13, 22, June 2, 1946; Clay, *Decision*, pp. 76–78; Rostow quoted in Gimbel, *Marshall Plan*, pp. 136–37.
23. Clay, *Decision*, pp. 130–31; Curry, *James Byrnes*, pp. 234–35, interviews with James Riddleberger and Benjamin Cohen; Kindleberger to deWilde, August 3, 1946 (letter one), Kindleberger papers. For the British, CAB 128/7, p. 16, Cabinet papers.
24. Clay to Joseph Dodge, July 31, 1946, Dodge papers; Kindleberger to de Wilde, August 3, 1946 (letter two for Clay on reparations), Kindleberger papers; for reply to Eisenhower, Smith, *Clay*, vol. 2, pp. 243–44. The retroactive claim that Clay at this time saw USSR as primary problem in Germany is also belied by notes made by James Forrestal in July when he descended on Berlin in the course of a round-the-world trip. "Talking from his own experience and contacts with the Russian military," Clay said that "the Russians did not want a war" and "we should find it possible to get along with them." Forrestal could not shake Clay's opinion even by citing Stalin's February 1946 election speech and what he saw as its message — that "the world revolution was still on" (entry on world trip, July 16, 1946, Box 69, Forrestal papers). Clay to Joseph Dodge on July 25, 1946, "While I appreciate the great difficulties involved in working with the Russians, I still refuse to be a pessimist and I am apprehensive that the old 'red scare' is receiving too much emphasis at home these days" (Dodge papers).
25. Interview with Benjamin Cohen; Curry, *James Byrnes*, pp. 248–49; Clay, *Decision*, pp. 78–80; *Department of State Bulletin*, September 15, 1946, p. 496; for the letter to Snyder, see Gimbel, "Implementation of Potsdam Agreement," *Political Science Quarterly* 87 (June 1972): 248; Byrnes to Truman, September 2, 1946, Box 52, President's secretary's file, Truman papers.
26. Byrnes, *Speaking Frankly*, p. 194; Curry, *James Byrnes*, pp. 236–37.
27. Byrnes to Ball, July 22, 1946, Box 225, Byrnes papers; Harold Nicolson, *Diaries and Letters 1945–62*, pp. 65–73; Sulzberger, *Long Row*, p. 316.
28. *FR: 1946*, VII, pp. 827–36; Anglo-Soviet political conversations, October 9, 17, 1944, pp. 6–7, 42, VI/10, Ismay papers.
29. *FR: Potsdam*, II, pp. 1015, 1422, 1496–97; *USSR: Tehran, Yalta and Potsdam Conferences*, p. 340; *FR: 1946*, VII, p. 837.
30. Forrestal diary, August 14, 1946, p. 1202; Millis, *Forrestal Diaries*, p. 193.
31. *FR: 1946*, VII, pp. 840–47, 857–58; Millis, *Forrestal Diaries*, p. 192; Jones, *Fifteen Weeks*, pp. 62–63; Acheson, *Present at the Creation*, pp. 261–65.
32. Forrestal diary, August 21, 1946, pp. 1217–18. The Yugoslavs had protested several times over violation of their air space and, in the context of continuing tension over Trieste, claimed to have evidence of hundreds of such violations (Dedijer, *Tito Speaks*, pp. 259–61). The British, worried that the United States was preparing for war, recommended direct Turkish-Soviet talks, a course the Turks did not want to follow. The secretary-general of the Turkish Foreign Office assured the American ambassador that Soviet agents were "spreading stories in cof-

fee houses that difficulties between Turkey and Russia could easily be arranged by direct conversations" (*FR: 1946*, VII, pp. 849, 879).

33. *FR: 1946*, VII, pp. 894–98. Some policymakers had always believed events would move in this direction. Russia's "determined economic infiltration" in Hungary, John McCloy had cabled from Europe in October 1945, "emphasizes again the supreme importance of the economic element in the whole picture. The political is even less important for without the former there is nothing on which to build politically" (McCloy to Hilldring et al., October 10, 1945, Eisenhower papers).

34. *FR: 1946*, V, p. 422; Forrestal diary, April 19, 1946, p. 1020. Clayton claimed, in the face of criticism, that the economic grounds for the loan were sufficient, but admitted he "had great difficulty in separating political from economic considerations in thinking about Europe" (*FR: 1946*, I, p. 1426; V, pp. 432, 443–45).

35. Kolko, *Limits of Power*, pp. 160–62; *FR: 1946*, I, pp. 1435, 1446–47. For export controls see Secretaries of War and Navy to the chairman of the State-War-Navy Coordinating Committee, June 26, 1946, CCS, 091.31 (9/28/45), Section 1, RG 218, Modern Military records.

36. *FR: 1946*, VI, pp. 216–17, 225, 235–36; VII, pp. 223–24; Byrnes, *Speaking Frankly*, pp. 143–44; interview with Benjamin Cohen. For reaction of a noncommunist Czech, see Hubert Ripka, *Czechoslovakia Enslaved*, p. 49.

37. Lilienthal, *Atomic Energy Years*, pp. 30, 55, 59, 43; Margaret Coit, *Mr. Baruch*, pp. 567, 572, 576; Baruch, *The Public Years*, p. 367; Baruch memorandum to D. F. Fleming, July 10, 1946, Box 62, Baruch papers. For insistence on sanctions, see memorandum of June 7, 1946, meeting with Byrnes and Truman, Baruch papers. For Baruch's "boom" and attitudes on monopoly, see Herken, "Atomic Bomb," pp. 302, 312. For concern about loss of private control of uranium mines, see ibid., pp. 309, 311, 316, 325–26, and John Hancock, "U.S. Plan for Control of Atomic Energy," Lecture, National War College, September 13, 1946, pp. 8–9, Baruch papers.

38. Eberstadt to Baruch, May 23, 1946, Baruch to Joint Chiefs of Staff, May 23, 1946, Eisenhower to Baruch, June 14, 1946, Box 52, Baruch papers. Also see Spaatz to Baruch, undated, Box 52, Baruch papers.

39. Hancock memorandum, July 29, 1946, Box 52, Baruch papers; Lilienthal, *Atomic Energy*, p. 123; *FR: 1946*, I, p. 965; Joseph Lieberman, *The Scorpion and the Tarantula*, p. 274.

40. For the "hidden veto," Lloyd Gardner, *Architects*, p. 193; Lieberman, *Scorpion*, p. 328.

41. *FR: 1945*, II, p. 82–84; Coit, *Mr. Baruch*, p. 572; the scholar is Luard, *Peace and Opinion*, pp. 8–9. On the incompatibility of approaches, see Baruch to Truman, July 2, 1946, Baruch papers. For a discussion of the "leap of faith" the Americans were asking the Russians to make, see Herken, "Atomic Bomb," pp. 350, 331.

42. Hancock memorandum, July 29, 1946, Box 52, Baruch memorandum to Fleming, July 10, 1946, Box 62, Baruch papers; *FR: 1946*, I, p. 805. See Lilienthal, *Atomic Energy*, pp. 43, 49, 69.

43. Notes on conference with General McNaughton and Mr. Ignatieff, August 1, 1946, Box 52, general staff meeting, August 23, 1946, Baruch

papers; Coit, *Baruch*, p. 595; Lieberman, *Scorpion*, pp. 338–44; John Hancock, "U.S. Plan for Control of Atomic Energy," Lecture, National War College, September 13, 1946, p. 21, Baruch papers. For Eberstadt, see Eberstadt to Baruch, September 13, 1946, Baruch papers, and Herken, "Atomic Bomb," p. 400.

44. Gardner, *Architects*, p. 173; *FR: 1946*, I, pp. 1017–19, 1103–4; Herken, "Atomic Bomb," p. 350. For Britain's unsuccessful drive to maintain postwar atomic collaboration, see Margaret Gowing, *Independence and Deterrence.*

45. Clifford letters to Secretary of State and others, July 18, 1946, Clifford papers; Elsey notes, July 18, 1946, Box 63, "L'Affaire Wallace," September 17, 1946, Elsey papers. Initially, Truman asked Clifford merely to prepare a comprehensive list of agreements broken by the Soviet Union. George Elsey oral history, p. 263. Truman quote from David Lilienthal, *Atomic Energy Years*, p. 434.

46. James Forrestal to the President, July 25, 1946, with memorandum from C. W. Nimitz, "Discussion of Recent Activities of the Soviet Union," July 23, 1946, Box 15, Clifford papers.

47. Robert Patterson to the President, July 27, 1946; "Estimate of Soviet Policy Relating to the Soviet Army and Air Force"; "Excerpt from a Discussion of Recent Activities of the Soviet Union," Box 15, Clifford papers. Army officials saw a threat in the fact that the Danes "inexplicably" refused entry to American personnel on the island of Bornholm, after Soviet evacuation. As they saw it, there could be no middle ground. Patterson denounced Soviet efforts "to discredit American intentions in securing bases necessary to our national security in the Atlantic and Pacific — as though the Americans had never denounced Soviet efforts to establish a military presence in the Dardanelles.

48. Department of State, "USSR: Policy and Information Statement," May 15, 1946; Dean Acheson to Clark Clifford, August 6, 1946, and list of agreements, Box 15, Clifford papers. Smith's June 15, 1946, telegram is printed in *FR: 1946*, VI, pp. 761–62. Also see Office of Intelligence Coordination and Liaison, "Soviet Observance of Treaty Obligations," August 2, 1946, 711.61/7–1846, State Department papers.

49. Patterson to Truman, July 27, 1946, Pauley to Clifford, July 24, 1946, Pauley memorandum for President, July 24, 1946, Box 15, Clifford papers.

50. "American Relations with the Soviet Union," published as Appendix A in Arthur Krock, *Memoirs: Sixty Years on the Firing Line*, pp. 419, 422, 425, 431, 468, 470–73, 481–82.

51. For the Clifford anecdote, Richard Freeland, *Truman Doctrine and the Origins of McCarthyism*, p. 67, and Margaret Truman, *Truman*, p. 347. Also see "L'Affaire Wallace," September 17, 1946, Elsey papers.

52. Rosenman, *Working With Roosevelt*, p. 213; see Norman Markowitz, *The Rise and Fall of the People's Century;* for "Post War Dream Boys," J. Samuel Walker, *Henry A. Wallace and American Foreign Policy*, p. 92.

53. Blum, ed., *Wallace Diary*, pp. 512, 531–33; Markowitz, *People's Century*, pp. 52, 174; Wallace to Stanley Isaacs, October 16, 1945, to Josiah Bailey, April 12, 1945, Wallace papers.

54. Blum, *Wallace Diary*, pp. 9–10, 250, 488. Wallace himself seemed

shocked, for instance, when Truman joked at a White House dinner "that what he really ought to have been was not a President but a piano player in a whorehouse" (Blum, *Wallace Diary*, p. 478).

55. Harry Truman to Henry Wallace, July 25, 1944, Wallace papers; Blum, *Wallace Diary*, pp. 475, 490–91, 524, 551.
56. Morgenthau presidential diary, June 6, 1945, p. 1652; "Interview with the President," June 10, 1946, Part I, Box 11, Bowles papers. Of Bowles, Truman said, "Bowles is a grand guy, but he makes me as mad as the devil sometimes. He has a headline in every Monday morning paper, and I sometimes think he makes entirely too many speeches. He has access to the OPA and some of the other agencies, and he is inclined to overdo the publicity job" (Harold Smith diary, May 15, 1946).
57. Wallace telephone conversation with Edwin Smith, October 29, 1945, Wallace papers; Blum, *Wallace Diary*, p. 528. Also see Wallace's suggestions for the State of the Union message, December 28, 1945, Wallace papers.
58. At a dinner in his own home on January 2, columnist Joseph Alsop, insisting he was "distressed as hell," kept declaring, "We had to know the Russian intentions." But he was sure Russia's intentions were those of Hitler's Germany. Another guest, William Gaud, wanted "to kick the Russians in the balls." Wallace called his statements "crap." "Well, then we are even," Gaud replied. Wallace argued, supported by Supreme Court Justice Hugo Black and, more tepidly, Ben Cohen, that the Russians were not without a case and that some of America's "intentions" might also appear questionable. Scatology continued to fly. Such views, said Alsop, were "a barrel of horseshit" (Blum, *Wallace Diary*, pp. 536–38).
59. Ibid., pp. 497, 503, 538; suggestions for the State of the Union message, December 28, 1945, pp. 2–3, Wallace to Stinnes ("competitive rearmament), April 3, 1946, Wallace papers. In fact, Farmer Wallace had opposed recognition of Russia in 1933, partly because of Stalin's war on the kulaks (Markowitz, *People's Century*, pp. 164–66, 193, footnote 8).
60. Blum, *Wallace Diary*, pp. 513, 525, 528–29, 535, 553; Wallace to Eisenhower, August 15, 1945, Wallace papers.
61. Wallace-Pepper telephone conversation, March 25, 1946, Wallace papers.
62. Blum, *Wallace Diary*, pp. 565–68.
63. Markowitz, *People's Century*, pp. 179–80; Blum, *Wallace Diary*, pp. 557–63, 572, 577, 582; Wallace letter and memorandum to Truman, March 21, 1946, Wallace papers. Wallace was excessively impressed by his 1944 visit to Siberia. He commented, for instance, with some enthusiasm on the economic progress in Magadan without realizing that it was the site of one of the most notorious slave labor camps in the USSR. Only some years later did he learn how good a job at setting up Potemkin villages the Russians had done. Telltale wooden guard towers were dismantled just before his arrival; prisoners were relieved of work duties and kept out of sight with three days of movies. Consumer goods suddenly appeared in shop windows. Wallace's later discovery casts an ironic light on a diary note he made during the trip. One of his Soviet hosts, Wallace wrote, "says the whole idea of developing the Magadan

area was Stalin's" (Blum, *Wallace Diary*, p. 337). For the artful stage management, see Walker, *Wallace and Foreign Policy*, pp. 107–8.

64. Blum, *Wallace Diary*, pp. 589–601; Elsey notes, July 24, 1946, Box 63, Elsey papers; Truman to Wallace, August 8, 1946, Box 156, President's secretary's file, Truman papers; Hippelhauser to Hauser, July 17, 1946, Wallace papers. For Ickes, see Hamby, *Beyond the New Deal*, pp. 71–73.
65. Wallace-Hippelhauser telephone conversation, September 10, 1946, Wallace to Parsons, November 12, 1946, Wallace to Richard Patterson (for "making sore"), September 12, 1946, Wallace papers; Blum, *Wallace Diary*, pp. 602, 612–13; Markowitz, *People's Century*, pp. 181–84; Millis, *Forrestal Diaries*, pp. 206–9; James Riddleberger oral history, p. 39. Truman's own later claim that there was "no time for me to read the speech" seems an example of wishful recollection. Truman, *Decisions*, pp. 557–58.
66. Blum, *Wallace Diary*, pp. 661–69.
67. Wallace-Hannegan telephone conversation, September 20, 1946, Wallace papers; Blum, *Wallace Diary*, pp. 613–29; Markowitz, *People's Century*, pp. 185–93; Margaret Truman, *Truman*, pp. 317–20; Truman, *Decisions*, pp. 559–60; Byrnes, *All in One Lifetime*, pp. 374–75; Vandenberg, *Private Papers*, pp. 300–301; Matthews to Murphy, September 19, 1946, Matthews file, State Department papers. Truman to Garner, September 21, 1946, Russian folder, Box 187, and two Byrnes communications, Box 84, President's secretary's file, Truman papers. For Wallace's not being the source of the July letter leak, see, for instance, Wallace–Charles Ross and Wallace–Ralph Ingersoll telephone conversations, September 17, 1946, Wallace papers. The press conference in Ayers diary, September 20, 1946.
68. Byrnes to Forrestal, September 20, 1946, Box 289, Russell to Byrnes, September 20, 1946, Box 552, Ethridge to Byrnes, September 24, 1946, Box 514, Byrnes papers; Dulles to Irving Fisher, September 23, 1946, Box 140, Dulles papers.
69. "L'Affaire Wallace," September 17, 1946, Elsey papers; Clifford to Truman, in Krock, *Sixty Years*, p. 419.
70. Patterson to Vandenberg, July 29, 1946, Box 27, Patterson papers; George Kennan, Lecture, September 17, 1946, Kennan papers; George Kennan, "Trust as a Factor in International Relations," Lecture at Yale Institute of International Studies, October 1, 1946, Box 20, Forrestal papers; for "hog wild," Davies diary, September 10, 1946.

X. The End of Diplomacy

1. Hickerson to Matthews, February 17, 1947, Box 3, European Affairs file, State Department papers; speech, January 17, 1947, Box 11, Dulles papers.
2. Lane to Keith, October 14, 1946, Lane papers; Dalton diary, September 10, 1946; Nicolson, *Diaries and Letters 1945–62*, p. 73.
3. Durbrow to Secretary of State, October 31, 1946, 861.00/10–3146, Heath to Riddleberger, November 25, 1946, 861.5048/11–2546, State Department papers. But it should be noted that Byrnes and John Hilldring,

Assistant Secretary of State for Occupied Areas, confidentially explained to Senate investigators in October 1946 that France had been the major obstacle to economic unity in Germany, but that France had received both less criticism than it deserved as well as (in Hilldring's phrase) "every extra ton of coal" mined in Germany — both in order to undercut the electoral appeal of the French communists. Perhaps Hilldring's willingness to apportion blame to the French resulted from the fact that he had recently come over to State from the War Department, where he had been director of the Civil Affairs Division. John Gimbel, "Implementation of the Potsdam Agreement," *Political Science Quarterly* 87 (June 1972): 261–63.

4. Forrestal diary, December 8, 1946, pp. 1389–90; *FR: 1946*, II, pp. 1264–69; Bohlen, *Witness*, pp. 255–56.
5. Interview with Benjamin Cohen; Bohlen, *Witness*, p. 256; Walter Lippmann, "A Year of Peacemaking," *Atlantic Monthly*, December 1946, pp. 36–38.
6. Ismay to Smith, December 18, 1945, Ismay papers; Melby, *Mandate of Heaven*, pp. 85, 92, 212, 218; Robert Ferrell, *George C. Marshall*, pp. 26–36. Marshall's ambivalence and frustration regarding his 1946 China mission are clear from a brief memoir he wrote for Harry Truman in 1954: "There now followed a serious dispute over the representation of delegates to the Constitutional Convention scheduled for May 5. This provoked added bitterness both in the field and among the workers behind the scenes politically. The Generalissimo then postponed the meeting of the Constitutional Convention because he stated he could not find a satisfactory basis for the representation of delegates. This was a very serious blow and, from then on, matters proceeded from difficult, to bad, to worse. During most of the period following January 10, I found the Communist representation and most of their forces in the field to be more responsive to the dictates of the Committee of Three than the Nationalists. It seemed to me the Communists felt that they could win their battle on political grounds more easily than on tactical fighting grounds because they had a more tightly held organization, whereas on the Nationalist side there were many contentious elements. The Communists continued on this line quite definitely, in my opinion, until early in June, after the postponement of the Constitutional Convention. The Nationalist commanders all seemed to be determined to pursue a policy of force . . . [From the spring onward] there developed a series of incidents provoked in turn by the Chinese Government and by the Communist forces, which led to a complete rupture of the relationships established to terminate hostilities . . . From here on out, the Communists were completely distrustful, in fact rather scornful, of any proposition I made or the Nationalist Government put forward toward finding an adjustment of differences. On the other hand, the Generalissimo, for the Nationalist Government, represented a varying role. At times his attitude was one of sincere endeavor to bring about some reasonable basis of adjustment, but invariably, it seemed to me, behind the scenes, his attitude with his leaders was one provocative of force." Marshall went on to add, "It has been a great misfortune that throughout this period the Generalissimo has had associated with him individuals who

had grown steadily in power from the time of the Generalissimo's march from Canton to the line of the Yangtse. Originally, these young men, [were] presumably animated with a very fine spirit to free China from the toils and treacheries of the past. But their steady acquisition of great power with virtually no opposition led naturally to a changed attitude until they were opposed to any effort along the line indicated by American policy. Partially discredited in 1946, they steadily regained their power, and found the development of the China political battle in the United States greatly to their advantage." George Marshall, memorandum on China, May 18, 1954, Box 174, President's secretary's file, Truman papers.

7. Stimson diary, February 22, 1943; Frankfurter diary, November 4, 1947.
8. Hickerson to Dunn, February 15, 1947, "Relations with the Soviet Union," memorandum for Secretary Marshall, January 17, 1947, European Affairs file, State Department papers; Lenin, "One Step Forward, Two Steps Back," *Collected Works*, vol. 7, pp. 414–15.
9. See, for instance, the comments of Senators Austin and Connally in NBC, "Our Foreign Policy: Our Relations with Russia," April 6, 1946, pp. 6–7, Box 564, Connally papers.
10. Truman to Committee on Expenditures, April 20, 1946, Box 145, President's secretary's file, Truman papers; Patterson to Bush, April 23, 1946, Box 18, War Council minutes, May 16, 1946, Box 23, Patterson to Austin, October 17, 1946, Patterson to Conant, October 17, 1946, Patterson to Brown, January 20, 1947, Box 27, Patterson papers; Millis, *Forrestal Diaries*, pp. 222–31; Byrnes to Forrestal, October 28, 1946, Box 289, Byrnes papers. A memo Forrestal sent to the President in January 1947 still warned that "the foreign examples of merged armed forces have an unbroken record of never winning a war." With covering letter, Foskett to Truman, January 14, 1947, Box 145, President's secretary's file, Truman papers.
11. Both Hewlett and Anderson (*New World*, p. 581) and Herken ("Atomic Bomb," p. 363) emphasize the immediate disappointment. For Patterson's subsequent enthusiasm, War Council minutes, August 1, 1946, Box 23, Patterson papers.
12. Eisenhower to Baruch, June 14, 1946, Spaatz to Baruch, June 11, 1946, Box 58, Baruch papers.
13. Herken, "Atomic Bomb," p. 426; Hewlett and Anderson, *New World*, p. 631; Conant's estimate of October 1946, in Box 27, Patterson papers. For confidence in the duration of the atomic monopoly, see Herken, "Atomic Bomb," p. 408; Joint Staff Planners, "Estimate of Probable Developments in World Political Situation up to 1956," November 8, 1946, p. 12, CCS 092 (10-9-46), RG 218, Modern Military records. On April 3, 1947, the Atomic Energy Commission warned President Truman that "the present supply of atomic bombs is very small," that none were assembled, that the core of the most important bomb type had never been tested, that production of critical materials like plutonium and uranium was "badly out of balance," and that a shortage of uranium loomed in the near future. "We found that the Joint Chiefs of Staff had not been informed of the foregoing facts," said the commissioners. "Whatever corrective measures are adopted, they are certain to call at

the earliest possible moment for extraordinary efforts in terms of money, materials, equipment and human energy." They concluded with an appeal for action anachronistic in its imagery: "In several critical fields there is need for a full head of steam." Box 200, President's secretary's file, Truman papers.

14. John Hancock, "U.S. Plan for Control of Atomic Energy," Lecture, National War College, September 13, 1946, Box 62, Baruch papers; Patterson to Vandenberg, July 29, 1946, to de Seversky, February 8, 1947, (for 58 percent), Box 27, Bush to Patterson, January 3, 1947, Box 18, War Council minutes, January 15, 1947, Box 23, Patterson papers; Herken, "Atomic Bomb," pp. 417–24, 430–32. For Shockley, see "National Power and Foreign Policy," second meeting and appendix, November 30, 1945, Council on Foreign Relations Study Group.
15. Vannevar Bush, *Pieces of the Action*, p. 288; Kolko, *Limits of Power*, pp. 96–97; Patterson to Chief of Staff, March 17, 1946, Box 27, War Council minutes, December 5, 1946, Box 23, Patterson papers; Yarmolinsky, *The Military Establishment*, pp. 291–93; Bush to Patterson, May 21, 1946, 334 Joint Research and Development Board, July 3, 1946, RG 218, Modern Military records; Hewlett and Anderson, *New World*, p. 625; *Fortune*, September 1946, p. 223. For 1947 R&D, see *Business Week*, September 6, 1947, p. 30. For "threshold" quote, memorandum with covering letter, Foskett to Truman, January 14, 1947, Box 145, President's secretary's file, Truman papers. Of course, the Navy was hardly about to endorse the "striking force," and this same Forrestal-sponsored memorandum informed Truman: "The American public has already gone overboard for the so-called push-button warfare, and is responding to the AAF's campaign that airpower (probably the least stable element in the evolution of weapons) can alone keep this country secure. Reliance on one idea — the Maginot Line — was fatal to France. We can fall in the same error."
16. *Aviation News*, September 2, 1946, p. 20, October 28, 1946, pp. 17–18, March 10, 1947, p. 12, May 5, 1947, p. 7.
17. Patterson to Truman, June 23, 1947, Truman to Patterson, June 26, 1947, Box 157, President's secretary's file, Truman papers; *Aviation Week*, April 2, 1947, p. 34. An Air Force intelligence analysis, sober in tone presumably because it was not to be used in either the budgetary or unification campaigns, declared: "The USSR will remain predominantly a land power. The traditional conception of the Army as the only sure shield in defense and the only fully effective weapon in the attack will persist in the future." The Soviet Air Force "will remain essentially 'tactical' in design" (to General George McDonald, November 12, 1946, Box 21, Spaatz papers). A similar conclusion, though obscured by stridency, is to be found in Robert Kilmarx, *A History of Soviet Air Power*, pp. 220–27.
18. Leahy to Secretary of War and Secretary of Navy, August 23, 1946, Joint Chiefs, "United States Strategic Interest in Iran," JCS 1714/3, October 14, 1946, CCS 092, Sec. 1, RG 218, Modern Military records; for assistance to Latin America, Patterson to Acheson, April 17, 1947, Box 27, Patterson papers.
19. Joint Staff Planners, "Estimate of Probable Developments in the World

Political Situation up to 1956," November 8, 1946, pp. 7–8, CCS 092 (10–9–46), RG 218, Modern Military records; Baruch to Secretary of State, April 28, 1947, 711.614–2847, State Department papers.

20. John R. Deane, Lecture, Washington, D.C., October 1946; Joint Working Committee, Moscow Embassy, "Soviet Strength and Weakness," September 1946; also see Joint Intelligence Committee, "Capabilities and Intentions of the USSR in the Post-War Period," February 1946; Hanson Baldwin, "Analysis of Russian Military Strength," *Army and Navy Bulletin,* April 27, 1946, p. 7; Patterson to President, July 27, 1946, p. 2, Clifford papers. For Austin's estimate, see NBC, "Our Foreign Policy: Our Relations with Russia," April 6, 1946, p. 6, Box 564, Connally papers.
21. C. C. Lototzky, ed., *The Soviet Army,* pp. 313–14; Huntington, *Common Defense,* p. 133; for the British, "National Power and Foreign Policy," Thirteenth Meeting, October 31, 1946, Council on Foreign Relations Study Group; Joint Staff Planners, "Estimate of Probable Developments," November 8, 1946, pp. 2, 7–8, 10, CCS 092 (10–9–46), RG 218, Modern Military records. In finding political and strategic significance in the disparity between the manpower in the Soviet and American military establishments, Thomas Wolfe, like many other commentators, overlooks the British. See his *Soviet Power and Europe,* pp. 10–11.
22. Hanson Baldwin, "Special Articles," *Armed Force,* July 26, 1947, p. 3; Patterson to Hopper, June 16, 1947, Box 27, Patterson papers.
23. Hickerson to Matthews, February 17, 1947, Hickerson to Acheson, February 25, 1947, Box 3, European Affairs file, State Department papers. Hickerson's comments followed upon several examples of "conciliatory" Soviet behavior. Prior to this, in a seven-chart briefing for President Truman, Air Force General Lauris Norstad had declared: "We consider it unlikely, however, that the Soviets deliberately plan to engage in a major clash of arms within the next five to ten years. The period 10 to 15 years from the present appears to be the most critical." The reasons for this lack of haste? "Depleted war potential; an incomplete assimilation of the satellite nations; lack of a strategic Air Force or an effective defense against such a force; and our possession of the atomic bomb" ("Postwar Military Establishment," October 29, 1946, Box 52, Hoyt Vandenberg papers).

XI. The All-Out Speech

1. Acheson in U.S. Congress, Senate, Committee on Foreign Relations, *The Legislative Origins of the Truman Doctrine* (Executive Session), 80th Cong., 2nd sess., 1947, p. 95; Davies diary, February 11, 1947.
2. Central Intelligence Group, "Revised Soviet Tactics in International Affairs," ORE 1/1, January 6, 1947, Byrnes papers.
3. The historian is Gaddis Smith, *Dean Acheson,* p. 414. I have drawn on his graceful biography, especially chapters 1, 2, and 16.
4. Dean Acheson, *Morning and Noon,* p. 52.
5. Ibid., pp. 267–78; Smith, *Acheson,* pp. 15–16, 417; Acheson, *Morning and Noon,* p. 219, 269–70. Also see Ronald Steel, *Imperialists and Other Heroes,* pp. 27–28.

6. Acheson, *Present*, pp. 132, 154; interview with Dean Rusk.
7. Acheson, *Present*, pp. 170, 270; Dean Acheson, "Formulation of Policy in the United States," Lecture, Washington, D.C., December 1947; interview with Eugene Rostow.
8. *FR: 1945*, II, pp. 48–50; Acheson, "Formulation of Policy," Lecture, Washington, D.C., December 1947; Acheson 1946 quote cited in *Fortune*, April 1949, p. 174.
9. Ibid.; Hickerson to Dunn, February 15, 1947, Hickerson file, Box 6, State Department papers.
10. Jones to Benton, February 26, 1947, Jones papers; *FR: 1947*, V, pp. 2–3.
11. Interviews with Mark Ethridge and Paul Porter; *FR: 1947*, V, pp. 17, 24–25. Also see ibid., pp. 17–22, 28.
12. Norman Ness, "Current Situation in Greece," Lecture, Washington, D.C., March 1947; *FR:* 1947, V, pp. 29–30.
13. Byrnes to Taft, March 19, 1947, Box 790, Taft papers; Dalton to Prime Minister, November 28, 1946, and "Notes on a Difference of Opinion," January 20, 1947, Miscellaneous, III-4, 1943–46, Dalton papers; Dalton diary, February 6, 7, March 14, 1947; memorandum of February 16, 1947, in Liddell Hart papers.
14. Dalton diary, March 14, 1947; interview with Loy Henderson; *FR: 1947*, V, pp. 32–37.
15. Jones, *Fifteen Weeks*, p. 133; memorandum and chronology on drafting of President's message, Jones papers; *FR: 1947*, V, p. 66; Senate Committee on Foreign Relations, *Origins of the Truman Doctrine*, pp. 12, 142. John Lewis Gaddis argues that the Truman Doctrine does not constitute a significant turning point, and that the real commitment came in Korea in 1950, not in the Near East in 1947. He discounts, however, not only the universal conviction among policymakers that a new departure was at hand, but also that with the Doctrine, U.S. leaders had at last found a coordinated approach and method with which to act on their ideology. Also, of course, there can be more than one turning point. See John Lewis Gaddis, "Was the Truman Doctrine a Real Turning Point?" *Foreign Affairs*, January 1974, pp. 386–402.
16. *FR: 1947*, V, pp. 56–58, 96–98; Senate Foreign Relations Committee, *Origins of the Truman Doctrine*, p. 20. Millis, *Forrestal Diaries*, pp. 251–52.
17. *FR: 1947*, V, pp. 59–61, 107–8 (italics added); Acheson, *Present*, p. 293; Jones, *Fifteen Weeks*, p. 141.
18. John Hilldring, Lecture, Washington, D.C., December 5, 1946. *FR: 1947*, V, p. 47.
19. George Kennan, Lecture, February 20, 1947, Kennan papers; Kennan, *Memoirs*, pp. 332–38; Bohlen, *Witness*, p. 261; Elsey to Clifford, March 7, 1947, Greece folder, Clifford papers.
20. Truman, *Public Papers: 1947*, p. 178–79.
21. Joyce and Gabriel Kolko suggest that the speech was little more than a "cynical" maneuver, intended to manipulate public opinion, and that "what was really in the mind of the President and his advisers" was the President's message in a speech on free trade and an open economic world on March 6, 1947. Kolko, *Limits of Power*, pp. 331, 341. This conclusion represents a misreading of a great deal of evidence. These

policymakers may have perceived events incorrectly, they may have exaggerated, but they did *believe*, they were not simply calculating profit-seekers. Their interpretation points to what is a basic problem both in *Limits of Power* and the earlier book by Gabriel Kolko, *Politics of War*, a substantial distortion that undercuts works of great scale and many individual insights. The Kolkos write with an assumption of a simple economic determinism, which they assert, but never prove. For them, something called "capitalism" is the source of all action. They assume that policymakers are sincere only when they express economic motives, but never demonstrate why this assumption should be accepted. Nor do they consider that economic arguments may themselves be sales talk, meant to drag Congress along. There is further distortion in their tendency to elevate officials of secondary importance to first rank in order to have quotes that substantiate their thesis. However, they are right to point out that the Truman Doctrine meant a renunciation of diplomacy. See *Limits of Power*, p. 343. Richard Freeland correctly recognizes that the Truman Doctrine combined salesmanship and sincerity; although, persuaded by the similarity between the internal Administration discussion and the public presentation, I place heavier emphasis on the sincerity. See Freeland, *Truman Doctrine*, p. 101.

22. "American Attitudes on U.S. Policy Towards Russia," attached to Russell memorandum, February 21, 1947, 711.61/2–2147, State Department papers; Lane to Durbrow, June 4, 1945, Lane to Matthews, March 1, 1946, Lane memorandum on Truman conversation, March 21, 1947, Lane papers.

23. Taft statement, March 12, 1947, Box 1260, Taft papers; Patterson, *Mr. Republican*, pp. 369–72; "The Responsibility of Power," speech, May 31, 1947, Herter papers; Alonzo Hamby, *Beyond the New Deal*, pp. 173–78. Mrs. Roosevelt's views in Russell to Acheson, March 27, 1947, 711.61/3–2747 and draft letter attached to Acheson memorandum to Hassett, May 5, 1947, 711.61/5–647, State Department papers; Schlesinger in Hickerson to Acheson, April 17, 1947, Hickerson file, State Department papers. For the Administration's efforts in 1947 to cope with rising domestic anticommunism, see Alan Harper, *The Politics of Loyalty*, pp. 48, 255–63, 34–35; Richard Fried, *Men Against McCarthy*, pp. 3–6; Susan Hartmann, *Truman and the 80th Congress*, pp. 20, 28; Norman Thomas in W. A. Swanberg, *Norman Thomas*, p. 304. For the postwar search for traitors in the Soviet Union, see Ulam, *Stalin*, pp. 642–50; Medvedev, *Let History Judge*, pp. 480–85, 491. Richard Freeland argues a strong thesis — in part, that the Truman Administration sought to use the loyalty program to create "the impression of widespread subversive activity" and so stir up anticommunist passions in order to get its foreign aid program through Congress. However, Freeland contradicts himself when he points out (correctly) that the loyalty program was meant to placate the new Republican Congress so that it would prove more amenable to the Administration's other programs. It is a very different matter to try to calm things down rather than stir them up. See his *Truman Doctrine*, pp. 10, 129–30.

24. *FR: 1947*, V, p. 114, 361; Senate Foreign Relations Committee, *Origins of the Truman Doctrine*, pp. 46, 131.

25. Ibid., pp. 134, 160. Also see Marshall to Bowles, July 15, 1947, Bowles papers.
26. George Kennan, "Russia's National Objectives," Lecture, April 10, 1947, Kennan papers.
27. Interviews with Paul Porter and Mark Ethridge; for MacVeagh, Senate Foreign Relations Committee, *Origins of the Truman Doctrine*, pp. 67, 39–40. MacVeagh's letter quoted by John Iatrides, "The United States and Greece: 1945–1963," paper presented at Harvard University, April 18, 1975, pp. 9–10.
28. *FR: 1947*, V, pp. 21–22; interview with Paul Porter.
29. Interview with Mark Ethridge.
30. Interview with Paul Porter.
31. John Iatrides, *Revolt in Athens*, pp. 6, 22, 74–76, 149, 199, 221–24; L. S. Stavrianos, *Greece*, pp. 78–79, 89–90, 123–24, 145; William H. McNeill, "The Greek Problem," p. 6, Box 177, Connally papers. Iatrides' balanced and thorough *Revolt in Athens* is the key book to date for understanding the Greek Civil War. Iatrides' quote is from "The United States and Greece: 1945–1963," p. 12.
32. McNeill, "The Greek Problem," p. 5, Box 177, Connally papers; interview with David Balfour; Iatrides, *Revolt in Athens*, pp. 257, 261–62, 283–84; Stavrianos, *Greece*, pp. 148–50. David Balfour, British chargé in this period, maintains that the British, while providing weapons and training to the Greek security and military forces, were unable to exert any control over command and promotion. Interview with David Balfour.
33. McNeill, "Greek Problem," pp. 7, 12, Box 177, Connally papers; interview with David Balfour; Iatrides, *Revolt in Athens*, p. 267; Stavrianos, *Greece*, pp. 168–71, 174–76; Bevin quoted in Dalton diary, September 10, 1946; MacVeagh quoted by Iatrides, "The United States and Greece: 1945–1963," p. 10.
34. Dominique Eudes, in *The Kapetanios* (especially pp. 100–103, 110–12, 116–21, 181–84, 234–40), emphasizes the split between the urban communist leadership and the guerrillas in the countryside.
35. Subhi Sadi, memorandum on Greece, July 25, 1947, Box 10, Aldrich papers; McNeill, "Greek Problem," p. 2, Box 177, Connally papers.
36. Acheson, "Formulation of Policy," Lecture, Washington, D.C., December 1947; Subhi Sadi, report, October 24, 1947, Box 10, Aldrich papers; Lovett quoted in *FR: 1947*, V, p. 314.
37. Interview with Paul Porter; *FR: 1947*, V, p. 295. For the drive for a Third Force, see Don Kingsley to Clifford, undated, Elsey papers; Averell Harriman, Lecture, Washington, D.C., December 1947. Samuel Popkin makes the argument about the paradoxical effects of intervention in a forthcoming book about the Vietnam war.
38. Dulles to Vandenberg, August 28, 1947, Vandenberg papers; *FR: 1947*, V, pp. 440–42, 468, 472–73. "The military situation has deteriorated to a marked degree since the initial allocation of funds was made to the military and economic programs," Eisenhower wrote to the Secretary of the Army on October 22, 1947. "Until the military situation is improved, it appears extremely unlikely that the economic program, as originally planned, can be implemented successfully" (CCS 092, 8–22–46, Section 8, RG 218, Modern Military records).

39. For the documents and carbons, see Iatrides, "United States and Greece: 1945–1963," p. 11; for the Yugoslavs, see Dedijer, *Battle Stalin Lost*, pp. 269–70; for the splits within the Greek movement, see Eudes, *Kapetanios*, pp. 307–55; for a discussion "why big nations lose small wars," see Andrew Mack, "The Politics of Asymmetric Conflict," *World Politics* 24 (January 1975) 175–200; for analyses of the military defeat of the guerrillas, George Kousoulas, *Revolution and Defeat*, pp. 248, 270, and Edgar O'Ballance, *The Greek Civil War*, pp. 194–220. In an important reassessment, Kousoulas suggests that Stalin opposed the expansion of the guerrilla movement (as well as the Yugoslavian support for it) because he feared that it would "provoke a determined reaction on the part of the Americans," would lead to the establishment of an American presence in Greece that "could be augmented as a response to increasing provocation" and which could "conceivably jeopardize the Soviet plans for a system of Moscow-controlled states in eastern Europe." In addition, Kousoulas, with the Greek Civil War in mind, finds that the circumstances of the Stalin-Tito split "brings into question the validity of the notion that a pro-Communist revolutionary movement in a particular country is necessarily part of a broad, co-ordinated scheme for expansion, directed by the major Communist power in the area." See "The Truman Doctrine and the Stalin-Tito Rift: A Reappraisal," *The South Atlantic Quarterly* 72 (Summer 1973): 431–32, 438.
40. Leahy diary, February 27, 1947; George Kennan, "Orientation and Comments on National Security Problem," March 14–28, 1947, Kennan papers.
41. Churchill in Pickersgill, *Mackenzie King Record*, vol. 3, p. 236; Stalin in Djilas, *Conversations*, p. 141.
42. Acheson in Senate Foreign Relations Committee, *Origins of the Truman Doctrine*, p. 22; explanation to Mrs. Roosevelt in Russell to Acheson, March 27, 1947, 711.61/3–2747, State Department papers; interview with Mark Ethridge.
43. Acheson in Senate Foreign Relations Committee, *Origins of the Truman Doctrine*, p. 95; Bidault, *Resistance*, p. 145; for Bevin, Williams, *Nothing So Strange*, pp. 243–44.
44. Sulzberger, *Long Row*, p. 347; Howard K. Smith transcript, March 16, 1947, Box 15, Dulles papers; Murphy, *Diplomat*, p. 342; *FR: 1947*, II, p. 169; interview with Frederick Reinhart, Dulles oral history. For briefer, Visson to Conant, February 27, 1947, McNaughton papers; for Bohlen, *Witness*, pp. 258–60.
45. Draper to Hoover, April 25, 1947, Hoover post-presidential papers. Dulles wrote to Arthur Vandenberg on March 29, 1947, "The insistence of the Soviet Union on reparations from current production out of the Western zones continues to be the outstanding feature" (Vandenberg papers). Also see Edward Mason, "Reflections on the Moscow Conference," *International Organization* 1 (September 1947): 475–87.
46. *FR: 1947*, II, p. 259; Werth, *Post-War Russia*, pp. 217–19, 229, 233; Stalin-Stassen transcript, April 9, 1947, Box 549, Taft papers; Nove, *Economic History of the USSR*, pp. 287–93; Strobe Talbott, ed., *Khrushchev Remembers*, pp. 227–44.
47. Clay to Dodge, March 24, 1947, Dodge papers; Werth, *Post-War Russia*, p. 226; Dulles to Vandenberg, March 29, 1947, Dulles papers; GRJ and

CPK to deWilde, March 29, 1947, and see Mason to Thorpe, March 26, 1947, Kindleberger to deWilde, March 24, 1947, Kindleberger papers.

48. *FR: 1947*, II, pp. 141, 273, 304, 336, 394–96; Kindleberger to deWilde, April 1, 1947, Kindleberger papers; Kennan, "Russia's National Objectives," Speech, April 10, 1947, Kennan papers. An "estimate of Soviet intentions in Germany," prepared by the intelligence branch of the U.S. Military Government in Germany, warned in early March that the Soviets aimed at "the complete inclusion of all of Germany within the Soviet sphere of influence." Reparations from current production, the report said, would provide "the means by which the Soviets intend to achieve economically what they failed to achieve politically" (Director of Intelligence, "Soviet Russia in Germany: Special Intelligence Summary," March 8, 1947, Pollack papers). For Dulles' influence on Marshall and the clash with Clay, see Gimbel, *American Occupation*, pp. 120–23, and Kindleberger to deWilde, March 24, 1947, Kindleberger papers.

49. Dulles to Vandenberg, April 10, 1947, Dulles papers. For Clay, see Kindleberger to deWilde, March 29, 1947, Kindleberger papers, and Smith, *Clay Papers*, p. 332. For Marshall and Stalin, *FR: 1947*, II, pp. 337–44; Stalin's appearance, in Reston to Krock, Black Book, Spring 1947, Krock papers; for Bevin's singing, Werth, *Post-War Russia*, p. 247.

50. Hickerson to Dunn, May 26, 1947, Box 6, Hickerson file, State Department papers; Bohlen, *Witness*, pp. 262–63; Forrestal diary, April 28, 1947, pp. 1600–1602.

51. Edward Mason, "Reflections on the Moscow Conference," *International Organization* 1 (September 1947): 475–87; Dulles, Speech, April 29, 1947, Box 11, discussion meeting, Council on Foreign Relations, June 6, 1947, Dulles papers.

XII. The Margin of Safety

1. Telephone transcript, March 13, 1947, Jones papers.
2. *Truman Public Papers: 1947*, p. 212. Also see Elsey to Freeland, May 11, 1967, Elsey papers.
3. Colonel Behn in Wasson to Lamont, February 25, 1946, Lamont papers; Stimson diary, April 19, July 25, 1945. For another eyewitness reaction to Europe's dislocation, see Lane to Dewey, August 14, 1945, Lane to Durbrow, August 3, 1945, Lane papers. The studies of multilateral planning are many, for instance, R. Gardner, *Sterling-Dollar Diplomacy*, and Freeland, *Truman Doctrine*.
4. Penrose, *Economic Planning for Peace*, pp. 321–33; Edward Mason oral history, pp. 29–31. For the concern on U.S. public opinion and international relief, Lubin to Hopkins, January 6, 1944, and report to Lubin by Cantril and Lambert, November 15, 1943, Post-War Planning file, Hopkins papers.
5. War Council minutes, November 7, 1945, Box 23, Patterson papers; Penrose, *Economic Planning*, p. 320; Williams, *Twilight of Empire*, p. 136; Truman, *Decisions*, p. 236; Byrnes quoted in *FR: 1946*, I, p. 1441; Clayton-Wallace telephone conversation, April 15, 1946, Wallace papers.
6. Blum, *Wallace Diary*, p. 554; memo on world trip, May 7, 1947, Gibson memorandum, February 21, 1947, Box 220, Hoover papers; War Council minutes, May 16, 1946, Box 23, Patterson papers.

7. Dalton diary, October 5, 1946.
8. United Nations, *Economic Report: World Economic Situation 1945–47*, pp. 123–25; Ingvar Svennilson, *Growth and Stagnation in the European Economy*, pp. 253, 246; United Nations, *Economic Situation and Prospects of Europe*, p. 5. Also see Richard Mayne, *The Recovery of Europe*, pp. 117–18, and *Business Week*, August 2, 1947.
9. United Nations, *Situation and Prospects of Europe*, pp. 53–55, 62–74, 44; Harry Price, *The Marshall Plan and Its Meaning*, pp. 29–32; Dirk Stikker, *Men of Responsibility*, pp. 163–65; Nourse to Truman, May 7, 19, October 18, 1948, Nourse papers; "Some Aspects of Foreign Aid Program," October 18, 1948, Salant papers.
10. "Overseas Deficit," May 2, 1947, III-4, miscellaneous papers, Dalton papers. Also see memorandum to Mr. Rowen for Prime Minister, July 29, 1947, Attlee papers.
11. Dobney, *Clayton*, p. 198; Cleveland to Jones, July 2, 1947, Jones papers. Also see Salant to Clark, May 12, 1947, Salant papers. *FR: 1947*, III, pp. 210–11. Freeland argues (*Truman Doctrine*, p. 154) that plans for aiding Europe had been deferred for domestic political reasons. On the contrary, policymakers did not recognize the economic problems until the winter and spring of 1946–47.
12. Acheson speech, April 18, 1947, Box 1, Jones papers.
13. Bohlen and Marshall interviews in Harry Price oral history collection; Gimbel, *American Occupation*, pp. 123, 150; Lovett to Lamont, July 31, 1947, Lamont papers; James Reston notes, vol. 1, Black Book, Krock papers. For Marshall's early emphasis upon Europe-wide approach, see Marshall to Bowles, February 17, 1947, Bowles papers. Kennan, in charge of drawing up the program as head of the Policy Planning Staff, had been keenly interested in a Europe-wide approach for some time. In 1942, he had suggested, "We endeavor to take over the whole system of control which the Germans have set up for the administration of European economy, preserving the apparatus, putting people of our own into the key positions to run it, and that we then apply this system to the execution of whatever policies we may adopt for continental Europe, in the immediate postwar period." Two years later he observed that European integration, in the form of some kind of federation, seemed to be the best solution to the problem of Germany and "the only way out of this labyrinth of conflict which is Europe today." Kennan to Burleigh, June 18, 1942, remarks to staff at Lisbon, June 1944, Kennan papers.
14. United Nations, *Situation and Prospects of Europe*, p. 61; Council of Economic Advisers, "Third Quarter Review," October 1, 1947, Nourse papers; Harriman and Hoover cited in Forrestal diary, April 9, 1947, pp. 1566–67. The Kolkos mistakenly argue: "As a capitalist nation unable to expand its internal market by redistributing its national income to absorb the surplus, the United States would soon plunge again into the depression that only World War II brought to an end. The alternative was to export dollars, primarily through grants rather than loans" (*Limits of Power*, p. 360).
15. *FR: 1947*, II, p. 240, III, p. 220; Dobney, *Clayton*, p. 202. Smith talk in F.P.M. to Peterson, May 16, 1947, ASW 091 Russia, RG 107, Modern Military records. "I agree with the general object of the Marshall Plan to help maintain the Western European countries in their battle against

Communism," Taft wrote on November 28, 1947, to Harry Bannister, Box 786, Taft papers.

16. Leffingwell to Lamont, May 21, 1947, Lamont papers; Smith, *Clay Papers*, pp. 356, 361; Keyes to Hoover, May 21, 1947, Hoover papers.
17. Djilas, *Conversations*, p. 141.
18. Dalton diary, September 10, 1946; *FR: 1947*, III, p. 894.
19. Kolko, *Limits of Power*, pp. 212–15; Hugh Seton-Watson, *The East European Revolution*, pp. 190–202; Vedeler to Steinhardt, August 12, 1947, Box 55, Steinhardt papers; Hughes to Booth, June 11, 1947, Hughes papers. For "moderate coalition," "Secret Summary for Secretary," June 2, 1947, with Marshall to Truman, June 2, 1947, Box 180, President's secretary's file, Truman papers.
20. *FR: 1947*, III, pp. 224–25, 237–38; memorandum on June 5, 1947, speech, Jones papers.
21. Marshall and Bohlen interviews, Price oral history collection; Forrestal conversations with Ploesser, July 2, 1947, Box 92, Forrestal papers. For the writing off of the Economic Commission for Europe, see George Kennan, "Problems of U.S. Foreign Policy," Lecture, Washington, D.C., May 6, 1947.
22. B. Ponomaryov, *History of Soviet Foreign Policy, 1945–70*, p. 163; Bohlen interview in Price oral history collection; Price, *Marshall Plan*, pp. 26–29; Djilas, *Conversations*, pp. 99–100.
23. *FR: 1947*, III, p. 235; Hickerson to Acheson, April 11, 1947, Hickerson to Labouisse, April 5, 1947, Winiewicz-Thompson conversation, April 3, 1947, Box 3, Hickerson files, State Department papers; Paterson, *Soviet-American Confrontation*, pp. 210–11; Robert Elson, "New Strategy in Foreign Policy," *Fortune*, December 1947, p. 222.
24. *FR: 1947*, III, pp. 260–61; notes on Poland, September 10, 1947, Herter papers; Pate to Lane, March 21, 1947, with UNRRA memo, Lane papers. Gomulka quoted in Nicholas Bethell, *Gomulka*, p. 135; Karel Jech, ed., *The Czechoslovak Economy, 1945–48*, p. 54. For the initially keen Polish interest in the Marshall Plan, also see Eugen Loebl, *Sentenced & Tried*, p. 25.
25. Interview with Halvard Lange, Price oral history collection.
26. *FR: 1947*, III, pp. 318–22; Ripka, *Czechoslovakia Enslaved*, pp. 56–71; Jech, *Czechoslovak Economy*, pp. 55–56.
27. Vedeler to Steinhardt, August 12, 1947, Box 55, Steinhardt papers; *FR: 1947*, III, pp. 335, 327.
28. Eisenhower to Clay, March 1, 1946, Clay folder, Eisenhower papers.
29. Clay to Warburg, September 21, 1946, Box 26, Warburg papers; War Council minutes, November 7, 1946, Box 23, Patterson papers.
30. John Hilldring, Lecture, Washington, D.C., December 5, 1946; Clay to Dodge, December 23, 1946, Dodge papers; Clay to Hoover, April 7, 1947, Hoover papers.
31. Memorandum of Hoover-McNeil conversation, February 20, 1947, Hoover papers; Dulles to Vandenberg, March 29, 1947, Dulles papers.
32. Forrestal diary, April 28, 1947, pp. 1600–1601; Hoover to Taber, May 26, 1947, Taber papers.
33. Smith, *Clay Papers*, pp. 387–91, 345, 372, 375, 412–13; Clay to Hoover, June 8, 1947, Hoover papers; Gimbel, *American Occupation*, pp. 156–

58, 170; Forrestal diary, May 17, 1947, p. 1618; Pauley to Truman, April 15, 1947, Steelman to Truman, n.d., Box 133, President's secretary's file, Truman papers. For Hoover's report, see Gimbel, *Marshall Plan*, pp. 182–84. Bizonia clearly posed a policy dilemma for the British. For their effort to balance off their heavy financial burden in Germany against the fears that the U.S. would undercut their plans for socialization of heavy industry in the Ruhr, see CAB 128/6, pp. 45, 126–28, Cabinet papers.

34. Royall to Taber, August 8, 1947, Taber papers; Smith, *Clay Papers*, p. 416; Gimbel, *American Occupation*, p. 195. In his excellent new study, *The Origins of the Marshall Plan*, John Gimbel argues that the "American economic dilemma in Germany" provided "the primary motivation for the Marshall Plan" (p. 279). Only by linking Germany to an overall Western European recovery could the U.S. overcome French resistance to a revivified Germany. He convincingly documents that, contrary to later memories, the Four-Power occupation broke down because of French obstructionism — not the Soviets'. See pp. 33–34, 48–49, 85–97, 112, 127–31, 138–39. In effect, he rightly says that the history of the German occupation in 1945 and 1946 was rewritten in 1947 and thereafter. He gives serious attention to the reparations issue and the role of "hidden reparations" from the Western zones. He also puts emphasis on the continuing clash between the State Department, worried about France and the rest of Western Europe, and Clay and the War Department, anxious to get out of the occupation business by getting Germany back onto its feet. Despite my agreement with his thesis that the Marshall Plan provided a "solution" to the German problem, as well as the considerable skill and care with which he makes his argument, I find his focus too narrow. The Marshall Plan was an effort to cope with the "problem" of Europe, which had three dimensions — Germany, the Western European economy, and the Soviet Union. Gimbel is right that an incorrect interpretative framework — what I have called the Riga axioms — was applied to Germany. Nevertheless, the fears and misperceptions of the Soviet Union among U.S. policymakers were very genuine. Second, their alarm about the German economy was more than matched by their alarm about what was happening in the economy of the rest of Western Europe, and he pays practically no attention to the latter. Finally, in developing his State-War controversy, he overlooks the significance of the close personal relationship between Byrnes and Clay. And it is not surprising that he finds no "plan" in the spring and summer of 1947. What existed — and from this emerged the plan — was a perception of crisis, a sense of danger and responsibility, and some general intentions and some thoughts about the need for a comprehensive response. All this said, Gimbel's book is a major addition to the literature, and is important for directing attention to the way in which the Marshall Plan was meant to provide a solution for Germany. But neither in the minds of its originators nor in fact was the plan separated from the confrontation with the Soviet Union.

35. Dalton diary, July 30, June 26, 1947; Bonesteel to Lovett, August 27, 1947, 740.00119 Control (Germany) 8–2747, State Department papers; for "friendly aid" and Clayton, *FR: 1947*, III, pp. 223–30, 370; for

France, Gimbel, *Marshall Plan,* pp. 252–54. On June 23, General Albert Wedemeyer, in reporting on a trip to Europe the previous month, observed that he had noted "restrained anti-American feeling" in Britain. "Lew Douglas the ambassador confirmed this. It is understandable — no people feel friendly toward creditors and many look to us as Shylocks. Life is very austere." Wedemeyer added, however, "There can be no doubt about the almost universal British desire to remain close to America in a political, economic and military sense." Attached to memo by Humelsine, July 15, 1947, FW 740.00119 Control (Germany) 7–749, State Department papers. The disastrous five weeks between July 15, when the British made the pound convertible in accord with the Anglo-American loan agreement, and August 20, when Britain suspended convertibility, fueled British antagonism. See R. Gardner, *Sterling-Dollar Diplomacy*, pp. 306–25, 337–42.

36. Elsey quoted in Paterson, *Soviet-American Confrontation*, p. 207; Patterson to Hoyt, June 23, 1947, Patterson papers.
37. Forrestal to Lippmann, January 7, 1946, Mosely to Forrestal, October 14, 1947, Box 70, Strausz-Hupe to Forrestal, March 14, 1946, Box 71, Forrestal papers; Forrestal diary, October 15, 1946, p. 1301.
38. Kennan, "Psychological Background," Box 18, O'Connor memo, October 7, 1946, Box 68, Forrestal papers; Kennan, *Memoirs*, pp. 373–76.
39. George Kennan, "The Sources of Soviet Conduct," *Foreign Affairs*, July 1947; Riddleberger to Steinhardt, August 29, 1947, Box 55, Steinhardt papers.
40. Vandenberg to Roberts, August 12, 1947, Arthur Vandenberg papers; Laurence Steinhardt, Lecture, Washington, D.C., December 1947.
41. See Dedijer, *Tito Speaks*, pp. 302–6; Bethell, *Gomulka*, pp. 135–38, 146–47; Djilas, *Conversations*, pp. 99–101; Shulman, *Stalin's Foreign Policy Reappraised*, pp. 14–17, 84; Werth, *Post-War Russia*, pp. 294–326; Sobolev, *Communist International*, pp. 512–15; Ulam, *The Rivals*, pp. 131–34; for the German communists, see Leonhard, *Child of the Revolution*, pp. 458–61; for a Western survey of the Polish road, John Scott, "Report on Poland," June 1, 1947, Box 55, Steinhardt papers.
42. *FR: 1947*, III, pp. 350–51; Taber to Hoover, May 21, 1947, Hoover papers; Taft to Bannister, November 28, 1947, Box 786, Taft papers; Hinshaw to Aldrich, October 27, 1947, Box 82, Aldrich papers.
43. Marshall interview in Price oral history collection; Vandenberg to Roberts, August 12, 1947, Arthur Vandenberg papers.
44. Forrestal diary, July 26, 1947, p. 1751; Lovett to Lamont, July 31, 1947, Lamont papers; Ford to Johnston, Air Policy Commission papers; Margaret Truman, *Truman*, p. 352.
45. Southard to Snyder, August 12, 1947, Snyder papers; "Notes on Boat Trip Coming Over" and London, September 3, 1947, Herter papers; Lovett to Taber, September 21, 1947, Taber papers; *Business Week*, August 9, 1947, p. 86, September 6, 1947, p. 102.
46. *FR: 1947*, III, pp. 344–46, 361, 470–71, 475–76; Leahy diary, September 29, 1947; Margaret Truman, *Truman*, p. 354.
47. For the dialogue, McNaughton file to Bermingham, October 4, 1947, McNaughton papers; memorandum, October 15, 1947, Box 4, Clifford papers.

48. Truman, *Truman*, p. 356; *Truman: Public Papers, 1947*, pp. 475–76, 492–98; Leahy diary, November 17, 1947.
49. *FR: 1947*, II, pp. 684, 680, 687, 713.
50. Robert Murphy, "The Current Situation in Germany," Lecture, Washington, D.C., October 1947; Smith, *Clay Papers*, pp. 351, 440, 448, 458–60, 463–64, 491; Marshall's presentation with Humelsine to Secretary of Agriculture, November 12, 1947, 711.61/11–1247, secret file, State Department papers.
51. *FR: 1947*, II, pp. 732, 738, 749, 756; *FR:USSR*, pp. 57–60; Acheson, *Present at the Creation*, p. 313.
52. *FR: 1947*, II, pp. 731, 757, 759, 817–18; Nicolson, *Diaries*, pp. 107–8.
53. Dulles, *War or Peace*, pp. 106–7; Sulzberger, *Long Row of Candles*, p. 373.
54. *FR: 1947*, II, pp. 751–73, 764–65. On Marshall's lack of patience, see John Hickerson interview, Dulles oral history.
55. *FR: 1947*, II, pp. 769–72, 826, 812.
56. Ibid., pp. 819, 823, 827, 815–17. Smith, *Clay*, pp. 501–2 (misdated).
57. Pauley in *FR: 1947*, II, p. 715, Clay to Patterson, December 23, 1947, Box 30, Patterson papers; Leahy diary, December 16, 1947.

XIII. Rebuilding the Arsenal

1. *Fortune*, March 1948, p. 95, December 1948, p. 209.
2. Webb letter of April 3, 1957, cited by Paul Hammond in "Super Carriers and B-36 Bombers: Appropriations, Strategy and Politics," in Harold Stein, ed., *American Civil-Military Decisions*, pp. 472–73; Whitehead to Spaatz, December 9, 1947, Box 28, Spaatz papers.
3. Symington to Kenney, May 30, 1947, Box 28, Spaatz papers. Also see War Council Meeting, March 19, 1947, Box 23, Patterson papers; Forrestal diary, April 18, 1947, pp. 1580–81; Caraley, *Military Unification*, pp. 174–82.
4. Millis, *Forrestal Diaries*, pp. 294–96, 299.
5. Ira Eaker, "Army Air Forces," Lecture, June 5, 1947, p. 4, National War College, Box 259, Spaatz papers.
6. Spaatz to Symington, December 30, 1947, Box 28, Spaatz papers. The student is Paul Hammond, "Super-Carriers," in Stein, *Civil-Military Decisions*, p. 483.
7. Sullivan testimony, December 2, 1947, Air Policy Commission papers; "USSR Submarines," McDonald to Spaatz, December 30, 1947, Box 28, Spaatz papers. Forrestal and the three secretaries of the services had agreed in October 1947 that "we should eliminate wherever possible any competitive publicity" (memorandum, meeting of three secretaries with Forrestal, October 13, 1947, Box 2, Hoyt Vandenberg papers). That agreement held virtually not at all. Moreover, the projection of Soviet threats, real and imaginary, was one of the most effective forms of competitive publicity. Occasionally, a conscious falsity would glimmer through. When General Spaatz went before the Air Policy Commission, he reported several alarming statistics: that the Soviet total armed forces had exceeded the American by 98 percent in 1946, by 134 percent in 1947; that 23 percent fewer personnel had manned the Soviet Air Force

than the American Air Force in 1946, but 33 percent more personnel than had manned the USAF in 1947. Then his most dramatic statistic in favor of Air Force buildup: "Thus, while her [Soviet] relative numerical superiority in total forces has increased 36 percent in the interim period, the relative increase in air forces personnel has amounted to 56 percent." Showing an inadvertent candor, as well as some confusion, he concluded: "These relative figures prove little, nevertheless they do show a trend, and, perhaps a strategic intention" (Air Policy Board briefing, September 16, 1947, p. 2, Box 29, Spaatz papers).

8. Patterson to Hopper, June 16, 1947, Box 27, Patterson papers. Hammond points to the popular support, "Super Carriers," in Stein, *Civil-Military Decisions*, p. 476.
9. As a pro–Air Force document, see President's Air Policy Commission, *Survival in the Air Age*, p. 25; Symington to Finletter, October 28, 1947, Air Policy Commission papers; *Fortune*, March 1948, pp. 151–52.
10. Forrestal statement, December 3, 1947, Air Policy Commission papers.
11. Air Policy Commission, *Survival in Air Age*, pp. 4–8, 133.
12. Air Policy Board briefing, September 16, 1947, Box 29, Spaatz papers. One of Spaatz' assistants outlined the Air Force's strategic outlook: "As I understand our Air Force concepts of operations in a war which might take place within the next 4 to 15 years, we will first employ our long range strategic bombers in a retaliatory action as expeditiously as possible. Atomic bombs will be used and the system of targets to be attacked will be those which would produce the maximum 'blunting' effect. That is, the results we would hope to obtain would be those that will produce the greatest immediate damage and destruction to the enemy, thus reducing his capability to operate against vital objectives of the United States or its allies . . . Concurrently with this retaliatory action or 'blunting' phase, the results of which it is hoped will provide the time necessary to assemble our over-all forces, we must seize and hold forward bases from which it will be possible to conduct around-the-clock operations necessary to establish control of the air . . . Our air intelligence estimates indicate that the potential enemy could over-run Europe as far as the English Channel and the Pyrenees in approximately ten days. And, in addition, we could be deprived of the use of the Middle East area as a base for air operations even though the potential enemy did not occupy the area in force. Moreover, their satellites in southeast Europe complete the perimeter of a defense in depth." Such a concept, naturally, called for an intense and expensive acceleration in development and production of new generations of aircraft. "Requirements Based upon U.S. Air Force Concept for the Employment of Air Power," Landry to Spaatz, January 27, 1948, Box 28, Spaatz papers.
13. Brodie made his point in "The Atomic Bomb and American Security," Memorandum No. 18, Yale Institute of International Studies, 1945: "Thus far the chief purpose of our military establishment has been to win wars. From now on its chief purpose must be to avert them. It can have no other useful purpose." Brodie's essay appeared in a collection he edited the following year, *The Absolute Weapon*. Arnold Wolfers also had an essay in the volume. Samuel Huntington (*The Common Defense*, pp. 45–46, 451) calls it "a remarkably prescient volume," add-

ing, "Determent was Wolfers' word. He had his suffix wrong but his concept right." Also see Michael Howard. *Studies in War and Peace*, pp. 159–60; Bernard Brodie, *War and Politics*, pp. 376–79.

14. Harriman testimony, September 8, 1947, Air Policy Commission papers. Thomas Wolfe writes: "There is perhaps some question whether the concept of nuclear deterrence, as it is generally understood today, was yet a well-developed notion in U.S. strategic thinking in the late forties" (*Soviet Power and Europe*, p. 34). The appropriate answer is that the concept was evolving; some held it; some, including those in the Air Force enraptured by the doctrine of strategic bombing, did not.
15. President's Air Policy Commission, *Survival in the Air Age*, pp. 6, 133.
16. See, for instance, *Aviation Week*, January 5, 1948, p. 11, February 16, 1948, p. 9.
17. *Aviation Week*, February 23, 1948, pp. 35, 26, 21–22, 42–44, January 15, 1948, p. 15, February 28, 1949, p. 20.
18. *Fortune*, January 1948, pp. 77, 80; *Aviation Week*, October 6, 1947, p. 11, January 12, 1948, p. 14; *Aviation News*, June 2, 1947, p. 7.
19. Ira Eaker, "Army Air Forces," Lecture, June 5, 1947, p. 16, National War College, Box 259, Spaatz papers; *Fortune*, March 1948, p. 95, January 1948, pp. 157, 81.
20. *Aviation Week*, February 23, 1948, p. 11.
21. *Aviation Week*, January 19, 1948, p. 11, February 23, 1948, p. 52, February 16, 1948, p. 9. For the "dim" chances, *Aviation Week*, January 5, 1948, p. 11.
22. Masaryk, in *FR: 1947*, IV, p. 243; Riddleberger to Steinhardt, December 2, 1946, Box 51, Steinhardt papers; Loebl, *My Mind on Trial*, pp. 70–73; for forced labor, Jiri Pelikan, *The Czechoslovak Political Trials: 1950–54*, p. 53.
23. Riddleberger to Steinhardt, December 2, 1946, Box 51, Steinhardt to Riddleberger, June 1947, Box 84, Steinhardt papers.
24. For the harvest, Jech, *The Czechoslovak Economy*, p. 57; for the efforts to obtain American grain, *FR: 1947*, IV, pp. 243, 247, 251. Ripka on Soviet grain quoted by Werth, *Postwar Russia*, pp. 328–29. "The move of Stalin's has received great publicity," reported *Business Week*. "The Communist press loses no opportunity of pointing out the advantages of the 'Molotov Plan' over the slower-starting Marshall Plan" (December 27, 1947, p. 74).
25. Laurence Steinhardt, Lecture, December 15, 1947, pp. 18–19, National War College, Steinhardt papers.
26. Ludek Pachman, *Checkmate in Prague*, p. 38; Steinhardt to Williamson, October 1, 1947, Box 85, Laurence Steinhardt, Lecture, December 15, 1947, p. 17, National War College, Steinhardt papers; Marshall's comments attached to Humelsine to Secretary of Agriculture, November 12, 1947, 711.61/11-1247, Secret, State Department papers. It is surprising that the Kolkos uncritically and without documentation accept Communist-pressed charges of a major reactionary plot in Slovakia. *Limits of Power*, p. 390.
27. Ripka, *Czechoslovakia Enslaved*, gives the inside view of one of the leading noncommunist politicians.
28. *FR: 1948*, IV, pp. 741–42.

29. Pelikan, *The Czechoslovak Political Trials:* pp. 64, 112–13. Artur London's *The Confession* is the powerful memoir of a believing Communist — one of Stalin's "honest fools" — caught up in this terror. So is Eugen Loebl's *My Mind on Trial.*
30. For Bevin, Marshall, and Steinhardt, *FR: 1948*, pp. 735–37, 749–50. For Soviet forces in Czechoslovakia, Ismay to Prime Minister, October 23, 1946, Box 22, Attlee papers; Joint Intelligence Committee, "Estimated Strength," June 4, 1948, CCS 091.711 (4–30–46), RG 218, Modern Military records. The information about the "comical" minutes comes from an interview.
31. Kennan, *Memoirs*, pp. 399, 423–25. Kennan was not quite as calm about Russian aims as his memoirs might lead the reader to think. He had told a group at the National War College on December 18, 1947: "Their immediate plans today probably envisage the consolidation of their power in Czechoslovakia as soon as possible and the actual seizure of power by violent means in Greece and Italy and France" ("What Is Policy?" Lecture, National War College, Kennan papers). Paul Hammond ("Super Carriers," in Stein, *Civil-Military Decisions*, p. 473) adds that the Spring Crisis "thus had two origins, a general movement of events affecting the strategic position of the United States and arousing the American public, and certain specific potential demands upon the military forces to which only the executive branch was privy."
32. Margaret Truman, *Truman*, pp. 358–60; Kennan, *Memoirs*, p. 422; Clay's message and background in Smith, *Clay*, pp. 568–69.
33. Notes on March 17, 1948, speech, Box 20, Elsey papers; Elsey to Clifford, March 5, 1948, Box 31, Clifford papers; Lilienthal, *Atomic Energy Years*, p. 302; memorandum by Chief of Naval Operations, March 9, 1948, CCS 334, Armed Forces Policy Council, Modern Military records.
34. Kennan, *Memoirs*, p. 422; for speculation on Masaryk's death, *FR: 1948*, IV, pp. 743–44. Claire Sterling is the investigator, author of *The Masaryk Case.* Prime Minister Mackenzie King of Canada observed, upon hearing of Masaryk's death over the radio: "One thing is certain. It has proven there can be no collaboration with Communists" (Pickersgill, *Mackenzie King*, vol. 4, p. 165).
35. For the emergency plans review, Smith, *Clay Papers*, II, p. 569; Leahy diary, March 14, 1948; for Forrestal, Millis, *Forrestal Diaries*, p. 393.
36. Notes on March 17, 1948, speech, Box 20, Elsey papers; Millis, *Forrestal Diaries*, pp. 394–95.
37. *Truman: Public Papers: 1948*, pp. 182–86; Pickersgill, *Mackenzie King*, vol. 4, pp. 170, 175–76; Leahy diary, March 17, 1948; Ayers diary, March 16, 1948.
38. Hamby, *Beyond the New Deal*, pp. 202–7, 230–31; Richard Walton, *Henry Wallace, Harry Truman, and the Cold War*, ch. 4; Truman to Folger, April 19, 1947, Box 141, Hoover to Vaughan, March 29, 1947, Box 167, Hoover to Allen, June 3, 1946, Hoover to Vaughan, November 19, 1945, October 5, 1945, January 27, 1948, December 31, 1948, Box 169, President's secretary's file, Truman papers. For Truman's suspicion of Hoover and the FBI, see Freeland, *Truman Doctrine*, pp. 205–6. Lillian Hellman, *Scoundrel Time*, p. 121; for diary, Hillman, *Mr. President*, p. 135. Clifford and historian, Robert Divine, *Foreign Policy and*

U.S. Presidential Elections, pp. 172–74, 179–84. In a kindred essay, Divine observes, "The conquest of Wallace marked the beginning of Truman's political resurrection." In "The Cold War and Election of 1948," *Journal of American History* 59 (June 1972): 96–99. On the Clifford-Rowe memorandum, Joseph Goulden, *The Best Years*, p. 363.

39. Lilienthal, *Atomic Energy Years*, pp. 305, 313; for Forrestal to National Security Council, March 30, 1948, and Forrestal query, Symington to Spaatz, March 31, 1948, Box 28, Spaatz papers; *Business Week*, April 24, 1948, pp. 19–23.
40. Nourse, Keyserling, and Clark to Truman, March 24, 1948, memorandum, May 10, 1948, Nourse papers; Millis, *Forrestal Diaries*, p. 409.
41. Millis, *Forrestal Diaries*, p. 436; *Truman: Public Papers: 1948*, p. 198; organization file, Box 262, Spaatz papers.
42. Memorandum, May 10, 1948, Nourse papers; Webb, in Lilienthal, *Atomic Energy Years*, pp. 350–51.
43. *Business Week*, April 10, 1948, pp. 15, 120; for the regular reports on Soviet developments, *Aviation Week*, April 19, 1948, p. 15; May 17, 1948, p. 13; June 14, 1948, pp. 14–15; for further campaigning, ibid., April 5, 1948, p. 11, April 12, 1948, p. 11. *Business Week*, May 1, 1948, p. 30. For the Navy, *Aviation Week*, May 10, 1948, p. 11.
44. Marshall's warning and Forrestal's complaint, in Millis, *Forrestal Diaries*, pp. 432, 438; Truman diary, May 7, 1948, Box 269, President's secretary's file, Truman papers; Webb, in Lilienthal, *Atomic Energy Years*, pp. 350–51; for Forrestal's impending breakdown, *New York Times Magazine*, August 29, 1948, p. 148; for "muttonheads" and "getting damn sore," Ayers diary, April 21, 26, 1948.
45. *Aviation Week*, March 29, 1948, p. 8, June 7, 1948, p. 11; *Business Week*, June 19, 1948, p. 26.
46. For the 1949 fiscal budget, *Aviation Week*, July 5, 1948, p. 10; for the increase in airframe weight, the new generations, ibid., February 28, 1949, pp. 10–12, 20; for the long-term buying spree, ibid., September 6, 1948, p. 9; for Forrestal's prediction, ibid., February 14, 1949, p. 12.
47. *Aviation Week*, February 23, 1948, p. 43.
48. For RAND's mandate, Secretary of Defense, *Second Annual Report: Fiscal Year 1949*, pp. 286–87; Bruce L. R. Smith, *The Rand Corporation*, p. 47. Bowles and Weaver, quoted in ibid., pp. 35, 51.
49. How significant was this development? Smith, writing in 1966, begins his book: "The emergence of the nonprofit research or advisory corporation is one of the most striking phenomena of America's postwar defense organization. A small but influential community, made up largely of civilian researchers and strategists, now provides defense policy makers with advice on a wide range of important problems. Leading members of this community have come to play a role in defense policy formation scarcely imaginable several decades ago. Struck by the phenomenon, one foreign observer remarked that representatives of certain U.S. research organizations roam through the corridors of the Pentagon 'rather as the Jesuits through the courts of Madrid and Vienna three centuries ago' " (Smith, *Rand*, p. 1).
50. *Aviation Week*, February 23, 1948, pp. 42, 44, February 28, 1949, p. 23. For the comparisons with the past, Secretary of Defense, *Second Annual*

Report: Fiscal 1949, p. 49; for the GNP, Alvin Hansen, *The Postwar Economy*, pp. 24–30. But note that military expenditures were 10 percent of GNP in 1948, and 12.5 percent in 1962.

51. Lovett, in *FR: 1948*, III, pp. 150, 153; Sargent to Prime Minister, January 2, 1948, with Draft Cabinet Paper, Box 28, Attlee papers.
52. *FR: 1948*, III, pp. 3–6, 8–12; Marshall to Truman, February 11, 1948, Box 178, President's secretary's file, Truman papers.
53. Bevin, in Dixon, *Double Diploma*, p. 255; Hickerson, in *FR: 1948*, III, p. 40. For the effects of Czechoslovakia on planning the alliance, also see Lord Gladwyn, *Memoirs*, p. 213.
54. Raymond Dennett and Robert Turner, *Documents on American Foreign Relations: 1948*, pp. 585–88.
55. For the efforts at secrecy, *FR: 1948*, III, pp. 59–61; Lord Gladwyn, *Memoirs*, pp. 215–16. The best sources on Maclean and Burgess, as well as Kim Philby, are two serious journalistic studies: Patrick Seale and Maureen McConville, *Philby: The Road to Moscow*, p. 194; and Bruce Page, David Leitch, and Phillip Knightley, *Philby: The Spy Who Betrayed a Nation*, pp. 201–2, 224. When the question of the consequences of Maclean's participation was put to Gladwyn Jebb three decades later, he replied: "I really have no idea to what extent Maclean's reports — which I think consisted mainly in verbal information and not in the passing on of actual documents — though here I may be wrong — were of assistance to the Soviet Government. If they confirmed impressions from other sources that the Western democracies were going to combine in order to create a defensive front in Europe and elsewhere, they may possibly have been useful from the Western point of view" (letter to author, August 24, 1976).
56. Bidault, in *FR: 1948*, III, p. 142; for participation in an alliance as a canon of national security, see ibid., p. 85; Lovett in *FR: 1948*, II, p. 233.
57. Vandenberg, *Papers of Senator Vandenberg*, pp. 399–411.
58. *Fortune*, December 1948, p. 209; Lilienthal, *Atomic Energy Years*, pp. 350–51; Walter Lippmann, "The Finletter Report," *New York Herald Tribune*, January 15, 1948.

XIV. The End of the Peace

1. Clay-Royall, in Smith, *Clay*, p. 702.
2. Robertson, in *FR: 1948*, II, p. 8; Clay, *Decision*, p. 348.
3. Marshall, in *FR: 1948*, II, pp. 71–73; Bohlen, *Witness*, p. 274.
4. For reparations as central Soviet objective and how it conflicted with other possible goals, see Gottlieb, *Berlin Crisis*, pp. 178–81, and Nettl, *Eastern Zone*, pp. 282, 299, 302–6. Gimbel, *American Occupation*, pp. 203–5, reflects on mutual perception of master plans. For some time the British had been aware of the contradictions in Soviet policy in Germany. William Strang, the political adviser to the British commander in Germany, observed on December 3, 1946 that "the impoverishment of the Soviet zone will be most repugnant to the Germans, even to those Germans upon whom the Soviet authorities most rely to further their influence in Germany. This is the dilemma which has constantly faced

the Russians in Germany. Their economic and security requirements are inconsistent with certain of their political objectives. This is the explanation of some of the hesitations and reversals in Soviet policy in Germany, and we may expect these to continue." CAB 129/15, pp. 207–8, Cabinet papers.

5. For Soviet apparently conciliatory moves, *Business Week*, February 7, 1948, pp. 15, 103; memorandum from Fuller, January 13, 1948, 740.00119 Control (Germany)/1–1348, State Department papers.
6. Smith, *Clay*, p. 548; *FR: 1948*, II, pp. 142–45.
7. *Business Week*, October 11, 1947, p. 105; Harriman to Truman, August 12, 1947, Box 28, Spaatz papers.
8. *FR: 1948*, II, pp. 871–73; Clay, *Decision*, pp. 211–12.
9. Wisner and Lovett, *FR: 1948*, II, pp. 879–80; Murphy and doodling, ibid., pp. 878–79, 892, 901. Indeed, Clay had felt for some time that German economic recovery was being frustrated by currency problems. On December 23, 1946, he had written that the March 1947 Moscow Council of Foreign Ministers meeting would be "the absolute deadline and if it does not bring agreement, we propose to proceed with the establishment of a new currency for the British and American zones" (to Joseph Dodge, Dodge papers).
10. *FR: 1948*, II, pp. 339, 341, 349, 352–53, 360, 363.
11. Saltzman to Lovett, April 8, 1948, 740.00119 Control (Germany)/4–848, State Department papers; Gimbel, *American Occupation*, p. 205; *FR: 1948*, II, pp. 889, 892–93.
12. Strang, Bidault, Marshall, and Douglas, in *FR: 1948*, II, pp. 218, 281, 71, 110.
13. Marshall, Douglas, agreements, Couve, in ibid., pp. 101, 138, 304–14, 169–70; Jean Chauvel, *Commentaire*, p. 199. For peace offensive, *Business Week*, May 15, 1948, pp. 9, 15, May 22, 1948, pp. 15–16; Divine, *Foreign Policy*, pp. 201–5. Just prior to the Molotov and Stalin bids, one State Department officer observed, "Evidence is slowly accumulating that since the Italian elections Soviet officials abroad, below the top level, are delicately probing for reactions to suggestions that major problems between the east and west can be ironed out through direct negotiations on a high level" (Stevens to Thompson, May 6, 1948, 711.61/5–648, State Department papers). But Truman did not like summit diplomacy and by this point simply believed that it was impossible to secure any workable agreements with the Russians. The Soviet Union "has never kept any of the agreements she has made," he told staff aides. Since "there is nothing to negotiate," there was no point in holding a high-level meeting. "What can you do?" he asked. Ayers diary, May 18, 1948.
14. For Clay and Royall, Smith, *Clay*, p. 602; memorandum by Lightner, acting chief, Division of Central European Affairs, December 26, 1947, 740.00119 Control (Germany)/12–2647, Saltzman to Lovett, April 8, 1948, 740.00119 Control (Germany)/4–848, State Department papers; Royall to Stimson, April 21, 1948, Stimson papers. In order to advance their argument that the Americans wanted "a manageable crisis that did not lead to war" and which would have "useful domestic consequences in spurring on Congress" (which, of course, accords with their overall

approach), the Kolkos argue that American leaders were by April "fairly confident that they could supply Berlin by air" (*Limits of Power,* p. 491). The Kolkos' apparent source for this contention is Royall's letter to Stimson. But Royall was not talking about supplying the entire city, only the American contingent in the city.

15. Smith, *Clay,* I, pp. xxxi–xxxii; *New York Times Magazine,* July 4, 1948, July 15, 1945; for the criticism of the Long Telegram, Murphy to Matthews, April 3, 1946, 861.00/4–346, State Department papers. See pp. 212–13 above. Interview with James Riddleberger. "Clay commenced to have more and more influence," Riddleberger also recalled.
16. Smith, *Clay,* vol. 1, p. xxx; McCloy, quoted in ibid., p. xxv; Kennan, Lecture, National War College, May 6, 1947, p. 30, Kennan papers; Murphy to Hickerson, January 5, 1948, 740.00119 Control (Germany)/1–548, State Department papers; Kindleberger to deWilde, August 16, 1946, Kindleberger papers.
17. Smith, *Clay,* p. 517. On April 10, 1948, Hickerson asked Murphy for his "frank views" of the effect of the establishment of a West German government on the Western position in Berlin. Murphy's reply: "In view of attitude and conduct of USSR at Berlin recently our position in Berlin would not in my opinion be adversely effected by establishment of a western German government in advance of similar Soviet step" (*FR: 1948,* II, pp. 176, 179).
18. Douglas and Lovett, *FR: 1948,* II, pp. 266–67, 272; Clay and Bradley, Smith, *Clay,* p. 623.
19. Truman, in Millis, *Forrestal Diaries,* p. 454; Bevin, in *FR: 1948,* II, p. 982; William Draper oral history, pp. 64–70.
20. Murphy, *Diplomat,* p. 352; Smith, *Clay,* vol. 2, pp. 709–10; Clay, *Decision,* pp. 372–73; "Berlin Situation: Air," Donnelly to Landry, July 8, 1948, Box 178, President's secretary's file, Truman papers.
21. Bevin, in Lord Strang, *Home and Abroad,* p. 298; Ismay to Eisenhower, July 8, 1948, Ismay papers.
22. Truman, *Years of Trial,* pp. 124–26; *FR: 1948,* II, pp. 925, 928, 130, 977, 982; Leahy diary, July 22, 1948.
23. Millis, *Forrestal Diaries,* pp. 453–56; Forrestal to Marshall, August 9, 1948, 740.00119 Control (Germany)/8–948, August 20, 1948, 740.00119 Control (Germany)/8–2048, State Department papers; W. Phillips Davison, *The Berlin Blockade,* pp. 129–30, 155–57; *Aviation Week,* August 2, 1948, p. 10. The historian is Walter Millis, *Arms and Men,* p. 323. For the June 28 decision and modification of the B-29s, Gowing, *Independence and Deterrence,* vol. 1, pp. 310–11.
24. See Smith, *Clay,* pp. 623, 677; *FR: 1948,* II, pp. 176–77, 179. "The initiative, the impetus, the guide, the force of anything that was done, was coming more from General Clay and the Secretary of the Army, than it was from the President and the National Security Council," recalled Charles Saltzman, Assistant Secretary of State for Occupied Areas in the years 1947–49. Saltzman oral history, p. 23.
25. Smith, *Clay,* pp. 697, 734–37; *FR: 1948,* II, pp. 918, 957–58; Millis, *Forrestal Diaries,* pp. 459–60; Murphy, *Diplomat,* p. 354.
26. For the Joint Chiefs, see Leahy diary, June 30, 1948; Howley to Bowles, April 5, 1948, June 23, 1948, Bowles papers.
27. Forrestal to Marshall, July 28, 1948 (with Reber memorandum),

740.00119 Control (Germany)/7–2848, State Department papers; "U.S. Military Action with Respect to Berlin," report to National Security Council, p. 2, July 28, 1948, Box 204, Landry to Truman, September 28, 1948, Box 126, President's secretary's file, Truman papers.

28. Dedijer, *Battle Stalin Lost*, pp. 198, 34, 73–96; Ulam, *Titoism and the Cominform*, pp. 77–84. For the Soviet economic operation in East Germany, see Nettl, *The Eastern Zone*. For Soviet forces, Joint Intelligence Committee, "Estimated Strengths," June 4, 1948, CCS 091.711 (4-30-46), RG 218, Modern Military records.
29. Dedijer, *Tito Speaks*, pp. 327, 333, 343; *Battle Stalin Lost*, p. 106; Ulam, *Titoism*, pp. 115–30.
30. Dedijer, *Battle Stalin Lost*, pp. 40–43, 93–94; *Tito Speaks*, p. 337. "I'm absolutely sure that if the Soviet Union had a common border with Yugoslavia, Stalin would have intervened militarily," Khrushchev later said. "As it was, though, he would have had to go through Bulgaria, and Stalin knew we weren't strong enough to get away with that. He was afraid that the American imperialists would have actively supported the Yugoslavs — not out of sympathy with the Yugoslav form of socialism, but in order to split and demoralize the socialist camp" (Talbott, *Khrushchev Remembers: The Last Testament*, p. 205).
31. For the debate among U.S. officials, *FR: 1948*, IV, pp. 1076–81, 1083, 1085–88, 1092–99, 1105–6, 1110; Talbott, *Khrushchev: Last Testament*, pp. 217–18.
32. For relationship between Berlin crisis and the double challenge to Truman from Dewey and Wallace, see Robert Divine, "The Cold War and the Election of 1948," *Journal of American History* 59 (June 1972): 90–110. Clifford quoted, ibid., p. 93.
33. Bevin, in Bohlen, *Witness*, p. 279; Smith, in *FR: 1948, II*, pp. 1194–97; Howley to Bowles, June 23, 1948, Bowles papers. On July 30, Marshall passed to Truman a State Department report showing public opinion overwhelmingly against America's being "coerced" out of Berlin, but also favoring negotiations so long as "a solution does not violate our principles and national interests" (Box 171, President's secretary's file, Truman papers).
34. Clay-Royall, in Smith, *Clay*, p. 702; *FR: 1948*, III, p. 207; *FR: 1948*, II, p. 928.
35. *FR: 1948*, II, pp. 381, 991, 999–1006; for Bohlen, Bohlen to Marshall, August 4, 1948, 740.00119 Control (Germany)/8–448, State Department papers.
36. Smith and Clay, in *FR: 1948*, II, pp. 1006–7, 1032; Bohlen to Marshall, August 4, 1948, 740.00119 Control (Germany)/8–448; Gimbel, *American Occupation*, p. 225.
37. For Marshall, *FR: 1948*, II, pp. 1083–85; for Smith's dissent, ibid., pp. 1160, 1194–97; for Kennan's, ibid., pp. 1287–97, 1320–38, Kennan, *Memoirs*, pp. 443–49; for Walter Bedell Smith's interest in the job in Germany that went to Clay in 1945, see Smith, *Clay*, pp. xxxi, xxxiv.
38. For Moscow agreements and Soviet concessions, see Leahy diary, August 31, 1948; Smith, *Clay*, pp. 835–36, 846, 850, 866; Bohlen to Marshall, August 20, 1948, Box 188, President's secretary's file, Truman papers. For the directive, Dennett and Turner, *Documents on American Foreign Relations: 1948*, pp. 95–97. The most difficult question for the

military governors involved Four-Power control over Berlin's currency. "The matter is of central importance and may prove to be the breaking point of the discussions," Marshall informed Truman on September 2, 1948. "We feel that these negotiations should not break down in Berlin on what would appear to be a technical point but rather in Moscow on the basic issue reflected in the technical point . . . [that] the entire financial life of the city would pass to unilateral Soviet control" (Box 178, President's secretary file, Truman papers).

39. Clay, in Smith, *Clay*, p. 859; for the Constituent Assembly, Konrad Adenauer, *Memoirs*, pp. 121, 125.
40. Clay, in Smith, *Clay*, pp. 867, 875; Marshall, in *FR: 1948*, II, pp. 1178. Clay reiterated his view a month later in conversation with Forrestal and Leahy: "We can continue to feed the population in the American Zone in Berlin by air lift indefinitely unless the Soviets use force to stop it which he does not expect" (Leahy diary, October 21, 1948).
41. Clay, *Decision*, pp. 382, 386; *Fortune*, November 1948, pp. 89, 220, 223; *Aviation Week*, February 29, 1948, p. 80. The scholar is Shulman, *Stalin's Foreign Policy*, p. 66. The point needs to be made, as Paul Hammond does, that the airlift was "a major achievement in air power, though not simply U.S. Air Force air power, for approximately 25 percent of the payload was carried by the Navy, and the RAF was an active participant also" (Hammond, "Super Carriers," in Stein, *Civil-Military Decisions*, p. 485).
42. Marshall, in *FR: 1948*, II, p. 1178; Smith, *Clay*, p. 858; Leahy diary, October 21, 1948. Charles Kindleberger points out that the credit given to the currency reform is somewhat exaggerated; output was already increasing prior to the reform, but it was going into hoarding. "The initial impact of the reform was to turn the black market white and to bring goods out of the back room into the front window." Charles Kindleberger, "The Marshall Plan and the Cold War," *International Journal* 23 (Summer 1968): 379–81.
43. For Kennan, *Memoirs*, p. 431, *FR: 1948*, III, pp. 157, 177; for Bohlen, *FR: 1948*, III, pp. 193, 186; for Washington paper and Wrong, ibid., pp. 237–49.
44. Ibid., pp. 270, 285.
45. Ibid., p. 177; *FR: 1948*, II, pp. 1287–97, 1320–38; Kennan, *Memoirs*, pp. 443–50; Bohlen, *Witness*, p. 175.
46. Robert Divine suggests that the 1948 election was much more of a referendum on Truman's foreign policy than is customarily perceived, but also that it was an incomplete referendum — by reviving bipartisanship, the Berlin crisis deprived Thomas Dewey of potentially his most effective issue, Truman's conduct of the Cold War. "In retrospect, it is apparent that the Berlin crisis was Truman's greatest asset in the 1948 election. Just as the Soviet move in Czechoslovakia in February had enabled him to repudiate Wallace, so the Soviet blockade of Berlin helped Truman block Dewey from waging an all-out attack on the containment policy. There can be little doubt that such an assault would have been effective. Public opinion polls taken in the summer of 1948 showed massive discontent with Truman's handling of the Cold War . . . Instead of suffering from a Republican attack on foreign policy, Truman

was able to regain public confidence by his careful handling of the Berlin blockade. He rightly sensed the desire of the American people for a tough policy that stopped short of war." Divine, "The Cold War and the Election of 1948," *Journal of American History* 59 (June 1972): 109.

47. *FR: 1948*, II, pp. 1083–85. As an indication of public support on the elite level, a group of influential outside consultants on the German question advised the State Department in mid-September: "We must recognize that there is practically no possibility that we could get Russian agreement at this juncture" on a program for re-establishing a united Germany "on conditions acceptable to us. We must be prepared, therefore, to proceed vigorously with the Western German arrangements, trying to overcome the mistakes we have made in the past, and to achieve real success with the Germans and not worrying too much about the possible long-term complications." Kennan to Marshall, September 17, 1948, 740.00119 Control (Germany)/9–1748, State Department papers.
48. For Smith, *FR: 1948*, II, p. 1161, and Walter Bedell Smith, Lecture, Washington, D.C., October 1948, Hillman, *Mr. President*, p. 141.

Epilogue: The National Security State from Blockade to Détente

1. Shulman, *Stalin's Foreign Policy*, pp. 12–20, 27–30, 64–68; Adenauer, *Memoirs*, pp. 125–38. For Lippmann, see *The Cold War*, p. 50. Lucius Clay, Lecture, October 26, 1949, Council on Foreign Relations papers. Clay added, "The airlift and our damaging counterblockade had the effect of showing the French where the major threat to their security lay, and inducing them at long last to join in the establishment of a West German government and to take steps toward a Franco-German rapprochement."
2. Shulman, *Stalin's Foreign Policy*, pp. 74–75; Acheson, *Present*, pp. 352–63, 383–96; memorandum addressed to Webb, May 26, 1949, Box 163, President's secretary's file, Truman papers; Ayers diary, January 1949.
3. H. Alexander Smith diary, March 13, 1947. For Eastern Europe, see, for instance, Eugen Loebl, *My Mind on Trial*, Jiri Pelikan, *The Czechoslovak Political Trials*, and Artur London, *The Confession*.
4. Elbridge Durbrow, "The Objectives of Soviet Policy," Lecture, Washington, D.C., October 21, 1948.
5. Millis, *Forrestal Diaries*, pp. 462–69, 475–79, 497–500, 506, 510–17; Lilienthal, *Journals*, pp. 351, 385–86.
6. Forrestal to Truman, July 10, 1948 (with memo for National Security Council), Truman to Forrestal, July 13, 1948, Box 156, President's secretary's file, Truman papers.
7. Transcript, meeting at Pentagon, August 24, 1948, p. 6, CCS, 337, 7–6–48, 5.1, Modern Military records; Forrestal to Truman, November 9, 1948, Box 120, President's secretary's file, Truman papers; Millis, *Forrestal Diaries*, pp. 498, 510, 535. For Forrestal's approach to Marshall, see *FR: 1948*, I, pp. 644–55.
8. Truman statement to National Security Council and the Joint Chiefs, Spring 1949, Box 150, President's secretary's file, Truman papers. For

Johnson, see Hammond, "NSC-68: Prologue to Rearmament," in Schilling, Hammond, and Snyder, *Strategy, Politics, and Defense Budgets*, pp. 280, 292–93.

9. Richard Hewlett and Francis Duncan, *Atomic Shield*, pp. 362–69. The Long Range Detection Program had only been in operation a year or so. The Atomic Energy Commission had to push the Air Force hard to get it to cooperate in setting up such a program, even going so far as to "loan" the Air Force the money at one point. Perhaps this Air Force sluggishness signified its conviction that a successful Russian test was still some years ahead. See "History of Long Range Detection Program," July 21, 1948, Box 199, President's secretary's file, Truman papers.
10. For the hydrogen bomb debate, Hewlett and Duncan, *Atomic Shield*, chapter 12; Lilienthal, *Journals*, pp. 580–635. For the order, Truman to Lilienthal, January 31, 1950, and Report by Special Committee, subsequent but no date, Box 202, President's secretary's file, Truman papers. A few days after ordering the hydrogen bomb project to go ahead, Truman commented that the decision had really been made the preceding autumn when the budget was made up for the Atomic Energy Commission. There was, in any event, no real choice, he said. "We had got to do it," Ayers diary, February 4, 1950.
11. For the history of the drafting of NSC-68, see Hammond, "NSC-68," in Schilling, *Strategy*, pp. 298–330. Hammond, however, was apparently not aware of Forrestal's 1948 suggestion. Gaddis Smith calls the document "a thoroughly Achesonian exposition" (*Acheson*, p. 161).
12. NSC-68, Report to the National Security Council, April 14, 1950, Record group 341, Modern Military records, pp. 6, 9, 10, 13, 14, 25, 30, 34, 63–65.
13. Smith, *Acheson*, p. 160.
14. Hammond, "NSC-68," in Schilling, *Strategy*, pp. 308–18; Kennan, *Memoirs*, pp. 450, 490–94, 526–28. Kennan's change of heart was dramatically clear in a prescient talk he gave to the Council on Foreign Relations on February 16, 1949. He said he was trying to look beyond the point when Russia ceased to be a "desperately acute" problem, to what today would be called environmental and ecological issues. He suggested that Stalin would prefer a "nationalist Germany with which he had a 'dicker' than a communist Germany which would not be subject to his control." Kennan already saw signs of tensions between the Soviets and Chinese communists. He warned that the United States would need some humility in approaching world problems. "We must be careful about talking in big words, about using too carelessly such words as 'world leadership,' 'raising the world standard of living.' " There could be no question of his disagreement with Acheson and other colleagues when he said: "We must refrain as much as possible from making the present East-West line a hard and fast one and should continually engage in negotiations with the Russians, even though we must recognize that they will consume needless time and that we cannot hope for success except in terms of years." Council on Foreign Relations papers.
15. Murphy in Margaret Truman, *Truman*, p. 431, and Charles Murphy oral history, pp. 184–87; Leon Keyserling oral history, pp. 155–60; Webb to Truman, March 5, 1950, Box 141, President's secretary's file, Truman

papers; Hammond, "NSC-68," in Schilling, *Strategy*, 333–34; Edward Flash, *Economic Advice and Presidential Leadership: The Council of Economic Advisers*, pp. 27–39. Webb had for some time been regarded as the villain holding down the military budgets. On October 17, 1946, one general complained in the War Council that "Mr. Webb, through the budget, had mixed into business which was not his own" (War Council Minutes, Box 23, Patterson papers).

16. On Vietnam: *Pentagon Papers*, Book 1, pp. A–45–46, Book 8, pp. 85, 97–103, 218, 266, 271, 288, 321; on military aid, Chester Cooper, *The Lost Crusade*, p. 88. David McLellan argues that American policy shifted in the spring of 1950 from wanting the colonial power (France) out of Vietnam to wanting it to stay so that the United States — in line with its imposition of a global framework on the local struggle — would not have to step in directly to contain "communism." See Dean Acheson, *Present At the Creation*, pp. 263–65. On McCarthy: Fried, *Men Against McCarthy*, pp. 20, 43–46, 74; for Acheson quotes, *Creation*, pp. 462, 470; Truman quoted in his daughter's *Truman*, p. 419; Clifford to Truman, April 1949, Clifford files.

17. Huntington, *Common Defense*, p. 54; *Aviation Week*, December 18, 1950, p. 20, February 26, 1951, pp. 11, 25. "We came, I think, to a firm judgment that our course ought to be sharply changed from what it had been," Charles Murphy later recalled. "And so the next question was, 'How do you explain this to Congress and to the American people?' And we were wrestling with that question in 1950, in June, when the North Koreans invaded South Korea, and from then on we explained it in terms of the Korean problem, which I think was permissible. It got kind of muddied, but we had in mind, I think, a clear belief that the general necessities, so far as defense was concerned, required a large increase in our defense strength as well as the Korean fighting" (Charles Murphy oral history). General Marshall told a group of congressional leaders in December 1950 that the Pentagon had been working on the assumption of a four-year buildup in U.S. strength, but now planned to move much faster — trying to procure by 1952 what had been planned for 1954. Acheson in the same briefing certainly did muddy the waters when he said, "Since the end of June, it had been clear that the Soviet Union has begun an all-out attack against the power position of the United States. It was clear that the Soviet leaders recognized that their policy might bring on a general war, and it was equally clear that they were prepared to run this risk." Meeting of President with congressional leaders, December 13, 1950, Box 164, President's secretary's file, Truman papers, pp. 3, 8. On December 20, 1950, Air Force Secretary Thomas Finletter said that 18.5 percent of national income was then going for military expenditures. Council on Foreign Relations papers.

18. Kennan, *Memoirs*, p. 527.

19. Carter in *New York Times* January 1, 1980, p. A4. See Zbigniew Brezinski, *Power and Principle: Memoirs of the National Security Assistant 1977–1981* (New York: Farrar, Straus, Giroux, 1985), pp. 156–66; Cyrus Vance, *Hard Choices: Critical Years in America's Foreign Policy* (New York: Simon and Schuster).

20. Reagan in *New York Times*, December 12, 1987, p. A8. On the formation of Reagan's views towards the Russians, see Lou Cannon, *Reagan*, (New York: G.P. Putnam's Sons, 1982), Chapter 7.
21. Thatcher in *New York Times*, November 18, 1988, p. A6; Bush on "previous opportunity" in *Ibid.*, May 13, 1989, p. 6. Malta Summit, Ibid., December 4, 1989. Winston Churchill, *Triumph and Tragedy* Vol. 12 of the Second World War, p. 9.
22. Mr. X., "The Sources of Soviet Conduct," *Foreign Affairs*, Spring 1987, pp. 867–68. Arguably, Kennan's essay is the most influential article ever published in the influential *Foreign Affairs*; it is, indubitably, the only article ever published twice in *Foreign Affairs*.
23. "Dry bread" in Jacob D. Beam, *Multiple Exposure: An American Ambassador's Unique Perspective on East-West Issues* (New York: Norton, 1978), p. 299.
24. George Elsey, "Some White House Recollections, 1942–1953," *Diplomatic History* 12 (Summer 1988): p. 364.
25. George Kennan, *Memoirs 1925–1950* (New York: Bantam, 1969), p. 527.

Bibliographical Note to the Revised Edition

Historical writing both affects and encapsulates worldviews. The writing of the late 1980s and early 1990s reflects the fading of the focus on the Vietnam War, the revelations about and self-criticism of the Soviet Union, and greater confidence in capitalism and democracy. The new cast of scholarship also reflects the fact that the romantic hopes and ardor for Third World "revolution"—which made a critical stance toward U.S. policies almost automatic—have turned to disillusionment, in the face of the grim and widespread legacy of dictatorship, repression, waste, and economic mismanagement. The new synthesis is most clearly expressed in the work of John Lewis Gaddis, in *Strategies of Containment* and, more recently, in his book *The Long Peace.* The biographer of George Kennan, he develops a general Kennanesque realpolitik view of the origins of the Cold War. Gaddis, as much as anyone, has become the arbiter of the Cold War debate. Currently the most vigorous exposition of an opposing and revisionist view is to found in a number of articles and a forthcoming book by Melvin Leffler. In explaining the origins of the Cold War, Leffler focuses on the expanionist ambitions of American leaders, and particularly on their pursuit of national security, which he argues fueled Stalin's paranoia. His explanation of the driving forces of American foreign policy is not so much economic as ideological. A perceptive and engaging biographically oriented study of the origins of the Cold War is to be found in the superbly written *Wise Men*, by Walter Isaacson and Evan Thomas. Ronald Steel's magisterial biography of Walter Lippmann also provides important insight into the origins of the Cold War.[1] These two books may be contrasted in their view of the "wisdom" of America's postwar leaders.

In addition to the broad views, four more specific strands can be identified in the recent discussions about the origins of the Cold War.

One reflects what might be described as "rolling thunder." That is, the timetable of archive openings helps to establish focus for scholarly work. By the early 1980s, the main U.S. archives had been open sufficiently long to have been fairly thoroughly plumbed for the broad issues of the Cold War origins. To be sure, some important subjects will be illuminated further. One of the most fruitful still to be examined concerns the activities and organization of the large communist parties in Western Europe and their interaction with the overall development of the Cold War and Western policy, especially in contributing to the apprehensions from 1947 onward.

Meanwhile, new archives have been opening up, in particular those of the Foreign Office in London, providing much new material for analysis, offering new perspectives, and broadening the understanding of British policy in those years. What is generally emerging is that British diplomacy was very alarmed by Soviet expansionism, primarily on grounds of balance of power and realpolitik, though not by any means exclusively. Poland was, after all, the reason that Britain went to war in 1939. The British labored hard to persuade Roosevelt and then Truman of the dangers of Stalin's policies and the need for timely response by the West. As the British considered the balance of power and recognized their own frail economic position, they found themselves also quite fearful of a resurgent American isolationism. Finally, they were perplexed by what they saw as the naive, knee-jerk, and uninformed anticolonialism of Washington. They knew they were not capable of the grand designs and great grabs that some in the United States attributed to them. Already, during World War II, Harold Macmillan, then minister resident in North Africa, had sketched out the postwar role for Britain. "We," he said to another official, "are Greeks in this American empire. You will find the Americans much as the Greeks found the Romans—great big, vulgar, bustling people, more vigorous than we are and also more idle, with more unspoiled virtues but also more corrupt."

Churchill, though out of office, played a prominent role in addressing the Americans after World War II, but he was hardly alone. The Labour government was to take the lead in organizing the common European response that led to the Marshall Plan and then the movement toward collective security in Western Europe that culminated in the North Atlantic Treaty Organization. For the latter, the galvanizing moment was the "March Crisis" of 1948. The Prague coup, which seemed about to be followed by one in Helsinki, persuaded British Foreign Secretary Ernest Bevin that, as he told the Cabinet, nothing less than a fundamental "threat to Western Civilization" was now at hand: "It has really become a matter of the defense of Western civilization, or everyone will be swamped by this Soviet method of infiltration. . . . After all the efforts that have been made and the appeasement that we followed to try and get a real friendly settlement on a four-Power basis, not only is the Soviet government not prepared at the present stage to co-operate in any real sense with any non-Communist or non-Communist-controlled government, but it is actively preparing to extend its hold over the remaining part of continental Europe and, subsequently, over the Middle East and no doubt the bulk of the Far East as well. In other words, physical control of the Eurasian land mass and eventual control of the whole World Island is what the Politburo is aiming at—no less a thing than that." Bevin sought and won approval to "proceed urgently with the active organization of all those countries who believe in parliamentary government and free institutions."[2]

A second growing strand is composed of area studies. The Middle East, Scandinavia, and Germany have benefitted from such analysis.[3] Vietnam provided stimulus to study the origins of the Cold War in East Asia. The results have sometimes imbued American policy with a strategy grander than may well have been the case, as well as to underplay the immediate issue, which was how to cope with the defeated remnants of the militaristic Japanese state and the upheaval and disorder throughout Asia in the wake of Japan's surrender. The occupation of Japan and the building of a new U.S.-Japanese relationship constituted one of the more extraordinary achievements of postwar U.S. policy. To be sure, even before the Korean War, concerns did shift as a consequence of the global intensification of the Cold War and the emerging communist victory in China. Economic recovery, stability, and preservation of Japan within a Western system—all these became of the highest priority. There is nothing surprising that, for instance, the Joint Chiefs of Staff should in 1949 have regarded Japan as "the key strategic position in East Asia for the United States." After all, it was. Japan's rise to today's status of economic superpower—and the shifting nature of U.S.-Japanese relations—call for a fresh perspective on the postwar years in East Asia and America's role in the region, but no doubt it will be a few years before this is reflected in historical writing.[4]

The third major focus concerns the postwar economy and the origins of the Cold War. There has been a retreat from various interpretations that tended to blame all and everything on rapacious American capitalism and to shut eyes tightly against both the realities of Soviet power under Stalin's rule and the vast economic and political disruption that followed the global conflagration. The actual evidence has always been weak for the economic interpretation of the Cold War origins. While some of these interpretations harked back to a Jeffersonian past; others were based upon various utopian, socialist, and Marxist frameworks and visions. That last approach, however, has lost its force at a time when Marxism is in retreat even in its staunchest homelands. The "God that failed"—Marxism—has been joined by the economic model that failed—the Soviet economy; and that in turn has had its effects on historical writing.

This is not to say that there is not considerable attention to the economic aspects of postwar politics, but rather that it is following different paths. Michael Hogan has analyzed the Marshall Plan through the framework of what has become known as the "corporatist" school. He sees it as the product of public-private cooperation, reflecting a "neo-capitalist" New Deal synthesis—and also a reasonable defense of American interests carried out in a positive fashion. Yet, though the goal was to make Europe over in America's "way," the Europeans proved quite adept at pursuing their own interest and, in the process, partly making America over in Europe's way. In his thoughtful study, Robert Pollard emphasizes reconstruction in the pursuit of economic growth and as the basis for U.S. security policy. The aim was a "sounder world political and economic structure" than that which had precipitated World War II.[5]

Finally, there are the efforts to understand Soviet policy—as seen from Moscow. Vojtech Mastny argues that the basis for Stalin's postwar policies were really laid out in the Nazi-Soviet Pact of 1939—both in terms of territorial objectives and in the mechanics of cynicism and ruthlessness. By this interpretation, Soviet expansion into Central Europe was facilitated by Western complacency. Stalin's hands, Mastny writes, "were tied by the Soviet system which had bred him and which he felt compelled to perpetuate by his execrable methods: that system was the true cause of the Cold War."[6] But now we must await what may emerge from the archives in Moscow themselves.

Bibliographical Note to the Revised Edition

1. John Lewis Gaddis, *The Long Peace: Inquiries into the History of the Cold War* (New York: Oxford University Press, 1987), and *Strategies of Containment: A Critical Appraisal of Postwar American National Security Policy* (New York: Oxford University Press, 1982). Melvin P. Leffler, "The United States and the Strategic Dimensions of the Marshall Plan," *Diplomatic History* 12 (Summer 1988), pp. 277–306, and "The American Conception of National Security and the Beginnings of the Cold War, 1945–1948," *American Historical Review* 89 (April 1984): 346–81. See his forthcoming *Global Predominance: The Truman Administration, The Cold War, and American National Security 1945–1952*. Walter Isaacson and Evan Thomas, *The Wise Men: Six Friends and the World They Made* (New York: Touchstone, 1988); Ronald Steel, *Walter Lippmann and the American Century* (Boston: Little Brown, 1980). Also see Forrest C. Pogue, *George C. Marshall: Statesman 1945–1959* (New York: Viking, 1987); On the place of the atomic bomb, Gregg Herkin, *The Winning Weapon: The Atomic Bomb in the Cold War 1945–1950* (New York: Vintage, 1982). Hugh de Santis offers a different view of the Foreign Service in *The Diplomacy of Silence: The American Foreign Service, the Soviet Union, and the Cold War* (Chicago: University of Chicago Press, 1980).
2. British policy is examined in Fraser J. Harbutt, *The Iron Curtain: Churchill, America, and the Origins of the Cold War* (Oxford: Oxford University Press, 1986); and Terry Anderson, *The United States, Great Britain, and the Cold War 1944–1947* (Columbia: University of Missouri Press, 1981). Harbutt further argues that the Cold War started not because of Soviet actions in Eastern Europe but because "Stalin stepped *outside* the East European theater. . . . By moving beyond this protected sphere, however, Stalin exposed the Soviet Union to the danger of Anglo-American political and public mobilization." (Harbutt, *Iron Curtain*, p. 283). Two important biographies are Alan Bullock, *Ernest Bevin: Foreign Secretary 1945–1951* (London: Heineman, 1984); and Alastair Horne, *Harold Macmillan 1891–1956, Vol. 1* (New York: Viking, 1989). (Macmillan quoted, *ibid.*, p. 160.) Bevin in "The Threat to Western Civilization," C.P. (48) 72/March 3, 1948/CAB 129, 25/Public Record Office.
3. Bruce Kuniholm explores how Soviet pressure on the "Northern Tier" countries—for both offensive and defensive reasons—stimulated the United States to step into the vacuum created by British weakness and launch a series of commitments, including the Truman Doctrine, aimed at preserving the balance of power in the region. Bruce H. Kuniholm, *The Origins of the Cold War in the Near East: Great Power Conflict and Diplomacy in Iran, Turkey, and Greece* (Princeton: Princeton University Press, 1980). William Roger Lewis, in his monumental and superb work on British foreign policy, makes excellent use of the Foreign Office archives to analyze the developments from the perspective of the retreat of British power. Wm. Roger Louis, *The British Empire in the Middle East 1945–1951: Arab Nationalism, the United States, and Postwar Imperialism* (Oxford: Oxford University Press, 1984). Also Barry Rubin, *The Great Powers in the Middle East 1941–1947: The Road to the Cold War* (London: Frank Cass, 1980). Geir Lundestad examines how the United States was "invited" into Scandinavia in *America,*

Scandinavia, and The Cold War (New York: Columbia University Press, 1980). An important new study on the central subject of contention, Germany, is in the forthcoming Thomas A. Schwartz, *America's Germany: John J. McClay, the Federal Republic of Germany, and the Creation of the American Empire, 1949–1955*. (Cambridge: Harvard University Press, 1990).

4. Joint Chiefs quoted in Robert J. McMahon, "The Cold War in Asia: Toward a New Synthesis," *Diplomatic History* 12 (Summer 1988): 321 See Michael Schaller, *The American Occupation of Japan: The Origins of the Cold War in Asia* (New York: Oxford, 1985). William S. Borden emphasizes the "reverse course" of 1947 in U.S. policy towards Japan, aimed at stimulating recovery in a derelict economy and how the military procurement boom launched the postwar Japanese economic takeoff. *The Pacific Alliance: United States Foreign Policy and Japanese Trade Recovery, 1947–1955* (Madison: University of Wisconsin, 1984). On the Vietnam War, see George C. Herring, *America's Longest War: The United States and Vietnam, 1950–1975* (New York: Knopf, 1986); and Gary R. Hess, *The United States' Emergence as a Southeast Asian Power, 1940–1950* (New York: Columbia University Press, 1987). Marc Gallichio argues that the Cold War in Asia was set in motion by the character of the Japanese surrender throughout the region, and the clashing forces of nationalism, communism, and colonialism. In this mix, its resources terribly strained and objectives unclear, the United States improvised and responded to changing circumstances. Marc S. Gallichio, *The Cold War Begins in Asia: American East Asian Policy and the Fall of the Japanese Empire* (New York: Columbia, 1988).

5. Michael J. Hogan, *The Marshall Plan: America, Britain, and the Reconstruction of Western Europe, 1947–1952* (Cambridge: Cambridge University Press, 1987); Robert A. Pollard, *Economic Security and the Origins of the Cold War, 1945–1950* (New York: Columbia University Press, 1985), p. 4. The corporatist view has been skillfully and thoughtfully pursued in David S. Painter, *Oil and the American Century: The Political Economy of U.S. Foreign Oil Policy, 1941–1954* (Baltimore: Johns Hopkins, 1986). The intersection of oil, the Middle East, and the Cold War is also examined in several other stimulating new books: Aaron David Miller, *Search for Security: Saudi Arabian Oil and American Oil Policy, 1939–1949* (Chapel Hill: University of North Carolina Press, 1980); Michael B. Stoff, *Oil, War, and American Security: The Search for a National Policy on Foreign Oil, 1941–1947* (New Haven: Yale University Press, 1980); and Irvine H. Anderson, *Aramco, the United States, and Saudi Arabia: A Study in the Dynamics of Foreign Oil Policy, 1933–1950* (Princeton: Princeton University Press, 1981). Anderson does a particularly good job in capturing the attitudes, roles, and complexities of private companies—something sometimes skipped over by diplomatic historians. Also see Daniel Yergin, *The Prize: The Epic Quest for Oil, Money, and Power* (New York: Simon and Schuster, 1990).

6. Vojtech Mastny, *Russia's Road to the Cold War* (New York: Columbia University Press, 1979) p. 301. Also see William Taubman, *Stalin's American Policy: From Entente to Détente to Cold War* (New York: Norton, 1982). Taubman argues that the character of Stalin and his system made cooperation impossible.

Bibliography

Major Archives

Churchill College, Cambridge, England

A. V. Alexander papers
Clement Attlee Papers
Edward Halifax papers (microfilm)

Harvard University, Cambridge, Massachusetts

Winthrop Aldrich papers
Joseph Grew papers
Christian Herter papers
Thomas Lamont papers

Library of Congress, Washington, D.C.

Tom Connally papers
Herbert Feis papers
Felix Frankfurter papers
Phillip Jessup papers
Robert Patterson papers
Carl Spaatz papers
Laurence Steinhardt papers
Robert A. Taft papers
Hoyt Vandenberg papers

National Archives, Washington, D.C.

Modern Military records (RG 218)
Claude Pepper papers
State Department Decimal Series
State Department: H. Freeman Matthews and John Hickerson files

Princeton University, Princeton, New Jersey

Bernard Baruch papers
John Foster Dulles papers
James Forrestal papers
George Kennan papers
Arthur Krock papers
David Lilienthal papers
Adlai Stevenson papers

Franklin D. Roosevelt Library, Hyde Park, New York

John Carmody papers
Oscar Cox papers
William D. Hassett papers
Leon Henderson papers
Harry L. Hopkins papers
Isador Lubin papers
R. Walton Moore papers
Henry M. Morgenthau, Jr., papers
President's Soviet Protocol Committee
Franklin Roosevelt: Map Room file
Franklin Roosevelt: Official file
Franklin Roosevelt: President's secretary's file
Samuel Rosenman papers

Harry S. Truman Library, Independence, Missouri

Dean Acheson papers
George V. Allen papers
Assistant Secretary of State for Economic Affairs papers
Eben Ayers papers
Thomas Blaisdell papers
William Clayton papers.
Clark Clifford files and papers

Harry S.Truman Library (contd.)

Jonathan Daniels papers
Robert Dennison papers
George Elsey files and papers
Ellen Clayton Garwood papers
William D. Hassett papers
Herschell Johnson papers
Joseph M. Jones papers
David D. Lloyd papers
Edwin Locke files and papers
Frank McNaughton papers
Charles Murphy papers
National Security Committee papers
Edwin G. Nourse papers
J. Anthony Panuch papers
President's Advisory Commission on Universal Training papers
President's Air Policy Commission papers
President's Committee on Foreign Aid papers
Harry B. Price notes
Samuel Rosenman papers
Charles Ross papers
Walter S. Salant papers
Alfred Schindler papers
John W. Snyder papers
Sidney Souers papers
Steven Springarn papers
John Steelman papers
Harry S. Truman papers: Central files
Harry S. Truman papers: Confidential files
Harry S. Truman papers: Official file
Harry S. Truman papers: President's secretary's file
Harry Vaughan papers
James Webb papers

Yale University, New Haven, Connecticut

Hanson Baldwin papers
Chester Bowles papers
Jerome Frank papers
Arthur Bliss Lane papers
Henry Stimson papers
Arnold Wolfers papers

I should also like to thank the National War College for their assistance.

OTHER MANUSCRIPT COLLECTIONS

Clement Attlee papers, University College, Oxford, England
James Byrnes papers, Clemson University, Clemson, South Carolina
Council on Foreign Relations papers, Council on Foreign Relations, New York
Hugh Dalton papers, London School of Economics
Joseph Dodge papers, Detroit Public Library
Dwight Eisenhower papers, Eisenhower Library, Abilene, Kansas
Foreign Office and Cabinet papers, Public Record Office, London
Samuel Harper papers, University of Chicago
Herbert Hoover papers, Herbert Hoover Library, West Branch, Iowa
Hastings Ismay papers, Liddell Hart Military Archives, King's College, London
James Pollock papers, University of Michigan
Sam Rayburn papers, Rayburn Library
Richard Scandrett papers, Columbia University
Edward Stettinius, Jr., papers, University of Virginia
John Taber papers, Cornell University, Ithaca, New York
Charles Tobey papers, Dartmouth College, Hanover, New Hampshire

Arthur Vandenberg papers, University of Michigan
Henry Wallace papers, University of Iowa
James Warburg papers, John F. Kennedy Library, Waltham, Massachusetts

I should also like to express special appreciation to Lady Liddell Hart, H. Stuart Hughes, and Charles Kindleberger for their kindness in allowing me to do research in papers in their private possession.

Unpublished Diaries

Eben Ayers diary, Truman Library
Walter Brown diary, Byrnes papers, Clemson University
Hugh Dalton diary, London School of Economics
Joseph Davies diary and journal, Library of Congress
James Forrestal diary, Princeton University
Felix Frankfurter diary, Library of Congress
Lord Halifax diary, Hickleton papers, Garrowby, York
William Leahy diary, Library of Congress
Henry Morgenthau diary and presidential diary, Roosevelt Library
James Pollock diary, University of Michigan
H. Alexander Smith diary, Princeton University
Harold Smith diary, Truman Library
Henry Stimson diary, Yale University

Interviews

The following people were kind enough to make themselves available to me for interviews, generally of between one and two hours in duration. Many of the interviews were tape-recorded.

Frank Altschul
David Balfour
Abram Bergson
Bernard Brodie
Benjamin V. Cohen
Elbridge Durbrow
George Elsey
Mark Ethridge
J. William Fulbright
Myron Gilmore
Loy Henderson
H. Stuart Hughes
Joseph E. Johnson
George Kistiakowsky
Foy Kohler
Elting Morison
Paul Porter
James Riddleberger
Eugene V. Rostow
Dean Rusk
Raymond Vernon
Victor Weisskopf

Oral Histories

Columbia University Oral History Collection
Harvey Bundy
Will Clayton
Isador Lubin
Marshall Plan Oral Histories
DeWitt Clinton Poole

Cornell University
Richard Scandrett oral history

Dulles Oral Histories (Princeton)

Theodore Achilles
Elliott Bell
James Byrnes
Thomas Dewey
Allen Dulles
Averell Harriman
Joseph C. Harsch
John Hickerson
Henry Luce
Carl McCardle
John McCloy
Frederick Reinhardt

Truman Library Oral History Collections

John Abbott
Theodore Achilles
George E. Allen
Willis Armstrong
David E. Bell
Ralph Block
Charles Bohlen
Bruce C. Clarke
William Draper
George Elsey
Thomas Finletter
William D. Hassett
Loy Henderson
Leon Keyserling
Halvard Lange
David Lawrence
Marx Leva
Edwin Locke
Max Lowenthal
Isador Lubin
George Marshall
Edward Mason
Clifford Matlock
H. Freeman Matthews
Charles Murphy
Frank Pace
James Reston
James Riddleberger
Samuel I. Rosenman
Charles Saltzman
John Sullivan
Harry Vaughan

Documents

Commission for the Publication of Diplomatic Documents. *Correspondence Between the Chairman of the Council of Ministers of the USSR and the Presidents of the USA and the Prime Ministers of Great Britain During the Great Patriotic War of 1941–5*. Moscow: Foreign Language Publishing House, 1957; New York: Capricorn Books, 1965.

Great Britain, Parliament. *Hansard's Parliamentary Debates*.

Great Britain, Secretary of State for Foreign Affairs. *Selected Documents on Germany and the Question of Berlin: 1944–1961*. Cmnd. 1552, December 1961.

The Pentagon Papers. *New York Times* Edition. New York: Bantam, 1971.

The Tehran, Yalta & Potsdam Conferences: Documents. Moscow: Progress Publishers, 1969.

Harry S. Truman: Public Papers. 1945–50.

United Nations, Department of Economic Affairs. *Economic Report: Salient Features of the World Economic Situation 1945–7*. New York: 1948.

United Nations, Economic Commission for Europe. *A Survey of the Economic Situation and Prospects of Europe*. Geneva: United Nations, 1948.

U.S. Congress. *Congressional Record*.

U.S. Congress. House. *Armed Services Committee*. *U.S.-Vietnam Relations*. By the Department of Defense. Series Print. Vol. 1. 1971 (Pentagon Papers.)

U.S. Congress. House. Select Committee on Post-War Military Policy. *Proposal to Establish a Single Department of Defense: Hearings*. 78th Cong., 2nd sess., 1944.

U.S. Congress. Senate. Committee on Foreign Relations. *Causes, Origins, and Lessons of the Vietnam War: Hearings*. 92nd Cong., 2nd sess., 1972.

———. *Documents on Germany: 1944–61*. Prepared by the Historical Office, Department of State, Washington, D.C.: Government Printing Office, 1961.

———. *Foreign Relief Aid: 1947. Hearings Held in Executive Session before the Senate Committee on Foreign Relations on S.1774.* 80th Cong., 1st sess., 1947. Historical series, 1973.

———. *Foreign Relief Assistance Act of 1948. Hearings Held in Executive Session.* 80th Cong., 2nd sess., 1948. Historical Series, 1973.

———. *Legislative Origins of the Truman Doctrine. Hearings Held in Executive Session on S.938.* 80th Cong., 1st sess., 1947. Historical Series, 1973.

———. *The Vandenberg Resolution and the North Atlantic Treaty. Hearings Held in Executive Session on S. Res. 239 and on Executive L.* 80th Cong., 2nd sess., 1948; 81st Cong., 1st sess., 1949. Historical Series, 1973.

U.S. Congress. Senate. Committee on Foreign Relations and Committee on Armed Services. *Military Assistance Program: 1949. Joint Hearings Held in Executive Session on S.2388.* 81st Cong., 1st sess., 1949. Historical Series, 1974.

U.S. Congress. Senate. Committee on Naval Affairs. *Unification of the War and Navy Departments and Postwar Organization for National Security: Report to James Forrestal.* 79th Cong., 1st sess., 1945. (Eberstadt Report.)

U.S. Congress. Senate. Military Affairs Committee. *Department of Armed Forces, Department of Military Security: Hearings.* 79th Cong., 1st sess., 1945.

U.S. Congress. Senate. Select Committee to Study Governmental Operations with Respect to Intelligence Activities. *Final Report: Supplementary Detailed Staff Reports on Foreign and Military Intelligence.* Book IV. 94th Cong., 2nd sess., 1976.

U.S. Congress. Senate. Special Committee Investigating Petroleum Resources. *American Petroleum Interests in Foreign Countries: Hearings.* 79th Cong., 1st sess., 1945.

———. *Wartime Petroleum Policy: Hearings.* 79th Cong., 1st sess., 1945.

U.S. Council of Economic Advisers. *Annual Report to the President,* 1946–8.

———. *The Impact of Foreign Aid upon the Domestic Economy.* Washington: Government Printing Office, October 1947.

U.S. Department of State. *Foreign Relations of the United States* (cited as *FR*).

U.S. National Military Establishment. *Annual Report of the Secretary of the Army: 1948.* Washington: Government Printing Office, 1949.

———. *First Report of the Secretary of Defense: 1948.* Washington: Government Printing Office, 1949.

United States Strategic Bombing Survey. *The Effects of Strategic Bombing on the German War Economy.* Washington, D.C.: 1945.

Books

Abell, Tyler, ed. *Drew Pearson: Diaries 1949–1959.* New York: Holt, Rinehart and Winston, 1974.

Acheson, Dean. *Morning and Noon.* Boston: Houghton Mifflin, 1965.
———. *Present at the Creation: My Years in the State Department.* New York: New American Library, 1970.
———. *Sketches from Life.* New York: Harper & Brothers, 1960.
Adenauer, Konrad. *Memoirs 1945–1953.* Translated by Beate Ruhm von Oppen. Chicago: Henry Regnery, 1965.
Albion, Robert G., and Connery, Robert H. *Forrestal and the Navy.* New York: Columbia University Press, 1962.
Alexander, Harold. *The Alexander Memoirs.* London: Cassell, 1962.
Alliluyeva, Svetlana. *Twenty Letters to a Friend.* Translated by Priscilla Johnson McMillan. New York: Harper & Row, 1967.
Almond, Gabriel. *The American People and Foreign Policy.* New York: Harcourt, Brace 1950.
Alperovitz, Gar. *Atomic Diplomacy: Hiroshima and Potsdam.* New York: Vintage Books, 1967.
———. *Cold War Essays.* New York: Anchor Books, 1970.
Ambrose, Stephen E. *Rise to Globalism: American Foreign Policy Since 1938.* London, Allen Lane, Penguin Press, 1971.
Anderson, Clinton, and Viorst, Milton. *Outsider in the Senate.* New York: World Publishing, 1970.
Anderton, David. *Strategic Air Command.* New York: Scribner's, 1976.
Arkes, Hadley. *Bureaucracy, the Marshall Plan and the National Interest.* Princeton: Princeton University Press, 1972.
Arnold, H. H. *Global Mission.* London: Hutchinson, 1951.
Auty, Phyllis. *Tito.* London: Penguin, 1974.

Baldwin, Hanson W. *The Price of Power.* New York: Harper & Brothers, 1947.
Barnet, Richard J. *Roots of War: The Men and Institutions behind U.S. Foreign Policy.* Baltimore: Penguin, 1973.
Barraclough, Geoffrey. *An Introduction to Contemporary History.* London: Pelican Books, 1969.
Baruch, Bernard. *The Public Years.* New York: Holt, Rinehart and Winston, 1960.
Beard, Charles. *The Idea of National Interest.* New York: Macmillan, 1934.
Beitzell, Robert. *The Uneasy Alliance.* New York: Knopf, 1972.
Bell, Quentin. *Virginia Woolf.* New York: Harcourt Brace Jovanovich, 1972.
Berle, Adolph. *Navigating the Rapids 1918–1971.* New York: Harcourt Brace Jovanovich, 1973.
Bernstein, Barton, ed. *Politics and Policies of the Truman Administration.* Chicago: Quadrangle, 1970.
———, ed. *Towards a New Past: Dissenting Essays in American History.* New York: Pantheon, 1968.
Bethell, Nicholas. *Gomulka.* London: Penguin, 1972.
Bialer, Seweryn, ed. *Stalin and His Generals.* New York: Pegasus, 1969.
Bidault, Georges. *Resistance: The Political Autobiography.* Translated by Marianne Sinclair. New York: Praeger, 1965.
Birkenhead, Earl of. *Halifax.* London: Hamish Hamilton, 1965.
Bishop, Donald G. *The Roosevelt-Litvinov Agreements.* Syracuse: Syracuse University Press, 1965.

Blum, John Morton. *From the Morgenthau Diaries: Years of Crisis, 1928–38.* Boston: Houghton Mifflin, 1959.
———. *From the Morgenthau Diaries: Years of War, 1941–45.* Boston: Houghton Mifflin, 1967.
———. *V Was for Victory.* New York: Harcourt Brace Jovanovich, 1976.
———, ed. *The Price of Vision: The Diary of Henry A. Wallace.* Boston: Houghton Mifflin, Boston, 1973.
Bohlen, Charles. *The Transformation of American Foreign Policy.* New York: W.W. Norton, 1969.
———. *Witness to History 1929–69.* New York: W. W. Norton, 1973.
Bowles, Chester. *Promises to Keep: My Years in Public Life, 1941–1969.* New York: Harper & Row, 1971.
Brandt, Heinz. *The Search for a Third Way.* Translated by Salvator Attanasio. New York: Doubleday, 1970.
Brodie, Bernard. *Strategy in the Missile Age.* Princeton: Princeton University Press, 1959.
———, ed. *The Absolute Weapon.* New York: Harcourt, Brace, 1946.
Browder, Robert Paul. *The Origins of Soviet-American Diplomacy.* Princeton: Princeton University Press, 1953.
Bryant, Sir Arthur. *Triumph in the West: Based on the Personal Diaries of Field Marshal Lord Alanbrooke.* Garden City: Doubleday, 1959.
Brzezinski, Zbigniew. *The Soviet Bloc.* Cambridge: Harvard University Press, 1969.
Bullitt, Orville H., ed. *For the President: Personal and Secret: Correspondence Between Franklin Roosevelt and William C. Bullitt.* Boston: Houghton Mifflin, 1972.
Burns, James MacGregor. *Roosevelt: The Soldier of Freedom.* New York: Harcourt Brace Jovanovich, 1970.
Bush, Vannevar. *Pieces of the Action.* New York: William Morrow, 1970.
Byrnes, James F. *All in One Lifetime.* New York: Harper & Brothers,1958.
———. *Speaking Frankly.* New York: Harper & Brothers, 1947.

Calleo, David P., and Rowland, Benjamin M. *America and the World Political Economy: Atlantic Dreams and National Realities.* Bloomington: Indiana University Press, 1973.
Calvocoressi, Peter, and Wint, Guy. *Total War.* London: Allen Lane, Penguin Press, 1972.
Cantril, Hadley. *Public Opinion 1935–1946.* Princeton: Princeton University Press, 1951.
Caraley, Demetrios. *The Politics of Military Unification.* New York: Columbia University Press, 1966.
Carr, Edward Hallett. *The Bolshevik Revolution 1917–23.* 3 vols. London: Pelican Books, 1966.
———. *Socialism in One Country 1924–26.* Vol. 1. London: Pelican Books, 1970.
———. *The Twenty-Years Crisis 1919–39.* London: Macmillan, 1939; New York: Harper Torchbook, 1964.
Chadwin, Mark Lincoln. *The Hawks of World War II.* Chapel Hill: University of North Carolina Press, 1968.
Chauvel, Jean. *Commentaire: D'Alger à Berne 1944–1952.* Paris: Fayard, 1972.

Chuikov, Vasili I. *The End of the Third Reich.* Translated by Ruth Kisch. London: MacGibbon & Kee, 1967.
Churchill, Winston. *Triumph and Tragedy.* Boston: Houghton Mifflin, 1953.
Clay, Lucius D. *Decision in Germany.* Garden City: Doubleday, 1950.
Clemens, Diane Shaver. *Yalta.* New York: Oxford University Press, 1970.
Cochran, Bert. *Harry Truman and the Crisis Presidency.* New York: Funk & Wagnalls, 1973.
Cohen, Stephen F. *Bukharin and the Bolshevik Revolution.* New York: Vintage Books, 1975.
Cohen, Warren I. *America's Response to China.* New York: John Wiley, 1971.
Coit, Margaret L. *Mr. Baruch.* Boston: Houghton Mifflin, 1957.
Conquest, Robert. *The Great Terror.* Rev. ed. New York: Collier Books, 1973.
Cooper, Chester L. *The Lost Crusade: America in Vietnam.* Greenwich: Fawcett Premier Book, 1972.
Cooper, Duff. *Old Men Forget.* London: Rupert Hart-Davis, 1953.
Cottam, Richard W. *Nationalism in Iran.* Pittsburgh: University of Pittsburgh Press, 1964.

Daniels, Jonathan. *Frontier on the Potomac.* New York: Macmillan, 1946.
———. *The Man of Independence.* Philadelphia: J. B. Lippincott, 1950.
———. *White House Witness.* New York: Doubleday, 1975.
Davies, Joseph. *Mission to Moscow.* New York: Pocket Books, 1943.
Davis, Lynn Etheridge. *The Cold War Begins.* Princeton: Princeton University Press, 1974.
Davis, Vincent. *Postwar Defense Policy and the US Navy, 1943–1946.* Chapel Hill: University of North Carolina Press, 1966.
Davison, W. Phillips. *The Berlin Blockade.* Princeton: Princeton University Press, 1958.
Deane, John R. *The Strange Alliance: The Story of Our Efforts at Wartime Cooperation with Russia.* New York: Viking, 1947.
DeConde, Alexander, ed. *Isolation and Security.* Durham: Duke University Press, 1957.
Dedijer, Vladimir. *The Battle Stalin Lost: Memoirs of Yugoslavia 1948–53.* New York: Viking Press, 1970.
———. *Tito Speaks.* London: Weidenfeld and Nicolson, 1954.
de Gaulle, Charles. *The Complete War Memoirs.* New York: Simon and Schuster, 1964.
Dehio, Ludwig. *The Precarious Balance: Four Centuries of the European Power Struggle.* Translated by Charles Fullman. New York: Knopf, 1962.
Dennett, Raymond, and Johnson, Joseph E., eds. *Negotiating with the Russians.* Boston: World Peace Foundation, 1951.
Dennett, Raymond, and Turner, Robert K., eds. *Documents on American Foreign Relations.* Vols. 8–10. Princeton: Princeton University Press, 1948–50.
Deutscher, Isaac. *Stalin: A Political Biography.* Rev. ed. London: Pelican Books, 1966.

Dilks, David, ed. *The Diaries of Sir Alexander Cadogan 1938–45.* London: Cassell, 1971.

Divine, Robert. *Foreign Policy and U.S. Presidential Elections.* New York: Franklin Watts, 1974.

———. *Roosevelt and World War II.* Baltimore: Johns Hopkins Press, 1969.

———. *Second Chance: The Triumph of Internationalism in America during World War II.* New York: Atheneum, 1967.

Dixon, Piers. *Double Diploma: The Life of Sir Pierson Dixon.* London: Hutchinson, 1968.

Djilas, Milovan. *Conversations with Stalin.* Translated by Michael B. Petrovich. London: Pelican Books, 1969.

Dobney, Frederick J., ed. *Selected Papers of Will Clayton.* Baltimore: Johns Hopkins Press, 1971.

Dolgun, Alexander, and Watson, Patrick. *Alexander Dolgun's Story: An American in the Gulag.* New York: Ballantine Books, 1976.

Druks, Herbert M. *Harry S. Truman and the Russians 1945–53.* New York: Robert Speller & Sons, 1966.

Dulles, Allen W. *The Craft of Intelligence.* New York: Harper & Row, 1963.

———. *The Secret Surrender.* New York: Harper & Row, 1966.

Dulles, John Foster. *War, Peace, and Change.* New York: Harper & Brothers, 1939.

———. *War or Peace.* New York: Macmillan, 1950.

Eden, Anthony. *The Eden Memoirs: The Reckoning.* London: Cassell, 1965.

Earle, Edward Mead, ed. *Makers of Modern Strategy.* Princeton: Princeton University Press, 1943.

Ehrman, John. *Grand Strategy.* Vol. 6. London: Her Majesty's Stationery Office, 1956.

Elliott, William Y., ed. *The Political Economy of American Foreign Policy.* New York: Henry Holt, 1955.

Elson, Robert T. *The World of Time Inc.* Vol. 2. New York: Atheneum, 1973.

Elwell-Sutton, L. P. *Persian Oil.* London: Lawrence and Wishart, 1955.

Erickson, John. *The Road to Stalingrad: Stalin's War with Germany.* Vol. 1. New York: Harper & Row, 1975.

Eudes, Dominique. *The Kapetanios.* Translated by John Howe. New York: Monthly Review Press, 1972.

Feis, Herbert. *The Atomic Bomb and the End of World War II.* Princeton: Princeton University Press, 1966.

———. *Between War and Peace: The Potsdam Conference.* Princeton: Princeton University Press, 1960.

———. *The China Tangle.* Princeton: Princeton University Press, 1953.

———. *Churchill-Roosevelt-Stalin.* Princeton: Princeton University Press, 1957.

———. *From Trust to Terror.* New York: Norton, 1970.

———. *Petroleum and American Foreign Policy.* Palo Alto: Stanford University Press, 1944.

———. *Three International Episodes Seen from EA*. New York: Norton, 1946; reprinted in Norton Library, 1966.
Feld, Mischa Jac, and Peterman, Ivan H. *The Hug of the Bear*. New York: Holt, Rinehart and Winston, 1961.
Ferrell, Robert. *George C. Marshall*. Vol. 15. The American Secretaries of State and their Diplomacy, ed. by Robert Ferrell. New York: Cooper Square Publishers, 1966.
Fischer, Louis. *Men and Politics*. New York: Duell, Sloan and Pearce, 1941.
Flash, Edward. *Economic Advice and Presidential Leadership*. New York: Columbia University Press, 1965.
Fleming, D. W. *The Cold War and Its Origins 1917–60*. 2 vols. Garden City: Doubleday, 1961.
Fontaine, André. *History of the Cold War*. Translated by D. D. Paige. Vol. 1. New York: Knopf, 1968.
Fox, William T. R. *The American Study of International Relations*. Columbia: University of South Carolina Press, 1968.
———. *The Super-powers*. New York: Harcourt, Brace, 1944.
Freedman, Max, ed. *Roosevelt and Frankfurter: Their Correspondence 1928–45*. Boston: Little, Brown, 1967.
Freeland, Richard M. *The Truman Doctrine and the Origins of McCarthyism*. New York: Knopf, 1972.
Freidel, Frank. *FDR: Launching the New Deal*. Boston: Little, Brown, 1973
Friedman, Otto. *The Break-up of Czech Democracy*. London: Victor Gollancz, 1950.

Gaddis, John Lewis. *The United States and the Origins of the Cold War*. New York: Columbia University Press, 1972.
Galbraith, John Kenneth. *The New Industrial State*. Boston: Houghton Mifflin, 1967.
Gallup, George. *The Gallup Poll: Public Opinion 1935–71*. Vol. 1. New York: Random House, 1972.
Gannon, Robert I. *The Cardinal Spellman Story*. Garden City: Doubleday, 1962.
Gardner, Lloyd C. *Architects of Illusion*. Chicago: Quadrangle, 1972.
Gardner, Lloyd C., Schlesinger, Arthur, Jr., and Morgenthau, Hans J. *The Origins of the Cold War*. Waltham: Ginn, 1970.
Gardner, Richard N. *Sterling Dollar Diplomacy*. New York: Oxford University Press, 1956. Rev. ed. New York: McGraw-Hill, 1969.
Gimbel, John. *The American Occupation of Germany: Politics and the Military 1945–49*. Stanford: Stanford University Press, 1968.
———. *The Origins of the Marshall Plan*. Stanford: Stanford University Press, 1976.
Ginzburg, Eugenia. *Into the Whirlwind*. Translated by Paul Stevenson and Manya Harari. London: Penguin, 1968.
Gladwyn, Lord. *The Memoirs of Lord Gladwyn*. London: Weidenfeld and Nicolson, 1972.
Gottlieb, Manuel. *The German Peace Settlement and the Berlin Crisis*. New York: Paine-Whitman, 1960.

Goulden, Joseph C. *The Best Years: 1945–1950.* New York: Atheneum, 1976.
Gowing, Margaret. *Independence and Deterrence: Britain and Atomic Energy 1945–52.* 2 vols. London: Macmillan, 1974.
Greene, Graham. *The Quiet American.* New York: Viking, 1956; Bantam, 1974.
Greenfield, Kent Roberts. *American Strategy in World War II: A Reconsideration.* Baltimore: Johns Hopkins Press, 1973.
Grew, Joseph C. *Turbulent Era.* 2 vols. Boston: Houghton Mifflin, 1952.

Halifax, Earl of. *Fulness of Days.* London: Collins, 1957.
Halle, Louis J. *The Cold War as History.* New York: Harper & Row, 1967.
Hamby, Alonzo L. *Beyond the New Deal: Harry S. Truman and American Liberalism.* New York: Columbia University Press, 1973.
Hamilton, John, ed. *The Federalist.* Philadelphia: J. B. Lippincott, 1866.
Hammond, Paul Y. *Organizing for Defense.* Princeton: Princeton University Press, 1961.
Hansen, Alvin H. *The Postwar American Economy.* New York: Norton, 1964.
Harper, Samuel. *The Russia I Believe In.* Chicago: University of Chicago Press, 1945.
Harriman, W. Averell. *America and Russia in a Changing World.* Garden City: Doubleday, 1971.
Harriman, W. Averell, and Abel, Elie. *Special Envoy to Churchill and Stalin 1941–1946.* New York: Random House, 1975.
Hartmann, Susan M. *Truman and the 80th Congress.* Columbia: University of Missouri Press, 1971.
Hartz, Louis. *The Liberal Tradition in America: An Interpretation of American Political Thought Since the Revolution.* New York: Harcourt, Brace & World, 1955.
Hassett, William D. *Off the Record with FDR, 1942–5.* New Brunswick: Rutgers University Press, 1958.
Heinrichs, Waldo H. *American Ambassador: Joseph Grew and the Development of the United States Diplomatic Tradition.* Boston: Little, Brown, 1966.
Hellman, Lillian. *Scoundrel Time.* Boston: Little, Brown, 1976.
Henderson, Hubert. *The Inter-War Years and Other Papers.* Edited by Henry Clay. Oxford: Oxford University Press, 1955.
Herring, George. *Aid to Russia 1941–46.* New York: Columbia University Press, 1973.
Herz, Martin. *Beginnings of the Cold War.* Bloomington: University of Indiana Press, 1966.
Hewlett, Richard G., and Anderson, Oscar E., Jr. *The New World: 1939–46.* University Park: Pennsylvania State University Press, 1962.
Hewlett, Richard G., and Duncan, Francis. *Atomic Shield: 1947–52.* University Park: Pennsylvania State University Press, 1969.
Hillman, William. *Mr. President.* New York: Farrar, Straus & Young, 1952.
Hinsley, F. H. *Nationalism and the International System.* London: Hodder & Stoughton, 1973.

———. *Power and the Pursuit of Peace.* Cambridge: Cambridge University Press, 1967.

Hoopes, Townsend. *The Devil and John Foster Dulles.* Boston: Atlantic-Little, Brown, 1973.

Horowitz, David, ed. *Containment and Revolution.* Boston: Beacon Press, 1968.

Howard, Michael. *Studies in War and Peace.* New York: Viking Press, 1971.

Hughes, H. Stuart. *The United States and Italy.* Cambridge, Mass.: Harvard University Press, 1965.

Hull, Cordell. *Memoirs.* 2 vols. New York: Macmillan, 1948.

Huntington, Samuel. *The Common Defense.* New York: Columbia University Press, 1961.

Iatrides, John. *Revolt in Athens: The Greek Communist "Second-Round," 1944–1945.* Princeton: Princeton University Press, 1972.

Israel, Fred., ed. *The War Diaries of Breckinridge Long.* Lincoln: University of Nebraska Press, 1966.

Issraeljan, Victor. *The Anti-Hitler Coalition.* Moscow: Progress Publishers, 1971.

Janeway, Eliot. *The Struggle for Survival.* New York: Weybright and Talley, 1968.

Janis, Irving L. *Victims of Groupthink: A Psychological Study of Foreign-Policy and Fiascoes.* Boston: Houghton Mifflin, 1972.

Jech, Karel, ed. *The Czechoslovak Economy 1945–1948.* Prague: State Pedagogical Publishing House, 1968.

Jones, Joseph M. *The Fifteen Weeks.* New York: Harcourt, Brace & World, 1964.

Kaiser, Robert G. *Cold Winter, Cold War.* New York: Stein and Day, 1974.

Kennan, George. *Memoirs 1925–50.* New York: Bantam, 1969.

———. *Memoirs 1950–63.* Boston: Atlantic-Little, Brown, 1972.

———. *Russia and the West Under Lenin and Stalin.* New York: New American Library, 1961.

Kilmarx, Robert. *A History of Soviet Air Power.* New York: Praeger, 1962.

Kirkendall, Richard S., ed. *The Truman Period as a Research Field: A Reappraisal 1972.* Columbia: University of Missouri Press, 1974.

Knebel, Fletcher, and Bailey, Charles W., II. *No High Ground.* New York: Bantam, 1961.

Kolko, Gabriel. *The Politics of War.* London: Weidenfeld and Nicolson, 1968.

———. *The Roots of American Foreign Policy.* Boston: Beacon Press, 1969.

Kolko, Joyce, and Kolko, Gabriel. *The Limits of Power: The World and United States Foreign Policy, 1945–54.* New York: Harper & Row, 1972.

Kousoulas, D. George. *Revolution and Defeat: The Story of the Greek Communist Party.* London: Oxford University Press, 1965.

Krock, Arthur. *Memoirs: Sixty Years on the Firing Line.* New York: Funk & Wagnalls, 1968.

Kuklick, Bruce. *American Policy and the Division of Germany.* Ithaca: Cornell University Press, 1972.

Kuusinen, Aino. *The Rings of Destiny: Inside Soviet Russia from Lenin to Brezhnev.* Translated by Paul Stevenson. New York: William Morrow, 1974.

LaFeber, Walter. *America, Russia and the Cold War.* 3rd ed. New York: John Wiley and Son, 1976.

———. *The New Empire.* Ithaca: Cornell University Press, 1963.

Lane, Arthur Bliss. *I Saw Poland Betrayed.* Reprint ed. Boston: Western Islands, 1965.

Lash, Joseph. *Eleanor and Franklin.* New York: New American Library, 1971.

———. *Eleanor: The Years Alone.* New York: New American Library, 1973.

Leahy, William. *I Was There.* New York: Whittlesey House, 1950.

Lenin, Vladimir Ilyich. *Collected Works.* Vol. 7. Moscow: Progress, 1966.

Leonhard, Wolfgang. *Child of the Revolution.* Translated by C. M. Woodhouse. Chicago: Henry Regnery, 1958. Gateway edition.

Levin, N. Gordon. *Woodrow Wilson and World Politics.* New York: Oxford University Press, 1967.

Levine, Isaac Don, ed. *Plain Talk: An Anthology.* New Rochelle: Arlington House, 1976.

Lewin, M. *Russian Peasants and Soviet Power: A Study of Collectivization.* Translated by Irene Nove. New York: W. W. Norton, 1975.

Liddell Hart, Basil. *The History of the Second World War.* New York: Putnam's, 1971.

Lie, Trygve. *In the Cause of Peace.* New York: Macmillan, 1954.

Lieberman, Joseph I. *The Scorpion and the Tarantula: The Struggle to Control Atomic Weapons 1945–9.* Boston: Houghton Mifflin, 1970.

Lilienthal, David. *Journals: The Atomic Energy Years 1945–50.* New York: Harper & Row, 1964.

Link, Arthur. *Wilson the Diplomatist.* Baltimore: Johns Hopkins, 1957.

Lippmann, Walter. *The Cold War.* Ronald Steel, ed. New York: Harper & Row, 1972.

———. *U.S. Foreign Policy: Shield of the Republic.* New York: Pocket Books, 1943.

Loebl, Eugen. *My Mind on Trial.* New York: Harcourt Brace Jovanovich, 1976.

———. *Sentenced & Tried: The Stalinist Purges in Czechoslovakia.* London: Elek Books, 1969.

London, Artur. *The Confession.* Translated by Alastair Hamilton. New York: William Morrow, 1970.

Lototzky, C. C., ed. *The Soviet Army.* Moscow: Progress, 1971.

Luard, Evan. *Peace and Opinion.* London: Oxford University Press, 1962.

Maddox, Robert James. *The New Left and the Origins of the Cold War.* Princeton: Princeton University Press, 1973.

Maier, Charles S. "Revisionism and the Interpretation of Cold War Origins." *Perspectives in American History IV.* Cambridge, Mass.: Harvard University Press, 1970.

Maisky, Ivan. *Memoirs of a Soviet Ambassador.* Translated by Andrew Rothstein. New York: Scribner's, 1968.

Mandelstam, Nadezhda. *Hope Abandoned.* Translated by Max Hayward. London: Collins and Harvill, 1974.

———. *Hope Against Hope.* Translated by Max Hayward. London: Collins and Harvill, 1971.

Marchetti, Victor, and Marks, John D. *The CIA and the Cult of Intelligence.* New York: Knopf, 1974.

Markowitz, Norman D. *The Rise and Fall of the People's Century: Henry A. Wallace and American Liberalism.* New York: The Free Press, 1973.

Mason, Edward S., and Asher, Robert E. *The World Bank Since Bretton Woods.* Washington, D.C.: Brookings Institution, 1973.

May, Ernest R. *American Imperialism: A Speculative Essay.* New York: Atheneum, 1968.

———. *"Lessons" of the Past.* New York: Oxford University Press, 1973.

Mayer, Arno. *Politics and Diplomacy of Peacemaking.* New York: Vintage Books, 1969.

———. *Wilson versus Lenin: The Political Origins of the New Diplomacy 1917–18.* Cleveland: World Publishing, 1964.

Mayne, Richard. *The Recovery of Europe 1945–73.* Rev. ed. New York: Anchor Books, 1973.

McIntire, Ross T. *White House Physician.* New York: G. P. Putnam's, 1946.

McLellan, David S. *Dean Acheson: The State Department Years.* New York: Dodd, Mead, 1976.

McNeill, William H. *America, Britain & Russia: Their Cooperation and Conflict, 1941–46.* New York: Oxford, 1953.

Medvedev, Roy A. *Let History Judge: The Origins and Consequences of Stalinism.* Translated by Colleen Taylor. Edited by David Joravsky and Georges Haupt. New York: Knopf, 1972.

Mee, Charles. *Meeting at Potsdam.* New York: M. Evans, 1975.

Melby, John F. *The Mandate of Heaven: Record of a Civil War in China 1945–49.* Garden City: Anchor Books, 1971.

Mikolajczyk, Stanislaw. *The Rape of Poland.* New York: McGraw-Hill, 1948.

Miller, Lynn H., and Pruessen, Ronald W. *Reflections on the Cold War.* Philadelphia: Temple University Press, 1973.

Millis, Walter. *Arms and Men.* New York: G. P. Putnam's, 1956.

Millis, Walter, ed. *The Forrestal Diaries.* New York: Viking, 1951.

Millis, Walter; Mansfield, Harvey C.; and Stein, Harold. *Arms and the State.* New York: Twentieth Century Fund, 1958.

Moore, Barrington. *Reflections on the Causes of Human Misery and Upon Certain Proposals to Eliminate Them.* Boston: Beacon Press, 1973.

Moran, Lord. *Churchill: The Struggle for Survival.* Boston: Houghton Mifflin, 1966.

Morison, Elting E. *Turmoil and Tradition: A Study of the Life and Times of Henry B. Stimson.* Boston: Houghton Mifflin, 1960.

Murphy, Robert. *Diplomat Among Warriors.* New York: Pyramid Books, 1965.

Nettl, J. P. *The Eastern Zone and Soviet Policy in Germany 1945–50.* London: Oxford University Press, 1951.

Nicolson, Harold. *Diaries and Letters 1945–62*. Edited by Nigel Nicolson. London: Fontana, 1971.

Nixon, Edgar B., ed. *Franklin D. Roosevelt and Foreign Affairs*. 3 vols. Cambridge, Mass.: Harvard University Press, 1969.

Notter, Harley. *Postwar Foreign Policy Preparation 1939–45*. Washington: Department of State, 1949.

Nove, Alec. *An Economic History of the USSR*. London: Allen Lane, Penguin Press, 1969.

O'Ballance, Edgar. *The Greek Civil War, 1944–49*. New York: Praeger, 1966.

Offner, Arnold. *American Appeasement: United States Foreign Policy and Germany 1933–1938*. New York: Norton, 1976.

Pachman, Ludek. *Checkmate in Prague*. Translated by Rosemary Brown. New York: Macmillan, 1975.

Page, Bruce; Leitch, David; and Knightley, Phillip. *Philby: The Spy Who Betrayed a Generation*. London: Penguin, 1969.

Paterson, Thomas. *Soviet-American Confrontation*. Baltimore: Johns Hopkins Press, 1973.

———, ed. *Cold War Critics*. Chicago: Quadrangle, 1971.

Patterson, James T. *Mr. Republican: A Biography of Robert A. Taft*. Boston: Houghton Mifflin, 1972.

Pelikan, Jiri, ed. *The Czechoslovak Political Trials, 1950–1954*. London: Macdonald, 1971.

Penrose, E. F. *Economic Planning for the Peace*. Princeton: Princeton University Press, 1953.

Phillips, Cabell. *The Truman Presidency*. New York: Macmillan, 1966.

Pickersgill, J. W., and Forster, D. F. *The Mackenzie King Record*. Vols. 2, 3, 4. Toronto: University of Toronto Press, 1968, 1970.

Pogue, Forrest C. *Education of a General*. New York: Viking, 1963.

———. *George C. Marshall: Ordeal and Hope*. New York: Viking, 1966.

———. *George C. Marshall: Organizer of Victory*. New York: Viking, 1973.

Ponomaryov, B.; Gromyko, A.; and Khvostov, V., eds. *History of Soviet Foreign Policy 1917–1945*. Moscow: Progress, 1969.

———, eds. *History of Soviet Foreign Policy 1945–70*. Moscow: Progress, 1974.

President's Air Policy Commission. *Survival in the Air Age*. Washington, D.C.: U.S. Government Printing Office, 1948.

Price, Harry Bayard. *The Marshall Plan and Its Meaning*. Ithaca: Cornell University Press, 1955.

Radosh, Ronald. *American Labor and United States Foreign Policy*. New York: Random House, 1969.

Range, Willard. *Franklin Roosevelt's World Order*. Athens: University of Georgia Press, 1959.

Ransom, Harry Howe. *The Intelligence Establishment*. Cambridge, Mass.: Harvard University Press, 1970.

Ratchford, B. U., and Ross, W. D. *Berlin Reparations Assignment*. Chapel Hill: University of North Carolina Press, 1947.

Ridgway, Matthew B. *Soldier: The Memoirs of Matthew B. Ridgway*. New York: Harper, 1956.

Ripka, Hubert. *Czechoslovakia Enslaved*. London: Victor Gollancz, 1950.

Roberts, Henry. *Eastern Europe: Politics, Revolution and Diplomacy*. New York: Knopf, 1970.

Rogow, Arnold. *Victim of Duty*. London: Rupert Hart-Davis, 1966.

Roosevelt, Eleanor. *This I Remember*. New York: Harper & Brothers, 1949.

Roosevelt, Elliott, ed. *Franklin Roosevelt: His Personal Letters 1928–1945*. 2 vols. New York: Duell, Sloan & Pearce, 1950.

Rosenau, James, ed. *Domestic Sources of Foreign Policy*. New York: Free Press, 1967.

Rosenman, Samuel I., *Working With Roosevelt*. New York: Harper & Brothers, 1952.

Rosenman, Samuel I., ed. *The Public Papers and Addresses of Franklin D. Roosevelt*. New York: Harper & Brothers, Macmillan, Random House, 1938–50.

Rostow, W. W. *How It All Began: Origins of the Modern Economy*. New York: McGraw-Hill, 1975.

Rothchild, Joseph. *East Central Europe between the Two World Wars*. Seattle: University of Washington Press, 1974.

Rozek, Edward J. *Allied Wartime Diplomacy: A Pattern in Poland*. New York: John Wiley, 1958.

Samuelson, Paul. *The Collected Scientific Papers*. Vol. 2. Edited by Joseph Stiglitz. Cambridge, Mass.: MIT Press, 1966.

Schilling, Warner; Hammond, Paul Y.; and Snyder, Glenn H. *Strategy, Politics, and Defense Budgets*. New York: Columbia University Press, 1962.

Schlesinger, Arthur, Jr. *The Imperial Presidency*. Boston: Houghton Mifflin, 1973.

Schurmann, Franz. *The Logic of World Power*. New York: Pantheon, 1974.

Scott, Otto J. *The Creative Ordeal: The Story of Raytheon*. New York: Atheneum, 1974.

Seale, Patrick, and McConville, Maureen. *Philby: The Long Road to Moscow*. London: Hamish Hamilton, 1973.

Senate Judiciary Committee. *Morgenthau Diaries: Germany*. Washington: Government Printing Office, 1967.

Serge, Victor. *From Lenin to Stalin*. New York: Monad Press, 1973.

———. *Memoirs of a Revolutionary*. Translated by Peter Sedgwick. London: Oxford University Press, 1975.

Seton-Watson, Hugh. *The East European Revolution*. 3rd ed. New York: Praeger, 1956.

Sharp, Tony. *The Wartime Alliance and the Zonal Division of Germany*. London: Oxford University Press, 1975.

Sherwin, Martin. *A World Destroyed*. New York: Knopf, 1975.

Sherwood, Robert E. *Roosevelt and Hopkins*. Rev. ed. in 2 vols. New York: Bantam, 1950.

Shtemenko, S. M. *The Soviet General Staff at War*. Moscow: Progress, 1970.

Shulman, Marshall D. *Beyond the Cold War*. New Haven: Yale University Press, 1966.

———. *Stalin's Foreign Policy Reappraised.* Cambridge, Mass.: Harvard University Press, 1963.

Slusser, Robert, ed. *Soviet Economic Policy in Postwar Germany.* New York: Research Program on the USSR, 1953.

Smith, Bruce L. R. *The Rand Corporation: Case Study of a Nonprofit Advisory Corporation.* Cambridge, Mass.: Harvard University Press, 1966.

Smith, Gaddis. *Dean Acheson.* The American Secretaries of State and Their Diplomacy, vol. 16. Edited by Robert H. Ferrell. New York: Cooper Square Publishers, 1972.

Smith, Jean Edward, ed. *The Papers of General Lucius D. Clay: Germany 1945–49.* 2 vols. Bloomington: Indiana University Press, 1974.

Smith, Perry McCoy. *The Air Force Plans for Peace, 1943–45.* Baltimore: Johns Hopkins Press, 1970.

Smith, R. Harris. *OSS: The Secret History of America's First Central Intelligence Agency.* Berkeley: University of California Press, 1972.

Smith, Walter Bedell. *My Three Years in Moscow.* Philadelphia: J. B. Lippincott, 1950.

Smyth, Henry D. *Atomic Energy for Military Purposes: The Official Report on the Development of the Atomic Bomb.* Princeton: Princeton University Press, 1945.

Sobolev, A. I. *Outline History of the Communist International.* Moscow: Progress, 1971.

Solzhenitsyn, Alexander I. *The Gulag Archipelago: 1918–1956.* Translated by Thomas Whitney. New York: Harper & Row, 1974.

Spaak, Paul-Henri. *The Continuing Battle: Memoirs of a European.* Translated by Henry Fox. Boston: Little, Brown, 1972.

Spanier, John W. *American Foreign Policy Since World War II.* 3rd ed. New York: Praeger, 1968.

Sprout, Harold, and Sprout, Margaret, eds. *Foundations of National Power.* Princeton: Princeton University Press, 1945.

Spykman, Nicholas John. *America's Strategy in World Politics.* New York: Harcourt, Brace, 1942.

Stavrianos, L. S. *Greece: American Dilemma and Opportunity.* Chicago: Henry Regnery, 1952.

Steel, Ronald. *Imperialists and Other Heroes: A Chronicle of the American Empire.* New York: Random House, 1971.

Stein, Harold, ed. *American Civil-Military Decisions.* Birmingham: University of Alabama, 1963.

Sterling, Claire. *The Masaryk Case.* New York: Harper & Row, 1970.

Stettinius, Edward R., Jr. *Roosevelt and the Russians.* Garden City: Doubleday, 1949.

Stikker, Dirk. *Men of Responsibility.* New York: Harper & Row, 1966.

Stimson, Henry L., and Bundy, McGeorge. *On Active Service in Peace and War.* New York: Harper, 1947.

Strang, Lord. *Home and Abroad.* London: Andre Deutsch, 1956.

Strauss, Lewis L. *Men and Decisions.* Garden City: Doubleday, 1962.

Sulzberger, C. L. *A Long Row of Candles: Memoirs and Diaries 1934–54.* New York: Macmillan, 1969.

Svennilson, Ingvar. *Growth and Stagnation in the European Economy.* Geneva: U.N. Economic Commission for Europe, 1954.

Talbott, Strobe, ed. and trans. *Khrushchev Remembers.* Boston: Little, Brown, 1970.

———, ed. and trans. *Khrushchev Remembers: The Last Testament.* New York: Bantam Books, 1976.

Taylor, A. J. P., et al. *Churchill Revised: A Critical Assessment.* New York: Dial Press. 1969.

Taylor, Maxwell. *The Uncertain Trumpet.* New York: Harper & Brothers, 1960.

Thayer, Charles. *Bears in the Caviar.* Philadelphia: J. B. Lippincott, 1951.

Theoharis, Athan. *Seeds of Repression: Harry S. Truman and the Origins of McCarthyism.* Chicago: Quadrangle, 1971.

———. *The Yalta Myths: An Issue in U.S. Politics 1945–50.* Columbia: University of Missouri Press, 1970.

Thorne, Christopher. *The Limits of Foreign Policy.* New York: Putnam's, 1973.

Thruelsen, Richard. *The Grumman Story.* New York: Praeger, 1976.

Truman, Harry S. *Memoirs: Year of Decisions.* Garden City: Doubleday, 1955.

———. *Memoirs: Years of Trial and Hope.* Garden City: Doubleday, 1956.

Truman, Margaret. *Harry S. Truman.* New York: William Morrow, 1973.

Tsoucalas, Constantine. *The Greek Tragedy.* London: Penguin, 1969.

Tucker, Robert W. *The Radical Left and American Foreign Policy.* Baltimore: Johns Hopkins Press, 1971.

Tugwell, Rexford Guy. *The Democratic Roosevelt.* Reprint ed. with new preface. Baltimore: Penguin, 1969.

———. *In Search of Roosevelt.* Cambridge, Mass.: Harvard University Press, 1972.

Ulam, Adam B. *The Bolsheviks.* New York: Collier Books, 1965.

———. *Expansion and Coexistence: The History of Soviet Foreign Policy 1917–67.* New York: Praeger, 1968.

———. *The Rivals.* New York: Viking, 1971.

———. *Stalin: The Man and His Era.* New York: Viking, 1973.

———. *Titoism and the Cominform.* Cambridge: Harvard University Press, 1952.

Upton, A. F. *Communism in Scandinavia and Finland.* Garden City: Anchor Books, 1973.

Vandenberg Arthur, Jr., ed. *The Private Papers of Senator Vandenberg.* Boston: Houghton Mifflin, 1972.

Vernon, Raymond. *Sovereignty at Bay.* New York: Basic Books, 1971.

Walker, J. Samuel. *Henry A. Wallace and American Foreign Policy.* Westport, Conn.: Greenwood Press, 1976.

Walker, Richard L., and Curry, George. *E. R. Stettinius, Jr., and James F. Byrnes.* The American Secretaries of State and Their Diplomacy, vol. 14. Edited by Robert H. Ferrell and Samuel Flagg Bemis. New York: Cooper Square Publishers, 1965.

Walton, Richard J. *Henry Wallace, Harry Truman, and the Cold War.* New York: Viking, 1976.

Waltz, Kenneth. *Man, the State and War.* New York: Columbia University Press, 1959.

Wedemeyer, Albert C. *Wedemeyer Reports.* New York: Henry Holt, 1958.

Welch, William. *American Images of Soviet Foreign Policy.* New Haven: Yale University Press, 1970.

Welles, Sumner. *Seven Decisions That Shaped History.* New York: Harper & Brothers, 1951.

Werth, Alexander. *Russia: The Post-War Years.* New York: Taplinger Publishing Company, 1971.

———. *Russia at War.* New York: Avon Books, 1965.

Wheeler-Bennett, John, and Nicholls, Anthony. *The Semblance of Peace.* New York: St. Martin's Press, 1972.

Willcox, William B., and Hall, Robert B., eds. *The United States in the Postwar World.* Ann Arbor: University of Michigan Press, 1947.

Williams, Francis. *Nothing So Strange.* London: Cassell, 1970.

———. *Twilight of Empire: Memoirs of Prime Minister Clement Attlee.* New York: Barnes, 1962.

Williams, William Appleman. *The Tragedy of American Diplomacy.* Rev. ed. New York: Delta Books, 1962.

Williamson, Harold F., et al. *The American Petroleum Industry.* Vol. 2. Evanston: Northwestern University, 1963.

Winch, Donald. *Economics and Policy: A Historical Study.* London: Fontana, 1972.

Wohlstetter, Roberta. *Pearl Harbor: Warning and Decision.* Stanford: Stanford University Press, 1962.

Wolfe, Bertram. *Khrushchev and Stalin's Ghost.* New York: Praeger, 1957.

Wolfe, Thomas. *Soviet Power and Europe.* Baltimore: Johns Hopkins, 1970.

Wolfers, Arnold. *Britain and France between Two Wars.* New York: Harcourt, Brace, 1940; Reprint ed., Norton, 1966.

———. *Discord and Collaboration.* Baltimore: Johns Hopkins Press, 1962.

Woodward, Sir Llewellyn. *British Foreign Policy in the Second World War.* London: Her Majesty's Stationery Office, 1962.

Xydis, Stephen G. *Greece and the Great Powers.* Thessaloniki: Institute for Balkan Studies, 1963.

Yarmolinsky, Adam. *The Military Establishment.* New York: Harper & Row, 1971.

Zhukov, Georgei K. *Memoirs of Marshal Zhukov.* New York: Delacorte, 1971.

PERIODICALS

American Academy of Political Science Proceedings

American Historical Review

American Journal of International Law

American Political Science Review

Annals of American Academy of Political and Social Sciences

Armed Force

Army and Navy Bulletin

Atlantic Monthly
Aviation News
Aviation Week
Business Week
Collier's
Commentary
Daedalus
Economist
Foreign Affairs
Foreign Policy
Fortune
Harper's
International Affairs (London)
International Affairs (Moscow)
International Journal
International Organization
Journal of American History
Journal of Contemporary History
Journal of Public Law
Life
Look
Military Review
Mirovoe Khoziaistov i Mirovaia Politika
Monthly Review
New Republic
Newsweek
New Times (Moscow)
New Times (New York)
New Yorker
New York Herald Tribune
New York Review of Books
New York Times
Political Science Quarterly
Pravda
Proceedings of Institute of World Affairs
Proceedings of the Academy of Political Science
Public Opinion Quarterly
Saturday Evening Post
Saturday Review
Slavic Review
South Atlantic Quarterly
United States Naval Institute Proceedings
U.S. State Department Bulletin
University of Virginia Quarterly
Vital Speeches
World Politics
Yale Law Journal
Yale Review

Other Unpublished Materials

Acheson, Dean. "Formulation of Policy in the United States." Lecture, Washington, D.C., December 1947.

Barnes, Maynard. "Current Situation in Bulgaria." Lecture, Washington, D.C., June 3, 1947.

———. Lecture, Washington, D.C., October 31, 1947.

Black, Cyril E. "Witnesses to the Start of the Cold War in Eastern Europe: The View from Bulgaria." Paper, October 1975.

Bohlen, Charles. "U.S.-Soviet Relations Today." Lecture, Washington, D.C., February 20, 1948.

Brown, Irving. "The Role of Communism in the European Labor Movement." Lecture, Washington, D.C., October 31, 1946.

Council on Foreign Relations. *American Interests in the War and the Peace.* Mimeographed series.

Deane, John. "Military Power and Organization in the USSR." Lecture, Washington, D.C., October 19, 1946.

Dinerstein, Herbert. "The Cold War from the Soviet Point of View: The Soviet Union and the Reordering of the International System after World War II." Paper, 1976.

Durbrow, Elbridge. "Contemporary Russia." Lecture, Washington, D.C., February 7, 1947.

———. "Objectives of Soviet Policy." Lecture, Washington, D.C., October 21, 1948.

Eberstadt, Ferdinand. "Mobilization of War Potential." Lecture, Washington, D.C., October 8, 1946.

Fairchild, Muir S. "Russian Air Power." Lecture, Washington, D.C., October 7, 1946.

Harriman, Averell. "Background to American-Soviet Relations." Lecture, Washington, D.C., December 1, 1947.

Herken, Gregg. "American Diplomacy and the Atomic Bomb, 1945–1946." Ph.D. dissertation, Princeton University, 1973.

———. "Under a Most Deadly Illusion: Politics and Diplomacy of U.S. Atomic Energy Policy: 1942–1949." Paper, n.d.

Hilldring, John. "Occupation Policies and Problems." Lecture, Washington, D.C., December 5, 1946.

Iatrides, John. "The United States and Greece, 1945–1963: Politics of Alliance and Penetration." Paper, April 18, 1975.

Johnson, Joseph. "Problems of Security in the Period Following World War II." Lecture, Washington, D.C., November 1946.

Joint Intelligence Committee of Joint Chiefs of Staff. "Capabilities and Intentions of the USSR in the Post-War Period." Washington, D.C., February 7, 1946.

Joint Working Committee. U.S. Moscow Embassy. "Soviet Strength and Weakness." September 1946.

Kennan, George. "Problems of U.S. Foreign Policy." Lecture, National War College, May 6, 1947.

———. "What Is Policy?" Lecture. National War College, Washington, D.C., December 15, 1947.

Kent, Sherman. "Strategic Intelligence." Lecture, Washington, D.C., January 6, 1947.

Legere, Lawrence J. "Unification of the Armed Forces." Ph.D. dissertation, Harvard University, 1951.

Lifka, Thomas. "The Concept of Totalitarianism and American Foreign Policy 1933–1949." Ph.D. dissertation, Harvard University, 1973.

Lytle, Mark H. "American-Iranian Relations 1941–7 and the Redefinition of National Security." Ph.D. dissertation, Yale University, 1973.

MacIsaac, David. "The United States Strategic Bombing Survey 1944–47." Ph.D. dissertation, Duke University, 1969.

Maddux, Thomas R. "American Relations with the Soviet Union, 1933–41." Ph.D. dissertation, University of Michigan, 1969.

Maier, Charles. Papers for seminars on "The United States and European Reorganization in the Wake of World War II." Lehrman Institute, New York, 1975–76 (Xeroxed).

Mastny, Vojtech. Papers for seminars on "Aims and Motives of Soviet Policies 1944–1945." Lehrman Institute, New York, 1974–75 (Xeroxed).

Murphy, Robert. "Current Situation in Germany." Lecture, Washington, D.C., October 20, 1947.

Ness, Norman. "Current Situation in Greece." Lecture, Washington, D.C., March 20, 1947.

Patterson, Robert. "Pressing War Department Problems." Lecture, Washington, D.C., June 12, 1947.

Smith, Walter Bedell. "Current Situation in USSR." Lecture, Washington, D.C., October 1, 1948.
Vandenberg, Hoyt. "Central Intelligence Group and Its Mission." Lecture, Washington, D.C., April 8, 1947.
Weil, Martin. "The American Military and the Cold War."
Yale Institute of International Affairs. Memoranda. Mimeographed series.
Yergin, Daniel H. "The Rise of the National Security State: Anti-Communism and the Origins of the Cold War." Ph.D. dissertation, Cambridge University, 1974.

Index